统计年鉴

重庆·2005

重庆市统计局 编
CHONGQING MUNICIPAL BUREAU OF STATISTICS

重庆统计年鉴

CHONGQING STATISTICAL YEARBOOK

2005年(总第16期 NO. 16)

重庆市统计局 编

CHONGQING MUNICIPAL BUREAU OF STATISTICS

中国统计出版社

China Statistics Press

图书在版编目（CIP）数据

重庆统计年鉴.2005/重庆市统计局编
北京：中国统计出版社,2005.7
ISBN 7-5037-4655-6

Ⅰ.重…
Ⅱ.重…
Ⅲ.统计资料—重庆市—2005—年鉴
Ⅳ.C832.719-54

中国版本图书馆CIP数据核字(2005)第052385号

重庆市统计年鉴 2005

作　　者：重庆市统计局
责任编辑：蔡启新
E--mail：yearbook@stats.gov.cn
责任校对：周丽娟　励　娜
封面设计：颐合企业形象设计
出版发行：中国统计出版社
通信地址：北京市西城区三里河月坛南街75号　中国统计出版社
邮政编码：100826
电　　话：(010) 63262295
印　　刷：豪森印务
开　　本：890×1240毫米　1/16
字　　数：180万字
印　　张：41
印　　数：1-2800
版　　别：2005年7月第1版
版　　次：2005年7月第1次印刷
书　　号：ISBN 7-5037-4655-6/F·2055
定　　价：260.00 元

本书附同版本CD-ROM一张，光盘内容以书面文字为准。
中国统计版图书，如有印装错误，请在购买处调换。

ISBN 7-5037-4655-6
9 787503 746550 >

重庆统计年鉴 • CHONGQING STATISTICAL YEARBOOK 2005

努力把重慶建設
成為長江上游的
經濟中心

江澤民
一九九四年十月十三日于重慶

春江水暖
鸭先知

辛巳小雪 王鸿举

《重庆统计年鉴—2005》
编辑委员会

CHONGQING STATISTICAL YEARBOOK 2005
EDITORIAL BOARD

编　辑　部

EDITORIAL DEPARTMENT

编 者 说 明

一、《重庆统计年鉴—2005》是由重庆市统计局编纂、中国统计出版社公开出版发行的一部全面记录重庆市经济建设和社会发展情况的大型资料性年刊。本书收录了重庆市历史重要年份和2004年经济和社会各方面的统计数据、各区县（自治县、市）主要统计资料，以及全国和各省区市的主要统计资料。

二、全书内容由二十三章和附录组成，包括1. 综合 2. 国民经济核算 3. 人口与就业 4. 固定资产投资 5. 能源消费 6. 财政 7. 人民生活和物价 8. 城镇建设和环境保护 9. 要素市场 10. 农业和农村经济 11. 工业 12. 建筑业 13. 运输和邮电 14. 国内贸易 15. 对外经济贸易和旅游业 16. 金融业 17. 教育、科技和文化业 18. 卫生、体育和其他社会活动 19. 区县（自治县、市）和开发区资料 20. 各类企业统计资料 21. 高新技术产业 22. 企业集团、景气调查 23. 三峡工程重庆库区移民；附录，收录了全国及各省区市的主要统计资料。每章前设《简要说明》，介绍本章节的主要内容和资料来源，章末附有《主要统计指标解释》。

三、本年鉴GDP核算和部分社会统计资料采用GB/T4754-84行业分类标准，其余资料采用新的国民经济行业分类标准（GB/T4754-2002）。

四、本年鉴的统计资料来源：大部分来自统计年报，部分来自抽样调查；附录中的有关全国及各省区市的统计资料来自中国统计出版社当年编印的《中国统计摘要》。

五、资料中所使用的度量衡单位均采用国际统一标准计量单位。

六、本年鉴部分数据的合计数或相对数，由于计量单位取舍不同而产生的计算误差未作机械调整。

七、本年鉴各表的部分指标注解位于该表下方或最后一张续表的下方。

八、本年鉴中符号的使用说明：“…”表示数据不足本表最小单位数；“空格”表示该项统计指标数据不详或无该项数据；“#”表示其中的主要项。

九、本年鉴在编辑、翻译过程中得到诸多单位和同志的大力支持，在此深表谢意。限于我们的水平，加之时间仓促，各界人士在使用资料时如发现错误和不足，恳请提出批评指正。

PREFACE

Ⅰ. *Chongqing Statistical Yearbook 2005* is a large annual statistical publication compiled by Chongqing Municipal Bureau of Statistics and issued by China Statistics Press openly, which covers not only comprehensive data on Chongqing's social and economic development in 2004 and some selected data series in historically important years, but also the major statistics on all districts (counties), as well as main data of the state, provinces, autonomous regions, municipalities directly under the jurisdiction of central government.

Ⅱ. The yearbook contains 23 chapters and the appendix, including (1) Comprehensive Statistics, (2) National Economic Accounting, (3) Population and Employment, (4) Investment in Fixed Assets, (5) Energy Consumption, (6) Government Finance, (7) People's Livelihood and Prices, (8) Urban Construction and Environmental Protection, (9) Markets of Key Factors, (10) Agriculture and Rural Economy, (11) Industry, (12) Construction, (13) Transportation, Postal and Telecommunication Services, (14) Domestic Trade, (15) Foreign Economic Relations, Trade and Tourism, (16) Financial Statistics, (17) Education, Science, Technology and Culture, (18) Public Health, Sports and Other Social Activities, (19) Districts (Counties) and Development Zones, (20) Enterprises, (21) High-tech Industry, (22) Enterprises Groups and Business Survey, (23) Resettlement of Chongqing Reservoir Area of Three Gorges Project; and the APPENDIX appends main data of the state, provinces, autonomous regions, municipalities directly under the jurisdiction of central government. Brief Introduction is at the beginning of each chapter, includes main coverage of this chapter and data sources. Explanatory Notes on Main Statistical Indicators are provided at the end of each part.

Ⅲ. Data of GDP and some social statistics are on basis of classification of national economic sectors (GBT/4754-84). Other data are adopted new classification of economic sectors (GB/T4754-2002).

Ⅳ. The major data sources of this publication are obtained from annual statistical reports, and some from sample surveys. Statistics in the APPENDIX come from China Statistical Summary complied by China Statistics Press in this year.

Ⅴ. The units of measurement used in this yearbook are international standard measurement units.

Ⅵ. Statistical discrepancies due to rounding are not adjusted in this yearbook.

Ⅶ. The notes concerning individual indicators are placed at the lower part of the table or the last page.

Ⅷ. Notations used in this yearbook: "…" indicates that the figure is not large enough to be measured with the smallest unit in the table; " (blank)" indicates that the date not available; "#" indicates that the major items of total.

Ⅸ. We are particularly grateful to vigorous assistances of various circles during edition and translation. Due to our limited level and hasty time, faults and shortage are unavoidable. Any criticism or suggestion is appreciated.

重庆统计年鉴

贰零零伍

chongqing statistical yearbook 2005

目 录 CONTENTS

CHONGQING STATISTICAL YEARBOOK 2005

一 综 合 COMPREHENSIVE STATISTICS

二 国民经济核算 NATIONAL ECONOMIC ACCOUNTING

三 人口与就业

POPULATION AND EMPLOYMENT

四 固定资产投资

INVESTMENT IN FIXED ASSETS

五 能源消费

ENERGY CONSUMPTION

六 财 政

GOVERNMENT FINANCE

七 人民生活与物价

PEOPLE'S LIVELIHOOD AND PRICES

八 城镇建设和环境保护

URBAN CONSTRUCTION AND ENVIRONMENTAL PROTECTION

九 要素市场

MARKETS OF KEY FACTORS

十 农业和农村经济

AGRICULTURE AND RURAL ECONOMY

十一 工 业

INDUSTRY

十二 建筑业

CONSTRUCTION

十三 运输和邮电

TRANSPORTATION, POSTAL AND TELECOMMUNICATION SERVICES

十四 国内贸易

DOMESTIC TRADE

十五 对外经济贸易和旅游业

FOREIGN ECONOMIC RELATIONS, TRADE AND TOURISM

十六 金融业

FINANCIAL STATISTICS

十七 教育、科技和文化业

EDUCATION, SCIENCE, TECHNOLOGY AND CULTURE

十八 卫生、体育和其他社会活动

PUBLIC HEALTH, SPORTS AND OTHER SOCIAL ACTIVITIES

十九 区县（自治县、市）和开发区

DISTRICTS (COUNTIES) AND DEVELOPMENT ZONES

二十 各类企业资料

VARIOUS ENTERPRISES

二十一 高新技术产业

HIGH—TECH INDUSTRY

二十二 企业集团、景气调查

ENTERPRISE GROUPS AND BUSINESS SURVEY

二十三 三峡工程重庆库区移民情况

RESETTLEMENT OF CHONGQING RESERVOIR AREA OF THREE GORGES PROJECT

附 录

APPENDIX

一 综 合
COMPREHENSIVE STATISTICS

简要说明　Brief Introduction

本章主要包括重庆市行政区划、自然地理、自然资源、气象、国民经济和社会发展综合资料，由市统计局综合处根据有关部门资料进行整理和编辑。

行政区划资料由市民政局提供；自然资源中土地、矿产资源数据由市国土资源和房屋管理局提供，林木资源数据由市林业局提供，水资源数据由市水利局提供；气象状况由市气象局提供。

This chapter mainly covers the data of Chongqing's administrative divisions, natural environment, natural resources, climate, national economic and social development. Data of this chapter are compiled by Division of Comprehensive Statistics, Municipal Bureau of Statistics using information from relevant bureaus and agencies.

Data of administrative divisions are provided by Municipal Bureau of Civil Affairs; Data of land and mineral resources are provided by Municipal Administration of Land, Resources and Buildings; Data of forest resource are prepared by Municipal Bureau of Forestry; Data of water resource are provided by Municipal Bureau of Water Conservancy; and data of climate are provided by Municipal Meteorological Bureau.

1—1 行政区划（2004年）
Administrative Divisions (2004)

单位：个 (unit)

地 区	Region	乡 Townships	镇 Towns	街道办事处 Urban Sub--district Offices	居委会 Neighborhood Committees	村委会 Village Committees
全市总计	**Total**	**418**	**626**	**106**	**1916**	**10137**
万州区	Wanzhou District	14	28	11	183	448
涪陵区	Fuling District	22	18	5	63	353
渝中区	Yuzhong District			13	108	
大渡口区	Dadukou District		3	5	38	32
江北区	Jiangbei District		3	9	67	51
沙坪坝区	Shapingba District		12	13	112	87
九龙坡区	Jiulongpo District		11	7	64	107
南岸区	Nan'an District		9	6	70	69
北碚区	Beibei District		14	5	59	119
万盛区	Wansheng District	1	7	2	24	57
双桥区	Shuangqiao District		2	1	7	14
渝北区	Yubei District		22	6	52	221
巴南区	Ba'nan District		19	2	75	275
黔江区	Qianjiang District	12	15	3	50	172
长寿区	Changshou District		16	2	19	228
綦江县	Qijiang County		19		50	314
潼南县	Tongnan County	9	22		22	282
铜梁县	Tongliang County	8	25		48	568
大足县	Dazu County	2	20	2	50	242
荣昌县	Rongchang County		20		42	209
璧山县	Bishan County	1	10	2	34	151
梁平县	Liangping County	8	25		23	316
城口县	Chengkou County	17	7		15	188
丰都县	Fengdu County	12	19		26	340
垫江县	Dianjiang County	11	14		26	275
武隆县	Wulong County	15	11		26	187
忠 县	Zhongxian County	19	23		32	331
开 县	Kaixian County	27	28		60	448
云阳县	Yunyang County	40	25		63	655
奉节县	Fengjie County	14	16		20	366
巫山县	Wushan County	30	11		27	315
巫溪县	Wuxi County	47	10		24	348
石柱土家族自治县	Shizhu County	20	12		17	224
秀山土家族苗族自治县	Xiushan County	18	14		32	231
酉阳土家族苗族自治县	Youyang County	25	14		8	270
彭水苗族土家族自治县	Pengshui County	29	10		26	274
江津市	Jiangjin City		23	3	85	340
合川市	Hechuan City		36	3	82	524
永川市	Yongchuan City		19	3	44	211
南川市	Nanchuan City	17	14	3	11	245

注：居委会个数包含社区居委会数；高新区、经开区的居委会和村委会数未分别分解到九龙坡区、南岸区和渝北区。

Note: Neighborhood committees includes community neighborhood committees. Neighborhood committees and village committees of High-tech Development Zone and Economic & Technology Development Zone aren't divided into Jiulongpo District, Nan'anDistrict and Yubei District respectively.

1－2 自然地理（2004年）

位置：重庆位于北纬28度10分-32度13分，东经105度11分-110度11分之间，地处较为发达的东部地区和资源丰富的西部地区的结合部，东邻湖北、湖南，南靠贵州，西接四川，北连陕西，是长江上游最大的经济中心、西南工商业重镇和水陆交通枢纽。1997年3月14日，第八届全国人民代表大会第五次会议通过了设立重庆直辖市的决议，与北京、天津、上海同为四大直辖市。

面积：重庆幅员面积8.24万平方公里，南北长450公里，东西宽470公里。2004年全市共辖15个区：万州区、涪陵区、渝中区、大渡口区、江北区、沙坪坝区、九龙坡区、南岸区、北碚区、万盛区、双桥区、渝北区、巴南区、黔江区、长寿区；4个县级市：江津市、合川市、永川市、南川市；21个县：綦江县、潼南县、铜梁县、大足县、荣昌县、璧山县、开县、忠县、梁平县、云阳县、奉节县、巫山县、巫溪县、城口县、垫江县、武隆县、丰都县、石柱县、彭水县、酉阳县、秀山县。

地势：重庆地势由南北向长江河谷逐级降低，西北部和中部以丘陵、低山为主，东南部靠大巴山和武陵山两座大山脉。

河流：主要河流有长江、嘉陵江、乌江、涪江、綦江、大宁河等。

气候：重庆属中亚热带湿润季风气候区，具有夏热冬暖，光热同季，无霜期长，雨量充沛，湿润多阴等特点。2004年平均气温18.4℃，年总降雨量1182.1毫米。

Natural Environment (2004)

Location:

Chongqing locates at. 28° 10'～32° 13' north latitude and 105° 11'～110° 11' east longitude. Chongqing has a favorable geographical location with a vast hinterland. With Hubei Province and Hu'nan Province to the east, Guizhou Province to the south, Sichuan Province to the west, Shaanxi Province to the north, Chongqing is a large commercial and industrial center, and enjoys convenient communications. Chongqing municipality was established on March 14, 1997.

Area:

Covering an area of 0.0824 million square kilometers, the municipality is 470 kilometers wide from east to west and 450 kilometers long from north to south. There was a total of 15 districts in Chongqing in 2004: Wanzhou, Fuling Yuzhong (center of Chongqing), Dadukou, Jiangbei, Shapingba, Jiulongpo, Nan'an, Beibei, Wansheng, Shuangqiao, Yubei, Ba'nan, Qianjiang, Changshou；4 cities at county level in Chongqing: Jiangjin, Hechuan, Yongchuan, Nanchuan. And 21 counties in Chongqing: Qijiang, Tongnan, Tongliang, Dazu, Rongchang, Bishan, Kaixian, Zhongxian, Liangping, Yunyang, Fengjie, Wushan, Wuxi, Chengkou, Dianjiang, Wulong, Fengdu, Shizhu, Pengshui, Youyang, Xiushan.

Topography:

Chongqing's eastern is lower than the western, lots of hills in the northwest and the middle areas, with Daba Mountain and Wuling Mountain to the southeast.

River:

The main rivers are Yangtze River, Jialing River, Wujiang River, Fujiang River, Qijiang River and Daning River.

Climate:

Chongqing has a subtropical humid monsoon climate with four distinct seasons. Summer of Chongqing is hot and winter is warm, with a long frost-free period. In 2004 Annual average temperature was 18.4℃ and annual precipitation was 1182.1mm.

1—3 自然资源（2003—2004年）
Natural Resources (2003-2004)

项　目	Item	2003	2004
土地资源(万公顷)	**Land Resources (10 000 hectares)**		
#农用地	Agricultural Land	695.39	694.40
#耕地	Cultivated Land	234.76	228.74
园地	Garden Land	21.00	22.09
林地	Forest Land	319.02	325.13
牧草地	Grassland	23.84	23.81
建设用地	Construction Land	54.00	55.89
未利用地	Unused Land	73.30	72.39
林木资源	**Forest Resources**		
活立木总蓄积量(万立方米)	Total Standing Stock Volume (10 000 cu.m)	11999	11999
森林面积(万公顷)	Forest Area (10 000 hectares)	223.73	223.73
森林蓄积量(万立方米)	Stock Volume of Forest (10 000 cu.m)	11173	11173
森林覆盖率(%)	Forest-coverage Rate (%)	27.1	27.1
水资源（当年量）	**Water Resources (current quantity)**		
降水深（毫米）	Depth of Precipitation (mm)	1229.80	1196.60
地表径流量(亿立方米)	Surface Runoff (100 million cu.m)	590.74	558.77
地下水量（亿立方米）	Shallow Ground Water Volume (100 million cu.m)	109.88	104.80
入境水资源总量(亿立方米)	Water Volume Entry (100 million cu.m)	3515.90	3590.39
水力资源蕴藏量(万千瓦)	Hydropower Resources (10 000 kw)	1388	1388
#可开发量	Developable Resources	760	760
主要矿产资源(基础储量)	**Major Mineral Resources (basic reserves)**		
天然气（亿立方米）	Natural Gas (100 million cu.m)	1043.32	1127.32
煤（万吨）	Coal (10 000 tons)	163604	162863
铁（矿石万吨）	Iron Ore (ore, 10 000 tons)	112	112
锰（矿石万吨）	Manganese Ore (ore, 10 000 tons)	1780	1791
锌（金属万吨）	Zinc Ore (metal, 10 000 tons)	15	15
铝土（矿石万吨）	Aluminum Ore (ore, 10 000 tons)	3639	3639
汞（吨）	Mercury (ton)	1672	1656
锶（天青石万吨）	Strontium Ore (ore, 10 000 tons)	25	25
熔剂用灰岩（矿石万吨）	Limestone for Flux (ore, 10 000 tons)	10178	10178
冶金用白云岩（矿石万吨）	Dolomite for Metallurgy (ore, 10 000 tons)	4546	4546
冶金用石英砂岩（矿石万吨）	Quartzite for Metallurgy (ore, 10 000 tons)	382	382
陶瓷用砂岩（矿石万吨）	Sandstone for Ceramics (ore, 10 000 tons)	495	495
耐火粘土（矿石万吨）	Refractory Clay (ore, 10 000 tons)	169	169
重晶石（矿石万吨）	Barytes (ore, 10 000 tons)	184	184
毒重石（矿石万吨）	Witherite (ore, 10 000 tons)	295	588
盐矿（矿石万吨）	Salt Mine (ore, 10 000 tons)	100562	100296

注：1）林木资源数据为2002年森林资源二类调查数，该调查一般五年一次。

2）煤和天然气数据为保有储量。

Note: a) Data of forest resources are from Class II survey in 2002. This kind of survey is carried out every 5 years ordinarily.

b) Data of natural gas are remained reserves.

1－4 气象基本情况（1951－2004年） Basic Statistics on Climate (1951-2004)

年 份 Year	降水量（毫米） Precipitation (mm)	平均气温（℃） Average Temperature (℃)	日照时数（时） Sunshine Hours (hour)	平均相对湿度(%) Average Relative Humidity (%)	平均风速(米/秒) Average Wind Speed (m/s)	平均气压（百帕） Average Air Pressure (100 pa)
1951	1043.4	18.4		81	1.0	
1952	1227.9	18.5	1198.6	81	1.0	
1953	852.1	18.8	1245.6	80	0.9	
1954	1112.8	17.9	1061.2	81	0.9	981.2
1955	927.4	18.2	1388.6	77	0.8	982.0
1956	1497.4	18.2	1433.2	76	1.4	982.8
1957	1171.9	17.9	1094.2	80	1.3	983.3
1958	740.7	18.6	1260.7	77	1.4	983.3
1959	915.7	18.7	1378.3	76	1.4	983.0
1960	1026.0	18.4	1102.0	78	1.4	983.5
1961	787.7	18.7	1338.8	77	1.5	982.8
1962	1210.4	18.0	1323.9	80	1.4	983.3
1963	1072.8	18.9	1370.4	77	1.4	982.4
1964	1031.6	18.2	1170.4	80	1.5	982.9
1965	1318.9	18.1	1009.5	81	1.4	983.4
1966	958.9	18.6	1278.9	78	1.4	982.7
1967	1046.0	18.1	1216.3	79	1.4	983.4
1968	1384.5	17.7	1054.6	82	1.2	983.5
1969	1080.5	18.6	1357.1	76	1.2	982.8
1970	1097.5	18.1	1197.9	79	1.1	983.5
1971	854.3	18.6	1370.6	76	1.3	983.4
1972	1171.8	18.4	1284.1	78	1.3	982.9
1973	1092.3	18.9	1349.4	78	1.3	983.2
1974	1258.0	17.8	1068.3	79	1.3	983.0
1975	1025.4	18.5	1202.5	78	1.2	982.9
1976	1044.9	17.7	1129.2	79	1.1	983.5
1977	1151.2	18.1	1234.8	79	1.1	984.0
1978	1057.2	18.8	1495.7	77	1.2	983.5

1-4 续表 CONTINUED

年 份 Year	降水量（毫米） Precipitation (mm)	平均气温（℃） Average Temperature (℃)	日照时数（时） Sunshine Hours (hour)	平均相对湿度(%) Average Relative Humidity (%)	平均风速(米/秒) Average Wind Speed (m/s)	平均气压（百帕） Average Air Pressure (100 pa)
1979	1160.0	18.4	1222.2	80	1.1	983.4
1980	1062.6	18.2	1071.8	79	1.4	983.6
1981	1157.9	18.1	1188.0	79	1.4	983.5
1982	1185.2	17.7	992.3	81	1.1	983.6
1983	1138.1	18.1	954.4	80	0.9	983.9
1984	1035.1	17.8	1028.7	79	1.1	983.1
1985	1004.0	17.9	997.1	79	1.3	983.3
1986	1141.4	17.8	946.1	80	1.3	984.2
1987	910.2	18.6	946.3	78	1.2	983.4
1988	1254.0	18.0	840.6	80	1.1	983.6
1989	1137.4	17.7	855.0	81	1.0	983.8
1990	956.7	18.7	1083.7	79	1.2	983.2
1991	1180.6	18.2	874.8	81	1.1	983.5
1992	987.4	18.1	975.0	78	1.6	984.0
1993	1164.3	17.8	894.6	81	1.5	984.0
1994	982.5	18.7	1063.8	80	1.4	983.2
1995	923.5	18.3	993.6	79	1.3	983.7
1996	1398.3	17.7	899.4	81	1.3	983.6
1997	898.8	18.5	943.0	79	1.4	983.8
1998	1508.0	19.2	941.9	79	1.5	983.0
1999	1305.6	18.5	833.6	81	1.5	983.2
2000	1010.9	18.2	961.1	80	1.4	983.0
2001	814.8	18.8	1050.4	78	1.6	983.3
2002	1430.6	18.8	1117.1	80	1.6	983.3
2003	1025.0	18.9	875.7	80	1.6	983.2
2004	1182.1	18.4	974.7	78	1.3	984.0

注：此表为重庆市区资料。

Note: This table is the data of Chongqing downtown.

1—5 国民经济和社会发展总量与速度指标

指　　标	Item	总量指标 Aggregate Indicators 1995	1996
人口与就业	**Population and Employment**		
人　口(万人)(抽样调查)	**Population (10 000 persons) (sample survey)**		
年末常住人口	Year-end Resident Population		
#城镇人口	Urban		
乡村人口	Rural		
#男性人口	Male		
女性人口	Female		
就　业(万人)	**Employment (10 000 persons)**		
就业人员数	Employment	1709.26	1674.90
#职工人数	Staff and Workers	294.25	294.63
城镇登记失业人数	Registered Urban Unemployment	10.47	10.95
宏观经济	**Macroeconomic Indicators**		
国民经济核算	**National EconomicAccounting**		
本市生产总值(现价)(亿元)	Gross Domestic Product (current prices)(100 million yuan)	1009.47	1179.09
第一产业	Primary Industry	261.52	284.89
第二产业	Secondary Industry	427.19	493.21
#工　业	Industry	368.17	423.01
第三产业	Tertiary Industry	320.76	400.99
固定资产投资(亿元)	**Investment in Fixed Assets (100 million yuan)**		
全社会固定资产投资总额	Total Investment in Fixed Assets	270.97	320.73
#基本建设	Capital Construction	69.27	88.40
更新改造	Innovation	68.41	67.16
房地产开发	Real Estate Development	46.88	55.62
财　政(亿元)	**Government Finance (100 million yuan)**		
地方预算内财政收入	Local Budgetary Financial Revenue	46.01	54.94
地方预算内财政支出	Local Budgetary Financial Expenditures	66.22	79.42
物价总指数(上年=100)	**Price Indices (preceding year=100)**		
居民消费价格总指数	General Consumer Price Index	119.4	109.7
商品零售价格总指数	General Retail Price Index	116.3	106.1
产　　业	**Industry**		
农　业	**Agriculture**		
年末常用耕地面积(万公顷)	Year-end Common Cultivated Area (10 000 hectares)	162.91	162.21
乡村从业人员(万人)	Rural Employment (10 000 persons)	1349.34	1330.44
农林牧渔业总产值(现价)(亿元)	Gross Output Value of Farming, Forestry, Animal Husbandry and Fishery (current prices) (100 million yuan)	377.83	424.99
#农　业	Farming	227.89	271.38
林　业	Forestry	10.67	11.55
牧　业	Animal Husbandry	130.42	131.17
渔　业	Fishery	8.84	10.89
主要农产品产量(万吨)	Output of Major Farm Products (10 000 tons)		
粮　食	Grain	1153.68	1172.14

注：1）本表数据除本市生产总值、农林牧渔业总产值、工业增加值速度指标按可比价计算，财政指标2004年比2003年为同口径指数，其余指标均为自然增长（下表同）。

2）1998年及以后职工人数为在岗职工口径（下表同）。

3）乡村从业人员是指乡村劳动力从业人员，包括外出务工人员（下表同）。

Principal Aggregate Indicators of National Economic and Social Development and Their Related Indices and Growth Rates

总量指标 Aggregate Indicators			速度指标（%） Indices and Growth Rate						
			指 数（2004为以下各年） Index (2004 as percentage of the following years)				平均增长速度 Average Growth Rate		
2000	2003	2004	1995	1996	2000	2003	1996-2000	2001-2004	1997-2004
2826.27	2777.47	2770.98			98.0	99.8		-0.5	
935.50	1163.76	1205.70			128.9	103.6		6.5	
1890.77	1613.71	1565.28			82.8	97.0		-4.6	
1466.83	1378.74	1388.01			94.6	100.7		-1.4	
1359.44	1398.73	1382.97			101.7	98.9		0.4	
1690.00	1726.36	1715.62	100.4	102.4	101.5	99.4	-0.2	0.4	0.3
208.87	204.99	208.04			99.6	101.5		-0.1	
10.15	16.16	16.76	160.1	153.1	165.1	103.7	-0.6	13.4	5.5
1589.34	2250.56	2665.39	234.9	211.3	150.4	112.2	9.3	10.7	9.8
283.00	336.36	423.70	131.5	125.2	116.0	104.7	2.5	3.8	2.8
657.51	977.30	1181.24	282.0	251.6	171.5	116.2	10.5	14.4	12.2
527.48	768.37	927.51	275.4	245.6	172.2	116.9	9.8	14.5	11.9
648.83	936.90	1060.45	256.1	222.9	143.9	110.4	12.2	9.5	10.5
655.81	1269.35	1621.92	598.6	505.7	247.3	127.8	19.3	25.4	22.5
262.93	665.49	891.32	1286.7	1008.3	339.0	133.9	30.6	35.7	33.5
92.03	122.01	153.43	224.3	228.5	166.7	125.8	6.1	13.6	10.9
139.63	327.89	405.08	864.1	728.3	290.1	123.5	24.4	30.5	28.2
104.46	206.93	302.44	657.3	550.5	289.5	140.6	17.8	30.4	23.8
202.46	391.36	485.12	732.6	610.8	239.6	124.0	25.0	24.4	25.4
96.7	100.6	103.7							
95.5	99.5	101.4							
158.32	135.32	140.06	86.0	86.3	88.5	103.5	-0.6	-3.0	-1.8
1352.60	1340.25	1361.54	100.9	102.3	100.7	101.6	…	0.2	0.3
412.63	488.57	612.77	125.8	122.4	114.8	105.7	1.9	3.5	2.6
244.74	270.12	332.95	123.3	121.1	115.8	105.5	1.3	3.7	2.4
10.82	14.58	18.48	108.7	107.3	145.9	108.8	-5.7	9.9	0.9
141.99	177.64	230.94	136.7	131.9	119.3	104.9	2.8	4.5	3.5
15.08	18.33	21.25	205.9	177.2	120.2	108.4	11.4	4.7	7.4
1131.21	1087.20	1144.57	99.2	97.6	101.2	105.3	-0.4	0.3	-0.3

Note: a) Indices and growth rate in this table are natural growth except that of gross domestic product, value of farming, forestry, animal husbandry and fishery, value-added of industry are at constant prices, and government finance in 2004 over 2003 is in same terms .

b) Number of staff and worker and wages since 1998 are on-post staff and worker (the same below).

c) Rural employment refers to rural able-bodied laborers, including laborers working outside Chongqing (the same below).

1-5 续表1

指　　标	Item	总量指标 Aggregate Indicators 1995	1996
油　料	Oil-bearing Crops	25.12	23.60
烟　叶	Tobacco	7.80	13.24
茶　叶	Tea	1.75	1.55
水　果	Fruit	59.29	56.62
肉　类	Meat	127.22	133.22
#猪　肉	Pork	112.27	114.18
水产品	Aquatic Products	12.13	14.07
工　业（国有及规模以上）	**Industry (State-owned Industrial Enterprises and Non-state-owned Industrial Enterprises above Desingated Size)**		
工业总产值（现价）（亿元）	Gross Output Value of Industry (current prices)(100 million yuan)		
工业增加值（现价）（亿元）	Value-added of Industry (current prices) (100 million yuan)		
主营业务收入（亿元）	Major Sales Value (100 million yuan)		
利税总额（亿元）	Total Pre-tax Profits (100 million yuan)		
经济效益综合指数	Comprehensive index of Economic Efficiency		
产品销售率（%）	Ratio of Sales to Products (%)		
全员劳动生产率（元/人年）	Overall Labor Productivity (yuan/person-year)		
主要工业产品产量	Output of Major Industrial Products		
原　煤（万吨）	Coal (10 000 tons)		
天然气（亿立方米）	Natural Gas (100 million cu.m)		
发电量（亿千瓦时）	Electricity (100 million kwh)		
钢　材（万吨）	Steel Products (10 000 tons)		
铝　材（万吨）	Aluminum Products (10 000 tons)		
水　泥（万吨）	Cement (10 000 tons)		
汽　车（万辆）	Motor Vehicles (10 000 vehicles)		
摩托车（万辆）	Motorcycles (10 000 vehicles)		
啤　酒（万千升）	Beer (10 000 kiloliters)		
卷　烟（亿支）	Cigarettes (100 million units)		
建筑业（资质等级四级以上）	**Construction (Grade 4 and above)**		
建筑业总产值（亿元）	Gross Output Value of Construction (100 million yuan)		205.30
建筑业增加值（亿元）	Value-added of Construction (100 million yuan)		56.43
房屋施工面积（万平方米）	Floor Space Under Construction (10 000 sq.m)		4065.24
房屋竣工面积（万平方米）	Floor Space Completed (10 000 sq.m)		2276.97
交通运输业	**Transportation**		
客运量（万人）	Passenger Traffic (10 000 persons)	39731	43123
铁　路	Railway	1962	1725
公　路	Highway	34379	37410
水　运	Waterway	3352	3900
民　航	Civil Aviation	38	88
货运量（万吨）	Freight Traffic (10 000 tons)	22795.70	25818.20
#铁　路	Railway	2960	3112
公　路	Highway	18253	20214
水　运	Waterway	1582	2491
民　航	Civil Aviation	0.70	1.20
港口货物吞吐量（万吨）	Freight handled at Ports (10 000 tons)	853.00	1076.00

注：1）工业总产值的绝对值和指数按现价计算；工业增加值的绝对值按现价计算，指数按可比价计算，

2）建筑业2003年起的所有数据均不包括劳务分包企业；其增加值2003年前按工程结算利润计算，从2003年起按营业利润算（下表同）。

3）从2000年起民航货运量按新制度统计，旅客行李不再计入货运（下表同）。

1-5 CONTINUED-1

总量指标 Aggregate Indicators			速度指标（%） Indices and Growth Rate						
			指　　数（2004为以下各年） Index (2004 as percentage of the following years)				平均增长速度 Average Growth Rate		
2000	2003	2004	1995	1996	2000	2003	1996-2000	2001-2004	1997-2004
31.06	38.27	41.75	166.2	176.9	134.4	109.1	4.3	7.7	7.4
10.41	8.60	8.50	109.0	64.2	81.7	98.8	5.9	-4.9	-5.4
1.45	1.43	1.61	92.0	103.9	111.0	112.6	-3.7	2.7	0.5
81.68	128.59	137.22	231.4	242.4	168.0	106.7	6.6	13.8	11.7
143.91	159.51	167.01	131.3	125.4	116.1	104.7	2.5	3.8	2.9
122.45	131.82	136.43	121.5	119.5	111.4	103.5	1.8	2.7	2.3
20.03	22.49	23.93	197.3	170.1	119.5	106.4	10.6	4.5	6.9
962.32	1588.99	2142.73				129.9			
287.50	477.85	588.32				125.3			
959.36	1595.07	2108.84			219.8	132.2		21.8	
85.57	191.09	242.02			282.8	126.7		29.7	
87.10	129.73	140.90							
99.10	97.83	99.87							
31081	55957	65329			210.2	116.7		20.4	
1149.90	1484.20	1738.19			151.2	117.1		10.9	
38.98	47.29	51.57			132.3	109.1		7.2	
167.90	188.64	232.82			138.7	123.4		8.5	
156.98	235.24	288.10			183.5	122.5		16.4	
13.98	21.60	26.23			187.6	121.4		17.0	
1402.78	1927.00	1906.23			135.9	98.9		8.0	
24.59	40.45	43.42			176.6	107.3		15.3	
191.07	441.32	473.07			247.6	107.2		25.4	
	44.42	46.21				104.1			
	387.50	386.32				99.7			
348.66	586.21	690.28				117.8			
94.52	128.72	151.98				118.1			
6088.49	9754.10	10184.46				104.4			
3083.72	4939.62	5167.65				104.6			
57852	59170	64675	162.8	150.0	111.8	109.3	7.8	2.8	5.2
2140	1949	2346	119.6	136.0	109.6	120.4	1.8	2.3	3.9
53170	55673	60833	176.9	162.6	114.4	109.3	9.1	3.4	6.3
2425	1417	1304	38.9	33.4	53.8	92.0	-6.3	-14.4	-12.8
117	131	192	505.3	218.2	164.1	146.6	25.2	13.2	10.2
28022.40	34113.20	38168.37	167.4	147.8	136.2	111.9	4.2	8.0	5.0
2848	3491	3731	126.0	119.9	131.0	106.9	-0.8	7.0	2.3
23646	28406	31515	172.7	155.9	133.3	110.9	5.3	7.4	5.7
1526	2214	2918	184.4	117.1	191.2	131.8	-0.7	17.6	2.0
2.40	2.20	2.64			110.0	120.0		2.4	
2448.00	3243.76	4539.00	532.1	421.8	185.4	139.9	23.5	16.7	19.7

Note: a) Data of industry are calculated at current prices except that index of industrial value-add is at comparable prices.

b) All data of construction since 2003 exclude construction enterprises of work subcontractors. Value-added is calculated in terms of profits of project settled accounts before 2003, whereas in terms of business profits since 2003. (the same below).

b) Freight traffic of civil aviation since 2000 exclude the baggages in accordance with new statistical system (the same below).

1-5 续表2

指　　标	Item	总量指标 Aggregate Indicators 1995	1996
邮电通信业	**Postal and Telecommunication Services**		
邮电业务总量（亿元）	Business Volume (100 million yuan)	10.96	15.99
本地电话用户（万户）	Local Telephone Subscribers (10 000 subscribers)	37.24	66.50
移动电话用户（万户）	Mobile Telephone Subscribers (10 000 subscribers)	3.62	9.00
国际互联网络用户（万户）	Subscribers of Internet Services (10 000 subscribers)		0.03
国内商业	**Domestic Trade**		
社会消费品零售总额（亿元）	Retail Sales of Consumer Goods (100 million yuan)	371.81	445.48
＃批发零售贸易业	Wholesale and Retail Trade	225.06	260.45
餐饮业	Catering Trade	28.69	33.45
对外贸易	**Foreign Trade**		
进出口总值（亿美元）	Total Imports and Exports (USD 100 million)	14.19	15.85
进口总值	Imports	5.71	9.92
出口总值	Exports	8.48	5.93
利用外资	**Utilization of Foreign Capital**		
实际利用外资额(亿美元)	Foreign Capital Actually Utilized (USD 100 million)	6.16	4.42
＃外商直接投资额	Foreign Direct Investment	3.79	2.19
国际旅游	**International Tourism**		
国际旅游人数（万人）	International Tourists (10 000 persons)	14.29	16.18
旅游外汇收入（万美元）	Foreign Exchange Earnings from International Tourism (USD 10 000)	6333	7090
金　融（亿元）	**Finance (100 million yuan)**		
金融机构人民币存款年末余额	Deposit Balance in RMB of Financial Institutions	676.70	846.43
＃城乡居民储蓄存款	Saving Deposits of Urban and Rural Residents	401.45	500.71
金融机构人民币贷款年末余额	Loan Balance of in RMB of Financial Institutions	755.39	913.93
保险公司保费收入	Insurance Premium of Insurance Companies		12.82
保险公司赔款及给付	Indemnity Expenditure and Payment of Insurance Companies		6.48
教育、科技、文化	**Education, Science, Technology and Culture**		
教　育	**Education**		
专任教师（人）	Full-time Teachers (person)		
＃普通高等学校	Regular Institutions of Higher Education	9409	9400
普通中等专业学校	Specialized Secondary Schools	4542	4505
普通中学	Regular Secondary Schools	67498	69503
小　学	Primary Schools	117497	117711
在校学生数（万人）	Student Enrollment (10 000 persons)		
＃普通高等学校	Regular Institutions of Higher Education	7.34	7.99
普通中等专业学校	Specialized Secondary Schools	6.27	6.95
普通中学	Regular Secondary Schools	97.71	101.27
小　学	Primary Schools	263.86	273.71
科　技	**Science and Technology**		
技术市场成交额（万元）	Transaction Value of Technology Exchanges (10 000 yuan)	32466	34344

注：邮电业务总量2001年前为1990年不变价，2001年及以后为2000年不变价口径（下表同）。

1-5 CONTINUED-2

总量指标 Aggregate Indicators			速度指标（%） Indices and Growth Rate						
			指数（2004为以下各年） Index (2004 as percentage of the following years)				平均增长速度 Average Growth Rate		
2000	2003	2004	1995	1996	2000	2003	1996-2000	2001-2004	1997-2004
85.82	121.31	168.65	1538.8	1054.7	196.5	139.0	50.9	18.4	34.2
268.43	533.40	642.39	1725.0	966.0	239.3	120.4	42.2	24.4	32.8
160.00	619.40	811.61	22420.2	9017.9	507.3	131.0	113.3	50.1	75.5
10.00	88.65	122.16		407200.0	1221.6	137.8		87.0	182.6
643.58	835.53	1061.49	285.5	238.3	164.9	127.0	11.6	13.3	11.5
383.19	719.13	902.30	400.9	346.4	235.5	125.5	1.4	23.9	16.8
54.56	107.32	144.29	502.9	431.4	264.5	134.4	-2.1	27.5	20.0
17.85	25.95	38.57	271.8	243.3	216.1	148.6	4.7	21.2	11.8
7.90	10.10	17.66	309.3	178.0	223.5	174.9	6.7	22.3	7.5
9.95	15.85	20.91	246.6	352.6	210.2	131.9	3.3	20.4	17.1
3.45	5.67	6.82	110.7	154.3	197.7	120.3	-10.9	18.6	5.6
2.44	3.11	4.05	106.9	184.9	166.0	130.2	-8.4	13.5	8.0
26.61	23.45	43.44	304.0	268.5	163.2	185.2	13.2	13.0	13.1
13837	11323	20308	320.7	286.4	146.8	179.4	16.9	10.1	14.1
1904.71	3438.61	4039.61	597.0	477.3	212.1	117.5	23.0	20.7	21.6
1085.36	1896.56	2189.73	545.5	437.3	201.8	115.5	22.0	19.2	20.3
1881.29	2774.81	3246.28	429.7	355.2	172.6	117.0	20.0	14.6	17.2
27.71	57.93	66.51	518.8	240.0	240.0	114.8	24.5	24.5	22.8
8.27	14.53	16.25		250.8	196.5	111.8		18.4	12.2
10449	16013	18214	193.6	193.8	174.3	113.7	2.1	14.9	8.6
4125	2656	2821	62.1	62.6	68.4	106.2	-1.9	-9.1	-5.7
81766	89560	92051	136.4	132.4	112.6	102.8	3.9	3.0	3.6
119014	115212	114007	97.0	96.9	95.8	99.0	0.3	-1.1	-0.4
13.25	25.53	30.39	414.0	380.4	229.4	119.0	12.5	23.1	18.2
8.45	9.51	9.95	158.7	143.2	117.8	104.6	6.1	4.2	4.6
147.79	166.37	170.75	174.8	168.6	115.5	102.6	8.6	3.7	6.7
276.13	277.94	271.90	103.0	99.3	98.5	97.8	0.9	-0.4	-0.1
296594	555083	596186	1836.3	1735.9	201.0	107.4	55.6	19.1	42.9

Note: Data on total business volume from postal and telecommunication services before 2001 were in terms of 1990 constant price, and since 2001 were in terms of 2000 constant price (the same below).

1-5 续表3

指标	Item	总量指标 Aggregate Indicators 1995	1996
文 化	**Culture**		
图书出版数量（万册、万张）	Books Published (10 000 copies)	15219	13023
杂志出版数量（万册）	Magazines Published (10 001 copies)		
报纸出版数量（万份）	Newspaper Published (10 002 copies)		
电视人口覆盖率（%）	Viewer Rating of TV Programs (%)	75.00	78.90
广播人口覆盖率（%）	Listener Rating of Radio Programs (%)	85.00	86.30
家庭、生活	**Family and Living Standards**		
家 庭（抽样调查）	**Family (sample survey)**		
家庭户户数（万户）	Households (10 000 households)		
城市居民平均每户家庭人口(人)	Population of Per Urban Household (person)	3.01	3.08
农村居民平均每户家庭人口(人)	Population of Per Rural Household (person)	3.90	3.85
婚 姻	**Marital Statistics**		
内地居民登记结婚对数（万对）	Marriages of Inland Residents (10 000 couples)		26.44
内地居民登记离婚对数（万对）	Divorces of Inland Residents (10 000 couples)		1.68
居 住（抽样调查）	**Residence (sample survey)**		
城市居民人均房屋建筑面积（平方米）	Per Capita Residential Space of Urban Households (sq.m)	8.13	8.00
农村居民人均住房面积(平方米)	Per Capita Residential Space of Rural Households (sq.m)	23.50	24.44
工资和收入	**Wages and Income**		
城镇经济单位职工工资总额(亿元)	Total Wages of Staff and Workers (100 million yuan)	130.93	145.49
城镇经济单位职工平均工资(元)	Average Annual Wages of Staff and Workers (yuan)	4508	5010
城市居民人均可支配收入(元)	Per Capita Disposable Income of Urban Households (yuan)	4375.43	5022.96
农村居民人均纯收入(元)	Per Capita Net Income of Rural Households (yuan)	1270.41	1479.05
城乡居民人均人民币储蓄存款余额(元)	Per Capita Saving Deposits of Urban and Rural Residents (yuan)	1337	1656
卫 生	**Public Health**		
医院、卫生院（个）	Hospitals (unit)	2505	2567
卫生技术人员（人）	Medical Technical Personnel (person)	86041	87542
#执业（助理）医师	Certified (Assistant) Doctors	31169	30733
卫生机构床位数（张）	Hospital Beds (bed)	67243	66339
市政建设	**Municipal Engineering**		
供水总量（万立方米）	Water Supply (10 000 cu.m)		84548
天然气供气总量（万立方米）	Natural Gas Supply (10 000 cu.m)		111980
排水管道长度（公里）	Length of Sewer Pipelines (km)		1857
公共汽(电)车总数(辆)	Number of Public Buses and Trolley Buses (vehicles)		3019
道路长度（公里）	Length of Urban Roads (km)		2652
公共绿地面积(公顷)	Public Green Areas (hectare)		1104

注：1）“城市居民人均房屋建筑面积”2002年前数据为“人均房屋居住面积”（下表同）。
2）城镇经济单位职工工资总额和平均工资1998年及以后为在岗职工口径（下表同）。
3）2002年起卫生统计指标名称变更，统计口径变化，不可与往年同比：2002年起卫生技术人员和床位不包括医学院校、卫生学校和计生站；执业（助理）医师2002年以前统计口径为“医生”（下表同）。

1-5 CONTINUED-3

总量指标 Aggregate Indicators			速度指标（%） Indices and Growth Rate						
			指数（2004为以下各年） Index (2004 as percentage of the following years)				平均增长速度 Average Growth Rate		
2000	2003	2004	1995	1996	2000	2003	1996-2000	2001-2004	1997-2004
11198	11175	11164	73.4	85.7	99.7	99.9	-6.0	-0.1	-1.9
3480	4191	4397			126.4	104.9		6.0	
48674	47420	47575			97.7	100.3		-0.6	
93.70	95.71	95.73							
89.90	92.26	92.26							
914.16	974.55	955.51			104.5	98.0		1.1	
3.05	2.97	3.02	100.3	98.1	99.0	101.7	0.3	-0.2	-0.2
3.70	3.65	3.67	94.1	95.3	99.2	100.5	-1.0	-0.2	-0.6
19.02	17.88	18.87		71.4	99.2	105.5		-0.2	-4.1
2.07	3.13	4.82		286.9	232.9	154.0		23.5	14.1
10.72	21.29	22.76				106.9			
29.58	31.45	32.49	138.3	132.9	109.8	103.3	4.7	2.4	3.6
173.23	253.51	293.98	224.5	202.1	169.7	116.0	5.8	14.1	9.2
8020	12440	14357	318.5	286.6	179.0	115.4	12.2	15.7	14.1
6176.30	8093.67	9220.96	210.7	183.6	149.3	113.9	7.1	10.5	7.9
1892.44	2214.55	2510.41	197.6	169.7	132.7	113.4	8.3	7.3	6.8
3511	6059	6964	520.9	420.5	198.3	114.9	22.0	18.7	19.7
2250	1682	1574				93.6			
88619	78628	77516				98.6			
44940	37122	36603				98.6			
65666	63287	63899				101.0			
70722	79935	81061		95.9	114.6	101.4		3.5	-0.5
75257	124408	164414		146.8	218.5	132.2		21.6	4.9
2806	4373	5033		271.0	179.4	115.1		15.7	13.3
4656	6251	7710		255.4	165.6	123.3		13.4	12.4
3299	4022	4272		161.1	129.5	106.2		6.7	6.1
1588	3155	4234		383.5	266.6	134.2		27.8	18.3

Note: a) Data of "per capita residential space of urban households" refer to "living space" before 2002 (thesame below) .

b) Total wages and average annual wages of staff and workers since 1998 refer to on-post staff and workers (the same below) .

c) Indices of health care since 2002 had been changed, and their range were not comparable with previous years. Medical technical personnel and hospital beds since 2002 didn't cover medical colleges & schools and family planning centers. Certified (assistant) doctors before 2002 refer to doctors (the same below) .

1－6 国民经济和社会发展结构指标
Structural Indicators of Natinal Economic and Social Development

单位：%　　(%)

指　　标	Item	1995	1996	2000	2003	2004
人口与就业	**Population and Employment**					
人　口（抽样调查）	**Population(sample survey)**					
城镇乡村人口结构	By Urban and Rural			100.0	100.0	100.0
城　镇	Urban			33.1	41.9	43.5
乡　村	Rural			66.9	58.1	56.5
性别结构	By Sex			100.0	100.0	100.0
男	Male			51.9	49.6	50.1
女	Female			48.1	50.4	49.9
就　业	**Employment**					
产业结构	By Industry	100.0	100.0	100.0	100.0	100.0
第一产业	Primary Industry	59.6	59.5	56.1	51.7	50.7
第二产业	Secondary Industry	18.2	20.3	16.3	17.3	17.5
第三产业	Tertiary Industry	22.2	20.2	27.6	31.0	31.8
登记注册类型结构	By Registration		100.0	100.0	100.0	100.0
国有经济	State-owned		11.8	8.8	7.3	7.3
集体经济	Collective-owned		74.5	68.5	62.9	60.9
私营和个体	Private and Individuals		12.9	21.0	26.2	27.6
其他经济	Others		0.8	1.7	3.6	4.2
宏观经济	**Macroeconomic Indicators**					
国民经济核算	**National EconomicAccounting**					
本市生产总值结构	GDP by Industry	100.0	100.0	100.0	100.0	100.0
第一产业	Primary Industry	25.9	24.2	17.8	15.0	15.9
第二产业	Secondary Industry	42.3	41.8	41.4	43.4	44.3
#工　业	Industry	36.5	35.9	33.2	34.1	34.8
第三产业	Tertiary Industry	31.8	34.0	40.8	41.6	39.8
固定资产投资	**Investment in Fixed Assets**					
管理渠道结构	By Channel of Management	100.0	100.0	100.0	100.0	100.0
基本建设	Capital Construction	25.6	27.6	40.1	52.4	54.9
更新改造	Innovation	25.2	20.9	14.0	9.6	9.5
房地产开发	Real Estate Development	17.3	17.3	21.3	25.8	25.0
其他投资	Others	31.9	34.2	24.6	12.2	10.6
产业结构	By Industry	100.0	100.0	100.0	100.0	100.0
第一产业	Primary Industry	0.6	0.7	1.4	2.1	2.2
第二产业	Secondary Industry	39.4	36.1	21.7	23.9	26.5
第三产业	Tertiary Industry	60.0	63.2	76.9	74.0	71.3
财　政	**Government Finance**					
财政收入结构	Financial Revenue	100.0	100.0	100.0	100.0	100.0
中　央	Central	45.1	41.7	36.0	39.5	34.7
地　方	Local	54.9	58.3	64.0	60.5	65.3

1-6 续表1 CONTINUED-1

单位：% (%)

指 标	Item	1995	1996	2000	2003	2004
能源消费	**Energy Consumption**					
能源消费总量结构	Total Energy Consumption	100.0	100.0	100.0	100.0	100.0
煤 炭	Coal	69.8	70.4	65.2	65.3	62.4
天然气	Natural Gas	14.5	13.9	13.4	13.0	12.0
油 料	Oil	5.8	5.2	8.7	8.2	12.7
电 力	Electricity	9.9	10.5	12.7	13.5	12.9
产 业	**Industry**					
农 业	**Agriculture**					
农林牧渔业产值结构	Gross Output Value of Farming, Forestry, Animal Husbandry and Fishery	100.0	100.0	100.0	100.0	100.0
农 业	Farming	60.3	63.9	59.3	55.3	54.3
林 业	Forestry	2.8	2.7	2.6	3.0	3.0
牧 业	Animal Husbandry	34.5	30.9	34.4	36.4	37.7
渔 业	Fishery	2.4	2.5	3.7	3.7	3.5
农林牧渔服务业	Agricultural Services				1.6	1.5
工 业	**Industry**					
规模以上工业增加值结构	Value-added of Industrial Enterprises above Designated Size			100.0	100.0	100.0
轻工业	Light Industry			36.1	35.4	32.0
重工业	Heavy Industry			63.9	64.6	68.0
运输业	**Transportation**					
货运量结构	Freight Traffic	100.0	100.0	100.0	100.0	100.0
#铁 路	Railway	13.0	12.1	10.2	10.2	9.8
公 路	Highway	80.1	78.3	84.4	83.3	82.6
水 运	Waterway	6.9	9.6	5.4	6.5	7.6
国内商业	**Domestic Trade**					
社会消费品零售总额结构	Retail Sales of Consumer Goods	100.0	100.0	100.0	100.0	100.0
市	City	57.8	58.1	56.2	57.7	61.5
县	County	13.5	12.9	13.8	13.5	11.3
县以下	Below County Level	28.7	29.0	30.0	28.8	27.2
对外经济贸易	**Foreign Relations and Trade**					
实际利用外资结构	Actual Utilization of Foreign Capital	100.0	100.0	100.0	100.0	100.0
对外借款	Foreign Loans	33.2	47.0	28.8	44.8	40.3
外商直接投资	Foreign Direct Investment	61.6	49.6	70.8	54.9	59.4
外商其他投资	Other Foreign Investment	5.2	3.4	0.4	0.3	0.3
进出口总值结构	Imports and Exports	100.0	100.0	100.0	100.0	100.0
进 口	Imports	40.3	62.6	44.3	38.9	45.8
出 口	Exports	59.7	37.4	55.7	61.1	54.2
旅 游	**Tourism**					
国际旅游人数结构	International Tourists	100.0	100.0	100.0	100.0	100.0
#外国人	Foreigners	65.5	66.9	72.5	77.5	78.0
港澳台同胞	Compatriots from Hongkong, Macao and Taiwan	34.3	32.9	27.5	22.5	22.0

1-6 续表2 CONTINUED-2

单位：% (%)

指 标	Item	1995	1996	2000	2003	2004
教育、科技、文化	**Education, Science,Technology and Culture**					
教 育	**Education**					
在校学生结构	Student Enrollment	100.0	100.0	100.0	100.0	100.0
大学生	Colleges and Universities	1.9	2.0	2.9	5.2	6.1
中学生	Secondary Schools	29.2	27.8	36.2	38.4	39.4
小学生	Primary Schools	68.9	70.2	60.9	56.4	54.5
专任教师结构	Full-time Teachers	100.0	100.0	100.0	100.0	100.0
大 学	Colleges and Universities	4.6	4.7	4.7	6.9	7.8
中 学	Secondary Schools	38.1	36.8	41.5	43.1	43.7
小 学	Primary Schools	57.3	58.5	53.8	50.0	48.5
生活、环境	**Living Standards and Environment**					
生 活（抽样调查）	**Living Standards (sample survey)**					
城市居民消费结构	Consumption of Urban Households	100.0	100.0	100.0	100.0	100.0
#服务性消费支出	Expenditure for service				28.4	30.7
#食 品	Food	48.7	49.0	40.4	38.0	37.8
衣 着	Clothing	14.0	14.5	10.1	10.3	9.8
居 住	Residence	5.5	5.5	9.0	10.4	11.3
农村居民生活消费结构	Consumption for Living of Rural Households	100.0	100.0	100.0	100.0	100.0
#食 品	Food	64.7	63.2	53.6	52.5	56.0
衣 着	Clothing	5.3	5.5	4.4	4.5	4.3
居 住	Residence	12.7	13.2	14.3	13.4	10.8
卫 生	**Public Health**					
卫生技术人员结构	Medical Technical Personnel (person)	100.0	100.0	100.0	100.0	100.0
#执业(助理) 医师	Certified (Assisstant) Doctors	36.2	35.1	50.7	47.2	47.2
注册护士	Registration Nurses	21.7	22.0	23.4	26.2	26.1
卫生机构床位结构	Beds in Health Institutions			100.0	100.0	100.0
#县及县以上医院	At County Level and above			59.0	69.2	68.5
环 境	**Environment**					
治理工业污染资金使用结构	Uses of Fund in Industrial Pollution Treatment			100.0	100.0	100.0
治理废水	Waste Water Treatment			48.1	55.7	46.8
治理废气	Waste Gas Treatment			41.9	43.4	49.4
治理固体废物	Solid Waste Treatment			3.8	0.2	3.5
治理噪声	Noise Abatement			0.8	0.7	0.2
其 他	Others			5.4	...	0.1

注：2002年卫生统计指标名称变更，统计口径变化，不可与往年同比。从2002年起卫生技术人员、床位统计范围不包括医学院校、卫生学校和计生站。卫生技术人员中，2002年以前统计口径为医生和护师、护士，2002年起为执业医师和注册护士。

Note: Indices of health care since 2002 had been changed, and their range were not comparable with previous years. Since 2002, institutes, hospital beds and medical technical personnel didn't cover medical colleges, medical schools and family planning centers. The statistical range refers to doctors and junior & senior nurses before 2002, whereas to doctors with authorization and registered nurses since 2002.

1—7 人均主要社会经济活动水平
Per Capita Main Social and Economic Activities

单位：元 (yuan)

指 标	Item	1995	1996	2000	2003	2004
国民经济核算	**National EconomicAccounting**					
本市生产总值(现价)	Gross Domestic Product (current prices)	3372	3914	5157	7209 (8077)	8496 (9608)
主要农产品产量（公斤）	**Output of Major Farm Products (kg)**					
粮 食	Grain	385	389	367	348	365
油 料	Oil-bearing Crops	8	11	10	12	13
肉 类	Meat	42	44	47	51	53
#猪 肉	Pork	38	38	40	42	43
水产品	Aquatic Products	4	5	6	7	8
水 果	Fruit	20	19	27	41	44
主要工业产品产量（国有及规模以上工业）	**Output of Major Industrial Product (State-owned and Non-state-owned Industrial Enterprises over Designated Size)**					
原 煤(公斤)	Coal (kg)			373	475	554
天然气(立方米)	Natural Gas (cu.m)			126	151	164
发电量(千瓦时)	Electricity (kwh)			545	604	742
钢 材(公斤)	Steel Products (kg)			51	75	92
铝 材(公斤)	Aluminum Products (kg)			5	7	8
水 泥(公斤)	Cement (kg)			455	617	608
啤 酒(千升)	Beer (kiloliters)				14	15
卷 烟(支)	Cigarettes (unit)				1241	1231
国内商业	**Domestic Trade**					
社会消费品零售总额	Retail Sales of Consumer Goods	1242	1479	2088	2676	3384
财政、金融	**Public Finance and Financial Statistics**					
地方预算内财政收入	Local Financial Budgetary Revenue	153	182	339	663	964
城乡居民储蓄存款余额	Saving Deposits of Urban and Rural Residents	1337	1656	3511	6059	6964
职工工资、居民收入	**Wages and Income**					
城镇经济单位职工平均工资	Average Annual Wages of Staff and Workers	4508	5010	8020	12440	14357
城市居民人均可支配收入	Per Capita Disposable Income of Urban Households	4375	5023	6176	8094	9221
农村居民人均纯收入	Per Capita Net Income of Rural Households	1270	1479	1892	2215	2510

注：本表中括号内的本市人均生产总值按常住人口计算，城镇经济单位职工平均工资1998年及以后为在岗职工口径，城市、农村居民收入为抽样调查数，其他人均数按户籍人口计算。

Note: Per capita GDP in brackets is in terms of resident population. Average annual wages of staff and workers since 1998 refer to on-post staff and workers. Per capita income of urban and rural households is on basis of sample survey. And other per capita figures in this talbe are in terms of registration statistics.

1－8 平均每天主要社会经济活动
Average Daily Level of Main Social and Economic Activities

指　　标	Item	1995	1996	2000	2003	2004
每天创造的财富	**Daily Production**					
本市生产总值(万元)	Gross Domestic Product (10 000 yuan)	27657	32304	43543	61659	73024
第一产业	Primary Industry	7165	7805	7753	9215	11608
第二产业	Secondary Industry	11704	13513	18014	26775	32363
#工　业	Industry	10087	11590	14452	21051	25411
第三产业	Tertiary Industry	8788	10986	17776	25668	29053
地方预算内财政收入(万元)	Local Financial Budgetary Revenue (10 000 yuan)	1254	1500	2862	5669	8286
粮　食（吨）	Grain (ton)	31608	32113	30992	29786	31358
油　料（吨）	Oil-bearing Crops (ton)	688	647	851	1048	1144
肉　类（吨）	Meat (ton)	3485	3560	3943	4370	4576
#猪　肉	Pork	3076	3128	3355	3612	3738
水产品（吨）	Aquatic Products (ton)	332	385	549	616	656
原　煤（吨）	Coal (ton)			31504	40663	47622
天然气(万立方米)	Natural Gas (10 000 cu.m)			1068	1296	1413
发电量(万千瓦小时)	Electricity (10 000 kwh)			4600	5168	6379
钢　材（吨）	Steel Products (ton)			4301	6445	7893
水　泥（吨）	Cement (ton)			38432	52795	52225
汽　车（辆）	Motor Vehicles (unit)			674	1108	1190
摩托车(辆)	Motorcycles (unit)			5235	12091	12961
每天消费量	**Daily Consumption**					
最终消费（万元）	Final Consumption Expenditures (10 000 yuan)			27244	38141	43274
居民消费	Household Consumption Expenditure			20822	26882	30905
农　村	Agricultural Households			9204	10445	11852
城　镇	Non-agricultural Households			11618	16437	19054
政府消费	Government Consumption Expenditure			6422	11258	12360
能源消费量（万吨标准煤）	Energy Consumption (10 000 tons of SCE)	4.87	5.13	6.39	7.36	8.05
地方预算内财政支出(万元)	Local Financial Budgetary Expenditures (10 000 yuan)	1814	2176	5547	10722	13291
社会消费品零售总额（万元）	Retail Sales of Consumer Goods (10 000 yuan)	10187	12205	17632	22891	29082
每天其他经济活动	**Other Daily Economic Activities**					
资本形成总额(万元)	Gross Capital Formation (10 000 yuan)			18920	36005	44954
固定资产形成	Fixed Capital Formation			17354	34105	42548
存货增加	Changes in Inventory			1566	1901	2406
客运量(万人)	Passenger Traffic (10 000 persons)	108.85	118.15	157.99	162.11	177.19
货运量(万吨)	Freight Traffic (10 000 tons)	62.45	70.73	76.41	93.46	104.57
港口货物吞吐量(万吨)	Freight Handled at Ports (10 000 tons)	2.34	2.95	6.71	8.89	12.44
邮电业务总量(万元)	Business Volume of Postal and Telecommunication Services (10 000 yuan)	300	438	2351	3324	4621
进出口总额(万美元)	Total Imports and Exports (USD 10 000)	388.77	434.25	489.04	710.96	1056.71
进口总额	Imports	156.44	271.78	216.44	276.71	483.84
出口总额	Exports	232.33	162.47	272.60	434.25	572.88
实际利用外资(万美元)	Actual Utilization of Foreign Capital (USD 10 000)	168.77	121.10	94.52	155.34	186.85
国际旅游人数(人)	International Tourists (person)	392	443	729	643	1190
居民新增储蓄额（万元）	Outstand Amount of Saving Deposits (10 000 yuan)	3179	2719	4829	8262	8032

注：1）本表价值指标除邮电业务总量按不变价计算外，其余均按当年价计算；邮电业务总量2001年前为1990年不变价，2001年及以后为2000年不变价口径。
2）工业产品产量为国有及规模以上非国有工业企业数。

Note: a) Figures in value terms in this table are at current prices, except that total business volume from postal and telecommunication services before 2001 were in terms of 1990 constant price, and since 2001 were in terms of 2000 constant price.
b) The output of industrial products is the figures of state-owned industrial enterprises and non-state-owned industrial enterprises above designated size.

主要统计指标解释

行政区划 指国家对行政区域的划分。根据宪法规定，我国的行政区划分如下：（1）全国分为省、自治区、直辖市；（2）省、自治区分为自治州、县、自治县、市；（3）自治州分为县、自治县、市；（4）县、自治县分为乡、民族乡、镇；（5）直辖市和较大的市分为区、县；（6）国家在必要时设立的特别行政区。

国土 指中华人民共和国国家管辖下的领土、领海和领空。

气候 指地球与大气之间长期能量交换与质量交换所形成的一种自然环境状态，它是多种因素综合作用的结果。气候既是人类生活和生产的环境要素之一，又是供给人类生活和生产的重要资源。气温、降水、湿度等气象要素的多年平均值是用来描述一个地区气候状况的主要参数，而各种气象要素某年、某月的平均值（或总量）则可以反映出该时期天气气候状况的重要特征。

自然资源 指人类可以直接从自然界获得，并用于生产和生活的物质资源。自然资源一般可以分成可再生资源和非再生资源两大类。可再生资源指在较短时间内可以再生、可以循环利用的资源，包括土地资源、水资源、气候资源、生物资源和海洋资源等。非再生资源指在使用后不能再生的资源，包括矿产资源和地热能源。

土地资源 土地指陆地的表层部分，它主要由岩石、岩石的风化物和土壤构成。土地资源按利用类型可以分为农用地、建筑用地和未利用地。农用地包括耕地、园地、林地、牧草地和水面。建筑用地包括居民点及工矿用地、交通用地和水利设施用地。未利用地指农用地和建筑用地以外的土地，包括滩涂、荒漠、戈壁、冰川和石山等。

耕地面积 指经过开垦用以种植各种农作物并经常进行耕耘的土地面积，包括有作物的土地面积、休闲地、新开荒地和抛荒未满三年的土地面积。

林业用地面积 指生长乔木、竹类、灌木、沿海红树林等林木的土地面积，包括有林地、灌木林、疏林地、未成林造林地、迹地、苗圃等。

草地面积 指牧区和农区用于放牧牲畜或割草，植被盖度在5%以上的草原、草坡、草山等面积。包括天然的和人工种植或改良的草地面积。

森林资源 指森林、林木、林地以及依托森林、林木、林地自下而上的野生动物、植物和微生物。林木指树木和竹子。森林指以乔木为主体的植物群落，是集生的乔木及与共同作用的植物、动物、微生物和土壤、气候等的总体。

活立木总蓄积量 指一定范围内土地上全部树木蓄积的总量，包括森林蓄积、疏林蓄积、散生木蓄积和四旁（村旁、路旁、水旁、宅旁）树蓄积。

森林面积 指由乔木树种构成，郁闭度0.2以上（含0.2）的林地或冠幅宽度10米以上的林带的面积，即有林地面积。森林面积包括天然起源和人工起源的针叶林面积、阔叶林面积、针阔混交林面积和竹林面积，不包括灌木林地面积和疏林地面积。

森林蓄积量 指一定森林面积上存在着的林木树干部分的总材积。它是反映一个国家或地区森林资源总规模和水平的基本指标之一，也是反映森林资源的丰富程度、衡量森林生态环境优劣的重要依据。

森林覆盖率 指一个国家或地区森林面积占土地面积的百分比。在计算森林覆盖率时，森林面积包括郁闭度 0.2 以上的乔木林地面积和竹林地面积、国家特别规定的灌木林地面积、农田林网以及四旁林木的覆盖面积。森林覆盖率是反映森林资源的丰富程度和生态平衡状况的重要指标。计算公式为：

森林覆盖率（%）=森林面积/土地总面积×100%

水资源 水在自然界中以固体、液体和气态三种聚集状态存在，分布于海洋、陆地（包括土壤）以及大气之中，通过水循环形成水资源。水资源包括经人类控制并直接可供灌溉、发电、给水、航运、养殖等用途的地表水和地下水，以及江河、湖泊、井、泉、潮汐、港湾和养殖水域等。水资源是发展国民经济不可缺少的重要自然资源。

地表水和地下水 陆地上的水因空间分布不同，可以分为地表水和地下水。地表水指分别存在于河流、湖泊、沼泽、冰川和冰盖等水体中水分的总称，又称陆地水。地下水指储存在地面以下饱和岩土孔隙、裂隙及溶洞中的水。

径流 指大气降水扣除损耗外，从地表和地下向流域出口断面汇集的水流。径流可分为地表径流、地下径流和壤中流。地表径流指沿地表向河流、湖泊、沼泽、海洋等汇集的水流；地下径流指沿潜水层或隔水层间的含水层，向河流、湖泊、沼泽、海洋等汇集的地下水水流。

径流量 指在一定时段内通过河流某一过水断面的水量，用以反映一个国家或地区水资源的丰歉程度。计算公式为：径流量=降水量－蒸发量

矿产资源 矿产指由地质作用形成，富集于地壳中或出露于地表达到工农业利用要求的有用矿物。矿产是一种重要的自然资源，是社会发展的重要物质基础。

矿产基础储量 基础储量是查明矿产资源的一部分。它能满足现行采矿和生产所需的指标要求，是控制的、探明的并通过可行性或预可行性研究认为属于经济的、边界经济的部分，用未扣除设计、采矿损失的数量表示。

气温 指空气的温度，我国一般以摄氏度（℃）为单位表示。气象观测的温度表是放在离地面约 1.5 米处通风良好的百叶箱里测量的，因此，通常说的气温指的是离地面 1.5 米处百叶箱的温度。其统计计算方法为：

月平均气温是全月各日的平均气温相加，除以该月的天数而得。

年平均气温是将 12 个月的月平均气温累加后除以 12 而得。

相对湿度 指空气中实际水气压与当时气温下的饱和水气压之比。其统计方法与气温相同。

降水量 指从天空降落到地面的液态或固态（经融化后）水，未经蒸发、渗透、流失而在地面上积聚的深度。其统计计算方法为：

月降水量是将全月各日的降水量累加而得。

年降水量是将 12 个月的月降水量累加而得。

日照时数 指太阳实际照射地面的时间。其统计方法与降水量相同。

可比价格 指计算各种总量指标所采用的扣除了价格变动因素的价格，可进行不同时期总量指标的对比。按可比价格计算总量指标有两种方法：一种是直接用产品产量乘某一年的不变价格计算；另一种是用价格指数进行缩减。

不变价格 指以同类产品某年的平均价格作为固定价格，用于计算各年的产品价值。按不变价格计算的产品价值消除了价格变动因素，不同时期对比可以反映生产的发展速度。新中国成立后，随着工农业产品价格水平的变化，国家统计局先后五次制定了全国统一的工业产品不变价格和农业产品不变价格。从 1952 年到 1957 年使用 1952 年工（农）业产品不变价格，从 1957 年到 1970 年使用 1957 年不变价格，从 1971 年到 1980 年使用 1970 年不变价格，从 1981 年到 1990 年使用 1980 年不变价格，从 1991 年开始使用 1990 年不变价格。

平均增长速度 我国计算平均增长速度有两种方法：一种是习惯上经常使用的"水平法"，又称几何平均法，是以间隔期最后一年的水平同基期水平对比来计算平均每年增长（或下降）速度；另一种是"累计法"，又称代数平均法或方程法，是以间隔期内各年水平的总和同基期水平对比来计算平均每年增长（或下降）速度。在一般正常情况下，两种方法计算的平均每年增长速度比较接近，但在经济发展不平衡、出现大起大落时，两种方法计算的结果差别较大。

本《年鉴》内所列的平均增长速度，一般使用"水平法"计算。从某年到某年平均增长速度的年份，均不包括基期年在内。如建国四十三年的平均增长速度是以 1949 年为基期计算的，则写为 1950—1992 年平均增长速度，其余类推。

国民经济行业分类 自 2003 年定期报表开始使用新的《国民经济行业分类》（GB/T4754-2002）该分类是由国家统计局组织修订，经国家质量监督检验检疫总局批准，于 2002 年 5 月 10 日发布实施。这次修订是在 1994 年分类标准的基础上，参照联合国《全部经济活动的国际标准产业分类》（ISIC/Rev.3）进行的。修订后的《国民经济行业分类》（GB/T4754-2002）共有门类 20 个，大类 95 个，中类 396 个，小类 913 个。新增门类 4 个，大类增加 3 个，中类增加 28 个，小类增加 67 个。

企业（单位）登记注册类型 是以在工商行政管理机关登记注册的各类企业为划分对象，以工商行政管理部门对企业登记注册的类型为依据，将企业登记注册类型分为内资企业、港澳台商投资企业和外商投资企业三大类。内资企业包括国有企业、集体企业、股份合作企业、联营企业、有限责任公司、股份有限公司、私营公司和其他企业，港澳台商投资企业和外商投资企业分别包括合资经营企业、合作经营企业、独资经营企业和股份有限公司。对不在工商行政管理部门进行登记注册的行政机关、事业单位和社会团体，主要按其经费来源和管理方式进行划分。

国有企业 指企业全部资产归国家所有，并按《中华人民共和国企业法人登记管理条例》规定登记注册的非公司制的经济组织。不包括有限责任公司中的国有独资公司。

集体企业 指企业资产归集体所有，并按《中华人民共和国企业法人登记管理条例》规定登记注册的经济组织。

股份合作企业 指以合作制为基础，由企业职工共同出资入股，吸收一定比例的社会资产投资组建，实行自主经营，自负盈亏，共同劳动，民主管理，按劳分配与按股份红相结合的一种集体经济组织。

联营企业 指两个及两个以上相同或不同所有制性质的企业法人或事业单位法人，按自愿、平等、互利的原则，共同投资组成的经济组织。联营企业包括国有联营企业、集体联营企业、国有与集体联营企业和其他联营企业。

有限责任公司 指根据《中华人民共和国公司登记管理条例》规定登记注册，由两个以上、五十个以下的股东共同出资，每个股东以其所认缴的出资额对公司承担有限责任，公司以其全部资产对其债务承担责任的经济组织。有限责任公司包括国有独资公司以及其他有限责任公司。

股份有限公司 指根据《中华人民共和国公司登记管理条例》规定登记注册，其全部注册资本由等额股份构成并通过发行股票筹集资本，股东以其认购的股份对公司承担有限责任，公司以其全部资产对其债务承担责任的经济组织。

私营企业 指由自然人投资设立或由自然人控股，以雇用劳动为基础的营利性经济组织。包括按照《公司法》、《合伙企业法》、《私营企业暂行条例》规定登记注册的私营有限责任公司、私营股份有限公司、私营合伙企业和私营独资企业。

其他内资企业 指上述企业之外的其他内资经济组织。

与港澳台商合资经营企业 指港澳台地区投资者与内地企业依照《中华人民共和国中外合资经营企业法》及有关法律的规定，按合同规定的比例投资设立、分享利润和分担风险的企业。

与港澳台商合作经营企业 指港澳台地区投资者与内地企业依照《中华人民共和国中外合作经营企业法》及有关法律的规定，依照合作合同的约定进行投资或提供条件设立、分配利润和分担风险的企业。

港澳台商独资经营企业 指依照《中华人民共和国外资企业法》及有关法律的规定，在内地由港澳台地区投资者全额投资设立的企业。

港澳台商投资股份有限公司 指根据国家有关规定，经外经贸部依法批准设立，其中港、澳、台商的股本占公司注册资本的比例达25%以上的股份有限公司。凡其中港、澳、台商的股本占公司注册资本的比例小于25%的，属于内资企业中的股份有限公司。

中外合资经营企业 指外国企业或外国人与中国内地企业依照《中华人民共和国中外合资经营企业法》及有关法律的规定，按合同规定的比例投资设立、分配利润和分担风险的企业。

中外合作经营企业 指外国企业或外国人与中国内地企业依照《中华人民共和国中外合作经营企业法》及有关法律的规定，依照合作合同的约定进行投资或提供条件设立、分配利润和分担风险的企业。

外资企业 指依照《中华人民共和国外资企业法》及有关法律的规定，在中国内地由外国投资者全额投资设立的企业。

外商投资股份有限公司 指根据国家有关规定，经外经贸部依法批准设立，其中外资的股本占公司注册资本的比例达25%以上的股份有限公司。凡其中外资股本占公司注册资本的比例小于25%的，属于内资企业中的股份有限公司。

行政机关、事业单位和社会团体 参照企业登记注册类型，主要按其经费来源和管理方式划分。具体规定如下：

（1）行政机关：包括国家机关和政党机关，原则上均列为"国有"。但有特殊规定的，如供销社等，列为"集体"。

（2）事业单位：包括经国家机构编制部门和有关业务主管部门批准成立的各类事业单位，不包括实行企业化管理的事业单位。事业单位的划分办法如下：

①由国家财政预算拨款或列入财政预算外资金管理以及经费主要来源于国有主管部门或国有上级单位的事

业单位，列为“国有”。

②经费主要来源于集体单位的事业单位，列为“集体”。

③公民个人（或个人合伙）开办的事业单位，列为“私营”。

④上述以外的其他事业单位，如果其经费来源不明确，按管理方式进行归类。

（3）社会团体：包括经民政部门批准成立以及未纳入社会团体管理条例范围的工会、妇联等各类社会团体。社会团体的划分办法如下：

①未纳入民政部社会团体管理条例范围的工会、妇联、共青团、青联、工商联、科协、侨联等社会团体，国家拨款设立的基金会或基金管理组织以及经费主要来源于国有业务主管部门或国有上级单位的社会团体，列为“国有”。

②经费主要来源于集体单位的社会团体。

③公民个人（或个人合伙）开办的社会团体，划为“私营”。

④上述以外的其他社会团体，如果其经费来源不明确，改按管理方式进行归类。

Explanatory Notes on Main Statistical Indicators

Administrative Division refers to the division of administrative areas by the state. The Constitution of the People's Republic of China stipulates that the administrative areas in China are divided as: 1) The whole country is divided into provinces, autonomous regions and municipalities directly under the central government; 2) Provinces and autonomous regions are divided into autonomous prefectures, counties, autonomous counties and cities; 3) Autonomous prefectures are divided into counties, autonomous counties and cities; 4) Counties and autonomous counties are divided into townships, nationality townships and towns; 5)Municipalities and large cities are divided into districts and counties, 6)The state shall, when necessary, establish special administrative regions.

Territory refers to territorial land, sea and air space under the administration of the People's Republic of China.

Climate refers to the natural environmental status formed by the long-time exchange of energy and mass between the earth and the air, and is the results of interaction of many factors. Climate is both one of the environment factors and the important resources for the living and production activities of the human being. The average values across several years of meteorological factors such as temperature, rainfall and humidity are used as important parameters to describe the climate of a region, while the average values (or total values) of a given year of month of meteorological factors reflect the key characteristics of climate for that period of time.

Natural Resources refer to material resources that could be obtained from the nature by human being and used for production and living. Natural resources in general can be classified as renewable resources and non-renewable resources. Renewable resources refer to resources that could be renewed and recycled during a relatively short period of time, including land resource, water resource, climate resource, biology resource and marine resource. Non-renewable resources include resources that could not be renewed, such as minerals and geothermal resource.

Land Resource Land refers to the surface of the earth, consisting of mainly rocks and its weathering and earth. Land resource can be classified, by its utilization, as land for agriculture, land for construction and unused land. Land for agriculture included cultivated land, plantation land, forestland, grassland and waters. Land for construction included land for residential purpose, for manufacturing and mining, for transportation and for water-conservancy projects. Unused land refers to land other than land for agriculture and construction, including beaches, deserts, Gobi glaciers and rock mountains.

Area of Cultivated Land refers to area of land reclaimed for the regular cultivation of various farm crops, including cropcover land, fallow, newly reclaimed land and land laid idle for less than 3 years.

Area of Afforestated Land refer of Land for trees Bamboo, bushes and mangrove, including forest-cover land, bush-covered land, sparse forest land, land planned for afforestation and nurseries of young trees.

Area of Grassland refers to areas of grassland, grass-slopes and grass-covered hills with a vegetation-covering rate of over 5% that are used for animal husbandry or harvesting of grass. It includes natural, cultivated and improved grassland areas.

Forest Resource refers to forests, trees, forestland and wild animals, plants and microorganism that live on forest and trees. Trees include trees and bamboo. Forest refers to the population of clusters of trees and other plants, animals and microorganism as well as the earth and climate that have interactions with the trees.

Total Standing Stock Volume refers to the total stock volume of trees growing in land, including trees in forest, tress in sparse forest, scattered trees and trees planted by the side of farm houses and along the roads, rivers and fields.

Forest Area refers to the area of forestland where trees and bamboo grow with canopy density above 0.2, including land of natural woods and planted woods, but excluding bush land and thin forestland. It reflects the total areas of afforestation.

Stock Volume of Forest refers to total stock volume of wood growing in forest area, which shows the total size and level of forest resources of a country or a region. It is also an important indicator illustration the richness of forest resource and the status of forest ecological environment.

Forest Coverage Rate refers to the ratio to the ratio of area of afforested land to total land area. This indicator shows the forest resources and afforestation progress of a country or a region. According to regulations of the government, in addition to afforested land, the area of bush forest, the area of forest land inside farm land and the area of trees planted by the side of farm houses and along the roads, rivers and fields should also be included in the area of afforested land in the calculation of the forest coverage-rate. The formula for calculation forest coverage rate is as follows.

Forestry coverage rate (%) = (Area of Afforested Land / Area of Total Land) × 100%

Water Resource Water exists in the nature in solid, liquid and gaseous states, is distributed in the ocean, land (including earth) and air, and constitutes the water resource through the circulation of water. Water resource includes the surface water and under-ground water that is controlled by the human being for irrigation, power-generation, water supply, navigation and cultivation. It also includes rivers, Lakes, wells, springs, tides, and gulf and water area for cultivation. Water resource as an important natural resource is indispensable for the development of the national economy.

Surface Water and Underground Water Water on earth can be divided into surface water and underground water according to its distribution. Surface water refers to moisture exists in rivers, lakes, swamps, glaciers, icecaps and so on. It is also called land water. The underground water refers to water deposited under-ground in the cranny and the hole of saturated rock soil and in the water-eroded cave.

Runoff refers to the water gathered at the way out of the cross section of drainage area either from the surface or underground after deducting the wastage of the precipitation. Runoff can be divided into surface runoff, underground runoff and within soil runoff. Surface runoff refers to water flow to the rivers, lakes, swamps, and seas on the surface of the earth. Underground runoff refers to water flow to rivers, swamps, and seas through the water-bearing stratum of confined layer or unconfined layer.

Volume of Runoff refers to the total volume of water running through a certain cross section of a river during a certain period of time, reflecting the water resource condition in a country or a region. The formula for calculating volume or runoff is as follows: *Runoff=Precipitation-Evaporation*

Mineral Resources refer to useful minerals that can be used for industrial or agricultural purposes enriched in lithosphere or on earth due to the geological process. Minerals are important natural resources, and important material base for social development.

Ensured Mineral Reserves refer to the actual mineral reserves, which equal to the proven mineral reserves (including industrial reserves and prospective reserves) minus extracted parts and underground losses.

Temperature refers to the air temperature. China uses centigrade (°C) as the unit. The thermometry used for weather observation is put in a breezy shutter, which is 1.5 meters high from the ground. Therefore, the commonly used temperature refers to the temperature in the breezy shutter 1.5 meters away from the ground. The calculation method is as follows:

Monthly average temperature is the summation of average daily temperature of one month divided by the actual days of that particular month.

Annual average temperature is the summation of monthly average of a year divided by 12 months.

Relative Humidity refers to the ratio of actual water vapor pressure to the saturation water vapor pressure under the current temperature. The calculation method is the same as that of temperature.

Volume of Precipitation refers to the deepness of liquid state of solid state (thawed) water falling from the sky to the ground that has not been evaporated, infiltrated or run off. The calculation method is as follows:

Monthly precipitation is the summation of daily precipitation of a month.

Annual precipitation is the summation of 12 months' precipitation of a year.

Sunshine Hours refer to the actual hours of sun irradiating the earth. The calculation method is the same as that of the precipitation.

Comparable Prices refer to prices that are used to remove the factors of price change in calculating economic aggregates, so as to facilitate comparison of aggregates over time. Two methods are used for calculating economic aggregates at comparable prices: (a) Multiplying the output of products by their constant prices of certain year. (b) Deflation of data at current prices by relevant price index.

Constant Price refers to the average price of a given product in certain year, which is used for comparison of output value over time. As the output value at constant prices removers the factor of price changes, it reflects the trend of production development over time. Since 1949,with the changes in general price level, the State Statistical Bureau has issued nationally unified constant prices five times: the 1952 constant prices for 1949-1957;the 1957 constant prices for 1957-1971;the 1970 constant prices for 1971-1981;the 1980 constant prices for 1981-1990; and the 1990 constant prices have been used since 1991.

Average Annual Growth Rate Two methods for calculating average annual growth rate are applied in China, one is often called level approach, or the method of calculating geometric average, which is derived by comparing the level of the last year of the interval with that of the beginning year; the other is called accumulative approach or algebraic average or equation method, which is derived by the summation of the actual figure of each year in the interval divided by the figure in the base year. Usually the results calculated by the two methods are fairly close, but they differed sharply when uneven economic development occurred with striking fluctuations in growth.

The average annual growth rates listed in this statistical yearbook are generally calculated by "level approach". The base years are not listed when the years are listed for average annual growth rates. For instance, the average annual growth rate of 43 years since 1949 is listed as average annual growth rate of 1950-1992 without listing the base year 1949.And the analogy of this is also the same for the rest of the years.

Industrial Classification of the National Economy The new *Industrial Classification of the National Economy*

(GB/T 4754-2002) is introduced starting from the compilation of 2003 annual statistics. The revision of the 1994 classification was organized by the National Bureau of Statistics taking into consideration of the *International Standards of the Industrial Classification of All Economic Activities (ISIC/Rev.3)* of the United Nations, and the new Classification was promulgated by the National Administration of Quality Supervision, Inspection and Quarantine on May 10, 2002. The revised version of the *Industrial Classification of the National Economy (GB/T 4754-2002)* is composed of 20 major divisions, 95 divisions, 396 major groups and 913 groups, including 4 new major divisions, 3 new divisions, 28 major groups and 67 groups.

Registration Status of Enterprises is classified into 3 categories, namely domestic-funded enterprises, enterprises with foreign investment, in the light of the registration status of an enterprise in industrial and commercial administration agencies. Domestic-funded enterprises include state-owned enterprises, collective-owned enterprises, cooperative enterprises, joint ownership enterprises, limited liability corporations, share-holding corporations Ltd., private enterprises and other enterprises. Included in the enterprises with investment from Hong Kong, Macao and Taiwan and enterprises with foreign investment are joint-venture enterprises, cooperative enterprises, sole investment enterprises and share-holding corporations Ltd. For government agencies, institutions and social organizations that are not requested to register in industrial and commercial administration agencies, they are classified mainly by their sources of funds and way of management.

State-owned Enterprises refer to non-corporation economic units where the entire assets are owned by the state and which have registered in accordance with the *Regulation of the People's Republic of China on the Management of Registration of Corporate Enterprises*. Excluded from this category are sole state-funded corporations in the limited liability corporations.

Collective-owned Enterprises refer to economic units where the assets are owned collectively and which have registered in accordance with the *Regulation of the People's Republic of China on the Management of Registration of Corporate Enterprises*.

Cooperative Enterprises refer to a form of collective economic units (enterprises) where capitals come mainly from employees as their shares, with certain proportion of capital from the outside, where production is organized on the basis of independent operation, independent accounting for profits and losses, joint work, democratic management, and a distribution system that integrates remuneration according to work with dividend according to capital share.

Joint Ownership Enterprises refer to economic units established by two or more corporate enterprises or corporate institutions of the same or different ownership, through joint investment on the basis of equality, voluntary participation and mutual benefits. They include state joint ownership enterprises, collective joint ownership enterprises, joint state-collective enterprises, other joint ownership enterprises.

Limited Liability Corporations refer to economic units established with investment from 2-50 investors and registered in accordance with the *Regulation of the People's Republic of China on the Management of Registration of Corporations*, each investor bearing limited liability to the corporation depending on its share of investment, and the corporation bearing liability to its debt to the maximum of its total assets. Limited liability corporations include exclusive state-funded limited liability corporations and other limited liability corporations.

Share holding Corporations Ltd. refer to economic units registered in accordance with the *Regulation of the People's Republic of China on the Management of Registration of Corporations*, with total registered capitals divided into equal shares and raised through issuing stocks. Each investor bears limited liability to the corporation depending on the holding of shares, and the corporation bears liability to its debt to the maximum of its total assets.

Private Enterprises refer to profit-making economic units invested and established by natural persons, or controlled by natural persons using employed labor. Included in this category are private limited liability corporations, private share-holding corporations Ltd., private partnership enterprises and private-funded enterprises registered in accordance with the *Corporation Law, Partnership Enterprises Law and Interim Regulations on Private Enterprise.*

Other Domestic-funded Enterprises refer to domestic-funded economic units other than those mentioned above.

Joint-venture Enterprises with Funds from Hong Kong, Macao and Taiwan refer to enterprises jointly established by invertors from Hong Kong, Macao and Taiwan with enterprises in the mainland of China in accordance with the *Law of the People's Republic of China on Sino-foreign Joint Venture Enterprises* and other relevant laws, where the share of investment, profits and risks is stipulated in the contract.

Cooperative Enterprises with Funds from Hong Kong Macau and Taiwan established by investors from Hong Kong, Macau and Taiwan with enterprises in the mainland of China in accordance with the *Law of the People's Republic of China on Sino-foreign Cooperative Enterprises* and other relevant laws, where the investment or provision of facilities, and the share of profits and risks is stipulated in the cooperative contract.

Enterprises with Sole (exclusive) Investment from Hong Kong, Macau and Taiwan refer to enterprises established in the mainland of China with exclusive investment from investors from Hong Kong, Macau and Taiwan in accordance with the *Law of the People's Republic of China on Foreign-Funded Enterprises* and other relevant laws.

Share-holding Corporations Ltd. with Investment from Hong Kong, Macau and Taiwan refer to share-holding corporations Ltd. established with the approval from the former Ministry of Foreign Trade and Economic Relations in line with relevant state regulations, where the share of investment from Hong Kong, Macau or Taiwan businessmen exceeds 25% of the total registered capital of the corporation. In case the share of investment from Hong Kong, Macau or Taiwan is less than 25% of the total registered capital, the enterprise is to be classified as domestic-funded share-holding corporation Ltd.

Joint-venture Enterprises with Foreign Investment refer to enterprises jointly established by foreign enterprises or foreigners with enterprises in the mainland of China in accordance with the *Law of the People's Republic of China on Sino-foreign Joint Venture Enterprises* and other relevant laws, where the share of investment, profits and risks is stipulated in the contract.

Cooperation Enterprises with Foreign Investment refer to enterprises jointly established by foreign enterprises or foreigners with enterprises in the mainland of China in accordance with the *Law of the People's Republic of China on Sino-foreign Cooperative Enterprises* and other relevant laws, where the investment or provision of facilities, and the share of profits and risks is stipulated in the cooperative contract.

Enterprises with Sole (exclusive) Foreign Investment refer to enterprises established in the mainland of China with exclusive investment from foreign investors in accordance with the *Law of the People's Republic of China on Foreign-Funded Enterprises* and other relevant laws.

Share-holding Corporations Ltd. with Foreign Investment refer to share-holding corporations Ltd. established with the approval from the Ministry of Foreign Trade and Economic Relations in line with relevant state regulations, where the share of investment from foreign investors exceeds 25% of the total registered capital of the corporation. In case the share of foreign investment is less than 25% of the total registered capital, the enterprise is to be classified as domestic-funded share-holding corporation Ltd.

Government Agencies, Institutions and Social Organizations are classified into following categories by source of funds and way of management taking reference of the registration status of enterprises:

(1) Government agencies: include state and party agencies, classified in principle as “state-owned”. There are exceptions, such as supply and marketing cooperatives, which are classified, as “collective”.

(2) Institutions: include institutions of various types established with the approval by organization and staffing departments of the government, but exclude institutions where enterprise management system is introduced. Institutions are further classified as follows:

(a) Institutions whose main budget is listed in the government budget appropriations or extra-budget funds, or allocated from the budget of their competent government agencies. Such institutions are classified as “state-owned”.

(b) Institutions whose budget mainly comes from collective units. Such institutions are classified as “collective”.

(c) Institutions other than those mentioned above whose source of budget are not clear. Such institutions are classified by way of management.

(3) Social organizations: include social organizations established with the approval from the Ministry of Civil Affairs, and organizations that are not covered by social organization management regulations such as trade unions, women’s federations etc. Social organizations are further classified as follows:

(a) Social organizations that are not covered by social organization management regulations of the Ministry of Civil Affairs such as trade unions, women’s federations, communist youth leagues, youth associations, industrial and commerce associations, scientists associations, overseas Chinese associations, etc., foundations and fund management organizations established with founds from the state, and social organizations whose funds mainly come from the budget of their competent government agencies. Such institutions are classified as “state-owned”.

(b) Social organizations whose budget mainly comes from collective units. Such institutions are classified as “collective”.

(c) Social organizations established by individual or a group of citizens, which are classified as “private”.

(d) Social organizations other than those mentioned above whose source of budget are not clear. Such organizations are classified by way of management.

二 国民经济核算

NATIONAL ECONOMIC ACCOUNTING

简要说明 Brief Introduction

本章由本市生产总值资料和2002年投入产出资料构成。

本市生产总值资料包括各年度本市生产总值的绝对值、构成和指数，本市生产总值项目结构，按支出法计算的本市生产总值，以及重庆市三大经济区生产总值的绝对值和指数；2002年投入产出资料包括2002年投入产出基本流量表、直接消耗系数表和完全消耗系数表。本章资料由市统计局核算处提供。

This chapter is consist of two parts: Gross Domestic Product (GDP) and input-output in 2002. The part of GDP includes absolute figures, composition and indices of GDP of Chongqing total and the three economic zones as well, and GDP by Expenditure Approach. The other part of input-output in 2002 includes 3 tables: basic flow of input-output table, direct input coefficients of input-output table and total input coefficients of input-output table. All data in this chapter are calculated by Division of National Economic Accounting, Municipal Bureau of Statistics.

2－1 重庆市生产总值（1949－1978年）
Gross Domestic Product (1949-1978)

单位：亿元 (100 million yuan)

年 份 Year	本市生产总值 Gross Domestic Product	第一产业 Primary Industry	第二产业 Secondary Industry	工 业 Industry	建筑业 Construction	第三产业 Tertiary Industry	#交通运输仓储邮电通信业 Transportation, Storage, Postal and Telecommunication Services	#批发和零售贸易及餐饮业 Wholesale & Retail Trade and Catering Trade	本市人均生产总值（元） Per Capita GDP (yuan)
1949	13.89	9.74	2.71	2.50	0.21	1.44	0.61	0.65	87
1950	14.98	10.23	2.96	2.73	0.23	1.79	0.70	0.72	91
1951	15.90	10.72	3.35	3.09	0.26	1.83	0.75	0.79	94
1952	17.85	11.86	3.90	3.55	0.35	2.09	0.85	0.88	102
1953	21.08	13.57	5.55	4.88	0.67	1.96	0.80	0.90	119
1954	22.54	13.89	6.40	5.88	0.52	2.25	0.90	0.97	123
1955	23.02	13.86	6.88	6.45	0.43	2.28	0.92	0.98	123
1956	25.97	15.01	8.11	7.48	0.63	2.85	1.13	1.16	133
1957	26.10	13.12	9.73	9.14	0.59	3.25	1.30	1.32	129
1958	34.13	15.43	14.04	13.02	1.02	4.66	1.86	1.88	167
1959	37.21	12.02	19.64	18.13	1.51	5.55	2.19	2.21	181
1960	37.90	11.10	20.50	19.00	1.50	6.30	2.20	2.23	188
1961	28.21	10.35	11.96	11.32	0.64	5.90	1.98	1.95	150
1962	24.42	9.92	9.20	8.92	0.28	5.30	1.76	1.75	135
1963	27.08	12.08	9.76	9.34	0.42	5.24	1.62	1.66	146
1964	31.53	13.37	12.34	11.72	0.62	5.82	1.89	1.92	164
1965	36.98	16.21	14.85	13.77	1.08	5.92	1.91	1.95	184
1966	38.18	16.18	16.63	15.37	1.26	5.37	1.59	1.72	184
1967	33.37	15.21	12.84	12.01	0.83	5.32	1.53	1.81	158
1968	27.11	15.18	7.26	6.84	0.42	4.67	1.39	1.54	126
1969	31.39	14.75	11.08	10.32	0.76	5.56	1.58	1.78	141
1970	38.18	15.96	16.06	14.74	1.32	6.16	1.64	1.91	164
1971	43.82	16.71	20.38	18.97	1.41	6.73	1.72	2.02	183
1972	43.16	16.67	19.06	17.86	1.20	7.43	1.89	2.23	176
1973	43.96	18.14	17.93	16.49	1.44	7.89	2.09	2.29	174
1974	43.29	18.43	16.35	15.17	1.18	8.51	2.18	2.30	168
1975	50.44	18.81	21.71	20.16	1.55	9.92	2.45	2.54	190
1976	50.39	19.07	21.12	19.64	1.48	10.20	2.35	2.55	188
1977	56.67	21.74	24.22	22.21	2.01	10.71	2.57	2.73	208
1978	67.32	24.81	30.80	27.92	2.88	11.71	2.92	2.96	257

注：本表按当年价格计算，其中本市人均生产总值为按户籍人口计算值。

Note: The data in value terms in this table are calculated at current prices. Per capita GDP is calculated by household registered population.

2－2 重庆市生产总值构成（1949－1978年）
Composition of Gross Domestic Product (1949-1978)

单位：% (%)

年 份 Year	本市生产总值 Gross Domestic Product	第一产业 Primary Industry	第二产业 Secondary Industry	工 业 Industry	建筑业 Construction	第三产业 Tertiary Industry	#交通运输仓储邮电通信业 Transportation, Storage, Postal and Telecommunication Services	#批发和零售贸易及餐饮业 Wholesale & Retail Trade and Catering Trade
1949	100.0	70.1	19.5	18.0	1.5	10.4	4.4	4.7
1950	100.0	68.3	19.8	18.2	1.6	11.9	4.7	4.8
1951	100.0	67.4	21.1	19.4	1.7	11.5	4.7	5.0
1952	100.0	66.4	21.9	19.9	2.0	11.7	4.8	4.9
1953	100.0	64.4	26.3	23.1	3.2	9.3	3.8	4.3
1954	100.0	61.6	28.4	26.1	2.3	10.0	4.0	4.3
1955	100.0	60.2	29.9	28.0	1.9	9.9	4.0	4.3
1956	100.0	57.8	31.2	28.8	2.4	11.0	4.4	4.5
1957	100.0	50.3	37.3	35.0	2.3	12.4	5.0	5.1
1958	100.0	45.2	41.1	38.1	3.0	13.7	5.4	5.5
1959	100.0	32.3	52.8	48.7	4.1	14.9	5.9	5.9
1960	100.0	29.3	54.1	50.1	4.0	16.6	5.8	5.9
1961	100.0	36.7	42.4	40.1	2.3	20.9	7.0	6.9
1962	100.0	40.6	37.7	36.5	1.2	21.7	7.2	7.2
1963	100.0	44.6	36.0	34.5	1.5	19.4	6.0	6.1
1964	100.0	42.4	39.1	37.2	1.9	18.5	6.0	6.1
1965	100.0	43.8	40.2	37.3	2.9	16.0	5.2	5.3
1966	100.0	42.4	43.6	40.3	3.3	14.0	4.2	4.5
1967	100.0	45.6	38.5	36.0	2.5	15.9	4.6	5.4
1968	100.0	56.0	26.8	25.2	1.6	17.2	5.1	5.7
1969	100.0	47.0	35.3	32.9	2.4	17.7	5.0	5.7
1970	100.0	41.8	42.1	38.6	3.5	16.1	4.3	5.0
1971	100.0	38.1	46.5	43.3	3.2	15.4	3.9	4.6
1972	100.0	38.6	44.2	41.4	2.8	17.2	4.4	5.2
1973	100.0	41.3	40.8	37.5	3.3	17.9	4.8	5.2
1974	100.0	42.6	37.7	35.0	2.7	19.7	5.0	5.3
1975	100.0	37.3	43.0	40.0	3.0	19.7	4.9	5.0
1976	100.0	37.9	41.9	39.0	2.9	20.2	4.7	5.1
1977	100.0	38.4	42.7	39.2	3.5	18.9	4.5	4.8
1978	100.0	36.8	45.8	41.5	4.3	17.4	4.3	4.4

注：本表按当年价格计算。

Note: The data in value terms in this table are calculated at current prices.

2-3 重庆市生产总值指数（1949-1978年）（上年=100）
Indices of Gross Domestic Product (1949-1978) (Preceding Year=100)

年份 Year	本市生产总值 Gross Domestic Product	第一产业 Primary Industry	第二产业 Secondary Industry	工业 Industry	建筑业 Construction	第三产业 Tertiary Industry	#交通运输仓储邮电通信业 Transportation, Storage, Postal and Telecommunication Services	#批发和零售贸易及餐饮业 Wholesale & Retail Trade and Catering Trade	本市人均生产总值 Per Capita GDP
1949	100.0	100.0	100.0	100.0	100.0	100.0	100.0	100.0	100.0
1950	105.4	103.0	111.0	110.4	118.2	118.6	128.2	105.6	102.2
1951	103.2	104.0	111.7	112.1	107.7	92.4	93.4	98.9	100.5
1952	109.0	107.0	114.9	113.2	135.7	118.8	112.9	116.0	105.3
1953	111.0	107.0	139.4	134.9	184.2	114.3	109.4	124.8	109.7
1954	110.3	107.9	121.7	127.1	82.9	113.5	109.5	106.6	109.1
1955	102.5	101.5	110.5	113.0	82.8	99.7	94.8	99.3	99.9
1956	113.2	107.0	129.2	127.0	162.5	120.3	118.3	113.9	109.2
1957	102.1	100.1	111.1	113.1	87.2	110.2	112.4	104.9	98.3
1958	118.6	106.4	144.6	142.8	173.5	143.9	138.6	137.8	118.3
1959	97.2	76.0	138.6	138.1	145.8	119.2	107.0	103.4	97.7
1960	110.8	84.0	149.5	150.0	143.0	113.9	102.3	102.9	112.9
1961	64.7	77.8	53.8	55.0	39.0	64.1	69.5	61.5	68.2
1962	99.8	122.5	75.2	77.0	43.8	94.1	92.2	92.3	102.5
1963	114.6	121.0	106.3	105.0	147.6	108.6	103.5	112.6	112.2
1964	114.7	109.7	127.9	127.0	148.4	112.5	102.1	98.1	111.2
1965	114.3	112.9	125.0	122.0	182.6	102.7	102.7	110.1	110.4
1966	105.7	105.1	116.4	116.0	121.4	88.6	96.7	106.9	102.8
1967	90.0	95.0	79.0	80.0	67.6	96.6	96.6	102.7	87.6
1968	84.2	96.0	59.6	60.0	53.6	87.5	98.6	84.8	81.8
1969	111.8	99.0	146.5	144.9	173.0	118.3	117.0	114.8	109.0
1970	120.5	110.0	148.1	146.0	176.6	111.5	109.7	108.1	116.5
1971	111.6	102.5	127.2	129.0	107.1	108.5	104.4	105.0	108.2
1972	99.9	100.9	94.4	95.0	86.0	110.4	110.1	110.4	97.1
1973	103.0	108.3	94.8	93.0	121.2	105.7	104.8	102.1	100.5
1974	101.4	101.4	98.1	99.0	88.1	107.8	107.3	100.4	98.9
1975	111.5	95.6	133.9	134.0	132.4	116.2	108.5	110.0	108.6
1976	94.9	97.6	87.9	88.1	86.4	102.8	105.1	100.4	93.9
1977	119.7	113.6	135.8	134.0	160.6	105.1	107.5	107.2	118.5
1978	116.8	111.2	126.9	125.7	140.2	107.6	101.7	103.5	116.7

注：本表按可比价格计算，其中本市人均生产总值为按户籍人口计算值。

Note: The indices in this table are calculated at comparable prices. Per capita GDP is calculated by household registered population.

2—4 重庆市生产总值指数（1949—1978年）（1949年=100）
Indices of Gross Domestic Product (1949-1978) (1949=100)

年份 Year	本市生产总值 Gross Domestic Product	第一产业 Primary Industry	第二产业 Secondary Industry	工业 Industry	建筑业 Construction	第三产业 Tertiary Industry	#交通运输仓储邮电通信业 Transportation, Storage, Postal and Telecommunication Services	#批发和零售贸易及餐饮业 Wholesale & Retail Trade and Catering Trade	本市人均生产总值 Per Capita GDP
1949	100.0	100.0	100.0	100.0	100.0	100.0	100.0	100.0	100.0
1950	105.4	103.0	111.0	110.4	118.2	118.6	128.2	105.6	102.2
1951	108.8	107.1	124.0	123.8	127.3	109.6	119.7	104.4	102.7
1952	118.6	114.6	142.5	140.1	172.7	130.2	135.2	121.1	108.2
1953	131.6	122.6	198.6	189.0	318.2	148.8	147.9	151.2	118.6
1954	145.2	132.3	241.7	240.2	263.8	168.9	161.9	161.2	129.4
1955	148.8	134.3	267.1	271.4	218.4	168.4	153.5	160.0	129.3
1956	168.4	143.7	345.0	344.7	354.9	202.6	181.6	182.3	141.2
1957	172.0	143.9	383.3	389.9	309.5	223.2	204.1	191.2	138.8
1958	204.0	153.1	554.3	556.7	537.0	321.2	282.9	263.5	164.2
1959	198.2	116.3	768.3	768.9	782.9	382.9	302.7	272.5	160.4
1960	219.7	97.7	1148.6	1153.3	1119.6	436.1	309.7	280.4	181.1
1961	142.1	76.0	617.9	634.3	436.6	279.6	215.2	172.4	123.5
1962	141.8	93.1	464.7	488.4	191.2	263.1	198.5	159.1	126.6
1963	162.5	112.7	494.0	512.8	282.3	285.7	205.4	179.2	142.1
1964	186.4	123.6	631.8	651.3	418.9	321.4	209.7	175.8	158.0
1965	213.1	139.6	789.7	794.6	764.9	330.1	215.4	193.6	174.4
1966	225.2	146.7	919.2	921.7	928.6	292.5	208.3	206.9	179.3
1967	202.7	139.3	726.2	737.4	627.7	282.5	201.2	212.5	157.1
1968	170.7	133.8	432.8	442.4	336.5	247.2	198.4	180.2	128.5
1969	190.8	132.4	634.1	641.1	582.1	292.4	232.1	206.9	140.0
1970	229.9	145.7	939.1	936.0	1028.0	326.1	254.6	223.6	163.1
1971	256.6	149.3	1194.5	1207.4	1100.9	353.8	265.8	234.8	176.5
1972	256.4	150.7	1127.6	1147.0	946.8	390.6	292.7	259.2	171.4
1973	264.1	163.2	1069.0	1066.7	1147.5	412.8	306.7	264.7	172.3
1974	267.7	165.5	1048.6	1056.1	1011.0	445.0	329.1	265.7	170.4
1975	298.5	158.2	1404.1	1415.1	1338.5	517.1	357.1	292.3	185.0
1976	283.3	154.4	1234.2	1246.7	1156.5	531.6	375.3	293.5	173.7
1977	339.1	175.4	1676.1	1670.6	1857.3	558.7	403.4	314.6	205.9
1978	396.1	195.0	2127.0	2100.0	2604.0	601.2	410.3	325.6	240.2

注：本表按可比价格计算，其中本市人均生产总值为按户籍人口计算值。

Note: The indices in this table are calculated at comparable prices. Per capita GDP is calculated by household registered population.

2－5 重庆市生产总值（1978－2004年）
Gross Domestic Product (1978-2004)

单位：亿元 (100 million yuan)

年 份 Year	本市生产总值 Gross Domestic Product	第一产业 Primary Industry	第二产业 Secondary Industry	工 业 Industry	建筑业 Construction	第三产业 Tertiary Industry	交通运输仓储邮电通信业 Transportation, Storage, Postal and Telecommunication Services	批发和零售贸易及餐饮业 Wholesale & Retail Trade and Catering Trade
1978	67.32	24.81	30.80	27.92	2.88	11.71	2.92	2.96
1979	75.84	28.76	34.07	30.89	3.18	13.01	3.24	3.29
1980	84.70	32.50	37.74	34.22	3.52	14.46	3.61	3.65
1981	90.56	36.20	38.79	35.16	3.63	15.57	3.92	3.99
1982	100.44	40.46	41.77	37.85	3.92	18.21	4.59	4.63
1983	111.24	45.23	44.72	40.30	4.42	21.29	6.22	5.31
1984	130.96	50.39	53.52	48.25	5.27	27.05	6.94	6.63
1985	151.54	53.39	64.73	57.35	7.38	33.42	7.40	9.76
1986	169.80	59.64	71.55	62.67	8.88	38.61	7.16	10.97
1987	189.68	62.24	79.70	68.63	11.07	47.74	7.39	13.23
1988	239.11	74.40	103.05	90.06	12.99	61.66	9.32	17.85
1989	277.27	81.32	118.87	106.35	12.52	77.08	12.27	22.22
1990	298.41	99.58	118.53	100.46	18.07	80.30	12.36	19.07
1991	339.81	108.60	134.43	115.26	19.17	96.78	13.97	22.10
1992	417.87	116.35	169.54	145.95	23.59	131.98	22.17	33.73
1993	549.79	140.64	236.71	204.61	32.10	172.44	26.01	48.68
1994	751.21	194.11	326.91	287.56	39.35	230.19	30.67	62.56
1995	1009.47	261.52	427.19	368.17	59.02	320.76	46.02	84.35
1996	1179.09	284.89	493.21	423.01	70.20	400.99	58.71	107.81
1997	1350.10	304.51	563.40	477.13	86.27	482.19	72.43	129.87
1998	1429.26	298.67	585.38	480.88	104.50	545.21	78.93	138.43
1999	1479.71	284.28	604.39	492.39	112.00	591.04	87.22	145.32
2000	1589.34	283.00	657.51	527.48	130.03	648.83	98.19	154.46
2001	1749.77	293.03	727.66	576.58	151.08	729.08	109.48	167.84
2002	1971.30	315.78	827.55	651.00	176.55	827.97	123.97	182.51
2003	2250.56	336.36	977.30	768.37	208.93	936.90	136.56	199.27
2004	2665.39	423.70	1181.24	927.51	253.73	1060.45	153.83	227.51

注：本表按当年价格计算。

Note: The data in value terms in this table are calculated at current prices.

2-5 续表 CONTINUED

单位：亿元 (100 million yuan)

年 份 Year	金融保险业 Finance and Insurance	房地产业 Real Estate	社会服务业 Social Services	卫生体育和社会福利 Public Health, Sports and Social Welfare	教育文艺和广播电影电视 Education, Culture, Art, Radio, Film and Television	科研综合技术服务 Scientific Research and Polytechnical Services	国家机关和社会团体 Government Agencies, Party Agencies and Social Organizations	本市人均生产总值（元） Per Capita GDP (yuan)
1978	1.21	0.88	0.76	0.45	1.34	0.34	0.85	257
1979	1.34	0.98	0.85	0.50	1.49	0.38	0.94	287
1980	1.49	1.09	0.94	0.56	1.66	0.42	1.04	319
1981	1.65	1.09	1.03	0.59	1.72	0.46	1.12	337
1982	1.81	1.24	1.36	0.67	2.00	0.59	1.32	371
1983	2.34	1.39	1.39	0.67	1.98	0.57	1.42	407
1984	4.02	1.72	1.72	0.88	2.36	0.70	2.08	477
1985	4.48	1.97	1.79	1.07	3.35	0.78	2.82	549
1986	5.23	2.44	2.41	1.09	4.11	1.40	3.80	609
1987	8.87	3.27	2.49	1.54	5.02	1.74	4.19	671
1988	10.65	4.03	3.15	1.98	6.39	2.62	5.67	836
1989	14.77	4.44	3.53	2.36	7.74	3.19	6.56	961
1990	15.37	5.01	4.78	2.60	8.57	4.58	7.96	1023
1991	18.36	6.20	7.57	3.24	9.87	4.93	10.54	1159
1992	23.72	6.30	12.09	3.74	11.90	4.81	13.52	1416
1993	30.87	7.74	18.13	4.17	14.00	5.29	17.55	1859
1994	43.14	9.16	27.90	8.55	17.62	8.72	21.87	2525
1995	56.72	14.46	44.71	9.84	23.94	13.23	27.49	3372
1996	60.66	20.89	56.80	12.86	30.35	17.24	35.67	3914
1997	68.31	26.86	66.46	16.58	37.22	24.03	40.43	4452
1998	73.84	36.57	79.98	18.42	43.30	26.54	49.20	4684
1999	69.79	40.68	92.39	20.53	48.78	30.94	55.39	4826
2000	68.62	51.92	101.67	23.40	51.09	35.39	64.09	5157
2001	73.36	60.47	114.62	27.91	62.46	40.14	72.80	5654
2002	78.25	70.90	133.89	30.37	83.79	43.87	80.42	6347 (7034)
2003	85.00	87.79	144.84	33.40	91.41	57.26	101.37	7209 (8077)
2004	93.45	98.42	163.66	42.18	99.25	66.24	115.91	8496 (9608)

注：1）本表按当年价格计算。

2）本市人均生产总值指标括号外的数据为按户籍人口计算值，括号内数据为按常住人口计算值。

Note: a) The data in value terms in this table are calculated at current prices.

b) Per capita GDP out of parentheses is calculated by household registered population, whereas in parentheses is by resident population.

2－6 重庆市生产总值构成（1978－2004年）
Composition of Gross Domestic Product (1978-2004)

单位：% (%)

年份 Year	本市生产总值 Gross Domestic Product	第一产业 Primary Industry	第二产业 Secondary Industry	工业 Industry	建筑业 Construction	第三产业 Tertiary Industry	交通运输仓储邮电通信业 Transportation, Storage, Postal and Telecommunication Services	批发和零售贸易及餐饮业 Wholesale & Retail Trade and Catering Trade
1978	100.0	36.8	45.8	41.5	4.3	17.4	4.3	4.4
1979	100.0	37.9	44.9	40.7	4.2	17.2	4.3	4.3
1980	100.0	38.4	44.6	40.4	4.2	17.0	4.2	4.3
1981	100.0	40.0	42.8	38.8	4.0	17.2	4.3	4.4
1982	100.0	40.3	41.6	37.7	3.9	18.1	4.6	4.6
1983	100.0	40.7	40.2	36.2	4.0	19.1	5.6	4.8
1984	100.0	38.5	40.8	36.8	4.0	20.7	5.3	5.1
1985	100.0	35.2	42.7	37.8	4.9	22.1	4.9	6.4
1986	100.0	35.1	42.1	36.9	5.2	22.8	4.2	6.5
1987	100.0	32.8	42.0	36.2	5.8	25.2	3.9	7.0
1988	100.0	31.1	43.1	37.7	5.4	25.8	3.9	7.5
1989	100.0	29.3	42.9	38.4	4.5	27.8	4.4	8.0
1990	100.0	33.4	39.7	33.7	6.0	26.9	4.1	6.4
1991	100.0	32.0	39.5	33.9	5.6	28.5	4.1	6.5
1992	100.0	27.8	40.6	34.9	5.7	31.6	5.3	8.1
1993	100.0	25.6	43.0	37.2	5.8	31.4	4.7	8.9
1994	100.0	25.8	43.5	38.3	5.2	30.7	4.1	8.3
1995	100.0	25.9	42.3	36.5	5.8	31.8	4.6	8.4
1996	100.0	24.2	41.8	35.9	5.9	34.0	5.0	9.1
1997	100.0	22.6	41.7	35.3	6.4	35.7	5.4	9.6
1998	100.0	20.9	41.0	33.7	7.3	38.1	5.5	9.7
1999	100.0	19.2	40.9	33.3	7.6	39.9	5.9	9.8
2000	100.0	17.8	41.4	33.2	8.2	40.8	6.2	9.7
2001	100.0	16.7	41.6	33.0	8.6	41.7	6.3	9.6
2002	100.0	16.0	42.0	33.0	9.0	42.0	6.3	9.3
2003	100.0	15.0	43.4	34.1	9.3	41.6	6.1	8.9
2004	100.0	15.9	44.3	34.8	9.5	39.8	5.8	8.5

注：本表按当年价格计算。

Note: The data in value terms in this table are calculated at current prices.

2-6 续表 CONTINUED

单位：% (%)

年 份 Year	金融保险业 Finance and Insurance	房地产业 Real Estate	社会服务业 Social Services	卫生体育和社会福利 Public Health, Sports and Social Welfare	教育文艺和广播电影电视 Education, Culture, Art, Radio, Film and Television	科研综合技术服务 Scientific Research and Polytechnical Services	国家机关和社会团体 Government Agencies, Party Agencies and Social Organizations
1978	1.8	1.3	1.1	0.7	2.0	0.5	1.3
1979	1.8	1.3	1.1	0.7	2.0	0.5	1.2
1980	1.7	1.3	1.1	0.7	2.0	0.5	1.2
1981	1.8	1.2	1.2	0.7	1.9	0.5	1.2
1982	1.8	1.2	1.3	0.7	2.0	0.6	1.3
1983	2.1	1.2	1.2	0.6	1.8	0.5	1.3
1984	3.1	1.3	1.3	0.7	1.8	0.5	1.6
1985	3.0	1.3	1.2	0.7	2.2	0.5	1.9
1986	3.1	1.4	1.4	0.7	2.4	0.8	2.3
1987	4.7	1.7	1.3	0.8	2.7	0.9	2.2
1988	4.5	1.7	1.3	0.8	2.7	1.1	2.3
1989	5.3	1.6	1.3	0.8	2.8	1.2	2.4
1990	5.1	1.7	1.6	0.9	2.9	1.5	2.7
1991	5.4	1.8	2.2	1.0	2.9	1.5	3.1
1992	5.7	1.5	2.9	0.9	2.8	1.2	3.2
1993	5.6	1.4	3.3	0.8	2.5	1.0	3.2
1994	5.8	1.2	3.7	1.1	2.4	1.2	2.9
1995	5.6	1.4	4.4	1.0	2.4	1.3	2.7
1996	5.1	1.8	4.8	1.1	2.6	1.5	3.0
1997	5.1	2.0	4.9	1.2	2.7	1.8	3.0
1998	5.2	2.5	5.6	1.3	3.0	1.9	3.4
1999	4.7	2.8	6.2	1.4	3.3	2.1	3.7
2000	4.3	3.3	6.4	1.5	3.2	2.2	4.0
2001	4.2	3.4	6.5	1.6	3.6	2.3	4.2
2002	4.0	3.6	6.8	1.5	4.3	2.2	4.0
2003	3.8	3.9	6.4	1.5	4.1	2.4	4.5
2004	3.5	3.7	6.1	1.6	3.7	2.5	4.3

注：本表按当年价格计算。

Note: The data in value terms in this table are calculated at current prices.

2－7 重庆市生产总值指数（1978－2004年）（上年=100）
Indices of Gross Domestic Product (1978-2004) (Preceding Year=100)

年份 Year	本市生产总值 Gross Domestic Product	第一产业 Primary Industry	第二产业 Secondary Industry	工业 Industry	建筑业 Construction	第三产业 Tertiary Industry	交通运输仓储邮电通信业 Transportation, Storage, Postal and Telecommunication Services	批发和零售贸易及餐饮业 Wholesale & Retail Trade and Catering Trade
1978	100.0	100.0	100.0	100.0	100.0	100.0	100.0	100.0
1979	110.9	108.5	111.2	111.2	111.3	110.5	110.4	110.3
1980	107.5	104.6	108.9	108.7	110.0	109.6	105.2	105.5
1981	106.0	106.1	105.4	103.1	106.8	109.0	107.8	108.5
1982	108.7	107.6	107.2	107.0	108.1	115.2	115.3	114.7
1983	110.1	105.8	108.4	108.2	110.7	114.9	128.9	114.6
1984	115.7	106.5	120.5	120.8	119.5	122.6	107.3	120.4
1985	108.4	109.5	105.4	102.1	120.2	114.1	98.9	136.0
1986	108.4	110.6	106.4	103.8	114.2	110.3	100.7	107.3
1987	105.1	98.1	109.8	108.6	120.1	114.1	108.3	111.4
1988	109.3	102.3	111.5	112.0	105.3	109.2	106.3	120.6
1989	104.7	104.7	102.2	104.4	95.4	109.9	116.2	109.5
1990	106.8	107.2	107.0	104.0	139.3	103.8	101.5	86.5
1991	109.0	106.6	109.0	110.5	102.2	111.7	105.6	108.3
1992	116.2	101.8	121.4	122.1	119.5	125.6	130.1	138.2
1993	115.3	105.0	121.5	122.3	118.8	116.7	104.6	136.6
1994	113.3	105.4	118.8	120.8	111.0	121.1	110.7	108.1
1995	112.1	105.2	114.6	114.4	116.0	116.1	121.3	117.1
1996	111.2	105.0	112.1	112.1	112.1	114.9	117.5	117.5
1997	111.0	103.4	112.4	111.4	119.1	114.5	116.1	116.7
1998	108.4	102.4	107.1	104.8	121.6	114.3	104.8	112.6
1999	107.6	100.4	110.3	110.7	108.3	108.1	106.4	107.1
2000	108.5	101.5	110.5	110.4	111.0	109.5	109.7	110.3
2001	109.0	102.2	111.8	111.2	114.4	109.1	108.8	109.8
2002	110.3	104.1	113.8	113.8	113.9	109.2	107.0	109.8
2003	111.5	104.2	116.0	116.4	114.1	109.4	108.0	109.0
2004	112.2	104.7	116.2	116.9	113.5	110.4	113.3	112.6

注：本表按可比价格计算。

Note: The indices in this table are calculated at comparable prices.

2-7 续表 CONTINUED

年 份 Year	金融保险业 Finance and Insurance	房地产业 Real Estate	社会服务业 Social Services	卫生体育和社会福利 Public Health, Sports and Social Welfare	教育文艺和广播电影电视 Education, Culture,Art, Radio, Film and Television	科研综合技术服务 Scientific Research and Polytechnic Services	国家机关和社会团体 Government Agencies, Party Agencies and Social Organizations	本市人均生产总值 Per Capita GDP
1978	100.0	100.0	100.0	100.0	100.0	100.0	100.0	100.0
1979	109.7	110.5	110.4	110.8	112.7	110.4	109.8	110.2
1980	105.4	105.6	105.7	106.0	105.8	105.5	105.2	106.6
1981	109.4	99.3	108.8	104.6	102.9	108.7	106.9	104.8
1982	108.0	112.0	129.8	111.8	114.5	126.3	110.0	107.9
1983	129.0	121.1	100.9	100.0	99.0	96.6	107.6	109.0
1984	165.6	119.3	121.0	126.6	114.9	118.4	141.2	115.2
1985	103.0	105.8	95.7	113.4	131.1	103.0	125.3	107.9
1986	110.9	118.3	129.3	97.3	117.2	158.4	127.9	107.4
1987	156.9	123.7	94.6	118.2	112.7	114.8	101.8	103.7
1988	101.5	104.1	107.4	108.7	107.6	127.3	114.3	108.0
1989	121.9	96.9	97.2	104.8	106.5	107.1	101.8	103.8
1990	104.9	113.7	129.5	108.0	109.6	139.7	119.3	105.8
1991	111.7	115.7	137.3	115.8	107.6	100.6	123.3	108.4
1992	120.1	96.8	148.4	104.8	108.9	96.7	116.5	115.4
1993	108.3	109.1	131.4	102.1	107.5	105.7	118.3	115.0
1994	115.4	103.6	128.1	172.1	120.9	135.4	111.3	112.7
1995	116.6	115.4	145.8	106.2	116.4	144.0	107.8	111.3
1996	103.8	132.1	127.3	110.2	110.9	115.4	108.9	110.6
1997	109.0	124.6	120.8	116.4	112.9	109.5	104.1	110.3
1998	110.0	122.9	124.1	115.6	120.7	113.1	118.9	107.8
1999	88.4	109.3	116.3	116.4	116.7	109.7	120.9	107.1
2000	100.2	110.7	108.7	114.8	106.5	114.8	117.0	107.9
2001	102.3	114.1	107.8	117.0	106.5	110.4	111.7	108.6
2002	107.0	113.6	109.0	109.5	111.0	105.6	110.9	109.9
2003	106.8	115.6	107.8	111.8	108.9	110.2	112.8	110.9 (112.1)
2004	105.3	103.8	108.5	112.4	108.0	113.7	113.3	111.6 (112.7)

注：1）本表按可比价格计算。

2）本市人均生产总值指标括号外的数据为按户籍人口计算值，括号内数据为按常住人口计算值。

Note: a) The indices in this table are calculated at comparable prices.

b) Per capita GDP out of parentheses is calculated by household registered population, whereas in parentheses is by resident population.

2－8 重庆市生产总值指数（1978－2004年）（1978年=100）
Indices of Gross Domestic Product (1978-2004) (1978=100)

年份 Year	本市生产总值 Gross Domestic Product	第一产业 Primary Industry	第二产业 Secondary Industry	工业 Industry	建筑业 Construction	第三产业 Tertiary Industry	交通运输仓储邮电通信业 Transportation, Storage, Postal and Telecommunication Services	批发和零售贸易及餐饮业 Wholesale & Retail Trade and Catering Trade
1978	100.0	100.0	100.0	100.0	100.0	100.0	100.0	100.0
1979	110.9	108.5	111.2	111.2	111.3	110.5	110.4	110.3
1980	119.2	113.5	121.1	120.9	122.4	121.1	116.1	116.4
1981	126.4	120.4	127.6	124.6	130.8	132.0	125.2	126.3
1982	137.4	129.6	136.8	133.3	141.3	152.1	144.4	144.8
1983	151.2	137.1	148.3	144.3	156.5	174.7	186.1	166.0
1984	175.0	146.0	178.7	174.3	187.0	214.2	199.7	199.8
1985	189.7	159.9	188.4	177.9	224.8	244.4	197.5	271.8
1986	205.6	176.8	200.4	184.7	256.7	269.6	198.8	291.6
1987	216.1	173.4	220.1	200.6	308.3	307.6	215.3	324.8
1988	236.2	177.4	245.4	224.7	324.6	335.9	228.9	391.7
1989	247.3	185.8	250.8	234.6	309.7	369.2	266.0	429.0
1990	264.1	199.1	268.3	243.9	431.4	383.2	270.0	371.1
1991	287.9	212.3	292.5	269.5	440.9	428.0	285.1	401.8
1992	334.5	216.1	355.1	329.1	526.8	537.6	370.9	555.4
1993	385.7	226.9	431.4	402.5	625.9	627.4	388.0	758.6
1994	437.0	239.2	512.5	486.2	694.7	759.8	429.5	820.1
1995	489.9	251.6	587.4	556.3	805.9	882.1	521.0	960.3
1996	544.8	264.2	658.4	623.6	903.4	1013.5	612.2	1128.3
1997	604.7	273.2	740.1	694.6	1075.9	1160.5	710.7	1316.8
1998	655.5	279.7	792.6	728.0	1308.3	1326.4	744.8	1482.7
1999	705.3	280.8	874.3	805.9	1416.9	1433.9	792.5	1588.0
2000	765.2	285.1	966.1	889.7	1572.8	1570.1	869.4	1751.5
2001	834.1	291.3	1080.0	989.3	1799.2	1713.0	945.9	1923.2
2002	920.0	303.2	1229.0	1125.8	2049.4	1870.6	1012.1	2111.7
2003	1025.8	315.9	1425.6	1310.4	2338.4	2046.4	1093.1	2301.8
2004	1150.9	330.7	1656.5	1531.9	2654.1	2259.2	1238.5	2591.8

注：本表按可比价格计算。

Note: The indices in this table are calculated at comparable prices.

2-8 续表 CONTINUED

年份 Year	金融保险业 Finance and Insurance	房地产业 Real Estate	社会服务业 Social Services	卫生体育和社会福利 Public Health, Sports and Social Welfare	教育文艺和广播电影电视 Education, Culture, Art, Radio, Film and Television	科研综合技术服务 Scientific Research and Polytechnic Services	国家机关和社会团体 Government Agencies, Party Agencies and Social Organizations	本市人均生产总值 Per Capita GDP
1978	100.0	100.0	100.0	100.0	100.0	100.0	100.0	100.0
1979	109.7	110.5	110.4	110.8	112.7	110.4	109.8	110.2
1980	115.6	116.7	116.7	117.4	119.2	116.5	115.5	117.5
1981	126.5	115.9	127.0	122.9	122.7	126.6	123.5	123.1
1982	136.6	129.8	164.8	137.3	140.5	159.9	135.8	132.8
1983	176.2	157.2	166.3	137.3	139.1	154.5	146.2	144.8
1984	291.8	187.5	201.2	173.9	159.8	182.9	206.4	166.8
1985	300.6	198.4	192.5	197.2	209.5	188.4	258.6	180.0
1986	333.4	234.7	249.0	191.9	245.5	298.4	330.7	193.3
1987	523.0	290.3	235.5	226.8	276.7	342.5	336.7	200.4
1988	530.9	302.2	252.9	246.5	297.8	436.1	384.8	216.5
1989	647.1	292.8	245.9	258.3	317.1	467.0	391.7	224.7
1990	678.9	332.9	318.4	279.0	347.5	652.4	467.3	237.7
1991	758.3	385.2	437.2	323.1	374.0	656.3	576.2	257.7
1992	910.7	372.9	648.7	338.6	407.2	634.7	671.3	297.4
1993	986.3	406.8	852.4	345.7	437.8	670.9	794.2	342.0
1994	1138.2	421.5	1092.0	595.0	529.3	908.3	883.9	385.5
1995	1327.1	486.4	1592.1	631.8	616.1	1308.0	952.9	429.0
1996	1377.5	642.5	2026.8	696.3	683.2	1509.4	1037.7	474.5
1997	1501.5	800.5	2448.3	810.5	771.4	1652.8	1080.2	523.4
1998	1651.7	983.8	3038.4	936.9	931.0	1869.4	1284.4	564.2
1999	1460.1	1075.3	3533.6	1090.6	1086.5	2050.7	1552.8	604.2
2000	1463.0	1190.4	3841.0	1252.0	1157.2	2354.2	1816.8	652.0
2001	1496.6	1358.2	4140.6	1464.8	1232.4	2599.0	2029.3	708.0
2002	1604.4	1542.9	4513.3	1604.0	1368.0	2744.5	2250.5	778.1
2003	1713.5	1783.6	4865.3	1793.3	1489.8	3024.4	2538.6	862.9
2004	1804.3	1851.4	5278.9	2015.7	1609.0	3438.7	2876.2	963.0

注：本表按可比价格计算。

Note: The indices in this table are calculated at comparable prices.

2－9 重庆市生产总值项目结构（2004年）
Composition of Gross Domestic Product (2004)

单位：亿元 (100 million yuan)

项　目	Item	增加值 Value-added	劳动者报酬 Compensa-tion of Laborers	生产税净额 Net Value of Production Tax	固定资产折旧 Deprecia-tion of Fixed Assets	营业盈余 Business Surplus
本市生产总值	**Gross Domestic Product**	**2665.39**	**1398.34**	**376.81**	**327.11**	**563.13**
第一产业	Primary Industry	423.70	378.69	15.05	7.75	22.21
第二产业	Secondary Industry	1181.24	454.81	260.76	150.54	315.13
工　业	Industry	927.51	280.19	223.79	137.02	286.51
建筑业	Construction	253.73	174.62	36.97	13.52	28.62
第三产业	Tertiary Industry	1060.45	564.84	101.00	168.82	225.79
农、林、牧、渔服务业	Services for Farming, Forestry, Animal Husbandry and Fishery	7.68	2.81	0.08	1.05	3.74
地质勘探、水利管理业	Geological Prospecting and Water Conservancy	4.69	3.93	0.05	0.27	0.44
交通运输、仓储、邮电通信业	Transportation, Storage, Postal and Telecommunication Services	153.83	71.67	15.20	52.06	14.90
交通运输业和仓储业	Transportation and Storage	94.89	60.28	10.35	22.35	1.91
邮电通信业	Postal and Telecommunication Services	58.94	11.39	4.85	29.71	12.99
批发和零售贸易、餐饮业	Wholesale & Retail Trade and Catering Trade	227.51	120.17	19.88	11.15	76.31
批发和零售贸易业	Wholesale & Retail Trade	186.56	98.88	18.65	7.46	61.57
餐饮业	Catering Trade	40.95	21.29	1.23	3.69	14.74
金融保险业	Finance and Insurance	93.45	37.24	11.63	9.73	34.85
金融业	Finance	58.30	32.06	10.49	9.33	6.42
保险业	Insurance	6.50	5.18	1.14	0.40	-0.22
其　他	Others	28.65				28.65
房地产业	Real Estate	98.42	13.19	25.18	46.37	13.68
房地产管理业	Real Estate Management	7.41	3.72	0.46	3.23	
房地产开发业	Real Estate Development	52.60	9.47	24.72	4.73	13.68
城镇居民自有住房	Urban Self-owned Buildings	15.10			15.10	
农村居民自有住房	Rural Self-owned Buildings	23.31			23.31	
社会服务业	Social Services	163.66	91.27	12.68	18.25	41.46
卫生、体育、社会福利事业	Public Health Sports and Social Welfare	42.18	29.63	0.02	4.80	7.73
教育、文艺、广播电影电视事业	Education, Culture, Art, Radio, Film and Television	99.25	82.38	0.99	12.90	2.98
科学研究和综合技术服务业	Scientific Research and Polytechnic Services	53.87	16.67	9.18	3.37	24.65
国家政党机关、社会团体	Government Agencies, Party Agencies and Social Organizations	115.91	95.88	6.11	8.87	5.05
其他行业	Others					

注：本表按当年价格计算。

Note: The data in value terms in this table are calculated at current prices.

2－10 按支出法计算的重庆市生产总值（2003－2004年）
Gross Domestic Product by Expenditure Approach (2003-2004)

单位：亿元 (100 million yuan)

项　　目	Item	2003	2004
本市生产总值	**Gross Domestic Product**	**2327.08**	**2745.35**
最终消费	Final Consumption Expenditure	1392.13	1579.50
居民消费	Household Consumption Expenditure	981.20	1128.05
农村居民	Agricultural Households	381.26	432.59
自给性消费	Self-using	112.43	127.12
商品性消费	Commerce	159.52	179.44
文化生活服务性消费	Culture and Services	72.98	87.10
住房及水电消费	Water, Electricity and Residence	36.33	38.93
#住房消费	Residence	21.79	25.91
城镇居民	Non-agricultural Households	599.94	695.46
商品性消费	Commerce	397.56	431.52
文化生活服务性消费	Culture and Service	137.48	179.32
住房及水电消费	Water, Electricity and Residence	64.90	84.62
#住房消费	Residence	28.58	44.91
政府消费	Government Consumption Expenditure	410.93	451.15
资本形成总额	Gross Capital Formation	1314.20	1640.82
固定资本形成总额	Gross Fixed Capital Formation	1244.83	1552.99
第一产业	Primary Industry	37.10	45.63
第二产业	Secondary Industry	297.46	418.63
第三产业	Tertiary Industry	910.27	1088.73
存货增加	Changes in Inventory	69.37	87.83
第一产业	Primary Industry	5.82	10.11
第二产业	Secondary Industry	21.24	28.25
第三产业	Tertiary Industry	42.31	49.47
货物和服务净出口	Net Export	-379.25	-474.67
出　口	Exports	247.15	291.56
进　口	Imports	626.40	766.23

注：本表数按当年价格计算。

Note: The figures in this table are calculated at current prices.

2－11 重庆市三大经济区生产总值（2003－2004年）
Gross Domestic Product of Three Economic Zones in Chongqing (2003-2004)

单位：亿元 (100 million yuan)

指标	Item	2003	2004	指数 上年=100 Index Preceding Year=100
本市生产总值	**Gross Domestic Product**	**2250.56**	**2665.39**	**112.2**
都市发达经济圈	Metropolitan Advanced Economic Sphere	887.01	1041.98	113.4
渝西经济走廊	West Chongqing Economic Corridor	686.84	821.93	111.3
三峡库区生态经济区	Ecological Economic Zone in Three Gorges Reservoir Area	676.71	801.48	111.5
第一产业	**Primary Industry**	**336.36**	**423.70**	**104.7**
都市发达经济圈	Metropolitan Advanced Economic Sphere	45.58	56.42	101.2
渝西经济走廊	West Chongqing Economic Corridor	141.94	177.71	105.0
三峡库区生态经济区	Ecological Economic Zone in Three Gorges Reservoir Area	148.84	189.57	105.5
第二产业	**Secondary Industry**	**977.30**	**1181.24**	**116.2**
都市发达经济圈	Metropolitan Advanced Economic Sphere	441.62	532.93	117.4
渝西经济走廊	West Chongqing Economic Corridor	265.93	327.75	115.2
三峡库区生态经济区	Ecological Economic Zone in Three Gorges Reservoir Area	269.75	320.56	115.3
第三产业	**Tertiary Industry**	**936.90**	**1060.45**	**110.4**
都市发达经济圈	Metropolitan Advanced Economic Sphere	399.81	452.63	110.0
渝西经济走廊	West Chongqing Economic Corridor	278.97	316.47	110.6
三峡库区生态经济区	Ecological Economic Zone in Three Gorges Reservoir Area	258.12	291.35	110.6
人均生产总值（元）	**Per Capita GDP (yuan)**	**8077**	**9608**	**112.7**
都市发达经济圈	Metropolitan Advanced Economic Sphere	14397	16703	112.2
渝西经济走廊	West Chongqing Economic Corridor	8127	9821	112.3
三峡库区生态经济区	Ecological Economic Zone in Three Gorges Reservoir Area	5106	6110	112.4

注：人均生产总值按常住人口计算。

Note: Per capita GDP is calculated by resident population.

2－12 投入产出基本流量表（2002年）

单位: 万元

投入 Output ＼ 产出 Input		总产出 Total Output
总投入合计	**Total Input**	**54815075**
中间投入合计	**Intermediate Input**	**54815075**
第一产业合计	Primary Industry	4787848
第二产业合计	Secondary Industry	32695927
工　业	Industry	25019927
采矿业	Mining and Quarrying	673496
制造业	Manufacturing	22945743
电力、燃气及水的生产和供应业	Electricity, Gas & Water Production and Supply	1400688
建筑业	Construction	7676000
第三产业合计	Tertiary Industry	17331300
交通运输、仓储及邮政业	Transportation, Storage, Postal Services	1953740
信息传输、计算机服务和软件业	Data Transmission, Computer Service and Software	769588
批发与零售业	Wholesale and Retail Trade	4226200
住宿和餐饮业	Hotels and Restaurants	848139
金融业	Financing	1036100
房地产业	Real Estate	2121500
租赁与商务服务业	Renting and Business Activities	1467805
科学研究、技术服务与地质勘查业	Scientific Research, Technical Services and Geological Prospecting	383157
水利、环境和公共设施管理业	Administration of Water Conservancy, Environment and Public Utilities	94885
居民服务和其他服务业	Personal Services and Other Services	722515
教　育	Education	1367481
卫生、社会保障和社会福利业	Public Health, Social Security and Social Welfare	558451
文化、体育与娱乐业	Culture, Sports and Entertainment	204539
公共管理与社会组织	Public Administration and Social Organizations	1577200
增加值合计	**Total Value-added**	
固定资产折旧	Depreciation of Fixed Assets	
劳动者报酬	Compensation for Laborers	
生产税净额	Net Taxes on Production	
营业盈余	Operating Surplus	

注：本表按当年生产者价格计算。

Basic Flow of Input-output Table (2002)

(10 000 yuan)

中间使用合计 Total Intermediate Use	第一产业 Primary Industry	第二产业 Secondary Industry	工　业 Industry	采矿业 Mining and Quarrying	制造业 Manufacturing
54815075	**4787848**	**32695927**	**25019927**	**673496**	**22945743**
35095572	**1563604**	**24402926**	**18492406**	**333243**	**17693103**
1601188	629538	851304	752584	3345	749217
25246216	849415	20371932	15130208	212516	14605472
24300371	846501	20363962	15122238	211736	14598602
1359832	49400	1283087	1001696	44630	821884
21194000	749772	17974349	13128355	126559	12928185
1746539	47329	1106526	992187	40547	848533
945845	2914	7970	7970	780	6870
8248168	84651	3179690	2609614	117382	2338414
1614565	20704	845869	705166	29512	663914
332765	2042	93927	68442	2955	62092
113590	74	50548	50548	25976	24545
952534	6023	186520	157343	6093	146291
1909233	23873	823357	757411	28225	610461
375677		28200	26824	238	25284
1304636	934	612662	463965	7789	452986
624471	128	359759	237822	2544	234447
12529		4507	4507	10	4493
288073	7061	94223	70566	8257	55274
77428	3372	26472	22431	1994	19349
129798	7355	18441	18441	2309	15824
328468	19	35205	26148	1480	23454
184401	13066				
19719503	**3224244**	**8293001**	**6527521**	**340253**	**5252640**
3243476	67906	2135013	1875712	75998	1315876
13802450	2848234	5276287	4185044	251910	3500505
775405	112962	147464	128296	3112	111624
1898172	195142	734237	338469	9233	324635

Note: The data in value terms in this table are calculated at producers' prices of 2002.

2-12 续表1

单位: 万元

投入 Output \ 产出 Input		电力、燃气及水的生产和供应业 Electricity, Gas & Water Production and Supply
总投入合计	**Total Input**	**1400688**
中间投入合计	**Intermediate Input**	**466060**
第一产业合计	Primary Industry	22
第二产业合计	Secondary Industry	312220
工　业	Industry	311900
采矿业	Mining and Quarrying	135182
制造业	Manufacturing	73611
电力、燃气及水的生产和供应业	Electricity, Gas & Water Production and Supply	103107
建筑业	Construction	320
第三产业合计	Tertiary Industry	153818
交通运输、仓储及邮政业	Transportation, Storage, Postal Services	11740
信息传输、计算机服务和软件业	Data Transmission, Computer Service and Software	3395
批发与零售业	Wholesale and Retail Trade	27
住宿和餐饮业	Hotels and Restaurants	4959
金融业	Financing	118725
房地产业	Real Estate	1302
租赁与商务服务业	Renting and Business Activities	3190
科学研究、技术服务与地质勘查业	Scientific Research, Technical Services and Geological Prospecting	831
水利、环境和公共设施管理业	Administration of Water Conservancy, Environment and Public Utilities	4
居民服务和其他服务业	Personal Services and Other Services	7035
教　育	Education	1088
卫生、社会保障和社会福利业	Public Health, Social Security and Social Welfare	308
文化、体育与娱乐业	Culture, Sports and Entertainment	1214
公共管理与社会组织	Public Administration and Social Organizations	
增加值合计	**Total Value-added**	**934628**
固定资产折旧	Depreciation of Fixed Assets	483838
劳动者报酬	Compensation for Laborers	432629
生产税净额	Net Taxes on Production	13560
营业盈余	Operating Surplus	4601

2-12 CONTINUED-1

(10 000 yuan)

建 筑 业 Construction	第三产业 Tertiary Industry	交通运输、仓储及邮政业 Transportation, Storage, Postal Services	信息传输、计算机服务和软件业 Data Transmission, Computer Service and Software	批发与零售业 Wholesale and Retail Trade	住宿和餐饮业 Hotels and Restaurants
7676000	**17331300**	**1953740**	**769588**	**4226200**	**848139**
5910520	**9129042**	**751579**	**410277**	**2670958**	**496483**
98720	120346	1680		144	105857
5241724	4024869	542493	71550	588605	310912
5241724	3089908	523136	70703	531603	306062
281391	27345	2925			13278
4845994	2469879	481309	62243	345100	232797
114339	592684	38902	8460	186503	59987
	934961	19357	847	57002	4850
570076	4983827	207406	338727	2082209	79714
140703	747992	54156	13102	356685	4987
25485	236796	21131	24031	46220	4374
	62968	10852	2231		875
29177	759991	11772	25616	434283	5672
65946	1062003	46199	242844	481260	36211
1376	347477	253	24	288143	3699
148697	691040	18163	11998	225123	15263
121937	264584	7481	1810	2765	1
	8022	1090			10
23657	186789	3934	1424	54577	5235
4041	47584	1910	5131	7418	666
	104002	4565		614	274
9057	293244	903	10511	185121	2444
	171335	24997	5		3
1765480	**8202258**	**1202161**	**359311**	**1555242**	**351656**
259301	1040557	407817	10453	67342	79047
1091243	5677929	359903	194753	1435351	200556
19168	514979	114044	12568	15628	16851
395768	968793	320397	141537	36921	55202

2-12 续表2

单位: 万元

投入 Output \ 产出 Input		金融业 Financing
总投入合计	**Total Input**	**1036100**
中间投入合计	**Intermediate Input**	**253845**
第一产业合计	Primary Industry	
第二产业合计	Secondary Industry	107926
工　业	Industry	97668
采矿业	Mining and Quarrying	
制造业	Manufacturing	80365
电力、燃气及水的生产和供应业	Electricity, Gas & Water Production and Supply	17304
建筑业	Construction	10258
第三产业合计	Tertiary Industry	145918
交通运输、仓储及邮政业	Transportation, Storage, Postal Services	28076
信息传输、计算机服务和软件业	Data Transmission, Computer Service and Software	22544
批发与零售业	Wholesale and Retail Trade	
住宿和餐饮业	Hotels and Restaurants	29048
金融业	Financing	6400
房地产业	Real Estate	25213
租赁与商务服务业	Renting and Business Activities	22212
科学研究、技术服务与地质勘查业	Scientific Research, Technical Services and Geological Prospecting	63
水利、环境和公共设施管理业	Administration of Water Conservancy, Environment and Public Utilities	1529
居民服务和其他服务业	Personal Services and Other Services	2464
教　育	Education	3334
卫生、社会保障和社会福利业	Public Health, Social Security and Social Welfare	825
文化、体育与娱乐业	Culture, Sports and Entertainment	3731
公共管理与社会组织	Public Administration and Social Organizations	480
增加值合计	**Total Value-added**	**782256**
固定资产折旧	Depreciation of Fixed Assets	194276
劳动者报酬	Compensation for Laborers	508014
生产税净额	Net Taxes on Production	27017
营业盈余	Operating Surplus	52949

2-12 CONTINUED-2

(10 000 yuan)

房地产业 Real Estate	租赁与商务服务业 Renting and Business Activities	科学研究、技术服务与地质勘查业 Scientific Research, Technical Services and Geological Prospecting	水利、环境和公共设施管理业 Administration of Water Conservancy, Environment and Public Utilities	居民服务和其他服务业 Personal Services and Other Services	教　育 Education
2121500	**1467806**	**383157**	**94885**	**722515**	**1367481**
1463847	**852063**	**207999**	**45428**	**398434**	**427485**
1571	10991	6			
889455	399524	154574	13132	228740	191194
200433	387815	92499	12916	172849	173274
726	8393	28	18		1493
111997	295259	84308	11005	153230	148629
87710	84163	8164	1893	19619	23153
689021	11709	62075	216	55891	17919
572821	441548	53419	32296	169694	236291
9977	102812	8170	6573	17153	46209
11124	35835	3281	3156	8146	13977
3361	29958	85		15359	
11448	42342	9073	5220	27800	51772
146620	62950	2868	1051	4956	5934
19123	2728	139		7569	
176622	123080	4895	4212	11277	14528
22115	147	11727	9360		38989
3649	238	4	3		305
5981	17191	1326	252	76506	11472
1269	7199	636	207	58	4935
125	3953	5332	1430		32926
23451	6879	5800	832	28	15212
137955	6236	83		842	32
657653	**615743**	**175158**	**49457**	**324081**	**939996**
127828	89140	9150	1641	32591	
130806	390505	108711	47456	206010	938435
181906	83368	11761	357	32915	627
217114	52730	45535	2	52565	935

2-12 续表3

单位: 万元

投入 Output \ 产出 Input		卫生、社会保障和社会福利业 Public Health, Social Security and Social Welfare
总投入合计	**Total Input**	**558451**
中间投入合计	**Intermediate Input**	**332705**
第一产业合计	Primary Industry	
第二产业合计	Secondary Industry	281283
工　业	Industry	280630
采矿业	Mining and Quarrying	54
制造业	Manufacturing	266797
电力、燃气及水的生产和供应业	Electricity, Gas & Water Production and Supply	13779
建筑业	Construction	653
第三产业合计	Tertiary Industry	51422
交通运输、仓储及邮政业	Transportation, Storage, Postal Services	3173
信息传输、计算机服务和软件业	Data Transmission, Computer Service and Software	2321
批发与零售业	Wholesale and Retail Trade	
住宿和餐饮业	Hotels and Restaurants	3382
金融业	Financing	2847
房地产业	Real Estate	
租赁与商务服务业	Renting and Business Activities	3836
科学研究、技术服务与地质勘查业	Scientific Research, Technical Services and Geological Prospecting	19945
水利、环境和公共设施管理业	Administration of Water Conservancy, Environment and Public Utilities	710
居民服务和其他服务业	Personal Services and Other Services	554
教　育	Education	3160
卫生、社会保障和社会福利业	Public Health, Social Security and Social Welfare	3650
文化、体育与娱乐业	Culture, Sports and Entertainment	7736
公共管理与社会组织	Public Administration and Social Organizations	108
增加值合计	**Total Value-added**	**225746**
固定资产折旧	Depreciation of Fixed Assets	4168
劳动者报酬	Compensation for Laborers	221159
生产税净额	Net Taxes on Production	150
营业盈余	Operating Surplus	269

2-12 CONTINUED-3

(10 000 yuan)

文化、体育与娱乐业 Culture, Sports and Entertainment	公共管理与社会组织 Public Administration and Social Organizations	最终使用合计 Total Final Use	最终消费 Final Consumption Expenditure	居民最终消费 Household Consumption Expenditure	农村居民 Agricultural Households
204539	**1577200**				
75927	**742014**	**19719503**	**12288900**	**8808600**	**3676900**
97		3186660	1601811	1437412	950201
22690	222792	7449711	5083041	5083041	2044422
21456	218863	719556	5083041	5083041	2044422
103	327	-686336	61785	61785	61426
17264	179577	1751743	4555278	4555278	1871531
4089	38959	-345851	465978	465978	111465
1234	3929	6730155			
53140	519222	9083132	5604048	2288147	682277
2210	94708	339175	460686	460686	220957
2301	38355	436823	298437	298437	
247		4112610	65046		
2136	100426	-104395	8360	8360	947
6242	15621	-873133			
586		1745823	64560	64560	2864
12818	47013	163169	28427		
14724	135458	-241314	156117		
21	463	82356	247919		
1372	4500	434442	133298	90200	28026
1167	10494	1290053	1161654	423175	423175
448	49860	428653	1187278	742485	
8868	21728	-123929	304269	200244	6308
	596	1392799	1487997		
128612	**835186**				
17104					
121931	814339				
7921	9866				
-18344	10981				

2-12 续表4

单位: 万元

投入 Output \ 产出 Input		城镇居民 Non-agricultural Households
总投入合计	**Total Input**	
中间投入合计	**Intermediate Input**	**5131700**
第一产业合计	Primary Industry	487211
第二产业合计	Secondary Industry	3038619
工　业	Industry	3038619
采矿业	Mining and Quarrying	359
制造业	Manufacturing	2683747
电力、燃气及水的生产和供应业	Electricity, Gas & Water Production and Supply	354513
建筑业	Construction	
第三产业合计	Tertiary Industry	1605870
交通运输、仓储及邮政业	Transportation, Storage, Postal Services	239729
信息传输、计算机服务和软件业	Data Transmission, Computer Service and Software	298437
批发与零售业	Wholesale and Retail Trade	
住宿和餐饮业	Hotels and Restaurants	7413
金融业	Financing	
房地产业	Real Estate	61696
租赁与商务服务业	Renting and Business Activities	
科学研究、技术服务与地质勘查业	Scientific Research, Technical Services and Geological Prospecting	
水利、环境和公共设施管理业	Administration of Water Conservancy, Environment and Public Utilities	
居民服务和其他服务业	Personal Services and Other Services	62174
教　育	Education	
卫生、社会保障和社会福利业	Public Health, Social Security and Social Welfare	742485
文化、体育与娱乐业	Culture, Sports and Entertainment	193936
公共管理与社会组织	Public Administration and Social Organizations	
增加值合计	**Total Value-added**	
固定资产折旧	Depreciation of Fixed Assets	
劳动者报酬	Compensation for Laborers	
生产税净额	Net Taxes on Production	
营业盈余	Operating Surplus	

2-12 CONTINUED-4

(10 000 yuan)

政府消费 Government Consumption Expenditure	资本形成总额 Capital Formation	固定资本形成总额 Gross Fixed Capital Formation	存货增加 Changes in Inventories	净流出及其他 Net Flow-out and Others
3480300	**9901006**	**9315300**	**585706**	**-2470403**
164399	164579		164579	1420270
	9736427	9315300	421127	-7369757
	9736427	9315300	421127	-14099912
	11309		11309	-759430
	9701599	9315300	386299	-12505134
	23519		23519	-835348
				6730155
3315901				3479084
				-121511
				138386
65046				4047564
				-112755
				-873133
				1681263
28427				134742
156117				-397431
247919				-165563
43098				301144
738479				128399
444793				-758625
104025				-428198
1487997				-95198

2－13 投入产出直接消耗系数表（2002年）

产出 Input / 投入 Output		农业 Agriculture	采矿业 Mining and Quarrying
农　业	Agriculture	0.1314866	0.0049666
采矿业	Mining and Quarrying	0.0103178	0.0662662
制造业	Manufacturing	0.1565990	0.1879135
电力、燃气及水的生产和供应业	Electricity, Gas & Water Production and Supply	0.0098852	0.0602038
建筑业	Construction	0.0006086	0.0011581
交通运输、仓储及邮政业	Transportation, Storage, Postal Services	0.0043243	0.0438191
信息传输、计算机服务和软件业	Data Transmission, Computer Service and Software	0.0004265	0.0043876
批发与零售业	Wholesale and Retail Trade	0.0000155	0.0385689
住宿和餐饮业	Hotels and Restaurants	0.0012580	0.0090468
金融业	Financing	0.0049862	0.0419082
房地产业	Real Estate		0.0003534
租赁与商务服务业	Renting and Business Activities	0.0001951	0.0115650
科学研究、技术服务与地质勘查业	Scientific Research, Technical Services and Geological Prospecting	0.0000267	0.0037773
水利、环境和公共设施管理业	Administration of Water Conservancy, Environment and Public Utilities		0.0000148
居民服务和其他服务业	Personal Services and Other Services	0.0014748	0.0122599
教　育	Education	0.0007043	0.0029607
卫生、社会保障和社会福利业	Public Health, Social Security and Social Welfare	0.0015362	0.0034284
文化、体育与娱乐业	Culture, Sports and Entertainment	0.0000040	0.0021975
公共管理与社会组织	Public Administration and Social Organizations	0.0027290	

Direct Input Coefficients of Input-output Table (2002)

制造业 Manufacturing	电力、燃气及水的生产和供应业 Electricity, Gas & Water Production and Supply	建筑业 Construction	交通运输、仓储及邮政业 Transportation, Storage, Postal Services	信息传输、计算机服务和软件业 Data Transmission, Computer Service and Software	批发与零售业 Wholesale and Retail Trade	住宿和餐饮业 Hotels and Restaurants
0.0326517	0.0000157	0.0128609	0.0008599		0.0000341	0.1248109
0.0358186	0.0965111	0.0366585	0.0014971			0.0156555
0.5634241	0.0525535	0.6313176	0.2463526	0.0808783	0.0816573	0.2744798
0.0369800	0.0736117	0.0148956	0.0199116	0.0109929	0.0441302	0.0707278
0.0002994	0.0002285		0.0099077	0.0011006	0.0134878	0.0057184
0.0289341	0.0083816	0.0183303	0.0277191	0.0170247	0.0843985	0.0058799
0.0027060	0.0024238	0.0033201	0.0108157	0.0312258	0.0109365	0.0051572
0.0010697	0.0000193		0.0055545	0.0028990		0.0010317
0.0063755	0.0035404	0.0038011	0.0060254	0.0332853	0.1027597	0.0066876
0.0266045	0.0847619	0.0085912	0.0236464	0.3155507	0.1138753	0.0426947
0.0011019	0.0009295	0.0001793	0.0001295	0.0000312	0.0681802	0.0043613
0.0197416	0.0022775	0.0193717	0.0092965	0.0155902	0.0532684	0.0179959
0.0102175	0.0005933	0.0158855	0.0038291	0.0023519	0.0006543	0.0000012
0.0001958	0.0000029		0.0005579			0.0000118
0.0024089	0.0050225	0.0030819	0.0020136	0.0018503	0.0129140	0.0061723
0.0008433	0.0007768	0.0005264	0.0009776	0.0066672	0.0017552	0.0007852
0.0006896	0.0002199		0.0023365		0.0001453	0.0003231
0.0010222	0.0008667	0.0011799	0.0004622	0.0136580	0.0438032	0.0028816
			0.0127944	0.0000065		0.0000035

2-13 续表

投入 Output ＼ 产出 Input		金融业 Financing	房地产业 Real Estate	租赁与商务服务业 Renting and Business Activities
农业	Agriculture		0.0007405	0.0074881
采矿业	Mining and Quarrying		0.0003422	0.0057181
制造业	Manufacturing	0.0775639	0.0527914	0.2011568
电力、燃气及水的生产和供应业	Electricity, Gas & Water Production and Supply	0.0167011	0.0413434	0.0573394
建筑业	Construction	0.0099006	0.3247806	0.0079765
交通运输、仓储及邮政业	Transportation, Storage, Postal Services	0.0270978	0.0047028	0.0700447
信息传输、计算机服务和软件业	Data Transmission, Computer Service and Software	0.0217585	0.0052435	0.0244140
批发与零售业	Wholesale and Retail Trade		0.0015843	0.0204101
住宿和餐饮业	Hotels and Restaurants	0.0280359	0.0053962	0.0288478
金融业	Financing	0.0061770	0.0691115	0.0428872
房地产业	Real Estate	0.0243345	0.0090139	0.0018586
租赁与商务服务业	Renting and Business Activities	0.0214371	0.0832534	0.0838531
科学研究、技术服务与地质勘查业	Scientific Research, Technical Services and Geological Prospecting	0.0000608	0.0104242	0.0001001
水利、环境和公共设施管理业	Administration of Water Conservancy, Environment and Public Utilities	0.0014757	0.0017200	0.0001621
居民服务和其他服务业	Personal Services and Other Services	0.0023781	0.0028197	0.0117120
教育	Education	0.0032178	0.0005982	0.0049046
卫生、社会保障和社会福利业	Public Health, Social Security and Social Welfare	0.0007963	0.0000589	0.0026931
文化、体育与娱乐业	Culture, Sports and Entertainment	0.0036010	0.0110540	0.0046866
公共管理与社会组织	Public Administration and Social Organizations	0.0004633	0.0650271	0.0042478

2-13 CONTINUED

科学研究、技术服务与地质勘查业 Scientific Research, Technical Services and Geological Prospecting	水利、环境和公共设施管理业 Administration of Water Conservancy, Environment and Public Utilities	居民服务和其他服务业 Personal Services and Other Services	教育 Education	卫生、社会保障和社会福利业 Public Health, Social Security and Social Welfare	文化、体育与娱乐业 Culture, Sports and Entertainment	公共管理与社会组织 Public Administration and Social Organizations
0.0000157					0.0004742	
0.0000731	0.0001897		0.0010918	0.0000967	0.0005036	0.0002073
0.2200351	0.1159825	0.2120786	0.1086882	0.4777447	0.0844044	0.1138581
0.0213046	0.0199505	0.0271538	0.0169311	0.0246736	0.0199913	0.0247014
0.1620093	0.0022764	0.0773562	0.0131037	0.0011693	0.0060331	0.0024911
0.0213255	0.0692733	0.0237407	0.0337913	0.0056818	0.0108048	0.0600482
0.0085631	0.0332613	0.0112745	0.0102210	0.0041561	0.0112497	0.0243184
0.0002218		0.0212577			0.0012076	
0.0236796	0.0550140	0.0384767	0.0378594	0.0060560	0.0104430	0.0636736
0.0074852	0.0110766	0.0068594	0.0043394	0.0050980	0.0305174	0.0099043
0.0003628		0.0104759			0.0028650	
0.0127754	0.0443906	0.0156080	0.0106246	0.0068690	0.0626678	0.0298079
0.0306063	0.0986457		0.0285108	0.0357149	0.0719863	0.0858851
0.0000104	0.0000316		0.0002230	0.0012714	0.0001027	0.0002936
0.0034607	0.0026558	0.1058885	0.0083891	0.0009920	0.0067078	0.0028532
0.0016599	0.0021816	0.0000803	0.0036088	0.0056585	0.0057055	0.0066536
0.0139160	0.0150709		0.0240778	0.0065359	0.0021903	0.0316130
0.0151374	0.0087685	0.0000388	0.0111241	0.0138526	0.0433560	0.0137763
0.0002140		0.0011654	0.0000234	0.0001934		0.0003779

2—14 投入产出完全消耗系数表（2002年）

产出 Input / 投入 Output		农业 Agriculture	采矿业 Mining and Quarrying
农　业	Agriculture	0.1710886	0.0349161
采矿业	Mining and Quarrying	0.0357943	0.1087728
制造业	Manufacturing	0.4851366	0.6481902
电力、燃气及水的生产和供应业	Electricity, Gas & Water Production and Supply	0.0373467	0.1098969
建筑业	Construction	0.0034582	0.0102238
交通运输、仓储及邮政业	Transportation, Storage, Postal Services	0.0242286	0.0811318
信息传输、计算机服务和软件业	Data Transmission, Computer Service and Software	0.0036606	0.0121979
批发与零售业	Wholesale and Retail Trade	0.0024374	0.0451546
住宿和餐饮业	Hotels and Restaurants	0.0073871	0.0253808
金融业	Financing	0.0267668	0.0883716
房地产业	Real Estate	0.0015256	0.0069198
租赁与商务服务业	Renting and Business Activities	0.0130915	0.0364509
科学研究、技术服务与地质勘查业	Scientific Research, Technical Services and Geological Prospecting	0.0060698	0.0128716
水利、环境和公共设施管理业	Administration of Water Conservancy, Environment and Public Utilities	0.0001585	0.0003463
居民服务和其他服务业	Personal Services and Other Services	0.0044104	0.0195867
教　育	Education	0.0016433	0.0047917
卫生、社会保障和社会福利业	Public Health, Social Security and Social Welfare	0.0026433	0.0051042
文化、体育与娱乐业	Culture, Sports and Entertainment	0.0012320	0.0066637
公共管理与社会组织	Public Administration and Social Organizations	0.0036815	0.0018066

Total Input Coefficients of Input-output Table (2002)

制造业 Manufacturing	电力、燃气及水的生产和供应业 Electricity, Gas & Water Production and Supply	建筑业 Construction	交通运输、仓储及邮政业 Transportation, Storage, Postal Services	信息传输、计算机服务和软件业 Data Transmission, Computer Service and Software	批发与零售业 Wholesale and Retail Trade	住宿和餐饮业 Hotels and Restaurants
0.1012024	0.0125406	0.0836592	0.0311902	0.0226808	0.0402457	0.1795177
0.1131427	0.1248102	0.1175460	0.0368765	0.0215087	0.0369365	0.0655182
1.5531605	0.2615618	1.6991380	0.7158122	0.3894724	0.5595905	0.8500791
0.1223960	0.1038052	0.1041447	0.0605684	0.0452138	0.1002381	0.1252003
0.0113788	0.0052026	0.0117590	0.0158033	0.0113914	0.0466998	0.0135683
0.0925735	0.0284948	0.0857898	0.0590896	0.0461052	0.1222448	0.0438854
0.0136869	0.0076756	0.0143632	0.0172237	0.0439491	0.0231713	0.0126785
0.0092300	0.0058189	0.0085164	0.0089202	0.0055568	0.0053838	0.0059707
0.0261165	0.0120846	0.0241209	0.0174775	0.0510897	0.1201380	0.0197383
0.0965820	0.1119822	0.0808722	0.0606138	0.3539215	0.1673660	0.0896703
0.0063926	0.0047158	0.0051828	0.0033255	0.0100155	0.0751048	0.0084306
0.0631988	0.0145933	0.0654582	0.0310741	0.0394220	0.0912469	0.0445553
0.0289895	0.0046017	0.0363055	0.0140387	0.0091060	0.0135122	0.0106038
0.0007243	0.0002506	0.0005277	0.0008425	0.0006551	0.0005820	0.0003628
0.0111773	0.0094683	0.0122261	0.0062819	0.0061234	0.0208492	0.0124522
0.0036308	0.0020366	0.0033868	0.0024876	0.0090123	0.0042606	0.0026776
0.0034098	0.0012274	0.0028654	0.0040395	0.0013544	0.0020959	0.0020407
0.0051911	0.0026753	0.0055118	0.0030811	0.0177954	0.0499644	0.0056492
0.0022105	0.0008320	0.0020021	0.0140285	0.0016516	0.0070538	0.0018520

2-14 续表

投入 Output \ 产出 Input		金融业 Financing	房地产业 Real Estate	租赁与商务服务业 Renting and Business Activities
农业	Agriculture	0.0177599	0.0436492	0.0450870
采矿业	Mining and Quarrying	0.0183414	0.0594462	0.0493555
制造业	Manufacturing	0.3167798	0.8554502	0.7428114
电力、燃气及水的生产和供应业	Electricity, Gas & Water Production and Supply	0.0411560	0.1069480	0.1142439
建筑业	Construction	0.0212889	0.3396526	0.0180511
交通运输、仓储及邮政业	Transportation, Storage, Postal Services	0.0443339	0.0601459	0.1140227
信息传输、计算机服务和软件业	Data Transmission, Computer Service and Software	0.0265148	0.0189940	0.0356876
批发与零售业	Wholesale and Retail Trade	0.0023184	0.0081119	0.0267421
住宿和餐饮业	Hotels and Restaurants	0.0350967	0.0283906	0.0476487
金融业	Financing	0.0342363	0.1249393	0.1006589
房地产业	Real Estate	0.0262616	0.0144084	0.0078262
租赁与商务服务业	Renting and Business Activities	0.0367176	0.1278969	0.1176532
科学研究、技术服务与地质勘查业	Scientific Research, Technical Services and Geological Prospecting	0.0054160	0.0338153	0.0109040
水利、环境和公共设施管理业	Administration of Water Conservancy, Environment and Public Utilities	0.0016695	0.0021808	0.0005647
居民服务和其他服务业	Personal Services and Other Services	0.0053033	0.0111760	0.0196448
教育	Education	0.0042425	0.0036926	0.0073201
卫生、社会保障和社会福利业	Public Health, Social Security and Social Welfare	0.0016768	0.0043301	0.0047588
文化、体育与娱乐业	Culture, Sports and Entertainment	0.0056501	0.0167753	0.0093425
公共管理与社会组织	Public Administration and Social Organizations	0.0029677	0.0675008	0.0069143

2-14 CONTINUED

科学研究、技术服务与地质勘查业 Scientific Research, Technical Services and Geological Prospecting	水利、环境和公共设施管理业 Administration of Water Conservancy, Environment and Public Utilities	居民服务和其他服务业 Personal Services and Other Services	教 育 Education	卫生、社会保障和社会福利业 Public Health, Social Security and Social Welfare	文化、体育与娱乐业 Culture, Sports and Entertainment	公共管理与社会组织 Public Administration and Social Organizations
0.0445615	0.0327160	0.0429013	0.0242140	0.0529680	0.0205211	0.0335131
0.0530539	0.0319104	0.0474892	0.0254669	0.0613719	0.0239821	0.0322035
0.9509250	0.5713563	0.8605663	0.4464111	1.2981456	0.4092922	0.5675423
0.0786990	0.0645526	0.0851732	0.0480928	0.0927354	0.0534501	0.0690401
0.1740887	0.0248975	0.0971402	0.0225240	0.0141144	0.0248492	0.0229686
0.0644018	0.1022130	0.0669040	0.0554734	0.0562348	0.0373460	0.0912724
0.0168596	0.0423773	0.0205336	0.0152810	0.0127540	0.0188834	0.0326377
0.0049024	0.0042448	0.0281550	0.0027082	0.0052001	0.0049599	0.0038511
0.0378844	0.0693695	0.0580354	0.0462996	0.0220338	0.0227252	0.0771141
0.0560796	0.0576902	0.0584471	0.0325492	0.0609212	0.0623983	0.0532048
0.0037005	0.0030358	0.0166986	0.0019899	0.0037462	0.0058466	0.0029118
0.0450003	0.0697381	0.0478726	0.0269713	0.0424898	0.0864926	0.0538235
0.0473759	0.1109181	0.0121859	0.0371713	0.0535880	0.0835349	0.0987766
0.0003547	0.0003306	0.0003342	0.0004341	0.0016780	0.0003343	0.0005989
0.0099261	0.0079829	0.1242275	0.0126120	0.0076544	0.0117918	0.0080520
0.0037266	0.0042117	0.0019177	0.0048761	0.0079125	0.0074878	0.0086417
0.0161230	0.0179939	0.0015501	0.0256383	0.0091554	0.0045027	0.0345332
0.0193861	0.0136868	0.0040009	0.0140576	0.0182149	0.0486989	0.0187882
0.0016431	0.0019553	0.0036042	0.0010867	0.0015328	0.0013437	0.0021184

主要统计指标解释

国内（地区）生产总值（GDP） 是一个国家（或地区）所有常住单位在一定时期内生产活动的最终成果。国内（地区）生产总值有三种表现形态，即价值形态、收入形态和产品形态。从价值形态看，它是所有常住单位在一定时期内所生产的全部货物和服务价值超过同期中间投入的全部非固定资产货物和服务价值的差额，即所有常住单位的增加值之和；从收入形态看，它是所有常住单位在一定时期内所创造并分配给常住单位和非常住单位的初次分配收入之和；从产品形态看，它是所有常住单位在一定时期内最终使用的货物和服务价值与货物和服务净出口价值之和。在实际核算中，国内（地区）生产总值的三种表现形态表现为三种计算方法，即生产法、收入法和支出法。三种方法分别从不同的方面反映国内（地区）生产总值及其构成。

国民生产总值（GNP） 是一个国家（或地区）所有常住单位在一定时期内收入初次分配的最终成果。一国常住单位从事生产活动所创造的增加值在初次分配过程中主要分配给该国的常住单位，但也有一部分以生产税及进口税（扣除生产和进口补贴）、劳动者报酬和财产收入等形式分配给非常住单位，同时，国外生产所创造的增加值也有一部分以生产税及进口税（扣除生产和进口补贴）、劳动者报酬和财产收入等形式分配给该国的常住单位，从而产生了国民生产总值的概念。它等于国内（地区）生产总值加上来自国外的净要素收入。与国内（地区）生产总值不同，国民生产总值则是个收入概念，而国内（地区）生产总值是一个生产概念。

三次产业 三产业的划分是世界上较为常用的产业结构分类，但各国的划分不尽一致。我国的三次产业划分是：

第一产业是指农、林、牧、渔业。

第二产业是指采矿业，制造业，电力、煤气及水的生产和供应业，建筑业。

第三产业是指除第一、二产业以外的其他行业。

劳动者报酬 是指劳动者因从事生产活动所获得的全部报酬。包括劳动者获得的各种形式的工资、奖金和津贴，既包括货币形式的，也包括实物形式的；还包括劳动者所享受的公费医疗和医药卫生费、上下班交通补贴和单位支付的社会保险费等。对于个体经济来说，其所有者所获得的劳动报酬和经营利润不易区分，这两部分统一作为劳动者报酬处理。

生产税净额 指生产税减生产补贴后的差额。生产税指政府对生产单位生产、销售和从事经营活动以及因从事生产活动使用某些生产要素（如固定资产、土地、劳动力）所征收的各种税、附加费和规费。生产补贴与生产税相反，是政府对生产单位的单方面收入转移，因此视为负生产税，包括政策亏损补贴、价格补贴等。

固定资产折旧 指一定时期内为弥补固定资产损耗按照核定的固定资产折旧率提取的固定资产折旧，或按国民经济核算统一规定的折旧率虚拟计算的固定资产折旧。它反映了固定资产在当期生产中的转移价值。各类企业和企业化管理的事业单位的固定资产折旧指实际计提并计入成本费用中的折旧费；不计提折旧的政府机关、非企业化管理的事业单位和居民住房的固定资产折旧则是按照统一规定的折旧率和固定资产原值计算的虚拟折旧。原则上，固定资产折旧应按固定资产的重置价值来计算，但是我国目前尚不具备对全社会固定资产进行重估价的基础，所以暂时只能采用上述方法来计算。

营业盈余 指常住单位创造的增加值扣除劳动者报酬、生产税净额和固定资产折旧后的余额。它相当于企业的营业利润加上生产补贴，但要扣除从利润中开支的工资和福利。

支出法国内（地区）生产总值　是从最终使用的角度反映一个国家(或地区)一定时期内生产活动最终成果的一种方法，包括最终消费、资本形成总额及货物和服务净出口三部分。计算公式为：

支出法国内生产总值=最终消费+资本形成总额+货物和服务净出口

最终消费　指常住单位为满足物质、文化和精神生活的需要，从本国经济领土和国外购买的货物和服务的支出。它不包括非常住单位在本国经济领土内的消费支出。最终消费分为居民消费和政府消费。

（一）居民消费：指常住住户在一定时期内对于货物和服务的全部最终消费支出。居民消费除了直接以货币形式购买的货物和服务的消费支出外，还包括以其他方式获得的货物和服务的消费支出，即所谓的虚拟消费支出。居民虚拟消费支出包括如下几种类型：单位以实物报酬及实物转移的形式提供给劳动者的货物和服务；住户生产并由本住户消费了的货物和服务，其中的服务仅指住户的自有住房服务和付酬的家庭雇员提供的家庭和个人服务；金融机构提供的金融媒介服务；保险公司提供的保险服务。

（二）政府消费：指政府部门为全社会提供的公共服务的消费支出和免费或以较低的价格向居民住户提供的货物和服务的净支出，前者等于政府服务的产出价值减去政府单位所获得的经营收入的价值，后者等于政府部门免费或以较低价格向居民住户提供的货物和服务的市场价值减去向住户收取的价值。

资本形成总额　指常住单位在一定时期内获得的减去处置的固定资产加存货的变动，包括固定资产形成总额和存货增加。

（一）固定资产形成总额：指生产者在一定时期内获得的固定资产减处置的固定资产的价值总额。固定资产是通过生产活动生产出来的，且其使用年限在一年以上、单位价值在规定标准以上的资产，不包括自然资产。可分为有形固定资本形成总额和无形固定资本形成总额。有形固定资本形成总额包括一定时期内完成的建筑工程、安装工程和设备工器具购置(减处置)价值，以及土地改良、新增役、种、奶、毛、娱乐用牲畜和新增经济林木价值。无形固定资本形成总额包括矿藏的勘探、计算机软件等获得减处置。

（二）存货增加：指常住单位在一定时期内存货实物量变动的市场价值，即期末价值减期初价值的差额，再扣除当期由于价格变动而产生的持有收益。存货增加可以是正值，也可以是负值，正值表示存货上升，负值表示存货下降。存货包括生产单位购进的原材料、燃料和储备物资等存货，以及生产单位生产的产成品、在制品和半成品等存货。

货物和服务净出口　指货物和服务出口减货物和服务进口的差额。出口包括常住单位向非常住单位出售或无偿转让的各种货物和服务的价值；进口包括常住单位从非常住单位购买或无偿得到的各种货物和服务的价值。由于服务活动的提供与使用同时发生，因此服务的进出口业务并不发生出入境现象，一般把常住单位从国外得到的服务作为进口，非常住单位从本国得到的服务作为出口。货物的出口和进口都按离岸价格计算。

直接消耗系数　也称为投入系数，记为 A_{ij} (ij=1,2,...,n)它是指在生产经营过程中第 j 产品(或产业)部门的单位总产出所直接消耗的第 i 产品部门货物或服务的价值量，将各产品(或产业)部门的直接消耗系数用表的形式表现出来，就是直接消耗系数表或直接消耗系数矩阵，通常用字母 A 表示。

完全消耗系数　指第 j 产品部门每提供一个单位最终使用时，对第 i 产品部门货物或服务的直接消耗和间接消耗之和。将各产品部门的完全消耗系数用表的形式表现出来，就是完全消耗系数表或完全消耗系数矩阵，通常用字母 B 表示。

Explanatory Notes on Main Statistical Indicators

Gross Domestic Product (GDP) refers to the final products of all resident unties in a country (or a region) during a certain period of time. Gross domestic product is expressed in three different forms, i.e. value added, income, and products respectively. The form of value added refers to the total value of all products and services produced by all resident units during a certain period of time minus total value of intimidate input of materials and services of the nature of non-fixed assets or the summation of the value added of all resident units; the form of income includes all the income created by all resident units and distributed primarily to all resident and non-resident units; the form of products refers to all final goods and services of final use by all resident units plus the value of net exports of goods and services. In the practice of national accounting, gross domestic product is calculated with three approaches, i.e. product approach, income approach and expenditure approach, which reflect gross domestic product and its composition from different aspects.

Gross National Product (GNP) refers to the final result of the primary distribution of the income created by all the resident units of a country (or a region) during a certain period of time. The value added created by the resident units of a country engaged in production activities is mainly distributed to the resident units of that country while a part of it is distributed to the non-resident units in the form of production tax and import duties (minus subsidies to production and import), remuneration for the laborers and property income. At the meantime, a part of the value-added created abroad is distributed to the resident unties of the country in the form of production tax and import duties (minus subsidies to production and import), remuneration for the laborers and property income. Thus the concept of gross national product is formed, which equals to gross domestic product plus net factor income from abroad. Unlike gross domestic product which is a concept of production, gross national product is a concept of income.

Three Industries Classification of economic activities into three branches of industries is a common practice in the world, although the grouping varies to some extent form country to country. In China economic activities are categorized into following industries:

Primary industry: refers to agriculture, forestry, animal husbandry and fishery.

Secondary industry: refers to mining and quarrying, manufacturing, production and supply of electricity, water and gas, and construction.

Tertiary industry: refers to all other economic activities not included in primary or secondary industry.

Laborers' Remuneration refers to the whole payment earned by the laborers from the productive activities they are engaged in. It includes wages, bonuses and allowances the laborers earned in various forms, including monetary form and form in kind. It also includes the free medical services provided to the laborers and the medicine expenses, traffic subsidies and social insurance fee paid by the laborers' working units for them. As the individual economy is concerned, since the laborers' remuneration is not easily distinguished from the operating profit, both are treated as laborers' remuneration.

Net Taxes on Production refers to the difference of the taxes on production minus the subsidies on production. The taxes on production refers to the various taxes, extra charges and fees levied on the production units on their production, sale and business activities as well as on some factors of production, such as fixed assets, land and labor force, used in the production activities they are engaged in. In contrast to the taxes on production, the subsidies on production is the unilateral transfer of part of the government's revenue to the production units and is therefore treated as the negative taxes on production, They include subsidies on the loss due to implementation of government policies, price subsidies, etc.

Depreciation of Fixed Assets refers to the depreciation of fixed assets drawn in accordance with the stipulated depreciation rate for the purpose of compensating the wear loss of the fixed assets or the depreciation of fixed assets calculated in a fictitious way in accordance with the stipulated unified depreciation rate in the national economic accounting system. It reflects the value of transfer of the fixed assets in the production of the current period. The depreciation of fixed assets in various enterprises and institutions managed as enterprises refers to the depreciation expenses actually drawn and calculated as part of the cost. In the units, which do not draw the depreciation expenses, such as government agencies, institutions not managed as enterprises as well as the houses of residents, the depreciation of fixed assets is the fictitious depreciation, which is calculated in accordance with the stipulated unified depreciation rate. In principle, the depreciation of fixed assets should be calculated on the basis of the re-purchased value of the fixed assets. However, there is no actual condition to re-evaluate all the fixed assets in China. Therefore, the above-mentioned methods are temporarily adopted at present.

Operating Surplus refers to the balance of the value added created by the resident units deducting the laborers' remuneration, net taxes on production ant the depreciation of fixed assets. It is equivalent to the business profit of the enterprises plus subsidies on production, but the wages and welfare expenses paid from the profits should be deducted.

GDP by Expenditure Approach refers to the method of measuring the final results of production activities of a country (region) during a given period from the perspective of final use. It includes final consumption, total capital formation and net export of goods and services, i.e.:

GDP by expenditure approach = final consumption + total capital formation + net export of goods and services

Final Consumption refers to the total expenditure of resident units on final consumption of goods and services in a certain period, namely the expenditure of the resident units for purchases of goods and services from domestic economic territory and abroad to meet the requirements of material, cultural and spiritual life. It excludes the expenditure of non-resident units on consumption in the economic territory of the country. The final consumption is classified into resident consumption and government consumption.

(1) Resident consumption refers to the total expenditure of resident households on the final consumption of goods and services. The expenditure of the residents on consumption is calculated at market prices, namely the purchasers' prices that the residents pay; the purchasers' prices of goods are the prices the residents pay when they obtain the goods, including the transport and commercial expenses paid by the residents. In addition to the expenditure on consumption of goods and services bought by the residents directly with money, the expenditure on goods and services obtained by the residents in other ways, i.e. the so-called fictitious expenditure on consumption is also included in the expenditure of the residents on consumption. The fictitious expenditure of the residents on consumption includes the following types:(a) the goods and services provided to the residents by the units in the form of payment in kind and transfer in kind;(b) the goods and services produced and consumed by the households themselves, in which the services refer only to the services provided by the residential buildings owned by the households;(c) the services of financial intermediary provided by the financial institutions;(d) the insurance services provided by the insurance companies.

(2) Government consumption refers to the expenditure on the consumption of the public services provided by the government to the whole society and the net expenditure on the goods and services provided by the government to the households for free charge or at lower prices. The former equals to the output value of the government services minus the

value of operating in come obtained by the government departments. (The output value of the government services equals to its current operating expenditure plus depreciation of fixed assets). The latter equals to the market value of the goods and services provided by the government to the households minus the value received by the government from the households.

Total Capital Formation refers to the net amount of the fixed assets and stock acquired minus those disposed, including the total fixed assets formation and the increase in stock.

(1) Total fixed capital formation refer to the value of fixed assets purchased, transferred in by the resident units and those produced and used by themselves deducting the value of fixed assets sold and transferred out. It can by classified into total tangible assets formation and total intangible assets formation. The total tangible assets formation include the value of the construction projects, installation projects completed and the equipment, apparatus and instruments purchased as well as the value of land improved, the value of draught animals, breeding stock, milk, wool and recreational animals and the newly increased economic forest in a certain period. The total intangible assets formation includes the prospecting of minerals, the acquisition of computer software, the originals of recreational works and works of literature and arts minus the disposal of them.

(2) Increase in stock refers to the market value of the change in stock, i.e., the difference of value between the beginning and the end of the period. The increase in stock can be positive or negative. A positive value indicates the increase in stock while a negative value indicates the decrease in stock. The stock includes the raw materials, fuels and reserve materials purchased by the production units as well as the stock of finished products, semi-finished products, work-in-progress, etc.

Net Export of Goods and Services refers to the difference of the exports of goods and services minus the imports of goods and services. The imports include the value of various goods and services sold or gratuitously transferred by the resident units to the non-resident units. The imports include the value of various goods and services purchased or gratuitously acquired by the resident units from the non-resident units. Because the provision of services and the use of them happen simultaneously, the import and export of services by the resident units from abroad is usually treated as import while the acquisition of services by non-resident units in this country is usually treated as export. The export and import of goods are calculated at FOB.

Direct Input Coefficient refers to the volume of products and services of industry i, which is consumed directly by industry j in the course of its production or business, recorded as A_{ij} (i,j=1,2, … ,n). The direct input coefficient table or direct input coefficient matrix, usually denoted as A, is a table that presents direct input coefficients of all industries.

Total Input Coefficient refers to the volume of products and services of industry i which is consumed directly and indirectly by industry j in producing each unit of final use. The total input coefficient table or total input coefficient matrix, usually denoted as B, is a table that presents total input coefficients of all industries.

三　人口与就业

POPULATION AND EMPLOYMENT

简要说明 Brief Introduction

本章内容主要包括全市的户籍人口、常住人口、五次人口普查的主要数据，以及计划生育、就业、工资等情况，由市统计局人口就业处整理编辑。

户籍统计人口资料由市公安局提供；计划生育资料由市计划生育委员会提供；失业和离退休资料由市社会劳动保障局提供；常住人口、人口普查主要数据、就业和工资资料由市统计局人口就业处提供。

The data in this chapter show the basic statistics on household registered population, resident population and 5 population censuses, and statistics on family planning, as well as employment and wages. They are prepared and edited by Division of Population and Employment Statistics, Municipal Bureau of Statistics.

The data on household registered population are provided by Municipal Bureau of Public Security. Data on family planning come from Municipal Family Planning Commission. And Data on unemployment and retired persons are provided by Municipal Bureau of Labor and Social Security. Main indicators of resident population, population censuses, employment and wages are provided by Division of Population and Employment Statistics, Municipal Bureau of Statistics.

3－1 主要年份总户数、总人口（户籍统计）
Total Households and Total Population in Major Years (Household Registration)

单位：万户、万人 (10 000 households, 10 000 persons)

年 份 Year	总户数 Total Households	总人口 Total Population	按性别分 By Sex 男 Male	女 Female	按农业、非农业分 By Agriculture and Non-agriculture 农业 Agriculture	非农业 Non-agriculture
1952	401.93	1776.52	927.91	848.61		
1957	434.66	2005.18	1040.82	964.36	1692.77	312.41
1962	442.01	1797.19	916.99	880.20	1528.95	268.24
1965	455.55	1974.89	1010.19	964.70	1685.08	289.81
1970	518.02	2289.64	1173.57	1116.07	1989.66	299.98
1975	579.36	2592.59	1332.89	1259.70	2280.39	312.20
1978	601.07	2635.56	1357.98	1277.58	2304.66	330.90
1980	610.19	2664.79	1376.22	1288.57	2291.51	373.28
1985	684.46	2768.26	1437.35	1330.91	2310.89	457.37
1986	716.53	2807.60	1458.75	1348.85	2343.23	464.37
1987	751.96	2845.14	1478.88	1366.26	2370.06	475.08
1988	784.83	2873.34	1494.20	1379.14	2390.36	482.98
1989	812.65	2897.01	1507.74	1389.27	2405.25	491.76
1990	833.78	2920.90	1520.83	1400.07	2427.92	492.98
1991	844.66	2938.99	1531.11	1407.88	2439.61	499.38
1992	849.77	2950.78	1538.46	1412.32	2438.94	511.84
1993	855.75	2964.92	1546.50	1418.42	2438.27	526.65
1994	870.20	2985.59	1558.05	1427.54	2440.41	545.18
1995	879.35	3001.77	1566.86	1434.91	2442.33	559.44
1996	888.56	3022.77	1577.97	1444.80	2445.65	577.12
1997	897.78	3042.92	1588.10	1454.82	2448.34	594.58
1998	907.17	3059.69	1596.88	1462.81	2445.66	614.03
1999	922.73	3072.34	1602.42	1469.92	2437.18	635.16
2000	938.87	3091.09	1611.68	1479.41	2430.20	660.89
2001	950.56	3097.91	1614.91	1483.00	2408.39	689.52
2002	961.69	3113.83	1623.13	1490.70	2392.38	721.45
2003	977.01	3130.10	1631.66	1498.44	2376.18	753.92
2004	988.59	3144.23	1637.18	1507.05	2358.40	785.83

3-2 主要年份人口自然变动（户籍统计）
Population Natural Changes in Major Years (Household Registration)

单位：万人、‰ (10 000 persons, ‰)

年份 Year	出生 Birth		死亡 Mortality		自然增长 Natural Growth	
	人口 Population	出生率 Birth Rate	人口 Population	死亡率 Mortality Rate	人口 Population	自然增长率 Natural Growth Rate
1957	54.20	27.32	21.78	10.98	32.42	16.34
1962	43.72	24.36	27.87	15.53	15.85	8.83
1965	74.01	38.03	21.43	11.01	52.58	27.02
1970	87.78	38.99	22.11	9.82	65.67	29.17
1975	72.03	28.06	21.33	8.31	50.70	19.75
1978	26.09	9.91	17.18	6.52	8.91	3.39
1980	29.68	11.16	17.19	6.46	12.49	4.70
1985	36.13	13.10	18.76	6.80	17.37	6.30
1986	54.47	19.54	18.36	6.59	36.11	12.95
1987	48.72	17.24	18.42	6.52	30.30	10.72
1988	38.58	13.49	19.43	6.79	19.15	6.70
1989	39.79	13.79	19.99	6.93	19.80	6.86
1990	42.53	14.62	19.59	6.73	22.94	7.89
1991	37.61	12.83	19.20	6.55	18.41	6.28
1992	35.62	12.09	20.89	7.09	14.73	5.00
1993	35.75	12.09	20.23	6.84	15.52	5.25
1994	40.05	13.46	19.95	6.70	20.10	6.76
1995	39.39	13.16	21.45	7.17	17.94	5.99
1996	41.06	13.63	21.62	7.18	19.44	6.45
1997	36.99	12.20	20.95	6.91	16.04	5.29
1998	35.51	11.64	21.64	7.09	13.87	4.55
1999	30.68	10.01	20.68	6.74	10.00	3.27
2000	35.22	11.43	24.59	7.98	10.63	3.45
2001	26.26	8.48	18.76	6.06	7.50	2.42
2002	28.65	9.20	18.07	5.80	10.58	3.40
2003	30.00	9.61	18.05	5.78	11.95	3.83
2004	33.72	10.74	23.44	7.47	10.28	3.27

3－3 各区县（自治县、市）常住人口（2000－2004年）
Resident Population by Region (2000-2004)

单位：万人 (10 000 persons)

地　区	Region	2000	2001	2002	2003	2004
全　市	**Total**	**2826.27**	**2809.94**	**2795.48**	**2777.47**	**2770.98**
万州区	Wanzhou District	155.06	153.95	153.10	151.49	150.67
涪陵区	Fuling District	104.36	103.15	102.63	100.88	100.67
渝中区	Yuzhong District	66.05	66.96	67.94	58.13	68.63
大渡口区	Dadukou District	24.93	25.13	25.20	25.43	25.70
江北区	Jiangbei District	61.64	62.42	63.78	62.51	63.51
沙坪坝区	Shapingba District	79.63	80.32	81.58	82.95	84.09
九龙坡区	Jiulongpo District	88.73	89.34	90.05	90.82	92.22
南岸区	Nan'an District	59.90	60.98	63.01	64.14	65.13
北碚区	Beibei District	65.20	65.25	65.29	65.37	66.20
万盛区	Wansheng District	26.84	25.93	25.23	24.57	24.86
双桥区	Shuangqiao District	4.50	4.52	4.56	4.60	4.64
渝北区	Yubei District	76.99	77.89	78.33	79.10	81.88
巴南区	Ba'nan District	79.95	79.56	79.23	79.38	79.80
黔江区	Qianjiang District	43.62	43.60	43.56	43.53	43.99
长寿区	Changshou District	76.28	75.77	74.69	74.49	74.69
綦江县	Qijiang County	87.36	86.25	84.55	83.55	83.32
潼南县	Tongnan County	73.65	72.64	72.13	71.69	70.68
铜梁县	Tongliang County	64.73	63.35	62.83	61.65	61.52
大足县	Dazu County	79.07	78.35	77.30	76.58	75.77
荣昌县	Rongchang County	65.60	65.56	65.54	65.50	64.74
璧山县	Bishan County	52.55	52.05	51.68	50.96	50.94
梁平县	Liangping County	74.20	73.83	72.88	72.07	71.28
城口县	Chengkou County	20.16	19.86	19.71	19.59	19.15
丰都县	Fengdu County	66.57	66.40	65.83	65.10	64.32
垫江县	Dianjiang County	76.53	75.89	74.82	73.60	72.71
武隆县	Wulong County	36.07	35.60	35.36	35.15	34.63
忠　县	Zhongxian County	76.68	75.69	75.23	74.97	74.21
开　县	Kaixian County	120.80	119.45	117.75	116.14	116.10
云阳县	Yunyang County	105.46	104.71	103.97	102.30	101.21
奉节县	Fengjie County	86.83	86.80	86.77	86.79	85.78
巫山县	Wushan County	52.32	51.45	50.65	50.49	49.85
巫溪县	Wuxi County	47.59	46.97	45.53	44.96	44.25
石柱县	Shizhu County	45.87	44.98	44.40	43.88	43.36
秀山县	Xiushan County	50.34	50.28	50.30	50.32	50.12
酉阳县	Youyang County	58.72	58.69	58.50	58.60	57.38
彭水县	Pengshui County	56.60	55.81	55.42	55.09	54.05
江津市	Jiangjin City	130.88	129.46	128.44	126.68	125.87
合川市	Hechuan City	130.66	129.23	127.96	127.65	126.90
永川市	Yongchuan City	95.61	94.56	93.77	92.09	91.98
南川市	Nanchuan City	57.74	57.31	55.98	54.68	54.18

3－4 人口抽样调查（2003－2004年）
Sample Survey of Population (2003-2004)

单位：万人 (10 000 persons)

项　　目	Item	2003	2004
家庭户户数（万户）	Family Households (10 000 households)	974.55	955.51
常住人口	Resident Population	2777.47	2770.98
#城镇	Urban	1163.76	1205.70
乡村	Rural	1613.71	1565.28
#男性	Male	1378.74	1388.01
女性	Female	1398.73	1382.97
#0-14岁	Age 0-14	609.93	587.45
15-64岁	Age 15-64	1877.02	1881.49
65岁以以上	Age 65 and Over	290.52	302.04
外出人口	Population Going outside Residential Area	556.50	593.68
#外出至市外	Going outside Chongqing	386.80	407.01
市外外来人口	Population Going to Chongqing	51.30	56.10
城镇化率（%）	Rate of Urban Population (%)	41.9	43.5
都市发达经济圈	Metropolitan Advanced Economic Sphere	84.4	85.0
渝西经济走廊	West Chongqing Economic Corridor	36.0	37.7
三峡库区生态经济区	Ecological Economic Zone in Three Gorges Reservoir Area	25.8	27.3
出生人口	Birth Population	27.50	26.32
出生率（‰）	Birth Rate (‰)	9.9	9.5
死亡人口	Mortality Population	20.00	18.29
死亡率（‰）	Mortality Rate (‰)	7.2	6.6
自然增长人口	Natural Growing Population	7.50	8.03
自然增长率（‰）	Natural Growth Rate (‰)	2.7	2.9

注：人口抽样调查样本比例2003年为千分之一，自2004年起为百分之一。
Note: Population sampling fraction in 2003 is 1‰, whereas since 2004 is 1%.

3－5 第四次、第五次人口普查基本情况
Basic Statistics on Population Censuses in 1990 and 2000

指　　标	Item	1990	2000
总人口（万人）	**Total Population (10 000 persons)**	**2886.62**	**3051.28**
男	Male	1499.83	1584.15
女	Female	1386.79	1467.13
性别比（女=100）	Sex Ratio (female=100)	108.15	107.98
家庭户户数（万户）	**Family Households (10 000 households)**	**788.84**	**914.16**
家庭户规模（人/户）	**Average Family Size (person/household)**	**3.56**	**3.23**
各年龄组人口（万人）	**Population by Age Group (10 000 persons)**		
0-14岁	Age 0-14	626.27	666.29
15-64岁	Age 15-64	2092.06	2140.45
65岁及以上	Age 65 and Over	168.29	244.54
预期寿命（岁）	**Life Expectancy (years old)**	**67.9**	**71.9**
城乡人口（万人）	**Population by Residence (10 000 persons)**		
城镇人口	Urban Population	842.11	1009.55
乡村人口	Rural Population	2044.51	2041.73
民族人口（万人，%）	**Nationality Population (10 000 persons, %)**		
汉族	Han Nationality	2737.58	2853.92
占总人口比重	Percentage as Total Population	94.8	93.5
少数民族	Minority Nationalities	149.04	197.36
占总人口比重	Percentage as Total Population	5.2	6.5
每十万人拥有的各种受教育程度人口（人）	**Population with Various Education Attainment Per 100 000 Population (person)**		
大专及以上	Junior College and Above	1070	2819
高中和中专	Senior Secondary/Secondary Technical School	6235	8600
初中	Junior Secondary School	22857	29474
小学	Primary School	44999	43357
文盲人口及文盲率	**Illiterate Population and Illiterate Rate**		
文盲人口（万人）	Illiterate Population (10 000 persons)	404.54	212.24
文盲率（%）	Illiterate Rate (%)	17.9	8.9

3—6 五次人口普查主要指标
Main Indicators of Five Population Censuses

单位：万人、% (10 000 persons, %)

普查时间	Census Time	总人口 Total Population			性别比（女=100） Sex Ratio (female=100)	年平均增长率 Annual Average Growth Rate
		合计 Total	男 Male	女 Female		
第一次人口普查（1953年7月1日）	First Population Census (July 1, 1953)	1766.39	924.56	841.83	109.83	
第二次人口普查（1964年7月1日）	Second Population Census (July 1, 1964)	1889.17	969.02	920.15	105.31	0.61
第三次人口普查（1982年7月1日）	Third Population Census (July 1, 1982)	2705.89	1402.46	1303.43	107.60	2.02
第四次人口普查（1990年7月1日）	Fourth Population Census (July 1, 1990)	2886.62	1499.83	1386.79	108.15	0.81
第五次人口普查（2000年11月1日）	Fifth Population Census (November 1, 2000)	3051.28	1584.15	1467.13	107.98	0.66

3—7 计划生育基本情况（1986—2004年）
Basic Statistics on Family Planning (1986-2004)

单位：万人、% (10 000 persons, %)

年份 Year	计划生育率 Birth Control Rate	已婚育龄妇女人数 Married Women at Childbearing Age	领独生子女证人数 Women with Only-child Certificates	领证率 Coverage of Only-child Certificates	采取节育措施人数 Women under Contraception	避孕率 Contraception Rate
1986	90.88	481.28	109.56	68.74	424.89	88.28
1987	90.16	503.67	126.44	71.91	451.19	89.58
1988	93.83	523.17	141.28	72.14	480.27	91.80
1989	92.78	540.80	151.72	70.35	491.35	90.86
1990	94.15	560.09	166.56	70.53	512.38	91.48
1991	95.11	577.54	178.27	69.31	527.88	91.40
1992	95.83	589.35	188.00	68.34	538.37	91.35
1993	93.23	599.23	199.97		548.27	91.50
1994	86.58	611.48	206.76		559.62	91.52
1995	89.22	625.71	220.32		573.38	91.64
1996	88.73	637.31	227.59	65.45	587.93	92.25
1997	91.94	644.56	230.99	64.11	588.75	91.34
1998	85.06	644.68	219.05	59.69	589.28	91.40
1999	94.09	640.70	214.79	57.43	587.94	91.77
2000	91.26	639.20	217.43	57.11	589.95	92.29
2001	91.15	632.25	203.30	53.04	583.65	92.31
2002	92.19	620.38	180.36	47.65	571.18	92.07
2003	92.39	622.26	195.38	51.11	571.87	91.90
2004	90.41	615.20	200.49	52.42	564.60	91.77

3－8 就业人员基本情况（1985－2004年）
Basic Statistics on Employment (1985-2004)

单位：万人 (10 000 persons)

年 份 Year	就业人员总计 Total Employment	#城 镇 Urban	按经济类型分 By Ownership			
			国 有 State-owned	集 体 Collective-owned	私营和个体 Private and Individuals	其 他 Others
1985	1432.03	269.37				
1986	1469.13	275.35				
1987	1507.33	282.39				
1988	1512.49	288.70				
1989	1540.03	291.29				
1990	1569.34	296.92				
1991	1620.67	307.87				
1992	1662.58	313.51				
1993	1658.95	310.05				
1994	1729.55	326.75				
1995	1709.26	347.06				
1996	1674.90	424.99	198.16	1248.51	215.80	12.43
1997	1679.91	442.30	189.07	1239.67	236.11	15.06
1998	1686.71	456.90	175.52	1207.66	279.77	23.76
1999	1688.73	473.30	161.15	1190.67	308.02	28.89
2000	1690.00	496.20	149.28	1157.80	354.86	28.06
2001	1697.00	525.00	136.63	1122.39	394.06	43.92
2002	1710.50	540.42	130.66	1102.46	425.07	52.31
2003	1726.36	557.19	125.88	1085.03	452.72	62.73
2004	1715.62	582.79	124.72	1044.97	473.22	72.71

3-8 续表 CONTINUED

年 份 Year	按产业分 By Industry			分产业比重（%） Compositon By Industry		
	第一产业 Primary Industry	第二产业 Secondary Industry	第三产业 Tertiary Industry	第一产业 Primary Industry	第二产业 Secondary Industry	第三产业 Tertiary Industry
1985	1042.22	223.37	166.44	72.78	15.60	11.62
1986	1048.32	241.66	179.15	71.36	16.45	12.19
1987	1064.06	258.93	184.34	70.59	17.18	12.23
1988	1056.49	262.83	193.17	69.85	17.38	12.77
1989	1082.41	263.81	193.81	70.29	17.13	12.58
1990	1103.04	263.86	202.44	70.29	16.81	12.90
1991	1130.47	275.72	214.48	69.75	17.01	13.24
1992	1118.59	277.77	266.22	67.28	16.71	16.01
1993	1088.70	287.88	282.37	65.63	17.35	17.02
1994	1062.90	301.13	365.52	61.46	17.41	21.13
1995	1018.30	310.88	380.08	59.58	18.19	22.23
1996	996.37	340.89	337.64	59.49	20.35	20.16
1997	995.15	335.29	349.47	59.24	19.96	20.80
1998	987.47	311.92	387.32	58.55	18.49	22.96
1999	981.33	281.24	426.16	58.11	16.65	25.24
2000	948.42	276.04	465.54	56.12	16.33	27.55
2001	924.78	284.71	487.51	54.49	16.78	28.73
2002	908.76	287.62	514.12	53.13	16.81	30.06
2003	892.23	298.42	535.71	51.68	17.29	31.03
2004	869.30	301.42	544.90	50.67	17.57	31.76

3－9 就业人员年末人数（2003－2004年）
Total Employment at Year-end (2003-2004)

单位：万人 (10 000 persons)

指标	Item	2003	2004
就业人员总计	**Total Employment**	**1726.36**	**1715.62**
城镇	Urban	557.19	582.79
乡村	Rural	1169.17	1132.83
按经济类型分	**By Ownership**		
国有经济	State-owned	125.88	124.72
集体经济	Collective-owned	1085.03	1044.97
私营	Private	89.09	93.64
个体	Individual	363.63	379.58
其他经济	Others	62.73	72.71
#联营	Joint Ownership	5.78	6.84
股份制	Share Holding	15.72	16.71
外商投资	Foreign-funded	3.23	4.16
港澳台投资	Funded by Hong Kong, Macao and Taiwan	2.55	2.33
按行业分	**By Sector**		
第一产业	Primary Industry	892.23	869.30
第二产业	Secondary Industry	298.42	301.42
采矿业	Mining and Quarrying	13.76	13.90
制造业	Manufacturing	164.81	165.72
电力、燃气及水的生产和供应业	Electricity, Gas & Water Production and Supply	6.25	6.30
建筑业	Construction	113.60	115.50
第三产业	Tertiary Industry	535.71	544.90
交通运输、仓储及邮政业	Transportation, Storage, Postal Services	44.98	45.28
信息传输、计算机服务和软件业	Data Transmission, Computer Service and Software	5.88	6.56
批发与零售业	Wholesale and Retail Trade	125.05	126.73
住宿和餐饮业	Hotels and Restaurants	73.11	74.05
金融业	Financing	6.59	6.63
房地产业	Real Estate	5.43	5.59
租赁与商务服务业	Renting and Business Activities	20.80	21.27
科学研究、技术服务与地质勘查业	Scientific Research, Technical Services and Geological Prospecting	8.77	8.97
水利、环境和公共设施管理业	Administration of Water Conservancy, Environment and Public Utilities	5.54	5.69
居民服务和其他服务业	Personal Services and Other Services	167.72	171.73
教育	Education	33.22	33.58
卫生、社会保障和社会福利业	Public Health, Social Security and Social Welfare	13.36	13.46
文化、体育与娱乐业	Culture, Sports and Entertainment	2.87	2.93
公共管理与社会组织	Public Administration and Social Organizations	22.39	22.43

3－10 城镇就业人员年末人数（2003－2004年）
Total Urban Employment at Year-end (2003-2004)

单位：万人 (10 000 persons)

指　　标	Item	2003	2004
就业人员总计	**Total Employment**	**557.19**	**582.79**
按经济类型分	**By Ownership**		
国有经济	State-owned	125.88	124.72
集体经济	Collective-owned	148.98	138.08
私　营	Private	62.88	69.86
个　体	Individual	156.92	177.42
其他经济	Others	62.53	72.71
#联　营	Joint Ownership	5.78	6.84
股份制	Share Holding	15.72	16.71
外商投资	Foreign-funded	3.23	4.16
港澳台投资	Funded by Hong Kong, Macao and Taiwan	2.55	2.33
按行业分	**By Sector**		
第一产业	Primary Industry	99.48	96.70
第二产业	Secondary Industry	188.34	200.66
采矿业	Mining and Quarrying	9.62	10.19
制造业	Manufacturing	107.35	113.31
电力、燃气及水的生产和供应业	Electricity, Gas & Water Production and Supply	6.25	6.30
建筑业	Construction	65.12	70.86
第三产业	Tertiary Industry	269.37	285.43
交通运输、仓储及邮政业	Transportation, Storage, Postal Services	22.43	24.26
信息传输、计算机服务和软件业	Data Transmission, Computer Service and Software	5.26	5.88
批发与零售业	Wholesale and Retail Trade	77.55	77.78
住宿和餐饮业	Hotels and Restaurants	47.29	48.02
金融业	Financing	6.59	6.63
房地产业	Real Estate	5.43	5.59
租赁与商务服务业	Renting and Business Activities	9.89	10.61
科学研究、技术服务与地质勘查业	Scientific Research, Technical Services and Geological Prospecting	6.87	7.25
水利、环境和公共设施管理业	Administration of Water Conservancy, Environment and Public Utilities	3.55	3.71
居民服务和其他服务业	Personal Services and Other Services	29.15	30.67
教　育	Education	21.12	30.58
卫生、社会保障和社会福利业	Public Health, Social Security and Social Welfare	11.85	11.95
文化、体育与娱乐业	Culture, Sports and Entertainment	2.52	2.59
公共管理与社会组织	Public Administration and Social Organizations	19.87	19.91

3－11 主要年份城镇经济单位职工人数
Staff and Workers of Urban Economic Units in Major Years

单位：万人 (10 000 persons)

年 份	合 计	按产业业分 By Industry			按经济类型分 By Registration		
		第一产业	第二产业	第三产业	国 有	集 体	其 他
Year	Total	Primary Industry	Secondary Industry	Tertiary Industry	State-owned	Collective-owned	Others
1949	5.34				5.34		
1952	47.62				47.62		
1957	71.19				71.19		
1962	80.79				80.79		
1965	91.96				91.96		
1970	109.98				109.98		
1975	127.99				127.99		
1978	154.44				154.44		
1980	220.06				162.97	57.09	
1985	257.63	4.80	144.90	107.93	186.74	70.81	0.08
1986	264.01	4.79	151.13	108.09	191.47	72.43	0.11
1987	270.46	5.39	153.80	111.27	196.79	73.36	0.31
1988	277.70	5.45	157.28	114.97	201.88	75.42	0.40
1989	280.69	5.66	158.65	116.38	205.98	74.01	0.70
1990	285.68	5.68	159.47	120.53	209.61	75.16	0.91
1991	293.59	5.68	163.94	123.97	215.78	76.58	1.23
1992	297.07	5.46	165.35	126.26	218.41	76.94	1.72
1993	290.02	4.16	164.74	121.12	215.05	70.79	4.18
1994	293.23	4.24	162.90	126.09	212.02	71.03	10.18
1995	294.25	4.35	160.58	129.32	212.34	69.85	12.06
1996	294.63	4.43	159.37	130.83	214.01	67.47	13.15
1997	289.29	4.13	153.73	131.43	211.13	61.64	16.52
1998	236.61	3.83	115.89	116.89	172.24	40.91	23.46
1999	222.34	3.58	106.07	112.69	158.64	35.54	28.16
2000	208.87	3.43	96.01	109.43	146.91	29.74	32.22
2001	201.23	2.94	91.73	106.56	134.79	23.77	42.67
2002	199.93	2.64	92.63	104.66	128.41	20.82	50.70
2003	204.99	2.46	97.56	104.97	121.27	18.94	64.78
2004	208.04	2.35	100.50	105.19	120.85	16.85	70.34

注：1998年及以后为在岗职工数（以下各表同）。

Note: Data since 1998 are the figures of on-post staff and workers (the same as in the following tables).

3－12 主要年份城镇经济单位职工工资总额
Total Wages of Staff and Workers of Urban Economic Units in Major Years

单位：万元 (10 000 yuan)

年 份 Year	合 计 Total Wages	按产业分 By Industry 第一产业 Primary Industry	第二产业 Secondary Industry	第三产业 Tertiary Industry	按经济类型分 By Registration 国 有 State-owned	集 体 Collective-owned	其 他 Others
1949	1368				1368		
1952	18577				18577		
1957	37710				37710		
1962	45532				45532		
1965	51159				51159		
1970	60866				60866		
1975	74645				74645		
1978	91615				91615		
1980	159426				125305	34121	
1985	259688	4528	149468	105692	195684	63939	65
1986	300882	4960	177126	118796	233311	67396	175
1987	349808	5802	206458	137548	271210	78190	408
1988	435140	6771	256248	172121	340494	94048	598
1989	497553	7713	294228	195612	392179	104065	1309
1990	573310	8232	335056	230022	454776	116718	1816
1991	637968	9313	373271	255384	501204	134105	2659
1992	728780	10757	415886	302137	577638	146315	4827
1993	831520	8623	489684	333213	664939	152705	13876
1994	1144546	12990	618503	513053	902585	190980	50981
1995	1309344	15878	715405	578061	1016056	222720	70568
1996	1454905	18116	782060	654729	1132844	237500	84561
1997	1581684	17286	829211	735187	1226641	244245	110798
1998	1540831	18140	769026	753665	1176479	201028	163324
1999	1606804	19304	760591	826909	1207329	184757	214718
2000	1732318	20606	777295	934417	1290215	176693	265410
2001	1941508	21510	833110	1086888	1381940	158228	401340
2002	2196175	21857	921105	1253213	1520518	159655	516002
2003	2535070	22059	1104724	1408287	1661336	160049	713685
2004	2939800	23358	1291498	1624944	1904154	164332	871314

注：1998年及以后为在岗职工工资总额（以下各表同）。

Note: Data since 1998 refer to total wages of on-post staff and workers (the same as in the following tables).

3—13 主要年份城镇经济单位职工平均工资
Average Wages of Staff and Workers of Urban Economic Units in Major Years

单位：元 (yuan)

年份 Year	平均工资 Average Wages	按产业分 By Industry 第一产业 Primary Industry	 第二产业 Secondary Industry	 第三产业 Tertiary Industry	按经济类型分 By Registration 国有 State-owned	 集体 Collective-owned	 其他 Others
1949	284				284		
1952	330				330		
1957	535				535		
1962	448				448		
1965	588				588		
1970	581				581		
1975	588				588		
1978	632				632		
1980	737				783	606	
1985	1038				1110	930	861
1986	1154	1034	1197	1100	1234	941	1842
1987	1309	1140	1354	1254	1397	1073	1943
1988	1588	1249	1647	1522	1708	1264	1685
1989	1782	1388	1863	1691	1923	1393	2380
1990	2025	1452	2106	1942	2189	1565	2256
1991	2203	1640	2308	2089	2356	1768	2485
1992	2468	1931	2526	2415	2661	1906	3273
1993	2833	1793	2967	2694	3068	2067	4704
1994	3925	3093	3776	4151	4227	2693	7100
1995	4508	3657	4423	4527	4789	3162	6346
1996	5010	4127	4889	5033	5352	3603	6607
1997	5502	4188	5412	5649	5828	4016	6845
1998	6433	4713	6529	6394	6732	4891	6907
1999	7182	5296	7184	7240	7541	5200	7641
2000	8020	5884	7704	8372	7431	4534	7450
2001	9523	6521	8925	10053	10035	6614	9503
2002	10960	7587	9905	11905	11745	7601	10339
2003	12440	8877	11425	13462	13616	8552	11316
2004	14357	9871	13125	15624	15847	9839	12831

注：1998年及以后为在岗职工平均工资（以下各表同）。

Note: Data since 1998 refer to average wages of on-post staff and workers (the same as in the following tables).

3－14 城镇经济独立核算单位数（2003－2004年）
Urban Economic Units with Independent Accounting System (2003-2004)

单位：个 (unit)

指标	Item	2003	2004
总　计	**Total**	**28012**	**26169**
按登记注册类型分	**By Registration**		
国有经济	State-owned	18799	18097
集体经济	Collective-owned	4750	3717
其他经济	Other Types of Urban Ownership	4463	4355
按企业、事业、机关分	**By Enterprise Institution and Agency**		
企　业	Enterprises	10307	9232
事　业	Institutions	13321	12653
机　关	Agencies & Organizations	4384	4284
按行业分	**By Sector**		
第一产业	Primary Industry	2046	1846
第二产业	Secondary Industry	3757	3452
采矿业	Mining and Quarrying	161	169
制造业	Manufacturing	2517	2149
电力、燃气及水的生产和供应业	Electricity, Gas & Water Production and Supply	246	241
建筑业	Construction	833	893
第三产业	Tertiary Industry	22209	20871
交通运输、仓储及邮政业	Transportation, Storage, Postal Services	682	623
信息传输、计算机服务和软件业	Data Transmission, Computer Service and Software	173	171
批发与零售业	Wholesale and Retail Trade	2756	2271
住宿和餐饮业	Hotels and Restaurants	281	250
金融业	Financing	675	544
房地产业	Real Estate	876	739
租赁与商务服务业	Renting and Business Activities	403	305
科学研究、技术服务与地质勘查业	Scientific Research, Technical Services and Geological Prospecting	1618	1571
水利、环境和公共设施管理业	Administration of Water Conservancy, Environment and Public Utilities	419	443
居民服务和其他服务业	Personal Services and Other Services	105	120
教　育	Education	5822	5465
卫生、社会保障和社会福利业	Public Health, Social Security and Social Welfare	2386	2199
文化、体育与娱乐业	Culture, Sports and Entertainment	725	627
公共管理与社会组织	Public Administration and Social Organizations	5288	5543

3－15 城镇经济单位职工人数（2003－2004年）
Staff and Workers of Urban Economic Units (2003-2004)

单位：万人 (10 000 persons)

指 标	Item	合 计 Total		#国 有 State-owned		#集 体 Collective-owned	
		2003	2004	2003	2004	2003	2004
总 计	**Total**	**204.99**	**208.04**	**121.27**	**120.85**	**18.94**	**16.85**
按企业、事业、机关分	**By Enterprise, Institution and Agency**						
企 业	Enterprises	137.42	140.12	56.11	55.18	16.53	14.60
事 业	Institutions	50.22	50.54	47.84	48.32	2.38	2.22
机 关	Agencies	17.35	17.38	17.32	17.35	0.03	0.03
按行业分	**By Sector**						
第一产业	Primary Industry	2.46	2.35	1.81	1.71	0.62	0.60
第二产业	Secondary Industry	97.56	100.50	35.29	34.11	12.81	11.41
采矿业	Mining and Quarrying	6.99	8.42	4.37	5.64	0.22	0.26
制造业	Manufacturing	54.09	52.04	21.74	19.87	6.43	4.99
电力、燃气及水的生产和供应业	Electricity, Gas & Water Production and Supply	5.77	5.61	3.67	3.43	0.18	0.25
建筑业	Construction	30.71	34.42	5.51	5.18	5.98	5.90
第三产业	Tertiary Industry	104.97	105.19	84.17	85.03	5.51	4.84
交通运输、仓储及邮政业	Transportation, Storage, Postal Services	14.35	14.13	11.27	11.29	1.02	0.87
信息传输、计算机服务和软件业	Data Transmission, Computer Service and Software	1.82	2.17	1.44	1.74	0.01	0.01
批发与零售业	Wholesale and Retail Trade	10.09	9.30	4.64	4.22	1.43	1.11
住宿和餐饮业	Hotels and Restaurants	2.47	2.45	1.04	1.00	0.09	0.11
金融业	Financing	5.02	5.13	2.90	2.86	0.83	0.78
房地产业	Real Estate	2.95	2.75	0.93	0.89	0.13	0.17
租赁与商务服务业	Renting and Business Activities	1.60	1.40	0.73	0.66	0.11	0.04
科学研究、技术服务与地质勘查业	Scientific Research, Technical Services & Geologic Prospecting	5.76	5.70	2.55	2.47	0.01	0.02
水利、环境和公共设施管理业	Administration of Water Conservancy, Environment and Public Utilities	2.30	2.25	2.03	2.00	0.16	0.12
居民服务和其他服务业	Personal Services and Other Services	0.38	0.46	0.25	0.32	0.04	0.03
教 育	Education	29.64	30.60	29.47	30.29	0.05	0.07
卫生、社会保障和社会福利业	Public Health, Social Security and Social Welfare	8.30	8.28	6.73	6.84	1.56	1.42
文化、体育与娱乐业	Culture, Sports and Entertainment	1.63	1.52	1.57	1.46	0.03	0.03
公共管理与社会组织	Public Administration and Social Organizations	18.66	19.05	18.62	18.99	0.04	0.06

3－16 城镇经济单位女职工人数（2003－2004年）
Female Staff and Workers of Urban Economic Units (2003-2004)

单位：万人 (10 000 persons)

指 标	Item	合 计 Total		#国 有 State-owned		#集 体 Collective-owned	
		2003	2004	2003	2004	2003	2004
总 计	**Total**	**67.83**	**67.16**	**41.98**	**41.87**	**6.31**	**5.04**
按企业、事业、机关分	**By Enterprise, Institution and Agency**						
企 业	Enterprises	42.77	41.62	17.88	17.23	5.35	4.14
事 业	Institutions	20.77	21.24	19.81	20.35	0.95	0.89
机 关	Agencies	4.29	4.30	4.29	4.29	0.01	0.01
按行业分	**By Sector**						
第一产业	Primary Industry	0.64	0.60	0.51	0.47	0.12	0.12
第二产业	Secondary Industry	27.77	26.71	10.74	10.03	4.00	3.04
采矿业	Mining and Quarrying	1.57	1.65	0.91	1.00	0.10	0.10
制造业	Manufacturing	20.33	19.14	7.65	6.99	3.04	2.18
电力、燃气及水的生产和供应业	Electricity, Gas & Water Production and Supply	2.06	1.94	1.31	1.23	0.07	0.07
建筑业	Construction	3.81	3.98	0.87	0.81	0.79	0.69
第三产业	Tertiary Industry	39.42	39.85	30.73	31.37	2.19	1.88
交通运输、仓储及邮政业	Transportation, Storage, Postal Services	4.06	4.04	3.19	3.20	0.24	0.18
信息传输、计算机服务和软件业	Data Transmission, Computer Service and Software	0.58	0.69	0.46	0.59	0.01	…
批发与零售业	Wholesale and Retail Trade	4.51	4.11	1.75	1.60	0.60	0.45
住宿和餐饮业	Hotels and Restaurants	1.34	1.31	0.58	0.55	0.05	0.07
金融业	Financing	2.26	2.41	1.28	1.29	0.35	0.33
房地产业	Real Estate	0.93	0.88	0.33	0.30	0.02	0.03
租赁与商务服务业	Renting and Business Activities	0.71	0.60	0.26	0.21	0.05	0.01
科学研究、技术服务与地质勘查业	Scientific Research, Technical Services & Geologic Prospecting	1.85	1.84	0.72	0.71	…	…
水利、环境和公共设施管理业	Administration of Water Conservancy, Environment and Public Utilities	0.98	0.90	0.86	0.81	0.08	0.06
居民服务和其他服务业	Personal Services and Other Services	0.10	0.13	0.04	0.06	0.01	0.01
教 育	Education	12.38	13.13	12.30	12.96	0.03	0.04
卫生、社会保障和社会福利业	Public Health, Social Security and Social Welfare	4.43	4.45	3.70	3.76	0.73	0.68
文化、体育与娱乐业	Culture, Sports and Entertainment	0.60	0.58	0.58	0.56	0.01	0.01
公共管理与社会组织	Public Administration and Social Organizations	4.69	4.78	4.68	4.77	0.01	0.01

3－17 城镇经济单位就业人员劳动报酬（2003－2004年）
Earnings of Employment of Urban Economic Units (2003-2004)

单位：万元 (10 000 yuan)

指　标	Item	合　计 Total		#国　有 State-owned		#集　体 Collective-owned	
		2003	2004	2003	2004	2003	2004
总　计	**Total**	**2591959**	**3022988**	**1686555**	**1938853**	**164245**	**168157**
按企业、事业、机关分	**By Enterprise, Institution and Agency**						
企　业	Enterprises	1683369	1979250	800689	918277	141521	144995
事　业	Institutions	658482	758082	636157	735361	22325	22721
机　关	Agencies	250108	285656	249709	285215	399	441
按行业分	**By Sector**						
第一产业	Primary Industry	22134	23479	16997	17680	4773	5128
第二产业	Secondary Industry	1120882	1320189	475830	528267	105859	107280
采矿业	Mining and Quarrying	71944	103109	47231	73116	1138	1904
制造业	Manufacturing	654178	736151	297826	313366	52096	47828
电力、燃气及水的生产和供应业	Electricity, Gas & Water Production and Supply	95268	110425	67479	75921	1658	3621
建筑业	Construction	299492	370504	63294	65864	50967	53927
第三产业	Tertiary Industry	1448943	1679320	1193728	1392906	53613	55749
交通运输、仓储及邮政业	Transportation, Storage, Postal Services	183798	212283	157913	182928	8146	8466
信息传输、计算机服务和软件业	Data Transmission, Computer Service and Software	45714	64174	35019	54167	150	129
批发与零售业	Wholesale and Retail Trade	108371	117974	58869	64680	10066	8301
住宿和餐饮业	Hotels and Restaurants	24060	26736	9638	9990	625	928
金融业	Financing	132931	158003	69602	80330	13860	16796
房地产业	Real Estate	37827	38445	12196	12205	794	1651
租赁与商务服务业	Renting and Business Activities	19988	18004	10833	9402	1331	549
科学研究、技术服务与地质勘查业	Scientific Research, Technical Services & Geologic Prospecting	87168	102209	53201	62727	165	295
水利、环境和公共设施管理业	Administration of Water Conservancy, Environment and Public Utilities	20999	23263	18819	21330	1192	952
居民服务和其他服务业	Personal Services and Other Services	3867	5347	2262	3406	385	394
教　育	Education	380618	443365	378819	439670	380	658
卫生、社会保障和社会福利业	Public Health, Social Security and Social Welfare	113375	133466	97378	117452	15845	15694
文化、体育与娱乐业	Culture, Sports and Entertainment	25911	30427	25274	29626	264	305
公共管理与社会组织	Public Administration and Social Organizations	264316	305624	263905	304993	410	631

3－18 城镇经济单位职工工资总额（2003－2004年）
Total Wages of Staff and Workers of Urban Economic Units (2003-2004)

单位：万元 (10 000 yuan)

指 标	Item	合计 Total		#国有 State-owned		#集体 Collective-owned	
		2003	2004	2003	2004	2003	2004
总 计	**Total**	**2535070**	**2939800**	**1661336**	**1904154**	**160049**	**164332**
按企业、事业、机关分	**By Enterprise, Institution and Agency**						
企 业	Enterprises	1635920	1911905	784577	898871	137658	141720
事 业	Institutions	650497	744379	628504	722195	21993	22184
机 关	Agencies	248653	283516	248255	283088	398	428
按行业分	**By Sector**						
第一产业	Primary Industry	22059	23358	16937	17596	4760	5102
第二产业	Secondary Industry	1104724	1291498	472125	523942	102469	104644
采矿业	Mining and Quarrying	71561	102417	46891	72520	1135	1902
制造业	Manufacturing	643909	713865	295766	311054	50153	46276
电力、燃气及水的生产和供应业	Electricity, Gas & Water Production and Supply	95080	109965	67365	75656	1637	3549
建筑业	Construction	294174	365251	62103	64712	49544	52917
第三产业	Tertiary Industry	1408287	1624944	1172274	1362616	52820	54586
交通运输、仓储及邮政业	Transportation, Storage, Postal Services	181524	207172	155801	178295	8026	8331
信息传输、计算机服务和软件业	Data Transmission, Computer Service and Software	45035	63295	34477	53308	150	129
批发与零售业	Wholesale and Retail Trade	106795	116351	58192	64298	9920	8192
住宿和餐饮业	Hotels and Restaurants	22925	25365	9349	9759	621	923
金融业	Financing	112095	131873	62828	71598	13745	16581
房地产业	Real Estate	35722	36272	11946	12043	749	1496
租赁与商务服务业	Renting and Business Activities	17669	17182	9008	9234	1322	531
科学研究、技术服务与地质勘查业	Scientific Research, Technical Services & Geologic Prospecting	84040	96037	50214	56728	163	239
水利、环境和公共设施管理业	Administration of Water Conservancy, Environment and Public Utilities	20825	23065	18665	21156	1175	950
居民服务和其他服务业	Personal Services and Other Services	3636	5235	2213	3400	346	392
教 育	Education	377954	439081	376214	435724	380	609
卫生、社会保障和社会福利业	Public Health, Social Security and Social Welfare	111811	130794	96150	115273	15552	15282
文化、体育与娱乐业	Culture, Sports and Entertainment	25643	29937	25013	29143	262	303
公共管理与社会组织	Public Administration and Social Organizations	262613	303285	262204	302657	409	628

3－19 城镇经济单位职工平均工资（2003－2004年）
Average Wages of Staff and Workers of Urban Economic Units (2003-2004)

单位：元 (yuan)

指　标	Item	合计 Total		#国有 State-owned		#集体 Collective-owned	
		2003	2004	2003	2004	2003	2004
总　计	**Total**	**12440**	**14357**	**13616**	**15847**	**8552**	**9839**
按企业、事业、机关分	**By Enterprise, Institution and Agency**						
企　业	Enterprises	11977	13902	13705	16292	8457	9808
事　业	Institutions	13011	14869	13206	15095	9150	9994
机　关	Agencies	14455	16505	14461	16512	11703	13083
按行业分	**By Sector**						
第一产业	Primary Industry	8877	9871	9200	10186	7662	8490
第二产业	Secondary Industry	11425	13125	13378	15251	7999	9335
采矿业	Mining and Quarrying	9725	12432	10072	13108	4856	7172
制造业	Manufacturing	11883	13751	13325	15461	7799	9104
电力、燃气及水的生产和供应业	Electricity, Gas & Water Production and Supply	16372	19580	18257	22058	8852	14090
建筑业	Construction	10028	11194	11038	12270	8802	9433
第三产业	Tertiary Industry	13462	15624	13927	16207	9586	11161
交通运输、仓储及邮政业	Transportation, Storage, Postal Services	12506	14806	13620	15958	7800	9473
信息传输、计算机服务和软件业	Data Transmission, Computer Service and Software	25298	30607	24422	32515	11364	10109
批发与零售业	Wholesale and Retail Trade	10497	12560	12039	15088	6664	7061
住宿和餐饮业	Hotels and Restaurants	9412	10705	9135	10463	7110	8101
金融业	Financing	2230	25882	21427	24963	16467	21615
房地产业	Real Estate	12174	13518	12706	13869	5989	8854
租赁与商务服务业	Renting and Business Activities	10805	12296	11763	14074	11378	14225
科学研究、技术服务与地质勘查业	Scientific Research, Technical Services & Geologic Prospecting	14478	16928	19253	23040	13040	12860
水利、环境和公共设施管理业	Administration of Water Conservancy, Environment and Public Utilities	9359	10454	9575	10814	7366	7976
居民服务和其他服务业	Personal Services and Other Services	1292	12187	14053	11743	8216	12655
教　育	Education	12865	14506	12879	14534	7274	9075
卫生、社会保障和社会福利业	Public Health, Social Security and Social Welfare	13472	15937	14344	17035	9795	10747
文化、体育与娱乐业	Culture, Sports and Entertainment	15537	19800	15741	20135	9313	10070
公共管理与社会组织	Public Administration and Social Organizations	14215	16100	14222	16120	10626	9979

3－20 城镇经济单位专业技术人员年末人数（2003－2004年）
Year-end Scientific and Technical Personnel of Urban Economic Units (2003-2004)

单位：人 (person)

指　　标	Item	2003	2004
总　计	**Total**	**620415**	**616604**
按登记注册类型分	**By Registration**		
国有经济	State-owned	449935	451628
集体经济	Collective-owned	41477	39870
其他经济	Other Types of Urban Ownership	129003	125106
按企业、事业、机关分	**By Enterprise, Institution and Agency**		
企　业	Enterprises	276154	265495
事　业	Institutions	332504	341393
机　关	Agencies	11757	9716
按行业分	**By Sector**		
第一产业	Primary Industry	10879	10106
第二产业	Secondary Industry	188909	180396
采矿业	Mining and Quarrying	9880	10340
制造业	Manufacturing	97724	95069
电力、燃气及水的生产和供应业	Electricity, Gas & Water Production and Supply	12528	10737
建筑业	Construction	68777	64250
第三产业	Tertiary Industry	420627	426102
交通运输、仓储及邮政业	Transportation, Storage, Postal Services	19779	18497
信息传输、计算机服务和软件业	Data Transmission, Computer Service and Software	3227	3439
批发与零售业	Wholesale and Retail Trade	17284	15407
住宿和餐饮业	Hotels and Restaurants	3026	2835
金融业	Financing	23643	22245
房地产业	Real Estate	8772	8105
租赁与商务服务业	Renting and Business Activities	3247	2721
科学研究、技术服务与地质勘查业	Scientific Research, Technical Services and Geological Prospecting	22430	22503
水利、环境和公共设施管理业	Administration of Water Conservancy, Environment and Public Utilities	2013	2204
居民服务和其他服务业	Personal Services and Other Services	396	646
教　育	Education	235697	246186
卫生、社会保障和社会福利业	Public Health, Social Security and Social Welfare	60070	60907
文化、体育与娱乐业	Culture, Sports and Entertainment	5895	5788
公共管理与社会组织	Public Administration and Social Organizations	15148	14619

3－21 城镇经济单位新增就业人员及构成（2003－2004年）
New Employment in Urban Economic Units and Its Composition (2003-2004)

单位:万人、% (10 000 persons, %)

项　目	Item	新增就业人员 New Employment 2003	2004	构　成 Composition 2003	2004
总　计	**Total**	**22.06**	**24.97**	**100.0**	**100.0**
按就业人员来源分	**By Source**				
城　镇	Urban	3.33	5.00	15.1	20.0
农　村	Rural	9.06	11.14	41.1	44.6
大中专技校毕业生	Graduates from Universities Specialized Secondary Schools and Technical Training Schools	3.18	3.54	14.4	14.2
其　他	Others	6.49	5.29	29.4	21.2
按就业人员去向分	**By Assignment**				
国有经济单位	State-owned Units	8.37	9.05	37.9	36.2
集体经济单位	Collective-owned Units	2.76	2.25	12.5	9.0
其他经济单位	Other Types of Urban Ownership	10.93	13.67	49.6	54.8

3－22 城镇经济单位离退休人员（1985－2004年）
Retired, VCSR and RRSW of Urban Economic Units (1985-2004)

单位：万人 (10 000 persons)

年　份 Year	合　计 Total	离　休 VCSR	退　休 Retired	退　职 RRSW
1985	51.08	1.08	49.12	0.88
1990	62.24	1.74	59.06	1.44
1991	63.63	1.84	60.44	1.35
1992	66.63	1.78	63.47	1.38
1993	72.95	1.87	69.85	1.23
1994	86.05	2.15	82.36	1.54
1995	85.89	1.93	82.47	1.49
1996	85.55	1.78	82.20	1.57
1997	84.04	1.74	80.64	1.66
1998	83.11	1.54	79.81	1.76
1999	88.57	1.64	85.27	1.66
2000	92.66	1.54	89.22	1.90
2001	108.50	1.51	105.07	1.92
2002	104.03	1.35	100.86	1.82
2003	106.58	1.34	103.23	2.01
2004	112.40	1.27	109.31	1.82

3－23 城镇登记失业人员（1985－2004年）
Registered Unemployment in Urban Areas (1985-2004)

单位：万人、% (10 000 persons, %)

年 份 Year	登记失业人数 Registered Unemployment	#女 性 Female	按失业时间分 By Unemployment Period 6个月以上 Over 6 Months	6个月以下 Less than 6 Months	登记失业率 Rate of Registered Unemployment
1985	6.46				2.3
1986	6.00				2.1
1987	6.29				2.2
1988	6.25				2.1
1989	8.43				2.8
1990	8.81				2.9
1991	9.42				3.0
1992	10.01				3.1
1993	10.23				3.2
1994	10.80				3.2
1995	10.47				2.9
1996	10.95				3.0
1997	10.85	6.18	6.92	3.93	3.5
1998	10.10	5.71	6.46	3.64	3.5
1999	10.08	5.48	6.15	3.93	3.5
2000	10.15	5.26	5.30	4.85	3.5
2001	13.72	7.24	7.72	6.00	3.9
2002	16.18	7.70	7.79	8.39	4.1
2003	16.16	8.20	8.62	7.54	4.1
2004	16.76	8.19	9.44	7.32	4.12

主要统计指标解释

人口数 指一定时点、一定地区范围内的有生命的个人的总和。

年度统计的年末人口数是指每年12月31日24时的人口数。

城镇人口和乡村人口的划分 城镇人口是指居住在城镇范围内的全部人口；乡村人口是除上述人口以外的全部人口。

历年城乡人口数据是按照当时国家《关于统计上划分城乡的规定》计算的。

三次普查之间年份的城乡人口根据1990年和2000年人口普查数据进行了调整。

常住人口 指全年经常在家或在家居住6个月以上，而且经济和生活与本户连成一体的人口。外出从业人员在外居住时间虽然在6个月以上，但收入主要带回家中，经济与本户连为一体，仍视为家庭常住人口；在家居住，生活和本户连成一体的国家职工、退休人员也为家庭常住人口。但是现役军人、中专及以上(走读生除外)的在校学生、以及常年在外(不包括探亲、看病等)且已有稳定的职业与居住场所的外出从业人员，不算家庭常住人口。

出生率（又称粗出生率） 指在一定时期内（通常为一年）一定地区内出生人数与同期内平均人数（或期中人数）之比，一般用千分率表示。本资料中的出生率指年出生率。计算公式为：

出生率=年出生人数/年平均人数×1000‰

式中：出生人数是指活产婴儿，即胎儿脱离母体时（不管怀孕月数），有过呼吸或其他生命现象。年平均人数是年初、年底人口数的平均数，也可用年中人口数代替。

死亡率（又称粗死亡率） 指在一定时期内（通常为一年）一定地区的死亡人数与同期平均人数（或期中人数）之比，一般用千分率表示。本资料中的死亡率指年死亡率。计算公式为：

死亡率=年死亡人数/年平均人数×1000‰

人口自然增长率 指在一定时期内（通常为一年）人口自然增加数（出生人数减死亡人数）与该时期内平均人数（或期中人数）之比，一般用千分率表示。计算公式为：

人口自然增长率=(本年出生人数-本年死亡人数)/年平均人数×1000‰

=人口出生率-人口死亡率

就业人员 指从事一定社会劳动并取得劳动报酬或经营收入的人员。包括在岗职工、再就业的离退休人员、私营业主、个体户主、私营和个体就业人员、乡镇企业就业人员、农村就业人员、其他从业人员（包括民办教师、宗教职业者、现役军人等）。这一指标反映了一定时期内全部劳动力资源的实际利用情况，是研究我国基本国情国力的重要指标。

各单位的就业人员 指在各级国家机关、政党机关、社会团体及企业、事业单位中工作，并取得工资或其他形式的劳动报酬的全部人员。包括在岗职工、再就业的离退休人员、民办教师以及在各单位中工作的外方人员和港澳台方人员、兼职人员、借用的外单位人员和第二职业者。不包括离开本单位仍保留劳动关系的职工。各单位的就业人员反映了各单位实际参加生产或工作的全部劳动力。

城镇私营和个体就业人员 城镇私营就业人员指在工商管理部门注册登记，其经营地址设在县城关镇（含城关镇）以上的私营企业从业人员；包括私营企业投资者和雇工。城镇个体就业人员指在工商管理部门注册登记，并持有城镇户口或在城镇长期居住，经批准从事个体工商经营的就业人员；包括个体经营者和在个体工商户劳动的家庭帮工和雇工。

城镇登记失业人员 指有非农业户口，在一定的劳动年龄内(16 岁以上及男 50 岁以下、女 45 岁以下)，有劳动能力，无业而要求就业，并在当地就业服务机构进行求职登记的人员。

城镇登记失业率 城镇登记失业人员与城镇单位就业人员(扣除使用的农村劳动力、聘用的离退休人员、港澳台及外方人员)、城镇单位中的不在岗职工、城镇私营业主、个体户主、城镇私营企业和个体就业人员、城镇登记失业人员之和的比。计算公式为：

城镇登记失业率=城镇登记失业人数/[（城镇单位就业人员-使用的农村劳动力-聘用的离退休人员-聘用的港澳台及外方人员）+不在岗职工+城镇私营业主+城镇个体户主+城镇私营企业及个体就业人员+城镇登记失业人数]×100%

职工 指在国有、城镇集体、联营、股份制、外商和港、澳、台投资、其他单位及其附属机构工作，并由其支付工资的各类人员。不包括下列人员：(1)乡镇企业就业人员；(2)私营企业就业人员；(3)城镇个体劳动者；(4)离休、退休、退职人员；(5)再就业的离、退休人员；(6)民办教师；(7)在城镇单位中工作的外方及港、澳、台人员；(8)其他按有关规定不列入职工统计范围的人员。(1998 年及以后的数据均为在岗职工数据，其他相关指标如职工工资总额，职工平均工资等指标也从 1998 年按此口径进行了相应调整)。

国有单位 指资产归国家所有的经济组织。包括按《中华人民共和国企业法人登记管理条例》规定登记注册的非公司制的经济组织，以及中央、地方各级国家机关、事业单位和社会团体。

集体单位 指生产资料归集体所有，并按《中华人民共和国企业法人登记管理条例》规定登记注册的经济组织。

其他单位 包括股份合作单位、联营单位、有限责任公司、股份有限公司、港澳台商投资单位以及外商投资单位等其他登记注册类型单位。

在岗职工 指在本单位工作并由单位支付工资的人员，以及有工作岗位，但由于学习、病伤产假等原因暂未工作，仍由单位支付工资的人员。

职工工资总额 指各单位在一定时期内直接支付给本单位全部职工的劳动报酬总额。工资总额的计算原则应以直接支付给职工的全部劳动报酬为根据。各单位支付给职工的劳动报酬以及其他根据有关规定支付的工资，不论是计入成本的还是不计入成本的，不论是按国家规定列入计征奖金税项目的，还是未列入计征奖金税项目的，不论是以货币形式支付的还是以实物形式支付的，均包括在工资总额内。

职工平均工资 指企业、事业、机关单位的职工在一定时期内平均每人所得的货币工资额。它表明一定时期职工工资收入的高低程度，是反映职工工资水平的主要指标，计算公式为：

职工平均工资=报告期实际支付的全部职工工资总额/报告期全部职工平均人数

专业技术人员 指从事专业技术工作的人员以及从事专业技术管理工作且已在 1983 年以前评定了专业技术职称或在 1984 年以后聘任了专业技术职务的人员。

专业技术人员具体指工程技术人员、农业技术人员、科研人员(自然科学研究、社会科学研究及实验技术人员)、卫生技术人员、教学人员(含高等院校、中等专业学校、技工学校、中学、小学)、民用航空飞行技术人员、船舶技术人员、经济人员、会计人员、统计人员、翻译人员、图书资料、档案、文博人员、新闻、出版人员、律师、公证人员、广播电视播音人员、工艺美术人员、体育人员、艺术人员及政工人员。

专业技术管理人员具体指企业、事业单位的领导；企业、事业单位下设的职能机构、企业的生产车间和辅助车间(或附属辅助生产单位)中从事生产、技术、经济管理和政治工作人员。

按照公务员管理或参照公务员管理的人员不统计为专业技术人员。

离休、退休、退职人员 指正式办理了离休、退休、退职手续，并享受相应的离休、退休、退职待遇人员。

Explanatory Notes on Main Statistical Indicators

Total population refers to the total number of people alive at a certain point of time within a given area.

The annual statistics on total population is taken at midnight, the 3lst of December.

Urban Population and Rural Population Urban population refer to all people residing in cities and towns, while rural population refer to population other than urban population.

Statistics on urban and rural population over the years are compiled in line with the regulations of statistical classification on urban and rural population stipulated by the government, which were in effect at different times.

Figures on urban/rural population for the years between the 3 censuses are adjusted in accordance with the 1990 and 2000 population census data.

Resident Population refers to population staying at home permanently or for over 6 months during a year and sharing life economically with the household. Members of the household staying away from the household for over 6 months but keeping a close economic relation with the household by sending the majority of income to the household are regarded as resident population of the household. Government staff and workers or retirees living as close members of the household are also considered as resident population. However, servicemen, students of secondary technical schools or schools of higher education and persons with stable jobs and residence outside the household (excluding those visiting relatives or seeking medical service) are not included as resident population of the household.

Birth Rate (or Crude Birth Rate) refers to the ratio of the number of births to the average population during a certain period of time (usually a year), which is often expressed in ‰. Birth rate in the chapter refers to annual birth rate. The following formula is used:

Birth Rate = Number of Births /Average Number of Population× 1000‰

Number of Births refers to live births, i.e. the births when babies had showed any vital phenomena regardless of the length of pregnancy.

Annual Average Number of Population is the average of the number of population at the beginning of the year and that at the end of the year. Sometimes it is substituted for with the mid-year population.

Death Rate (or Crude Death Rate) refers to the ratio of the number of deaths to the average population (or mid-year population) during a certain period of time (usually a year), which is often expressed in ‰. Death rate in the chapter refers to annual death rate. The following formula is used:

Death Rate =Number of Deaths/Annual Average Number of Population ×1000‰

Natural Growth Rate of Population refers to the ratio of natural increase in population (number of births minus number of deaths) in a certain period of time (usually a year) to average population (or mid-year population) of the same period, which is often expressed in ‰. The following formulas are applied:

Natural Growth of Population =Number of Births-Number of Deaths /Average number of Population×1000‰

Natural Growth Rate of Population=Birth Rate - Death Rate

Employees refers to the persons who are engaged in social labor and receive remuneration payment or earn business income, including: total staff and workers, re-employed retirees, employers of private enterprises, self-employed workers, employers in private and individual economy, employees in township, employed persons in the rural areas, and other employed persons (including teachers in the schools run by the local people, people engaged in religious profession and the servicemen, etc.). This indicator reflects the actual utilization of total labor force during a certain period of time and is often used for the research on China's economic affairs and national power.

Persons Employed in Various Units refer to all the persons working in government agencies of various levels, political and party organizations, social organizations, and enterprises and institutions and receiving payment, including staff and workers, reemployed retirees, teachers in schools run by the local people, foreigners, and Chinese compatriots from Hong Kong, Macao, and Taiwan working in various units, part-time employees, employees of other units working temporarily at current posts, and employees holding the second job, but exclude staff and workers who have left their working units while keeping their labor contract (employment relation) unchanged. This indicator reflects the total number of laborers actually engaged in production or other operations in various units.

Persons Employed in Private Enterprises and Self-Employed Individuals in Urban Areas: Persons employed in private enterprises refer to the persons employed in the private enterprises which have been registered at the departments of industrial and commercial administration and are situated at a county town (i.e. a town where the county government is located) for business operation or at urban areas with the level higher than a county town. The self-employed individuals in urban areas refer to persons who hold the certificates of residence in urban areas or have resided in the urban areas for a long time and have been registered at the departments of industrial and commercial administration and approved to be engaged in individual industrial or commercial business, including self - employed persons as well as helpers and hired laborers who work in the individual households engaged in industrial or commercial business.

Registered Urban Unemployed Persons refer to the persons with non-agricultural household registration at certain working ages (16-50 years for male and 16-45 years for females), who are capable of work, unemployed and willing to work, and have been registered at the local employment service agencies to apply for a job.

Registered Urban Unemployment Rate refers to the ratio of the number of the registered unemployed persons to the sum of the number of persons employed in various units (minus the rural labor force, retirees, and Hong Kong, Macao, Taiwan or foreign employees they employ) laid-off workers in urban units, owners and employees in urban private enterprises, urban self-employed individuals and the registered urban unemployed persons. The formula is as follows:

Registered urban unemployment rate = number of registered urban unemployed persons÷(number of persons employed in urban units - rural labor force employed – retirees employed - Hong Kong, Macao, Taiwan or foreign employees employ + laid-off workers + owners and employees in urban private enterprises + self-employed individuals in urban areas + registered urban unemployed persons) × 100%

Staff and Workers refer to persons working in, and receive payment from units of state ownership, collective ownership, joint ownership, share holding ownership, foreign ownership, and ownership by entrepreneurs from Hong Kong, Macao, and Taiwan, and other types of ownership and their affiliated units. They exclude 1) persons employed in township enterprises, 2) persons employed in private enterprises, 3) urban self-employed persons, 4) retirees, 5) re-employed retirees, 6) teachers in the schools run by the local people, 7) foreigners and persons from Hong Kong, Macao and Taiwan who work in urban units, 8) other persons not to be included by relevant regulations. (Data of 1998 and afterward refer to fully employed staff and workers. Other related statistics such as total wage bill and average wage are adjusted since 1998 accordingly).

State-owned Units refer to economic units whose assets are owned by the state. Included are non-corporation units registered according to Regulation of the People's Republic of China on the Registration of Enterprises and Corporations, state organs, institutions and social organizations at the central and local levels.

Collective Units refer to economic units registered according to Regulation of the People's Republic of China on the Registration of Enterprises and Corporations where the means of production are collectively owned.

Units of Other Types of Ownership refer to units registered with other types of ownership, including cooperative units, joint ownership units, limited companies, share holding corporations, units invested by entrepreneurs from Hong Kong, Macao, and Taiwan, and foreign-invested units.

Staff and Workers at Post refer to persons who work in, and receive wages from their working units, as well as persons who have their work posts, but are temporarily absent from work for reasons of study or on sick, injury or maternal leave and still receive wages from their working units.

Total Wages of Staff and Workers refer to the total remuneration payment to staff and workers in various units during a certain period of time. The calculation of total wages is based on the total remuneration payment to the staff and workers. Therefore, all the wages and salaries and other payments to staff and workers are included in the total wages regardless of their sources, category, and forms (in kind or cash).

Average Wage of Staff and Workers refers to the average wage in money terms per person during a certain period of time for staff and workers in enterprises, institutions, and government agencies, which reflects the general level of wage income during a certain period of time and is calculated as follows:

Average Wage of Staff and Workers=Total Wages of Staff and Workers in Reference Period/Average Number of Staff and Workers in Reference Period

Professional Personnel refers to the persons who are engaged in special professional work or in professional management who got the titles of professional post before 1983 or who were appointed to professional positions since 1984.

Professional personnel specifically refers to engineering professionals, agricultural professionals, scientific research professionals (natural science researchers, social science researchers and laboratory technicians), health professionals, teaching professionals (including institutions of higher education, specialized secondary schools, technical schools, regular secondary schools, and primary schools), civil aviation professionals, nautical professionals, economic professionals, accounting professionals, statistical professionals, interpretation professionals, library professionals, archives professionals, professionals of culture, arts and cultural relics, newsman and publishing professionals, lawyers, notary professionals, radio and television announcers, industrial arts professionals, sports professionals, artists and political professionals.

Professional management personnel specifically refers to the managers of enterprises and institutions, the personnel engaged in management of production, techniques, economic and political aspects in functional departments under enterprise and institution, production workshops and accessorial workshops (or accessorial production units) under enterprises.

Professional personnel excluded the personnel managed by or according to the system of civil servants.

Retired or Resigned Personnel refers to the persons who have formally gone through the formalities for their retirement or quitting work and enjoy the corresponding treatments.

四　固定资产投资

INVESTMENT IN FIXED ASSETS

简要说明　Brief Introduction

本章内容主要包括全社会固定资产投资、基本建设投资、更新改造投资，以及渝房景气指数、房地产开发和商品房销售情况，由市统计局固定资产投资处整理提供。

The statistics on the investment in fixed assets cover total investment in fixed assets, the investment in capital construction, the investment in innovation, business survey of real estate development, and sales of commercial buildings. The data in this chapter are prepared and provided by Division of Statistics of Investment in Fixed Assets, Municipal Bureau of Statistics.

4－1 主要年份全社会固定资产投资
Total Investment in Fixed Assets in Major Years

单位：万元 (10 000 yuan)

年 份 Year	固定资产投资额总计 Total Investment in Fixed Assets	新增固定资产 New Fixed Assets	固定资产投资按构成分 Investment in Fixed Assets by Use of Funds		
			建筑安装工程 Construction and Installation	设备工具器具购置 Purchase of Equipment and Instruments	其他费用 Others
1949	39	37	39		
1952	9535	7107	7027	1751	757
1957	21330	20591	12563	6636	2131
1962	7769	7650	5853	1654	262
1965	37677	32844	24658	10280	2739
1970	62448	44331	26528	31658	4262
1975	64359	29973	26446	26539	11374
1978	59026	46834	37630	16958	4438
1980	102789	101499	71220	26265	5304
1985	364822	265993	238027	101461	25334
1986	420675	343008	265430	124895	30350
1987	482445	345528	329053	114844	38548
1988	558331	378150	374833	148913	34585
1989	547540	405769	370687	140033	36820
1990	693140	462056	450344	192115	50681
1991	851614	636525	548518	234255	68841
1992	1063852	871892	703962	261333	98557
1993	1550546	1036205	1008107	389367	153072
1994	2029178	1377025	1336181	509362	183635
1995	2709663	1886888	1707448	737819	264396
1996	3207278	2306996	2076949	733537	342156
1997	3709485	3143528	2418273	879477	411735
1998	4981452	3693019	3248271	1083808	649373
1999	5628679	3706704	3860379	1080062	688238
2000	6558116	4364464	4599909	1055220	902987
2001	8018228	4722181	5460064	1435621	1122543
2002	9956645	6868792	6961365	1482391	1512889
2003	12693544	7244753	8608006	1594910	2490628
2004	16219203	8377655	10155324	2512064	3551815

4-1 续表1 CONTINUED-1

单位：万元 (10 000 yuan)

年 份 Year	固定资产投资按报表种类分 Investment in Fixed Assets by Type of Forms					
	基本建设 Capital Construction	更新改造 Innovation	房地产开发 Real Estate Development	城乡集体 Urban and Rural Collective-owned	城乡私人 Urban and Rural Individual	其 他 Others
1949	39					
1952	9535					
1957	21330					
1962	7769					
1965	37677					
1970	62448					
1975	64359					
1978	57324			1702		
1980	64353	30024		4718	3692	2
1985	131698	105342		66862	51444	9476
1986	137212	150257		60497	56012	16696
1987	153420	164988		58155	75233	30649
1988	164972	219784		56588	88464	28523
1989	207620	169757		46813	92688	30662
1990	276365	201809	17503	49525	110063	37875
1991	343108	239822	19185	69943	136846	42710
1992	345182	315625	33868	137945	185997	45235
1993	417023	425852	123151	276425	231216	76842
1994	579314	513433	279089	353815	278365	25162
1995	692686	684065	468845	392390	425657	46020
1996	884040	671647	556185	462120	598918	34368
1997	1208667	654264	675022	488250	635175	48107
1998	1864898	892886	973014	526638	637275	86741
1999	2114327	917501	1125135	579339	769361	123016
2000	2629302	920341	1396327	648947	829063	134136
2001	3283225	1080419	1966684	640442	942900	104558
2002	4747585	1150785	2459130	679000	779588	140557
2003	6654920	1220100	3278881	651544	750003	138096
2004	8913181	1534319	4050791	732088	802274	186550

注：1）城乡私人包括农村私人投资和城镇工矿区私人建房投资。

2）自2003年起基本建设和更新改造包括城镇集体和城镇私营个体投资，城乡集体只包括农村集体投资。

Note: a) Urban and rural individual investment includes rural individual investment, housing construction by individuals in cities, towns, industrial and mining areas.

b) Investment in capital construction and innovation since 2003 includes urban collective and individual investment. Data of urban and rural collective-owned since 2003 only refer to investment by rural collective-owned.

4-1 续表2 CONTINUED-2

单位：万元 (10 000 yuan)

年份 Year	固定资产投资按登记注册类型分 Investment in Fixed Assets by Registration						
	国有 State-owned	集体 Collective-owned	联营 Joint-owned	股份制 Share Holding	港澳台及外商投资 Foreign-funded	私营个体 Individuals	其他 Others
1949	39						
1952	9535						
1957	21330						
1962	7769						
1965	37662	15					
1970	62447	1					
1975	64355	4					
1978	56823	2203					
1980	91150	4718				3692	
1985	243927	66862				44712	9321
1986	301256	60497				48260	10662
1987	345509	58155				67033	11748
1988	410106	56588				78012	13625
1989	405239	46813				82058	13430
1990	528648	49525				92235	22732
1991	639554	69943				120515	21602
1992	739230	137945				165300	21377
1993	979597	276425	2798	32512	25320	206511	27383
1994	1364920	353815	2598	8013	13340	243119	43373
1995	1433244	424399	5834	101846	232079	370479	141782
1996	1597680	513195	6857	100805	278214	598918	111609
1997	1763147	550970	11428	354040	154602	669117	31148
1998	2598535	599304	7963	691371	402084	637275	44920
1999	2839011	664552	9951	612007	353199	1097082	52877
2000	3132534	730555	31555	877503	319730	1381098	85141
2001	3849113	821206	65544	1077977	432826	1715384	56178
2002	4603442	884409	45739	1678915	731767	1989250	23123
2003	5517224	845591	30177	3055216	648829	2514803	81704
2004	6625116	958051	30942	4199655	1174341	3114906	116192

4-1 续表3 CONTINUED-3

单位：万元、万平方米 (10 000 yuan, 10 000 sq.m)

年 份 Year	固定资产投资按三次产业分 Investment in Fixed Assets byIndustry 第一产业 Primary Industry	第二产业 Secondary Industry	第三产业 Tertiary Industry	本年房屋施工面积 Floor Space Under Construction	#住 宅 Residential Buildings	本年房屋竣工面积 Floor Space Completed	#住 宅 Residential Buildings
1949						0.50	
1952	37	4616	4882			5.05	1.26
1957	203	15421	5706			153.06	84.07
1962	314	6080	1375			17.81	7.29
1965	5130	25482	7065			103.23	42.52
1970	1291	56173	4984			121.46	48.82
1975	2716	54692	6951			95.10	38.60
1978	3790	45516	9720			121.27	39.40
1980	2101	69188	31500			322.56	165.76
1985	4848	184918	175056	2536.18		1340.52	679.97
1986	3359	238569	178747	2595.60		2141.05	1445.41
1987	4794	282515	195136	2752.10		2168.82	1474.41
1988	5490	346847	205994	2631.50		1969.68	1478.48
1989	5919	314655	226966	2400.41		1850.52	706.20
1990	13220	413776	266144	2522.36		2057.35	1620.48
1991	19966	487813	343835	2753.33		2258.20	1756.46
1992	20329	558021	485502	3227.87		2473.16	1947.05
1993	14208	701890	834448	3619.35		2631.21	1993.87
1994	14449	839691	1175038	4045.16		2926.46	2119.02
1995	17117	1066810	1625736	4964.40		3305.92	2503.18
1996	23128	1156837	2027313	6026.39	4163.82	4208.66	3313.32
1997	33820	1309109	2366556	6145.25	4197.97	4301.95	3363.04
1998	44133	1418980	3518339	6587.09	4474.14	4284.85	3267.26
1999	65652	1217277	4345750	7170.15	4798.52	4659.64	3527.28
2000	89657	1423981	5044478	8493.97	5931.11	5337.33	4087.44
2001	108038	1462479	6447711	8812.23	6055.41	4938.55	3664.49
2002	191128	1956665	7808852	10643.21	7305.16	6402.69	4664.91
2003	264249	3033987	9395308	10961.76	7397.58	5958.80	4292.79
2004	360891	4301999	11556313	11796.95	7835.24	5559.80	3962.33

4－2 全社会固定资产投资（2003－2004年）
Total Investment in Fixed Assets (2003-2004)

指　　标	Item	投资额 Investment		构成 (%) Composition	
		2003	2004	2003	2004
投资总额(万元)	**Total Investment (10 000 yuan)**	**12693544**	**16219203**	**100.0**	**100.0**
按隶属关系分	**By Administrative Relationship**				
中央项目	Central	1576869	2553467	12.4	15.7
地方项目	Local	11116675	13665736	87.6	84.3
(包括无隶属关系的)	(including non-relationship)				
按登记注册类型分	**By Registration**				
内　资	Domestic-funded	12044715	15044862	94.9	92.8
#国　有	State-owned	5517224	6625116	43.5	40.8
集　体	Collective-owned	845591	958051	6.7	5.9
联　营	Joint-owned	30177	30942	0.2	0.2
股份制	Share Holding	3055216	4199655	24.1	25.9
私营个体	Individual	2514803	3114906	19.8	19.2
其　他	Others	81704	116192	0.6	0.7
港澳台投资经济	Funded by Entrepreneurs from Hong Kong, Macao and Taiwan	336270	508011	2.6	3.1
外商投资经济	Foreign-funded	312559	666330	2.5	4.1
按报表种类分	**By Report Sort**				
基本建设	Capital Construction	6654920	8913181	52.4	55.0
更新改造	Innovation	1220100	1534319	9.6	9.5
房地产开发	Real Estate Development	3278881	4050791	25.8	25.0
其他投资	Others	1539643	1720912	12.2	10.6
按构成分	**By Use of Funds**				
建筑工程	Construction	7824230	9300386	61.6	57.3
安装工程	Installation	783776	854938	6.2	5.3
设备工具器具购置	Purchase of Equipment and Instruments	1594910	2512064	12.6	15.5
其他费用	Others	2490628	3551815	19.6	21.9
新增固定资产(万元)	**Newly Increased Fixed Assets (10 000 yuan)**	**7244753**	**8377655**		
固定资产交付使用率(%)	**Rate of Fixed Assets Put into Use (%)**	**57.1**	**51.7**		
房屋建筑面积(万平方米)	**Floor Space of Buildings (10 000 sq.m)**				
施工面积	Floor Space under Construction	10961.76	11796.95		
#住　宅	Residential Buildings	7397.58	7835.24		
竣工面积	Floor Space Completed	5958.80	5559.80		
#住　宅	Residential Buildings	4292.79	3962.33		

4-3 按行业分的全社会固定资产投资（2003-2004年）
Total Investment in Fixed Assets by Sector (2003-2004)

单位：万元 (10 000 yuan)

行业	Sector	2003	2004
总计	**Total**	**12693544**	**16219203**
第一产业	Primary Industry	264249	360891
第二产业	Secondary Industry	3033987	4301999
工业	Industry	2624388	3982985
采矿业	Mining and Quarrying	144014	387040
制造业	Manufacturing	1632568	2519120
电力、燃气及水的生产和供应业	Electricity, Gas & Water Production and Supply	847806	1076825
建筑业	Construction	409599	319014
第三产业	Tertiary Industry	9395308	11556313
交通运输、仓储及邮政业	Transportation, Storage, Postal Services	1822835	2062096
信息传输、计算机服务和软件业	Information Transmission, Computer Service and Softwares	415738	487891
批发与零售业	Wholesale and Retail Trade	155448	251324
住宿和餐饮业	Hotels and Restaurants	87855	70739
金融业	Financing	22654	15075
房地产业	Real Estate	4275942	5470966
租赁与商务服务业	Renting and Business Activities	52814	65175
科学研究、技术服务与地质勘查业	Scientific Research, Technology Services and Geological Prospecting	39470	11929
水利、环境和公共设施管理业	Administration of Water Conservancy, Environment and Public Facilities	1487596	1863778
居民服务和其他服务业	Household Services and Other Services	17897	29098
教育	Education	335599	474832
卫生、社会保障和社会福利业	Health, Social Security and Social Welfare	90098	139002
文化、体育与娱乐业	Culture, Sports and Entertainment	95700	121891
公共管理与社会组织	Public Administration and Social Organizations	495662	492517

4－4 按资金来源分的全社会固定资产投资（2003－2004年）
Total Investment in Fixed Assets by Source of Fund (2003-2004)

单位：万元 (10 000 yuan)

指　标	Item	总计 Total		#基本建设 Capital Construction	
		2003	2004	2003	2004
本年资金来源合计	**Total Fund in this Year**	**14353280**	**17992820**	**7387860**	**9741575**
上年末结余资金	Surplus Fund of 2000's End	1809148	1671420	1087788	643088
本年资金来源小计	Sources of Fund in this Year	12544132	16321400	6300072	9098487
国家预算内资金	State Budgetary Appropriation	1314525	1041203	1230746	955039
国内贷款	Domestic Loans	3330585	4041197	2008171	2800638
债　券	Bonds	82287	174311	82287	169760
利用外资	Foreign Investment	256842	463775	194548	337006
自筹资金	Fundraising	4758783	6698725	2072057	3648973
其他资金来源	Others	2801110	3902189	712263	1187068

指　标	Item	#更新改造 Innovation		#房地产 Real Estate	
		2003	2004	2003	2004
本年资金来源合计	**Total Fund in this Year**	**1365928**	**1805081**	**4793499**	**6220133**
上年末结余资金	Surplus Fund of 2000's End	137350	123737	570236	902564
本年资金来源小计	Sources of Fund in this Year	1228578	1681344	4223263	5317569
国家预算内资金	State Budgetary Appropriation	46181	60865	1000	6562
国内贷款	Domestic Loans	281759	423152	949504	781531
债　券	Bonds		51		
利用外资	Foreign Investment	18861	22273	41458	104096
自筹资金	Fundraising	805314	1088677	1371847	1836902
其他资金来源	Others	76463	86329	1859454	2588478

注：本表不含城乡私人投资。

Note: Town and rural private investment is not contained in this table.

4—5 全社会房屋竣工面积（2003—2004年）
Total Floor Space of Completed Buildings (2003-2004)

单位：万平方米 (10 000 sq.m)

指　　标	Item	房屋竣工面积 Floor Space of Buildings Completed 2003	2004	#住　宅 Residential Buildings 2003	2004
总　　计	**Total**	**5958.80**	**5559.79**	**4292.79**	**3962.33**
基本建设	Capital Construction	1319.86	1245.88	684.47	525.49
更新改造	Innovation	61.44	64.80	5.95	3.91
房地产开发	Real Estate Development	1676.97	1585.98	1231.75	1227.66
城镇集体	Urban Collective				
农村集体	Rural Collective	342.02	294.81	89.12	69.05
城镇私人	Urban Individual	181.75	190.10	160.55	159.52
农村私人	Rural Individual	2342.04	2139.50	2098.43	1947.86
其　　他	Others	34.72	38.72	22.51	28.84

注：城镇私人建房不含城关镇以下的建制镇数据。

Note: Data of housing construction by urban individuals should excludes that at towns with county governments stationed below.

4—6 全社会房屋造价（2003—2004年）
Total Cost of Completed Buildings (2003-2004)

单位：元/平方米 (yuan/sq.m)

指　　标	Item	每平方米造价 Per Sq.m Cost of Buildings Completed 2003	2004	#住　宅 Residential Buildings 2003	2004
总　　计	**Total**	**574**	**608**	**491**	**537**
基本建设	Capital Construction	663	677	566	581
更新改造	Innovation	776	783	520	525
房地产开发	Real Estate Development	937	1008	827	929
城镇集体	Urban Collective				
农村集体	Rural Collective	487	540	460	480
城镇私人	Urban Individual	478	454	443	455
农村私人	Rural Individual	281	290	277	288
其　　他	Others	522	630	444	542

注：城镇私人建房不含城关镇以下的建制镇数据。

Note: Data of housing construction by urban individuals should excludes that at towns with county governments stationed below.

4－7 基本建设投资（2003－2004年）
Investment in Capital Construction (2003-2004)

指　　标	Item	2003	2004
投资总额(万元)	**Total Investment (10 000 yuan)**	**6654920**	**8913181**
按隶属关系分	By Administrative Relationship		
中央项目	Ministerial Projects	991089	1172299
地方项目	Local Projects	5663831	7740882
按构成分	By Use of Funds		
建筑工程	Construction	4356356	5269813
安装工程	Installation	306902	412572
设备、工具、器具购置	Purchase of Equipment and Instrument	650746	1103131
其他费用	Others	1340916	2127665
按建设性质分	By Type of Construction		
#新　建	New Construction	4630391	6443037
扩　建	Expansion	817706	1159701
改　建	Reconstruction	686846	815873
#住　宅	Residential Buildings	516443	478662
按规模分	By Project Size		
大中型项目	Large & Medium-sized Projects	1413687	2079744
小型项目	Small Sized Projects	5203408	6779216
按国民经济行业分	By Sector		
第一产业	Primary Industry	190999	257988
第二产业	Secondary Industry	1783885	2805290
#工　业	Industry	1401412	2563325
第三产业	Tertiary Industry	4680036	5849903
新增固定资产(万元)	**New Fixed Assets (10 000 yuan)**	**2950717**	**3546250**
建设项目(个)	**Construction Project (unit)**		
施工项目	Project under Construction	3402	4076
全部建成投产项目	Project Completed and Put into Use	1918	2130
房屋建筑面积(万平方米)	**Floor Space of Buildings (10 000 sq.m)**		
施工面积	Floor Space under Construction	2515.49	2666.34
#住　宅	Residential Buildings	1196.58	1045.76
竣工面积	Floor Space Completed	1319.86	1245.88
#住　宅	Residential Buildings	684.47	525.49

注：1）此表数据不包括农村集体、城镇工矿区私人建房及农村私人投资。

2）大中型项目包括中央级大中项目和地方级大中项目。

Note: a) Data on this table exclude investment by rural collective-owned units, urban individuals in industrial & mining areas and rural individuals;

b) Large and medium sized projects includes Large and medium sized projects at both central level and local level.

4－8 按行业分的基本建设投资（2004年）
Investment in Capital Construction by Sector (2004)

单位：万元 (10 000 yuan)

行　　业	Sector	施工项目个数(个) Project under Construction (unit)	计划总投资 Planned Total Investment	本年完成投资 Investment Completed in Current Year
总　　计	Total	4076	33955909	8913181
第一产业	Primary Industry	336	1195159	257988
第二产业	Secondary Industry	1501	9081513	2805290
工　业	Industry	1303	8501226	2563325
采矿业	Mining and Quarrying	183	292483	263278
#石油和天然气开采业	Petroleum and Natural Gas Mining	9	199236	190026
制造业	Manufacturing	891	3369357	1356910
#化学原料及化学制品制造业	Raw Chemical Materials and Chemical Products	42	177719	101792
医药制造业	Medical Materials and Medicines	33	146193	59749
通用设备制造业	Ordinary Equipment	46	96305	39059
专用设备制造业	Special Equipment	34	215878	41472
交通设备制造业	Transport Equipment	155	879100	296306
电力、燃气及水的生产和供应业	Electricity, Gas & Water Production and Supply	229	4839386	943137
电力、热力的生产和供应业	Electricity & Hot Power Production and Supply	114	3844392	720867
燃气生产和供应业	Gas Production and Supply	30	132690	30852
水的生产和供应业	Water Production and Supply	85	862304	191418
建筑业	Construction	248	580287	241965
第三产业	Tertiary Industry	2239	23679247	5849903
交通运输、仓储及邮政业	Transportation, Storage, Postal Services	343	8826056	1904410
#邮政业	Postal Services	6	11452	5618
信息传输、计算机服务和软件业	Data Transmission, Computer Service and Software	28	263611	63651
#电信和其他信息传输服务业	Telecommunications and Other Information Transmission Services	27	258611	61551
批发与零售业	Wholesale and Retail Trade	141	515136	208204
住宿和餐饮业	Hotels and Restaurants	62	163156	44730
金融业	Financing	17	12305	5951
房地产业	Real Estate	131	1324674	603240
租赁与商务服务业	Renting and Business Activities	15	211804	52897
科学研究、技术服务与地质勘查业	Scientific Research, Technical Services and Geological Prospecting	14	28898	10302
水利、环境和公共设施管理业	Administration of Water Conservancy, Environment and Public Utilities	553	9429696	1829444
居民服务和其他服务业	Household Services and Other Services	21	63252	22436
教　育	Education	293	1089687	446247
卫生、社会保障和社会福利业	Public Health, Social Security and Social Welfare	131	203699	108040
#卫　生	Public Health	115	186249	99562
文化、体育与娱乐业	Culture, Sports and Entertainment	71	348803	107781
公共管理与社会组织	Public Administration and Social Organizations	419	1198460	442570

注：此表数据不包括农村集体、城镇工矿区私人建房及农村私人投资。

Note: Data on this table exclude investment by rural collective-owned units, urban individuals in industrial & mining areas and rural individuals.

4－9 更新改造投资（2003－2004年）
Investment in Innovation (2003-2004)

指　　标	Item	2003	2004
投资总额(万元)	**Total Investment (10 000 yuan)**	**1220100**	**1534319**
按隶属关系分	**By Administrative Relationship**		
中央项目	Ministerial Projects	569218	676077
地方项目	Local Projects	650882	858242
按构成分	**By Use of Funds**		
建筑工程	Construction	281748	267259
安装工程	Installation	222758	154865
设备、工具、器具购置	Purchases of Equipment and Instruments	607276	1003497
其他费用	Others	108318	108698
按建设性质分	**By Type of Construction**		
#新　建	New Construction	34425	88681
扩　建	Expansion	834445	866745
改　建	Reconstruction	234169	398687
按规模分	**By Project Size**		
大中型项目	Large & Medium-sized Projects	144487	170180
小型项目	Small Sized Projects	1075613	1364139
按国民经济行业分	**By Sector**		
第一产业	Primary Industry	616	2400
第二产业	Secondary Industry	775372	926526
#工　业	Industry	771366	915721
第三产业	Tertiary Industry	444112	605393
新增固定资产(万元)	**New Fixed Assets (10 000 yuan)**	**977482**	**1351517**
建设项目(个)	**Construction Project (unit)**		
施工项目	Project under Construction	810	816
全部建成投产项目	Project Completed and Put into Use	537	539
房屋建筑面积(万平方米)	**Floor Space of Buildings (10 000 sq.m)**		
施工面积	Floor Space under Construction	115.50	107.04
#住　宅	Residential Buildings	8.22	5.84
竣工面积	Floor Space Completed	61.44	64.80
#住　宅	Residential Buildings	5.95	3.91

注：此表数据不包括农村集体、城镇工矿区私人建房及农村私人投资。

Note: Data on this table exclude investment by rural collective-owned units, urban individuals in industrial & mining areas and rural individuals.

4—10 按行业分的更新改造投资（2004年）
Investment in Innovation by Sector (2004)

单位：万元 (10 000 yuan)

行　　业	Sector	施工项目个数(个) Project under Construction (unit)	计划总投资 Planned Total Investment	本年完成投资 Investment Completed in Current Year
总　　计	**Total**	**816**	**3334617**	**1534319**
第一产业	Primary Industry	6	2400	2400
第二产业	Secondary Industry	673	2606276	926526
工　业	Industry	658	2595302	915721
采矿业	Mining and Quarrying	97	76089	53921
#石油和天然气开采业	Petroleum and Natural Gas Mining	9	9800	3288
制造业	Manufacturing	508	2172158	755209
#化学原料及化学制品制造业	Raw Chemical Materials and Chemical Products	53	115286	50761
医药制造业	Medical Materials and Medicines	19	178840	29469
通用设备制造业	Ordinary Equipment	15	47609	25039
专用设备制造业	Special Equipment	12	31761	19088
交通设备制造业	Transport Equipment	87	636812	198899
电力、燃气及水的生产和供应业	Electricity, Gas & Water Production and Supply	53	347055	106591
电力、热力的生产和供应业	Electricity & Hot Power Production and Supply	35	327186	95433
燃气生产和供应业	Gas Production and Supply	4	4681	4280
水的生产和供应业	Water Production and Supply	14	15188	6878
建筑业	Construction	15	10974	10805
第三产业	Tertiary Industry	137	725941	605393
交通运输、仓储及邮政业	Transportation, Storage, Postal Services	37	110480	96507
#邮政业	Postal Services	7	9099	5967
信息传输、计算机服务和软件业	Data Transmission, Computer Service and Software	52	498973	423518
#电信和其他信息传输服务业	Telecommunications and Other Information Transmission Services	52	498973	423518
批发与零售业	Wholesale and Retail Trade	11	35999	20205
住宿和餐饮业	Hotels and Restaurants	2	1854	1554
金融业	Financing		6372	6372
房地产业	Real Estate	1	509	473
租赁与商务服务业	Renting and Business Activities	6	2214	2049
科学研究、技术服务与地质勘查业	Scientific Research, Technical Services and Geological Prospecting	1	1526	1526
水利、环境和公共设施管理业	Administration of Water Conservancy, Environment and Public Utilities	10	10580	4171
居民服务和其他服务业	Household Services and Other Services		700	700
教　育	Education	6	12705	12602
卫生、社会保障和社会福利业	Public Health, Social Security and Social Welfare	1	15950	15950
#卫　生	Public Health	1	15950	15950
文化、体育与娱乐业	Culture, Sports and Entertainment	5	6653	3196
公共管理与社会组织	Public Administration and Social Organizations	5	21426	16570

注：此表数据不包括农村集体、城镇工矿区私人建房及农村私人投资。

Note: Data on this table exclude investment by rural collective-owned units, urban individuals in industrial & mining areas and rural individuals.

4－11 基本建设新增主要产品生产能力（2003－2004年）
Newly Increased Production Capacity through Capital Construction (2003-2004)

能力名称	Production Capacity	2003	2004
铁合金（万吨/年）	Iron Alloy, Electric Furnace (10 000 tons/year)		10
原煤开采（万吨/年）	Coal Mining (10 000 tons/year)	8	193
发电机组容量（万千瓦）	Capacity of Power Generating Sets (10 000 kw/year)	11	44
#火　电	Thermal Power		3
水　电	Hydropower	11	41
汽车制造（万辆/年）	Motor Vehicles (10 000 units/year)		58
水泥（万吨/年）	Cement (10 000 tons/year)	61	168
化学纤维（万吨/年）	Chemical Fiber (10 000 tons/year)		1
棉纺锭（万锭）	Cotton Spindles (10 000 units)	1	8
机制纸及纸板（万吨/年）	Machine-made Paper and Paperboards (10 000 tons/year)	6	105
新建铁路主线正线交付营业里程（公里）	Length of Newly Built Railways Put into Operation (km)		6
新(扩)建港口码头	Newly Built or Expanded Ports		
年吞吐量（万吨）	Annual Handling Capacity (10 000 tons)	53	23
泊　位（个）	Number of Berth (unit)	1	6
新建公路（公里）	Length of New Highways (km)	454	770
改建公路（公里）	Length of Reconstructed Highways (km)	1442	1372
粮食仓库（万平方米）	Grain Storehouses (10 000 sq.m)		300
粮食仓库（万公斤）	Grain Storehouses (10 000 kg)		30
高等院校：学生席位（个）	Students Capacity of Universities and Colleges (unit)	800	37567
医院病床床位（张）	Number of Hospital Beds (bed)	2972	1533
城市自来水供水能力（万吨/日）	Tap Water Supply Capacity (10 000tons/day)	33	28

4－12 更新改造新增主要产品生产能力（2003－2004年）
Newly Increased Production Capacity through Innovation (2003-2004)

能力名称	Production Capacity	2003	2004
炼　钢（万吨/年）	Steel-making (10 000 tons/year)		170
初　轧（万吨/年）	Rough Rolling (10 000 tons/year)	2	
原煤开采（万吨/年）	Coal Mining (10 000 tons/year)	100	48
烧　碱（万吨/年）	Caustic Soda (10 000 tons/year)	2	
合成氨（万吨/年）	Synthetic Ammonia (10 000 tons/year)	8	3
化　肥（万吨/年）	Chemical Fertilizer (10 000 tons/year)	10	4
发电机组容量（万千瓦）	Capacity of Power Generating Sets (10 000 kw/year)	3	32
#火　电	Thermal Power	2	32
水　电	Hydropower	1	…
汽车制造（辆/年）	Motor Vehicles (unit/year)	800	203000
#载重汽车制造	Trucks	800	
胶合板（万立方米/年）	Plywood (10 000 cu.m/year)		2
水　泥（万吨/年）	Cement (10 000 tons/year)	231	361
卷　烟（万箱/年）	Cigarettes (10 000 cases/year)	…	
酒（吨/年）	Liquors (10 000 tons/year)	200	200
化学纤维（吨/年）	Chemical Fiber (ton/year)	1600	
棉纺锭（万锭）	Cotton Spindles (10 000 units)	5	1
棉印染布（万米/年）	Printed and Dyed Cloth (10 000 m/year)	900	
新(扩)建港口码头	Newly Built or Expanded Ports		
年吞吐量（万吨）	Annual Handling Capacity (10 000 tons)		50
泊　位（个）	Number of Berths (unit)		1
新建公路（公里）	Length of New Highways (km)		61
改建公路（公里）	Length of Reconstructed Highways (km)	7	43
医院病床床位（张）	Number of Hospital Beds (unit)	46	
城市自来水供水能力（万吨/日）	Tap Water Supply Capacity (10 000 tons/day)	4	

4－13 城镇和工矿区个人建房（2003－2004年） Building Construction by Individuals in Cities & Towns and in Industrial & Mining Areas (2003-2004)

指　　标	Item	2003	2004
城镇工矿区个数（个）	Number of Cities, towns, Industrial and Mining Areas (unit)	71	60
建房户数（户）	Households with Building Construction (household)	10895	10583
竣工房屋建筑面积（万平方米）	Floor Space of Buildings Completed (10 000 sq.m)	181.75	190.10
#住　宅	Residential Buildings	160.55	159.52
竣工房屋价值（万元）	Value of Buildings Completed (10 000 yuan)	83603	86323
#住　宅	Residential Buildings	68522	72626

4－14 渝房景气指数（1996－2004年） Business Survey of Real Estate Development in Chongqing (1996-2004)

年　份 Year	1 月 January	2 月 February	3 月 March	4 月 April	5 月 May	6 月 June
1996	100.93	101.69	100.00	99.50	102.31	102.56
1997	105.81	98.29	101.00	104.09	99.74	95.62
1998	102.96	112.03	114.38	108.84	111.86	112.16
1999	109.08	106.38	101.61	105.14	103.02	106.24
2000	108.59	103.50	109.48	109.19	108.63	105.83
2001	102.77	103.11	107.95	110.18	108.35	110.94
2002	102.66	101.42	105.64	103.72	103.82	104.41
2003	113.40	114.57	113.96	115.87	115.42	110.89
2004	112.55	113.49	114.05	116.18	117.44	113.76

年　份 Year	7 月 July	8 月 August	9 月 September	10 月 October	11 月 November	12 月 December
1996	104.88	105.33	102.95	104.14	104.30	101.95
1997	94.64	94.24	96.67	96.63	96.93	103.07
1998	111.36	115.07	116.97	119.31	120.12	112.46
1999	104.78	102.12	100.78	98.81	97.98	97.44
2000	107.76	108.80	109.77	109.25	108.92	107.25
2001	112.12	112.87	113.60	115.05	115.56	110.38
2002	102.64	102.38	102.72	103.51	103.91	106.65
2003	114.06	115.06	114.03	115.04	114.04	110.15
2004	109.45	110.70	109.44	109.25	110.53	104.93

4－15 房地产开发基本情况（1990－2004年）
Basic Statistics on Real Estate Development (1990-2004)

单位：万平方米 (10 000 sq.m)

年份 Year	企业数（个） Number of Enterprises (unit)	从业人员（人） Employment (person)	本年完成土地开发面积 Land Space Developed in This Year	本年土地购置面积 Land Space Purchased in This Year	本年完成投资总额（万元） Investment Completed in This Year (10 000 yuan)	#商品房屋建设投资 Investment in Commercial Building Construction	#住宅 Residential Buildings	资金来源（万元） Total Funds (10 000 yuan)
1990					17503	16351	10600	17568
1991					19185	18983	14040	18042
1992					33868	33628	21239	33148
1993					123151	121419	66833	107210
1994					279089	277355	196411	377959
1995					468845	457742	252085	612121
1996	635	22512	93.84	588.65	556185	400859	259881	836655
1997	622	24911	183.31	259.49	675022	477218	282592	1060761
1998	991	50088	205.98	521.48	973014	781839	440889	1391253
1999	1073	50526	211.12	624.53	1125135	893899	523357	1504042
2000	1339	63925	384.68	619.21	1396327	1138097	728125	1784950
2001	1474	78961	518.00	870.34	1966684	1630362	1107126	2373982
2002	1559	76582	661.94	1320.26	2459130	2027530	1306998	3148171
2003	1597	54148	842.35	1637.19	3278881	2247433	1774341	4793499
2004	1828	70711	852.02	1137.61	4050791	2842003	2171303	6220133

年份 Year	房屋施工面积 Floor Space under Construction	#住宅 Residential Buildings	房屋竣工面积 Floor Space Completed of Commercial Buildings	#住宅 Residential Buildings	商品房销售面积 Floor Spaces Sold of Commercial Buildings	#住宅 Residential Buildings	商品房销售额（万元） Sales Value of Commercial Buildings (10 000 yuan)	#住宅 Residential Buildings
1990	107.80	65.48	46.16	34.16	23.29		17648	
1991	112.57	83.54	37.33	28.61	27.48		20007	
1992	160.91	94.56	45.90	30.48	32.87		29583	
1993	437.73	293.03	81.05	66.01	37.39		42221	
1994	650.71	394.43	141.27	115.05	46.32		55336	
1995	1267.96	810.36	258.25	208.70	114.61		116657	
1996	1424.35	855.64	351.76	275.62	166.21	142.98	189856	145507
1997	1652.32	904.18	459.92	358.36	260.78	215.33	313111	222376
1998	2058.35	1223.66	600.04	422.61	416.82	359.73	554786	417609
1999	2103.76	1285.41	619.56	438.56	429.98	364.56	591992	393569
2000	2833.42	1896.18	849.42	622.08	579.96	491.09	783709	528698
2001	3653.71	2508.30	1020.63	738.41	746.05	635.04	1076534	719196
2002	4414.96	3081.57	1390.73	1033.60	1016.58	870.41	1581505	1111929
2003	5287.80	3747.34	1676.97	1231.75	1316.83	1132.95	2102260	1499915
2004	6247.86	4544.54	1585.98	1227.66	1329.32	1157.95	2327978	1817280

4－16 房地产开发主要指标（2003－2004年）
Main Indicators of Real Estate Development (2003-2004)

指　　标	Item	2003	2004
企业个数（个）	**Number of Enterprises (unit)**	**1597**	**1828**
内资企业	Domestic Funded	1486	1714
#国　有	State-owned	81	90
集　体	Collective-owned	36	41
港、澳、台投资企业	Funded by Entrepreneurs from Hong Kong, Macao and Taiwan	78	83
外商投资企业	Foreign Funded	33	31
从业人员（人）	**Employment (person)**	**54148**	**70711**
内资企业	Domestic Funded	49072	64906
#国　有	State-owned	2903	5457
集　体	Collective-owned	964	1555
港、澳、台投资企业	Funded by Entrepreneurs from Hong Kong, Macao and Taiwan	4075	4168
外商投资企业	Foreign Funded	1001	1637
土地开发及购置（万平方米）	**Land Development and Purchase (10 000 sq.m)**		
本年完成土地开发面积	Land Space Developed in This Year	842.35	852.02
本年土地购置面积	Land Space Purchased in This Year	1637.19	1137.61
本年完成投资总额(万元)	**Investment Completed in This Year (10 000 yuan)**	**3278881**	**4050791**
#土地开发投资	Land Development Investment	341766	209549
商品房屋建设投资	Commercial Building Construction Investment	2247433	2842003
按工程用途分	By Use of Projects		
住　宅	Residential Buildings	1774341	2171303
#别墅、高档公寓	Villas and Senior Flats	116952	113601
经济适用房屋	Economical Houses	163154	134071
办公楼	Office Buildings	118569	114328
商业营业用房	Commercial Buildings	508227	621105
其　他	Others	877744	1144055
资金来源（万元）	**Total Funds by Source (10 000 yuan)**	**4793499**	**6220133**
#国内贷款	Domestic Loans	949504	781531
利用外资	Foreign Investment	41458	104096
自筹资金	Fundraising	1371847	1836902
房屋建筑面积(万平方米)	**Floor Space of Buildings (10 000 sq.m)**		
施工面积	Floor Space under Construction	5287.80	6247.86
#住　宅	Residential Buildings	3747.34	4544.54
竣工面积	Floor Space Completed	1676.97	1585.98
#住　宅	Residential Buildings	1231.75	1227.66
本年新开工面积	Floor Space Started in This Year	2098.24	2190.99
#住　宅	Residential Buildings	1580.04	1691.63
商品房销售	**Sales of Commercial Buildings**		
商品房销售面积（万平方米）	Floor Space of Sales (10 000 sq.m)	1316.83	1329.32
#住　宅	Residential Buildings	1132.95	1157.95
商品房销售额（万元）	Total Sales of Commercial Buildings (10 000 yuan)	2102260	2327978
#住　宅	Residential Buildings	1499915	1817280
实收资本合计（万元）	**Total Capital Hold (10 000 yuan)**	**2895894**	**3198841**
#国家资本金	State Capital	121331	299492
资产负债率（%）	Ratio of Liabilities to Assets (%)	71.4	69.9
房地产开发经营情况（万元）	**Real Estate Development and Management (10 000 yuan)**		
经营总收入	Total Revenue	2469860	3091509
#土地转让收入	Land Transferred	37242	48308

4－17 商品房销售情况和空置面积（2003－2004年）
Sales of Commercial Buildings and Vacant Space (2003-2004)

单位：万平方米 (10 000 sq.m)

指标	Item	2003	2004
商品房实际销售面积	**Floor Space of Commercial Buildings Actually Sold**	**1316.83**	**1329.32**
#住　宅	Residential Buildings	1132.95	1157.95
#别墅、高档公寓	Villas and Good Apartments	26.12	15.90
经济适用房屋	Economical Houses	126.69	107.78
办公楼	Office Buildings	32.00	29.63
商业营业用房	Houses for Business Use	135.93	125.46
个人购买商品住宅面积	Area of Personal Purchases of Commercials Buildings	1076.78	1096.69
商品房屋销售额(亿元)	**Sales Revenue of Commercial Buildings (100 million yuan)**	**210.23**	**232.80**
#住　宅	Residential Buildings	150.00	181.73
#别墅、高档公寓	Villas and Good Apartments	8.78	8.30
经济适用房屋	Economical Houses	11.28	14.81
办公楼	Office Buildings	7.93	7.20
商业营业用房	Houses for Business Use	49.77	41.01
个人购买商品住宅额（亿元）	Amount of Personal Purchases of Commercials Buildings (100 million yuan)	143.21	170.71
商品房空置面积	**Vacant Space of Commercial Buildings**	**551.28**	**567.68**
#住　宅	Residential Buildings	225.62	191.16
#别墅、高档公寓	Villas and Good Apartments	2.59	6.24
经济适用房屋	Economical Houses	8.80	5.59
办公楼	Office Buildings	44.72	48.75
商业营业用房	Houses for Business Use	224.68	246.39
其中：空置一年以上	Vacant over 1 Year	331.34	319.48
#住　宅	Residential Buildings	110.85	75.63
#别墅、高档公寓	Villas and Good Apartments	2.30	1.79
经济适用房屋	Economical Houses	4.26	3.31
办公楼	Office Buildings	36.10	37.39
商业营业用房	Houses for Business Use	148.85	160.97

4－18 房地产开发企业资产负债情况（2003－2004年）
Asset Balance of Enterprises for Real Estate Development (2003-2004)

单位：万元 (10 000 yuan)

指　标	Item	2003	2004
实收资本合计	Total Capital Hold	2895894	3198841
#国家资本金	State Capital	121331	299492
资产总计	Total Assets	12968949	14987769
累计折旧	Total Depreciation	206505	216365
#本年折旧	Depreciation in This Year	42805	41543
负债总计	Total Liabilities	9257357	10483699
所有者权益	Creditors' Equity	3711592	4504071
资产负债率（%）	Ratio of Liabilities to Assets (%)	71.4	69.9

4－19 房地产开发企业经营情况（2003－2004年）
Real Estate Development and Management (2003-2004)

单位：万元 (10 000 yuan)

指　标	Item	2003	2004
经营总收入	Total Revenue	2469860	3091509
土地转让收入	Land Transferred	37242	48308
商品房屋销售收入	Commercial Houses Sold	1914342	2762452
房屋出租收入	Houses Leased	43603	65653
其他收入	Others	474673	215097
经营税金及附加	Business Tax and Extra Charges	128979	171690
利润总额	Total Profits	72736	172773

主要统计指标解释

全社会固定资产投资 以货币形式表现的在一定时期内全社会建造和购置固定资产的工作量以及与此有关的费用的总称。该指标是反映固定资产投资规模、结构和发展速度的综合性指标,又是观察工程进度和考核投资效果的重要依据。全社会固定资产投资按登记注册类型可分为国有、集体、个体、联营、股份制、外商、港澳台商、其他等。按照管理渠道，可分为基本建设、更新改造、房地产开发投资和其他固定资产投资四个部分。

新增固定资产 指报告期内已经完成建造和购置过程，并已交付生产或使用单位的固定资产价值。该指标是表示固定资产投资成果的价值指标，也是反映建设进度，计算固定资产投资效果的重要指标。

基本建设投资 基本建设是企业、事业、行政单位以扩大生产能力或工程效益为主要目的的新建、扩建工程及有关活动。其综合范围为总投资 50 万元以上（含 50 万元，下同）的基本建设项目。具体包括（1）列入中央和各级地方本年基本建设计划的建设项目，以及虽未列入本年基本建设计划，但使用以前年度基建计划内结转投资（包括利用基建库存设备材料）在本年继续施工的建设项目；（2）本年基本建设计划内投资与更新改造计划内投资结合安排的新建项目和新增生产能力（或工程效益）达到大中型项目标准的扩建项目，以及为改变生产力布局而进行的全厂性迁建项目；（3）国有单位既未列入基建计划，也未列入更新改造计划的总投资 50 万元以上的新建、扩建、恢复项目和为改变生产力布局而进行的全厂性迁建项目，以及行政、事业单位增建业务用房和行政单位增建生活福利设施的项目。

更新改造投资 更新改造是指企业、事业单位对原有设施进行固定资产更新和技术改造，以及相应配套的工程和有关工作（不包括大修理和维护工程）。其综合范围为总投资 50 万元以上（含 50 万元，下同）的更新改造项目。具体包括：（1）列入中央和各级地方本年更新改造计划的项目和虽未列入本年更新改造计划，但使用上年更新改造计划内结转的投资在本年继续施工的项目；（2）本年更新改造计划内投资与基本建设计划内投资结合安排的对企、事业单位原有设施进行技术改造或更新的项目，和增建主要生产车间、分厂等其新增生产能力（或工程效益）未达到大中型项目标准的项目，以及由于城市环境保护和安全生产的需要而进行的迁建工程；（3）国有企、事业单位既未列入基建计划也未列入更新改造计划，总投资 50 万元以上属于改建或更新改造性质的项目，以及由于城市环境保护和安全生产的需要而进行的迁建工程。

房地产开发投资 指房地产开发公司、商品房建设公司及其他房地产开发法人单位和附属于其他法人单位实际从事房地产开发或经营的活动单位统一开发的包括统代建、拆迁还建的住宅、厂房、仓库、饭店、宾馆、度假村、写字楼、办公楼等房屋建筑物和配套的服务设施，土地开发工程（如道路、给水、排水、供电、供热、通讯、平整场地等基础设施工程）的投资；不包括单纯的土地交易活动。

其他固定资产投资 全社会固定资产投资中未列入基本建设，更新改造和房地产开发投资的建造和购置固定资产的活动。包括：

（1）国有单位未纳入基本建设计划和更新改造计划管理的项目和工程投资：①用油田维护费和石油开发基金进行的油田维护和开发工程；②煤炭、铁矿、森工等采掘采伐业用维简费进行的开拓延伸工程；③交通部门用公路养路费对原有公路、桥梁进行改建的工程；④商业部门用简易建筑费建造的仓库工程。

（2）城镇集体固定资产投资：指所有隶属城市、县城（城关镇）领导的集体单位（乡镇企业局管理的除外）建造和购置固定资产计划总投资（或实际需要总投资）在 50 万元及 50 万元以上，未列入基本建设和更新改造计划的单位（项目）投资。

（3）除上述以外的其他各种企业、事业单位、个体建造和购置固定资产总投资在 50 万元及 50 万元以上，未列入基本建设和更新改造计划的单位（项目）。

（4）城镇和工矿区私人建房投资：包括市、县城、镇、工矿区所辖范围内的全部私人建房，不论其房主是否系本地的常住户口均应包括。

（5）农村投资：包括农村区域范围内进行固定资产投资活动的企业及农村个人投资。

固定资产投资的资金来源 根据固定资产投资的资金来源不同，分为国家预算内资金、国内贷款、利用外资、自筹资金和其他资金来源。

（1）国家预算内资金　分为财政拨款和财政安排的贷款两部分，包括中央财政的基本建设基金（分经营性基金和非经费性基金两部分），专项支出、收回再贷、贴息资金、财政安排的挖潜改造和新产品试制支出、城建支出、商业部门简易建筑支出，不发达地区发展基金等资金中用于固定资产投资的资金；地方财政中由国家统筹安排的固定资产投资资金等。

（2）国内贷款　指报告期固定资产投资单位向银行及非银行金融机构借入的用于固定资产投资的各种国内借款，包括：银行贷款，上级主管部门拨入的国内贷款、国家专项贷款（包括煤代油贷款、劳改煤矿专项贷款等），地方财政专项资金安排的贷款、国内储备贷款、周转贷款等。

（3）利用外资　指报告期收到的用于固定资产投资的国外资金。包括对外借款（外国政府、国际金融组织贷款、出口信贷、外国银行商业贷款、对外发行债券和股票）外商直接投资，外商其他投资（包括利用外商投资收益在国内进行固定资产再投资活动的资金）。

（4）自筹资金　指固定资产投资单位报告期收到的，由各地区、各部门及企事业单位筹集用于固定资产投资的预算外资金。

（5）其他资金来源　指在报告期收到的除以上各种资金以外其他用于固定资产投资的资金，包括群众集资，个人资金、无偿损赠的资金及其他单位拨入的资金等。

固定资产投资按国民经济行业分 建设项目归哪个行业，按其建成投产后的主要产品或主要用途及社会经济活动性质来确定，基本建设按建设项目划分国民经济行业，更新改造、国有经济单位其他固定资产投资及城镇集体投资根据整个企业、事业单位所属的行业来划分。一般情况下，一个建设项目或一个企业、事业单位只能属于一种国民经济行业。为了更准确地反映国民经济各行业之间的比例关系，联合企业（总厂）所属分厂属于不同行业的，原则上按分厂划分行业。

固定资产投资按建设性质分 建设项目的性质一般分为新建、扩建、改建、迁建、恢复。基本建设按建设项目划分建设性质，更新改造、国有经济单位其他固定资产投资及城镇集体投资按整个企业、事业单位的情况确定建设性质。房地产开发单位、农村投资、城镇工矿区私人建房等投资不划分建设性质。

（1）新建：一般是指从无到有、“平地起家”开始建设的企、事业和行政或独立的工程单位。有的单位原有的基础很小，经过建设后其新增加的固定资产价值超过原有固定资产价值（原值）三倍以上的也算新建。

（2）扩建：是指为扩大原有产品的生产能力、在厂内或其他地点增建主要生产车间（或主要工程）、独立的生产线或总厂之下的分厂的企业；事业单位和行政单位在原单位增建业务用房（如学校增建教学用房、医院增建门诊部或病床用房、行政机关增建办公楼等）也作为扩建。

（3）改建：一般是指现有企业、事业单位为了技术进步，提高产品质量，增加花色品种，促进产品升级换代，降低消耗和成本，加强资源综合利用和三废治理、劳保安全等，采用新技术、新工艺、新设备、新材料等对现有设施、工艺条件进行技术改造或与更新（包括相应配套的辅助性生产、生活福利设施）。有的企业充分发挥现有生产能力，进行填平补齐而增建不增加本单位主要产品生产能力的车间等，也属于改建。

固定资产投资按构成分 固定资产投资活动按其工作内容和实现方式分为建筑安装工程，设备、工具、器具购置，其他费用三个部分。

（1）建筑安装工程（建筑工作量）：指各种房屋、建筑物的建造工程和各种设备、装置的安装工程。包括各种房屋建造工程，各种用途设备基础和各种工业窑炉的砌筑工程；为施工而进行的各种准备工作和临时工程以及完工后的清理工作等；铁路、道路的铺设，矿井的开凿及石油管道的架设等；水利工程；防空地下建筑等特殊工程；以及各种机械设备的安装工程；为测定安装工程质量，对设备进行的试运行工作。在安装工程中，不包括被安装设备本身的价值。

（2）设备、工具、器具购置：指购置或自制达到固定资产标准的设备、工具、器具的价值。新建单位、扩建单位的新建车间按照设计和计划要求购置或自制的全部设备、工具、器具，不论是否达到固定资产标准均计入"设备、工具、器具购置"中。

（3）其他费用：指在固定资产建造和购置过程中发生的，除建筑安装工程和设备、工具、器具购置以外的各种应摊入固定资产的费用。

施工项目 指报告期内曾进行建筑或安装工程施工活动的建设项目。包括报告期内新开工项目、报告期以前开工跨入报告期继续施工的项目以及报告期施过工并在报告期内全部建设投产或停缓建的项目。

全部建成投产项目 工业项目是指设计文件规定形成生产能力的主体工程及其相应配套的辅助设施全部建成，经负荷试运转，证明具备生产设计规定合格产品的条件，并经过验收鉴定合格或达到竣工验收标准，与生产性工程配套的生产福利设施可以满足近期正常生产的需要，正式移交生产的建设项目。非工业项目是指设计文件规定的主体工程和相应的配套工程全部建成，能够发挥设计规定的全部效益，经验收鉴定合格或达到竣工验收标准，正式移交使用的建设项目。

新增生产能力(或工程效益) 指通过固定资产投资活动而增加的设计能力(或工程效益)，该指标是以实物形态表现的反映固定资产投资成果的指标，也是考核投资经济效果的重要依据之一。

新增生产能力(或工程效益)一般有以下几种表现形式：

（1）用产品数量表示，以工程在单位时间内(一般是一年)所能生产的产品数量(即年产量)表示。如原煤开采用万吨／年表示，化学农药用吨／年表示，拖拉机制造用台／年表示等。某些化工产品由于含量差别较大，按其设计含量计算折合量表示，如硫酸、纯碱、烧碱等。

（2）用单位时间内所能处理的原料数量表示，以工程每天(或小时)所能处理原料的数量表示。如机制糖工程日处理原料吨，食用植物油日处理原料吨，城市污水处理能力用万吨／日表示等。

（3）用新增加的主要设备的数量或容量表示，如新增棉布织机、丝织机等台数，毛纺锭等锭数，发电厂新增发电机组容量用千瓦表示等。

（4）以节约的原材料、燃料、动力实物量表示，适用于反映更新改造节约项目的效益。

（5）用建筑物容积、容量、面积、长度表示，是非工业项目或工程新增效益的一种表现形式。如铁路里程、公路里程、水库容量、仓库容量、房屋建筑面积、学校学生席位、医院病床、灌区灌溉面积等。

根据工程的特点，有时需要用两种或两种以上的复合计量单位表示新增生产能力(或工程效益)，如新增内燃机生产能力同时用年产台数、千瓦数表示等。

房屋建筑面积 指房屋建筑物勒脚以上外墙外围的水平截面面积，包括房屋建筑物的有效面积和结构面积。该指标是从实物形态上反映建设规模和建设成果的重要指标之一，也是检查工程形象进度、计算工程造价、分析投资效果、研究施工任务和建筑材料之间平衡情况的重要依据。

住宅建筑面积 指施工和竣工房屋建筑面积中供居住用的施工和竣工房屋建筑面积。

房屋施工面积　指报告期内施工的全部房屋建筑面积。包括本期新开工的面积和上期开工跨入本期继续施工的房屋面积，以及上期已停建在本期恢复施工的房屋面积。本期竣工和本期施工后又停缓建的房屋，其建筑面积仍计入本期房屋施工面积中。

房屋竣工面积　指报告期内房屋建筑按照设计要求已全部完工，达到入住和使用条件，经验收鉴定合格（或达到竣工验收标准），可正式移交使用的各栋房屋建筑面积的总和。

固定资产交付使用率　指一定时期新增固定资产与同期完成投资额的比率。该指标是反映固定资产动用速度，衡量建设过程中宏观投资效果的综合指标。由于新增固定资产是较长时期内形成的结果，而投资额则是当年完成的，因此，该指标一般适宜于反映较长时期内固定资产的动用情况。

渝房景气指数　是重庆房地产开发景气指数的简称，也就是国房重庆指数。它是综合反映重庆房地产业发展景气状况的总体指数，该指数配合“国房指数”的发布，准确反映重庆房地产发展态势，正确引导重庆房地产业健康有序地发展，为重庆市政府宏观决策提供科学依据，为本市广大房地产开发商和经济建设服务。

别墅、高档公寓　指建筑造价和销售价格明显高于一般商品住宅的商品住宅。别墅一般指地处郊区，独立成栋的商品住宅；高档公寓一般指地处市内高尚社区，高层或多层的商品住宅。别墅、高档公寓的确定标准：一是经有房地产投资计划审批权的主管部门审批建设的别墅、高档公寓开发项目；二是销售价格高于当地同等地段商品住宅平均销售价格一倍以上的别墅、公寓开发项目。该指标可以分析房地产投资结构，反映高收入家庭商品住宅的供求平衡情况。

经济适用房　指根据国家经济适用房计划安排建设的政策性住宅。经济是指房屋建筑造价和销售价格低于一般商品住宅；适用是指适合中低收入家庭购买使用。经济适用房主要是由国家统一下达投资计划，房地产公司开发，对外销售；用地一般采用行政划拨或招标投标方式，免收土地出让金；对各种经批准的收费减半征收，开发利润不超过3%；销售价格实行政府指导价。该指标可以分析房地产投资结构，反映中低收入家庭商品住宅的供求平衡情况。

实际销售房屋面积　指已签订房屋销售合同并在报告期正式交付购房者使用的商品房屋面积，即报告期现房销售面积。不包括已签订预售合同尚在建设过程中的商品房屋面积，但包括报告期或报告期以前签订了预售合同，在报告期又竣工并交付使用的商品房屋面积。

销售给个人　指实际销售给国内私人的商品房屋面积，不包括外销中销售给个人的部分。

商品房建设投资额　是指房地产开发企业（单位）开发建设的供出售、出租用的住宅、厂房、仓库、饭店、度假村、写字楼、办公楼等房屋工程及其配套的服务设施所完成的投资额。

完成开发土地面积　指报告期内对土地进行开发并已完成七通一平等前期开发工程，具备进行房屋建筑物施工或达到出让条件的土地面积。

本年购置土地面积　指在本年内通过各种方式获得土地使用权的土地面积。

Explanatory Notes on Main Statistical Indicators

Total Investment in Fixed Assets refers to the volume of activities in construction and purchases of fixed assets and related fees, expressed in monetary terms. It is a comprehensive indicator which shows the size, structure and growth of the investment in fixed assets, providing basis for observing the progress of construction projects and evaluating results of investment. Total investment in fixed assets in the whole country includes, by type of ownership, the investment by the state-owned units, collective units, individuals, joint ownership units, share-holding units, as well as investment by businessmen from foreign countries and from Hong Kong, Macao and Taiwan, and by other units. According to China's current management system, the investment in fixed assets is classified into the following four parts: investment in capital construction, investment in innovation, investment in real estates development and other investment in fixed assets.

Newly Increased Fixed Assets refer to the newly increased value of fixed assets, constructed or purchased, that have been transferred to the investors. This is an indicator that demonstrates the results of investment in fixed assets in monetary terms, and an important indicator to reflect the speed of construction and to calculate the efficiency of investment.

Investment in Capital Construction Capital construction refers to the new construction projects or extension projects and the related work of the enterprises, institutions or administrative units mainly for the purpose of expanding production capacity or improving project efficiency covering only projects each with a total investment of 500,000 RMB yuan and over. It includes: (1) projects listed in the capital construction plan of the current year of the central government and the local governments at various levels as well as the projects, though not listed in the capital construction plan of the current year, but continued to be constructed in this year, using the investment listed in the plan of capital construction of previous years and carried forward to this year (also using the equipment and materials kept in stock of the capital construction); (2) new construction projects arranged both in the plan of capital construction and the plan of innovation; extension projects with the newly increased production capacity (or project efficiency) up to the standard of a large and medium - sized project; and the projects of moving the whole factory to a new site so as to improve the distribution of productive forces; (3) new construction projects, extension projects or restoration projects with the total investment more than 500,000 RMB yuan by the state - owned units, though listed neither in the plan of capital construction nor in the plan of innovation; the projects in the state - owned units of moving the whole factory to a new site so as to improve the distribution of productive forces; and the projects of building additional business houses by the administrative units and institutions and building welfare facilities by the administrative units.

Investment in Innovation Innovation refers to the renewal of fixed assets and technological innovation of the original facilities by the enterprises and institutions as well as the corresponding supplementary projects and the related work (excluding major overhaul and maintenance projects), It includes: (1) projects listed in the innovation plan of the current year of the central government and the local governments at various levels as well as the projects, though not listed in the innovation plan of the current year, but continued to be constructed in this year, using the investment listed in the plan of innovation of previous years and carried forward to the year; (2) projects of technological innovation or renewal of the original facilities, arranged both in the plan of innovation and in the plan of capital construction; extension projects (main workshops or a branch of the factory) with the newly increased production capacity (or project efficiency) not up to the standard of a large and medium - sized project; and the projects of moving the whole factory to a new site so as to meet the requirements of urban environmental protection or safe production; (3) projects of reconstruction or technological innovation by the state - owned units, though listed neither in the plan of capital construction nor in the plan of innovation; the projects in the state - owned units of moving the whole factory to a new site so as to meet the requirements of urban environmental protection or safe production.

Investment in Real Estate Development It includes the investment by the real estate development companies, commercial buildings construction companies and other real estate development units of various types of ownership in the construction of house buildings, such as residential buildings, factory buildings, warehouses, hotels, guesthouses, holiday villages, office buildings, and the complementary service facilities and land development projects, such roads, water supply, water drainage, power supply, heating, telecommunications, land leveling and other projects of infrastructure. It excludes the activities in simple land transactions.

Other Investment in Fixed Assets refers to the construction and purchases of fixed assets not listed in the investment in capital construction, investment in innovation and investment in real estate development. It includes:

(I) The following projects of the state - owned units, which are not included in the plan of capital construction and the plan of innovation: (a) projects of oil fields maintenance and exploitation with the oil field maintenance funds and petroleum development funds; (b) opening and extending projects with the maintenance funds in coal, ore and other mining enterprises and logging enterprises; (c) project of reconstruction of the original highways and bridges with the highway maintenance funds in the department of communication; (d) projects of construction of warehouses with the funds of simple construction in the commercial department.

(II) The investment in fixed assets by urban collective units: including the projects of construction and purchases of fixed assets over 50 thousand RMB in plan or actually demanded by the urban collective units, excluding the projects not listed in the plan of capital construction and the plan of innovation.

(III) The projects with total investment over 50 thousand RMB by different enterprises, institutions, (excludes the projects above) and not listed in the plan of capital construction and the plan of innovation.

(IV) The private house construction in the urban areas and industrial and mining areas includes all the private house construction under the jurisdiction of cities, counties, towns and industrial and mining areas, no matter whether the owner of the house is registered as the permanent resident in the locality or not.

(V) The individual investment in the rural areas includes the investment in house construction and purchase of productive fixed assets by the individuals in the rural areas.

Sources of Funds for Investment in Fixed Assets are classified into: (a) balance of funds brought forward from the previous year, (b) subtotal of the sources of funds in this year and (c) various payable funds. The subtotal of the sources of funds in this year is further divided into six categories, i.e. state budgetary appropriation, domestic loans, bonds, foreign investment, self - raised funds, and others.

(I) State budgetary appropriation includes the appropriation for capital construction fund of the central government, which are appropriated to or entrusted the banks to lend to the construction enterprises by state budget, local finance, responsible department and state specialized investment companies; the appropriations for innovation which are appropriated to the enterprises and the special appropriation for capital construction, which is arranged in the finance of central government.

(II) Domestic loans refer to various funds borrowed by enterprises and institutions from banks and non-bank financial institutions during the reference period for the purpose of investment in fixed assets. Domestic loans include loans issued by banks from their self-owned funds and deposit, loans appropriated by higher responsible authorities, special loans by government (including loan for replacing petroleum with coal, special loan for reform-through-labor coal mines), loans arranged by local government from special funds, domestic reserve loan, and working loan, etc.

(III) Foreign Investment refers to foreign funds borrowed and managed by the government refer to foreign loan borrowed by the government from foreign governments, organizations, or financial institutions under official agreements signed by both parties and the government is responsible for the repayment of both the principal and interests of the foreign loans.

(IV) Self-raised funds refer to funds received by construction enterprises from their higher responsible authorities, local governments, and raised within enterprises for the purpose of investment in fixed assets during the reference period.

(V) Others refer to received during the reference period which are not included in the above - mentioned sources.

Investment in Fixed Assets by Sector The classification of construction projects buy sector is determined by the major products or the purpose of the projects when they are put into production or use, and by the nature of their social economic activities. The investment in capital construction is classified by construction projects, while investment in innovation, other investment by state - owned units and urban collective units are classified according to the sector which the whole enterprise or institution belongs to. In general, one project or one enterprise or institution can only belong to one sector. In order to reflect more accurately the proportions among various sectors, the branch factories of integrated complex are classified into deferent sectors according to their economic activities.

Investment in Fixed Assets by Type of Construction The constructing projects in general can be classified by the type of construction into new construction, expansion, reconstruction and moving away. In capital construction, the type of construction is determined by the condition of the project. In investment in innovation, in other investment by state - owned units and investment by collective - owned units, the type of construction is determined by the condition of the whole enterprise and institutions. Investment by type of construction is not applied to investment by real-estate development units, investment in rural areas and investment in housing by urban individuals.

(I) New construction in general refers to newly constructed units. In the case in which the value of the original fixed assets is quite small, and the value of newly added fixed assets exceed the original ones by three times, the expansion construction is considered as new construction.

(II) Expansion refers to construction of new major production workshop or independent production line within a factory or in other locations, or construction branch of a factory so as to increase the production capacity of the original products. Newly constructed business houses in institutions and administrative organizations (such as the newly constructed teaching buildings in schools, clinic or bed building in hospitals, and office buildings in administrative agencies, etc.) are classified as expansion.

(III) Reconstruction refers to technical innovation and transformation of the existing equipment and technical conditions undertaken by enterprises and institutions for the purposes of technological advancement, improvement in product quality, enlarging variety of products, promoting new generation of products, reducing production consumption and cost, promoting comprehensive utilization of resources, strengthening treatment of waste gas, waste water and solid wastes, and safety in production, etc. through application of new technologies and techniques, use of new equipment and new materials (including accessory facilities for production or for living and welfare purposes). Construction of new workshops for improving existing production capacity rather than increasing production capacity is also considered as reconstruction.

Investment in Fixed Assets by Structure refers to the three major parts of investment activities, i.e. construction and installation, purchase of equipment and instrument, and other expenses.

(I) Construction and installation (work volume of construction) refers to the construction of various houses and buildings and installation of various kinds of equipment and instruments, including construction of various houses, equipment foundations and industrial kilns and stoves, preparation works for project construction, and clearing up works post project construction, pavement of railways and roads, drilling of mines and putting up of oil pipes, construction of projects of water conservancy, underground constructions for air defense and construction of other special projects, installation of various machinery equipment, testing operation for protesting the quality of installation projects. The value of equipment installed is not included in the value of installation projects.

(II) Purchase of equipment and instruments refers to the total value of equipment, tools, and vessels purchased or self - produced. Equipment, tools and vessels purchased or self - produced for new workshops by newly established or expanded units are categorized as "purchase of equipment and instruments" no matter whether they come up to the standards for fixed assets or not.

(III) Other expenses refer to expenses occurring during the construction or purchase of fixed assets other than construction, installation or purchase of equipment and instruments.

Projects Under Construction refer to projects having construction and installation activities undertaken in the reference period, including projects started in the reference period, or continued from the previous period, or completed and put into production or suspended in the reference period.

Projects Completed and Put into Use Industrial projects refer to the major projects and accessory facilities completed which result in forming production capacity and have been checked and accepted while the living and welfare facilities have been completed and can ensure normal production and formally put into production. Non - industrial projects refer to the major projects and accessory facilities completed which possess the designed capacity and have been checked, accepted and formally put into production.

Newly Increased Production Capacity (or Project Efficiency) refers to the increase of designed capacity (or project efficiency) through investment in fixed assets, which reflects the accomplishment of investment in fixed assets in kind and serves as important basis for evaluating the economic efficiency of investment.

The newly increased production capacity (project efficiency) is usually expressed in one of the following forms:

(1) Output of products, i.e. the output that the project can produce during a given period (usually a year). For instance, the capacity in coal mining is expressed in 10,000 tons/year, the capacity in producing chemical pesticides expressed in ton/year, the capacity in producing tractors in tractor/year, etc. For some chemical products where the effective contents differ significantly, the production capacity is expressed as the designed effective content equivalent, such as in the case of sulphuric acid, soda ash, caustic soda, etc.

(2) Raw materials processing capacity, i.e. the volume of raw materials that could be processed by the project per day (or per hour), such as tons of materials processed per day by a sugar refining project or edible vegetable oil project, or tons of urban sewage processed per day.

(3) Number or capacity of major equipment increased, such as number of cotton or silk looms increased, wool spindles increased, or capacity (in kilowatts) of power generators increased.

(4) Saved raw materials, fuels or power, which are mainly used for the efficiency of innovation and transformation projects.

(5) Physical measures (volume, capacity, area, and length) of construction, which is typical for non-industrial projects, for instance, the length of new railways or highways, the capacity of reservoirs, the floor space of housing projects, capacity for new students in schools or beds in hospitals, areas under new irrigation project, etc.

Features of projects sometimes call for combined use of two or more measurement to reflect the increased production capacity (or project efficiency), for instance, the new capacity for the production of internal combustion engines are expressed in sets per year and kilowatts per year simultaneously.

To standardize the nomenclature and unit of measurement for new production capacity (or project efficiency), the National Bureau of Statistics has developed Nomenclature for New Production Capacity (Project Efficiency) and Nomenclature for Saving Raw Materials, Fuels and Power. All reporting units with investment activities are required to follow these two nomenclatures in reporting statistics on new production capacity (project efficiency).

Floor Space of Buildings under Construction and Completed refers to total floor space of the horizontal section of outer walls above the plinth of the building, including the effective area and the area occupied by the structure. This indicator is one of the important indicators in physical terms to reflect the scale and accomplishment of the construction industry, and important basis for monitoring the progress, calculating the cost, analyzing the efficiency and studying the supply of building materials in relation with the construction projects.

Floor Space of Residential Buildings refers to the floor space of the residential buildings under construction and completed among the total space of buildings under construction and completed.

Floor Space of Buildings under Construction refers to total floor space of all buildings under construction during the reference period, including floor space of newly started buildings during the reference period, floor space of construction extended from the previous period to the current period, and floor space of construction suspended during the previous period and resumed in the current period. Floor space of construction completed in the current period, and floor space of construction started and then suspended in the current period are also included in the floor space under construction of the current year.

Floor Space of Buildings Completed refers to the floor space of buildings completed in the reference period, which have come up to the designed standards and have been put into use.

Rate of Projects of Fixed Assets Completed and Put into Operation refers to the ratio of the newly increased fixed assets to the total investment made in the same period. This is a comprehensive indicator reflecting the speed of the employment of fixed assets and the investment efficiency at the macro-level. As the newly increase fixed assets is the result of a long period while the investment is completed in the current year, this indicator is expected to be used to reflect the employment of fixed assets over a long period of time.

Business Survey of Real Estate Development in Chongqing Business survey of real estate development in Chongqing is the general climate index comprehensively reflecting real estate development in Chongqing, indicating the developing trends of real estate.

Villas, High-Grade Apartments refers to commercial houses whose construction costs and marketing prices are significantly higher than ordinary housing. Villas are independent structures generally located in the suburbs; high-grade apartments are multi-story buildings located in elegant urban neighborhoods. Criteria for villas and high-grade apartments include: 1) projects for the construction of villas or high-grade apartments have to be approved by competent departments in charge of real estate development and investment plans, and 2) prices for projects on villas or high-grade apartments are higher by over 100% compared with the average prices of ordinary commercial housing projects in similar location. This indicator helps to analyze the investment structure of the real estate industry and the demand and supply of housing for high-income households.

Economically Affordable Housing refers to housing constructed according to the state plan for economically affordable housing. Houses of this category featured in low cost in construction and low prices, and therefore are affordable to mid-income or low income households. Economically affordable housing projects are developed by real estate companies under the state investment plan, with the land provided through government allocation or tendering procedures. Developers are exempted from land utilization fees and enjoy another 50% exemption of all other legitimate fees, while their profits are limited to less than 3%, and the completed houses are sold under the government-guided prices. This indicator helps to analyze the investment structure of the real estate industry and the demand and supply of housing for mid or low income households.

Floor Space of Buildings Actually Sold refers to the sold floor space of buildings on hand in reporting period.

Sales to Individuals refers to floor space of commercial buildings sold to individuals at home.

Investment in Commercial Buildings refers to the investment in residential buildings, workshops, warehouses, hotels, official buildings and related service establishment for sale or rent by real estate development enterprises.

Developed Land Area Completed refers to the land area of land development and prophase development projects completed, which can carry out construction or remise.

Purchased Land Area in Current Year refers to the land area accessible by various means in current year.

五　能源消费

ENERGY CONSUMPTION

简要说明　Brief Introduction

本章主要内容包括能源消费及品种构成，能源消费弹性系数，平均每万元GDP能源消费量及日均能源消费量，综合能源平衡表，按工业行业分的能源消费量和工业产值综合能耗。本章资料由市统计局工业交通处根据有关资料和调查结果编制。

The data in this chapter cover mainly the energy consumption and their composition, the elasticity ratio of energy consumption, average per 10,000 yuan GDP energy consumption, and average daily energy consumption, the overall balance of energy, energy consumption by industrial sector, and overall energy consumption of surveyed industrial enterprises. This chapter is compiled by Division of Industry and Transport Statistics, Municipal Bureau of Statistics on the basis of data from surveys and from input-output tables.

5－1 主要年份能源消费总量
Total Consumption of Energy in Major Years

单位：万吨标准煤 (10 000 tons of SCE)

年 份 Year	能源消费总量 Total Consumption of Energy	煤 炭 Coal	天然气 Natural Gas	油 料 Oil	电 力 Electricity
1949	91.71	88.97		2.06	0.68
1952	155.47	150.64		3.43	1.40
1957	263.73	247.95	3.41	7.00	5.37
1962	476.37	429.30	18.20	14.21	14.66
1965	342.88	295.00	19.65	9.85	18.38
1970	469.56	379.80	50.13	14.04	25.59
1975	651.21	514.03	78.58	21.99	36.61
1978	889.20	703.87	103.87	32.20	49.26
1980	985.59	752.60	129.08	40.53	63.38
1981	1004.30	766.33	137.82	33.83	66.32
1982	1050.33	794.01	138.62	48.30	69.40
1983	1110.05	838.14	148.22	51.06	72.63
1984	1160.49	872.47	151.97	60.05	76.00
1985	1241.40	938.21	160.83	62.83	79.53
1986	1271.14	938.66	173.38	75.61	83.49
1987	1395.65	1036.28	195.61	76.12	87.64
1988	1513.18	1157.08	183.73	80.37	92.00
1989	1565.46	1194.44	190.36	84.08	96.58
1990	1516.59	1130.76	196.44	88.00	101.39
1991	1558.56	1151.68	197.06	96.63	113.19
1992	1601.01	1172.98	198.32	103.34	126.37
1993	1644.85	1194.68	200.89	108.20	141.08
1994	1696.72	1216.78	216.74	105.70	157.50
1995	1776.91	1239.85	258.36	102.87	175.83
1996	1871.09	1317.32	260.86	97.39	195.52
1997	2030.13	1383.98	282.80	145.47	217.88
1998	2119.46	1393.43	291.30	183.62	251.11
1999	2278.42	1495.55	308.19	196.34	278.34
2000	2330.82	1519.80	312.20	202.17	296.65
2001	2463.68	1590.43	322.51	206.20	344.54
2002	2532.66	1638.51	331.87	213.84	348.44
2003	2686.85	1755.37	349.11	220.81	361.56
2004	2937.31	1832.71	351.03	373.73	379.84

5－2 能源消费弹性系数（1985－2004年） Elasticity Ratio of Energy Consumption (1985-2004)

年　份 Year	能源消费比上年增长% Growth Rate of Energy Consumption over Preceding Year (%)	本市生产总值比上年增长% Growth Rate of GDP over Preceding Year (%)	能源消费弹性系数 Elasticity Ratio of Energy Consumption
1985	7.0	8.4	0.83
1986	2.4	8.4	0.29
1987	9.8	5.1	1.92
1988	8.4	9.3	0.90
1989	3.5	4.7	0.74
1990	-3.1	6.8	-0.46
1991	2.8	9.0	0.31
1992	2.7	16.2	0.17
1993	2.7	15.3	0.18
1994	3.2	13.3	0.24
1995	4.7	12.1	0.39
1996	5.3	11.2	0.47
1997	8.5	11.0	0.77
1998	4.4	8.4	0.52
1999	7.5	7.6	0.99
2000	2.3	8.5	0.27
2001	5.7	9.0	0.63
2002	2.8	10.3	0.27
2003	6.1	11.5	0.53
2004	9.3	12.2	0.76

注：本市生产总值增长速度按可比价格计算。

Note: Growth rate of GDP is calculated at comparable prices.

5－3 平均每万元本市生产总值能源消费量（2003－2004年） Average 10 000 Yuan GDP Energy Consumption (2003-2004)

品　　种	Type	2003	2004
能源总消费量（吨标煤/万元）	**Total Energy Consumption (SCE/10 000 yuan)**	**1.19**	**1.10**
#煤　炭	Coal	0.78	0.69
天然气	Natural Gas	0.16	0.13
油　料	Oil	0.10	0.14
电　力	Electricity	0.16	0.14

注：各年能源品种均已折合为吨标准煤。

Note: Energy types of each year are converted into SCE.

5－4 平均每天主要能源消费量（2003－2004年）
Average Daily Energy Consumption (2003-2004)

品　　种	Type	2003	2004
能源总消费量（万吨标煤/天）	**Total Energy Consumption (10 000 tons of SCE/day)**	**7.36**	**8.05**
#煤　炭	Coal	4.81	5.02
天然气	Natural Gas	0.96	0.96
油　料	Oil	0.60	1.02
电　力	Electricity	0.99	1.04

注：各年能源品种均已折合为吨标准煤。
Note: Energy types of each year are converted into SCE.

5－5 综合能源平衡表（2003－2004年）
Overall Energy Balance (2003-2004)

单位：万吨标准煤 (10 000 tons of SCE)

项　　目	Item	2003	2004
可供消费的能源总量	**Total Energy Available for Consumption**	**2686.85**	**2937.31**
#一次能源生产量	Output of Primary Energy	2613.76	2697.31
调进量	Transfer in	435.62	589.03
调出量(-)	Transfer out	-692.52	-347.73
能源消费总量	**Total Energy Consumption**	**2686.85**	**2937.31**
终端消费	Final Consumption	2208.26	2340.30
第一产业	Primary Industry	190.76	163.93
第二产业	Secondary Industry	1574.03	1558.81
第三产业	Tertiary Industry	173.77	351.27
生活消费	Residential Consumption	269.70	266.29
城　镇	Urban	120.15	121.78
乡　村	Rural	149.55	144.51
加工转换投入(-)产出(+)量	Input(-) and Output(+) in Processing and Transformation	-448.86	-566.37
#火力发电	Thermal Power	-418.13	-470.39
洗　煤	Coal Washing and Dressing	-14.82	-72.63
损失量	Losses	29.73	30.64

5－6 按工业行业分的能源消费量（2004年）

行　业	Sector	原煤(吨) Coal (ton)	焦炭(吨) Coke (ton)	汽油(吨) Gasoline (ton)	煤油(吨) Kerosene (ton)	柴油(吨) Diesel Oil (ton)	天然气(万立方米) Natural Gas (10 000 cu.m)	电力(万千瓦时) Electricity (10 000 kwh)
工业消费总量	**Total Industry Consumption**	**20358234**	**1791238**	**48166**	**6035**	**88270**	**224910**	**1809364**
采矿业	Mining and Quarrying	6122930	150491	1594	93	10177	2523	90580
#煤炭开采和洗选业	Coal Mining and Dressing	5786647	450	1193	93	3057	155	68233
石油和天然气开采业	Petroleum and Natural Gas Extraction			60		51	2300	1458
黑色金属矿采选业	Ferrous Metals Mining and Dressing	128288	147984	262		3200	68	9542
有色金属矿采选业	Nonferrous Metals Mining and Dressing							32
非金属矿采选业	Nonmetal Minerals Mining and Dressing	207995	2057	79		3869		11316
制造业	Manufacturing	6312207	1640747	42174	5931	64355	222063	1319442
农副食品加工业	Farm Products and By-food Processing	29611		279	3	1069	606	8743
食品制造业	Food Production	118490		957		2165	1844	10364
饮料制造业	Beverage Production	75682	57	422	7	1005	575	10207
烟草制品业	Tobacco Products	22175		199	1	249	416	4779
纺织业	Textile Industry	281799	80	510	41	251	947	43883
纺织服装、鞋、帽制造业	Garments, Shoes and Hats Production	4366		397		168	73	947
皮革、毛皮、羽毛（绒）及其制品业	Leather, Furs, Down and Related Products	2379	5	147	9	68	2	2024
木材加工及木、竹、藤、棕、草制品业	Timber Processing, Bamboo Cane Palm Fiber and Straw Products	19049		42		55	6	1340
家具制造业	Furniture Manufacturing			195	1	258	1	1294
造纸及纸制品业	Papermaking and Paper Products	163164		8941	19	931	839	18702
印刷业、记录媒介的复制	Printing and Record Medium Reproduction	427		1718	95	166	31	2168
文教体育用品制造业	Cultural Educational and Sports Goods			6		17	3	18
石油加工、炼焦及核燃料加工业	Petroleum, Coking and Nuclear Fuel Processing	23903		50	35	313	104	4153

Energy Consumption by Industrial Sector (2004)

行业	Sector	原煤(吨) Coal (ton)	焦炭(吨) Coke (ton)	汽油(吨) Gasoline (ton)	煤油(吨) Kerosene (ton)	柴油(吨) Diesel Oil (ton)	天然气(万立方米) Natural Gas (10 000 cu.m)	电力(万千瓦时) Electricity (10 000 kwh)
化学原料及化学制品制造业	Raw Chemical Materials and Chemical Products	1227640	54500	2170	407	8025	153329	280630
医药制造业	Medical and Pharmaceutical Products	186895		1081	79	654	2057	15112
化学纤维制造业	Chemical Fiber	1225		15		17		832
橡胶制品业	Rubber Products	21979		840	2	206	779	6011
塑料制品业	Plastic Products	20438	13	359	25	364	268	10024
非金属矿物制品业	Nonmetal Mineral Products	3558351	96	1434	227	21306	22782	241994
黑色金属冶炼及压延加工业	Smelting and Pressing of Ferrous Metals	355868	1523772	548	104	2853	10183	209884
有色金属冶炼及压延加工业	Smelting and Pressing of Nonferrous Metals	22172	5145	561	16	2787	5631	184496
金属制品业	Metal Products	16821	2607	788	59	552	647	11874
通用设备制造业	Ordinary Equipment	15662	16033	2015	1003	4120	2816	40815
专用设备制造业	Special Equipment	31897	583	1606	146	1765	2786	31666
交通运输设备制造业	Transportation Equipment	80013	37128	14365	3237	12906	14497	151866
电气机械及器材制造业	Electric Equipment and Machinery	6045	287	1120	294	620	730	14225
通信设备、计算机及其他电子设备制造业	Communication Equipment, Computers and Other Electronic Equipment	11	20	361	14	122	9	3350
仪器仪表及文化、办公用机械制造业	Instruments, Meters, Cultural and Office Machinery	2269	420	941	101	411	96	6502
工艺品及其他制造业	Handicraft and Other Production	23873		88	5	63	7	663
废弃资源和废旧材料回收加工业	Recovery and Processing of Waste Resources and Materials			17		872		873
电力、燃气及水的生产和供应业	Electricpower, Gas & Water Production and Supply	7923097		4398	11	13738	324	399342
电力、热力的生产和供应业	Electricpower and Hot Power Production and Supply	7923096		3628	2	13474	81	359605
燃气生产和供应业	Gas Production and Supply			516		109	241	1665
水的生产和供应业	Water Production and Supply	1		254	9	155	2	38072

5－7 调查工业企业工业产值综合能耗（2004年）
Overall Energy Consumption of Surveyed Industrial Enterprises (2004)

行业	Sector	综合能源消费量(吨标准煤) Overall Energy Consumption (ton of SCE)	工业总产值(现价)(万元) Gross Output Value of Industry (current price) (10 000 yuan)	产值能耗(吨标准煤/万元) Output Value to Energy Consumption (ton of SCE/ 10 000 yuan)
工业消费总量	**Total Industry Consumption**	**18890519**	**21373131**	**0.88**
采矿业	Mining and Quarrying	1880620	634307	2.96
#煤炭开采和洗选业	Coal Mining and Dressing	1381865	435276	3.17
石油和天然气开采业	Petroleum and Natural Gas Extraction	33912	30609	1.11
黑色金属矿采选业	Ferrous Metals Mining and Dressing	275787	82945	3.32
有色金属矿采选业	Nonferrous Metals Mining and Dressing	129	190	0.68
非金属矿采选业	Nonmetal Minerals Mining and Dressing	188926	85287	2.22
制造业	Manufacturing	14771574	19035590	0.78
农副食品加工业	Farm Products and By-food Processing	64748	572912	0.11
食品制造业	Food Production	92248	220444	0.42
饮料制造业	Beverage Production	102759	239661	0.43
烟草制品业	Tobacco Products	36089	423185	0.09
纺织业	Textile Industry	354299	384629	0.92
纺织服装、鞋、帽制造业	Garments, Shoes and Hats Production	7865	58455	0.13
皮革、毛皮、羽毛（绒）及其制品业	Leather, Furs, Down and Related Products	9903	138979	0.07
木材加工及木、竹、藤、棕、草制品业	Timber Processing, Bamboo Cane Palm Fiber and Straw Products	19175	29537	0.65
家具制造业	Furniture Manufacturing	5538	92650	0.06
造纸及纸制品业	Papermaking and Paper Products	203931	196486	1.04
印刷业、记录媒介的复制	Printing and Record Medium Reproduction	11741	95195	0.12
文教体育用品制造业	Cultural Educational and Sports Goods	142	1402	0.10
石油加工、炼焦及核燃料加工业	Petroleum, Coking and Nuclear Fuel Processing	135936	73142	1.86

5-7 续表 CONTINUED

行 业	Sector	综合能源消费量(吨标准煤) Overall Energy Consumption (ton of SCE)	工业总产值(现价)(万元) Gross Output Value of Industry (current price) (10 000 yuan)	产值能耗(吨标准煤/万元) Output Value to Energy Consumption (ton of SCE/ 10 000 yuan)
化学原料及化学制品制造业	Raw Chemical Materials and Chemical Products	4190422	1376165	3.04
医药制造业	Medical and Pharmaceutical Products	211756	533530	0.40
化学纤维制造业	Chemical Fiber	4196	12899	0.33
橡胶制品业	Rubber Products	48030	109407	0.44
塑料制品业	Plastic Products	58398	125696	0.46
非金属矿物制品业	Nonmetal Mineral Products	3875573	966819	4.01
黑色金属冶炼及压延加工业	Smelting and Pressing of Ferrous Metals	3013986	1373254	2.19
有色金属冶炼及压延加工业	Smelting and Pressing of Nonferrous Metals	836406	900884	0.93
金属制品业	Metal Products	69798	258656	0.27
通用设备制造业	Ordinary Equipment	228301	868385	0.26
专用设备制造业	Special Equipment	176440	561059	0.31
交通运输设备制造业	Transportation Equipment	889443	7876476	0.11
电气机械及器材制造业	Electric Equipment and Machinery	71211	750090	0.09
通信设备、计算机及其他电子设备制造业	Communication Equipment, Computers and Other Electronic Equipment	12908	375810	0.03
仪器仪表及文化、办公用机械制造业	Instruments, Meters, Cultural and Office Machinery	27387	369063	0.07
工艺品及其他制造业	Handicraft and Other Production	8053	30559	0.26
废弃资源和废旧材料回收加工业	Recovery and Processing of Waste Resources and Materials	4890	20158	0.24
电力、燃气及水的生产和供应业	Electricpower, Gas & Water Production and Supply	2238325	1703234	1.31
电力、热力的生产和供应业	Electricpower and Hot Power Production and Supply	2075689	1472680	1.41
燃气生产和供应业	Gas Production and Supply	8737	145539	0.06
水的生产和供应业	Water Production and Supply	153899	85016	1.81

主要统计指标解释

能源消费总量 指一定时期内全国（地区）物质生产部门、非物质生产部门和生活消费的各种能源的总和，是观察能源消费水平、构成和增长速度的总量指标。能源消费总量包括：煤和原油及其制品、天然气、电力。不包括：低热值燃料、生物质能和太阳能等的利用。能源消费总量分为终端能源消费量、能源加工转换损失量和损失量三部分。

（1）终端能源消费量 指一定时期内全国（地区）生产和生活消费的各种能源在扣除了用于加工转换二次能源消费量和损失量以后的数量。

（2）能源加工转换损失量 指一定时期内全国（地区）投入加工转换的各种能源数量之和与产出各种能源产品之和的差额，是观察能源在加工转换过程中损失量变化的指标。

（3）能源损失量 指一定时期内能源在输送、分配、储存过程中发生的损失和由客观原因造成的各种损失量。不包括各种气体能源放空、放散量。

能源消费弹性系数 是反映能源消费增长速度与国民经济增长速度之间比例关系的指标。计算公式为：

能源消费弹性系数=能源消费量平均增长速度/国民经济年平均增长速度

Explanatory Notes on Main Statistical Indicators

Total Energy Consumption refers to the total consumption of energy of various kinds by material production sectors, non-material production sectors and households in the country (region) in a given period of time. It is a comprehensive indicator to show the scale, composition and development of energy consumption. The total energy consumption includes that of coal, crude oil and their products, natural gas and electricity. However, it excludes the consumption of fuel of low calorific value, bioenergy and solar energy. Total domestic energy consumption can be divided into three parts:

(1) Final Energy Consumption: It refers to the total energy consumption by material production sectors, non-material production sectors and households in the country (region) in a given period of time, but excludes the consumption in conversion of the primary energy into the secondary energy and the loss in the process of energy conversion.

(2) Loss During the Process of Energy Conversion: It refers to the total input of various kinds of energy for conversion, minus the total output of various kinds of energy in the country in a given period of time. It is an indicator to show the loss that occurs during the process of energy conversion.

(3) Loss: It refers to the total of the loss of energy during the course of energy transport, distribution and storage and the loss caused by any objective reason in a given period of time. The loss of various kinds of gas due to gas discharges and stocktaking is excluded.

Elasticity Ratio of Energy Consumption is an indicator to show the relationship between the growth rate of energy consumption and the growth rate of the national economy. The formula is:

Elasticity Ratio of Energy Consumption=Average annual Growth Rate of Energy Consumption/ Average Annual Growth Rate of National Economy.

六 财政

GOVERNMENT FINANCE

简要说明 Brief Introduction

本章资料包括我市财政收入和支出情况、国税和地税税收收入情况，由市统计局综合处分别根据市财政局、市国税局和市地税局的有关资料整理编辑。

The data in this chapter include the financial revenue and expenditures, revenue of national taxation and local taxation. All information is prepared by Division of Comprehensive Statistics, Municipal Bureau of Statistics using data from Municipal Bureau of Finance, Municipal Bureau of National Taxation, Municipal Bureau of Local Taxation.

6－1 财政收入及支出（1994－2004年）
Financial Revenue and Expenditures (1994-2004)

单位：万元 (10 000 yuan)

年 份 Year	财政收入 Financial Revenue	#地方财政收入 Local Financial Revenue	#一般预算收入 General Budgetary Revenue	#中央两税（四税）收入 Revenue of Two/Four Central Level Taxes	地方财政支出 Local Financial Expenditures	#一般预算支出 General Budgetary Expenditures
1994	716172	366325	366325	349847	560818	560818
1995	837748	460052	460052	377696	662235	662235
1996	942682	549412	549412	393270	794216	794216
1997	1180555	745296	593060	435259	1151627	1010110
1998	1338867	858046	711287	480821	1359474	1257608
1999	1402935	898912	767341	504023	1623685	1502365
2000	1632353	1044570	872442	587783	2024606	1876433
2001	1961761	1264090	1061243	697671	2555530	2375486
2002	2632891	1578651	1260674	991445	3450674	3058591
2003	3422639	2069315	1615618	1205457	3913564	3415775
2004	4629591	3024439	2006241	1435206	4851221	3957233

注：1）财政收入2002年前为地方财政收入与中央两税（增值税和消费税）之和，2002年起为地方财政收入、中央四税收入和其他中央收入之和。
2）其他中央收入不含关税，自2003年起包含车辆购置税。

Note: a) Financial revenue before 2002 is the sum of local financial revenue and two central level tax revenue (value-added tax and consumption tax), whereas since 2002 it is the sum of local financial revenue, four central level tax revenue and other central level revenue.
b) Other central level revenue excludes tariff, however since 2003 vehicle purchasing tax is also included.

6－2 财政收入与本市生产总值的比重（1994－2004年）
Financial Revenue as Percentage of Gross Domestic Product (1994-2004)

年 份 Year	财政收入（亿元） Finance Revenue (100 million yuan)	本市生产总值（亿元） Gross Domestic Product (100 million yuan)	财政收入相当于本市生产总值的比重（%） Finacial Revenue as Percentage of GDP (%)
1994	71.62	751.21	9.5
1995	83.77	1009.47	8.3
1996	94.27	1179.09	8.0
1997	118.06	1350.10	8.7
1998	133.89	1429.26	9.4
1999	140.29	1479.71	9.5
2000	163.24	1589.34	10.3
2001	196.18	1749.77	11.2
2002	263.29	1971.30	12.2
2003	342.26	2250.56	13.4
2004	462.96	2665.39	17.4

注：本表财政收入口径同表6-1。

Note: The finance revenue in this table is in terms of 6-1.

6－3 财政收入（2003－2004年）
Financial Revenue (2003-2004)

单位：万元 (10 000 yuan)

项目	Item	2003	2004	指数 上年同口径数=100 Index Preceding Year in Same Terms=100.
财政收入	**Financial Revenue**	**3422639**	**4629591**	**135.3**
一、地方财政收入	**Local Financial Budgetary Revenue**	**2069315**	**3024439**	**140.6**
其中：市级	Of Which at Municipal Level	1036491	1586609	136.8
一般预算收入	**General Financial Revenue**	**1615618**	**2006241**	**125.9**
其中：市级	Of Which at Municipal Level	685683	900507	127.3
工商各税	Industrial and Commercial Taxes	1058932	1282024	123.9
#增值税	Value-added Tax	246601	259481	119.1
营业税	Operation Tax	466392	585417	125.5
企业所得税	Enterprise Income Tax	87694	111487	127.1
个人所得税	Personal Income Tax	78711	89359	113.5
资源税	Resource Tax	20172	24742	122.7
城市维护建设税	Tax on City Maintenance and Construction	86520	111971	124.3
房产税	Tax on Real Estates	42134	46536	110.4
印花税	Stamp Tax	12939	17915	138.5
农业四税	4 Taxes on Agriculture	134757	167490	124.3
#农业税	Agricultural Tax	62348	49115	78.8
契税	Contract Tax	41920	83035	198.1
非税收入	Non-taxation Revenue	421929	556727	131.3
#国有资产经营收益	Profits of State-owned Assets	36510	48055	131.6
国有企业计划亏损补贴	Planning Subsidies to Loss-suffering State-owned Enterprises	-23319	-21114	90.5
行政性收费收入	Revenue of Administrative Fees	259343	333932	128.8
罚没收入	Revenue of Penalties	79978	88337	110.4
专项收入	Expert Project Revenue	48764	84495	168.3
基金预算收入	**Fund Budgetary Revenue**	**453697**	**1018198**	**199.5**
#工业交通部门基金收入	Fund Revenue of Departments of Industry and Transportation	102819	118555	115.3
土地有偿使用收入	Revenue of Compensable Use of Land	275267	788709	263.0
地方财政税费附加收入	Additional Revenue of Local Financial Fees	64579	78930	122.2
二、中央四税收入	**Revenue of 4 Central Level Taxes**	**1205457**	**1435206**	**119.1**
增值税收入	Revenue of Value-added Tax	739803	879564	118.9
消费税收入	Revenue of Consumption Tax	217832	257358	118.1
企业所得税收入	Revenue of Enterprise Income Tax	129760	164252	126.6
个人所得税收入	Revenue of Personal Income Tax	118062	134032	113.5
三、其他中央收入	**Other Central Level Revenue**	**147867**	**169946**	**114.9**
#车辆购置税	Tax of Vehicle Purchasing	67966	77886	114.6

注：其他中央收入不含关税。
Note: Other central level revenue excludes tariff.

6－4 财政支出（2003－2004年）
Financial Expenditures (2003-2004)

单位：万元 (10 000 yuan)

项　目	Item	2003	2004	指数 上年同口径数=100 Index Preceding Year in Same Terms=100.
地方财政支出	**Local Budgetary Expenditures**	**3913564**	**4851221**	**124.0**
其中：市级	Of Which at Municipal Level	1471246	1668881	123.5
一般预算支出	**General Budgetary Expenditures**	**3415775**	**3957233**	**124.9**
其中：市级	Of Which at Municipal Level	1246523	1214182	114.5
生产性支出	Productive Expenditures	917670	982931	139.4
基本建设支出	Expenditrue for Capital Construction	640685	529594	122.4
企业挖潜改造资金	Expenditure for Enterprise Technical Updates and Innovation	72583	76144	112.2
地质勘探费	Expenditure for Geological Prospecting	6609	7379	111.7
科技三项费用	Expenditure for Science and Technology Promotion	27969	39668	141.8
支援农村生产支出及农业综合开发支出（含农林水气）	Expenditures for Supporting Rural Production and Agricultural Comprehensive Development (including agriculture, forestry, water conservancy and meteorology)	169824	330146	194.4
各项事业费支出	Expenditures for Various Causes	708600	834791	117.8
#教育支出	Education	429462	497847	115.9
医疗卫生支出	Public Health	108218	120564	111.4
行政事业单位离退休支出	Expenditure for Retired Persons in Administrative Department	240926	288870	119.9
抚恤和社会福利救济	Expenditure for Pensions and Relief Funds for Social Welfare	128237	144578	112.7
社会保障补助支出	Social Security Subsidies	339682	327589	113.0
行政管理费及外交外事支出	Expenditur for Government Administration and Foreign Affairs	369027	452275	122.6
公检法司、武警及国防支出	Expenditure for Public Security Agency, Procuratorial Agency, Court of Justice, Armed Police and National Defense	250933	289703	115.5
城市维护费	Expenditure for City Maintenance	198820	274108	137.9
政策性补贴支出	Price Subsidies	53581	58897	109.9
支援不发达地区支出	Expenditure for Supporting Under-developed Areas	39372	43436	110.3
专项支出	Expenditure for Special Items	47287	75797	160.3
其他支出	Others	121640	184258	151.5
基金预算支出	**Fund Budgetary Expenditures**	**497789**	**893988**	**155.5**
#工业交通部门基金支出	Fund Expenditure of Department of Industry and Transport	102757	113612	110.6
土地有偿使用支出	Expenditure of Compensable Use of Land	229356	682561	271.2
地方财政税费附加支出	Additional Expenditure of Local Financial Fees	43074	49207	114.2

6—5 国税和地税税收收入（1996—2004年）
Revenue of National and Local Taxation (1996-2004)

单位：万元 (10 000 yuan)

年份 Year	国税税收收入 National Taxation	#增值税 Value-added Tax	#消费税 Consumption Tax	地税税收收入 Local Taxation	#营业税 Operation Tax	#企业所得税 Enterprise Income Tax	#个人所得税 Personal Income Tax
1996	535564	379277	92920	266486	130952	33616	17747
1997	608114	450942	108409	323862	155607	47121	29468
1998	686805	501336	123845	382948	195747	41808	42562
1999	850898	661868	120669	436999	218101	52873	54910
2000	872759	623788	144361	500530	243476	68614	72133
2001	1091211	795789	164879	602387	278516	97553	105450
2002	1243874	915425	193646	732964	367458	91953	120326
2003	1491119	1112204	217868	894415	466393	100102	148386
2004	1822591	1366125	257385	1115549	585415	125572	168282

6—6 国税税收收入（2003—2004年）
Revenue of National Taxation (2003-2004)

单位：万元 (10 000 yuan)

项目	Item	2003	2004
税收收入合计	**Total**	**1491119**	**1822591**
按税种分	By Classification		
#增值税	Value-added Tax	1112204	1366125
其中：一般纳税人	Of Which: Ordinary Taxpayers	896650	1113809
消费税	Consumption Tax	217868	257385
营业税	Operation Tax	2465	1422
企业所得税	Enterprise Income Tax	69488	82533
外商投资企业和外国企业所得税	Tax on Foreign-funded Enterprise Income	40710	60020
个人所得税	Personal Income Tax	48384	55106
按行业分	By Sector		
第一产业	Primary Industry	2	15
第二产业	Secondary Industry	1179692	1451591
工　业	Industry	1179400	1449780
建筑业	Construction	292	1811
第三产业	Tertiary Industry	311425	370985
交通运输仓储及邮政业	Transportation, Storage and Postal Services	1902	2072
批发和零售业	Wholesale and retail Trade	188571	247056
金融业	Financing	16450	17178
信息传输、计算机服务和软件业	Data Transmission, Computer Service and Software	15481	19603
租赁和商务服务业	Renting and Business Activities	165	2223
房地产业	Real Estate	3140	6981
其他行业	Other Sectors	85716	75872

6－7 按企业类型分的国税税收收入（2004年）
National Taxation by Registration (2004)

单位：万元 (10 000 yuan)

项　目	Item	合　计 Total	内资企业 Domestic-funded					
			小　计 Sub-total	国有企业 State-owned	集体企业 Collective-owned	股份合作企业 Coopera-tive	联营企业 Joint Ownership	有限责任公司 Limited Liability Corp.
总　计	**Total**	**1822591**	**1243291**	**368720**	**40682**	**13436**	**5315**	**486164**
#增值税	Value-added Tax	1366125	962977	305432	40416	12941	4887	354755
消费税	Consumption Tax	257385	196359	40818	133	440	5	109636
营业税	Operation Tax	1422	1422	1392	5			1
企业所得税	Enterprise Income Tax	82533	82533	21078	128	55	423	21772
外商投资企业和外国企业所得税	Tax on Foreign-funded Enterprise Income	60020						
个人所得税	Personal Income Tax	55106						
资源税	Resource Tax							
固定资产投资方向调节税	Tax on Adjustment Investment in Fixed Assets							
城市维护建设税	Tax on City Maintenance and Construction							

项　目	Item	内资企业 Domestic-funded			港澳台投资企业 Funded By Hong Kong, Macao & Taiwan	外商投资企业 Foreign-funded	个体经营 Individuals	附列资料：乡(镇)企业 Township Enterprises
		股份有限公司 Share-holding	私营企业 Private	其他企业 Others				
总　计	**Total**	**224036**	**104931**	**7**	**92515**	**385214**	**101571**	**222018**
#增值税	Value-added Tax	145249	99297		76217	281148	45783	212338
消费税	Consumption Tax	41248	4079		6184	54160	682	7794
营业税	Operation Tax	24						
企业所得税	Enterprise Income Tax	37515	1555	7				1886
外商投资企业和外国企业所得税	Tax on Foreign-funded Enterprise Income				10114	49906		
个人所得税	Personal Income Tax						55106	
资源税	Resource Tax							
固定资产投资方向调节税	Tax on Adjustment Investment in Fixed Assets							
城市维护建设税	Tax on City Maintenance and Construction							

6－8 地税税收收入（2003－2004年）
Revenue of Local Taxation (2003-2004)

单位：万元 (10 000 yuan)

项　　目	Item	2003	2004
税收收入合计	**Total**	**894415**	**1115549**
其中：中央级	Of Which: Central Level	149092	176309
重庆市级	Chongqing Municipal Level	301053	451720
区（市）县级	Disitrct (county) Level	444270	487520
按税种分	By Classification		
营业税	Operation Tax	466393	585415
企业所得税	Enterprise Income Tax	100102	125572
外商投资企业和外国企业所得税	Tax on Foreign-funded Enterprise Income		
个人所得税	Personal Income Tax	148386	168282
资源税	Resource Tax	20172	24742
固定资产投资方向调节税	Tax on Adjustment Investment in Fixed Assets		
城市维护建设税	Tax on City Maintenance and Construction	86520	111972
房产和城市房地产税	Tax on Real Estates and Land	42134	46535
印花税	Stamp Tax	12939	17914
城镇土地使用税	Tax on Using Urban Land	11890	15877
土地增值税	Value-added Tax on Land	4104	15688
车船使用和牌照税	Tax on Using Vehicles & Vessels and Licences	1775	3552
屠宰税	Slaughter Tax		
按行业分	By Sector		
第一产业	Primary Industry	4	
第二产业	Secondary Industry	341601	413053
工　业	Industry	160220	198168
建筑业	Construction	181381	214885
第三产业	Tertiary Industry	552810	702496
交通运输仓储及邮政业	Transportation, Storage and Postal Services	39228	65053
批发和零售业	Wholesale and retail Trade	53896	67302
金融业	Financing	77508	91190
信息传输、计算机服务和软件业	Data Transmission, Computer Service and Software	33936	36317
租赁和商务服务业	Renting and Business Activities	126585	139374
房地产业	Real Estate	120012	185732
其他行业	Other Sectors	101645	117528

6－9 按企业类型分的地税税收收入（2004年）
Local Taxation by Registration (2004)

单位：万元 (10 000 yuan)

项　目	Item	合计 Total	内资企业 Domestic-funded 小计 Sub-total	国有企业 State-owned	集体企业 Collective-owned	股份合作企业 Coopera-tive	联营企业 Joint Ownership	有限责任公司 Limited Liability Corp.
总　计	**Total**	**1115549**	**962415**	**282281**	**76763**	**8026**	**4433**	**345869**
营业税	Operation Tax	585415	499049	150413	40019	4550	2712	185672
企业所得税	Enterprise Income Tax	125572	125572	23495	12045	874	217	51405
外商投资企业和外国企业所得税	Tax on Foreign-funded Enterprise Income							
个人所得税	Personal Income Tax	168282	124749	40239	9528	782	792	37587
资源税	Resource Tax	24742	20361	5310	3392	96	72	2658
固定资产投资方向调节税	Tax on Adjustment Investment in Fixed Assets							
城市维护建设税	Tax on City Maintenance and Construction	111972	107738	37668	5577	805	328	36381
房产和城市房地产税	Tax on Real Estates and Land	46535	39673	13656	3256	518	141	13199
印花税	Stamp Tax	17914	14525	4253	672	125	44	4485
城镇土地使用税	Tax on Using Urban Land	15877	15632	5034	991	176	58	6474
土地增值税	Value-added Tax on Land	15688	12743	1421	807	92	37	7386
车船使用和牌照税	Tax on Using Vehicles & Vessels and Licences	3552	2373	792	476	8	32	622
屠宰税	Slaughter Tax							

项　目	Item	内资企业 Domestic-funded 股份有限公司 Share-holding	私营企业 Private	其他企业 Others	港澳台投资企业 Funded By Hong Kong, Macao & Taiwan	外商投资企业 Foreign-funded	个体经营 Individuals	附列资料：乡(镇)企业 Township Enterprises
总　计	**Total**	**118856**	**104919**	**21268**	**29994**	**44018**	**79122**	**76591**
营业税	Operation Tax	49997	54134	11552	21808	25661	38897	39545
企业所得税	Enterprise Income Tax	19918	17086	532				12008
外商投资企业和外国企业所得税	Tax on Foreign-funded Enterprise Income							
个人所得税	Personal Income Tax	17945	11505	6371	3115	12921	27497	8818
资源税	Resource Tax	5048	2958	827	17	231	4133	3478
固定资产投资方向调节税	Tax on Adjustment Investment in Fixed Assets							
城市维护建设税	Tax on City Maintenance and Construction	15835	10327	817			4234	6099
房产和城市房地产税	Tax on Real Estates and Land	5226	3301	376	2673	2557	1632	3418
印花税	Stamp Tax	2600	1880	466	608	2018	763	797
城镇土地使用税	Tax on Using Urban Land	1360	1448	91			245	1142
土地增值税	Value-added Tax on Land	830	2100	70	1760	605	580	810
车船使用和牌照税	Tax on Using Vehicles & Vessels and Licences	97	180	166	13	25	1141	476
屠宰税	Slaughter Tax							

主要统计指标解释

财政收入 指国家财政参与社会产品分配所取得的收入，是实现国家职能的财力保证。财政收入所包括的内容几经变化，目前主要包括：

(1)各项税收：包括增值税、营业税、消费税、土地增值税、城市维护建设税、资源税、城市土地使用税、企业所得税、个人所得税、关税、证券交易印花税、车辆购置税、农牧业税和耕地占用税等。

(2)专项收入：包括排污费收入、城市水资源费收入、矿产资源补偿费收入、教育费附加收入等。

(3)其他收入：包括利息收入、基本建设贷款归还收入、基本建设收入、捐赠收入等。

(4)国有企业亏损补贴：此项为负收入，冲减财政收入。主要包括对工业企业、商业企业、粮食企业的补贴。

中央财政收入和地方财政收入指按现行分税制财政体制划分的中央本级收入和地方本级收入。1994 年实行分税制财政体制以后，属于中央财政的收入包括关税、海关代征消费税和增值税，消费税，中央企业所得税，地方银行和外资银行及非银行金融企业所得税，铁道部门、各银行总行、各保险总公司等集中缴纳的营业税、利润和城市维护建设税，车辆购置税，船舶吨税，增值税的 75%部分，证券交易税(印花税)94%部分，个人所得税中的利息所得税，利息所得税之外的个人所得税中央分享的部分，海洋石油资源税。属于地方财政的收入包括营业税，地方企业所得税，利息所得税之外的个人所得税地方分享的部分，城镇土地使用税，固定资产投资方向调节税，城镇维护建设税，房产税，车船使用税，印花税，屠宰税，农牧业税，农业特产税，耕地占用税，契税，土地增值税、国有土地有偿使用收入，增值税 25%部分，证券交易税(印花税)6%部分和除海洋石油资源税以外的其他资源税。

财政支出 国家财政将筹集起来的资金进行分配使用，以满足经济建设和各项事业的需要，主要包括：

(1)基本建设支出：指按国家有关规定，属于基本建设范围内的基本建设有偿使用、拨款、资本金支出以及经国家批准对专项和政策性基建投资贷款，在部门的基建投资额中统筹支付的贴息支出。

(2)企业挖潜改造资金：指国家预算内拨给的用于企业挖潜、革新和改造方面的资金。包括各部门企业挖潜改造资金和企业挖潜改造贷款资金，为农业服务的县办“五小”企业技术改造补助，挖潜改造贷款贴息资金。

(3)地质勘探费用：指国家预算用于地质勘探单位的勘探工作费用，包括地质勘探管理机构及其事业单位经费、地质勘探经费。

(4)科技三项费用：指国家预算用于科技支出的费用，包括新产品试制费、中间试验费、重要科学研究补助费。

(5)支援农村生产支出：指国家财政支援农村集体(户)各项生产的支出。包括对农村举办的小型农田水利和打井、喷灌等的补助费，对农村水土保持措施的补助费，对农村举办的小水电站的补助费，特大抗旱的补助费，农村开荒补助费，扶持乡镇企业资金，支援农村合作生产组织资金、农村农技推广和植保补助费，农村草场和畜禽保护补助费，农村造林和林木保护补助费，农村水产补助费，发展粮食生产专项资金。

(6)农林水利气象等部门的事业费用：指国家财政用于农垦、农场、农业、畜牧、农机、林业、森工、水利、水产、气象、乡镇企业的技术推广、良种推广(示范)、动植物(畜禽、森林)保护、水质监测、勘探设计、资源调查、干部训练等项费用，园艺特产场补助费，中等专业学校经费，飞播牧草试验补助费，营林机构、气象机构经费，渔政费以及农业管理事业费等。

(7)工业交通商业等部门的事业费：指国家预算支付给工交商各部门用于事业发展的人员和公用经费支出，包括勘探设计费、中等专业学校经费、技术学校经费、干部训练费。

(8)文教科学卫生事业费：指国家预算用于文化、出版、文物、教育、卫生、中医、公费医疗、体育、档案、地震、海洋、通讯、电影电视、计划生育、党政群干部训练、自然科学、社会科学、科协等项事业的人员和公用经费支出以及高技术研究专项经费。主要包括工资、补助工资、福利费、离退休费、助学金、公务费、设备购置费、修缮费、业务费、差额补助费。

(9)抚恤和社会福利救济费：指国家预算用于抚恤和社会福利救济事业的经费。包括由民政部门开支的烈士家属和牺牲病残人员家属的一次性、定期抚恤金，革命伤残人员的抚恤金，各种伤残补助费，烈军属、复员退伍军人生活补助费，退伍军人安置费，优抚事业单位经费，烈士纪念建筑物管理、维修费，自然灾害救济事业费和特大自然灾害灾后重建补助费等。

(10)行政事业单位离退休支出：指实行归口管理的行政事业单位离退休经费。

(11)社会保障补助支出：指国家预算用于社会保障的补助支出，包括对社会保险基金的补助、促进就业补助、国有企业下岗职工补助、补充全国社会保障基金等。

(12)国防支出：指国家预算用于国防建设和保卫国家安全的支出，包括国防费、国防科研事业费、民兵建设以及专项工程支出等。

(13)行政管理费：包括行政管理支出，党派团体补助支出，外交支出，公安安全支出，司法支出，法院支出，检察院支出和公检法办案费用补助。

(14)政策性补贴支出：指经国家批准，由国家财政拨给用于粮棉油等产品的价格补贴支出。主要包括粮、棉、油差价补贴，平抑物价和储备糖补贴，农业生产资料价差补贴，粮食风险基金，副食品风险基金，地方煤炭风险基金等。

(15)债务利息支出：指国家预算中用于偿还国内外债务利息的支出。

中央财政支出和地方财政支出指根据政府在经济和社会活动中的不同职责，划分中央和地方政府的责权，按照政府的责权划分确定的支出。中央财政支出包括国防支出，武装警察部队支出，中央级行政管理费和各项事业费，重点建设支出以及中央政府调整国民经济结构、协调地区发展、实施宏观调控的支出。地方财政支出主要包括地方行政管理和各项事业费，地方统筹的基本建设、技术改造支出，城市维护费等。

预算外资金收支　预算外资金是指国家机关、事业和社会团体为履行或代行政府职能，依据国家法律、法规和具有法律效力的规章而收取、提取和安排使用的未纳入国家预算管理的各种财政性资金。其范围主要包括：法律、法规规定的行政事业性收费、基金和附加收入等；国务院或省级人民政府及其财政、计划（物价）部门审批的行政事业性收费；国务院及财政部审批建立的基金、附加收入等；主管部门所属单位集中上缴资金；用于乡镇政府开支的乡自筹和乡统筹资金；其他未纳入预算管理的财政性资金。社会保障基金在国家财政尚未建立社会保障预算制度以前，先按预算外资金管理制度进行管理，专款专用。财政部门在银行开设统一的专户，用于预算外资金收入和支出管理。部门和单位的预算外收入必须上缴同级财政专户，支出由同级财政按预算外资金收支计划和单位财务收支计划统筹安排，从财政专户中拨付，实行收支两条线管理。

Explanatory Notes on Main Statistical Indicators

Government Revenue refers to the revenue of the government finance by means of participating in the distribution of the social products, which are the financial resources for ensuring the government to function. The contents of government revenue have been changed several times. Now it includes the following main items:

(1) Various tax revenues, including value added tax, business tax, consumption tax, land value added tax, tax on city maintenance and construction, resources tax, tax on use of urban land, enterprise income tax, personal income tax, tariff, stamp tax on security transactions, tax on purchase of motor vehicles, tax on agriculture and animal husbandry and tax on occupancy of cultivated land, etc.

(2) Special revenues, including revenues from the fee on sewage treatment, fee on urban water resources, fee for the compensation of mineral resources and extra-charges for education, etc.

(3) Other revenues, including revenue from interest, revenue from the repayment of capital construction loan, revenue from capital construction projects, and donations and grants.

(4) Subsidies for the losses of the state-owned enterprises. This is an item of negative revenue, consisting of subsidies to industrial, commercial and grain purchasing and supply enterprises.

Revenue of the central government and revenue of the local governments refers to the revenue of the central government and that of the local governments as defined by the decentralized taxation system starting from 1994. In accordance with this system, the revenue of the central government includes tariff, consumption tax and value added tax levied by the customs, consumption tax, income tax of the enterprises subordinate to the central government, income taxes of the local banks, foreign-funded banks and non-bank financial institutions, business tax and profits of railways, head offices of banks, head office of insurance company , which are handed over to the government in a centralized way, tax on city maintenance and construction, tax on purchasing motor vehicles, tonnage tax of ships, 75% of the value added tax, 94% of the tax on stock dealing (stamp tax), interest income tax in the personal income tax, proportion of the personal income tax (other that interest income tax) to be shared by the central government, and tax on ocean petroleum resources,. The revenue of the local governments includes business tax, income tax of the enterprises subordinate to the local government, proportion of the personal income tax (other that interest income tax) to be shared by the central government, tax on the use of urban land, tax on the adjustment of the investment in fixed assets, tax on town maintenance and construction, tax on real estates, tax on the use of vehicles and ships, stamp tax, slaughter tax, tax on agriculture and animal husbandry, tax on special agricultural products, tax on the occupancy of cultivated land, contract tax, value-added tax on land, income from charges on use of state-owned land, 25% of the value added tax, 6% of the tax on stock dealing (stamp tax) and tax on resources other than the ocean petroleum resources.

Government Expenditure refers to the distribution and use of the funds the government finance has raised, so as to meet the needs of economic construction and various causes. It includes the following main items:

(1) Expenditure for capital construction: It refers to the non-gratuitous use and appropriation of funds for capital construction in the range of capital construction, outlay of capital as well as the loans on capital construction approved by the government for special purpose or policy purpose and the expenditure with discount paid in an overall way within the amount of the funds appropriated to the departments for capital construction.

(2) Innovation funds of the enterprises: They refer to the funds appropriated from the government budget for the enterprises to tap the latent power, upgrade the technology and carry out innovation, including the innovation fund of the

departments, loan of the enterprises for innovation, subsidies on the innovation of the small fertilizer plant, small cement plant, small coal mines, small machinery plant and small steel plant, the expenditure of interest for the loan for innovation.

(3) Geological prospecting expenses: They refer to the expenses appropriated from the government budget to the geological prospecting units for the expenditure of the prospecting work, including the expenditures of the administrative agencies for geological prospecting and their institutional units as well as the geological prospecting expenditure.

(4) Expenditures for science and technology promotion: They refer to the expenses appropriated from the government budget for the scientific and technological expenditure, including new products development expenditure, expenditure for intermediate trial and subsidies on important scientific researches.

(5) Expenditure for supporting rural production: It refers to the expenditures appropriated from the government budget for supporting the various expenditures of the rural collective units or households for production, including the subsidies to the small water conservancy projects and well drilling, sprinkling irrigation projects run by the villages; subsidies on the rural water and soil conserving measures; subsidies to the small power stations run by the villages; subsidies to the expenditure for fighting against particularly severe draughts; subsidies on the rural waste land exclamation; fund for supporting the township enterprises; fund for supporting rural cooperative production organizations, subsidies to the expenditure for popularization of the agricultural technologies and plant protection in the rural areas; subsidies to the expenditure for the protection of grasslands and cattle and fowls; subsidies on afforestation and forest protection in rural areas; subsidies on the rural aquatic products industry; special fund for developing grain production.

(6) Operating expenses of the departments of farming, forestry, water conservancy and meteorology etc.: They refer to the expenses appropriated from the government budget for the expenditures of agricultural exclamation, farms, agriculture, animal husbandry, agricultural machinery, forestry, timber industry, water conservancy, aquatic products industry, meteorology, technology popularization in township enterprises, popularization (demonstration) of improved varieties, plant (cattle and fowls, forest) protection, water quality monitoring, prospecting and designing, resources investigation, cadres training, subsidies to horticulture gardens, expenditure of specialized secondary schools. subsidies on the experiments of sowing herbage seeds by flights, expenditures of afforestation agencies and meteorology agencies, expenses for fishery administration and operating expenses for agricultural administration, etc.

(7) Operating expenses of the departments of industry, transport and commerce: They refer to the expenses appropriated from the government budget to cover the expenditure on salaries and operational expenditure of the departments of industry, transport and commerce for the expenditure of business development, including expenses for prospecting and designing, expenditures of specialized secondary schools, expenditures of the technical training schools and expenditures for cadres training, etc.

(8) Operating expenses of the departments of culture, education, science and public health: They refer to the expenses appropriated from the government budget for the expenditures on salaries and operational expenditure of the causes of culture, publication, cultural relics, education, public health, traditional Chinese medical science, free medical services, sports, archives, earthquake, ocean, communications, broadcasting, film and television, family planning; expenditure for training of cadres of government, party and mass organization; expenditures for natural sciences, social sciences, associations for science and technology and the special expenditure for the high-tech researches. They include mainly wages, extra wages, welfare funds, pension for the retirees, stipend, expenses for official business, expenses for equipment purchases, expenses for repairs, business expenses and subsidies to the units which are unable to support their expenditures by their own earnings.

(9) Pension for the disabled or for the families of the bereaved and relief funds for social welfare: They refer to the funds appropriated from the government budget for the expenditures of pension for the disabled or for the families of the

bereaved and relief funds for social welfare, including the lump-sum or regular pension paid by the departments of civil affairs to the members of martyrs families and families of those who died for the public interest, pension to the revolutionary disabled, subsidies for permanent disability of various kinds, subsidies to the military martyrs dependents and the demobilized servicemen, expenditure for settling down the demobilized servicemen, operating expenses of the consoling institutions, expenses for management and repair of the commemorative buildings for the martyrs, the expenses managed by the departments of civil affairs for the retirees and those who have quitted their work, expenses for social relief in rural and urban areas, operating expenses for providing relief to the areas of natural calamity and subsidies on the reconstruction after the particularly severe natural calamities, etc.

(10) Expenditure on retirees: It refers to the expenditure on retirees of government agencies and institutions that are covered by the state budget.

(11) Expenses on subsidies to social security system: It refers to expenditure from the state budget for subsidies to social security system, including subsidies to the social insurance fund, subsidies to promoting employment, subsidies to laid-off workers of state-owned enterprises, supplement to national social security funds, etc.

(12) Expenditures for national defence: They refer to the funds appropriated from the government budget for the expenditures for building up national defence and safeguarding national security, including expenses of national defence, expenses of scientific researches on national defence, expenses for building up people militia and expenditure for special projects, etc.

(13) Administrative expenses: They include expenditure for administration, subsidies to the parties and mass organizations, diplomatic expenditure, expenditure for public security, judicial expenditure, law court expenditure, procuratorial expenditure and subsidies to the expenses for treating the cases by the public security departments, procuratorial organs and law courts.

(14) Expenditure on policy-related subsidies: It refers to the expenditure appropriated, with the approval of the government, from the state budget for price subsidies on such products as grain, cotton and edible oil. More specifically, it includes subsidies to the difference between the selling prices and purchasing prices of grains, cotton and edible oil, subsidies for curtaining prices and for sugar reserve, subsidies to the difference between the selling prices and purchasing prices of means pf agricultural production, risk fund for grains, risk fund for non-staple food, risk fund for local production of coal, etc.

(15) Expenditure on interest of debts: It refers to expenses from the state budget on paying interest of domestic and foreign debts.

Expenditure of the central government and expenditure of he local governments: According to the different functions of the central government and local governments in the economic and social activities, the rights of affairs administration are classified between the central government and local governments; and the classification of the expenditure between the central government and local governments are made on the basis of the classification of the rights of affairs administration between them. The expenditure of the central government includes the expenditure for national defense, expenditure for armed police forces, the administrative expenses and various operating expenses at the level of central government, expenditure for key projects and the expenditure of the central government for adjusting the national economic structure, coordinating the development among different regions and exercising the macro-economic regulation and control. The expenditure of the local governments includes mainly the administrative expenses and various operating expenses at the level of local governments, the expenditure for capital construction and technological innovation with the funds raised by the local government, and expenditure for city maintenance, etc.

Extra-Budgetary Revenue and Expenditure Extra-budgetary fund refers to financial fund of various types not covered by the regular government budgetary management, which is collected, allocated or arranged by government agencies, institutions and social organizations while performing duties delegated to them or behalf of the government in accordance with laws, rules and regulations. It mainly covers following items: administrative and institutional fees, funds and extra charges that are stipulated by laws and regulations; administrative and institutional fees approved by the State Council and provincial governments and their financial and planning (price management) departments; funds and extra chares established by the State Council and the Ministry of Finance; funds turned over to competent compartments by their subordinate institutions; self-raised and collected funds by township governments for their own expenditure; and other financial funds that not covered in budgetary fund and managed for its exclusive use, given the circumstance that separate government budgetary system for social security is yet to be designed. Special accounts are opened by the financial departments in banks for the management of revenue and expenditure of extra-budgetary fund. Extra-budgetary revenue and expenditure is managed separately, namely, revenue of institutions and departments must enter into the special accounts of the financial departments at the same administrative level, and their extra-budgetary expenditure is arranged in line with the extra-budget plans and appropriated from these accounts.

七　人民生活与物价

PEOPLE'S LIVELIHOOD AND PRICES

简要说明 Brief Introduction

本章资料反映我市城乡居民生活状况，主要内容包括城乡居民家庭基本情况、恩格尔系数、居民储蓄、年收入支出及其构成、主要商品购买数量、耐用消费品的拥有量，以及居民消费价格指数、商品零售价格指数、原材料、燃料、动力购进价格指数和工业品出厂价格指数等。居民住户调查资料是抽样调查汇总的结果，价格指数采用分层抽样调查方法取得。

城市居民生活状况的数据来源于市城市社会经济调查队，农村居民生活的数据来源于市农村社会经济调查队。城乡居民物质生活情况和居民储蓄由市统计局综合处整理编辑。

The data in this chapter show the livelihood of urban and rural households, including basic statistics on urban and rural households, Engle coefficient, saving deposits, and annual income and expenditures and their compositions, purchases of major commodities, possession of durable consumer goods, consumer price indices, retail price indices, purchasing price indices of raw material, fuel and power, and ex-factory price indices of industrial products. The data on urban and rural households are collected by the sample surveys. The data on price indices are collected with the stratified sampling method.

The data on the livelihood of urban residents come from Urban Socio-economic Survey Organization, and that on rural residents come from Rural Socio-economic Survey Organization. Data on material & cultural life and saving deposits of urban & rural residents are edited by Division of Comprehensive Statistics, Municipal Bureau of Statistics.

7－1 城乡居民物质文化生活情况（2003－2004年）
Material and Cultural Life of Urban & Rural Residents (2003-2004)

指　　标	Item	2003	2004
就　　业	**Employment**		
每一城市就业者负担人数(人)（抽样调查）	Number of Dependents Per Urban Employee (person) (sample survey)	1.83	1.88
每一农村劳动力负担人数(人)（抽样调查）	Number of Dependents Per Rural Labor (person) (sample survey)	1.36	1.35
城镇登记失业率（%）	Urban Registered Unemployment Rate (%)	4.1	4.12
收入和支出	**Income and Expenditure**		
职工平均工资(元)	Annual Average Wages of Staff and Workers (yuan)	12440	14357
城市居民人均可支配收入(元)	Annual Per Capita Disposable Income of Urban Households (yuan)	8093.67	9220.96
农民人均纯收入(元)	Annual Per Capita Net Income of Rural Households (yuan)	2214.55	2510.41
城市居民人均消费性支出（元）	Annual Per Capita Consumption Expenditure of Urban Households (yuan)	7118.06	7973.05
农村居民人均生活消费支出（元）	Annual Per Capita Living Expenditure of Rural Households (yuan)	1583.31	1853.94
城市居民家庭恩格尔系数（%）	Engle Coefficient of Urban Households (%)	38.0	37.8
农村居民家庭恩格尔系数（%）	Engle Coefficient of Rural Households (%)	52.5	56.0
人均储蓄存款余额(元)	Per Capita Balance of Saving Deposits (yuan)	6059	6964
住房(抽样调查)	**Housing (sample survey)**		
城市人均房屋建筑面积(平方米)	Per Capita Residential Floor Space of Urban Residents (sq.m)	21.29	22.76
农村人均住房面积(平方米)	Per Capita Floor Space of Rural Residents (sq.m)	31.45	32.49
交通邮电	**Transportation, Postal and Telecommunication Services**		
城镇每万人拥有公共车辆（标台）	Number of buses Per 10 000 Persons in Cities and Towns (unit)	5.50	6.94
人均道路面积(平方米)	Per Capita Area of Paved Roads (sq.m)	6.00	6.33
每万人拥有电话(部)	Number of Telephones Per 10 000 Persons (unit)	4151	5247
每人平均交寄函件(件)	Number of Letters Mailed Per Person (unit)	7.38	6.65
城市公用事业	**Public Utilities in Urban Areas**		
用水普及率（%）	Percentage of Population with Access to Tap Water (%)	76.8	77.4
燃气普及率（%）	Percentage of Population with Access to Gas (%)	60.4	63.2
人均公共绿地面积（平方米）	Per Capita Public Green Land (sq.m)	3.10	4.09
教　　育	**Education**		
学龄儿童入学率（%）	Enrollment Ratio of School-age Children (%)	99.9	99.9
每万人口中在校大学生(人)	Number of Undergraduates Per 10 000 Persons (person)	81.76	96.86
文　　化	**Culture**		
每百户城市家庭拥有彩色电视机(台)	Number of Color TV Sets Per 100 Urban Households (unit)	150.67	153.33
每百户农村家庭拥有电视机(台)	Number of TV Sets Per 100 Rural Households (unit)	102.39	104.28
广播人口覆盖率（%）	Broadcasting Covering Rate of Population (%)	92.26	92.26
电视人口覆盖率（%）	TV Covering Rate of Population (%)	95.71	95.73
卫　　生	**Public Health**		
每万人拥有医院、卫生院病床(张)	Number of Hospital Beds Per 10 000 Persons (unit)	19.22	19.31
每万人拥有执业（助理）医师(人)	Number of Certified (Assistant) Doctors Per 10 000 Persons (person)	11.89	11.66

7－2 城乡居民人民币储蓄存款年末余额（1980－2004年） Year-end Saving Deposits of RMB of Urban and Rural Households (1980-2004)

年份 Year	城乡居民人民币储蓄存款年末余额（亿元） Year-end Saving Deposits of RMB of Urban and Rural Households (100 million yuan)	定期 Time	活期 Demand	人均人民币储蓄存款余额（元） Per Capita Balance of Saving Deposits of RMB (yuan)
1980	6.22			23
1981	8.35			31
1982	10.56			39
1983	13.34			49
1984	18.39			67
1985	25.41			92
1986	34.79			124
1987	44.46			156
1988	50.50	40.65	9.85	176
1989	68.17	55.75	12.42	235
1990	92.17	77.63	14.54	316
1991	121.95	103.36	18.59	415
1992	154.45	128.64	25.81	523
1993	198.05	160.51	37.54	668
1994	285.40	231.23	54.17	956
1995	401.45	331.09	70.36	1337
1996	500.71	403.84	96.87	1656
1997	580.67	454.04	126.63	1908
1998	724.54	552.72	171.82	2368
1999	909.10	672.96	236.14	2959
2000	1085.36	774.38	310.98	3511
2001	1317.17	929.37	387.80	4252
2002	1595.01	1082.90	512.11	5122
2003	1896.56	1265.52	631.04	6059
2004	2189.73	1469.99	719.74	6964

7－3 城乡居民家庭恩格尔系数（1978－2004年）
Engle Coefficient of Urban and Rural Households (1978-2004)

年 份 Year	农村居民家庭人均纯收入 Per Capital Annual Net Income of Rural Households		城市居民家庭人均可支配收入 Per Capital Annual Disposable Income of Urban Households		农村居民家庭恩格尔系数（%） Engle Coefficient of Rural Households (%)	城市居民家庭恩格尔系数（%） Engle Coefficient of Urban Households (%)
	绝对数（元） Value (yuan)	指数 (1978=100) Index	绝对数（元） Value (yuan)	指数 (1979=100) Index		
1978	126.01	100.0			74.0	
1979	150.18	119.2	354.54	100.0	72.9	61.9
1980	163.33	129.6	411.47	116.1	68.1	52.8
1985	325.24	258.1	812.40	229.1	63.9	51.8
1986	358.86	284.8	983.99	277.5	63.4	53.1
1987	385.82	306.2	1108.71	312.7	62.2	52.4
1988	457.54	363.1	1277.89	360.4	60.5	51.6
1989	510.09	404.8	1448.98	408.7	61.7	57.4
1990	586.73	465.6	1691.13	477.0	63.6	54.6
1991	628.89	499.1	1891.90	533.6	63.8	52.9
1992	677.46	537.6	2195.33	619.2	62.8	54.3
1993	748.08	593.7	2780.62	784.3	61.3	52.9
1994	1018.24	808.1	3634.33	1025.1	63.5	53.7
1995	1270.41	1008.2	4375.43	1234.1	64.7	50.6
1996	1479.05	1173.8	5022.96	1416.8	63.2	50.2
1997	1692.36	1343.0	5302.05	1495.5	65.8	46.7
1998	1801.17	1429.4	5442.84	1535.2	61.3	45.6
1999	1835.54	1456.7	5828.43	1643.9	60.7	42.8
2000	1892.44	1501.8	6176.30	1742.1	53.6	42.2
2001	1971.18	1564.3	6572.30	1853.8	54.1	40.8
2002	2097.58	1664.6	7238.07	2041.5	55.8	38.0
2003	2214.55	1757.4	8093.67	2282.9	52.5	38.0
2004	2510.41	1992.2	9220.96	2600.2	56.0	37.8

注：因统计制度变更，1985-2001年城市居民家庭可支配收入、消费支出和恩格尔系数等指标按2002年制度调整（下表同）。

Note: For the reason of system changes, disposable income, consumption expenditures and Engle coefficient of urban households were readjusted in accordance with system of 2002 (the same below).

7－4 城市居民家庭基本情况（1985－2004年）
Basic Statistics on Urban Households (1985-2004)

年 份 Year	平均每户家庭人口(人) Population Per Household (person)	平均每户就业人口(人) Average Number of Employees Per Household (person)	平均每一就业者负担人数(人) Number of Persons Supported by Each Employee (person)	平均每人可支配收入(元) Per Capita Disposable Income (yuan)	平均每人消费性支出(元) Per Capita Living Expenditures for Consumption (yuan)	平均每人房屋建筑面积（平方米） Per Capita Residential Floor Space of Buildings (sq.m)
1985	3.49	2.01	1.73	812.40	711.13	6.58
1986	3.41	2.01	1.70	983.99	893.84	6.68
1987	3.40	2.00	1.70	1108.71	1043.86	7.28
1988	3.31	1.87	1.77	1277.89	1323.17	7.64
1989	3.18	1.71	1.86	1448.98	1382.66	8.40
1990	3.12	1.73	1.81	1691.13	1569.97	8.90
1991	3.10	1.88	1.65	1891.90	1754.20	7.06
1992	3.16	2.04	1.55	2195.33	1928.63	6.75
1993	3.11	1.94	1.61	2780.62	2397.08	6.98
1994	3.03	1.89	1.61	3634.33	3126.56	7.30
1995	3.01	1.87	1.61	4375.43	4051.53	8.13
1996	3.08	2.00	1.54	5022.96	4467.12	8.00
1997	3.06	1.92	1.60	5302.05	4919.63	8.65
1998	3.01	1.86	1.62	5442.84	4956.80	9.21
1999	3.03	1.77	1.71	5828.43	5376.69	9.51
2000	3.05	1.72	1.78	6176.30	5471.70	10.72
2001	3.05	1.69	1.80	6572.30	5724.90	11.47
2002	3.05	1.50	2.03	7238.07	6360.20	19.56
2003	2.97	1.62	1.83	8093.67	7118.06	21.29
2004	3.02	1.61	1.88	9220.96	7973.05	22.76

注：因统计制度变更，指标“平均每人房屋建筑面积”2002年前的数据为“平均每人房屋居住面积”数。

Note: For the reason of system changes, data of "per capita residential floor space of buildings" refers to "living floor space" before 2002.

7-5 城市居民家庭基本情况（2003-2004年）
Basic Statistics on Urban Households (2003-2004)

指　　标	Item	2003	2004
调查户数(户)	**Surveyed Households (household)**	**300**	**300**
平均每户就业人数(人)	**Average Number of Employees Per Household (person)**	**1.62**	**1.61**
#国有经济单位	State-owned	1.10	0.99
城镇集体经济单位	Urban Collective-owned	0.12	0.11
城镇个体私营经济	Urban Individual and Private	0.18	0.23
平均每人全年总收入(元)	**Per Capita Total Annual Income (yuan)**	**8671.91**	**9910.09**
#可支配收入	Disposable Income	8093.67	9220.96
工薪收入	Income from Wages	6288.55	7162.69
#工资及补贴收入	Wage and Subsidies	6147.90	7009.97
经营净收入	Net Business Income	114.13	228.53
财产性收入	Property Income	80.80	109.67
转移性收入	Transfer Income	2188.43	2409.20
平均每人全年消费支出(元)	**Per Capita Annual Living Expenditures for Consumption (yuan)**	**7118.06**	**7973.05**
其中：服务性消费支出	Of Which: Expenditure for Services	2019.74	2443.77
食品	Food	2702.34	3015.32
#粮食	Grain	168.39	225.84
衣着	Clothing	735.01	779.68
#服装	Garments	526.98	579.31
家庭设备用品及服务	Household Appliances & Articles and Services	475.36	474.15
医疗保健	Medicine and Medical Services	459.69	537.95
交通和通讯	Transportation and Communications	790.26	865.45
教育娱乐文化服务	Educational, Recreational and Cultural Services	1025.99	1200.52
#教育	Education	565.07	667.79
居住	Residence	741.60	903.22
#住房	Housing	249.19	387.28
杂项商品与服务	Miscellaneous Commodities and Services	187.81	196.77

7－6 按可支配收入分组的城市居民家庭情况（2004年）
Statistics on Urban Households by Disposable Income (2004)

项目	Item	合计 Total	按平均每人每月可支配收入分组 By Per Capita Monthly Disposable Income		
			200元以下 Below 200 yuan	200-400元 200-400 yuan	400-600元 400-600 yuan
调查户数(户)	Survey Households (household)	300	1.00	30.42	78.25
比　重(%)	Composition (%)	100.0	0.3	10.1	26.1
平均每户家庭人口数(人)	Population Per Household (person)	3.02	4.00	3.21	3.24
平均每户就业人口数(人)	Average Number of Employees Per Household (person)	1.61		1.21	1.67
平均每户就业面(%)	Percentage of Employed Persons Per Household (%)	53.3		37.7	51.5
平均每一就业者负担人数(人)	Number of Persons Supported by Each Employee (person)	1.88		2.65	1.94
平均每人每月总收入(元)	Per Capita Monthly Total Income (yuan)	825.84	196.04	347.02	550.15
#可支配收入	Disposable Income	768.41	193.75	317.55	512.70
平均每人每月消费性支出(元)	Per Capita Monthly Living Expenditures for Consumption (yuan)	664.42	186.64	318.04	506.02
#服务性消费支出	Expenditure for Services	203.65	20.98	80.42	155.38

项目	Item	按平均每人每月可支配收入分组 By Per Capita Monthly Disposable Income			
		600-800元 600-800 yuan	800-1000元 800-1000 yuan	1000-1500元 1000-1500 yuan	1500元以上 Over 1500 yuan
调查户数(户)	Survey Households (household)	66.91	63.67	43.08	16.67
比　重(%)	Composition (%)	22.3	21.2	14.4	5.6
平均每户家庭人口数(人)	Population Per Household (person)	3.18	2.81	2.77	7.24
平均每户就业人口数(人)	Average Number of Employees Per Household (person)	1.59	1.59	1.79	5.53
平均每户就业面(%)	Percentage of Employed Persons Per Household (%)	50.0	56.6	64.6	76.4
平均每一就业者负担人数(人)	Number of Persons Supported by Each Employee (person)	2.00	1.77	1.55	1.31
平均每人每月总收入(元)	Per Capita Monthly Total Income (yuan)	748.61	947.40	1328.20	7292.02
#可支配收入	Disposable Income	697.01	887.19	1220.64	6809.00
平均每人每月消费性支出(元)	Per Capita Monthly Living Expenditures for Consumption (yuan)	627.95	727.51	1033.09	3899.69
#服务性消费支出	Expenditure for Services	174.88	213.38	366.34	1393.73

注：1）2002年统计制度变更后，“可支配收入”为家庭总收入扣除各种社会保障金，因此按月分组计算各组平均户数，部分分组的调查户数为小数。

2）本表资料按全年平均每人每月可支配收入分组汇总。

Note: a) For the reason of system changes, "disposable income" refers to total income minus various social security revenue in accordance with the system of 2002. So data of some groups of surveyed households by monthly and by yearly average household was decimal.

b) Data in 2003 were classified by average monthly disposable income.

7—7 城市居民家庭平均每人全年收入及构成（2004年）
Per Capita Annual Income of Urban Households and Its Composition (2004)

项　目	Item	总平均 Overall Average	最低收入户 Lowest Income Households	#困难户 Difficult Households	低收入户 Low Income Households	中等偏下户 Medium Income by Lower Households
全年总收入(元)	**Annual Total Income (yuan)**	**9910.09**	**4017.32**	**3469.99**	**5727.12**	**7323.16**
#可支配收入	Disposable Income	9220.96	3683.87	3091.00	5362.20	6789.50
工薪收入	Income from Wages	7162.69	2161.87	1806.53	3871.83	5356.09
#工资及补贴收入	Wage and Subsidies	7009.97	1978.83	1783.69	3757.31	5333.64
经营净收入	Net Business Income	228.53	331.90	516.64	183.73	73.02
财产性收入	Property Income	109.67	4.92		11.24	57.22
转移性收入	Transfer Income	2409.20	1518.63	1146.82	1660.31	1836.82
全年总收入构成(%)	**Composition of Annual Total Income (%)**	**100.0**	**100.0**	**100.0**	**100.0**	**100.0**
工薪收入	Income From Wages	72.3	53.8	52.1	67.6	73.1
#工资及补贴收入	Wage and Subsidies	70.7	49.3	51.4	65.6	72.8
非工薪收入	Income From Non-wages	27.7	46.2	47.9	32.4	26.9

项　目	Item	中等收入户 Medium Income Households	中等偏上户 Medium Income by Upper Households	高收入户 High Income Households	最高收入户 Highest Income Households
全年总收入(元)	**Annual Total Income (yuan)**	**9229.36**	**11402.39**	**14803.80**	**22005.52**
#可支配收入	Disposable Income	8614.42	10676.06	13598.56	20523.36
工薪收入	Income from Wages	6165.76	8339.17	11139.45	17447.01
#工资及补贴收入	Wage and Subsidies	6034.18	8186.18	10943.42	16965.11
经营净收入	Net Business Income	252.01	149.67	367.44	518.75
财产性收入	Property Income	107.37	54.95	178.68	542.22
转移性收入	Transfer Income	2704.21	2858.59	3118.22	3497.55
全年总收入构成(%)	**Composition of Annual Total Income (%)**	**100.0**	**100.0**	**100.0**	**100.0**
工薪收入	Income From Wages	66.8	73.1	75.2	79.3
#工资及补贴收入	Wage and Subsidies	65.4	71.8	73.9	77.1
非工薪收入	Income From Non-wages	33.2	26.9	24.8	20.7

7—8 城市居民家庭平均每人全年消费支出及构成（2004年）
Per Capita Annual Expenditures of Urban Households and Its Composition (2004)

项　目	Item	总平均 Overall Average	最低收入户 Lowest Income Households	#困难户 Difficult Households	低收入户 Low Income Households	中等偏下户 Medium Income by Lower Households
消费支出(元)	**Expenditures for Consumption (yuan)**	**7973.05**	**3640.96**	**3203.92**	**5673.82**	**6510.41**
其中：服务性消费支出	Of Which: Expenditure for Services	2443.77	814.01	707.65	1613.50	2134.70
食品	Food	3015.32	1968.45	1711.98	2360.32	2748.24
#粮油类	Grain and Oils	404.12	391.97	353.42	382.82	385.16
#粮食	Grain	225.84	217.01	195.27	213.11	213.67
肉禽蛋水产品类	Meat, Poultry, Eggs and Aquatic Products	862.52	688.92	583.20	809.32	785.91
#肉类	Meat	457.60	391.47	331.24	425.49	415.98
蔬菜类	Vegetable	297.99	306.17	297.05	262.88	268.99
糖烟酒饮料类	Sugar, Cigarettes, Alcohol and Drinks	320.90	146.73	127.85	225.32	264.39
糕点、奶及奶制品	Cakes, Milk and Dairy Products	234.18	110.18	98.92	132.06	217.38
衣着	Clothing	779.68	218.22	188.12	329.81	576.85
#服装	Garments	579.31	146.15	113.05	225.23	393.61
家庭设备用品及服务	Household Appliances & Articles and Services	474.15	151.18	173.60	263.74	246.41
医疗保健	Medicine and Medical Services	537.95	176.36	81.39	449.75	430.48
交通和通讯	Transportation and Communications	865.45	227.68	175.87	580.62	726.00
教育娱乐文化服务	Educational, Recreational and Cultural Services	1200.52	431.62	452.14	703.09	1094.77
#教育	Education	667.79	366.25	395.69	420.20	790.01
居住	Residence	903.22	390.65	374.83	857.99	575.14
#住房	Housing	387.28	37.08	56.38	451.62	160.18
杂项商品与服务	Miscellaneous Commodities and Services	196.77	76.79	46.00	128.50	112.52
消费支出构成(%)	**Composition of Living Expenditures for Consumption (%)**	**100.0**	**100.0**	**100.0**	**100.0**	**100.0**
其中：服务性消费支出	Of Which: Expenditure for Services	30.7	22.4	22.1	28.4	32.8
食品	Food	37.8	54.1	53.4	41.6	42.2
衣着	Clothing	9.8	6.0	5.9	5.8	8.9
家庭设备用品及服务	Household Appliances & Articles and Services	5.9	4.2	5.4	4.7	3.8
医疗保健	Medicine and Medical Services	6.7	4.8	2.5	7.9	6.6
交通和通讯	Transportation and Communications	10.9	6.3	5.5	10.2	11.2
教育娱乐文化服务	Educational, Recreational and Cultural Services	15.1	11.8	14.1	12.4	16.8
居住	Residence	11.3	10.7	11.7	15.1	8.8
杂项商品与服务	Miscellaneous Commodities and Services	2.5	2.1	1.5	2.3	1.7

7-8 续表 CONTINUED

项　　目	Item	中等收入户 Medium Income Households	中等偏上户 Medium Income by Upper Households	高收入户 High Income Households	最高收入户 Highest Income Households
消费支出(元)	**Expenditures for Consumption (yuan)**	**7608.36**	**8749.23**	**10440.66**	**16290.81**
其中：服务性消费支出	Of Which: Expenditure for Services	2029.51	2582.20	3287.74	5973.94
食品	Food	3198.57	3421.90	3267.92	4219.77
#粮油类	Grain and Oils	439.76	436.72	348.76	397.57
#粮食	Grain	244.05	241.02	210.65	224.26
肉禽蛋水产品类	Meat, Poultry, Eggs and Aquatic Products	941.70	960.75	846.48	949.49
#肉类	Meat	508.70	516.86	426.21	467.79
蔬菜类	Vegetable	337.54	311.10	275.88	310.40
糖烟酒饮料类	Sugar, Cigarettes, Alcohol and Drinks	413.38	435.86	253.31	401.96
糕点、奶及奶制品	Cakes, Milk and Dairy Products	272.24	285.29	265.87	329.78
衣着	Clothing	751.64	912.62	1228.35	1851.75
#服装	Garments	552.94	711.46	936.18	1421.77
家庭设备用品及服务	Household Appliances & Articles and Services	379.46	516.09	972.89	1303.09
医疗保健	Medicine and Medical Services	715.12	622.47	494.61	805.48
交通和通讯	Transportation and Communications	800.80	1068.42	1186.98	1712.97
教育娱乐文化服务	Educational, Recreational and Cultural Services	792.49	1239.75	1392.18	3636.35
#教育	Education	460.90	504.44	750.81	1780.57
居住	Residence	788.00	748.00	1658.45	2192.51
#住房	Housing	249.26	164.71	1060.40	1376.04
杂项商品与服务	Miscellaneous Commodities and Services	182.29	219.98	239.27	568.88
消费支出构成(%)	**Composition of Living Expenditures for Consumption (%)**	**100.0**	**100.0**	**100.0**	**100.0**
其中：服务性消费支出	Of Which: Expenditure for Services	26.7	29.5	31.5	36.7
食品	Food	42.0	39.1	31.3	25.9
衣着	Clothing	9.9	10.4	11.8	11.4
家庭设备用品及服务	Household Appliances & Articles and Services	5.0	5.9	9.3	8.0
医疗保健	Medicine and Medical Services	9.4	7.1	4.7	4.9
交通和通讯	Transportation and Communications	10.5	12.2	11.4	10.5
教育娱乐文化服务	Educational, Recreational and Cultural Services	10.4	14.2	13.3	22.3
居住	Residence	10.4	8.6	15.9	13.5
杂项商品与服务	Miscellaneous Commodities and Services	2.4	2.5	2.3	3.5

7—9 主要年份居民消费价格总指数和商品零售价格总指数
General Indices of Consumer Price and Retail Price in Major Years

年份 Year	以1950年为100 1950=100		以1978年为100 1978=100		以上年为100 Preceding Year=100	
	居民消费价格总指数 General Consumer Price Index	商品零售价格总指数 General Retail Price Index	居民消费价格总指数 General Consumer Price Index	商品零售价格总指数 General Retail Price Index	居民消费价格总指数 General Consumer Price Index	商品零售价格总指数 General Retail Price Index
1952	106.1	108.7			97.3	97.2
1957	114.0	116.5			104.6	103.9
1962	145.8	158.1			95.2	95.0
1965	125.1	133.1			98.0	98.2
1970	129.2	137.9			99.6	99.5
1975	131.2	140.2			100.3	100.3
1978	135.4	145.1	100.0	100.0	102.9	103.2
1980	148.3	160.1	109.5	110.3	107.9	108.6
1985	179.4	191.7	132.4	132.0	109.9	110.0
1986	186.9	199.8	138.0	137.5	104.2	104.2
1987	205.2	220.8	151.5	151.9	109.8	110.5
1988	251.8	272.2	185.9	187.3	122.7	123.3
1989	294.9	317.1	217.7	218.2	117.1	116.5
1990	299.0	317.4	220.7	218.4	101.4	100.1
1991	319.9	336.8	236.1	231.7	107.0	106.1
1992	355.7	369.8	262.5	254.4	111.2	109.8
1993	422.2	430.1	311.6	295.9	118.7	116.3
1994	547.6	544.1	404.1	374.3	129.7	126.5
1995	653.8	632.8	482.5	435.3	119.4	116.3
1996	717.2	671.4	529.3	461.9	109.7	106.1
1997	741.2	682.6	546.8	470.4	103.3	101.7
1998	714.5	645.1	527.1	444.5	96.4	94.5
1999	709.5	622.5	523.4	428.9	99.3	96.5
2000	686.1	594.5	506.1	409.6	96.7	95.5
2001	697.8	588.6	514.7	405.5	101.7	99.0
2002	695.0	582.1	512.6	401.0	99.6	98.9
2003	699.2	579.2	515.7	399.0	100.6	99.5
2004	725.1	587.3	534.8	404.6	103.7	101.4

7－10 居民消费价格分类指数（2003－2004年）
Consumer Price Indices by Category (2003-2004)

（上年=100） (preceding year=100)

项　　目	Item	2003	2004
居民消费价格总指数	**General Consumer Price Index**	**100.6**	**103.7**
食品	Food	104.3	111.0
＃粮食	Grain	100.5	127.1
油脂	Oils and Fats	114.2	121.4
肉禽及其制品	Meat Poultry and Related Products	99.2	121.5
蛋	Eggs	98.3	117.2
水产品	Aquatic Products	104.7	111.6
菜	Vegetables	120.6	112.6
＃鲜菜	Fresh Vegetables	122.8	114.5
茶及饮料	Tea and Beverages	98.5	101.9
干鲜瓜果	Dried and Fresh Melons and Fruits	122.6	99.6
＃鲜果	Fresh Fruits	130.5	98.6
奶及奶制品	Milk and Dairy Products	100.5	100.1
在外用膳食品	Outward Dinner	101.3	100.1
其它食品及加工服务费	Other Foods and Manufacturing Services	102.5	101.3
烟酒及用品	Cigarettes, Alcohol and Relative Products	98.2	100.4
＃烟草	Tobacco	97.0	98.5
酒	Liquor	101.1	106.0
衣着	Clothing	94.2	91.2
＃服装	Garments	93.9	93.4
家庭设备用品及维修服务费	Household Appliances & Articles and Service Fees	95.5	98.5
＃耐用消费品	Durable Consumer Goods	94.2	95.6
家庭服务及加工维修服务费	Other Household Service and Manufacturing Upkeep	99.8	100.8
医疗保健和个人用品	Medicine, Medical Articles & Services and Personal Articles	99.3	99.4
医疗保健	Medicine, Medical Articles & Services	99.2	98.7
个人用品及服务	Personal Articles and Services	99.8	101.2
交通和通信	Transportation and Communications	98.7	99.2
交通	Transportation	100.2	100.8
通信	Telecommunication	97.7	98.0
娱乐教育文化用品及服务	Recreational, Educational & Cultural Articles and Services	99.6	103.2
＃教育	Education	102.2	107.2
旅游及外出	Tourism and Outing	98.7	105.5
居住	Residence	102.2	100.9

7－11 商品零售价格分类指数（2003－2004年）
Retail Price Indices By Category of Commodities (2003-2004)

（上年=100） (preceding year=100)

项　　目	Item	2003	2004
商品零售价格总指数	**General Retail Price Index**	**99.5**	**101.4**
食　品	Food	104.4	111.2
饮料、烟酒	Beverages, Tobacco and Liquor	98.6	101.4
服装、鞋帽	Garments, Shoes and Hats	94.0	91.1
纺织品	Textiles	100.5	99.8
家用电器及音像器材	Household Appliances and Video Materials	93.5	93.0
文化办公用品	Cultural and Office Articles	98.2	98.2
日用品	Articles for Daily Use	94.9	99.9
体育娱乐用品	Sports and Amusement Articles	98.9	96.7
交通、通信用品	Transport and Telecommunication Articles	90.8	89.6
家　具	Furniture	98.2	99.7
化妆品	Cosmetics	97.1	101.8
金银珠宝	Gold, Silver and Jewelry	110.5	106.5
中西药品及医疗保健用品	Traditional Chinese & Western Medicines and Medical Articles	97.8	93.2
书报杂志及电子出版物	Newspaper, Magazines and Electronic Publications	100.2	101.1
燃　料	Fuels	105.3	106.2
建筑材料及五金电料	Building Materials and Hardware & Electric Materials	100.1	99.0

7－12 原材料、燃料、动力购进价格指数（2003－2004年）
Purchasing Price Indices of Raw Material, Fuel and Power (2003-2004)

（上年=100） (preceding year=100)

指　　标	Item	2003	2004
原材料、燃料、动力购进价格指数	**Purchasing Price Indices of Raw Material, Fuel and Power**	**104.9**	**112.9**
燃料、动力类	Fuel and Power	103.6	114.8
黑色金属材料类	Ferrous Metals	109.3	119.9
有色金属材料类	Nonferrous Metals	106.8	121.0
化工原料类	Raw Chemical Materials	104.5	115.1
木材及纸浆类	Timber and Paper Pulp	100.5	103.7
建筑材料及非金属矿类	Building Materials and Non-metal Minerals	101.2	105.5
其他工业原材料及半成品类	Other Industrial Raw Material and Semi-products	102.0	105.1
农副产品类	Agricultural Products	108.1	110.5
纺织原料类	Textile Materials	100.7	101.5

7－13 工业品出厂价格指数（2003－2004年）
Ex-factory Price Indices of Industrial Products (2003-2004)

（上年=100） (preceding year=100)

指　标	Item	2003	2004
工业品出厂价格总指数	**Ex-factory Price Indices of Industrial Products**	**100.6**	**103.9**
#轻工业	Light Industry	99.9	102.4
以农产品为原料	Farm Products as Raw Materials	102.0	104.2
以非农产品为原料	Non-farm Products as Raw Materials	98.6	101.8
重工业	Heavy Industry	101.1	105.1
采掘工业	Minming and Quarrying	103.4	128.7
原材料工业	Raw Material Industry	103.6	113.0
加工工业	Manufacturing Industry	101.6	101.9
#生产资料	Means of Production	101.9	105.3
采掘工业	Minming and Quarrying	102.7	131.1
原材料工业	Raw Material Industry	103.0	110.9
加工工业	Manufacturing Industry	101.6	103.3
生活资料	Consumer Goods	97.7	99.6
食　品	Food	102.0	104.4
衣　着	Clothing	96.9	101.1
一般日用品	Articles for Daily Use	99.6	100.1
耐用消费品	Durable Consumer Goods	93.9	96.9

7－14 城市居民家庭平均每人全年购买的主要商品数量（2003－2004年）
Per Capita Purchases of Major Commodities in Urban Households (2003-2004)

指　标	Item	2003	2004
粮食（公斤）	Grain (kg)	64.35	67.16
鲜菜（公斤）	Fresh Vegetable (kg)	119.85	130.20
食用植物油（公斤）	Edible Plant Oil (kg)	12.16	11.96
猪肉（公斤）	Pork (kg)	30.49	33.29
牛羊肉（公斤）	Beef and Mutton (kg)	2.77	3.16
家禽（公斤）	Poultry (kg)	15.28	11.33
鲜蛋（公斤）	Fresh Eggs (kg)	10.02	9.41
鱼虾（公斤）	Fish and Shrimp (kg)	9.00	9.27
鲜乳品（公斤）	Fresh Dairy Products (kg)	23.36	23.38
酒类（公斤）	Wine (kg)	9.37	9.24
茶叶（公斤）	Tea (kg)	0.31	0.28
鲜瓜果（公斤）	Fresh Melons and Fruits (kg)	47.10	41.43
男士服装（件）	Men's Clothing (piece)	2.57	2.37
女士服装（件）	Women's Clothing (piece)	4.07	3.80
各式童装（件）	Children's Clothing (piece)	0.74	0.84
鞋类（双）	Shoes (pair)	3.11	2.60

7－15 城市居民家庭平均每百户年末耐用消费品拥有量（2003－2004年）
Number of Durable Consumer Goods Owned Per 100 Urban Households at Year-end (2003-2004)

指　　标	Item	2003	2004
成套家具（套）	Furniture (set)	92.00	98.33
摩托车（辆）	Motorcycles (vehicle)	2.00	2.33
电风扇（台）	Electric Fans (unit)	194.33	182.33
电冰箱(台)	Refrigerators (unit)	98.00	99.67
洗衣机（台）	Washing Machines (unit)	97.67	99.33
彩色电视机(台)	Color TV Sets (unit)	150.67	153.33
组合音响(套)	Hi-Fi Stereo Component System (set)	35.33	39.67
影碟机(台)	Radio Cassette Players (unit)	70.67	82.00
摄像机（架）	Pickup Cameras (unit)	3.67	4.67
照相机(架)	Cameras (unit)	48.33	52.67
钢琴（架）	Pianos (unit)	1.33	2.00
中高档乐器(件)	Medium and High Grade Musical Instruments (piece)	3.00	6.33
微波炉（台）	Micro-wave Ovens (unit)	58.67	66.33
空调器(台)	Air Conditioners (unit)	126.67	152.33
取暖器（台）	Room Heater (unit)	35.67	34.67
电炊具（台）	Electric Cooking Appliances (unit)	70.33	83.00
淋浴热水器（台）	Showers (unit)	92.00	96.33
排油烟机（台）	Smoke Absorbers (unit)	41.00	38.67
健身器材（套）	Health Equipments (set)	4.67	5.67
饮水机（台）	Drinking Machine (unit)	33.33	45.33
吸尘器（台）	Dust Catchers (unit)	14.67	12.00
家用电脑(台)	Personal Computers (unit)	34.67	43.67
普通电话(部)	Household Telephones (unit)	97.67	96.00
移动电话(部)	Mobile Telephones (unit)	95.67	128.33

7－16 农村居民家庭基本情况（1985－2004年）
Basic Statistics on Rural Households (1985-2004)

年 份 Year	平均每户常住人口（人） Average Permanent Population Per Household (person)	平均每户整半劳力（人） Average Able-bodied and Semi-Ablebodied Laborers Per Household (person)	平均每个劳动力负担人口(人) Average Number of Persons Supported By Each Laborer (person)	平均每人纯收入(元) Per Capita Average Net Income (yuan)	平均每人生活消费支出(元) Per Capita Living Expenditures for Consumption (yuan)	平均每人住房面积(平方米) Per Capita Floor Space of Residential Buildings (sq.m)
1985	4.63	2.81	1.65	325.24	275.81	18.04
1986	4.58	2.85	1.61	358.86	312.34	18.06
1987	4.51	2.87	1.57	385.82	346.40	18.23
1988	4.40	2.89	1.53	457.54	427.19	19.03
1989	4.31	2.92	1.47	510.09	463.47	19.29
1990	4.21	2.93	1.44	586.73	519.26	19.37
1991	4.20	2.88	1.46	628.89	558.44	21.52
1992	4.12	2.88	1.43	677.46	573.65	21.94
1993	4.05	2.90	1.39	748.08	694.60	22.01
1994	3.98	2.88	1.38	1018.24	879.26	22.55
1995	3.90	2.83	1.38	1270.41	1097.52	23.50
1996	3.85	2.70	1.43	1479.05	1328.18	24.44
1997	3.82	2.69	1.42	1692.36	1389.99	24.74
1998	3.71	2.61	1.42	1801.17	1417.08	26.50
1999	3.68	2.59	1.42	1835.54	1388.64	26.67
2000	3.70	2.63	1.41	1892.44	1395.53	29.58
2001	3.66	2.56	1.43	1971.18	1475.16	31.00
2002	3.65	2.62	1.39	2097.58	1497.72	31.02
2003	3.65	2.69	1.36	2214.55	1583.31	31.45
2004	3.67	2.72	1.35	2510.41	1853.94	32.49

7－17 农村居民家庭基本情况（2003－2004年）
Basic Statistics on Rural Households (2003-2004)

指　　标	Item	2003	2004
调查户数(户)	**Surveyed Households (household)**	**1800**	**1800**
调查户人口(人)	**Surveyed Population (person)**	**6566**	**6602**
常住人口	Residents Population	6566	6602
整半劳动力	Able-bodied and Semi-able-bodied Laborers	4833	4899
平均每户常住人口	Average Population Residents Per Household	3.65	3.67
平均每户整半劳力	Average Able-bodied and Semi-able-bodied Laborers Per Household	2.69	2.72
平均每个劳动力负担人口(含本人)	Average Number of Persons Supported By Each Laborer (including the laborer himself or herself)	1.36	1.35
平均每人年收入(元)	**Per Capita Annual Income (yuan)**	**2922.12**	**3341.19**
总收入	Total Income	2922.12	3341.19
纯收入	Net Income	2214.55	2510.41
现金收入	Cash Income	2019.62	2267.56
按纯收入分组户数占调查户比重(%)	**Percentage of Households By Per Capita Annual Net Income (%)**	**100.0**	**100.0**
600元以下	Below 600 Yuan	1.2	0.9
600-800元	600-800 Yuan	1.8	0.9
800-1000元	800-1000 Yuan	4.8	2.7
1000-1200元	1000-1200 Yuan	6.2	4.2
1200-1500元	1200-1500 Yuan	12.2	8.9
1500-2000元	1500-2000 Yuan	22.2	19.1
2000-2500元	2000-2500 Yuan	17.9	18.4
2500-3000元	2500-3000 Yuan	12.2	13.9
3000-4000元	3000-4000 Yuan	12.6	17.5
4000元以上	4000 Yuan and Over	8.9	13.5
平均每人年支出(元)	**Per Capita Annual Expenditure (yuan)**	**2333.87**	**2773.43**
总支出	Total Expenditure	2333.87	2773.43
现金支出	Cash Expenditure	1672.00	1896.91
平均每人经营耕地面积(亩)	**Per Capita Management Cultivated Area (mu)**	**0.95**	**0.95**
平均每人生产性固定资产原值(元)	**Per Capita Original Value of Productive Fixed Assets (yuan)**	**694.04**	**711.81**
第一产业	Primary Industry	558.19	599.17
#役畜、产品畜	Draught Animals and Commodity Animals	107.25	114.87
大中型铁木农具	Large and Medium Wood and Iron Farm Tools	54.84	58.36
农林牧渔机械	Machinery of Farming Forestry Animal Husbandry and Fishery	25.33	25.95
第二产业	Secondary Industry	10.99	13.54
第三产业	Tertiary Industry	124.86	99.10

7－18 农村居民家庭平均每人收入情况（2003－2004年）
Per Capita Annual Income of Rural Households (2003-2004)

单位：元 (yuan)

指　　标	Item	2003	2004
总收入	**Total Income**	**2922.12**	**3341.19**
工资性收入	Wages	858.50	931.69
＃在本地劳动得到收入	From Local Enterprises	290.68	276.58
常住人口外出从业得到收入	From Outwork of Permanent Population	487.28	588.83
家庭经营收入	Total Income from Household Business Operation	1821.44	2191.41
第一产业	Primary Industry	1652.87	2052.08
＃农　业	Farming	888.20	1051.31
牧　业	Animal Husbandry	715.16	942.41
第二产业	Secondary Industry	26.51	21.33
第三产业	Tertiary Industry	142.06	118.00
＃交通运输、邮电业	Transportation, Storage, Postal Services	53.67	46.83
批零贸易、餐饮业	Wholesale & Retail Trade and Catering Service	42.58	40.01
财产性收入	Property Income	34.17	33.06
转移性收入	Transfer Income	208.01	185.03
纯收入	**Net Income**	**2214.55**	**2510.41**
工资性收入	Wages	858.50	931.69
＃在本地劳动得到收入	From Local Enterprises	290.68	276.58
常住人口外出从业得到收入	From Outwork of Permanent Population	487.28	588.83
家庭经营收入	Total Income from Household Business Operation	1185.12	1418.84
第一产业	Primary Industry	1062.68	1327.83
＃农　业	Farming	693.43	838.9
牧　业	Animal Husbandry	336.22	446.45
第二产业	Secondary Industry	22.36	14.79
第三产业	Tertiary Industry	100.08	76.22
＃交通运输、邮电业	Transportation, Storage, Postal Services	24.77	19.26
批零贸易、餐饮业	Wholesale & Retail Trade and Catering Service	35.8	32.89
财产性收入	Property Income	34.17	33.06
转移性收入	Transfer Income	136.76	126.82
现金收入	**Cash Income**	**2019.62**	**2267.56**
工资性收入	Wages	857.81	931.57
＃在本地劳动得到收入	From Local Enterprises	290.63	276.51
常住人口外出从业得到收入	From Outwork of Permanent Population	486.65	588.83
家庭经营收入	Total Income from Household Business Operation	930.43	1129.56
第一产业	Primary Industry	761.88	990.79
＃农　业	Farming	229.89	269.39
牧　业	Animal Husbandry	492.94	675.50
第二产业	Secondary Industry	26.50	21.33
第三产业	Tertiary Industry	142.05	117.44
＃交通运输、邮电业	Transportation, Storage, Postal Services	53.67	46.83
批零贸易、餐饮业	Wholesale & Retail Trade and Catering Service	42.58	40.01
财产性收入	Property Income	33.82	30.87
转移性收入	Transfer Income	197.56	175.56

7－19 农村居民家庭平均每人支出情况（2003－2004年）
Per Capita Annual Expenditures of Rural Households (2003-2004)

单位：元 (yuan)

指　标	Item	2003	2004
总支出	**Total Expenditure**	**2333.87**	**2773.43**
家庭经营费用支出	Expenditure for Household Business Cost	550.56	696.42
第一产业	Primary Industry	515.16	657.03
第二产业	Secondary Industry	3.20	5.60
第三产业	Tertiary Industry	32.20	33.79
购置生产性固定资产支出	Expenditure for Purchasing Productive Fixed Assets	19.02	33.26
税费支出	Taxes and Fees	39.48	28.69
生活消费支出	Living Expenditures for Consumption	1583.31	1853.94
食　品	Food	831.63	1039.00
衣　着	Clothing	70.49	79.08
居　住	Residence	212.38	201.03
家庭设备、用品及服务	Household Appliances, Articles and Services	76.68	74.80
医疗保健	Medicines and Medical Services	89.42	115.31
交通和通讯	Transportation and Communications	102.40	119.67
文教娱乐用品及服务	Cultural Educational and Recreational Articles and Services	180.28	198.65
其他商品和服务	Other Commodities and Services	20.03	26.40
财产性支出	Property Expenditure	6.73	3.53
转移性支出	Transfer Expenditure	134.77	157.59
现金支出	**Cash Expenditure**	**1672.00**	**1896.91**
家庭经营费用支出	Expenditure for Household Business Cost	363.11	442.78
第一产业	Primary Industry	327.71	403.41
第二产业	Secondary Industry	3.20	5.60
第三产业	Tertiary Industry	32.20	33.77
购置生产性固定资产支出	Expenditure for Purchasing Productive Fixed Assets	19.00	33.26
税费支出	Taxes and Fees	38.65	28.55
生活消费支出	Living Expenditures for Consumption	1111.06	1231.90
食　品	Food	376.75	440.91
衣　着	Clothing	70.49	79.08
居　住	Residence	195.52	177.49
家庭设备、用品及服务	Household Appliances, Articles and Services	76.20	74.40
医疗保健	Medicines and Medical Services	89.42	115.31
交通和通讯	Transportation and Communications	102.40	119.67
文教娱乐用品及服务	Cultural Educational and Recreational Articles and Services	180.28	198.65
其他商品和服务	Other Commodities and Services	20.00	26.39
财产性支出	Property Expenditure	6.73	3.53
转移性支出	Transfer Expenditure	133.45	156.89

7－20 不同收入组农村居民家庭收入支出情况（2004年）
Per Capita Annual Income and Expenditures of Rural Households (2004)

单位：元 (yuan)

指标	Item	总平均 Total Average	低收入户 Low Income Households	中低收入户 Medium Income by Lower Households
平均每人总收入	**Per Capita Total Income**	**3341.19**	**1874.93**	**2519.88**
＃现金收入	Cash Income	2267.56	1051.92	1556.55
平均每人纯收入	**Per Capita Net Income**	**2510.41**	**1176.57**	**1827.74**
工资性收入	Income from Wages	931.69	394.95	621.14
家庭经营纯收入	Family Business Income	1418.84	734.13	1109.88
财产性收入	Property Income	33.06	8.14	11.79
转移性收入	Transfer Income	126.82	39.35	84.93
平均每人总支出	**Per Capita Total Expenditure**	**2773.43**	**2049.24**	**2165.57**
＃现金支出	Cash Expenditure	1896.91	1288.87	1348.14
生活消费总支出	**Per Capita Living Expenditures for Consumption**	**1853.94**	**1323.55**	**1438.51**
食　品	Food	1039.00	787.33	859.50
衣　着	Clothing	79.08	56.67	60.23
居　住	Residence	201.03	130.93	108.29
家庭设备用品及服务	Household Appliances, Articles and Services	74.80	51.36	50.60
医疗保健	Medicines and Medical Services	115.31	54.22	86.93
交通通讯	Transportation and Communications	119.67	86.27	84.33
文教娱乐用品及服务	Cultural Educational and Recreational Articles and Services	198.65	143.12	172.02
其他商品及服务	Other Commodities and Services	26.40	13.65	16.61

指标	Item	中等收入户 Medium Income Households	中高收入户 Medium Income by Upper Households	高收入户 High Income Households
平均每人总收入	**Per Capita Total Income**	**3157.33**	**3899.37**	**5979.05**
＃现金收入	Cash Income	2037.79	2734.52	4583.48
平均每人纯收入	**Per Capita Net Income**	**2363.01**	**3054.04**	**4759.67**
工资性收入	Income from Wages	867.45	1213.18	1817.98
家庭经营纯收入	Family Business Income	1393.35	1653.64	2508.62
财产性收入	Property Income	8.28	48.17	107.42
转移性收入	Transfer Income	93.93	139.05	325.65
平均每人总支出	**Per Capita Total Expenditure**	**2633.52**	**3069.17**	**4379.65**
＃现金支出	Cash Expenditure	1728.85	2140.67	3362.93
生活消费总支出	**Per Capita Living Expenditures for Consumption**	**1776.61**	**2141.96**	**2878.43**
食　品	Food	1035.27	1172.29	1465.69
衣　着	Clothing	76.72	91.55	122.64
居　住	Residence	151.42	242.89	429.86
家庭设备用品及服务	Household Appliances, Articles and Services	63.40	93.03	131.21
医疗保健	Medicines and Medical Services	126.35	152.48	178.81
交通通讯	Transportation and Communications	107.24	143.28	199.23
文教娱乐用品及服务	Cultural Educational and Recreational Articles and Services	194.11	219.85	289.63
其他商品及服务	Other Commodities and Services	22.10	26.59	61.36

7－21 农村居民家庭平均每人主要消费品消费量（2003－2004年）
Per Capita Consumption of Major Consumer Goods in Rural Households (2003-2004)

指　　标	Item	2003	2004
粮食(原粮)(公斤)	Grain (unprocessed) (kg)	216.51	213.66
蔬菜(公斤)	Fresh Vegetable (kg)	154.70	166.85
食用植物油(公斤)	Edible Plant Oil (kg)	2.17	1.95
肉类(公斤)	Meat (kg)	28.06	27.96
#猪　肉	Pork	27.91	27.85
牛羊肉	Beef and Mutton	0.15	0.11
家禽(公斤)	Poultry (kg)	2.21	2.78
鲜蛋(公斤)	Eggs (kg)	3.98	6.10
鱼虾(公斤)	Fish and Shrimp (kg)	1.84	2.05
鲜奶（公斤）	Milk and Dairy Products (kg)	0.06	0.09
卷烟（盒）	Cigarettes (pack)	29.83	29.66
酒类(公斤)	Alcohol (kg)	7.98	8.50

7－22 农村居民家庭平均每百户年末耐用消费品拥有量（2003－2004年）
Number of Durable Consumer Goods Owned Per 100 Rural Households at Year-end (2003-2004)

指　　标	Item	2003	2004
大型家具（件）	Large Furniture (unit)	403.78	416.85
洗衣机(台)	Washing Machines (unit)	15.89	18.83
电风扇(台)	Electric Fans (unit)	141.61	148.67
电冰箱(台)	Refrigerators (unit)	8.89	10.22
空调机（台）	Air Conditioners (unit)	0.39	0.94
抽油烟机（台）	Exhausts Fan (unit)	0.33	0.72
微波炉（台）	Micro-wave Ovens (unit)	0.39	0.44
热水器（台）	Showers (unit)	4.44	6.33
自行车(辆)	Bicycles (vehicle)	16.94	16.89
摩托车(辆)	Motorcycles (vehicle)	7.78	9.67
汽车（生活用）（辆）	Motor Vehicles for living (vehicle)	0.39	0.06
电话机（部）	Household Telephone (unit)	43.72	52.22
移动电话（部）	Mobile Telephones (unit)	20.06	27.89
彩色电视机(台)	Color TV Sets (unit)	53.33	63.22
黑白电视机(台)	Black and White TV Sets (unit)	49.06	41.06
影碟机(台)	Vedio Players (unit)	25.00	30.89
收录机(台)	Radio Cassette Players (unit)	5.89	4.39
照相机(架)	Cameras (unit)	1.50	1.00

主要统计指标解释

城乡居民储蓄存款余额 指某一时点城乡居民存入银行及农村信用社的储蓄金额，包括城镇居民储蓄存款和农民个人储蓄存款，不包括居民的手存现金和工矿企业、部队、机关、团体等单位存款。

城市居民家庭就业人口 指城市居民从事社会劳动并取得劳动报酬或经营收入的人口。就业人口包括通过国家统筹规划和指导由劳动部门介绍就业，自愿组织起来就业和自谋职业等方式，在国有、集体所有制、中外合资、中外合作、外资在华独资的企事业单位和私营企业单位工作或从事个体劳动的有固定性职业或临时性职业的人口。被聘用和留用的离退休人员也计入就业人口。本指标可以反映城市居民的就业情况，是计算就业面，负担系数的重要资料。

城市居民家庭总收入 指家庭成员得到的工薪收入、经营净收入、财产性收入、转移性收入之和，不包括出售财物收入和借贷收入。

城市居民家庭可支配收入 指家庭成员得到可用于最终消费支出和其它非义务性支出以及储蓄的总和，即居民家庭可以用来自由支配的收入。它是家庭总收入扣除交纳的所得税、个人交纳的社会保障支出以及记账补贴后的收入。计算公式为：

可支配收入=家庭总收入-交纳所得税-个人交纳的社会保障支出-记帐补贴

城市居民家庭总支出 指除借贷支出以外的全部家庭支出。包括消费性支出、购房建房支出、转移性支出、财产性支出、社会保障支出。

城市居民家庭消费性支出 指家庭用于日常生活的支出，包括食品、衣着、家庭设备用品及服务、医疗保健、交通和通信、娱乐教育文化服务、居住、杂项商品和服务等八大类支出。

城市居民家庭服务性消费支出 指被调查的城市居民家庭用于本家庭支付社会提供的各种文化和生活方面的非商品性服务费用。不包括为别人付款的服务。服务消费与商品消费不同，其特点在于其劳动过程和消费过程在时间与空间上的统一。

城市居民家庭收入分组方法 将所有调查户依户人均可支配收入由低到高排队，按10%，10%，20%，20%，20%，10%，10%的比例依次分成：最低收入户、低收入户、中等偏下收入户、中等收入户、中等偏上收入户、高收入户、最高收入户等七组。总体中最低5%的户为困难户。

恩格尔系数 指家庭或个人食物支出总额占全部消费支出总额的比重。计算公式为：

恩格尔系数 = 食物支出总额 / 消费支出总额×100%

农村居民家庭整半劳动力 整劳动力指男子18周岁到50周岁，女子18周岁到45周岁；半劳动力指男子16周岁到17周岁，51周岁到60周岁；女子16周岁到17周岁，46周岁到55周岁，同时具有劳动能力的人。虽然在劳动年龄之内，但已丧失劳动能力的人，不应算为劳动力；超过劳动年龄，但能经常参加劳动，计入半劳动力数内。常住人口中的职工，若这些职工为劳动力，就包括在本户的整半劳动力中。

农村居民家庭总收入 指调查期内农村住户和住户成员从各种来源渠道得到的收入总和。按收入的性质划分为工资性收入、家庭经营收入、财产性收入和转移性收入。

农村居民家庭现金收入 指农村住户和住户成员在调查期内得到以现金形态表现的收入。按来源分成工资性收入、家庭经营现金收入、财产性收入、转移性收入。

农村居民家庭纯收入 指农村住户当年从各个来源得到的总收入相应地扣除所发生的费用后的收入总和。纯收入主要用于再生产投入和当年生活消费支出，也可用于储蓄和各种非义务性支出。"农民人均纯收入"按人口平均的纯收入水平，反映的是一个地区或一个农户农村居民的平均收入水平。计算方法：

纯收入= 总收入-家庭经营费用支出-税费支出-生产性固定资产折旧

农村居民家庭总支出 指农村住户用于生产、生活和再分配的全部支出。家庭经营费用支出、购置生产性固定资产支出、生产性固定资产折旧、税费支出、生活消费支出、财产性支出和转移性支出。

农村居民家庭生活消费支出 指农村住户用于物质生活和精神生活方面的支出。生活消费支出包括食品、衣着、居住、家庭设备用品及服务、医疗保健、交通和通讯、文化教育娱乐用品及服务、其他商品和服务等消费。

农村居民家庭现金支出 指农村住户用于生产、生活和再分配所支付的现金。包括家庭经营费用支出、缴纳的税费、购买生产性固定资产、生活消费、财产性和转移性支出。

居民消费价格指数 居民消费价格指数是度量一组代表性消费商品及服务项目价格水平随着时间而变动的相对数，反映居民家庭购买的消费品及服务价格水平的变动情况。它是宏观经济分析和决策、价格总水平监测和调控以及国民经济核算的重要指标。其按年度计算的变动率通常被用来作为反映通货膨胀（或紧缩）程度的指标。

商品零售价格指数 商品的零售价格是商品在流通过程中最后一个环节的价格，是工业、商业、餐饮业和其他零售企业向城乡居民、机关团体出售生活消费品和办公用品的价格。通过系统地调查、搜集和整理市场商品零售价格资料，编制商品零售价格指数，以此反映市场商品零售价格的变动趋势和变动程度。其目的在于掌握商品价格的变动趋势，为国家宏观调控和国民经济核算提供参考依据。同时，还可在此基础上编制出其他各种派生价格指数。

原材料、燃料和动力购进价格指数 是反映工业企业作为生产投入，而从物资交易市场和能源、原材料生产企业购买原材料、燃料和动力产品时，所支付的价格水平变动趋势和程度的统计指标，是扣除工业企业物质消耗成本中的价格变动影响的重要依据。

工业品出厂价格指数 是反映一定时期内全部工业产品出厂价格总水平的变动趋势和程度的相对数，包括工业企业售给本企业以外所有单位的各种产品和直接售给居民用于生活消费的产品。该指数可以观察出厂价格变动对工业总产值及增加值的影响。

Explanatory Notes on Main Statistical Indicators

Saving Deposits of Urban and Rural Residents refer to the total value of savings deposits of urban and rural households in banks and rural credit cooperatives at a given point of time, including the saving deposits of urban residents and the saving deposits of rural residents. The cash in hand by residents and the deposits of organizations such as enterprises, military units, government agencies, institutions, etc. are not included.

Employed Population in Urban Households refers to urban residents engaged in certain work and receiving payment for their labor or income from their business operation, including those who work in state-owned or collective units, joint ventures, foreign-owned units and private units with permanent or temporary jobs. The self - employed individuals and reemployed retirees are also basic data for calculating employment rate and dependency ratio.

Total Income of Urban Households refers to the sum of wage and salary, net business income, income from properties, and income from transfers of members of the households, excluding income from selling of properties and income from borrowings.

Disposable Income of Urban Households refers to the actual income at the disposal of members of the households which can be used for final consumption, other non-compulsory expenditure and savings. This equals to total income minus income tax, personal contribution to social security and sample household subsidy for keeping dairies. Following formula is used: *Disposable income = total household income - income tax - personal contribution to social security –sample household subsidy for keeping dairies*

Total expenditure of Urban Households refer to all expenditure of the households except expenditure on leading. It includes expenditure on consumption, on purchasing or building houses, on transfers, on properties and on social security.

Consumption Expenditure of Urban Households refers to total expenditure of the sample households for consumption in daily life, including expenditure on eight categories such as food, clothing, household appliances and services, health care and medical services, transport and communications, recreation, education and cultural services, housing, miscellaneous goods and services.

Expenditure of Urban Households on Consumption of Services refers to expenditure of households on services of various kinds provided by the society.

Urban Households by Income Group All households in the sample are grouped, by per capita disposable income of the household, into groups of lowest income, low income, lower middle income, middle income, upper middle income, high income and highest income, each group consisting of 10%, 10%, 20%, 20%, 20%, 10% and 10% of all households respectively. The lowest 5% of households are also referred to as poor households.

Engel Coefficient refers to the percentage of family or individual's expenditure on food in the total consumption expenditure, using the following formula:

Engel Coefficient = (expenditure on food / total consumption expenditure) × 100%

Full/Semi Labour Force Full labor force refers to persons capable of work, aged 18-50 for males and 18-45 for females. Semi labor force refers to persons capable of work, aged 16-17 and 51-60 for males and 16-17 and 46-55 for females.

Persons at their working ages but not capable of work are not to be included as labor force. Persons not at working ages but participating regularly in work are included in semi labor force. For staff and workers as resident population of the household, they are included as full or semi labor force of the household if they are in the labor force.

Total Income of Rural Households refers to the sum of income earned from various sources by the rural households and their members during the reference period, and is classified as income from wages and salaries, income from household operations, income from properties and income from transfers.

Cash Income of Rural Households refers to income received by rural households and their members in the form of cash during the reference period. It is classified, by source of income, into income from wages and salaries, cash income from household operations, income from properties and income from transfers

Net Income of Rural Households refers to the total income of rural households from all sources minus all corresponding expenses. Net income is mainly used as input for reproduction and as consumption expenditure of the year, and also used for savings and non-compulsory expenses of various forms. "Per capita net income of farmers" is the level of net income averaged by population which reflects the average income level of rural households in a given area. The formula for calculation is as follows:

Net income = total income – household operation expenses – taxes and fees – depreciation of fixed assets for production

Total Expenditure of Rural Households refers to total expenses of rural households on production, consumption and redistribution, including expenditure on household operations, on purchase of productive fixed assets, depreciation of productive fixed assets, taxes and fees, expenses on household consumption, expenses on properties and expenses on transfers.

Expenditure on Household Consumption of Rural Households refers to expenditure by rural households on their material and cultural life, including expenditure on food; clothing; housing; household appliances, articles and services; health and medical service; transportation and communications; articles and services on culture, education and recreation; and other goods and services.

Cash Expenditure of Rural Households refers to cash expenditure by rural households for production, consumption and redistribution during the reference period, including cash expenses on household operations, taxes and fees, purchase of productive fixed assets, household consumption, and expenses on properties and transfers.

Consumer Price Index reflects the relative change in prices of consumer goods and services in a certain period of time, Formation of consumer price index aims to study the impact of consumer price changes on the actual living cost of urban and rural residents and to provide scientific basis for central government and relevant departments in drawing up consumer up consumer policy, price policy, wage policy and monetary policy and in accounting the nation economy. It is also a key index reflecting the fluctuation of inflation.

Retail Price Index refers to the prices at which industrial, commercial, catering and other retail enterprises sell daily consumer goods and products for office use to urban and rural residents and institutions and social organizátions. It reflects the general change in prices of retail commodities in a certain period of time. Formation of retail price index aims to keep abreast of price fluctuation of retail commodities and provide the reference basis for the central government in working out economic policies. Other derivative indexes can been formulate based on retail price index, providing the scientific bases for studying market circulation and the new accounting system of national economy.

Indices of Purchasing Prices of Raw Materials, Fuels and Power reflect changes in the level and degree of prices paid by industrial enterprises when they purchase production input such as raw materials, fuels and power from the market or from other energy or raw materials producing enterprises. These indices provide important basis for measuring the material consumption of industrial enterprises after removing influence of price changes.

Ex-factory Price Indices of Industrial Products reflect the trend and degree of changes in general ex-factory prices of all industrial products during a given period, including sales of industrial products by an industrial enterprise to all units outside the enterprise, as well as sales of consumer goods to residents. It can be used to analyze the impact of ex-factory prices on gross output value and value-added of the industrial sector.

八　城镇建设和环境保护

URBAN CONSTRUCTION AND ENVIRONMENTAL PROTECTION

简要说明　Brief Introduction

本章资料反映我市城镇建设和环境保护的基本情况。

城镇建设资料主要包括城镇建设用地、基础设施水平、市政设施、园林绿化、供水供气、公共交通、基础设施建设投资、房屋等，由市统计局固定资产投资处根据市建设委员会和市国土资源和房屋管理局资料整理提供。环境保护主要包括工业废水、废气、固体废物的排放处理和利用，工业污染治理投资，生活污染物排放，以及环境污染与破坏事故情况等，由市统计局社会科技处根据市环境保护局的资料整理提供。

Data in this chapter show the basic conditions of urban construction and environmental protection in Chongqing.

The statistics on urban construction cover land for urban construction, level of public facilities, civil engineering, afforestation, water and gas supply, public traffic, investment in infrastructure construction, and buildings and housing. The data of urban construction are provided by Division of Statistics of Investment in Fixed Assets, Municipal Bureau of Statistics according to information of Municipal Construction Commission and Municipal Administration of Land, Resources and Buildings. Environmental protection mainly includes discharge, treatment and utilization of industrial waste water, waste gas and solid wastes, investment in anti-industrial pollution projects, discharge of pollutants from daily life, and pollution accidents. The Data on environmental protection are prepared by Division of Social and Technology Statistics, Municipal Bureau of Statistics on basis of data from Municipal Environmental Protection Bureau.

8－1 城镇建设用地（2003－2004年）
Land for Urban Construction (2003-2004)

单位：平方公里 (sq.km)

项　目	Item	全　市 Total		#区市合计 Total of Districts (cities)	
		2003	2004	2003	2004
建成区面积合计	**Developed Area**	**654.95**	**647.78**	**523.71**	**516.49**
建设用地面积合计	**Area of Land for Urban Construction**	**550.61**	**555.97**	**433.63**	**437.45**
居住用地	Land for Residence	188.53	179.25	149.87	139.14
公共设施用地	Land for Public Utilities	79.04	77.68	62.26	60.63
工业用地	Land for Industry	107.20	105.35	93.09	91.65
仓储用地	Land for Storage	22.96	23.36	18.43	19.26
对外交通用地	Land for External Transportation	33.11	33.64	26.02	26.63
道路广场用地	Land for Roads and Squares	45.87	45.69	28.94	29.52
市政公用设施用地	Land for Municipal Public Utilities	16.49	17.78	10.22	11.98
绿　地	Land for Afforestation	39.20	53.76	29.26	41.89
特殊用地	Land for Special Purpose	18.21	19.46	15.54	16.75

注：1）“区市合计”数2002年前为14个市辖区和4个县级市合计，2002年起为15个市辖区（含长寿区）和4个县级市合计（下表同）。

2）2004年建成区面积为市规划局重新测定数。

Note: a) "Total of Districts (cities) " refers to total data of 14 districts and 4 cities at county level before 2002 whereas total data of 15 districts (including Changshou District) and 4 cities at county level since 2002 (the same below).

b) The developed area in 2004 was surveyed and readjusted by Municipal Bureau of Urban Planning.

8－2 城镇基础设施水平（2003－2004年）
Level of Public Facilities in Urban Area (2003-2004)

项　目	Item	全　市 Total		#区市合计 Total of Districts (cities)	
		2003	2004	2003	2004
人均日生活用水量（升）	Per Capita Daily Water Consumption for Living (liter)	147.50	147.72	155.24	155.82
用水普及率（%）	Percentage of Population with Access to Tap Water (%)	76.8	77.4	76.5	76.8
燃气普及率（%）	Percentage of Population with Access to Gas (%)	60.4	63.2	59.5	63.5
每万人拥有公共交通车辆（标台）	Public Transport Vehicles Owned Per 10 000 Persons (vehicle)	5.43	6.94	6.16	7.71
人均道路面积（平方米）	Per Capita Area of Paved Roads (sq.m)	5.96	6.33	5.86	6.20
污水处理厂集中处理率（%）	Intensive Treatment Rate of Polluted Water by Special Factories (%)	7.5	14.6	7.7	12.6
人均公共绿地面积（平方米）	Per Capita Public Green Land (sq.m)	3.12	4.09	3.09	4.06
建成区绿地率（%）	Rate of Green Area to Developed Area (%)	14.7	18.7	15.6	19.9
建成区绿化覆盖率（%）	Rate of Afforestation Covered Area to Developed Area (%)	16.6	20.9	17.0	21.7

注：人均数为户籍人口口径。

Note: Data of average population refer to registration statistics.

8－3 城镇市政设施（2003－2004年）
Urban Civil Engineering (2003-2004)

项　　目	Item	全　市 Total		#区市合计 Total of Districts (cities)	
		2003	2004	2003	2004
道路长度（公里）	Length of Roads (km)	4021.82	4271.93	3278.79	3448.39
道路面积（万平方米）	Area of Roads (10 000 sq.m)	6028.50	6559.70	4784.10	5206.05
#人行道	Sidewalk	1682.50	1938.20	1353.90	1532.20
桥梁数（座）	Number of Bridges (unit)	840	868	618	630
#立交桥	Stereoscopic Traffic Bridges	103	100	97	94
路灯盏数（盏）	Number of Street Lights (unit)	233182	246738	165155	179468
排水管道长度（公里）	Length of Drainpipes (km)	4372.60	5032.87	3267.50	3752.46
#污水管道	Waste Pipes	1590.79	1902.37	1100.71	1297.09
污水年排放量（万立方米）	Discharged Volume of Polluted Water (10 000 cu.m)	62859	66250	56057	59243
污水处理厂处理总量（万立方米）	Treated Volume of Polluted Water by Special Factories (10 000 cu.m)	4707	9650	4288	7459
防洪堤长度（公里）	Length of Flood Protecting Embankment (km)	407.04	417.14	297.76	299.66

注：1）自2001年起，道路面积为车行道与人行道面积之和。
　　2）2002年起桥梁范围调整为规划区范围内；由于库区移建原因，2004年立交桥数量比2003年减少。

Note: a) Since 2001, the area of roads is the summed area of carriageway and sidewalk
b) The statistical range of bridges has referred to planned area since 2002. Because of the movement of reservioir area, the number of stereoscopic traffic bridge is less than that of 2003.

8－4 城镇园林绿化（2003－2004年）
Parks, Gardens and Green Areas in Urban Area (2003-2004)

指　　标	Item	全　市 Total		#区市合计 Total of Districts (cities)	
		2003	2004	2003	2004
绿化覆盖面积（公顷）	Coverage Area of Afforestation (hectare)	15403	19256	12904	16282
#建成区	Developed Area	10851	13491	8884	11101
园林绿地面积（公顷）	Area of Gardens and Green Area (hectare)	13953	16616	12125	14325
#建成区	Developed Area	9614	12045	8190	10210
公共绿地面积（公顷）	Area of Public Green Area (hectare)	3155	4234	2523	3409
动物园、公园个数（个）	Number of Parks and Zoos (unit)	100	112	71	78
动物园、公园面积（公顷）	Area of Parks and Zoos (hectare)	1511	1769	1249	1357

8－5 城镇供水及供气情况（2003－2004年）
Water and Gas Supply in Urban Area (2003-2004)

指　标	Item	全　市 Total		#区市合计 Total of Districts (cities)	
		2003	2004	2003	2004
城镇供水	**Water Supply in Urban Area**				
年末供水综合生产能力（万立方米/日）	Year-end Comprehensive Productive Capacity of Water Supply (10 000 cu.m/day)	455.32	438.46	388.98	373.65
年末供水管道长度（公里）	Year-end Length of Water Supply Pipelines (km)	7948.36	8335.19	6082.66	6413.55
供水总量（万立方米）	Total Volume of Water Supply (10 000 cu.m)	79935	81061	71077	71653
生产运营用水	Production and Operation	30028	26404	28311	24618
公共服务用水	Public Services	7148	7080	6020	5899
居民家庭用水	Households	34664	36160	29370	30769
消防及其他用水	Fires and Other Purposes	8095	11417	7376	10367
用水户数（户）	Households with Access to Tap Water (household)	1469602	1539417	1096688	1106019
#家庭用户	Residential Households	1268706	1342648	934630	962617
用水人口（万人）	Number of Residents with Access to Tap Water (10 000 persons)	776.63	801.98	624.56	644.70
城镇供气	**Gas Supply in Urban Area**				
天然气供气总量（万立方米）	Total Natural Gas Supply (10 000 cu.m)	124408	164414	110438	135173
#家庭用量	Used by Residential Households	64697	66053	56666	52230
天然气用气户数（户）	Households with Access to Natural Gas (household)	1696669	1734743	1457252	1440259
#家庭用户	Residential Households	1672089	1695254	1446439	1419347
天然气用气人口（万人）	Population with Access to Natural Gas (10 000 persons)	512.80	548.45	437.98	458.01
天然气汽车加气站（个）	Natural Gas Stations for Motor Vehicles (unit)	29	43	29	38
液化石油气供气总量（吨）	Total Liquefied Petroleum Gas Supply (ton)	88995	123332	62519	96023
#家庭用量	Used by Residential Households	45433	66308	24024	43733
液化石油气用气户数（户）	Households with Access to Liquefied Petroleum Gas (household)	359594	600552	199321	396178
#家庭用户	Residential Households	273030	355387	142730	209051
液化石油气用气人口（万人）	Population with Access to Liquefied Petroleum Gas (10 000 persons)	96.84	123.46	46.07	75.14

注：2004年部分企业的自备小水厂被关停或兼并。

Note: Self-provided water factories of some enterprises were closed or merged in 2004.

8－6 城镇公共交通情况（2003－2004年）
Public Traffic in Urban Area (2003-2004）

指标	Item	全市 Total		#区市合计 Total of Districts (cities)	
		2003	2004	2003	2004
营运客车	**Operating Public Vehicles**				
公共汽车（含无轨电车）运营车数（辆）	Year-end Operating Public Buses (including trolley buses) (vehicle)	6251	7710	5333	6778
公共汽车	Public Buses	6168	7710	5250	6778
#小公共汽车	Mini Public Buses	1324	1718	540	945
天然气燃料车	Vehicles of Natural Gas	3882	5220	3846	5210
液化石油气燃料车	Vehicles of Liquid Petrol Gas	324	277	324	252
无轨电车	Trolley Buses	83		83	
年末营运线路网长度（公里）	Year-end Length of Public Transportation Routes (km)	2326	2465	2063	2255
客运总量（万人次）	Total Passenger Traffic (10 000 person-times)	95564	100290	90407	95174
公共汽车	Public Buses	89290	100290	84133	95174
#小公共汽车	Mini Public Buses	6504	7646	3277	3970
无轨电车	Trolley Buses	6274		6274	
缆 车	**Cable Cars**				
缆车道条数（条）	Number of Cable Car Line (line)	4	4	4	4
车辆数（辆）	Number of Vehicles (vehicle)	6	6	6	6
客运量（万人次）	Passengers Traffic (10 000 person-times)	382	290	382	290
客运架空索道	**Ropeway of Building on Stilts**				
索道条数（条）	Number of Ropeway (line)	2	2	2	2
客车数（辆）	Number of Vehicles (vehicle)	4	4	4	4
客运量（万人次）	Passengers Traffic (10 000 person-times)	234	163	234	163
轮 渡	**Ferries**				
年末实有轮渡总数（艘）	Year-end Total Ferries (vessel)	36	51	23	47
出租汽车	**Taxis**				
车辆数（辆）	Number of Vehicles (vehicle)	19647	18538	17233	15665

注：从2004年起重庆取消了无轨电车；2004年出租车数不含面的。

Note: Trolley buses have been stoped using in Ch… …er of taxis excludes minibus taxis in 2004.

9 …（2003－2004年）
Inves… …Construction (2003-2004)

单位：万元 (10 000 yuan)

指…		2003	2004
公用事业	**Publ…**	**156052**	**266934**
供　水	Water Supply	41552	66742
燃　气	Gas Supply	20460	26909
公共交通	Public Traffic	94040	173283
市政建设	**Municipal Construction**	**1058200**	**1295043**
园林绿化	Parks, Gardens and Green Areas	71861	85496
环境卫生	Environmental Sanitation	77210	48388
市政工程	Municipal Engineering	909129	1161159

8－8 基础设施建设投资额（2003－2004年）
Investment in Infrastructure Construction (2003-2004)

单位：万元 (10 000 yuan)

指　　标	Item	2003	2004
合　计	**Total**	**4897984**	**5959718**
水利管理业	Water Conservancy Management	154173	138363
电力、燃气及水的生产和供应业	Electricpower, Gas & Water Production and Supply	585068	827347
交通运输邮电业	Transportation, Postal and Telecommunication Services	2182668	2308168
#交通运输	Transportation	1758855	1811458
邮电通信	Postal and Telecommunication Services	423813	496710
教育文化艺术及广播电影电视	Education, Culture, Art, Broadcasting, Film and Television	418744	577859
城市基础设施	Urban Infrastructure	1557331	2107981

8－9 城镇房屋及居住情况（2003－2004年）
Statistics on Buildings and Housing in Urban Area (2003-2004)

指　　标	Item	全　市 Total		#区市合计 Total of Districts (cities)	
		2003	2004	2003	2004
房屋状况（万平方米）	**Conditions of Buildings (10 000 sq.m)**				
年末实有房屋建筑面积	Year-end Total Available Floor Space of Building Construction	26778.53	32323.19	20568.78	25252.25
#住　宅	Residential Buildings	16879.37	21210.13	12632.85	16274.61
#自有（私有）住宅	Self-owned (private)	11623.83	14974.03	8289.19	11268.28
年末实有住宅套数（套）	Year-end Total Number of Available Apartment Buildings (set)	1973956	2382053	1510172	1861992
年末成套住宅建筑面积	Year-end Total Floor Space of Apartment Buildings	13176.00	17102.07	9850.00	13111.59
年末危险房屋建筑面积	Year-end Total Floor Space of Dangerous Building Construction	694.30	587.43	637.73	543.55
#住　宅	Residential Buildings	462.77	327.21	424.81	297.57
居住状况	**Conditions of Housing**				
居住户数（万户）	Households of Housing (10 000 households)	219.97	260.76	165.23	204.77
人均住宅建筑面积（平方米/人）	Per Capita Floor Space of Residential Buildings (sq.m/person)	25.72	28.25	25.69	28.17
户均住宅套数（套/户）	Average Number of Apartments Per Household (set/household)	0.90	0.91	0.91	0.91

8－10 环境保护情况（2003－2004年）
Environmental Protection (2003-2004)

项　　目	Item	2003	2004
环保投资（亿元）	Investment in Environmental Protection (100 million yuan)	44.72	50.88
自然保护区数（个）	Number of Nature Reserves (unit)	46	49
自然保护区面积（万公顷）	Are of Nature Reserves (10 000 ha)	81.79	84.60
保护区面积占土地总面积比重（%）	Percentage of Nature Reserves in the Land Area (%)	9.94	10.27
生态示范区数（个）	Number of Demonstration Zone of Ecology (unit)	3	3
生态示范区面积（万公顷）	Area of Demonstration Zone of Ecology (10 000 ha)	72.60	72.60
工业污染治理施工项目数（个）	On-going Projects of Industrial Pollution Treatment (unit)	183	178
工业污染治理项目完成投资（万元）	Completed Investment in Projects of Industrial Pollution Treatment (10 000 yuan)	14192	28626
工业污染治理竣工项目数（个）	Completed Projects of Industrial Pollution Treatment (unit)	172	165
工业废水排放达标率（%）	Rate of Waste Water up to Discharge Standard (%)	89.9	93.4
工业固体废物综合利用率（%）	Rate of Industrial Solid Wastes Comprehensively Utilized (%)	68.4	70.9
生活污水排放量（万吨）	Discharged Volume of Sanitary Sewage (10 000 tons)	51988	52487
生活二氧化硫排放量（万吨）	Discharged Volume of SO2 from Living (10 000 tons)	13.53	15.42
烟尘控制区数（个/平方公里）	Number of Districts Where Dusts are under Control (unit/sq.km)	54/344.00	66/360.00
环境噪声达标区数（个/平方公里）	Number of Districts Where Noises are up to Standards (unit/sq.km)	37/173.40	44/227.20
主城区区域环境躁声平均值（分贝）	Average Noises in Downtown (db)	54.9	55.1
主城区道路交通噪声（分贝）	Traffic Noises in Downtown (db)	67.5	68.1
主城区大气可吸入颗粒年日均值（毫克/立方米）	Annual Average Daily Inhalable Motes in Atmosphere in Downtown (mg/cu.m)	0.147	0.142
主城区二氧化硫年日均值（毫克/立方米）	Annual Average Daily SO_2 Concentration in Downtown (mg/cu.m)	0.115	0.113
主城区二氧化氮年日均值（毫克/立方米）	Annual Average Daily NO_2 Concentration in Downtown (mg/cu.m)	0.046	0.067
饮用水源水质达标率（%）	Rate of Quality of Drinking Water Sources up to Standards (%)	96.1	96.3
地面水水质达标率（%）	Rate of Quality of Ground Water up to Standards (%)	100.0	100.0
汽车尾气达标率（%）	Rate of Motor Vehicle Exhaust up to Standards (%)	85.9	86.5

8－11 工业"三废"排放处理及综合利用情况（1995－2004年）
Discharge, Treatment and Utilization of Waste Gas, Waste Water and Solid Wastes by Industry (1995-2004)

年份 Year	工业废水（万吨） Industrial Waste Water (10 000 tons)			工业废气（万吨） Industrial Waste Gas (10 000 tons)			
	排放总量 Discharged Volume	排放达标量 Up to Discharge Standards	排放达标率（%） Rate up to Discharge Standard	工业废气排放总量（亿标立方米） Total Volume of Industrial Waste Gas Discharged (100 million cu.m)	工业二氧化硫排放量 Discharged Volume of SO_2	工业粉尘排放量 Discharged Volume of Industrial Dusts	工业粉尘去除量 Removed Volume of Industrial Dusts
1995	95590	57000	55.4	1979	71.45	22.39	25.30
1996	93889	46879	62.4	1697	72.16	22.36	23.43
1997	101324	67766	80.2	1794	71.43	33.18	22.60
1998	93997	58396	77.8	1712.76	73.64	28.65	28.92
1999	90220	58380	82.3	1839.33	75.88	26.44	33.33
2000	84344	63612	82.6	1907.90	66.42	22.01	44.61
2001	81214	66920	91.0	1856.24	56.94	21.41	37.42
2002	79872	71372	89.4	1978.89	55.18	20.31	40.18
2003	81973	73663	89.9	2276.94	59.97	22.23	33.49
2004	83031	77559	93.4	3540.86	64.11	21.98	36.76

年份 Year	工业废气 Industrial Waste Gas	工业固体废物（万吨） Industrial Solid Wastes (10 000 tons)					"三废"综合利用产品产值（万元） Output Value of Products Made from Comprehensive Utilization of Waste Water, Waste Gas and Solid Wastes (10 000 yuan)
	工业烟尘排放量（万吨） Discharged Volume of Industrial Soot (10 000 tons)	产生量 Produced Volume	排放量 Discharged Volume	处置量 Treated Volume	综合利用量 Utilized Volume	综合利用率（%） Rate of Utilization	
1995	16.12	1092	230	68.34	467.79	50.37	31138
1996	15.76	1174	229	61.06	510.06	58.10	52037
1997	14.90	1279	273	49.16	623.00	54.27	44737
1998	14.42	1368	229	43.75	597.00	61.78	48945
1999	14.07	1512	291	42.40	655.47	64.32	80554
2000	12.18	1305	238	37.64	626.01	71.00	59593
2001	11.01	1300	168	87.85	881.64	65.30	74642
2002	11.08	1348	160	68.78	960.95	68.20	72459
2003	11.98	1336	142	73.54	967.98	68.43	71512
2004	12.53	1489	118	62.09	1093.35	70.93	79932

8－12 重点调查工业分行业废气排放及处理情况（2004年）

行　业	Sector	汇总工业企业数（个）Number of Industrial Enterprises (unit)	废气治理设施数（套）Number of Facilities for Treatment of Waste Gas (set)	工业废气排放总量（亿标立方米）Total Discharged Volume of Industrial Waste Gas (100 million cu.m)
总　计	**Total**	**1368**	**2046**	**3540.86**
采矿业	Mining and Quarrying	121	140	46.31
煤炭开采和洗选业	Coal Mining and Dressing	94	50	24.20
石油和天然气开采业	Petroleum and Natural Gas Extraction	5	7	3.68
黑色金属矿采选业	Ferrous Metals Mining and Dressing	9	60	11.33
有色金属矿采选业	Nonferrous Metals Mining and Dressing	3	10	5.92
非金属矿采选业	Nonmetal Minerals Mining and Dressing	8	13	1.18
其他采矿业	Other Minerals Mining	2		…
制造业	Manufacturing	1139	1817	1946.66
农副食品加工业	Farm Products and By-food Processing	57	29	3.29
食品制造业	Food Production	41	20	10.36
饮料制造业	Beverage Production	28	31	10.29
烟草制品业	Tobacco Products	5	5	2.21
纺织业	Textile Industry	52	44	13.52
纺织服装、鞋、帽制造业	Garments, Shoes and Hats Production	3	1	0.09
皮革毛皮羽毛（绒）及其制品业	Leather, Furs, Down and Related Products	8	3	0.54
木材加工及木竹藤棕草制品业	Timber Processing, Bamboo, Cane, Palm, Straw Products	1	1	0.93
家具制造业	Furniture Manufacturing	2		0.34
造纸及纸制品业	Papermaking and Paper Products	60	63	22.17
印刷业、记录媒介的复制	Printing and Record Medium Reproduction	12	2	4.30
文教体育用品制造业	Cultural Educational and Sports Goods	2		
石油加工、炼焦及核燃料加工业	Petroleum, Coking and Nuclear Fuel Processing	9	5	4.09
化学原料及化学制品制造业	Raw Chemical Materials and Chemical Products	126	212	324.95
医药制造业	Medical and Pharmaceutical Products	46	41	20.31
化学纤维制造业	Chemical Fiber	1	5	58.70
橡胶制品业	Rubber Products	19	6	1.36
塑料制品业	Plastic Products	18	12	24.81
非金属矿物制品业	Nonmetal Mineral Products	303	904	779.22
黑色金属冶炼及压延加工业	Smelting and Pressing of Ferrous Metals	18	128	434.83
有色金属冶炼及压延加工业	Smelting and Pressing of Nonferrous Metals	38	28	57.76
金属制品业	Metal Products	59	21	12.92
通用设备制造业	Ordinary Equipment	56	51	11.17
专用设备制造业	Special Equipment	33	19	3.93
交通运输设备制造业	Transportation Equipment	98	157	142.89
电气机械及器材制造业	Electric Equipment and Machinery	17	12	1.22
通信设备、计算机及其他电子设备制造业	Communication, Computers and Other Electronic Equipment	8	1	0.34
仪器仪表及文化、办公用机械制造业	Instruments, Meters, Cultural and Office Machinery	11	13	0.02
工艺品及其他制造业	Handicraft and Other Production	6	3	0.04
废弃资源和废旧材料回收加工业	Recovery and Processing of Waste Resources and Materials	2		0.06
电力、燃气及水的生产和供应业	Electric power, Gas & Water Production and Supply	35	70	1531.87
电力、热力的生产和供应业	Electric power and Hot Power Production and Supply	28	70	1531.87
燃气生产和供应业	Gas Production and Supply			
水的生产和供应业	Water Production and Supply	7		
其　他	Others	73	19	16.02

Discharge and Treatment of Waste Gas of Major Surveyed Industrial Enterprises by Sector (2004)

燃料燃烧过程中废气排放量 Volume of Waste Gas in the Process of Fuel Burning	生产工艺过程中废气排放量 Volume of Waste Gas in the Process of Production	工业二氧化硫排放量(万吨) Volume of Sulphur Dioxide Discharged (10 000 ton)	工业二氧化硫去除量(万吨) Removed Volume of Sulphur Dioxide of Industry (10 000 ton)	工业烟尘排放量(万吨) Volume of Soot Discharged (10 000 ton)	工业烟尘去除量(万吨) Volume of Soot Removed (10 000 ton)	工业粉尘排放量(万吨) Volume of Dust Discharged (10 000 ton)	工业粉尘去除量(万吨) Volume of Dust Removed (10 000 ton)
2489.67	**1051.19**	**60.59**	**32.24**	**11.89**	**179.01**	**21.38**	**36.76**
38.75	7.55	1.93	1.99	0.33	1.86	0.07	0.08
17.62	6.57	1.52	0.19	0.15	0.40	0.02	
2.98	0.69	0.26	1.60	0.05	0.01	0.03	
11.33		0.11		0.11	1.26	0.02	0.08
5.92		0.02	0.20	0.02	0.18	…	…
0.90	0.29	0.02	…	…	0.01	…	
		…		…			
917.33	1029.31	25.99	10.55	5.62	24.86	21.11	36.65
3.29		0.12	…	0.03	0.04	0.01	
10.36		0.14	0.13	0.10	0.37	…	
10.29		0.19	0.10	0.05	0.08	…	
2.21		0.03	0.06	0.03	0.06	…	…
13.52		0.28	0.24	0.12	0.29	0.01	
0.09		…	…	…	…	…	
0.52	0.02	0.01	0.01	0.01	0.01	…	
0.93		0.02		…	0.06	…	
	0.34					…	…
22.17		0.55	0.07	0.17	0.36	…	
4.22	0.08	…		…			
		…		…			
0.69	3.40	0.04	0.01	0.01	0.05	…	0.02
160.83	164.12	2.72	2.93	0.99	2.41	0.31	0.95
20.30		0.27	0.39	0.08	1.30	…	…
53.30	5.40	2.06		0.18	11.37		
1.23	0.13	0.01	0.01	0.01	0.03	…	
0.57	24.24	0.02		0.01	…	…	
457.80	321.42	10.59	5.11	3.64	7.19	18.78	28.05
116.97	317.86	8.55	1.21	0.08	0.32	1.86	7.46
10.95	46.81	0.06	0.18	0.02	0.39	0.05	0.08
5.78	7.14	0.10	…	0.02	0.04	0.06	0.01
6.28	4.89	0.05	0.02	0.03	0.03	0.01	0.01
1.12	2.81	0.01	…	…	…	…	…
13.03	129.85	0.14	0.07	0.04	0.45	0.01	0.05
0.70	0.52	…	…	…	…	…	…
0.07	0.27	…		…	…	0.01	…
0.02		…		…	…		
0.03	0.01	…		…	…		
0.06		…		…			
1531.73	0.14	32.52	19.42	5.89	152.29	0.09	…
1531.73	0.14	32.52	19.42	5.89	152.29	0.09	…
1.86	14.19	0.14	0.28	0.04	…	0.12	0.03

8—13 重点调查工业分行业固体废物产生及处理利用情况（2004年）

行　业	Sector	汇总工业企业数（个） Number of Industrial Enterprises (unit)	工业固体废物产生量(万吨) Volume of Industrial Solid Waste Produced (10 000 tons)
总　计	**Total**	**1368**	**1353.31**
采矿业	Mining and Quarrying	121	402.36
煤炭开采和洗选业	Coal Mining and Dressing	94	380.46
石油和天然气开采业	Petroleum and Natural Gas Extraction	5	0.03
黑色金属矿采选业	Ferrous Metals Mining and Dressing	9	12.67
有色金属矿采选业	Nonferrous Metals Mining and Dressing	3	8.32
非金属矿采选业	Nonmetal Minerals Mining and Dressing	8	0.63
其他采矿业	Other Minerals Mining	2	0.25
制造业	Manufacturing	1139	541.70
农副食品加工业	Farm Products and By-food Processing	57	0.86
食品制造业	Food Production	41	4.24
饮料制造业	Beverage Production	28	8.35
烟草制品业	Tobacco Products	5	0.59
纺织业	Textile Industry	52	3.40
纺织服装、鞋、帽制造业	Garments, Shoes and Hats Production	3	0.02
皮革毛皮羽毛（绒）及其制品业	Leather, Furs, Down and Related Products	8	0.10
木材加工及木竹藤棕草制品业	Timber Processing, Bamboo, Cane, Palm, Straw Products	1	0.26
家具制造业	Furniture Manufacturing	2	
造纸及纸制品业	Papermaking and Paper Products	60	3.52
印刷业、记录媒介的复制	Printing and Record Medium Reproduction	12	0.03
文教体育用品制造业	Cultural Educational and Sports Goods	2	
石油加工、炼焦及核燃料加工业	Petroleum, Coking and Nuclear Fuel Processing	9	0.05
化学原料及化学制品制造业	Raw Chemical Materials and Chemical Products	126	188.46
医药制造业	Medical and Pharmaceutical Products	46	6.38
化学纤维制造业	Chemical Fiber	1	13.20
橡胶制品业	Rubber Products	19	0.13
塑料制品业	Plastic Products	18	0.11
非金属矿物制品业	Nonmetal Mineral Products	303	61.26
黑色金属冶炼及压延加工业	Smelting and Pressing of Ferrous Metals	18	179.70
有色金属冶炼及压延加工业	Smelting and Pressing of Nonferrous Metals	38	52.82
金属制品业	Metal Products	59	0.92
通用设备制造业	Ordinary Equipment	56	6.96
专用设备制造业	Special Equipment	33	0.50
交通运输设备制造业	Transportation Equipment	98	7.81
电气机械及器材制造业	Electric Equipment and Machinery	17	0.47
通信设备、计算机及其他电子设备制造业	Communication, Computers and Other Electronic Equipment	8	1.47
仪器仪表及文化、办公用机械制造业	Instruments, Meters, Cultural and Office Machinery	11	0.05
工艺品及其他制造业	Handicraft and Other Production	6	0.02
废弃资源和废旧材料回收加工业	Recovery and Processing of Waste Resources and Materials	2	0.02
电力、燃气及水的生产和供应业	Electric power, Gas & Water Production and Supply	35	406.90
电力、热力的生产和供应业	Electric power and Hot Power Production and Supply	28	406.90
燃气生产和供应业	Gas Production and Supply		
水的生产和供应业	Water Production and Supply	7	
其　他	Others	73	2.35

Discharge, Treatment and Utilization of Solid Wastes of Major Surveyed Industrial Enterprises by Sector (2004)

#危险废物产生量 Dangerous Wastes	工业固体废物综合利用量(万吨) Volume of Industrial Solid Wastes Utilized (10 000 tons)	工业固体废物贮存量(万吨) Volume of Industrial Solid Wastes Accumulated (10 000 tons)	工业固体废物处置量(万吨) Volume of Industrial Solid Wastes Treated (10 000 tons)	工业固体废物排放量(万吨) Volume of Industrial Solid Wastes Discharged (10 000 tons)	“三废”综合利用产品产值(万元) Output Value of Products Made from Comprehensive Utilization of Waste Water, Waste Gas and of Solid Wastes (10 000 yuan)
42.69	**1006.32**	**240.88**	**51.35**	**108.15**	**79932**
0.02	310.53	39.52	13.51	44.53	10446
	300.65	34.82	8.12	42.59	8954
	0.03				74
	0.89	4.60	5.39	1.79	113
0.02	8.24			0.08	338
	0.57			0.07	967
	0.15	0.10			
42.61	387.87	106.32	36.78	45.53	53896
	0.55	0.02	0.08	0.21	225
	2.96		1.24	0.04	43
	7.17		0.02	1.16	1280
	0.59				121
	2.79		0.19	0.42	123
	0.02				
	0.08	0.02			
	0.26				155
	3.32	0.10	0.06	0.03	540
	0.03				3
	0.04				24
41.14	91.79	56.44	17.74	23.91	15759
0.01	5.46	0.01	0.46	0.46	605
1.09	13.05		0.14		
	0.09	0.03		0.01	345
0.04	0.02		0.10		15
	92.60	0.59	0.10	1.35	26247
0.05	149.64	0.77	14.33	14.96	1572
	2.27	48.20	0.07	2.28	835
0.02	0.72		0.07	0.13	81
0.01	6.05	0.10	0.61	0.20	1087
0.01	0.21		0.29		292
0.24	6.33	0.04	1.25	0.23	4164
	0.36		0.01	0.09	24
	1.42			0.05	353
	0.04				1
			0.02		2
	0.01				
0.01	305.71	95.04	0.89	18.08	11067
0.01	305.71	95.04	0.89	18.08	11047
					20
0.05	2.21		0.16	0.01	4523

8－14 重点调查工业分行业废水排放及处理情况（2004年）
Discharge and Treatment of Waste Water of Major Surveyed Industrial Enterprises by Sector (2004)

单位：万吨 (10 000 tons)

行业	Sector	汇总工业企业数（个） Number of Industrial Enterprises (unit)	工业废水排放总量 Total Discharged Volume of Industrial Waste Water	#工业废水排放达标量 Up to Discharge Standards	废水治理设施数（套） Number of Facilities for Treatment of Waste Water (set)
总计	Total	1368	76691.02	73041.56	1205
采矿业	Mining and Quarrying	121	4608.72	4400.98	108
煤炭开采和洗选业	Coal Mining and Dressing	94	3473.08	3426.73	86
石油和天然气开采业	Petroleum and Natural Gas Extraction	5	70.81	68.78	4
黑色金属矿采选业	Ferrous Metals Mining and Dressing	9	373.91	265.12	5
有色金属矿采选业	Nonferrous Metals Mining and Dressing	3	658.50	608.00	6
非金属矿采选业	Nonmetal Minerals Mining and Dressing	8	31.58	31.57	7
其他采矿业	Other Minerals Mining	2	0.84	0.78	
制造业	Manufacturing	1139	54228.73	51162.23	979
农副食品加工业	Farm Products and By-food Processing	57	3041.63	2969.20	42
食品制造业	Food Production	41	2267.84	2038.20	21
饮料制造业	Beverage Production	28	454.87	420.39	21
烟草制品业	Tobacco Products	5	92.13	92.13	3
纺织业	Textile Industry	52	1111.37	837.51	41
纺织服装、鞋、帽制造业	Garments, Shoes and Hats Production	3	29.11	29.11	3
皮革毛皮羽毛（绒）及其制品业	Leather, Furs, Down and Related Products	8	240.85	210.70	5
木材加工及木竹藤棕草制品业	Timber Processing, Bamboo, Cane, Palm, Straw Products	1	8.40	8.40	2
家具制造业	Furniture Manufacturing	2	0.32		
造纸及纸制品业	Papermaking and Paper Products	60	5454.41	5063.83	59
印刷业、记录媒介的复制	Printing and Record Medium Reproduction	12	12.26	10.26	1
文教体育用品制造业	Cultural Educational and Sports Goods	2	2.02	0.19	2
石油加工、炼焦及核燃料加工业	Petroleum, Coking and Nuclear Fuel Processing	9	68.61	68.61	12
化学原料及化学制品制造业	Raw Chemical Materials and Chemical Products	126	16135.94	15139.46	167
医药制造业	Medical and Pharmaceutical Products	46	2612.12	2583.85	83
化学纤维制造业	Chemical Fiber	1	2319.90	2273.50	1
橡胶制品业	Rubber Products	19	49.05	48.94	4
塑料制品业	Plastic Products	18	426.95	386.02	10
非金属矿物制品业	Nonmetal Mineral Products	303	2875.06	2561.75	130
黑色金属冶炼及压延加工业	Smelting and Pressing of Ferrous Metals	18	6982.98	6615.23	27
有色金属冶炼及压延加工业	Smelting and Pressing of Nonferrous Metals	38	2425.51	2382.57	43
金属制品业	Metal Products	59	527.47	526.45	45
通用设备制造业	Ordinary Equipment	56	1388.29	1360.66	57
专用设备制造业	Special Equipment	33	164.79	164.45	38
交通运输设备制造业	Transportation Equipment	98	4512.95	4399.44	123
电气机械及器材制造业	Electric Equipment and Machinery	17	432.61	432.14	12
通信设备、计算机及其他电子设备制造业	Communication, Computers and Other Electronic Equipment	8	487.97	437.97	6
仪器仪表及文化、办公用机械制造业	Instruments, Meters, Cultural and Office Machinery	11	82.80	80.80	13
工艺品及其他制造业	Handicraft and Other Production	6	19.33	19.28	5
废弃资源和废旧材料回收加工业	Recovery and Processing of Waste Resources and Materials	2	1.19	1.19	3
电力、燃气及水的生产和供应业	Electric power, Gas & Water Production and Supply	35	16926.88	16568.77	38
电力、热力的生产和供应业	Electric power and Hot Power Production and Supply	28	15813.78	15465.67	35
燃气生产和供应业	Gas Production and Supply				
水的生产和供应业	Water Production and Supply	7	1113.10	1103.10	3
其他	Others	73	926.69	909.58	80

8－15 工业污染治理项目及投资情况（2003－2004年）
Investment in Anti-industrial Pollution Projects (2003-2004)

项　　目	Item	2003	2004
汇总工业企业数（个）	**Number of Industrial Enterprises (unit)**	**140**	**140**
施工项目数（个）	**Projects under Construction (unit)**	**183**	**178**
治理废水	Treatment of Waste Water	95	90
治理废气	Treatment of Waste Gas	75	74
治理固体废物	Treatment of Solid Wastes	3	5
治理噪声	Treatment of Noise Pollution	7	5
治理其他	Treatment of Other Pollution	3	4
资金来源合计（万元）	**Total Funds (10 000 yuan)**	**14192**	**28626**
国家预算内资金	National Budgetary Assets	40	
环境保护补助资金	Subsidies for Environmental Protection	1395	3852
环保贷款	Loans for Environmental Protection	354	129
其　他	Others	12403	24645
资金使用合计（万元）	**Total Expenditures (10 000 yuan)**	**14192**	**28626**
治理废水	Treatment of Waste Water	7908	13408
治理废气	Treatment of Waste Gas	6154	14129
治理固体废物	Treatment of Solid Wastes	21	1001
治理噪声	Treatment of Noise Pollution	97	53
治理其他	Treatment of Other Pollution	12	35
本年竣工项目数（个）	**Number of Projects Completed (unit)**	**172**	**165**
当年竣工项目新增设计处理利用“三废”能力	**Newly Designed Treatment and Utilization Capacity of Waste Water, Waste Gas & Solid Wastes of Completed Projects in the Year**		
废水(吨/日)	Waste Water (ton/day)	33988	52848
废气(万标立方米/时)	Waste Gas (10 000 cu.m/hour)	35.02	41.28
固体废物(吨/日)	Solid Wastes (ton/day)	118	166

8－16 生活污染物排放情况（2003－2004年）
Discharge of Pollutants from Daily Life (2003-2004)

项　　目	Item	2003	2004
生活污水排放量（万吨）	Volume of Waste Water Discharged from Daily Life (10 000 tons)	51988	52487
生活污水中化学需氧量排放量（吨）	Absorption of Oxygen by Waste Water from Daily Life (ton)	150590	153298
生活二氧化硫排放量（吨）	Discharge of Sulfur Dioxide from Daily Life (ton)	135339	154153
生活烟尘排放量（吨）	Discharge of Dust from Daily Life (ton)	73806	78640

8－17 环境污染与破坏事故情况（2003－2004年）
Pollution Accidents (2003-2004)

项　　目	Item	2003	2004
环境污染与破坏事故次数（次）	**Number of Pollution Accidents (time)**	**6**	**4**
按事故类型分（次）	**Pollution Accidents by Type (time)**		
水污染	Water Pollution	4	1
大气污染	Air Pollution	2	2
固体废物污染	Solid Waste Pollution		1
噪声与振动危害	Noises and Vibration Pollution		
其　他	Others		
污染直接经济损失（万元）	**Losses Converted into Cash (10 000 yuan)**	**18.6**	**2.2**
污染事故赔、罚款总额（万元）	**Amount of Reparations and Fines (10 000 yuan)**	**1.3**	**10.0**

主要统计指标解释

供水综合生产能力 指按供水设施取水、净化、送水、出厂输水干管等环节设计能力计算的综合生产能力。包括在原设计能力基础上，经挖、革、改增加的生产能力。计算时，以四个环节中最薄弱的环节为主确定能力。

供水管道长度 指从送水泵到用户水表之间所有管道的长度。不包括新安装尚未使用的管道。

供水总量 指报告期供水企业(单位)供出的全部水量。包括有效供水量和漏损水量。

生活用水量 包括公共服务用水和居民家庭用水。公共服务用水指为城市社会公共生活服务的用水。包括行政事业单位、部队营区和公共设施服务、社会服务业、批发零售贸易业、旅馆饮食业及其他公共服务业等单位用水。居民家庭用水指城市范围内所有居民家庭的日常生活用水。包括城市居民、农民家庭、公共供水站用水。

城市人口用水普及率 指城市用水人口数与城市人口总数之比。计算公式为：

用水普及率=（城市用水人口数/城市人口数）×100%

全年供气总量 指全年燃气企业(单位)向用户供应的燃气数量，包括销售量和损失量。

城市用气普及率 指报告期末使用燃气的城市人口数与城市人口总数的比率。计算公式为：

用气普及率=城市用气人口数/城市人口总数×100%

道路长度 指年末道路长度和与道路相通的广场、桥梁、隧道的长度，按车行道中心线计算。在统计时只统计路面宽度在3.5米(含3.5米)以上的各种铺装道路，包括开放型工业区和住宅区道路在内。

城市桥梁 指为跨越天然或人工障碍物而修建的构筑物。包括跨河桥、立交桥、人行天桥以及人行地下通道等。包括永久性桥和半永久性桥。

城市排水管道长度 指所有排水总管、干管、支管、检查井及连接井进出口等长度之和。

年末运营车数 指年末公交企业(单位)用于运营业务的全部车辆数。以企业(单位)固定资产台帐中已投入运营的车辆数为准。

城市园林绿地面积 指报告期末用作园林和绿化的各种绿地面积。包括公共绿地、居住区绿地、单位附属绿地、防护绿地、生产绿地、道路绿地和风景林地面积。不包括：

1. 屋顶绿化、垂直绿化、阳台绿化和室内绿化。
2. 以物质生产为主的林地、耕地、牧草地、果园和竹园等。
3. 城市总体规划中不列入绿地的水域。

公共绿地 指向公众开放的市级、区级、居住区级各类公园、街旁游园，包括其范围内的水域。其中居住区级公园应不小于1万平方米，街旁游园的宽度不小于8米，面积不小于400平方米。

工业废水排放量 指经过企业厂区所有排放口排到企业外部的工业废水量。包括生产废水、外排的直接冷却水、超标排放的矿井地下水和与工业废水混排的厂区生活污水，不包括外排的间接冷却水（清污不分流的间接冷却水应计算在内）。

工业废水排放达标量 指报告期内废水中各项污染物指标都达到国家或地方排放标准的外排工业废水量，

包括未经处理外排达标的，经废水处理设施处理后达标排放的，以及经污水处理厂处理后达标排放的。

工业废气排放量 指企业厂区内燃料燃烧和生产工艺过程中产生的各种排入空气的含有污染物的气体的总量，按标准状态（273K，101325Pa）计算。

工业二氧化硫排放量 指报告期内企业在燃料燃烧和生产工艺过程中排入大气的SO_2总量，计算公式为：

工业SO_2排放量=燃料燃烧过程中SO_2排放量+生产工艺过程中SO_2排放量

工业烟尘排放量 指企业厂区内的燃料燃烧产生的烟气中夹带的颗粒物数量。

工业粉尘排放量 指企业在生产工艺过程中排放的能在空气中悬浮一定时间的固体颗粒物排放量。如钢铁企业的耐火材料粉尘、焦化企业的筛焦系统粉尘、烧结机的粉尘、石灰窑的粉尘、建材企业的水泥粉尘等。不包括电厂排入大气的烟尘。

工业固体废物产生量 指企业在生产过程中产生的固体状、半固体状和高浓度液体状废弃物的总量，包括危险废物、冶炼废渣、粉煤灰、炉渣、煤矸石、尾矿、放射性废物和其他废物等；不包括矿山开采的剥离废石和掘进废石（煤矸石和呈酸性或碱性的废石除外）。酸性或碱性废石是指采掘的废石其流经水、雨淋水的ＰＨ值小于4或ＰＨ值大于10.5者。

工业固体废物综合利用量 指通过回收、加工、循环、交换等方式，从固体废物中提取或者使其转化为可以利用的资源、能源和其他原材料的固体废物量（包括当年利用往年的工业固体废物累计贮存量），如用作农业肥料、生产建筑材料、筑路等。综合利用量由原产生固体废物的单位统计。

工业固体废物贮存量 指以综合利用或处置为目的，将固体废物暂时贮存或堆存在专设的贮存设施或专设的集中堆存场所内的数量。专设的固体废物贮存场所或贮存设施必须有防扩散、防流失、防渗漏、防止污染大气、水体的措施。

工业固体废物处置量 指将固体废物焚烧或者最终置于符合环境保护规定要求的场所，并不再回取的工业固体废物量（包括当年处置往年的工业固体废物累计贮存量）。处置方法有填埋（其中危险废物应安全填埋）、焚烧、专业贮存场（库）封场处理、深层灌注、回填矿井等。

工业固体废物排放量 指将所产生的固体废物排到固体废物污染防治设施、场所以外的数量，不包括矿山开采的剥离废石和掘进废石（煤矸石和呈酸性或碱性的废石除外）。

"三废"综合利用产品产值 指利用"三废"（废液、废气、废渣）作为主要原料生产的产品产值（现行价），已经销售或准备销售的应计算产品产值，留作生产上自用的不应计算产品产值。

城镇生活污水排放量 指城镇居民每年排放的生活污水。用人均系数法测算。测算公式为：

城镇生活污水排放量=城镇生活污水排放系数×市镇非农业人口×365

生活及其他烟尘排放量 指除工业生产活动以外的所有社会、经济活动及公共设施的经营活动中燃烧所排放的烟尘纯重量。以生活及其他煤炭消费量为基础进行测算。

环境污染与破坏事故 指由于违反环境保护法规的经济、社会活动与行为，以及意外艺术的影响或不可抗拒的自然灾害等原因，致使环境受到污染，国家重点保护的野生动物、植物、自然保护区受到破坏，人体健康受到危害，社会经济和人民财产受到损失，造成不良社会影响的突发性事件。

Explanatory Notes on Main Statistical Indicators

Production Capacity of Water Supply refers to the designed comprehensive production capacity of water facilities, covering the 4 links of water collection, purification, conveyance, and outflow through trunk pipelines. Increase capacity through transformation and innovation projects is included as well. The capacity is determined mainly on the weakest of the above-mentioned 4 links.

Length of Water Supply Pipelines at the Year-end refers to the total length of all the pipelines between the water pumps and the user's water meters, excluding pipelines newly installed but not used yet.

Annual Volume of Water Supply refers to the total volume of water supplied by water-works (units) during the reference period, including both the effective water supply and loss during the water supply.

Consumption of Water for Residential Use refers to the water consumption of households for daily life and the water consumption of public service facilities. The latter refers to water consumption for urban public services, including the consumption of government agencies and public institutions, military barracks, public facilities, wholesale and retail outlets, restaurants, hotels, and other units providing public services. Household water consumption refers to consumption of water for daily life of all households in the boundary of cities, including households of urban residents and farmers, and public water supply stations.

Percentage of Urban Population with Access to Tap Water refers to the ratio of the urban population with access to tap water to the total urban population. The formula is:

Percentage of Population with access to Tap Water = Urban Population with Access to Tap Water / Urban Population ×100%

Volume of Gas Supply refers to the total volume of gas provided to users by gas-producing enterprises (units) in a year, including the volume sold and the volume lost.

Percentage of Urban Population with Access to Gas refers to the ratio of the urban population with access to gas to the total urban population at the end of the reference period. The formula is:

Percentage of population with access to gas = (Urban population with access to gas / Urban population) ×100%

Length of Paved Roads at the Year-end refers to the length of roads with paved surface including squares bridges and tunnels connected with roads by the end of the year. Length of the roads is measured by the central lines for vehicles for paved roads with a width of 3.5 meters and over, including roads in open-ended factory compounds and residential quarters.

Urban Bridges refer to bridges built to cross over natural or man-made barriers, including bridges over rivers, overpasses for traffic and for pedestrian, underpasses for pedestrian, etc. Both permanent and semi-permanent bridges are included.

Length of Urban Sewage Pipes refers to the total length of general drainage, trunks, branch and inspection wells, connection wells, inlets and outlets, etc.

Number of Vehicles under Operation at the Year-end refers to the total number of vehicles under operation by public transport enterprises (units) at year-end, based on the records of operational vehicles by the enterprises (units).

Area of Urban Gardens and Green Areas refers to the total area occupied for green projects at the end of the reference period, including public green land, green land in residential quarters, green land attached to institutions, protection green land, production green land, roadside green land and forest in scenic spots. It does not include the following:

(1) Greenery and plants on roofs, balconies, indoors and vertical green areas;

(2) Forest, cultivated land, grassland, orchards and bamboo grooves that are for production purpose; and

(3) Water areas that are not included in urban master plan as green land.

Public Green Area refers to green areas open to the public such as municipal, community and neighborhood parks and roadside parks, including waters within parks. Neighborhood parks should occupy an area larger than 10,000 square meters, and the width of roadside parks should occupy an area larger than 400 square meters, with a width of more that 8 meters.

Volume of Industrial Waste Water Discharged refers to the volume of industrial waste water discharged, through all outlets, to the outside of industrial enterprises, including waste water produced, direct - cooling water, underground water from mines that does not meet the standard of discharge, and the domestic sewage mixed up with industrial waste water when discharged, but excluding discharged indirect - cooling water.

Volume of Waste Water up to the Standard for Discharge refers to the volume of discharged industrial wastewater that, with or without treatment, has come up to the national or local standards for discharge.

Industrial Waste Air Emission refers to discharge into atmosphere of waste air containing pollutants generated from fuel burning and production process in enterprises within a given period of time. It is converted into standard (273K, 101325Pa).

Industrial SO_2 Emission refers to volume of sulphur dioxide emission from fuel burning and production process in premises of enterprises for a given period of time. Its calculation formula is:

Industrial SO_2 Emission = SO_2 Emission from fuel burning + SO_2 Emission from production process

Industrial Soot Emission refers to volume of soot in smoke emitted in process of fuel burning in premises of enterprises.

Industrial Dust Emission refers to volume of dust emitted by production process of enterprises and suspended in the air for a given period of time, including dust from refractory material of iron and steel works, dust from coke-screening systems and sintering machines of coke plants, dust from lime kilns and dust from cement production in building material enterprises, but excluding soot and dust emitted from power plants.

Volume of Industrial Solid Wastes Produced refers to the total volume of solid, semi-solid or high-concentration liquid residue produced by industrial enterprises in their production process, including dangerous wastes, residues from melting, slag, powdered coal ash, gangue, chemical residues, tailings, radioactive residues and other residues, but excluding stripped or dug stones in mining (except gangue and acid or alkali stones which are stones washed or soaked by water with a PH value smaller than 4 or larger than 10.5).

Volume of Industrial Solid Wastes Utilized in a Comprehensive Way refers to the volume of solid wastes from which useful materials can be extracted or which can be changed to be utilizable resources, energy or other materials, including the volume of industrial solid wastes stored up in the previous years and utilized in the current year, such as the solid wastes utilized as fertilizers, building materials, for making roads or for other purpose. Statistical date on utilization of industrial solid wastes is collected by solid wastes producing units.

Volume of Industrial Solid Wastes Stored up refers to the volume of industrial solid wastes temporarily stored up or piled with special facilities or piled in the special sites for the purpose of utilization or treatment in future. The special facilities or special sites for storing up solid wastes should have the measures against spreading or being washed away to other places, permeating the soil or causing air pollution or water contamination.

Volume of Industrial Solid Wastes Treated refers to solid wastes disposed of in a non-recoverable place that meet the requirement of environmental protection, such as burying (The dangerous wastes should be buried safely), burning, piling in designated sites, pouring water into the deep strata, filling of old mines, etc. (including treatment of solid wastes piled up in the previous years).

Volume of Industrial Solid Wastes Discharged refers to the volume of industrial solid wastes produced and discharged at the places outside the special facilities or special sites for preventing against pollution, excluding stripped or dug stones in mining (except gangue and acid or alkali waste stones).

Output Value of Products Made from Utilization of Waste Gas, Waste Water and Industrial Solid Wastes refers to the value of products (calculated at current prices) made by industrial enterprises using recovered waste water, waste gas or solid wastes as main raw materials. Only the value of the products, which have been sold or are ready, to be sold should be included. The value of the products, which will be used in the production of the enterprises, should not be included.

Urban Consumption Waste Water Discharge refers to annual discharge of consumption waste water by urban households. Its calculation formula is:

Discharge = Discharge of Consumption Wastewater by Urban Households × Urban Non-agricultural Population × 365

Soot Emission by Consumption and Others refers to net volume of soot emitted by fuel burning from all social and economic activities and operation of public facilities other than industrial activities. It is calculated on the basis of coal consumption by households and others.

Accidents of Environment Pollution and Destruction refer to sudden accidents, due to economic and social behavior or activities in contrast with environment protection legislation, unexpected factors or irresistible natural disasters, that cause the pollution of environment, the destruction of natural protection zones, wild plants and animals, the danger to the health of people, and the loss in the property of the society and people.

九 要素市场
MARKETS OF KEY FACTORS

简要说明　Brief Introduction

本章资料中的国有土地使用权出让与划拨、城市房产市场交易情况由市统计局固定资产投资处根据市国土资源和房屋管理局资料整理提供，亿元以上商品市场由市统计局贸易外经处提供，技术市场由市统计局社会科技处根据市科学技术委员会资料整理提供，人才市场、劳动力市场和证券市场情况由市统计局综合处根据市人才交流服务中心、市就业服务管理局和重庆证监局资料整理编辑。

货币流通、保险业务和有价证券的相关资料详见第十六章金融。

Data on transaction and allotment of right of use for state-owned land, real estate markets in urban areas are provided by Division of Statistics of Investment in Fixed Assets, Municipal Bureau of Statistics according to data of Municipal Administration of Land, Resources and Buildings. Commodity markets with transaction value over 100 million yuan are provided by Division of Trade and External Economic Relations Statistics, Municipal Bureau of Statistics. Transactions of technology exchanges are provided by Division of Social and Technology Statistics, Municipal Bureau of Statistics with data from Municipal Scientific and Technological Committee. Markets of human resources, Labors and securities are edited by Division of Comprehensive Statistics, Municipal Bureau of Statistics with data from Municipal Human Resource Exchanges Service Center, Municipal Administration of Employment Services and from China Securities Regulatory Commission Chongqing Bureau.

Data on currency, insurance and security are detailed in Chapter 16 Financial Statistics.

9－1 国有土地使用权出让与划拨情况（2003－2004年）
Transactions and Allotment of Right of Use for State-owned Land (2003-2004)

指　　标	Item	2003	2004
土地使用权出让	**Transaction of Right of Use for State-owned Land**		
地块（宗）	Land Site (case)	3547	2857
面积（公顷）	Land Area (hectare)	3548.40	4295.07
出让金总额（万元）	Total Value of Transaction (10 000 yuan)	492972.55	715145.39
土地使用权划拨	**Allotment of Right of Use for State-owned Land**		
地块（宗）	Land Site (case)	844	791
面积（公顷）	Land Area (hectare)	1387.56	2021.01

9－2 城市房产市场交易情况（2003－2004年）
Real Estate Markets in Urban Areas (2003-2004)

指　　标	Item	2003	2004
房产转让	**Housing Transactions**		
成交面积（万平方米）	Area (10 000 sq.m)	2417.17	2813.28
#住宅	Residential Buildings	2082.93	2433.78
#商品房	Commercial Buildings	1645.26	1918.75
存量房	Outstock Buildings	771.91	894.53
成交金额（亿元）	Amount (100 million yuan)	351.16	440.68
#住宅	Residential Buildings	267.28	343.51
#商品房	Commercial Buildings	284.84	356.65
存量房	Outstock Buildings	66.32	84.03
房产抵押	**Housing Mortgage**		
面积（万平方米）	Area (10 000 sq.m)	3269.44	4426.47
担保金额（亿元）	Amount Assured (100 million yuan)	424.30	578.48

注：本表为都市发达经济圈九区的数据。

Note: The data refers to metropolitan advanced economic sphere (9 districts).

9—3 亿元以上商品市场交易情况（2003—2004年）
Transaction of Commodity Markets with Transaction Value over 100 Million Yuan (2003-2004)

单位：万元 (10 000 yuan)

指标	Item	摊位数量（个） Number of Stands (unit)		总成交额 Total Volume of Transaction		#零售额 Retail Trade	
		2003	2004	2003	2004	2003	2004
合　计	**Total**	**45171**	**48613**	**4135749**	**6323735**	**699533**	**1096521**
食品、饮料、烟酒类	Food, Beverages, Tobacco and Liquor	13192	13974	1027402	1391743	233968	312628
#粮油果菜类	Grains, Oil, Fruits and Vegetables	7332	7805	443370	511876	125274	147950
服装鞋帽、针、纺织品类	Clothing, Shoes, Hats and Textiles	10809	13385	703389	994252	79505	178464
化妆品类	Cosmetics	294	380	140642	79867	6563	9206
日用品类	Articles for Daily Use	3188	2567	141017	206059	33642	59965
五金电料类	Hardwear and Electrical Materials	2832	2574	182014	179748	13449	9588
体育、娱乐用品类	Sports and Recreation Articles	17	142	374	2855	124	1238
书报杂志类	Newspapers and Magazines	3	5	5	95	1	37
电子出版物及音像制品类	E-journal and Video Products	91	99	1480	842	1421	683
家用电器和音像制品类	Household Appliances and Video Products	327	501	14142	18111	5704	3350
中西药品类	Traditional Chinese and Western Medicines	91	111	3117	7176	1564	3496
#中草药及中成药类	Traditional Chinese Medicines	29	33	227	624	126	230
文化办公用品类	Cultural and Official Goods	706	621	81478	35827	20991	16193
家具类	Furniture	785	1045	255664	323838	113847	138493
通讯器材类	Communication Appliances		148		38448		14591
煤炭及制品类	Coal and Related Products						
木材及制品类	Wood and Wooden Products	764	814	147911	209933	18991	20643
化工材料及制品类	Raw Chemical Materials	239	244	39044	53380	4770	5576
金属材料类	Metal Materials	1873	2849	510767	1463544	10283	14580
建筑及装潢材料类	Buildings and Decoration Materials	1683	2430	178075	385652	48266	128993
机电产品及设备类	Mechanical and Electrical Products	1845	1213	436052	514437	27994	65268
#农机类	Agricultural Machinery		3		251		77
汽车类	Automobile	400	460	290298	327918	7000	8485
其他类	Others	6432	5511	273176	417930	78450	113529
#旧货类	Old Goods	207		8445			

9-4 技术市场交易情况（2003-2004年）
Transactions of Technology Exchanges (2003-2004)

单位：项、万元 (item, 10 000 yuan)

指标	Item	技术买方 Purchases of Technology 项数 Number 2003	2004	金额 Value 2003	2004	技术卖方 Sales of Technology 项数 Number 2003	2004	金额 Value 2003	2004
总计	**Total**	**1925**	**1768**	**555083**	**596186**	**1925**	**1768**	**555083**	**596186**
#企业	Industrial Enterprises	1620	1524	480047	555853	301	264	395597	404527
科研机构	Research Institutions	146	120	8760	13065	1329	1029	60717	22444
大中专院校	Higher Education Institutions and Secondary Schools					228	330	64409	62994
技术贸易机构	Technical Business Institutions	1		260		32	73	8637	2068
个体私营	Individual and Private	14	5	6839	993	14	2	3842	14050

9-5 人才市场人才流动情况（2003-2004年）
Markets of Human Resources and Exchanges (2003-2004)

指标	Item	2003	2004
人才流动机构（个）	Number of Agencies of Human Resource Exchanges (unit)	83	96
政府人事部门所属	Belong to Official Departments	47	36
非政府人事部门所属	Belong to Un-official Departments	36	60
人才市场（个）	Number of Human Resource Markets (unit)	37	31
举办人才交流会（次）	Number of Assemblies of Human Resource Exchangeds (time)	609	664
登记要求流动人数（人）	Number of Registered Persons Desiring Exchanges (person)	484275	321951
参加人才交流会人数（人）	Number of Persons Attended the Assemblies (person)	440250	292683
参加人才交流会的招聘单位（个）	Number of Units Attended in Assemblies of Human Resource Exchanges for Job Applications (unit)	32722	29389
全年接收人事档案数量（份）	Number of Personal Files Received (copy)	29202	19312
现存人事档案总量（份）	Number of Personal Files Remained (copy)	103421	128372
当年流动人员职称评定（人）	Professional Titles of Exchanging Persons in Current Year (person)	2163	2704
评定高级职称人数	Senior Titles	120	168
评定中级职称人数	Medium Titles	655	814
评定初级职称人数	Junior Titles	1388	1722

注：本表指标除人才流动机构为全市口径，其余指标均为人事部门口径。

Note: Indices of this table refer to personnel departments except that agencies of human resource exchanges refer to Chongqing total.

9－6 劳动力市场职业介绍情况（2003－2004年）
Career Service of Labor Markets (2003-2004)

单位：人 (person)

指　　标	Item	2003	2004
年末职业介绍机构个数（个）	**Number of Career Service Agencies (unit)**	**281**	**303**
#劳动保障部门办	Run by Official Labor Securities	115	128
#县（区）及以上	Counties (districts) and above	43	47
登记招聘人数	**Number of Registered Job Applications**	**303734**	**291960**
登记求职人数	**Number of Registered Job-seekers**	**323736**	**304001**
#女性	Female	134710	148281
#下岗职工	Laid-off Workers	36036	24044
#失业人员	Unemployees	164474	185705
#获得职业资格人员	Persons with Certificates	55302	50533
职业指导人数	**Number of Person-times of Vocational Guidance**	**213082**	**272466**
介绍成功人数	**Number of Persons Employed**	**160725**	**193141**
#女性	Female	82964	95150
#下岗职工	Laid-off Workers	23441	14819
#失业人员	Unemployees	94603	113091
#获得职业资格人员	Persons with Certificates	35698	35655

9－7 证券市场基本情况（2003－2004年）
General Statistics on Security Markets (2003-2004)

指　　标	Item	2003	2004
境内上市公司数（A、B股）（家）	Number of Listed Companies (A and B Shares) in Mainland	27	29
境内上市外资股（B股）（家）	Number of Listed Companies of Foreign Fund (B Shares) in Mainland	2	2
境外上市公司数（H股）（家）	Number of Listed Companies (H Shares) Overseas	2	2
股票发行量（万股）	Issued Amount of Shares (10 000 shares)	3275	22285
股票总发行股本（万股）	Total Issued Capital of Shares (10 000 shares)	709678	832125
#流通股本	Negotiable Capital	266484	321809
股票市价总值（亿元）	Total Market Capitalization of Shares (100 million yuan)	580.67	402.26
#股票流通市值	Negotiable Market Capitalization	207.91	148.36
国债发行额（亿元）	T-bonds Issued Volume (100 million yuan)	34.12	19.67
企业债发行额（亿元）	Enterprise Bonds Issued Volume (100 million yuan)		
股票筹资额（亿元）	Raised Capital of Shares (100 million yuan)	3.74	15.65
投资者开户数（万户）	Total Investors (10 000 accounts)	85.62	91.95
期货总成交额（亿元）	Total Future Turnover (100 million yuan)	2765.06	3179.72

注：股票发行量、总发行股本、市价总值和筹资额均不含H股。

Note: Issued amount, total issued capital, total market capitalization and raised capital of shares don't include H share.

十 农业和农村经济

AGRICULTURE AND RURAL ECONOMY

简要说明　Brief Introduction

本章反映我市农业生产和农村经济的基本情况，内容主要包括农村基本情况、农业生产条件与生产情况、农作物播种面积、农林牧渔产品产量、耕地、农林牧渔业产值、农业商品产值和商品率、乡镇企业等方面的统计资料。

本章资料由市农村社会经济调查队根据市农业局、市林业局、市水利局、市乡镇企业管理局和市农村社会经济调查队等资料整理提供。

The data in this chapter show the basic conditions of agricultural production and rural economy, including basic statistics on rural areas, basic conditions of agricultural production, sown areas of farm crops, output of farming, forestry, animal husbandry and fishery products, cultivated land, gross output value of farming, forestry, animal husbandry and fishery, output value of agricultural commodities and corresponding commodity rate, and township-owned enterprises.

The data in this chapter are provided by Municipal Rural Socio-economic Survey Organization, according to data of Municipal Bureau of Agriculture, Municipal Bureau of Forestry, Municipal Bureau of Water Conservancy, Municipal Administration of Township-owned Enterprises and Municipal Rural Socio-economic Survey Organization.

10－1 主要年份农村基本情况
Basic Statistics on Rural Areas in Major Years

年 份 Year	乡村户数(万户) Number of Rural Households (10 000 households)	乡村人口(万人) Rural Population (10 000 persons)	乡村从业人员(万人) Rural Employment (10 000 persons)
1949		1446.24	650.59
1952		1546.01	692.81
1957		1685.98	762.15
1962		1506.16	692.19
1965		1676.21	755.99
1970		1977.85	857.78
1975		2264.67	921.67
1978		2316.54	926.32
1980	534.19	2294.08	980.75
1985	573.00	2355.39	1114.34
1986	596.13	2365.34	1154.26
1987	626.70	2391.29	1184.92
1988	650.27	2412.04	1218.03
1989	671.51	2427.70	1249.12
1990	686.26	2446.38	1273.06
1991	697.61	2471.48	1314.79
1992	699.94	2476.10	1350.71
1993	700.88	2463.53	1352.26
1994	710.34	2482.05	1356.59
1995	706.86	2454.17	1349.34
1996	709.86	2464.23	1330.44
1997	708.64	2452.75	1320.91
1998	709.84	2445.12	1316.95
1999	710.99	2442.47	1342.99
2000	710.28	2440.32	1352.60
2001	714.67	2438.79	1345.15
2002	718.31	2443.21	1342.17
2003	718.65	2436.47	1340.25
2004	714.99	2425.25	1361.54

注：乡村从业人员是指乡村劳动力从业人员，包括外出务工人员。

Note: Rural employment refers to rural able-bodied laborers, including laborers working outside Chongqing.

10－2 主要年份农业生产条件
Conditions for Agricultural Production in Major Years

年 份 Year	年末常用耕地面积（万公顷） Year-end Cultivated Area (10 000 hectares)	有效灌溉面积（万公顷） Effective Irrigated Area (10 000 hectares)	农业机械总动力（万千瓦） Total Power of Agricultural Machinery (10 000 kw)	农村用电量（万千瓦时） Electricity Consumption in Rural Areas (10 000 kwh)	农业化肥施用量（折纯）（万吨） Consumption of Chemical Fertilizer (net) (10 000 tons)	农膜使用量（万吨） Consumption of Farm Plastic Film (10 000 tons)	农药使用量（万吨） Consumption of Chemical Pesticides (10 000 tons)
1949	196.96	5.48					
1952	200.21	6.73					
1957	198.53	13.40					
1962	186.56	21.31	4	1852			
1965	187.50	26.10	10	3791			
1970	181.74	31.92	22	12655			
1975	177.80	42.84	54	21045			
1978	174.55	56.27	101	28542	21.63	0.33	0.64
1980	173.24	60.42	155	37953	29.21	0.37	0.71
1985	166.72	60.98	219	63309	31.76	0.50	0.73
1986	166.01	60.12	240	71471	36.70	0.51	0.79
1987	165.61	59.27	259	83229	38.26	0.57	0.78
1988	165.38	58.41	278	79637	38.29	0.61	0.81
1989	165.24	57.56	291	89611	44.72	0.65	0.81
1990	165.15	58.02	300	97091	48.13	0.80	0.87
1991	164.84	58.55	316	104430	52.08	0.97	1.01
1992	164.37	58.96	324	115831	52.75	1.07	1.05
1993	163.82	59.26	343	134027	54.51	1.18	1.27
1994	163.46	59.53	366	160197	58.55	1.28	1.29
1995	162.91	59.79	386.05	174847	62.02	1.43	1.46
1996	162.21	60.08	409.91	196788	65.55	1.53	1.69
1997	161.28	61.14	454.07	227302	69.64	1.59	1.68
1998	160.11	61.41	506.64	242934	71.18	1.77	1.82
1999	159.43	62.05	558.54	260029	71.03	1.86	1.84
2000	158.32	62.60	586.47	278728	72.00	1.96	1.85
2001	155.51	63.19	628.07	301140	72.58	1.94	1.91
2002	138.37	64.12	665.57	338717	73.37	2.53	1.93
2003	135.32	64.97	695.67	366535	71.59	2.42	1.95
2004	140.06	61.68	728.31	384627	77.02	2.68	1.95

10－3 农作物播种面积（1978－2004年）
Sown Areas of Farm Crops (1978-2004)

单位：公顷 (hectare)

年 份 Year	农作物播种总面积 Sown Areas of Farm Crops	＃粮食 Grain	＃稻谷 Rice	＃油料 Oil-bearing Crops	＃油菜籽 Rapeseeds	＃蔬菜 Vegetables	＃烟叶 Tobacco
1978	3498061	3177221	849243	92351	71374	95954	26582
1980	3345304	3048196	828317	116577	89369	78400	10416
1985	3214717	2748498	820140	176866	137367	140569	30956
1986	3232433	2710205	819858	183859	143792	159811	40897
1987	3241258	2697509	807797	180579	143292	160867	41729
1988	3287399	2727164	821305	185171	150612	171444	54056
1989	3381959	2788700	836231	188593	154505	177979	75726
1990	3438950	2847370	821986	203171	168751	183873	66607
1991	3526637	2889404	816684	224412	188989	197049	70859
1992	3522037	2874889	819262	215622	179402	200686	81258
1993	3513064	2870480	804560	184964	147692	222621	82461
1994	3493884	2877837	800342	174643	135505	225902	54997
1995	3526684	2876853	799482	201550	162572	236283	58939
1996	3585745	2889834	802279	202483	159584	257106	77657
1997	3605420	2881902	797955	191800	152222	267203	99482
1998	3614446	2900656	794636	192330	148896	290397	56603
1999	3592496	2862143	788576	197151	151801	301389	63969
2000	3590815	2773404	776636	226384	173185	327094	70775
2001	3555871	2714600	763964	225046	167911	366330	55210
2002	3464566	2606866	757195	236325	173930	359674	56012
2003	3307179	2410369	738486	236724	176836	386990	57237
2004	3435957	2516507	749300	244129	173815	390237	52995

10—4 主要年份农林牧渔产品产量
Output of Farming, Forestry, Animal Husbandry and Fishery Products in Major Years

年 份 Year	粮食(万吨) Grain (10 000 tons)	#稻谷 Rice	#豆类 Beans	油料(万吨) Oil-bearing Crops (10 000 tons)	#油菜籽 Rapeseeds	麻类(吨) Fiber Crops (ton)	甘蔗(万吨) Sugarcane (10 000 tons)
1949	402.68	246.57		0.90		1416	8.78
1952	470.97	281.33		3.19		1889	10.61
1957	596.55	316.39		5.13		1811	6.86
1962	378.23	191.26		1.40		598	1.04
1965	566.17	293.32		3.87		1048	14.47
1970	564.37	307.80		2.68		666	9.00
1975	603.72	325.84		4.13		632	24.87
1978	814.71	345.07	29.07	7.71	6.03	1659	31.20
1980	835.43	341.59	22.20	11.57	9.28	6172	36.64
1985	948.97	461.73	22.26	18.12	13.63	25787	30.24
1986	1004.92	493.41	25.02	20.91	15.85	21719	31.42
1987	1004.51	499.56	22.34	20.89	16.14	35995	29.43
1988	958.02	503.00	20.53	19.25	14.94	31013	29.32
1989	1044.88	541.81	17.25	18.78	14.38	18932	24.41
1990	1085.07	550.40	19.93	22.02	17.74	12707	20.55
1991	1115.28	535.90	21.53	26.92	22.81	11487	26.07
1992	1050.24	509.07	18.48	25.18	21.40	9716	14.33
1993	1052.72	479.90	21.90	21.70	17.22	9257	12.30
1994	1134.10	523.13	25.94	19.26	15.31	11471	9.39
1995	1153.68	532.63	30.38	25.12	20.54	11092	8.76
1996	1172.14	542.64	20.10	23.60	18.66	10898	8.27
1997	1184.63	552.44	21.90	23.34	18.34	11175	8.08
1998	1155.36	519.38	22.17	25.11	19.03	7541	7.28
1999	1143.05	533.01	21.93	24.09	17.33	6826	7.59
2000	1131.21	525.43	24.60	31.06	22.61	8406	9.06
2001	1035.35	466.45	23.32	29.96	21.91	8857	10.08
2002	1082.15	484.42	27.78	35.04	25.84	12139	12.06
2003	1087.20	494.29	32.21	38.27	28.51	9620	11.35
2004	1144.57	509.55	38.11	41.75	30.99	10209	11.77

10-4 续表1 CONTINUED-1

年 份 Year	烟叶(吨) Tobacco (ton)	蔬菜（万吨） Vegetables (10 000 tons)	茶叶(吨) Tea (ton)	蚕茧(吨) Silkworm Cocoons (ton)	水果(万吨) Fruit (10 000 tons)	牛奶(吨) Cow Milk (ton)	禽蛋(万吨) Poultry Eggs (10 000 tons)
1949	8535		916	761	6.02	1171	
1952	9238		1059	1236	7.75	1292	
1957	8247		1914	1588	7.14	2621	
1962	2566		1981	1325	8.80	3925	
1965	4654		2369	2306	6.83	6576	
1970	1667		2927	6608	4.54	9651	
1975	8146		4884	10477	7.12	11940	
1978	22528	243.95	8004	15404	7.91	15891	4.46
1980	8098	229.86	9217	25751	15.69	17277	5.51
1985	36239	390.86	16172	33130	24.70	29677	8.77
1986	46724	421.94	16893	32693	28.61	32665	9.44
1987	44992	439.00	18267	35755	29.57	36474	9.98
1988	68928	460.93	18676	41748	20.50	39126	10.17
1989	62093	469.31	18568	42063	37.19	40308	11.24
1990	74393	499.61	18103	43502	35.08	46293	12.01
1991	98156	533.00	18264	47757	40.75	51988	12.94
1992	124705	541.38	17178	50686	41.38	56579	14.61
1993	113208	558.23	19522	54505	56.85	54880	15.71
1994	68904	569.83	21920	57408	52.87	48514	17.32
1995	77981	593.91	17452	27000	59.29	39153	19.18
1996	132355	637.03	15536	27402	56.62	40297	20.85
1997	164736	668.44	14996	28072	60.72	45129	23.50
1998	79970	711.30	15299	29226	74.10	46587	24.46
1999	95653	737.11	14441	24177	71.70	46614	26.29
2000	104082	775.42	14526	29098	81.68	55989	27.89
2001	80064	779.96	14142	32396	82.61	67791	29.79
2002	87052	833.84	14093	33856	113.41	80952	31.58
2003	86048	840.17	14320	27802	128.59	90608	35.36
2004	85036	863.57	16064	29376	137.22	85143	36.55

10-4 续表2 CONTINUED-2

年 份 Year	水产品(吨) Aquatic Products (ton)	肉猪出栏头数(万头) Slaughtered Fattened Hogs (10 000 heads)	猪年末头数(万头) Year-end Hogs (10 000 heads)	大牲畜年末存栏头数(万头) Year-end Large Animals (10 000 heads)	#牛 Cattle and Buffaloes	肉类总产量(万吨) Gross Output of Meat (10 000 tons)	#猪肉 Pork
1949	3576	174.70		107.90		11.00	
1952	4119	254.80		122.50		16.00	
1957	6515	345.10		131.20		21.70	
1962	3791	76.90		115.60		6.90	
1965	6964	421.50		128.00		25.60	
1970	7649	414.50		150.20		23.10	
1975	10797	489.90		151.10		28.10	
1978	14362	542.70	914.98	142.15	141.58	40.51	37.38
1980	17734	797.63	1165.05	141.75	141.19	59.89	55.92
1985	42838	1140.06	1353.02	128.91	127.62	84.45	79.96
1986	47805	1190.22	1377.37	129.39	128.10	88.56	83.15
1987	51854	1243.78	1418.69	128.24	126.96	92.76	86.89
1988	58419	1345.77	1448.48	128.35	127.07	99.85	94.02
1989	65707	1375.38	1471.66	127.92	126.64	102.41	96.09
1990	65482	1375.79	1429.13	129.18	127.63	102.92	96.12
1991	71813	1429.45	1440.56	129.77	128.21	107.45	99.87
1992	74459	1469.47	1444.16	130.80	128.84	111.47	102.66
1993	89227	1492.99	1438.96	130.54	129.24	113.73	104.30
1994	103492	1555.69	1476.05	132.50	132.41	121.61	108.48
1995	121289	1610.14	1489.55	136.61	135.72	127.22	112.27
1996	140656	1637.51	1477.06	140.43	137.89	133.22	114.18
1997	160692	1699.74	1475.25	144.01	141.04	141.86	119.66
1998	178607	1720.14	1492.95	152.48	149.24	140.00	121.61
1999	191313	1703.19	1512.18	163.88	160.58	140.50	120.61
2000	200345	1724.96	1509.91	167.45	164.05	143.91	122.45
2001	196967	1746.85	1533.03	168.63	165.05	147.88	124.87
2002	211568	1781.69	1548.89	170.52	166.85	152.40	127.48
2003	224893	1828.49	1583.03	172.58	169.31	159.51	131.82
2004	239255	1909.32	1640.75	173.56	170.08	167.01	136.43

10－5 主要年份农林牧渔业总产值（现价）
Gross Output Value of Farming, Forestry, Animal Husbandry and Fishery in Major Years (Current Prices)

单位：万元 (10 000 yuan)

年 份 Year	农林牧渔业总产值 Gross Output Value	农 业 Farming	林 业 Forestry	牧 业 Animal Husbandry	渔 业 Fishery	农林牧渔服务业 Agricultural Services
1949	142123	111424	3837	26293	568	
1952	186367	140707	6523	38205	932	
1957	240351	176658	10816	51916	961	
1962	153506	120349	4605	28245	307	
1965	165688	122775	5799	36617	497	
1970	269234	192504	11128	64604	998	
1975	295062	210016	18048	65660	1338	
1978	357616	262881	17236	75731	1768	
1980	417925	296840	16160	102514	2411	
1985	739003	477570	43546	208842	9044	
1986	801998	516990	42045	231097	11867	
1987	902072	564063	40932	282816	14262	
1988	1104369	641751	49662	393394	19561	
1989	1243819	706771	49328	463300	24420	
1990	1460003	858133	55308	518757	27805	
1991	1595286	938353	60038	565193	31702	
1992	1713839	995009	70992	612498	35340	
1993	2073607	1197742	77531	749776	48558	
1994	2831816	1552652	86981	1127394	64789	
1995	3778259	2278927	106732	1304229	88371	
1996	4249903	2713807	115493	1311666	108937	
1997	4393508	2678892	117313	1468914	128389	
1998	4288839	2549365	150929	1444758	143787	
1999	4168780	2496237	115588	1409527	147428	
2000	4126272	2447376	108236	1419910	150750	
2001	4311666	2503968	112044	1544041	151613	
2002	4609755	2640760	135143	1661965	171887	
2003	4885655	2701156	145824	1776384	183251	79040
2004	6127723	3329516	184814	2309374	212464	91555

注：按照新国民经济行业分类标准（GB/T4754-2002），从2003年起增加了农林牧渔服务业（下表同）。

Note: According to GB/T4754-2002, the sector of agricultural services is added since 2003 (the same below).

10－6 主要年份农林牧渔业总产值指数（上年=100）
Indices of Gross Output Value of Farming, Forestry, Animal Husbandry and Fishery in Major Years (Preceding Year=100)

年份 Year	农林牧渔业总产值 Gross Output Value	农业 Farming	林业 Forestry	牧业 Animal Husbandry	渔业 Fishery	农林牧渔服务业 Agricultural Services
1952	119.9	116.8	123.7	135.7	111.2	
1957	129.0	126.7	144.5	133.4	156.4	
1962	63.9	69.9	58.0	39.4	49.5	
1965	151.1	137.2	125.4	275.5	194.9	
1970	101.5	100.3	88.5	109.7	107.3	
1975	108.2	110.6	129.7	94.6	134.0	
1978	123.2	126.7	119.1	109.7	121.2	
1980	115.3	105.9	99.6	165.8	121.0	
1985	144.1	130.9	210.2	169.8	292.2	
1986	105.8	106.3	83.9	109.3	119.4	
1987	102.7	102.1	89.0	106.3	110.3	
1988	101.8	97.3	99.1	111.7	115.2	
1989	106.4	108.4	99.9	103.0	111.0	
1990	102.7	101.1	96.4	106.4	106.8	
1991	106.2	105.3	102.1	108.2	113.9	
1992	101.9	98.7	110.4	107.3	100.9	
1993	104.1	103.4	104.8	104.6	120.8	
1994	105.6	103.5	101.8	109.0	115.4	
1995	106.3	105.1	106.7	107.7	116.8	
1996	102.8	101.8	101.3	103.6	116.2	
1997	103.3	102.0	95.8	105.4	115.7	
1998	102.4	101.5	117.2	101.6	112.4	
1999	99.8	100.7	75.7	100.4	108.5	
2000	101.0	100.3	86.6	102.9	104.5	
2001	102.1	100.3	109.7	104.1	101.9	
2002	101.7	99.7	102.3	104.2	105.6	
2003	104.6	103.5	119.6	104.8	106.8	
2004	105.7	105.5	108.8	104.9	108.4	116.5

注：本表指数按可比价计算；其中1952年以1949年为100。

Note: Indices of this table are calculated at comparable prices.1949 is considered as 100 percentage as index of 1952.

10－7 农林牧渔业总产值（2003－2004年）
Gross Output Value of Farming, Forestry, Animal Husbandry and Fishery (2003-2004)

单位：万元 (10 000 yuan)

指　　标	Item	农林牧渔业总产值 Gross Output Value 2003	2004	指数 上年=100 Index Preceding Year=100
总计	**Total**	**4885655**	**6127723**	**105.7**
农业	Farming	2701156	3329516	105.5
谷物及其他作物	Cereal and Other Crops	1667898	2160082	105.2
#谷物	Cereal	1031878	1427891	105.6
豆类	Bean	96464	120337	107.4
油料	Oil Crops	91629	134037	118.3
烟草	Tobacco	62326	80225	104.0
蔬菜园艺作物	Vegetables and Gardening	769773	851606	105.5
#蔬菜（含菜用瓜）	Vegetables (including Melons as Vegetables)	734786	801894	103.0
花卉	Flowers	19117	13788	82.1
水果、坚果、饮料和香料作物	Fruits, Nuts, Drinks and Spices	234880	274766	107.2
#水果、坚果（含果用瓜）	Fruits and Nuts (including Melons as Fruits)	216807	243187	106.4
茶及其他饮料	Tea and Other Drinks	14034	31579	127.7
#茶	Tea	14034	31579	127.7
中药材	Traditional Chinese Medical Materials	28604	43062	104.0
林业	Forestry	145824	184814	108.8
林木的培育和种植	Forest Cultivation	63330	55617	82.6
#造林	Afforestation	46890	26793	49.1
竹木采运	Bamboo Felling and Transportation	12268	29670	117.1
林产品	Forest Products	70226	99527	132.1
牧业	Animal Husbandry	1776384	2309374	104.9
牲畜饲养	Livestock Raising	138750	174006	121.5
#牛	Cattle	67496	88077	113.5
奶产品	Milk Products	36243	34926	142.8
猪的饲养	Hog Raising	1052196	1438281	104.6
#肉猪	Edible Hogs	1046846	1432696	104.6
家禽饲养	Poultry Raising	508858	609285	105.3
#禽蛋	Poultry Eggs	281959	285050	103.4
狩猎和捕捉动物	Animal Hunting	176		
其他畜牧业	Others	76404	87802	90.7
#蚕茧	Silkworm Cocoons	31972	36748	105.7
渔业	Fishery	183251	212464	108.4
#内陆水域水产品	Aquatic Products in Inland Water Areas	183251	212464	108.4
#养殖	By Breeding	172600	199948	108.6
#鱼类	Fish	176072	199029	104.6
农林牧渔服务业	Agricultural Services	79040	91555	116.5

注：本表数据绝对值按现价计算，指数按可比价计算。

Note: The absolute figures in this table are calculated at current prices whereas the indices are calculated at comparable prices.

10－8 农村基本情况（2003－2004年）
Basic Statistics on Rural Areas (2003-2004)

指　　标	Item	2003	2004
户数(万户)	**Households(10 000 households)**	**718.65**	**714.99**
人口(万人)	**Population(10 000 persons)**	**2436.47**	**2425.25**
乡村从业人员(万人)	**Rural Employment(10 000 persons)**	**1340.25**	**1361.54**
按性别分	By Sex		
男	Male	715.09	730.52
女	Female	625.16	631.02
按产业分	By Sector		
第一产业	Primary Industry	813.19	800.83
第二产业	Secondary Industry	180.81	206.83
第三产业	Tertiary Industry	346.25	353.88
农村基础设施（个）	**Rural Infrastructure (unit)**		
自来水受益村数	Number of Villages with Access to Tap Water	6690	5064
通汽车村数	Villages with Highways	13450	9755
通电话村	Villages with Post and Telecommunications Offices	13213	9853

注：从2001年起，民政部门调整乡、镇、村的区划，村个数均比往年减少。
Note: The number of villages is less than that in previous years for the administrative adjustment since 2001.

10－9 耕地面积情况（2003－2004年）
Statistics on Cultivated Land (2003-2004)

单位：公顷 (hectare)

指　　标	Item	2003	2004
年初耕地总资源	**Year-beginning Cultivated Area**	**2282525**	**2144365**
年内增加	Increase in the Year	4014	13893
#新开荒	Open up Undeveloped Land	2357	3447
年内减少	Decrease in the Year	142174	52406
#国家基建占地	Government Capital Construction	5624	7440
退耕还林还草占地	Green for Grain	126475	35189
年末耕地总资源	**Year-end Cultivated Land**	**2144365**	**2105852**
常用耕地面积	Regularly Cultivated Land	1353221	1400590
#水田	Paddy Fields	760000	761141
水浇地	Dry Fields	104	713
临时性耕地	Temporarily Cultivated Land	791144	705262
平均每个农村人口占有常用耕地（亩）	Cultivated Area Per Rural Person (mu)	0.83	0.87
平均每个农村劳动力占有常用耕地（亩）	Cultivated Area Per Rural Labor Force (mu)	1.51	1.54

注：自2002年起，耕地统计指标按新农业统计制度变更。
Note: Indicators on cultivated land have been changed in terms of new agricultural statistics since 2002.

10－10 农业生产条件（2003－2004年）
Conditions for Agricultural Production (2003-2004)

指　　标	Item	2003	2004
农业机械化情况	**Agricultural Mechanization**		
农业机械总动力(万千瓦)	Total Power of Agricultural Machinery (10 000 kw)	695.67	728.31
农用大中型拖拉机数(万台)	Large and Medium Agricultural Tractors (10 000 units)	0.29	0.27
农用大中型拖拉机动力(万千瓦)	Capacity of Large and Medium Agricultural Tractors (10 000 kw)	7.35	6.56
小型拖拉机数(万台)	Small and Walking Tractors (10 00 units)	0.93	0.84
小型拖拉机动力(万千瓦)	Capacity of Small and Walking Tractors (10 000 kw)	11.06	10.67
农用排灌动力机械台数(万台)	Drainage and Irrigation Machinery (10 00 units)	36.59	45.53
农用排灌动力机械动力(万千瓦)	Capacity of Drainage and Irrigation Machinery (10 000 kw)	106.17	115.07
农用水泵(万台)	Pumps (10 00 units)	39.04	52.43
机动脱粒机(万台)	Motorized Threshing Machines (10 00 units)	19.89	24.76
农用运输车(万辆)	Farm Tracks (10 00 vehicles)	3.39	3.25
渔用机动船(万艘)	Motorized Fishing Boats (10 00 vessels)	0.20	0.54
农业主要能源及物耗	**Main Agricultural Energy and Material Consumption**		
农村用电量(万千瓦时)	Electricity Consumption in Rural Areas (10 000 kwh)	366535	384627
乡村办电站(个)	Electricity Power Stations in Rural Areas (unit)	623	630
乡村办电站发电量(万千瓦时)	Generating Capacity of Electricity Station in Rural Areas (10 000 kwh)	81557	90313
有效灌溉面积(公顷)	Effective Irrigated Area (hectare)	649690	616790
占耕地面积比重(%)	Proportion of Cultivated Area (%)	48.0	44.0
化肥施用量(折纯量)(万吨)	Chemical Fertilizer (net) (10 000 tons)	71.60	77.02
#氮　肥	Nitrogenous Fertilizer	43.86	46.35
磷　肥	Phosphate Fertilizer	16.55	16.94
钾　肥	Potash Fertilizer	3.12	3.55
复合肥	Compound Fertilizer	8.07	10.04
每公顷耕地化肥施用量(公斤)	Chemical Fertilizer Per Hectare (kg)	529.12	549.91
农用塑料薄膜使用量(万吨)	Farm Plastic Film (10 000 tons)	2.42	2.68
#地膜使用量	Consumption of Farm Plastic Film	1.54	1.66
地膜覆盖面积(公顷)	Covered Area by Farm Plastic Film (hectare)	199053	269359
农用柴油使用量(万吨)	Consumption of Farm Diesel Oil (10 000 tons)	12.56	13.28
农药使用量(万吨)	Consumption of Chemical Pesticides (10 000 tons)	1.95	1.95

10－11 主要农作物播种面积及产量（2003－2004年）
Sown Areas and Output of Major Farm Crops (2003-2004)

指　标	Item	播种面积(公顷) Sown Areas (hectare)		总产量(吨) Total Output (ton)		单位产量(公斤/公顷) Yield Per Unit (kg/ha)	
		2003	2004	2003	2004	2003	2004
粮食	**Grain**	**2410369**	**2516507**	**10872037**	**11445661**	**4511**	**4548**
谷物	Cereal	1539598	1566568	7961695	8282562	5171	5287
稻谷	Rice	738486	749300	4942970	5095471	6693	6800
早稻	Early Rice	474	441	2522	2430	5321	5510
中稻	Middle Rice	736198	748307	4929708	5090028	6696	6802
双季晚稻	Late Rice	1814	552	10740	3013	5921	5458
小麦	Wheat	322734	280528	838423	783825	2598	2794
玉米	Corn	429966	460415	2062559	2278038	4797	4948
高粱	Sorghum	26326	37530	69986	80186	2658	2137
其他谷物	Other Cereal	22086	38795	47757	45042	2162	1161
豆类	Bean	203970	224279	322124	381081	1579	1699
#大豆	Soybean	79759	95094	100679	165380	1262	1739
薯类	Tuber	666801	725660	2588218	2782018	3882	3834
#马铃薯	Potato	282993	306039	746565	928397	2638	3034
油料	**Oil-bearing Crops**	**236724**	**244129**	**382742**	**417501**	**1617**	**1710**
#花生	Peanut	48284	52686	85950	96189	1780	1826
油菜籽	Rapeseed	176836	173815	285101	309876	1612	1783
芝麻	Sesame Seed	6941	6856	5935	6626	855	966
麻类	**Fiber Crops**	**7108**	**7573**	**9620**	**10209**	**1353**	**1348**
#苎麻	Ramie	6567	7054	9128	9766	1390	1384
黄红麻	Jute and Ambary Hemp	219	163	203	116	927	712
糖料(甘蔗)	**Sugar Crops (sugarcane)**	**2829**	**2800**	**113460**	**117734**	**40106**	**42048**
烟叶	**Tobacco**	**57237**	**52995**	**86048**	**85036**	**1503**	**1605**
#烤烟	Flue-cured Tobacco	46605	41361	68365	64470	1467	29167
蔬菜、瓜果	**Vegetables and Melons**	**403365**	**406985**	**8629225**	**8879565**	**21393**	**21817**
#蔬菜（含菜用瓜）	Vegetables (including Melons as Vegetables)	386990	390237	8401712	8635651	21710	22129

10－12 林牧渔业生产情况（2003－2004年）
Output of Forestry, Animal Husbandry and Fishery (2003-2004)

指　标	Item	2003	2004
林　业(公顷)	**Forestry (hectare)**		
当年造林面积	Current New Forest Areas	352619	107168
年末封山育林面积	Year-end Mountain Seal for Afforestation	245716	224276
零星（四旁）植树（万株）	Surrounding Tree Planting (10 000 plants)	8289	8415
育苗面积	Nursery Garden Areas	5313	5304
当年苗木产量（万株）	Output of Plants in Current Year (10 000 plants)	70590	48460
幼林抚育实际面积	Actual Nursery Areas	89279	219061
成林抚育面积	Forest Areas	27189	207379
牧　业	**Animal Husbandry**		
年末大牲畜总头数(万头)	Year-end Large Animals (10 000 heads)	172.58	173.56
＃农事劳役头数	Draught Animals	114.61	117.95
年末生猪存栏头数(万头)	Year-end Hogs Raised (10 000 heads)	1583.03	1640.75
年末羊只数(万只)	Year-end Sheep and Goats (10 000 heads)	233.21	365.11
年内出栏肥猪头数(万头)	Slaughtered Fattened Hogs (10 000 heads)	1828.49	1909.32
年内出栏羊只数(万只)	Slaughtered Sheep and Goats (10 000 heads)	235.86	284.55
年内出栏家禽(万只)	Slaughtered Poultry (10 000 heads)	12731.57	13737.37
渔　业(公顷)	**Fishery (hectare)**		
水产品养殖面积	Cultured Areas of Aquatic Products	68560	68880
＃池　塘	Ponds	31690	32390
水　库	Reservoirs	23210	23140

10－13 林牧渔业主要产品产量（2003－2004年）
Major Product Output of Forestry, Animal Husbandry and Fishery (2003-2004)

单位：吨 (ton)

指　标	Item	2003	2004
水果	Fruit	1285880	1372247
＃柑桔	Citrus	752374	799543
肉类	Meat	1595097	1670064
＃猪牛羊肉	Pork, Beef and Mutton	1383522	1457288
＃猪肉	Pork	1318198	1364335
禽肉	Meat of Poultry	179242	193581
兔肉	Meat of Rabbit	15231	16754
奶类	Milk	90608	86236
＃牛奶	Cow Milk	90608	85143
蜂蜜	Honey	6010	6231
水产品	Aquatic Products	224893	239255
＃养殖	Cultured Aquatic Products	212655	226343
年末实有茶园面积（公顷）	Area of Tea Plantations (year-end) (hectare)	23433	24027
＃本年采摘面积	Picked Area in Current Year	15183	17608
年末果园面积（公顷）	Area of Orchards (year-end) (hectare)	164766	164719
＃梨园	Pear	24383	26315
＃柑桔	Citrus	96273	98061

10－14 主要农产品产量与建国以来最高年产量的比较（2004年）
Output of Major Agricultural Products in Comparison with Peak Year since Foundation of PRC (2004)

单位：万吨 (10 000 tons)

指 标	Item	2004	建国以来最高产量年 Peak Year Since Foundation of PRC		2004年为建国以来最高年份（%）
			年 份 Year	产 量 Output	2004 as Percentage of Peak Year
粮食总产量	Gross Output of Grain	1144.57	1997	1184.63	96.6
#稻谷	Rice	509.55	1997	552.44	92.2
小麦	Wheat	78.38	1995	156.24	50.2
玉米	Corn	227.80	1997	208.87	109.1
豆类	Bean	38.11	1958	45.34	84.1
薯类	Tubers	278.20	1996	258.86	107.5
油菜籽	Rapeseed	30.99	2000	22.61	137.1
麻类	Fiber Crops	1.02	1985	2.60	39.2
甘蔗	Sugarcane	11.77	1980	36.64	32.1
烤烟	Cured Tobacco	6.45	1997	11.00	58.6
蔬菜类	Vegetable	863.57	2000	781.87	110.4
年末生猪存栏头数（万头）	Year-end Hogs Raised (10 000 heads)	1640.75	2001	1553.63	105.6
猪牛羊肉	Pork, Beef and Mutton	145.73	2001	131.65	110.7
#猪肉	Pork	136.43	2001	124.87	109.3
禽肉	Meat of Poultry	19.36	1997	16.65	116.3
奶类	Milk	8.62	2001	6.78	127.1
禽蛋	Poultry Eggs	36.55	2001	29.79	122.7
水产品	Aquatic Products	23.93	2000	20.03	119.5
蚕茧	Silkworm Cocoon	2.94	1995	5.21	56.4
茶叶	Tea	1.61	1990	1.81	89.0
水果	Fruit	137.22	2001	97.36	140.9

10－15 农业商品产值和商品率（2003－2004年）
Output Value of Agricultural Commodities and Corresponding Commodity Rate (2003-2004)

指 标	Item	农业商品产值（万元） Output Value of Agricultural Commodities (10 000 yuan)		农业商品率（%） Commodity Rate (%)	
		2003	2004	2003	2004
总计	**Total**	**2720544**	**3426843**	**56.6**	**57.0**
农业	Farming	1189703	1494853	44.0	45.0
#粮食作物	Grain Crops	335970	511114	25.7	27.8
经济作物	Cash Crops	160371	174655	86.4	75.3
蔬菜	Vegetables	371050	541858	57.1	68.0
茶、桑、水果	Tea, Mulberry and Fruits	192344	196654	74.1	70.7
林业	Forestry	77013	125512	52.8	68.0
牧业	Animal Husbandry	1321887	1645334	74.4	71.0
#猪	Hogs	715776	935086	68.0	65.0
活的畜禽产品	Livestocks and Relative Products	243850	254058	74.5	70.7
渔业	Fishery	131941	161145	72.0	76.0

10－16 乡镇企业主要指标（2003－2004年）
Main Indicators of Township-owned Enterprises (2003-2004)

单位：个、人、万元　　(unit, person, 10 000 yuan)

指　　标	Item	2003	2004
企业单位数	Number of Enterprises	73421	74597
#工业	Industry	34714	35495
#集体企业	Collective-owned Enterprises	2878	2413
私有企业	Private Enterprises	31836	33082
从业人数	Employment	1789890	1916309
#集体企业	Collective-owned Enterprises	367780	334151
私有企业	Private Enterprises	1422110	1582158
总产值(现价)	Gross Output Value (current prices)	16784095	21596726
#集体企业	Collective-owned Enterprises	2791855	2590873
私有企业	Private Enterprises	13992240	19005853
工业总产值(现价)	Gross Industrial Output Value (current prices)	10578543	13807827
#集体企业	Collective-owned Enterprises	1350022	1309962
私有企业	Private Enterprises	9228521	12497865
乡镇企业增加值	Value-added of Township Enterprises	4143664	5542260
#工业	Industry	2582826	3493062
营业收入	Business Income	16251011	22043626
#集体企业	Collective-owned Enterprises	2653379	2431174
私有企业	Private Enterprises	13597632	19612452
利润总额	Total Pre-tax Profits	599828	792048
实交税金	Taxes Payable	493485	657745
#所得税	Income-tax Payable	88980	94085
当地入库税金	Stored Taxes	493485	657745
工资总额	Total Wages	1302037	1599309
#集体企业	Collective-owned Enterprises	257446	267272
私有企业	Private Enterprises	1044591	1332037
年末固定资产原值	Original Value of Fixed Assets	5080359	6397903
#集体企业	Collective-owned Enterprises	738543	755875
私有企业	Private Enterprises	4341816	5642028
银行(信用社)贷款余额	Bank (credit cooperative) Loans	625308	781635

主要统计指标解释

农林牧渔业总产值 是以货币表现的农、林、牧、渔业全部产品的总量，以及为农、林、牧、渔业生产活动进行的支持性服务活动的总和，它反映一定时期内农业生产总规模和总成果。农业总产值的计算方法通常是按农林牧渔业产品及其副产品的产量分别乘以各自单位产品价格求得，少数生产周期较长，当年没有产品或产品产量不易统计的，则采用间接方法匡算其产值，然后将四业产品产值和农林牧渔业服务业产值相加即为农业总产值。

1957 年以前的农业总产值中包括了厩肥和农民自给性手工业（如农民自制衣服、鞋、袜，自己从事粮食初步加工等）。1958 年及以后的农业总产值，林业中增加了村及村以下竹木采伐产值；牧业中取消费厩肥产值；副业中取消了农民自给性手工业产值，增加了村及村以下办的工业产值；渔业中增加了海洋捕捞水产品产值。1980 年及以后的农业总产值，在副业中增加了农民家庭兼营工业商品部分的产值。从 1984 年起村及村以下办工业产值划归工业。从 1993 年起，取消副业。将野生动物的捕猎划入牧业，野生植物采集和农民家庭兼营商品性工业划归农业。1996 年第一次农业普查以后，由于畜牧业产品年报数据与普查数据数据之间存在一定的差距，重庆市统计局农调队对畜牧业年报数据与普查数据进行衔接，相应的畜牧业产值进行调整。从 2003 年起，农业总产值按照新的国民经济行业分类标准（GB/T4754-2002）进行计算，增加了农林牧渔业服务业，内部结构也进行了调整，同时开始采用价格指数缩减法计算农业发展速度。

粮食产量 指全社会的产量。包括国有经济经营的、集体统一经营的和农民家庭经营的粮食产量，还包括工矿企业办的农场和其他生产单位的产量。粮食除包括稻谷、小麦、玉米、高粱、谷子及其他杂粮外，还包括薯类和豆类。其产量计算方法，豆类按去豆荚后的干豆计算；薯类（包括甘薯和马铃薯，不包括芋头和木薯）1963 年以前按每 4 公斤鲜薯折 1 公斤粮食计算，从 1964 年开始及以后改为按 5 公斤鲜薯折 1 公斤粮食计算。城市郊区作为蔬菜的薯类（如：马铃薯等）按鲜品计算，并且不做为粮食统计。其他粮食一律按脱粒后的原粮计算。1989 年以前全国粮食产量数据主要靠全面报表取得，1989 年开始使用抽样调查数据。

油料产量 指全部油料作物的生产量。包括花生、油菜籽、芝麻、向日葵籽，胡麻籽（亚麻籽）和其他油料。不包括大豆，也不包括木本油料和野生油料。花生以带壳干花生计算。

水产品产量 指人工养殖的水产品和天然生长的水产品的捕捞量。包括海水的鱼类、虾蟹类、贝类和藻类以及内陆水域的鱼类、虾蟹类和贝类，不包括淡水生植物。水产品产量是通过各级水产和统计部门逐级上报取得数据。1995 年及以前，贝类中牡蛎按鲜肉计算；蚶、蛤、蛙按 5 斤鲜品折 1 斤计算。1996 年以后则统一按鲜品计算。

猪、牛、羊肉产量 指当年出栏并已屠宰后除去头蹄下水后带骨肉（即胴体重）的重量。

期初（末）畜禽存栏头（只）数 指报告期初（末）农村各种合作经济组织和国营农场、农民个人、机关、团体、学校、工矿企业，部队等单位以及城镇居民饲养的大牲畜、猪、羊、家禽等畜禽的存栏头（只）数。

农作物播种面积 指实际播种或移植有农作物的面积，凡是实际种植有农作物的面积，不论种植在耕地上还是种植在非耕地上，均包括在农作物播种面积中。在播种季节基本结束后，因遭灾而重新改种和补种的农作物面积，也包括在内。它是反映我国耕地面积利用情况的一个重要指标。目前，农作物播种面积主要包括粮食、棉花、油料、糖料、麻类、烟叶、蔬菜和瓜类、药材和其它农作物九大类。

常用耕地 指耕地总资源中专门种植农作物并经常进行耕种，能够正常收获的土地。包括当地实际耕种的熟地；弃耕、休闲不满三年，随时可以复耕的地；开荒利用三年以上的地。不包括临时种植农作物的坡度在25度以上的陡坡地；在河套、湖畔、库区临时开发的成片或零星土地；也不包括已列为国家和省（区、市）退耕计划但临时耕种的土地。

有效灌溉面积 指具有一定的水源，地块比较平整，灌溉工程或设备已经配套，在一般年景下当年能够进行正常灌溉的耕地面积。在一般情况下，有效灌溉面积应等于灌溉工程或设备已经配备，能够进行正常灌溉的水田和水浇地面积之和。

农用化肥施用量 指本年内实际用于农业生产的化肥数量，包括氮肥、磷肥，钾肥和复合肥。化肥施用量要求按折纯量计算数量。折纯法化肥施用量是把氮肥、磷肥和钾肥分别按含氮、含五氧化二磷、含氧化钾的百分之一百成份折算后的数量。复合肥按其所含主要成分折算。

农业机械总动力 指主要用于农、林、牧、渔业的各种动力机械的动力总和。包括耕作机械、排灌机械、收获机械、农用运输机械、植物保护机械、牧业机械、林业机械、渔业机械和其他农业机械［内燃机按引擎马力折成瓦（特）计算，电动机按功率折成瓦（特）计算］。不包括专门用于乡、镇、村、组办工业、基本建设、非农业运输、科学试验和教学等非农业生产方面用的动力机械与作业机械。

Explanatory Notes on Main Statistical Indicators

Gross Output Value of Farming Forestry, Animal Husbandry and Fishery refers to the total volume of products of farming, forestry, animal husbandry and fishery in value terms, and supporting services for the production of farming, forestry, animal husbandry and fishery, reflecting the total scale and total result of agricultural production during a given period of time. Gross output value of agriculture is obtained by first multiplying the output of each product or by-products by its price, resulting in the output value of each single item. For a small number of products, annual output of which is not available or difficult to get due to the long production/growing process involved, the output value is estimated through an indirect approach. The sum of output value of all products of farming, forestry, animal husbandry, fishery and agricultural services is then equal to the gross output value of agriculture.

Prior to 1957, China's gross agricultural output value included barnyard manure and handicraft products for self-consumption (clothes, shoes, stockings, and initial grain processing undertaken by peasants). Since 1958, cutting and felling of bamboo and trees by villages and other cooperative organizations under villages have been included in forestry; value of barnyard manure has been excluded from animal husbandry; self-consumed handicrafts has been excluded from sideline occupations, while the output value of industries run by villages and cooperative organizations under village had been included in sideline occupations and the output value of fish catches by motor fishing boats has been added to fishery. Since 1980, the value of handicraft products made for sale by individuals in households had been added to sideline occupations. Since 1984, industries run by villages and cooperative organizations under villages have been included in the sector of industry. Since 1993, the subdivision of sideline occupations has been canceled, and the hunting of wild animals has been classified into animal husbandry, and the gathering of wild plants and commodity industry run by rural household have been included in farming. The first agriculture census of China in 1996 revealed some discrepancy between the production of animal products from the annual reports and that from the census. Efforts were made by the Rural Socio-economic Survey Organization of Municipal Bureau of Statistics to adjust the output value of animal husbandry to make the figures from the annual reports consistent with the census data. Since 2003, gross output value of agriculture is calculated by new sector category of national economic (GB/T4754-2002). Farming, forestry, animal husbandry, fishery and agricultural services are added in it. As the same time, inner structure is adjusted too. The development rate is calculated by price reduction measure.

Grain Yield refers to the yield in the whole country including grains produced by state farms, collective units, industrial enterprises and mines. Grain includes rice, wheat, corn, sorghum, millet and other miscellaneous grains as well as tubers and beans. Output of beans refers to dry beans without pods. The output of tubers (sweet potatoes and potatoes, not including taros and cassava) was converted into that of grain at the ration 4:1, i.e. four kilograms of fresh tubers was equivalent to one kilogram of grain up to 1963. Since 1964 the ratio for conversion has been 5:1. Tubers supplied as vegetables (such as potatoes) in cities and suburbs are calculated as fresh vegetables and their output is not included in the output of grain. Output of all other grains refers to husked grain. Data on grain production before 1989 were obtained through Comprehensive Statistical Reporting System. Since 1989, data from sample surveys are used.

Yield of Oil-bearing Crops refers to the total yield of oil-bearing crops of various kinds, including peanuts, (dry, in shell) rapeseeds, sesame, sunflower seeds, flax seeds, and other oil-bearing crops. Soybeans, oil-bearing woody plants, and oil-bearing crops are not included.

Output of Aquatic Products refers to catches of both artificially cultured and naturally grown aquatic products, including fish, shrimps, crabs and shellfish in sea and inland water as well as seaweed. Freshwater plants are not included. Data on output of aquatic products are reported by aquatic product and statistical agencies level by level. Before 1995, among the shellfish, the oyster was counted as fresh meat; 5 kilograms of ark shell, clams and frogs are equivalent to 1 kilogram of fresh aquatic products; they are all counted as fresh aquatic products since 1996.

Output of Pork, Beef and Mutton refers to the meat of slaughtered hogs, cattle, sheep and goats with head, feet, and offal taken away.

Number of Livestock or Poultry in Hand at the Beginning (or End) of the Reference Period refers to the total number of large animals, pigs, sheep, fowls, etc., raised by rural cooperative organizations, state farms, rural individuals, government agencies, schools, industrial and mining enterprises, army, and urban residents at the beginning (or end) of the reference period.

Sown Area of Crops refers to area of land sown or trans-planted with crops regardless of being in cultivated area or non-cultivated area. Area of land resown due to natural disasters is also included. At present, the sown area of crops mainly include the following 9 categories of crops: grain, cotton, oil-bearing crops, sugar crops, fiber crops, Tobacco, Vegetables and melons, medicinal materials and other farm crops.

Regularly Cultivated Land refers to farmland among the total land resources which is exclusively used for farming and is under regular cultivation with harvest in normal years. Included are currently cultivated land, land that has been abandoned or put in idle for less than 3 years and could be re-used for cultivation at any time, and new-claimed land that has been put into cultivation for more than 3 years. Excluded under temporary cultivation, land (large or small plots) that is claimed along river bends, lake sides or banks of reservoirs, as well as land that has been designated under the "Green for Grain" programs of the state and provincial governments but is still temporarily under cultivation.

Irrigated Area refers to areas that are effectively irrigated, i.e. level land, which has water source and complete sets of irrigation facilities to lift and move adequate water for irrigation purpose under normal conditions. Under normal conditions, irrigated area is the sum of watered fields and irrigated fields where irrigation systems of equipment have been installed for regular irrigation purpose.

Consumption of Chemical Fertilizers for Farming refers to the quantity of chemical fertilizers applied in agriculture in the year, including nitrogenous fertilizer, phosphate fertilizer, potash fertilizer, and compound fertilizer. The consumption of chemical fertilizers is required in calculation to convert the gross weight into weight containing 100% effective component (e.g. 100% nitrogen content in nitrogenous fertilizer, 100% phosphorous pentoxide content in phosphate fertilizer, 100% potassium oxide content in potash fertilizer). Compound fertilizer is converted with its major component.

Total Power of Farm Machinery refers to total mechanical power of machinery used in farming, forestry, animal husbandry, and fishery, including sloughing, irrigation and drainage, harvesting, transport, plant protection, stockbreeding, forestry and fishery. The power of internal combustion engines is required to convert horsepower into watts and the power of electric motors is required to be converted into watts. Machinery employed for non-agricultural purposes, such as the machines used in township-run and village-run industry, construction, non-agricultural transport, scientific experiments and teaching, is excluded.

十一 工业

INDUSTRY

简要说明 Brief Introduction

本章资料主要包括工业企业主要指标，国有及规模以上（即指年产品销售收入在500万元以上）非国有工业企业单位数、增加值、主要经济指标和效益指标，国有及国有控股工业企业的主要经济指标和效益指标，大中型工业企业的主要经济指标和效益指标，主要工业产品产量以及占全国当年产量的比重。本章资料由市统计局工业交通处整理提供。

Data in this chapter cover the following data: major indicators of industrial enterprises, the number, value-added and main economic indicators and efficiency indicators of state-owned industrial enterprises and the non-state enterprises that are above designated size (referring to enterprises each with an annual sales of over 5 million yuan); main economic indicators and efficiency indicators of the state-owned and state holding industrial enterprises; main economic indicators and efficiency indicators of large and medium sized industrial enterprises; output of major industrial products and relative percentage of national total output in this year. Data in this chapter are provided by Division of Industry and Transport Statistics, Municipal Bureau of Statistics.

11－1 工业企业主要指标（1978－2004年）
Major Indicators of Industrial Enterprises (1978-2004)

单位：万元 (10 000 yuan)

年 份 Year	单位数（个） Number of Enterprises (unit)	从业人员平均人数（人） Average Emloyment (person)	工业总产值 Industrial Gross Output Value		工业增加值 Value-added of Industry	
			绝对值 Value	指数（上年=100） Index Preceding Year=100	绝对值 Value	指数（上年=100） Index Preceding Year=100
1978	8037	951217	643444	100.0		
1980	10963	998963	772307	104.6		
1985	9924	1251649	1408126	117.2		
1986	12454	1473491	1604215	104.1		
1987	11556	1511086	1921043	112.4		
1988	11303	1552189	2529674	116.1		
1989	10976	1587712	2991130	102.4		
1990	10763	1610473	2993490	100.7		
1991	10780	1652984	3424558	111.8		
1992	9693	1662144	4191279	116.3	1149187	100.0
1993	9083	1752822	5847377	118.2	1837033	159.9
1994	9713	1692108	7185418	115.4	2034142	110.7
1995	11474	1724173	7651109	115.2	1935522	95.2
1996	11077	1894816	8234700	111.1	2333652	120.6
1997	9185	1570400	8705521	110.1	2404660	103.0
1998	2000	1164200	7667894		2097535	
1999	1975	1004400	8585525	118.9	2407000	114.8
2000	2040	907900	9623226	113.6	2875000	119.4
2001	2054	841900	10728325	115.5	3329900	115.8
2002	2072	820103	12283741	119.8	3974400	119.4
2003	2243	843341	15889928	126.7	4778500	120.2
2004	2634	900546	21427261	129.9	5883198	125.3

注：1）本表统计口径1998年以前为全部独立核算工业企业，1998年及以后为全部国有及规模以上（即年产品销售收入在500万元以上）非国有工业企业（下表同）。

2）工业总产值、工业增加值的绝对值按现价计算。由于工业统计制度变更，工业总产值指数2003年及以前按可比价计算，2004年起按现价计算；工业增加值指数2003年及以前按现价计算，2004年起按可比价计算。

Note: a) In this table, the data on industry refer to total industrial enterprises with independent accounting system from 1978 to 1997 whereas refers to state-owned industrial enterprises and non-state-owned industrial enterprises over designated size since 1998 whose annual sales revenue is over 5 million yuan (the same below).

b) Gross output value of industry and value-added of industry are calculated at current prices. As industry statistic system has been changed, index of industrial gross output value was at comparable prices before 2003, which has been calculated at current prices since 2004. Index of value-added of industry was at current prices before 2003, which has been calculated at comparable prices since 2004.

11-1 续表 CONTINUED

单位：万元 (10 000 yuan)

年 份 Year	年末固定资产 Year-end Fixed Assets		流动资产年平均余额 Annual Average Balance of Value of Circulating Fund	主营业务收入 Sales Revenue	利税总额 Total Pre-tax Profits
	原 值 Original Value	净 值 Net Value			
1978	706016	475301	298093	595593	119300
1980	823370	540178	329897	708120	146213
1985	1339800	923111	604983	1449426	260677
1986	1445859	970019	743986	1559353	225749
1987	1635303	1135872	908572	1897962	251220
1988	1830786	1254850	1062157	2472560	358610
1989	2063326	1405200	1441939	2734475	365348
1990	2314886	1490850	1942657	2782262	253309
1991	2585930	1647544	2418353	3338105	291455
1992	2947902	1784094	2852708	4167995	365134
1993	3424857	2106423	3484050	6124846	551046
1994	4953046	2967592	4631636	6294911	573144
1995	7307273	4057468	5702467	7524836	580345
1996	8242796	5469742	6209179	7775698	474970
1997	9551992	6348348	7464835	8594769	466987
1998	9866758	6940364	7202796	7809127	393220
1999	10840971	7604150	7733524	8546131	572648
2000	11515782	7848443	8157646	9593576	855670
2001	12056356	7958216	8874861	10732455	1016889
2002	12730167	8282507	9228472	12357157	1320260
2003	13424490	8576299	10305605	15950727	1910901
2004	14970250	9738481	11641381	21088433	2420163

11－2 主要工业产品产量（1978－2004年）
Output of Major Industrial Products (1978-2004)

年 份 Year	原煤（万吨） Coal (10 000 tons)	天然气 （亿立方米） Natural Gas (100 million cu.m)	发电量 （亿千瓦时） Electricity (100 million kwh)	钢材（万吨） Steel Products (10 000 tons)	铝材（万吨） Aluminum Products (10 000 tons)	水泥（万吨） Cement (10 000 tons)
1978	1429.30	0.09	29.60	73.09	1.47	96.14
1980	1519.58	15.78	33.32	76.52	2.27	129.10
1985	2085.66	24.47	36.67	86.35	4.50	262.78
1986	2109.01	25.88	41.96	94.99	4.55	269.20
1987	2255.86	28.39	54.73	111.36	5.00	308.29
1988	2459.97	29.44	66.38	121.06	5.01	353.43
1989	2540.03	31.96	72.64	102.59	4.99	345.39
1990	2332.71	34.59	73.75	109.61	3.97	351.85
1991	2380.45	35.86	84.05	105.67	5.51	428.56
1992	2432.44	36.44	91.95	112.24	5.55	517.31
1993	2624.97	37.14	118.41	162.74	5.79	562.32
1994	2841.32	41.87	124.36	130.74	6.19	642.62
1995	3104.83	45.00	127.62	120.68	5.93	820.57
1996	2170.19	26.10	143.70	129.00	7.44	780.61
1997	2931.07	30.69	148.16	120.56	9.10	977.37
1998	2573.99	33.24	158.67	131.01	10.62	1173.59
1999	1183.22	34.74	158.27	135.10	12.11	1197.60
2000	1149.90	38.98	167.90	156.98	13.98	1402.78
2001	1154.67	41.88	170.41	161.42	16.82	1511.18
2002	1211.73	45.41	184.75	201.48	19.94	1679.52
2003	1484.20	47.29	188.64	235.24	21.60	1927.00
2004	1738.19	51.57	232.82	288.10	26.23	1906.23

11-2 续表 CONTINUED

年 份 Year	汽车（万辆） Motor Vehicles (10 000 vehicles)	摩托车（万辆） Motorcycles (10 000 vehicles)	变压器（万千伏安） Transformers (10 000 kilovolt-amperes)	硫酸（万吨） Sulphuric Acid (10 000 tons)	啤酒（万吨）（万千升） Beer (10 000 tons) (1000 kiloliters)	卷烟（万箱）（亿支） Cigarettes (10 000 cases) (100 million units)
1978	0.16		43.46	12.76		17.54
1980	0.23	0.27	51.65	15.85		23.15
1985	0.89	47.18	69.50	15.09	3.50	49.34
1986	0.61	31.94	90.72	20.86	4.20	62.98
1987	0.90	27.14	103.44	23.25	5.23	69.39
1988	1.66	44.47	102.96	25.31	6.32	71.13
1989	2.02	36.85	115.51	27.33	5.96	71.24
1990	2.18	38.22	81.91	25.24	5.97	71.57
1991	3.04	48.48	104.20	33.10	6.74	73.77
1992	4.56	69.37	172.60	34.28	7.82	87.82
1993	6.82	120.38	182.46	25.96	15.77	87.42
1994	8.77	170.23	235.08	25.31	16.86	86.13
1995	11.47	220.17	277.56	48.84	19.08	100.45
1996	12.42	179.00	308.86	51.36	29.12	90.95
1997	16.07	181.89	286.26	52.23	40.45	102.61
1998	15.74	126.90	151.99	59.47	51.17	73.87
1999	21.85	174.93	226.34	61.83	51.32	96.57
2000	24.59	191.07	684.27	50.65	50.92	68.70
2001	24.38	253.53	820.69	65.77	40.31	67.70
2002	33.13	323.42	1223.90	85.64	41.77	68.76
2003	40.45	441.32	2060.32	99.18	44.42	387.50
2004	43.42	473.07	2890.19	135.51	46.21	386.32

注：啤酒和卷烟的计量单位2003年前为万吨和万箱，2003年及以后为万千升和亿支。

Note: The units of beer and cigarettes before 2003 refers to 10 000 tons and 10 000 cases, whereas since 2003 refers to 1000 kiloliters and 100 million units.

11－3 工业企业经济效益指标（1992－2004年）
Economic Efficiency Indicators of Industrial Enterprises (1992-2004)

单位: % (%)

年 份	经济效益综合指数 Comprehensive Index of Economic Efficiency	总资产贡献率 Ratio of Total Assets to Industrial Output Value	资本保值增值率 Ratio of Creditors' Equity of Current Year to that of Previous Year	资产负债率 Ratio of Liabilities to Assets
1992	76.17			
1993	84.61			
1994	83.91			
1995	73.04			
1996	63.77	2.80	125.70	68.60
1997	60.25	2.70	113.90	68.40
1998	57.27	5.00	103.00	68.30
1999	67.66	5.50	101.40	67.10
2000	87.10	6.30	112.10	64.80
2001	95.24	6.90	108.30	62.70
2002	109.80	7.82	120.72	61.33
2003	129.73	9.91	115.83	60.82
2004	140.90	10.57	120.15	60.84

年 份	流动资产周转率（次） Turnover Ratio of Annual Circulating Funds (time)	成本费用利润率 Ratio of Profits to Cost	全员劳动生产率（元/人年） Overall Labor Productivity (yuan/person-year)	产品销售率 Ratio of Sales to Products
1992	1.40	3.20	7296	97.00
1993	1.60	3.10	10758	97.10
1994	1.40	2.70	12638	96.40
1995	1.20	0.70	11804	96.30
1996	1.30	-1.20	12298	96.20
1997	1.20	-1.80	13688	95.40
1998	1.10	-2.40	16690	97.20
1999	1.10	-1.10	23385	97.50
2000	1.20	1.70	31081	99.10
2001	1.20	2.30	37750	97.90
2002	1.32	3.42	46464	98.07
2003	1.54	5.71	55957	97.83
2004	1.81	5.82	65329	99.87

注：经济效益综合指数1997年前由资金利税率、增加值率、流动资产周转率、成本费用利润率、全员劳动生产率、产品销售率等六项指标计算求得，从1997年起由总资产贡献率、资本保值增值率、资产负债率、流动资产周转率、成本费用利润率、全员劳动生产率、产品销售率等七项指标计算求得。

Note: Comprehensive index of economic efficiency before 1997 are calculated with 6 items of ratio of pretax profits to total industrial assets, ratio of value-added to gross industrial output value, turnover ratio of annual circulating funds, ratio of profits to cost, overall labor productivity, ratio of sales to products, and since 1997 are calculated with 7 items of ratio of total assets to industrial output value, ratio of creditors' equity of current year to that of previous year, ratio of liabilities to assets, turnover ratio of output value, circulating funds, ratio of profits to cost, overall labor productivity, ratio of sales to products.

11－4 国有及规模以上非国有工业企业单位数（2003－2004年）
Number of State-owned Industrial Enterprises and Non-state -owned Industrial Enterprises above Designated Size (2003-2004)

单位：个 (unit)

指　　标	Item	2003	2004
总　　计	**Total**	**2243**	**2634**
#国有控股企业	State-owned and State Holding	573	529
#亏损企业	Lose-suffering	440	546
按登记注册类型分	**By Registration**		
内资企业	Domestic-funded Enterprises	2081	2453
国有企业	State-owned	264	244
集体企业	Collective-owned	208	178
股份合作企业	Cooperative Share Holding	93	74
国有联营	State Joint Ownership Enterprises	3	2
集体联营	Collective Joint Ownership Enterprises	1	2
国有与集体联营	Joint State-collective Enterprises	3	4
其他联营	Other Joint Ownership Enterprises	1	1
国有独资公司	State-funded Corporations	79	56
其他有限责任公司	Other Limited Liability Corporations	430	600
股份有限公司	Share-holding Corporations Ltd.	84	107
私营独资	Private-funded Enterprises	207	218
私营合作	Private Partnership Enterprises	38	61
私营有限责任公司	Private Limited Liability Corporations	607	797
私营股份有限公司	Private Share-holding Corporations Ltd.	62	100
其他内资	Other Enterprises	1	9
港澳台商投资企业	Enterprises Funded by Hong Kong, Macao and Taiwan	65	61
与港澳台商合资经营	Joint-venture (with Funds from Hong Kong, Macao and Taiwan)	46	42
与港澳台商合作经营	Cooperative Enterprises (with Funds from Hong Kong, Macao and Taiwan)	5	8
港澳台商独资	Enterprises with Sole Investment from Hong Kong, Macao and Taiwan	13	9
港澳台商投资股份有限公司	Share-holding Corporations Ltd.with Investment from Hong Kong, Macao and Taiwan	1	2
外商投资企业	Foreign-funded Enterprises	97	120
中外合资经营	Joint-venture Enterprises	81	91
中外合作经营	Cooperation Enterprises with Sole Foreign Investment	3	4
外资企业	Enterprises with Foreign Investment	11	21
外商投资股份有限公司	Share-holding Corporations Ltd.with Foreign Investment	2	4
按轻重工业分	**By Light and Heavy Industry**		
轻工业	Light Industry	947	1101
重工业	Heavy Industry	1296	1533
按企业规模分	**By Size**		
大型企业	Large	43	49
中型企业	Medium	353	386
小型企业	Small	1847	2199

注：国有控股为国有及国有控股（下表同）。

Note: State holding enterprises refer to state-owned and state holding enterprises (the same below).

11－5 国有及规模以上非国有工业企业增加值（2003－2004年）
Value-adder of State-owned Industrial Enterprises and Non-state--owned Industrial Enterprises above Designated Size (2003-2004)

单位：万元 (10 000 yuan)

指 标	Item	2003	2004
总 计	**Total**	**4778500**	**5883198**
#国有控股企业	State-owned and State Holding	2847600	3375128
按登记注册类型分	**By Registration**		
内资企业	Domestic-funded Enterprises	3884500	4723693
#国有企业	State-owned	579500	596521
集体企业	Collective-owned	175200	122681
港澳台投资企业	Funded by Hong Kong, Macao and Taiwan	375540	385910
外商投资企业	Foreign-funded	518460	773595
按轻、重工业分	**By Light and Heavy Industry**		
轻工业	Light Industry	1692000	1881206
重工业	Heavy Industry	3086500	4001992
按企业规模分	**By Size of Enterprise**		
大型企业	Large	1821813	2453463
中型企业	Medium	1763587	2012678
小型企业	Small	1193100	1417057
按行业分	**By Sector**		
采矿业	Mining and Quarrying		
煤炭开采和洗选业	Coal Mining and Dressing	113958	215656
石油和天然气开采业	Petroleum and Natural Gas Extraction	16430	19562
黑色金属矿采选业	Ferrous Metals Mining and Dressing	23514	42048
有色金属矿采选业	Nonferrous Metals Mining and Dressing	24	106
非金属矿采选业	Nonmetal Minerals Mining and Dressing	29538	41890
其他采矿业	Other Minerals Mining		
制造业	Manufacturing		
农副食品加工业	Farm Products and By-food Processing	69473	86032
食品制造业	Food Production	47574	64529
饮料制造业	Beverage Production	93066	89962
烟草制品业	Tobacco Products	263662	274180
纺织业	Textile Industry	75300	97529
纺织服装、鞋、帽制造业	Garments, Shoes and Hats Production	8070	17580
皮革、毛皮、羽毛（绒）及其制品业	Leather, Furs, Down and Related Products	14146	38387
木材加工及木竹藤棕草制品业	Timber Processing,Bamboo,Cane,Palm,Straw Products	5064	8832
家具制造业	Furniture Manufacturing	4937	17803
造纸及纸制品业	Papermaking and Paper Products	36899	57626
印刷业、记录媒介的复制	Printing and Record Medium Reproduction	30670	32046
文教体育用品制造业	Cultural Educational and Sports Goods	795	668
石油加工、炼焦及核燃料加工业	Petroleum, Coking and Nuclear Fuel Processing	6578	22281
化学原料及化学制品制造业	Raw Chemical Materials and Chemical Products	372919	458537
医药制造业	Medical and Pharmaceutical Products	147609	202465
化学纤维制造业	Chemical Fiber	397	3741
橡胶制品业	Rubber Products	17296	26264
塑料制品业	Plastic Products	26559	31814
非金属矿物制品业	Nonmetal Mineral Products	320903	351019
黑色金属冶炼及压延加工业	Smelting and Pressing of Ferrous Metals	292956	351440
有色金属冶炼及压延加工业	Smelting and Pressing of Nonferrous Metals	103542	156725
金属制品业	Metal Products	56858	73373
通用设备制造业	Ordinary Equipment	205079	259144
专用设备制造业	Special Equipment	97743	124682
交通运输设备制造业	Transportation Equipment	1526937	1707749
电气机械及器材制造业	Electric Equipment and Machinery	100170	145012
通信设备、计算机及其他电子设备制造业	Communication,Computers and Other Electronic Equipment	51811	110263
仪器仪表及文化、办公用机械制造业	Instruments, Meters,Cultural and Office Machinery	93481	113108
工艺品及其他制造业	Handicraft and Other Production	12145	11703
废弃资源和废旧材料回收加工业	Recovery and Processing of Waste Resources and Materials	369	5489
电力、燃气及水的生产和供应业	Electricpower, Gas & Water Production and Supply		
电力、热力的生产和供应业	Electricpower and Hot Power Production and Supply	441497	535595
燃气生产和供应业	Gas Production and Supply	23483	38850
水的生产和供应业	Water Production and Supply	47049	49508

11－6 国有及规模以上非国有工业企业主要经济指标（2004年）

单位:万元

指　标	Item	单位数(个) Number of Enterprises (unit)	从业人员平均人数（万人） Average Emloyment (10 000 persons)
总　计	**Total**	**2634**	**90.05**
#国有控股企业	State Holding	529	43.03
按登记注册类型分	**By Registration**		
内资企业	Domestic-funded Enterprises	2453	83.61
#国有企业	State-owned	244	13.49
集体企业	Collective-owned	178	4.18
港澳台投资企业	Funded by Hong Kong, Macao and Taiwan	61	2.41
外商投资企业	Foreign-funded	120	4.03
按轻、重工业分	**By Light and Heavy Industry**		
轻工业	Light Industry	1101	31.64
重工业	Heavy Industry	1533	58.41
按企业规模分	**By Size of Enterprise**		
大型企业	Large	49	22.36
中型企业	Medium	386	32.74
小型企业	Small	2199	34.95
按行业分	**By Sector**		
采矿业	Mining and Quarrying		
煤炭开采和洗选业	Coal Mining and Dressing	143	7.91
石油和天然气开采业	Petroleum and Natural Gas Extraction	2	0.13
黑色金属矿采选业	Ferrous Metals Mining and Dressing	16	0.61
有色金属矿采选业	Nonferrous Metals Mining and Dressing	1	…
非金属矿采选业	Nonmetal Minerals Mining and Dressing	22	0.70
其他采矿业	Other Minerals Mining		
制造业	Manufacturing		
农副食品加工业	Farm Products and By-food Processing	104	1.64
食品制造业	Food Production	49	1.34
饮料制造业	Beverage Production	40	0.96
烟草制品业	Tobacco Products	5	0.58
纺织业	Textile Industry	111	5.03
纺织服装、鞋、帽制造业	Garments, Shoes and Hats Production	19	0.48
皮革、毛皮、羽毛（绒）及其制品业	Leather, Furs, Down and Related Products	43	0.69
木材加工及木竹藤棕草制品业	Timber Processing, Bamboo, Cane, Palm, Straw Products	10	0.20
家具制造业	Furniture Manufacturing	20	0.29
造纸及纸制品业	Papermaking and Paper Products	58	0.92
印刷业、记录媒介的复制	Printing and Record Medium Reproduction	49	0.64
文教体育用品制造业	Cultural Educational and Sports Goods	3	0.01
石油加工、炼焦及核燃料加工业	Petroleum, Coking and Nuclear Fuel Processing	14	0.33
化学原料及化学制品制造业	Raw Chemical Materials and Chemical Products	164	5.68
医药制造业	Medical and Pharmaceutical Products	51	1.97
化学纤维制造业	Chemical Fiber	2	0.05
橡胶制品业	Rubber Products	26	0.87
塑料制品业	Plastic Products	71	0.78
非金属矿物制品业	Nonmetal Mineral Products	259	8.02
黑色金属冶炼及压延加工业	Smelting and Pressing of Ferrous Metals	76	3.12
有色金属冶炼及压延加工业	Smelting and Pressing of Nonferrous Metals	67	1.94
金属制品业	Metal Products	77	1.64
通用设备制造业	Ordinary Equipment	141	4.64
专用设备制造业	Special Equipment	50	4.67
交通运输设备制造业	Transportation Equipment	620	23.67
电气机械及器材制造业	Electric Equipment and Machinery	100	2.05
通信设备、计算机及其他电子设备制造业	Communication, Computers and Other Electronic Equipment	24	0.70
仪器仪表及文化、办公用机械制造业	Instruments, Meters, Cultural and Office Machinery	49	2.05
工艺品及其他制造业	Handicraft and Other Production	15	0.28
废弃资源和废旧材料回收加工业	Recovery and Processing of Waste Resources and Materials	4	0.06
电力、燃气及水的生产和供应业	Electricpower, Gas & Water Production and Supply		
电力、热力的生产和供应业	Electricpower and Hot Power Production and Supply	70	4.08
燃气生产和供应业	Gas Production and Supply	22	0.51
水的生产和供应业	Water Production and Supply	37	0.81

Main Economic Indicators of State-owned Industrial Enterprises and Non-state-owned Industrial Enterprises above Designated Size (2004)

(10 000 yuan)

工业总产值（现价）		工业销售产值	工业增加值	实收资本		
Gross Output Value (Current prices)	#新产品产值 Output Value of New Products	Sales Value of Industry	Value-added of Industry	Capital Obtained	#国家资本 State Capital	#外商资本 Foreign Capital
21427261	**5198017**	**21398773**	**5883198**	**6821412**	**1958544**	**589452**
11781904	3741133	11831276	3375128	4769601	1922746	333778
17267083	3561379	17302158	4723693	5699161	1810562	170157
1726158	316470	1742534	596521	808727	665736	464
440441	7805	443311	122681	62947	1250	
1343834	215616	1308968	385910	226243	73916	843
2816344	1421022	2787647	773595	896008	74066	418452
7326968	1464774	7285571	1881206	1442255	409577	104220
14100293	3733243	14113202	4001992	5379157	1548967	485232
9421947	3754188	9471541	2453463	2769585	890408	230469
6613924	1226248	6564083	2012678	2512203	735500	247234
5391390	217581	5363149	1417057	1539624	332636	111749
435575		438447	215656	237000	12225	
30609		30177	19562	13036	6324	
83394		103550	42048	23397	19421	
190		190	106	279	279	
85286	3961	97219	41890	22275	3390	
581078	26137	584032	86032	58604	13826	13474
220444	13985	224368	64529	55473	13594	18534
239661	35997	239648	89963	101350	17995	18834
423185	86960	423229	274180	83007	68457	
391986	55190	394289	97529	110686	50394	83
58455		51705	17580	12914		3209
138979		127913	38387	11795	130	225
30535	1787	29103	8833	6654	1020	
92650		95248	17803	18178	262	5807
196487	30037	194983	57626	48257	2754	1929
95195	5203	97119	32046	20944	7013	235
1402		1200	668	409	51	
73142	1355	70563	22281	32584	305	
1376593	253092	1377140	458537	536977	247769	50232
535128	181569	543086	202465	228565	60283	1231
12899	4159	12758	3741	497		
109407	16093	109469	26264	29420	488	11358
125696	3156	126833	31814	64168	6263	3371
969367	163196	978380	351019	433219	27514	68132
1373254	180728	1351299	351440	244309	131708	1700
901574	75063	885727	156725	421054	11367	35
258656	47322	254925	73373	86072	1954	4446
871162	224963	858045	259144	305307	51451	45156
561059	122412	663967	124682	260811	72269	150
7886738	3435091	7845157	1707749	1742663	190534	289615
752963	48200	704723	145011	137518	27970	26962
375810	101676	336405	110263	107993	30629	13420
370751	80476	361828	113108	121718	37481	4230
30559	9	27989	11702	8085	519	
20158		21856	5489	2685	50	
1481054	200	1485693	535595	1008555	664728	7084
150406		164205	38850	97326	82180	
85774		86305	49508	127628	95947	

11-6 续表1

单位:万元

指 标	Item	资产合计 Total Assets	#流动资产合计 Circulating Funds
总 计	**Total**	**27182505**	**12735008**
#国有控股企业	State Holding	18490358	8187917
按登记注册类型分	**By Registration**		
内资企业	Domestic-funded Enterprises	23078199	10834489
#国有企业	State-owned	2922904	1334996
集体企业	Collective-owned	350793	205728
港澳台投资企业	Funded by Hong Kong, Macao and Taiwan	1114338	542952
外商投资企业	Foreign-funded	2989968	1357567
按轻、重工业分	**By Light and Heavy Industry**		
轻工业	Light Industry	6930367	3840016
重工业	Heavy Industry	20252138	8894992
按企业规模分	**By Size of Enterprise**		
大型企业	Large	12646234	5893522
中型企业	Medium	9087297	4252614
小型企业	Small	5448974	2588872
按行业分	**By Sector**		
采矿业	Mining and Quarrying		
煤炭开采和洗选业	Coal Mining and Dressing	620201	226518
石油和天然气开采业	Petroleum and Natural Gas Extraction	42911	10911
黑色金属矿采选业	Ferrous Metals Mining and Dressing	93400	48351
有色金属矿采选业	Nonferrous Metals Mining and Dressing	378	119
非金属矿采选业	Nonmetal Minerals Mining and Dressing	101917	39774
其他采矿业	Other Minerals Mining		
制造业	Manufacturing		
农副食品加工业	Farm Products and By-food Processing	275061	133668
食品制造业	Food Production	191648	85454
饮料制造业	Beverage Production	359486	142270
烟草制品业	Tobacco Products	508644	322789
纺织业	Textile Industry	424903	169854
纺织服装、鞋、帽制造业	Garments, Shoes and Hats Production	43864	30427
皮革、毛皮、羽毛（绒）及其制品业	Leather, Furs, Down and Related Products	52112	29577
木材加工及木竹藤棕草制品业	Timber Processing, Bamboo, Cane, Palm, Straw Products	21719	9480
家具制造业	Furniture Manufacturing	72690	53121
造纸及纸制品业	Papermaking and Paper Products	180920	89648
印刷业、记录媒介的复制	Printing and Record Medium Reproduction	104472	52557
文教体育用品制造业	Cultural Educational and Sports Goods	1415	938
石油加工、炼焦及核燃料加工业	Petroleum, Coking and Nuclear Fuel Processing	78120	27598
化学原料及化学制品制造业	Raw Chemical Materials and Chemical Products	1853779	736894
医药制造业	Medical and Pharmaceutical Products	1008332	488689
化学纤维制造业	Chemical Fiber	15934	6504
橡胶制品业	Rubber Products	163696	78318
塑料制品业	Plastic Products	164695	79410
非金属矿物制品业	Nonmetal Mineral Products	1660077	663179
黑色金属冶炼及压延加工业	Smelting and Pressing of Ferrous Metals	1065314	507218
有色金属冶炼及压延加工业	Smelting and Pressing of Nonferrous Metals	819046	457181
金属制品业	Metal Products	290091	170102
通用设备制造业	Ordinary Equipment	1094604	670443
专用设备制造业	Special Equipment	1603137	581291
交通运输设备制造业	Transportation Equipment	7492067	4436393
电气机械及器材制造业	Electric Equipment and Machinery	697756	508585
通信设备、计算机及其他电子设备制造业	Communication, Computers and Other Electronic Equipment	389071	271242
仪器仪表及文化、办公用机械制造业	Instruments, Meters, Cultural and Office Machinery	510367	301405
工艺品及其他制造业	Handicraft and Other Production	29752	18930
废弃资源和废旧材料回收加工业	Recovery and Processing of Waste Resources and Materials	7559	5997
电力、燃气及水的生产和供应业	Electricpower, Gas & Water Production and Supply		
电力、热力的生产和供应业	Electricpower and Hot Power Production and Supply	4468655	1072904
燃气生产和供应业	Gas Production and Supply	260622	114751
水的生产和供应业	Water Production and Supply	414090	92518

11-6 CONTINUED-1

(10 000 yuan)

流动资产年平均余额 Annual Average Balance of Value of Circulating Fund	固定资产 Fixed Assets		固定资产净值年平均余额 Annual Average Balance of Net Value of Fixed Assets	负债合计	
	原　值 Original	净　值 Net		Total Liabilities	#流动负债合计 Total Circulating Liabilities
11641381	**14970250**	**9738481**	**9315003**	**16537398**	**12513705**
7446908	11175923	7006265	6680345	11178297	8262861
9826781	12273573	8239206	7804529	14222161	10966158
1243107	2061333	1170432	1111509	2220753	1631880
203178	177453	100188	101629	244034	211308
496436	735564	412457	409874	581245	473962
1318164	1961113	1086818	1100600	1733992	1073585
3478554	3033998	2037003	1977248	4637669	3838533
8162827	11936252	7701478	7337755	11899729	8675172
5108129	6924441	4373160	4125355	7248710	5615517
3980114	5193446	3301501	3175431	5724436	4264265
2553138	2852363	2063820	2014217	3564252	2633923
202255	472799	269686	260043	295900	214396
8905	33865	18592	13284	12643	8106
40127	50201	38756	34151	43426	40008
114	652	249	251	316	163
36454	40433	30909	29016	60195	42963
121854	127720	96243	97143	196946	146265
90440	133042	76567	73281	106773	85909
134379	229732	136455	139615	202419	168773
304960	245389	146781	140988	331717	267418
178432	269275	183371	189550	346046	209719
27859	11747	8722	8197	26857	24785
28851	13535	10106	10166	26372	24142
10407	10363	7492	7429	9758	7745
49020	25240	17324	16160	48142	45931
88467	74348	56587	54865	117820	86905
59669	60750	38118	38305	60241	48648
969	865	409	441	456	456
24396	44205	31862	26771	29711	23073
677600	1343545	724920	669115	969891	693173
432685	368341	276967	259338	560119	468444
6034	14223	7157	8805	11329	7718
79032	62599	48540	44599	125323	102992
77164	82446	55451	58639	105819	93048
622337	989910	687586	664917	1068377	703661
426277	695730	404510	401055	532497	453488
454325	607340	344610	344353	564622	449196
149192	122450	80954	76059	176452	161520
607369	508616	283751	256471	706459	601967
560731	673095	452128	441317	1279736	1158884
4031399	2873525	1937973	1814205	4242981	3915825
393462	193369	134068	122607	553783	529701
229287	91770	51375	47196	258486	226872
299622	178414	108521	109425	331807	291806
17914	6969	5632	5483	16111	12550
6185	741	684	640	4616	4256
974224	3838304	2624630	2523861	2777082	1051532
105274	138139	85710	83901	110033	72500
83710	336563	255085	243361	226137	69167

11-6 续表2

单位:万元

指标	Item	所有者权益 Creditors' Equity	主营业务收入 Major Business Revenue
总计	**Total**	**10645107**	**21088433**
#国有控股企业	State Holding	7312062	11765499
按登记注册类型分	**By Registration**		
内资企业	Domestic-funded Enterprises	8856037	17020556
#国有企业	State-owned	702151	1731395
集体企业	Collective-owned	106760	439805
港澳台投资企业	Funded by Hong Kong, Macao and Taiwan	533093	1280099
外商投资企业	Foreign-funded	1255977	2787778
按轻、重工业分	**By Light and Heavy Industry**		
轻工业	Light Industry	2292698	7105549
重工业	Heavy Industry	8352409	13982884
按企业规模分	**By Size of Enterprise**		
大型企业	Large	5397524	9467587
中型企业	Medium	3362861	6405625
小型企业	Small	1884722	5215221
按行业分	**By Sector**		
采矿业	Mining and Quarrying		
煤炭开采和洗选业	Coal Mining and Dressing	324301	436249
石油和天然气开采业	Petroleum and Natural Gas Extraction	30267	29841
黑色金属矿采选业	Ferrous Metals Mining and Dressing	49974	102800
有色金属矿采选业	Nonferrous Metals Mining and Dressing	61	190
非金属矿采选业	Nonmetal Minerals Mining and Dressing	41722	90901
其他采矿业	Other Minerals Mining		
制造业	Manufacturing		
农副食品加工业	Farm Products and By-food Processing	78115	573739
食品制造业	Food Production	84875	238674
饮料制造业	Beverage Production	157067	239204
烟草制品业	Tobacco Products	176927	420837
纺织业	Textile Industry	78857	393963
纺织服装、鞋、帽制造业	Garments, Shoes and Hats Production	17006	49600
皮革、毛皮、羽毛（绒）及其制品业	Leather, Furs, Down and Related Products	25740	126444
木材加工及木竹藤棕草制品业	Timber Processing, Bamboo, Cane, Palm, Straw Products	11961	27239
家具制造业	Furniture Manufacturing	24548	94925
造纸及纸制品业	Papermaking and Paper Products	63101	186004
印刷业、记录媒介的复制	Printing and Record Medium Reproduction	44231	90023
文教体育用品制造业	Cultural Educational and Sports Goods	959	1191
石油加工、炼焦及核燃料加工业	Petroleum, Coking and Nuclear Fuel Processing	48410	72152
化学原料及化学制品制造业	Raw Chemical Materials and Chemical Products	883887	1380495
医药制造业	Medical and Pharmaceutical Products	448213	458653
化学纤维制造业	Chemical Fiber	4605	11972
橡胶制品业	Rubber Products	38373	106437
塑料制品业	Plastic Products	58876	122989
非金属矿物制品业	Nonmetal Mineral Products	591700	939904
黑色金属冶炼及压延加工业	Smelting and Pressing of Ferrous Metals	532817	1360181
有色金属冶炼及压延加工业	Smelting and Pressing of Nonferrous Metals	254423	860981
金属制品业	Metal Products	113639	253578
通用设备制造业	Ordinary Equipment	388145	837615
专用设备制造业	Special Equipment	323401	643865
交通运输设备制造业	Transportation Equipment	3249087	7755987
电气机械及器材制造业	Electric Equipment and Machinery	143973	710398
通信设备、计算机及其他电子设备制造业	Communication, Computers and Other Electronic Equipment	130586	272306
仪器仪表及文化、办公用机械制造业	Instruments, Meters, Cultural and Office Machinery	178560	337317
工艺品及其他制造业	Handicraft and Other Production	13641	26486
废弃资源和废旧材料回收加工业	Recovery and Processing of Waste Resources and Materials	2943	21856
电力、燃气及水的生产和供应业	Electricpower, Gas & Water Production and Supply		
电力、热力的生产和供应业	Electricpower and Hot Power Production and Supply	1691574	1566311
燃气生产和供应业	Gas Production and Supply	150589	163835
水的生产和供应业	Water Production and Supply	187953	83291

11-6 CONTINUED-2

(10 000 yuan)

主营业务成本 Cost of Major Business	主营业务税金及附加 Tax and Extra Charges of Major Business	主营业务利润 Profit of Major Business	利润总额 Total After-tax Profits	利税总额 Total Pre-tax Profits	工资总额 Total Wages
17029097	**409377**	**3649958**	**1155898**	**2420163**	**1238422**
9191169	297250	2277080	649083	1519150	741474
13821006	352628	2846922	763949	1777368	1106255
1327141	55347	348907	24292	169993	194420
381180	3864	54762	14696	36437	42978
1067448	5746	206904	107278	173521	57258
2140643	51003	596132	284671	469274	74909
5651459	225451	1228639	215101	645949	350017
11377638	183926	2421319	940797	1774214	888405
7410116	277694	1779777	604685	1279366	451154
5134143	94203	1177278	354332	733411	435185
4484838	37480	692903	196881	407386	352083
322277	5418	108555	26957	62413	96122
20523	562	8756	6573	8982	2357
70330	1776	30694	19055	29334	12118
113	1	77	56	59	35
65027	2037	23837	9275	16185	8275
526553	1295	45891	12038	18841	15242
191259	1425	45990	11150	23296	13402
150660	14947	73597	10949	41565	14036
182832	149088	88918	27547	223047	19314
362955	1757	29251	-15148	-1443	37749
37934	260	11406	1947	3917	4801
107633	474	18337	7358	10249	8931
24097	149	2992	896	2147	2069
84441	256	10227	1334	4425	4380
161043	1164	23798	8938	16922	9084
76845	603	12575	3220	8378	6637
789	14	388	98	207	234
56030	609	15513	5834	9985	4042
1054365	8423	317707	143184	222443	79126
272472	4459	181722	39169	74252	29381
10285	45	1642	790	1164	392
87197	847	18392	2637	5851	8603
108800	326	13863	-927	2785	8164
736816	45468	157620	57369	157777	81122
1173472	2243	184466	99531	163076	63518
793075	3116	64790	21017	48807	34085
203148	1058	49371	13755	21307	18812
667017	5900	164697	47067	89925	65699
533408	10028	100429	10366	33002	80726
6503809	128705	1123473	418536	770863	320132
432877	2639	274882	29374	52326	28361
230576	390	41340	10646	15662	11720
253198	1770	82349	20346	35552	29545
19247	150	7090	4096	5082	2041
19511	104	2241	1657	2257	1079
1310354	9444	246513	77051	207583	89465
123361	1759	38714	11484	17568	13981
54768	668	27855	10673	14372	13642

11－7 国有及规模以上非国有工业企业经济效益指标（2004年）

单位：%

指 标	Item	增加值率 Ratio of Value-added to Gross Industrial Output Value	总资产贡献率 Ratio of Total Assets to Industrial Output Value
总 计	**Total**	**27.46**	**10.57**
#国有控股企业	State Holding	28.65	9.38
按登记注册类型分	**By Registration**		
内资企业	Domestic-funded Enterprises	27.36	9.34
#国有企业	State-owned	34.56	7.72
集体企业	Collective-owned	27.85	10.32
港澳台投资企业	Funded by Hong Kong, Macao and Taiwan	28.72	14.78
外商投资企业	Foreign-funded	27.47	18.56
按轻、重工业分	**By Light and Heavy Industry**		
轻工业	Light Industry	25.68	11.68
重工业	Heavy Industry	28.38	10.19
按企业规模分	**By Size of Enterprise**		
大型企业	Large	26.04	10.13
中型企业	Medium	30.43	12.39
小型企业	Small	26.28	8.65
按行业分	**By Sector**		
采矿业	Mining and Quarrying		
煤炭开采和洗选业	Coal Mining and Dressing	49.51	11.64
石油和天然气开采业	Petroleum and Natural Gas Extraction	63.91	16.93
黑色金属矿采选业	Ferrous Metals Mining and Dressing	50.42	36.17
有色金属矿采选业	Nonferrous Metals Mining and Dressing	55.60	16.13
非金属矿采选业	Nonmetal Minerals Mining and Dressing	49.12	18.41
其他采矿业	Other Minerals Mining		
制造业	Manufacturing		
农副食品加工业	Farm Products and By-food Processing	14.81	8.97
食品制造业	Food Production	29.27	11.60
饮料制造业	Beverage Production	37.54	13.21
烟草制品业	Tobacco Products	64.79	47.79
纺织业	Textile Industry	24.88	4.08
纺织服装、鞋、帽制造业	Garments, Shoes and Hats Production	30.07	6.46
皮革、毛皮、羽毛（绒）及其制品业	Leather, Furs, Down and Related Products	27.62	19.72
木材加工及木竹藤棕草制品业	Timber Processing, Bamboo, Cane, Palm, Straw Products	28.93	17.37
家具制造业	Furniture Manufacturing	19.22	6.75
造纸及纸制品业	Papermaking and Paper Products	29.33	9.21
印刷业、记录媒介的复制	Printing and Record Medium Reproduction	33.66	7.44
文教体育用品制造业	Cultural Educational and Sports Goods	47.64	14.14
石油加工、炼焦及核燃料加工业	Petroleum, Coking and Nuclear Fuel Processing	30.46	11.72
化学原料及化学制品制造业	Raw Chemical Materials and Chemical Products	33.31	13.07
医药制造业	Medical and Pharmaceutical Products	37.83	9.60
化学纤维制造业	Chemical Fiber	29.01	13.84
橡胶制品业	Rubber Products	24.01	6.19
塑料制品业	Plastic Products	25.31	3.49
非金属矿物制品业	Nonmetal Mineral Products	36.21	9.17
黑色金属冶炼及压延加工业	Smelting and Pressing of Ferrous Metals	25.59	15.54
有色金属冶炼及压延加工业	Smelting and Pressing of Nonferrous Metals	17.38	6.01
金属制品业	Metal Products	28.37	8.53
通用设备制造业	Ordinary Equipment	29.75	10.23
专用设备制造业	Special Equipment	22.22	3.98
交通运输设备制造业	Transportation Equipment	21.65	12.22
电气机械及器材制造业	Electric Equipment and Machinery	19.26	9.28
通信设备、计算机及其他电子设备制造业	Communication, Computers and Other Electronic	29.34	5.49
仪器仪表及文化、办公用机械制造业	Instruments, Meters, Cultural and Office Machinery	30.51	7.95
工艺品及其他制造业	Handicraft and Other Production	38.30	18.92
废弃资源和废旧材料回收加工业	Recovery and Processing of Waste Resources and Materials	27.23	10.44
电力、燃气及水的生产和供应业	Electricpower, Gas & Water Production and Supply		
电力、热力的生产和供应业	Electricpower and Hot Power Production and Supply	36.16	7.14
燃气生产和供应业	Gas Production and Supply	25.83	6.24
水的生产和供应业	Water Production and Supply	57.72	4.85

Economic Efficiency Indicators of State-owned Industrial Enterprises and Non-state-owned Industrial Enterprises above Designated Size (2004)

(%)

资本保值增值率 Ratio of Creditors' Equity of Current Year to that of Previous Year	资产负债率 Ratio of Liabilities to Assets	流动资产周转率（次） Turnover Ratio of Annual Circulating Funds (time)	成本费用利润率 Ratio of Profits to Cost	全员劳动生产率（元/人年） Overall Labor Productivity (yuan/person-year)	产品销售率 Ratio of Sales to Products
120.15	**60.84**	**1.81**	**5.82**	**65329**	**99.87**
112.54	60.45	1.58	5.85	78432	100.42
119.73	61.63	1.73	4.72	56497	100.20
113.85	75.98	1.39	1.41	44213	100.95
122.12	69.57	2.16	3.44	29383	100.65
115.35	52.16	2.58	9.18	159916	97.41
126.04	57.99	2.11	11.42	191869	98.98
117.01	66.92	2.04	3.32	59451	99.44
121.07	58.76	1.71	7.03	68513	100.09
110.85	57.32	1.85	6.90	109708	100.53
123.04	62.99	1.61	5.83	61478	99.25
140.83	65.41	2.04	3.92	40542	99.48
113.51	47.71	2.16	6.65	27247	100.66
98.14	29.46	3.35	26.37	149559	98.59
146.69	46.49	2.56	23.26	68315	124.17
1291.67	83.77	1.67	42.47	23556	100.00
134.71	59.06	2.49	11.52	60006	113.99
133.73	71.60	4.71	2.15	52388	100.51
117.91	55.71	2.64	4.89	47955	101.78
97.29	56.31	1.78	5.13	93516	99.99
114.87	65.22	1.38	11.17	475760	100.01
143.33	81.44	2.21	-3.72	19406	100.59
144.98	61.23	1.78	4.02	36624	88.45
168.93	50.61	4.38	6.07	55625	92.04
138.18	44.93	2.62	3.36	44926	95.31
125.32	66.23	1.94	1.42	60472	102.80
85.83	65.12	2.10	4.92	62610	99.23
118.59	57.66	1.51	3.63	49722	102.02
104.94	32.20	1.23	8.93	48040	85.58
222.96	38.03	2.96	8.97	67993	96.47
114.17	52.32	2.04	11.33	80754	100.04
128.54	55.55	1.06	9.39	102988	101.49
100.00	71.10	1.98	7.05	80806	98.91
144.68	76.56	1.35	2.58	30130	100.06
92.61	64.25	1.59	-0.76	40819	100.90
125.19	64.36	1.51	6.46	43743	100.93
154.94	49.99	3.19	7.90	112735	98.40
60.90	68.94	1.90	2.48	80591	98.24
131.85	60.83	1.70	5.72	44871	98.56
121.96	64.54	1.38	5.91	55909	98.49
103.53	79.83	1.15	1.17	26685	118.34
117.31	56.63	1.92	5.71	72150	99.47
137.15	79.37	1.81	6.03	70748	93.59
118.32	66.44	1.19	3.98	157160	89.51
139.74	65.01	1.13	6.25	55212	97.59
137.38	54.15	1.48	17.84	41483	91.59
277.43	61.06	3.53	8.22	94148	108.42
138.52	62.15	1.61	5.25	131434	100.31
107.45	42.22	1.56	7.31	76027	109.17
137.04	54.61	0.99	13.06	61501	100.62

11-7 续表

指　　标	Item	销售利润率 (%) Ratio of Profits to Sales
总　计	**Total**	**5.48**
#国有控股企业	State Holding	5.52
按登记注册类型分	**By Registration**	
内资企业	Domestic-funded Enterprises	4.49
#国有企业	State-owned	1.40
集体企业	Collective-owned	3.34
港澳台投资企业	Funded by Hong Kong, Macao and Taiwan	8.38
外商投资企业	Foreign-funded	10.21
按轻、重工业分	**By Light and Heavy Industry**	
轻工业	Light Industry	3.03
重工业	Heavy Industry	6.73
按企业规模分	**By Size of Enterprise**	
大型企业	Large	6.39
中型企业	Medium	5.53
小型企业	Small	3.78
按行业分	**By Sector**	
采矿业	Mining and Quarrying	
煤炭开采和洗选业	Coal Mining and Dressing	6.18
石油和天然气开采业	Petroleum and Natural Gas Extraction	22.03
黑色金属矿采选业	Ferrous Metals Mining and Dressing	18.54
有色金属矿采选业	Nonferrous Metals Mining and Dressing	29.62
非金属矿采选业	Nonmetal Minerals Mining and Dressing	10.20
其他采矿业	Other Minerals Mining	
制造业	Manufacturing	
农副食品加工业	Farm Products and By-food Processing	2.10
食品制造业	Food Production	4.67
饮料制造业	Beverage Production	4.58
烟草制品业	Tobacco Products	6.55
纺织业	Textile Industry	-3.84
纺织服装、鞋、帽制造业	Garments, Shoes and Hats Production	3.92
皮革、毛皮、羽毛（绒）及其制品业	Leather, Furs, Down and Related Products	5.82
木材加工及木竹藤棕草制品业	Timber Processing, Bamboo, Cane, Palm, Straw Products	3.29
家具制造业	Furniture Manufacturing	1.40
造纸及纸制品业	Papermaking and Paper Products	4.81
印刷业、记录媒介的复制	Printing and Record Medium Reproduction	3.58
文教体育用品制造业	Cultural Educational and Sports Goods	8.22
石油加工、炼焦及核燃料加工业	Petroleum, Coking and Nuclear Fuel Processing	8.09
化学原料及化学制品制造业	Raw Chemical Materials and Chemical Products	10.37
医药制造业	Medical and Pharmaceutical Products	8.54
化学纤维制造业	Chemical Fiber	6.60
橡胶制品业	Rubber Products	2.48
塑料制品业	Plastic Products	-0.75
非金属矿物制品业	Nonmetal Mineral Products	6.10
黑色金属冶炼及压延加工业	Smelting and Pressing of Ferrous Metals	7.32
有色金属冶炼及压延加工业	Smelting and Pressing of Nonferrous Metals	2.44
金属制品业	Metal Products	5.42
通用设备制造业	Ordinary Equipment	5.62
专用设备制造业	Special Equipment	1.61
交通运输设备制造业	Transportation Equipment	5.40
电气机械及器材制造业	Electric Equipment and Machinery	4.13
通信设备、计算机及其他电子设备制造业	Communication, Computers and Other Electronic Equipment	3.91
仪器仪表及文化、办公用机械制造业	Instruments, Meters, Cultural and Office Machinery	6.03
工艺品及其他制造业	Handicraft and Other Production	15.46
废弃资源和废旧材料回收加工业	Recovery and Processing of Waste Resources and Materials	7.58
电力、燃气及水的生产和供应业	Electricpower, Gas & Water Production and Supply	
电力、热力的生产和供应业	Electricpower and Hot Power Production and Supply	4.92
燃气生产和供应业	Gas Production and Supply	7.01
水的生产和供应业	Water Production and Supply	12.81

11-7 CONTINUED

资本积累率 (%) Ratio of Accumulated Capital to Original Capital	流动比率 Circulating Rate	速动比率 Speed Rate	产权比率 Ratio of Equity to Production	人均实现利税（元） Per Capita Pre-tax Profits (yuan)	从业人员人均工资（元） Per Capita Wages of Employees (yuan)
20.15	**1.02**	**0.75**	**1.55**	**26874**	**13752**
12.54	0.99	0.73	1.53	35302	17231
19.73	0.99	0.74	1.61	21258	13231
13.85	0.82	0.58	3.16	12599	14410
22.12	0.97	0.63	2.29	8727	10294
15.35	1.15	0.68	1.09	71905	23727
26.04	1.26	0.91	1.38	116390	18579
17.01	1.00	0.73	2.02	20414	11062
21.07	1.03	0.76	1.42	30374	15209
10.85	1.05	0.79	1.34	57207	20174
23.04	1.00	0.73	1.70	22402	13293
40.83	0.98	0.71	1.89	11655	10073
13.51	1.06	0.94	0.91	7886	12145
-1.86	1.35	1.10	0.42	68674	18023
46.69	1.21	0.94	0.87	47659	19688
1191.67	0.73	0.69	5.16	13111	7778
34.71	0.93	0.85	1.44	23184	11853
33.73	0.91	0.56	2.52	11473	9282
17.91	0.99	0.72	1.26	17313	9960
-2.71	0.84	0.49	1.29	43207	14591
14.87	1.21	0.54	1.87	387033	33515
43.33	0.81	0.40	4.39	-287	7511
44.98	1.23	0.58	1.58	8161	10002
68.93	1.23	0.67	1.02	14852	12941
38.18	1.22	0.93	0.82	10920	10523
25.32	1.16	0.99	1.96	15029	14878
-14.17	1.03	0.66	1.87	18386	9870
18.59	1.08	0.82	1.36	12998	10297
4.94	2.06	1.27	0.47	14856	16806
122.96	1.20	0.67	0.61	30470	12335
14.17	1.06	0.81	1.10	39175	13935
28.54	1.04	0.87	1.25	37770	14945
100.00	0.84	0.13	2.46	25149	8462
44.68	0.76	0.50	3.27	6712	9870
-7.39	0.85	0.57	1.80	3573	10474
25.19	0.94	0.70	1.81	19662	10109
54.94	1.12	0.61	1.00	52312	20375
-39.10	1.02	0.73	2.22	25097	17527
31.85	1.05	0.74	1.55	13030	11504
21.96	1.11	0.76	1.82	19401	14174
3.53	0.50	0.38	3.96	7063	17278
17.31	1.13	0.83	1.31	32568	13525
37.15	0.96	0.69	3.85	25528	13836
18.32	1.20	0.78	1.98	22323	16705
39.74	1.03	0.75	1.86	17354	14422
37.38	1.51	0.73	1.18	18013	7235
177.43	1.41	1.02	1.57	38708	18515
38.52	1.02	1.00	1.64	50941	21955
7.45	1.58	1.47	0.73	34380	27361
37.04	1.34	1.28	1.20	17854	16946

11－8 国有控股工业企业主要经济指标（2004年）

单位: 万元

指　　标	Item	单位数（个）Number of Enterprises (unit)	从业人员平均人数（万人）Average Emloyment (10 000 persons)
总　　计	**Total**	**529**	**43.03**
按轻、重工业分	**By Light and Heavy Industry**		
轻工业	Light Industry	174	9.45
重工业	Heavy Industry	355	33.58
按企业规模分	**By Size of Enterprise**		
大型企业	Large	40	19.68
中型企业	Medium	171	17.27
小型企业	Small	318	6.08
按行业分	**By Sector**		
采矿业	Mining and Quarrying		
煤炭开采和洗选业	Coal Mining and Dressing	28	4.98
石油和天然气开采业	Petroleum and Natural Gas Extraction	2	0.13
黑色金属矿采选业	Ferrous Metals Mining and Dressing	4	0.32
有色金属矿采选业	Nonferrous Metals Mining and Dressing	1	…
非金属矿采选业	Nonmetal Minerals Mining and Dressing	2	0.21
其他采矿业	Other Minerals Mining		
制造业	Manufacturing		
农副食品加工业	Farm Products and By-food Processing	13	0.39
食品制造业	Food Production	10	0.40
饮料制造业	Beverage Production	7	0.45
烟草制品业	Tobacco Products	4	0.49
纺织业	Textile Industry	15	2.58
纺织服装、鞋、帽制造业	Garments, Shoes and Hats Production		
皮革、毛皮、羽毛（绒）及其制品业	Leather, Furs, Down and Related Products		
木材加工及木竹藤棕草制品业	Timber Processing, Bamboo, Cane, Palm, Straw Products	1	0.01
家具制造业	Furniture Manufacturing	2	0.01
造纸及纸制品业	Papermaking and Paper Products	7	0.16
印刷业、记录媒介的复制	Printing and Record Medium Reproduction	15	0.27
文教体育用品制造业	Cultural Educational and Sports Goods	2	…
石油加工、炼焦及核燃料加工业	Petroleum, Coking and Nuclear Fuel Processing	2	0.11
化学原料及化学制品制造业	Raw Chemical Materials and Chemical Products	39	3.40
医药制造业	Medical and Pharmaceutical Products	19	1.30
化学纤维制造业	Chemical Fiber		
橡胶制品业	Rubber Products	4	0.29
塑料制品业	Plastic Products	6	0.06
非金属矿物制品业	Nonmetal Mineral Products	22	0.95
黑色金属冶炼及压延加工业	Smelting and Pressing of Ferrous Metals	11	2.07
有色金属冶炼及压延加工业	Smelting and Pressing of Nonferrous Metals	13	1.13
金属制品业	Metal Products	9	0.30
通用设备制造业	Ordinary Equipment	43	3.02
专用设备制造业	Special Equipment	21	4.32
交通运输设备制造业	Transportation Equipment	67	7.60
电气机械及器材制造业	Electric Equipment and Machinery	22	1.07
通信设备、计算机及其他电子设备制造业	Communication, Computers and Other Electronic Equipment	10	0.53
仪器仪表及文化、办公用机械制造业	Instruments, Meters, Cultural and Office Machinery	20	1.46
工艺品及其他制造业	Handicraft and Other Production	3	0.02
废弃资源和废旧材料回收加工业	Recovery and Processing of Waste Resources and Materials	1	0.04
电力、燃气及水的生产和供应业	Electricpower, Gas & Water Production and Supply		
电力、热力的生产和供应业	Electricpower and Hot Power Production and Supply	55	3.77
燃气生产和供应业	Gas Production and Supply	16	0.47
水的生产和供应业	Water Production and Supply	33	0.72

Main Economic Indicators of State Holding Industrial Enterprises (2004)

(10 000 yuan)

工业总产值（现价） Gross Output Value (Current prices)	#新产品产值 Output Value of New Products	工业销售产值 Sales Value of Industry	工业增加值 Value-added of Industry	实收资本 Capital Obtained	#国家资本 State Capital	#外商资本 Foreign Capital
11781904	**3741133**	**11831276**	**3375128**	**4769601**	**1922746**	**333778**
2368006	625058	2335266	814982	713177	397963	30535
9413898	3116075	9496010	2560146	4056424	1524783	303243
7989632	3096084	8035250	2157742	2671352	890408	229622
3064879	612315	3057850	1027256	1574229	717173	89467
727393	32734	738176	190130	524020	315165	14689
256087		248882	125746	205401	11618	
30609		30177	19562	13036	6324	
33602		52717	17973	19309	19171	
190		190	106	279	279	
32515	2266	34047	15291	13727	3390	
72200	22915	71382	14587	13353	12115	68
64305	8028	64547	15067	20662	13190	260
129872	27719	130606	54803	39595	10671	5000
418110	86959	416188	271287	74507	68457	
142585	42593	137939	31408	64241	50394	
1150		389	612	1050		
1148		1323	119	262	262	
46237		46949	14222	8004	2754	
19223	5203	19999	5604	8414	6898	
311		244	117	51	51	
32551	1355	29845	6242	16796	305	
804457	184736	805627	253310	361324	247744	8368
351739	137926	360234	125268	160520	59710	201
27328	3083	28528	5563	3763	488	
8590		8954	1802	8643	5195	1500
111007	36290	118861	44723	87659	18521	13779
1106972	172443	1100472	276597	176986	131698	
426278	62093	424156	73100	353756	11367	
40625	347	39318	9431	12391	1954	
592027	179233	580222	193611	237701	50791	34360
508634	114903	608190	106804	246331	72269	
4005993	2488317	3988007	910497	1268347	183209	242708
499863	17428	448535	97996	87566	26463	25510
103037	73629	105366	26230	76335	30629	300
287912	73467	282846	86023	64590	37162	1724
2239		1962	1029	419	419	
6016		7714	1968	150	50	
1407921	200	1412784	492945	927269	661071	
141855		155654	35194	93160	82180	
68716		68422	40291	104004	95947	

11-8 续表1

单位: 万元

指标	Item	资产合计 Total Assets	#流动资产合计 Circulating Funds
总　计	**Total**	**18490358**	**8187917**
按轻、重工业分	**By Light and Heavy Industry**		
轻工业	Light Industry	3471719	1833118
重工业	Heavy Industry	15018639	6354799
按企业规模分	**By Size of Enterprise**		
大型企业	Large	11796818	5350546
中型企业	Medium	5078051	2271485
小型企业	Small	1615489	565886
按行业分	**By Sector**		
采矿业	Mining and Quarrying		
煤炭开采和洗选业	Coal Mining and Dressing	515265	186069
石油和天然气开采业	Petroleum and Natural Gas Extraction	42910	10911
黑色金属矿采选业	Ferrous Metals Mining and Dressing	63863	30493
有色金属矿采选业	Nonferrous Metals Mining and Dressing	378	119
非金属矿采选业	Nonmetal Minerals Mining and Dressing	74203	26293
其他采矿业	Other Minerals Mining		
制造业	Manufacturing		
农副食品加工业	Farm Products and By-food Processing	73209	31683
食品制造业	Food Production	77130	36237
饮料制造业	Beverage Production	214620	75014
烟草制品业	Tobacco Products	491493	319831
纺织业	Textile Industry	238167	78558
纺织服装、鞋、帽制造业	Garments, Shoes and Hats Production		
皮革、毛皮、羽毛（绒）及其制品业	Leather, Furs, Down and Related Products		
木材加工及木竹藤棕草制品业	Timber Processing, Bamboo, Cane, Palm, Straw Products	2480	1114
家具制造业	Furniture Manufacturing	989	874
造纸及纸制品业	Papermaking and Paper Products	57972	30105
印刷业、记录媒介的复制	Printing and Record Medium Reproduction	34658	14859
文教体育用品制造业	Cultural Educational and Sports Goods	326	319
石油加工、炼焦及核燃料加工业	Petroleum, Coking and Nuclear Fuel Processing	29294	18100
化学原料及化学制品制造业	Raw Chemical Materials and Chemical Products	1157404	472875
医药制造业	Medical and Pharmaceutical Products	740645	344951
化学纤维制造业	Chemical Fiber		
橡胶制品业	Rubber Products	45150	24778
塑料制品业	Plastic Products	17018	7964
非金属矿物制品业	Nonmetal Mineral Products	297983	109739
黑色金属冶炼及压延加工业	Smelting and Pressing of Ferrous Metals	892811	423116
有色金属冶炼及压延加工业	Smelting and Pressing of Nonferrous Metals	585869	328298
金属制品业	Metal Products	46717	30239
通用设备制造业	Ordinary Equipment	804902	501732
专用设备制造业	Special Equipment	1536425	537656
交通运输设备制造业	Transportation Equipment	4859781	2724704
电气机械及器材制造业	Electric Equipment and Machinery	445088	332587
通信设备、计算机及其他电子设备制造业	Communication, Computers and Other Electronic Equipment	213775	123349
仪器仪表及文化、办公用机械制造业	Instruments, Meters, Cultural and Office Machinery	341672	217293
工艺品及其他制造业	Handicraft and Other Production	1641	1220
废弃资源和废旧材料回收加工业	Recovery and Processing of Waste Resources and Materials	912	436
电力、燃气及水的生产和供应业	Electricpower, Gas & Water Production and Supply		
电力、热力的生产和供应业	Electricpower and Hot Power Production and Supply	4044756	955389
燃气生产和供应业	Gas Production and Supply	238657	105059
水的生产和供应业	Water Production and Supply	302195	85953

11-8 CONTINUED-1

(10 000 yuan)

流动资产年平均余额 Annual Average Balance of Value of Circulating Fund	固定资产 Fixed Assets		固定资产净值年平均余额 Annual Average Balance of Net Value of Fixed Assets	负债合计 Total Liabilities	
	原值 Original	净值 Net			#流动负债合计 Total Circulating Liabilities
7446908	**11175923**	**7006265**	**6680345**	**11178297**	**8262861**
1673854	1697273	1065270	1037590	2416346	1931296
5773054	9478650	5940995	5642755	8761951	6331565
4719878	6705323	4207454	3986522	6749565	5174642
2155127	3431961	2067703	1978166	3263727	2324625
571903	1038639	731108	715657	1165005	763594
167286	410046	225318	217681	235702	159149
8905	33864	18592	13284	12643	8106
24573	41956	32934	28457	30157	29867
114	652	249	251	316	163
23593	23562	20289	18592	50738	35544
28832	40106	26793	27309	62218	43203
38454	48477	27758	28094	55229	39186
70509	139699	81176	82736	123785	102799
300805	228065	133796	127336	324619	260321
89460	167216	101486	113280	235400	114720
1114	585	362	362	410	410
944	250	115	106	835	835
37047	14417	12376	11964	43651	32777
21061	24413	13592	13991	22016	13700
319	21	8	8	28	28
16414	17605	9048	5342	12285	11658
437213	961034	464879	421696	619816	452280
313604	280355	206062	191996	434565	369088
24866	24563	15693	15849	39150	37590
8898	7520	3935	4135	8760	7697
118273	191515	141059	142204	209032	122899
347983	607660	331206	328655	437788	365448
265157	516152	267833	268651	417122	321101
27213	29070	14369	14168	44936	37697
450805	402580	212178	188284	523239	453371
520572	654481	439795	429731	1239168	1122538
2507070	2075884	1375920	1281062	2496371	2347143
235771	126378	85468	74816	384428	369647
114168	70594	36008	33730	128781	108406
206365	155972	93242	93338	262924	225814
889	322	256	249	891	876
431	512	476	425	760	760
863361	3518750	2371788	2270918	2467062	958301
96935	124021	75362	73627	98511	65529
77904	237626	166844	158018	154961	44210

11-8 续表2

单位: 万元

指　　标	Item	所有者权益 Creditors' Equity	主营业务收入 Major Business Revenue
总　计	**Total**	**7312062**	**11765499**
按轻、重工业分	**By Light and Heavy Industry**		
轻工业	Light Industry	1055374	2246202
重工业	Heavy Industry	6256688	9519297
按企业规模分	**By Size of Enterprise**		
大型企业	Large	5047253	8030695
中型企业	Medium	1814325	3028250
小型企业	Small	450484	706554
按行业分	**By Sector**		
采矿业	Mining and Quarrying		
煤炭开采和洗选业	Coal Mining and Dressing	279564	244119
石油和天然气开采业	Petroleum and Natural Gas Extraction	30267	29841
黑色金属矿采选业	Ferrous Metals Mining and Dressing	33706	52717
有色金属矿采选业	Nonferrous Metals Mining and Dressing	61	190
非金属矿采选业	Nonmetal Minerals Mining and Dressing	23465	35881
其他采矿业	Other Minerals Mining		
制造业	Manufacturing		
农副食品加工业	Farm Products and By-food Processing	10991	70671
食品制造业	Food Production	21902	80642
饮料制造业	Beverage Production	90835	131437
烟草制品业	Tobacco Products	166873	413796
纺织业	Textile Industry	2767	134672
纺织服装、鞋、帽制造业	Garments, Shoes and Hats Production		
皮革、毛皮、羽毛（绒）及其制品业	Leather, Furs, Down and Related Products		
木材加工及木竹藤棕草制品业	Timber Processing, Bamboo, Cane, Palm, Straw Products	2070	396
家具制造业	Furniture Manufacturing	154	1193
造纸及纸制品业	Papermaking and Paper Products	14320	43660
印刷业、记录媒介的复制	Printing and Record Medium Reproduction	12643	19815
文教体育用品制造业	Cultural Educational and Sports Goods	298	236
石油加工、炼焦及核燃料加工业	Petroleum, Coking and Nuclear Fuel Processing	17009	31446
化学原料及化学制品制造业	Raw Chemical Materials and Chemical Products	537589	817490
医药制造业	Medical and Pharmaceutical Products	306080	290159
化学纤维制造业	Chemical Fiber		
橡胶制品业	Rubber Products	6001	26661
塑料制品业	Plastic Products	8258	8518
非金属矿物制品业	Nonmetal Mineral Products	88951	116067
黑色金属冶炼及压延加工业	Smelting and Pressing of Ferrous Metals	455022	1106923
有色金属冶炼及压延加工业	Smelting and Pressing of Nonferrous Metals	168747	406651
金属制品业	Metal Products	1781	39117
通用设备制造业	Ordinary Equipment	281662	572023
专用设备制造业	Special Equipment	297256	591056
交通运输设备制造业	Transportation Equipment	2363411	3963100
电气机械及器材制造业	Electric Equipment and Machinery	60661	447605
通信设备、计算机及其他电子设备制造业	Communication, Computers and Other Electronic Equipment	84994	100886
仪器仪表及文化、办公用机械制造业	Instruments, Meters, Cultural and Office Machinery	78748	261199
工艺品及其他制造业	Handicraft and Other Production	750	1911
废弃资源和废旧材料回收加工业	Recovery and Processing of Waste Resources and Materials	152	7714
电力、燃气及水的生产和供应业	Electricpower, Gas & Water Production and Supply		
电力、热力的生产和供应业	Electricpower and Hot Power Production and Supply	1577693	1493928
燃气生产和供应业	Gas Production and Supply	140146	156288
水的生产和供应业	Water Production and Supply	147235	67491

11-8 CONTINUED-2

(10 000 yuan)

主营业务成本 Cost of Major Business	主营业务税金及附加 Tax and Extra Charges of Major Business	主营业务利润 Profit of Major Business	利润总额 Total After-tax Profits	利税总额 Total Pre-tax Profits	工资总额 Total Wages
9191169	**297250**	**2277080**	**649083**	**1519150**	**741474**
1440144	179076	626982	49052	340279	134542
7751025	118174	1650098	600031	1178871	606932
6237532	229586	1563577	522827	1130333	414133
2354161	62887	611202	135275	362543	253039
599476	4777	102301	-9019	26274	74302
190432	2768	50919	1983	23217	60963
20523	562	8756	6573	8983	2357
41422	1247	10048	6051	10588	8539
113	1	76	56	59	35
22570	932	12378	4266	8071	3158
59139	383	11149	1614	4330	3941
63856	608	16178	2394	5957	4971
71226	12045	48165	9484	32038	7965
178918	149011	85867	26403	220868	18271
123404	683	10585	-19794	-13802	20753
291	5	100		37	91
1179	9	5	-180	-107	112
37128	184	6349	1665	3448	1816
17109	141	2565	-1827	-635	2757
120	2	114	29	45	22
25256	128	6063	559	1957	1941
656117	4791	156582	58690	103434	53458
162621	3009	124529	22192	47523	21004
22042	469	4150	-2018	-475	3330
6627	38	1853	26	578	605
80080	839	35148	11601	18107	11063
946944	1019	158960	92271	145884	52087
359958	1069	45624	10449	21882	23735
34834	122	4161	-488	486	3999
442249	4575	125199	32344	66777	48129
493108	9699	88249	6884	26806	76935
3212576	89217	661307	270979	517938	150553
207415	1178	239011	17335	31122	15875
79296	234	21356	6471	8806	8617
191584	1340	68275	10677	22623	23124
1187	33	692	34	116	196
7371	70	274	32	210	719
1270981	8551	214397	56750	178273	85256
119530	1643	35114	9028	14737	13402
43963	645	22882	6549	9269	11695

11－9 国有控股工业企业经济效益指标（2004年）

单位：%

指　标	Item	增加值率 Ratio of Value-added to Gross Industrial Output Value	总资产贡献率 Ratio of Total Assets to Industrial Output Value
总　计	**Total**	**28.65**	**9.38**
按轻、重工业分	**By Light and Heavy Industry**		
轻工业	Light Industry	34.42	12.47
重工业	Heavy Industry	27.20	8.62
按企业规模分	**By Size of Enterprise**		
大型企业	Large	27.01	9.94
中型企业	Medium	33.52	10.24
小型企业	Small	26.14	3.46
按行业分	**By Sector**		
采矿业	Mining and Quarrying		
煤炭开采和洗选业	Coal Mining and Dressing	49.10	7.39
石油和天然气开采业	Petroleum and Natural Gas Extraction	63.91	16.93
黑色金属矿采选业	Ferrous Metals Mining and Dressing	53.49	21.86
有色金属矿采选业	Nonferrous Metals Mining and Dressing	55.60	16.13
非金属矿采选业	Nonmetal Minerals Mining and Dressing	47.03	25.56
其他采矿业	Other Minerals Mining		
制造业	Manufacturing		
农副食品加工业	Farm Products and By-food Processing	20.20	11.37
食品制造业	Food Production	23.43	8.17
饮料制造业	Beverage Production	42.20	15.93
烟草制品业	Tobacco Products	64.88	48.94
纺织业	Textile Industry	22.03	1.00
纺织服装、鞋、帽制造业	Garments, Shoes and Hats Production		
皮革、毛皮、羽毛（绒）及其制品业	Leather, Furs, Down and Related Products		
木材加工及木竹藤棕草制品业	Timber Processing, Bamboo, Cane, Palm, Straw Products	53.22	16.07
家具制造业	Furniture Manufacturing	10.35	0.72
造纸及纸制品业	Papermaking and Paper Products	30.76	4.52
印刷业、记录媒介的复制	Printing and Record Medium Reproduction	29.15	-1.11
文教体育用品制造业	Cultural Educational and Sports Goods	37.80	13.75
石油加工、炼焦及核燃料加工业	Petroleum, Coking and Nuclear Fuel Processing	19.18	7.69
化学原料及化学制品制造业	Raw Chemical Materials and Chemical Products	31.49	10.20
医药制造业	Medical and Pharmaceutical Products	35.61	8.22
化学纤维制造业	Chemical Fiber		
橡胶制品业	Rubber Products	20.36	0.27
塑料制品业	Plastic Products	20.98	3.37
非金属矿物制品业	Nonmetal Mineral Products	40.29	7.05
黑色金属冶炼及压延加工业	Smelting and Pressing of Ferrous Metals	24.99	15.91
有色金属冶炼及压延加工业	Smelting and Pressing of Nonferrous Metals	17.15	4.54
金属制品业	Metal Products	23.22	2.94
通用设备制造业	Ordinary Equipment	32.70	10.04
专用设备制造业	Special Equipment	21.00	3.66
交通运输设备制造业	Transportation Equipment	22.73	10.07
电气机械及器材制造业	Electric Equipment and Machinery	19.60	8.90
通信设备、计算机及其他电子设备制造业	Communication, Computers and Other Electronic Equipment	25.46	4.92
仪器仪表及文化、办公用机械制造业	Instruments, Meters, Cultural and Office Machinery	29.88	9.09
工艺品及其他制造业	Handicraft and Other Production	45.94	13.30
废弃资源和废旧材料回收加工业	Recovery and Processing of Waste Resources and Materials	32.71	11.65
电力、燃气及水的生产和供应业	Electricpower, Gas & Water Production and Supply		
电力、热力的生产和供应业	Electricpower and Hot Power Production and Supply	35.01	6.87
燃气生产和供应业	Gas Production and Supply	24.81	4.94
水的生产和供应业	Water Production and Supply	58.63	4.79

Economic Efficiency Indicators of State Holding Industrial Enterprises (2004)

(%)

资本保值增值率 Ratio of Creditors' Equity of Current Year to that of Previous Year	资产负债率 Ratio of Liabilities to Assets	流动资产周转率（次） Turnover Ratio of Annual Circulating Funds (time)	成本费用利润率 Ratio of Profits to Cost	全员劳动生产率（元/人年） Overall Labor Productivity (yuan/person-year)	产品销售率 Ratio of Sales to Products
112.54	**60.45**	**1.58**	**5.85**	**78432**	**100.42**
104.58	69.60	1.34	2.66	86236	98.62
114.19	58.34	1.65	6.49	76236	100.87
109.89	57.22	1.70	7.02	109627	100.57
114.63	64.27	1.41	4.66	59488	99.77
126.50	72.11	1.24	-1.22	31263	101.48
101.93	45.74	1.46	0.79	25233	97.19
98.14	29.46	3.35	26.37	149559	98.59
125.56	47.22	2.15	13.25	55989	156.89
1291.67	83.77	1.67	42.47	23556	100.00
125.38	68.38	1.52	13.75	72402	104.71
100.96	84.99	2.45	2.31	37587	98.87
106.67	71.60	2.10	3.02	38155	100.38
92.87	57.68	1.86	8.57	122491	100.56
113.26	66.05	1.38	10.97	549721	99.54
94.30	98.84	1.51	-12.80	12188	96.74
98.24	16.52	0.36		44673	33.86
87.84	84.40	1.26	-12.11	14143	115.29
32.57	75.30	1.18	4.03	87091	101.54
88.24	63.52	0.94	-8.28	20911	104.04
121.51	8.61	0.74	13.16	37742	78.64
176.02	41.94	1.92	1.80	58124	91.69
106.67	53.55	1.87	7.47	74525	100.15
117.02	58.67	0.93	8.24	96079	102.42
-22.44	86.71	1.07	-7.33	19163	104.39
103.64	51.48	0.96	0.29	29639	104.24
124.24	70.15	0.98	11.08	47281	107.07
145.12	49.03	3.18	9.08	133473	99.41
48.40	71.20	1.53	2.61	64903	99.50
-68.66	96.19	1.44	-1.20	31270	96.78
113.12	65.01	1.27	5.95	64067	98.01
102.45	80.65	1.14	0.83	24711	119.57
111.00	51.37	1.58	7.26	119791	99.55
157.63	86.37	1.90	7.38	91620	89.73
113.06	60.24	0.88	6.54	49820	102.26
110.23	76.95	1.27	4.23	58964	98.24
95.41	54.28	2.15	1.72	55607	87.60
46.37	83.32	17.88	0.42	47995	128.22
134.57	60.99	1.73	4.02	130772	100.35
107.30	41.28	1.61	5.98	74328	109.73
135.99	51.28	0.87	9.86	56391	99.57

11-9 续表

指　标	Item	销售利润率（%） Ratio of Profits to Sales
总　计	**Total**	**5.52**
按轻、重工业分	**By Light and Heavy Industry**	
轻工业	Light Industry	2.18
重工业	Heavy Industry	6.30
按企业规模分	**By Size of Enterprise**	
大型企业	Large	6.51
中型企业	Medium	4.47
小型企业	Small	-1.28
按行业分	**By Sector**	
采矿业	Mining and Quarrying	
煤炭开采和洗选业	Coal Mining and Dressing	0.81
石油和天然气开采业	Petroleum and Natural Gas Extraction	22.03
黑色金属矿采选业	Ferrous Metals Mining and Dressing	11.48
有色金属矿采选业	Nonferrous Metals Mining and Dressing	29.62
非金属矿采选业	Nonmetal Minerals Mining and Dressing	11.89
其他采矿业	Other Minerals Mining	
制造业	Manufacturing	
农副食品加工业	Farm Products and By-food Processing	2.28
食品制造业	Food Production	2.97
饮料制造业	Beverage Production	7.22
烟草制品业	Tobacco Products	6.38
纺织业	Textile Industry	-14.70
纺织服装、鞋、帽制造业	Garments, Shoes and Hats Production	
皮革、毛皮、羽毛（绒）及其制品业	Leather, Furs, Down and Related Products	
木材加工及木竹藤棕草制品业	Timber Processing, Bamboo, Cane, Palm, Straw Products	
家具制造业	Furniture Manufacturing	-15.04
造纸及纸制品业	Papermaking and Paper Products	3.81
印刷业、记录媒介的复制	Printing and Record Medium Reproduction	-9.22
文教体育用品制造业	Cultural Educational and Sports Goods	12.34
石油加工、炼焦及核燃料加工业	Petroleum, Coking and Nuclear Fuel Processing	1.78
化学原料及化学制品制造业	Raw Chemical Materials and Chemical Products	7.18
医药制造业	Medical and Pharmaceutical Products	7.65
化学纤维制造业	Chemical Fiber	
橡胶制品业	Rubber Products	-7.57
塑料制品业	Plastic Products	0.31
非金属矿物制品业	Nonmetal Mineral Products	10.00
黑色金属冶炼及压延加工业	Smelting and Pressing of Ferrous Metals	8.34
有色金属冶炼及压延加工业	Smelting and Pressing of Nonferrous Metals	2.57
金属制品业	Metal Products	-1.25
通用设备制造业	Ordinary Equipment	5.65
专用设备制造业	Special Equipment	1.16
交通运输设备制造业	Transportation Equipment	6.84
电气机械及器材制造业	Electric Equipment and Machinery	3.87
通信设备、计算机及其他电子设备制造业	Communication, Computers and Other Electronic Equipment	6.41
仪器仪表及文化、办公用机械制造业	Instruments, Meters, Cultural and Office Machinery	4.09
工艺品及其他制造业	Handicraft and Other Production	1.79
废弃资源和废旧材料回收加工业	Recovery and Processing of Waste Resources and Materials	0.42
电力、燃气及水的生产和供应业	Electricpower, Gas & Water Production and Supply	
电力、热力的生产和供应业	Electricpower and Hot Power Production and Supply	3.80
燃气生产和供应业	Gas Production and Supply	5.78
水的生产和供应业	Water Production and Supply	9.70

11-9 CONTINUED

资本积累率（%） Ratio of Accumulated Capital to Original Capital	流动比率 Circulating Rate	速动比率 Speed Rate	产权比率 Ratio of Equity to Production	人均实现利税（元） Per Capita Pre-tax Profits (yuan)	从业人员人均工资（元） Per Capita Wages of Employees (yuan)
12.54	**0.99**	**0.73**	**1.53**	**35302**	**17231**
4.58	0.95	0.68	2.29	36006	14236
14.19	1.00	0.75	1.40	35104	18073
9.89	1.03	0.77	1.34	57428	21041
14.63	0.98	0.71	1.80	20995	14653
26.50	0.74	0.56	2.59	4320	12218
1.93	1.17	1.04	0.84	4659	12233
-1.86	1.35	1.10	0.42	68674	18023
25.56	1.02	0.82	0.89	32986	26600
1191.67	0.73	0.69	5.16	13111	7778
25.38	0.74	0.70	2.16	38214	14950
0.96	0.73	0.44	5.66	11156	10154
6.67	0.92	0.74	2.52	15085	12589
-7.13	0.73	0.32	1.36	71608	17803
13.26	1.23	0.54	1.95	447554	37024
-5.70	0.68	0.32	85.08	-5356	8053
-1.76	2.72	2.00	0.20	2730	6642
-12.16	1.05	0.80	5.41	-12786	13321
-67.43	0.92	0.56	3.05	21114	11118
-11.76	1.08	0.82	1.74	-2370	10287
21.51	11.34	8.19	0.09	14645	7129
76.02	1.55	0.73	0.72	18225	18074
6.67	1.05	0.80	1.15	30431	15728
17.02	0.93	0.79	1.42	36450	16110
-122.44	0.66	0.42	6.52	-1636	11471
3.64	1.03	0.78	1.06	9515	9959
24.24	0.89	0.70	2.35	19142	11696
45.12	1.16	0.62	0.96	70397	25135
-51.60	1.02	0.74	2.47	19429	21074
-168.66	0.80	0.50	25.24	1610	13261
13.12	1.11	0.78	1.86	22097	15926
2.45	0.48	0.37	4.17	6202	17800
11.00	1.16	0.84	1.06	68144	19808
57.63	0.90	0.63	6.34	29097	14842
13.06	1.14	0.77	1.52	16725	16366
10.23	0.96	0.66	3.34	15507	15851
-4.59	1.39	1.11	1.19	6276	10622
-53.63	0.57	0.50	5.00	5124	17541
34.57	1.00	0.97	1.56	47294	22617
7.30	1.60	1.48	0.70	31123	28303
35.99	1.94	1.88	1.05	12973	16368

11－10 大中型工业企业主要经济指标（2004年）

单位：万元

指 标	Item	单位数（个） Number of Enterprises (unit)	从业人员平均人数（万人） Average Emloyment (10 000 persons)	工业总产值（现价） Gross Output Value (Current prices)	#新产品产值 Output Value of New Products
总 计	**Total**	**435**	**55.10**	**16035871**	**4980436**
#国有控股企业	State Holding	211	36.95	11054512	3708399
按登记注册类型分	**By Registration**				
内资企业	Domestic-funded Enterprises	386	50.41	12593534	3395035
#国有企业	State-owned	78	10.15	1535168	312292
集体企业	Collective-owned	11	1.10	129462	5287
港澳台投资企业	Funded by Hong Kong, Macao and Taiwan	12	1.78	1136265	210539
外商投资企业	Foreign-funded	37	2.91	2306073	1374862
按轻、重工业分	**By Light and Heavy Industry**				
轻工业	Light Industry	159	16.55	4962018	1414892
重工业	Heavy Industry	276	38.55	11073853	3565544

指 标	Item	固定资产净值 Net Value of Fixed Assets	固定资产净值年平均余额 Annual Average Balance of Net Value of Fixed Assets	负债合计 Total Liabilities	#流动负债合计 Total Circulating Liabilities
总 计	**Total**	**7674661**	**7300786**	**12973146**	**9879783**
#国有控股企业	State Holding	6275157	5964688	10013292	7499266
按登记注册类型分	**By Registration**				
内资企业	Domestic-funded Enterprises	6391756	6005747	11057836	8636202
#国有企业	State-owned	915548	865048	1685152	1251438
集体企业	Collective-owned	36037	37999	87973	80545
港澳台投资企业	Funded by Hong Kong, Macao and Taiwan	352599	350596	471366	374084
外商投资企业	Foreign-funded	930306	944443	1443944	869497
按轻、重工业分	**By Light and Heavy Industry**				
轻工业	Light Industry	1382309	1344741	3268083	2742601
重工业	Heavy Industry	6292352	5956045	9705063	7137182

Main Economic Indicators of Large & Medium-sized Industrial Enterprises (2004)

(10 000 yuan)

工业销售产值 Sales Value of Industry	工业增加值 Value-added of Industry	实收资本 Capital Obtained	#国家资本 State Capital	资产合计 Total Assets	#流动资产合计 Circulating Funds	流动资产年平均余额 Annual Average Balance of Value of Circulating Fund	固定资产原值 Original Value of Fixed Assets
16035624	**4466141**	**5281788**	**1625908**	**21733531**	**10146136**	**9088243**	**12117888**
11093100	3184999	4245580	1607581	16874869	7622031	6875005	10137284
12653396	3456952	4415481	1499854	18299842	8623688	7653513	9742884
1549043	543668	633980	516603	2338830	1134555	1027123	1665167
127410	38145	19614		115574	64912	64497	61439
1110488	324363	150817	65669	928259	434391	388727	637381
2271740	684826	715490	60385	2505430	1088057	1046003	1737623
4931382	1325013	906669	313415	4882137	2777255	2437852	2139664
11104242	3141128	4375119	1312493	16851394	7368881	6650391	9978224

所有者权益 Creditors' Equity	主营业务收入 Major Business Revenue	主营业务成本 Cost of Major Business	主营业务税金及附加 Tax and Extra Charges of Major Business	主营业务利润 Profit of Major Business	利润总额 Total After-tax Profits	利税总额 Total Pre-tax Profits	工资总额 Total Wages
8760385	**15873212**	**12544259**	**371897**	**2957055**	**959017**	**2012777**	**886339**
6861577	11058945	8591693	292474	2174779	658102	1492876	667171
7242006	12505106	9943085	315785	2246236	602360	1422713	778896
653678	1537529	1166854	53767	316908	51445	184393	154924
27601	134522	111765	1206	21551	5427	11836	13974
456893	1092918	905699	5637	181582	98579	158589	49281
1061486	2275188	1695475	50475	529237	258078	431475	58162
1614054	4813597	3618033	210652	984912	169668	534938	208801
7146331	11059615	8926226	161246	1972143	789349	1477839	677538

11－11 大中型工业企业经济效益指标（2004年）

指　标	Item	增加值率（%） Ratio of Value-added to Gross Industrial Output Value	总资产贡献率（%） Ratio of Total Assets to Industrial Output Value
总计	**Total**	**27.85**	**11.13**
#国有控股企业	State Holding	28.81	10.05
按登记注册类型分	**By Registration**		
内资企业	Domestic-funded Enterprises	27.45	9.50
#国有企业	State-owned	35.41	9.86
集体企业	Collective-owned	29.46	8.54
港澳台投资企业	Funded by Hong Kong Macao and Taiwan	28.55	16.68
外商投资企业	Foreign-funded	29.70	21.35
按轻、重工业分	**By Light and Heavy Industry**		
轻工业	Light Industry	26.70	13.53
重工业	Heavy Industry	28.37	10.42

指　标	Item	销售利润率（%） Ratio of Profits to Sales	资本积累率（%） Ratio of Accumulated Capital to Original Capital
总计	**Total**	**6.04**	**15.63**
#国有控股企业	State Holding	5.95	11.33
按登记注册类型分	**By Registration**		
内资企业	Domestic-funded Enterprises	4.82	14.34
#国有企业	State-owned	3.35	13.36
集体企业	Collective-owned	4.03	36.79
港澳台投资企业	Funded by Hong Kong Macao and Taiwan	9.02	15.10
外商投资企业	Foreign-funded	11.34	26.36
按轻、重工业分	**By Light and Heavy Industry**		
轻工业	Light Industry	3.52	13.14
重工业	Heavy Industry	7.14	16.24

Economic Efficiency Indicators of Large & Medium-sized Industrial Enterprises (2004)

资本保值增值率（%） Ratio of Creditors' Equity of Current Year to that of Previous Year	资产负债率（%） Ratio of Liabilities to Assets	流动资产周转率（次） Turnover Ratio of Annual Circulating Funds (time)	成本费用利润率（%） Ratio of Profits to Cost	全员劳动生产率（元/人年） Overall Labor Productivity (yuan/person-year)	产品销售率（%） Ratio of Sales to Products
115.63	**59.69**	**1.75**	**6.46**	**81053**	**100.00**
111.33	59.34	1.61	6.35	86196	100.35
114.34	60.43	1.63	5.08	68582	100.48
113.36	72.05	1.50	3.45	53548	100.90
136.79	76.12	2.09	4.20	34526	98.42
115.10	50.78	2.81	9.97	181981	97.73
126.36	57.63	2.18	12.90	235061	98.51
113.14	66.94	1.97	4.01	80067	99.38
116.24	57.59	1.66	7.44	81476	100.27

流动比率 Circulating Rate	速动比率 Speed Rate	产权比率 Ratio of Equity to Production	人均实现利税（元） Per Capita Pre-tax Profits (yuan)	从业人员人均工资（元） Per Capita Wages of Employees (yuan)
1.03	**0.76**	**1.48**	**36528**	**16086**
1.02	0.75	1.46	40402	18056
1.00	0.75	1.53	28225	15453
0.91	0.63	2.58	18162	15259
0.81	0.48	3.19	10713	12648
1.16	0.68	1.03	88975	27649
1.25	0.90	1.36	148100	19964
1.01	0.74	2.02	32325	12617
1.03	0.77	1.36	38333	17574

11－12 国有及规模以上非国有工业企业主要产品产量（2003－2004年）

产　　品	Products	2003	2004
化学纤维(万吨)	Chemical Fiber (10 000 tons)	1.47	2.34
纱(吨)	Yarn (ton)	67045	69446
布(万米)	Cloth (10 000 m)	29634.90	29418.63
印染布(万米)	Printed and Dyed Fabric (10 000 m)	8079.72	11200.84
毛线(吨)	Knitting Wool (ton)	957	833
丝(吨)	Silk (ton)	4553	5103
丝织品(万米)	Silk Products (10 000 m)	1197.59	1135.32
电视机(万部)	TV Sets (10 000 units)	60.30	59.92
#彩色电视机	Color TV Sets	60.30	59.92
摩托车(万辆)	Motorcycles (10 000 vehicles)	441.32	473.07
机制纸及纸板(吨)	Machine-made Paper and Paperboard (ton)	185087	227344
日用陶瓷制品(万件)	Household Ceramics (10 000 pcs)	8033	4486
日用玻璃制品(吨)	Daily-use Glassware (ton)	149114	29075
日用精铝制品(吨)	Fine Aluminum Products for Daily-use (ton)	2349	495
合成洗涤剂(吨)	Synthetic Detergents (ton)	94745	62780
肥　皂(吨)	Soap (ton)	4170	5321
干电池(折一号电池)(万只)	Dry Cells (10 000 units)	41645	49340
卷　烟(亿支)	Cigarettes (100 million units)	387.5	386.32
白　酒(万千升)	Liquor (1000 kiloliters)	4.84	5.45
啤　酒(万千升)	Beer (1000 kiloliters)	44.42	46.21
罐　头(吨)	Canned Food (ton)	21928	25985
食用植物油(吨)	Edible Vegetable Oil (ton)	6177	23916
布　鞋(万双)	Cloth Shoes (10 000 pairs)	892.35	243.08
皮　鞋(万双)	Leather Shoes (10 000 pairs)	295.96	1313.70
服　装(万件)	Garments (10 000 pcs)	233.79	325.46

注：本表部分产品与2003年年报口径不尽一致。

Note: Some data in this table aren't consistent with yearly data of 2003.

Output of Major Products of State-owned Industrial Enterprises and Non-state-owned Industrial Enterprises above Designated Size (2003-2004)

产　　品	Products	2003	2004
乳制品(万吨)	Dairy Products (10 000 tons)	7.54	10.93
无酒精饮料(软饮料)(吨)	Non-alcoholic Beverage (soft) (ton)	468145	494304
原　煤(万吨)	Coal (10 000 tons)	1484.20	1738.19
洗精煤(万吨)	Washed and Fine Coal (10 000 tons)	202.09	274.81
焦　炭(万吨)	Coke (10 000 tons)	149.97	188.36
发电量(万千瓦时)	Electricity (10 000 kwh)	1886430	2328247
天然气(万立方米)	Natural Gas (10 000 cu.m)	472910	515748
生　铁(万吨)	Pig Iron (10 000 tons)	203.50	247.45
铁矿石(成品矿)(万吨)	Mineral Iron (10 000 tons)	25.26	49.87
钢(万吨)	Steel (10 000 tons)	219.70	267.79
钢　材(万吨)	Steel Products (10 000 tons)	235.24	288.10
#大型钢材	Large	10.87	9.39
中小型钢材	Medium	11.07	10.41
中厚钢板	Medium Rolled-steel	94.43	100.30
无缝钢管	Seamless Steel Pipe	7.11	7.62
铝(吨)	Aluminum (ton)	61401	60639
硫　酸(吨)	Sulphuric Acid (ton)	991790	1355130
盐　酸(吨)	Hydrochloric Acid (ton)	39549	21462
烧　碱(吨)	Caustic Soda (ton)	102597	45985
电　石(折合量)(吨)	Calcium Carbide (equivalent) (ton)	27210	21992
精甲醇(商品量)(吨)	Fine Methyl Alcohol (commodities) (ton)	248348	307974
染　料(吨)	Dyestuff (ton)	1026	5348
油　漆(吨)	Paint (ton)	36439	35085
塑料制品(吨)	Plastics (ton)	80933	930034
合成橡胶(吨)	Synthetic Rubber (ton)	15258	18759
化学原料药(吨)	Chemical Raw Material (ton)	11249	12701

注：从2003年起天然气产量不包括四川省境内气矿的产量。

Note: Output of natural gas since 2003 excludes that of gas mining areas in Sichuan.

11-12 续表 CONTINUED

产　　品	Products	2003	2004
中成药(吨)	Traditional Chinese Medicine (ton)	25009	28754
轮胎外胎(万条)	Tire (10 000 units)	271.47	321.90
水　泥(万吨)	Cement (10 000 tons)	1927.00	1906.23
石棉制品(吨)	Asbestos Products (ton)	664	807
人造板(立方米)	Artificial Boards (cu.m)	4638	67888
矿山设备(吨)	Mining Equipment (ton)	10696	20552
化工设备(吨)	Chemical Industry Equipment (ton)	80	152
起重设备(吨)	Hoist and Derrick (ton)	25668	17001
制冷空调设备(套)	Freezing equipment (set)	240	565
发电设备(千瓦)	Generating Equipment (kw)	312801	572162
交流电动机(万千瓦)	Alternating Current Motors(10 000 kw)	151.90	252.29
电力变压器(万千伏安)	Electric Transformer Products (10 000 kva)	2060.32	2890.19
金属切削机床(台)	Metal-cutting Machines (unit)	3248	4095
汽　车(辆)	Motor Vehicles (vehicle)	404494	434209
内燃机(商品量)(万千瓦)	Internal Combustion Engines (commodities) (10 000 kw)	3635.13	517.91
钢芯铝绞线(吨)	Aluminum Twist Wire with Steel Core (ton)	24904	18271
裸铜元线及铜电车线(吨)	Copper Bare Wire and Trolleybus Wire (ton)	2388	4214
泵(台)	Industry Pumps (unit)	10167	31009
风　机(台)	Air Pumps (unit)	1683	3108
气体压缩机(台)	Gas Compressors (unit)	341	286
轴　承(万套)	Bearings (10 000 sets)	4314.97	4362.81
工业锅炉(蒸吨)	Industry Boilers (ton)	10	1538
民用钢质船舶(综合吨)	Civil Steel Ships (ton)	54820	50278
合成氨(吨)	Synthetic Ammonia (ton)	833788	842526
化肥(100%)(吨)	Chemical Fertilizer (100%) (ton)	899675	1074043
#氮　肥	Nitrogen Fertilizer	605154	679694
磷　肥	Phosphate Fertilizer	294521	394349
配混合饲料(吨)	Mingled Forage (ton)	717587	900185
农　膜(吨)	Farm-use Membrane (ton)	111	914
农　药(吨)	Chemical Pesticides (ton)	10926	5088

11－13 国有及规模以上非国有工业企业主要产品产量占全国的比重（2004年）

Output of Major Industrial Products of State-owned Industrial Enterprises and Non-state-owned Industrial Enterprises above Designated Sized as Percentage of Nation Total (2004)

产　　品	Products	全　国 Nation Total	重　庆 Chongqing	重庆占全国比重（%） Chongqing as % of Nation Total
维纶纤维(吨)	Polyvinyl Alcohol Fiber (ton)	35105	13021	37.1
布(亿米)	Cloth (100 million m)	294.75	2.94	1.0
丝(万吨)	Silk (10 000 tons)	10.26	0.51	5.0
合成洗涤剂(万吨)	Synthetic Detergents (10 000 tons)	436.36	6.28	1.4
合成洗衣粉(万吨)	Synthetic Washing Powder (10 000 tons)	272.67	4.30	1.6
原　盐(万吨)	Salt (10 000 tons)	3710.07	38.02	1.0
卷　烟(亿支)	Cigarettes (100 million units)	18745.10	386.32	2.1
白　酒(万千升)	Liquor (1000 kiloliters)	311.70	5.45	1.7
啤　酒(万千升)	Beer (1000 kiloliters)	2910.05	46.21	1.6
软饮料(万吨)	Soft Beverage (10 000 tons)	2620.17	49.43	1.9
乳制品(万吨)	Dairy Products (10 000 tons)	949.19	10.93	1.2
原　煤(亿吨)	Coal (100 million tons)	16.06	0.17	1.1
发电量(亿千瓦小时)	Electricity (100 million kwh)	21302.28	232.82	1.1
天然气(亿立方米)	Natural Gas (100 million cu.m)	407.69	51.57	12.6
生　铁(万吨)	Pig Iron (10 000 tons)	25185.05	247.45	1.0
钢(万吨)	Steel (10 000 tons)	27245.63	267.79	1.0
成品钢材(万吨)	Steel Products (10 000 tons)	29738.70	288.10	1.0
铝　材(万吨)	Aluminum Products (10 000 tons)	448.40	26.23	5.8
水　泥(万吨)	Cement (10 000 tons)	93368.62	1906.23	2.0
硫　酸(万吨)	Sulphuric Acid (10 000 tons)	3824.94	135.51	3.5
纯　碱(万吨)	Soda Ash (10 000 tons)	1266.79	10.03	0.8
烧　碱(万吨)	Caustic Soda (10 000 tons)	1060.26	4.60	0.4
农用化学肥料(万吨)	Chemical Fertilizer (10 000 tons)	4519.79	107.40	2.4
化学农药(万吨)	Chemical Pesticides (10 000 tons)	86.96	0.51	0.6
合成氨(万吨)	Synthetic Ammonia (10 000 tons)	4222.20	84.25	2.0
化学原料药(万吨)	Chemical Raw Material Medicine (10 000 tons)	93.44	1.27	1.4
中成药(万吨)	Traditional Chinese Medicine (10 000 tons)	61.58	2.88	4.7
冰醋酸(万吨)	Glacial Acetic Acid (10 000 tons)	115.16	21.44	18.6
精甲醇(万吨)	Refined Methanol (10 000 tons)	440.64	30.80	7.0
油　漆(万吨)	Paint (10 000 tons)	184.78	3.51	1.9
牙　膏(自然支)(亿支)	Toothpaste (100 million units)	47.96	1.74	3.6
卫生陶瓷(万件)	Toilet Wares (10 000 tons)	109400	257.31	0.2
变压器(万千伏安)	Transformers (10 000 kilovolt-amperes)	48970.11	2890.19	5.9
微波通信设备(部)	Microwave Communication Equipment (unit)	7854	1357	17.3
汽　车(万辆)	Motor Vehicles (10 000 vehicles)	519.65	43.42	8.4
摩托车(万辆)	Motorcycles (10 000 vehicles)	1581.55	473.07	29.9

主要统计指标解释

工业 指从事自然资源的开采，对采掘品和农产品进行加工和再加工的物质生产部门。具体包括：（1）对自然资源的开采，如采矿、晒盐、森林采伐等（不包括禽兽捕猎和水产捕捞）；（2）对农副产品的加工、再加工，如粮油加工、食品加工、轧花、缫丝、纺织、制革等；（3）对采掘品的加工、再加工，如炼铁、炼钢、化工生产、石油加工、机器制造、木材加工等，以及电力、自来水、煤气的生产和供应等；（4）对工业品的修理、翻新，如机器设备的修理、交通运输工具（包括小卧车）的修理等。1984 年以前农村的村及村以下办工业归属农业，1984 年以后划归工业。

本年鉴中涉及的企业登记注册类型：

（1）国有企业　指企业全部资产归国家所有，并按《中华人民共和国企业法人登记管理条例》规定登记注册的非公司制的经济组织。不包括有限责任公司中的国有独资公司。

（2）集体企业　指企业资产归集体所有，并按《中华人民共和国企业法人登记管理条例》规定登记注册的经济组织。

（3）股份合作企业　指以合作制为基础，由企业职工共同出资入股，吸收一定比例的社会资产投资组建，实行自主经营，自负盈亏，共同劳动，民主管理，按劳分配与按股份红相结合的一种集体经济组织。

（4）联营企业　指两个及两个以上相同或不同所有制性质的企业法人或事业单位法人，按自愿、平等、互利的原则，共同投资组成的经济组织。联营企业包括国有联营企业、集体联营企业、国有与集体联营企业和其他联营企业。

（5）有限责任公司　指根据《中华人民共和国公司登记管理条例》规定登记注册，由两个以上、五十个以下的股东共同出资，每个股东以其所认缴的出资额对公司承担有限责任，公司以其全部资产对其债务承担责任的经济组织。有限责任公司包括国有独资公司以及其他有限责任公司。

（6）股份有限公司　指根据《中华人民共和国公司登记管理条例》规定登记注册，其全部注册资本由等额股份构成并通过发行股票筹集资本，股东以其认购的股份对公司承担有限责任，公司以其全部资产对其债务承担责任的经济组织。

（7）私营企业　指由自然人投资设立或由自然人控股，以雇佣劳动为基础的营利性经济组织。包括按照《公司法》、《合伙企业法》、《私营企业暂行条例》以及《个人独资企业法》规定登记注册的私营有限责任公司、私营股份有限公司、私营合伙企业和私营独资企业。

（8）其他内资企业　指上述第 1 条至第 7 条之外的其他内资经济组织。

（9）与港澳台商合资经营企业　指港澳台地区投资者与内地企业依照《中华人民共和国中外合资经营企业法》及有关法律的规定，按合同规定的比例投资设立、分享利润和分担风险的企业。

（10）与港澳台商合作经营企业　指港澳台地区投资者与内地企业依照《中华人民共和国中外合作经营企业法》及有关法律的规定，依照合作合同的约定进行投资或提供条件设立、分配利润和分担风险的企业。

（11）港澳台商独资经营企业　指依照《中华人民共和国外资企业法》及有关法律的规定，在内地由港澳台地区投资者全额投资设立的企业。

（12）港澳台商投资股份有限公司　指根据国家有关规定，经原外经贸部依法批准设立，其中港、澳、台商的股本占公司注册资本的比例达 25% 以上的股份有限公司。凡其中港、澳、台商的股本占公司注册资本的比例小于 25%的，属于内资企业中的股份有限公司。

（13）中外合资经营企业　指外国企业或外国人与中国内地企业依照《中华人民共和国中外合资经营企业法》及有关法律的规定，按合同规定的比例投资设立、分享利润和分担风险的企业。

（14）中外合作经营企业　指外国企业或外国人与中国内地企业依照《中华人民共和国中外合作经营企业法》及有关法律的规定，依照合作合同的约定进行投资或提供条件设立、分配利润和分担风险的企业。

（15）外资企业　指依照《中华人民共和国外资企业法》及有关法律的规定，在中国内地由外国投资者全额投资设立的企业。

（16）外商投资股份有限公司　指根据国家有关规定，经原外经贸部依法批准设立，其中外资的股本占公司注册资本的比例达 25% 以上的股份有限公司。凡其中外资股本占公司注册资本的比例小于 25%的，属于内资企业中的股份有限公司。

国有控股企业　是对混合所有制经济的企业进行的“国有控股”分类。它是指这些企业的全部资产中国有资产(股份)相对其他所有者中的任何一个所有者占资(股)最多的企业。该分组反映了国有经济控股情况。

轻工业　指主要提供生活消费品和制作手工工具的工业。

重工业　指为国民经济各部门提供物质技术基础的主要生产资料的工业。

工业总产值　指以货币形式表现的，工业企业在一定时期内生产的工业最终产品或提供工业性劳务活动的总价值量。

工业增加值　指工业企业在报告期内以货币形式表现的工业生产活动的最终成果，是企业全部生产活动的总成果扣除了在生产过程中消耗或转移的物质产品和劳务价值后的余额，是企业生产过程中新增加的价值。

实收资本　指企业实际收到的投资人投入的资本。按投资主体可分为国家资本、集体资本、法人资本、个人资本、港澳台资本和外商资本等。

资产总计　指企业拥有或控制的能以货币计量的经济资源。包括各种财产、债权和其他权利。资产按其流动性划分为流动资产、长期投资、固定资产、无形及递延资产和其他资产。

（1）流动资产　指企业可以在一年内或者超过一年的一个营业周期内变现或耗用的资产。包括现金及各种存款、短期投资、应收及预付款项、存货等。

（2）固定资产　指使用期限较长，单位价值较高，并且在使用过程中保持原有实物形态的资产。

（3）无形资产　指企业长期使用而没有实物形态的资产。包括专利权、非专利技术、商标权、著作权、土地使用权、商誉等。

负债合计　指企业承担的能以货币计量，将以资产或劳务偿付的所有债务。负债一般按偿还期长短分为流动负债和长期负债。

（1）流动负债　指企业在一年内或者超过一年的一个营业周期内需要偿还的债务，包括短期借款、应付及预收款项、应付工资、应交税金和应付利润等。

（2）长期负债　指企业在一年以上或者超过一年的一个营业周期以上需要偿还的债务，包括长期借款、应付债务、长期应付款项等。

所有者权益　指企业投资者对企业净资产所拥有的权利。所有者权益等于企业全部资产减去全部负债后的余额，其中包括投资者对企业的最初投入，以及资本公积金、盈余公积金和未分配利润。

固定资产原价　指企业在建造、购置、安装、改建、扩建、技术改造某项固定资产时所支出的全部货币总额。它一般包括买价、包装费、运杂费和安装费等。

固定资产净值 指固定资产原价减去历年已提折旧额后的净额。

主营业务收入 指企业销售产品和提供劳务等主要经营业务取得的收入。

主营业务成本 指企业销售产品和提供劳务等主要经营业务过程中的实际成本。

主营业务税金及附加 指企业销售产品和提供劳务等主要经营业务应负担的城市维护建设税、消费税、资源税和教育费附加。

主营业务利润 指企业销售产品和提供劳务等主要经营业务收入扣除其成本、费用、税金后的利润。

利润总额 指企业在一定时期的最终经营成果，是企业的收入减去相关的成本与费用后的差额，收入大于相关的成本费用，企业就盈利，反之则亏损。

应交增值税 指企业在报告期内应交纳的增值税额。

利税总额 指企业利润总额、产品销售税金及附加、应交增值税之和。

工业经济效益综合指数 是综合衡量地区工业经济效益总体水平的一种特殊相对数，是反映一定时期工业经济运行质量的主要指标。工业经济效益综合指数由总资产贡献率、资本保值增值率、资产负债率、流动资产周转率、成本费用利润率、全员劳动生产率和产品销售率的实际数值分别除以该项指标的全国标准值，并乘以各自的权数，加总后除以总权数求得。该指标可从静态水平和动态趋势上较为全面地反映各地区工业经济效益的变化情况，并可在一定程度上消除地区对比的不可比因素。

工业增加值率 指在一定时期内工业增加值占同期工业总产值的比重，反映降低中间消耗的经济效益。计算公式为：

工业增加值率（%）=工业增加值（现价）/工业总产值（现价）×100%

总资产贡献率 反映企业全部资产的获利能力，是企业经营业绩和管理水平的集中体现，是评价和考核企业盈利能力的核心指标。计算公式为：

总资产贡献率（%）=（利润总额+税金总额+利息支出）/平均资产总额×100%

资产负债率 该指标既反映企业经营风险的大小，也反映企业利用债权人提供的资金从事经营活动的能力。计算公式为：资产负债率（%）=负债总额/资产总额×100%

流动资产周转次数 指在一定时期内流动资产完成的周转次数，反映流动资产的周转速度。计算公式为：

流动资产周转次数=产品销售收入/全部流动资产平均余额

工业成本费用利润率 指在一定时期内实现的利润与成本费用之比，是反映工业生产成本及费用投入的经济效益指标，同时也是反映降低成本的经济效益的指标。计算公式为：

工业成本费用利润率（%）=利润总额/成本费用总额×100%

全员劳动生产率 指根据产品的价值量指标计算的平均每一就业人员在单位时间内的产品生产量。是考核企业经济活动的重要指标，是企业生产技术水平、经营管理水平、职工技术熟练程度和劳动积极性的综合表现。目前，我国的全员劳动生产率是将工业企业的增加值除以同一时期全部就业人员的平均人数来计算的。计算公式为：

全员劳动生产率＝工业增加值/全部从业人员平均人数

产品销售率 指工业销售产值与同期全部工业总产值之比，反映工业产品已实现销售的程度，分析工业产销衔接情况，研究工业产品满足社会需求程度的指标。计算公式为：

产品销售率（%）＝现价工业销售产值/报告期现价工业总产值×100%

销售利润率 指企业利润与销售收入的比率。

计算公式为：销售利润率（%）＝利润/销售收入×100%

资本积累率 指企业所有者权益增长额与年初所有者权益的比率。计算公式为：

资本积累率（%）＝所有者权益增长额/年初所有者权益×100%

流动比率 指流动资产与流动负债的比率，它表明每一元流动负债有多少流动资产作为偿还的保证，反映企业用可在短期内转变为现金的流动资产偿还到期流动负债的能力。计算公式为：

流动比率＝流动资产/流动负债

速动比率 指企业速动资产与流动负债的比率。计算公式为：速动比率＝速动资产/流动负债

产权比率 指企业负债总额与所有者权益的比率，是企业财务结构稳健与否的重要标志，也称资本负债率。计算公式为：产权比率＝负债总额/所有者权益

Explanatory Notes on Main Statistical Indicators

Industry refers to the material production sector which is engaged in extraction of natural resources and processing and reprocessing of minerals and agricultural products, including (1) extraction of natural resources, such as mining, salt production, logging (but not including hunting and fishing); (2) processing and reprocessing of farm and sideline produces, such as rice husking, flour milling, wine making, oil pressing, cotton ginning, silk reeling, spinning and weaving, and leather making; (3) manufacture of industrial products, such as steel making, iron smelting, chemicals manufacturing, petroleum processing, machine building, timber processing; water and gas production and electricity generation and supply; (4) repairing of industrial products such as the repairing of machinery and means of transport (including cars). Prior to 1984, the rural industry run by villages and cooperative organizations under village was classified into agriculture. Since 1984, it has been grouped into industry.

Types of enterprise registration involved in this yearbook are as the following:

(1) State-owned Enterprises refer to non-corporation economic units where the entire assets are owned by the state and which have registered in accordance with the *Regulation of the People's Republic of China on the Management of Registration of Corporate Enterprises*. Excluded from this category are sole state-funded corporations in the limited liability corporations.

(2) Collective-owned Enterprises refer to economic units where the assets are owned collectively and which have registered in accordance with the *Regulation of the People's Republic of China on the Management of Registration of Corporate Enterprises.*

(3) Cooperative Enterprises refer to a form of collective economic units (enterprises) where capitals come mainly from employees as their shares, with certain proportion of capital from the outside, where production is organized on the basis of independent operation, independent accounting for profits and losses, joint work, democratic management, and a distribution system that integrates remuneration according to work with dividend according to capital share.

(4) Joint Ownership Enterprises refer to economic units established by two or more corporate enterprises or corporate institutions of the same or different ownership, through joint investment on the basis of equality, voluntary participation and mutual benefits. They include state joint ownership enterprises, collective joint ownership enterprises, joint state-collective enterprises, other joint ownership enterprises.

(5) Limited Liability Corporations refer to economic units established with investment from 2-50 investors and registered in accordance with the *Regulation of the People's Republic of China on the Management of Registration of Corporations*, each investor bearing limited liability to the corporation depending on its share of investment, and the corporation bearing liability to its debt to the maximum of its total assets. Limited liability corporations include exclusive state-funded limited liability corporations and other limited liability corporations.

(6) Share holding Corporations Ltd. refer to economic units registered in accordance with the Regulation of the *People's Republic of China on the Management of Registration of Corporations*, with total registered capitals divided into equal shares and raised through issuing stocks. Each investor bears limited liability to the corporation depending on the holding of shares, and the corporation bears liability to its debt to the maximum of its total assets.

(7) Private Enterprises refer to profit-making economic units invested and established by natural persons, or controlled by natural persons using employed labor. Included in this category are private limited liability corporations, private share-holding corporations Ltd., private partnership enterprises and private-funded enterprises registered in accordance with the *Corporation Law, Partnership Enterprises Law and Interim Regulations on Private Enterprise.*

(8) Other Domestic-funded Enterprises refer to domestic-funded economic units other than those mentioned above.

(9) Joint-venture Enterprises with Funds from Hong Kong, Macao and Taiwan refer to enterprises jointly established by invertors from Hong Kong, Macao and Taiwan with enterprises in the mainland of China in accordance with the *Law of the People's Republic of China on Sino-foreign Joint Venture Enterprises* and other relevant laws, where the share of investment, profits and risks is stipulated in the contract.

(10) Cooperative Enterprises with Funds from Hong Kong Macau and Taiwan established by investors from Hong Kong, Macau and Taiwan with enterprises in the mainland of China in accordance with the *Law of the People's Republic of China on Sino-foreign Cooperative Enterprises* and other relevant laws, where the investment or provision of facilities, and the share of profits and risks is stipulated in the cooperative contract.

(11) Enterprises with Sole (exclusive) Investment from Hong Kong, Macau and Taiwan refer to enterprises established in the mainland of China with exclusive investment from investors from Hong Kong, Macau and Taiwan in accordance with the *Law of the People's Republic of China on Foreign-Funded Enterprises* and other relevant laws.

(12) Share-holding Corporations Ltd. with Investment from Hong Kong, Macau and Taiwan refer to share-holding corporations Ltd. established with the approval from the former Ministry of Foreign Trade and Economic Relations in line with relevant state regulations, where the share of investment from Hong Kong, Macau or Taiwan businessmen exceeds 25% of the total registered capital of the corporation. In case the share of investment from Hong Kong, Macau or Taiwan is less than 25% of the total registered capital, the enterprise is to be classified as domestic-funded share-holding corporation Ltd.

(13) Joint-venture Enterprises with Foreign Investment refer to enterprises jointly established by foreign enterprises or foreigners with enterprises in the mainland of China in accordance with the *Law of the People's Republic of China on Sino-foreign Joint Venture Enterprises* and other relevant laws, where the share of investment, profits and risks is stipulated in the contract.

(14) Cooperation Enterprises with Foreign Investment refer to enterprises jointly established by foreign enterprises or foreigners with enterprises in the mainland of China in accordance with the *Law of the People's Republic of China on Sino-foreign Cooperative Enterprises* and other relevant laws, where the investment or provision of facilities, and the share of profits and risks is stipulated in the cooperative contract.

(15) Enterprises with Sole (exclusive) Foreign Investment refer to enterprises established in the mainland of China with exclusive investment from foreign investors in accordance with the *Law of the People's Republic of China on Foreign-Funded Enterprises* and other relevant laws.

(16) Share-holding Corporations Ltd. with Foreign Investment refer to share-holding corporations Ltd. established with the approval from the Ministry of Foreign Trade and Economic Relations in line with relevant state regulations, where the share of investment from foreign investors exceeds 25% of the total registered capital of the corporation. In case the share of foreign investment is less than 25% of the total registered capital, the enterprise is to be classified as domestic-funded share-holding corporation Ltd.

State-holding Enterprises refer to a classification of enterprises of mixed ownership. It means the state-owned asset of total assets is more than that of other owners. The classification shows the status of share held by state-owned economy.

Light Industry refers to the industry, which produces consumer goods and hand tools.

Heavy Industry refers to the industry which produces capital goods, and provides various sectors of the national economy with necessary material and technical basis.

According to the above principle of classification, the repairing trades which are engaged primarily in repairing products of heavy industry are classified into heavy industry while these engaged in repairing products of light industry are classified into light industry.

Gross Industrial Output Value is the total volume of industrial final products and industrial services in value terms within a certain time.

Value Added of Industry refers to the final results of industrial trade in money terms during the reference period. The value added is the balance that the total results of industrial production deduct the used or transferred products and their value. It is the newly increased value.

Capital Obtained refers to capital actually received by the enterprise from investors. It can be further classified by investors as state capital, capital from Hong Kong, Macao and Taiwan and foreign Capital.

Total Assets refer to all assets which are owned or controlled by enterprises, including circulating assets, long-term investment, fixed assets, intangible assets and deferred assets, other long-term assets, and deferred taxes, etc. The summation of above items is equal to total assets shown in the balance sheets of the enterprises.

(1) Circulating assets (working capital) refer to assets which can be cashed in or spent or consumed in an operating cycle of one year or over one year, including cash, all kinds of deposits, short term investment, receivables, advance payment, stock, etc.

(2) Fixed assets refer to the assets with high unit value can keep its original body in use and last for a long period.

(3) Intangible assets refer to the assets without material form used by enterprises over a long time, such as patents, non-patent technologies, trade marks, copyright, land use right, business reputation, etc.

Total Liabilities refer to the debts that enterprises are responsible for repayment, including liquid liabilities and long-term liabilities. Total liabilities correspond to the summation item of liabilities shown in the balance sheets of the enterprises.

(1) Liquid liabilities (also called quick liabilities or immediate liabilities) refer to enterprises total debt payable within an operating cycle of one year or over one year, including short term loans, payables and advance payments, wages payable, taxes payable and profit payable, etc.

(2) Long-term liabilities refers to total debt payable within an operating cycle of one year or over one year, including long-term loans, payable liabilities, long-term payables, etc.

Creditors' Equity refers to investors' ownership of net assets of the enterprise. It is equal to the total assets of the enterprise minus its total liabilities, including the primary input from investors, capital accumulation fund, surplus accumulation fund and undistributed profit.

Original Value of Fixed Assets refers to the original value of all fixed assets owned by industrial enterprises, calculated at the cost paid at the time of purchase, installation, reconstruction, expansion, and technical innovation and transformation of the said assets, which includes expenses on purchase, package, transportation, and installation, etc.

Net Value of Fixed Assets is obtained by deducting depreciation over years from the original value of fixed assets.

Major Business Revenue refers to the revenue from the sales of products by industrial enterprises and the revenue from services provided and etc.

Major Business Cost refers to the actual cost of products of industrial enterprises and industrial services provided, etc.

Tax and Extra Charges on Major Business refer to the tax on city maintenance and construction, consumption tax, resources tax and extra charges for education, which should be borne by the enterprises in selling products and providing industrial services.

Major Business Profit refers to the profit gained by the enterprises by deducting cost, charges and taxes from the business income of the enterprises obtained in selling products and providing industrial services.

Total Profits refer to the final results gained by the enterprises. It is got as using the total revenue taking off related costs and fees. Only if the revenue is more than the costs, the enterprises gain the profits.

Value Added Tax Payable refers to the amount of the value-added tax, which should be paid by the enterprises in the reporting period.

Total Value of Profit and Tax (Pre-tax Profits) refers to the sum of the total profits, products sales tax and surcharges and the value added tax payable of industrial enterprises. It is also called Pre-tax profits.

Industrial Comprehensive Index of Economic Efficiency is a special kind of relative figure to comprehensively measure overall economic efficiency of regional industry, showing the quality of industrial economic efficiency of the reference period. Industrial comprehensive index of economic efficiency is calculated with 7 items of ratio of total assets to industrial output value, ratio of creditors' equity of current year to that of previous year, ratio of liabilities to assets, turnover ratio of output value, circulating funds, ratio of profits to cost, overall labor productivity, ratio of sales to products. The actual figure of every indicator above is divided by responding national standard numerical value, and the results multiply correlative weight coefficients, then the total number is divided by general weight coefficient. The index comprehensively reflects the changes of regional industrial economic efficiency in static and dynamic status, eliminating the incomparable factors at a certain extent.

Value Added Rate of Industry refers to the ratio of value added of industry in a given period to the gross output value in the same period, which reflects the economic efficiency of cutting down the intermediate input and is calculated as follows:

Value Added Rate of Industry (%) =Value Added of Industry (at Current Prices)/Gross Output Value (at Current Prices)×100%

Ratio of Total Assets to Industrial Output Value reflects the profit-making capability of all assets of the enterprise and is a key indicator manifesting the performance and management and evaluating the profit-making potential of the enterprise. It is calculated as follows:

Ratio of Total Assets to Industrial Output (%) = [(Total profits + Total taxes + Interest payment) / average assets] × 100%

Ratio of Liabilities to Assets reflect both the operation risk and the capability of the enterprise in making use of the capital from the creditors. It is calculated as follows:

Ratio of liabilities to assets (%) = Total liabilities/total assets×100%

Turnover Ratio of Circulating Funds refers to times of turnover of circulating funds in a given period of time, which reflects the speed of the turnover of working capital and is calculated as follows:

Turnover Ratio of Circulating Funds (%) = Sales Revenue of Products/Average Balance of Total Circulating Funds×100%

Ratio of Profits to Costs refers to the ratio of profits realized in a given period to the total costs in the same period, which reflects the economic efficiency of input cost and is calculated as follows:

Ratio of Profits to Cost (%) =Total Profits/Total Costs×100%

Overall Labor Productivity refers to the average output per employed person in industrial enterprises in value terms. At present, the value added and the average number of staff and workers of an industrial enterprises in a given period are used to calculate the overall labor productivity. The formula used is:

Overall Labor Productivity = (Value Added of Industry) / (Average Number of Staff and Workers)

Ratio of Sales to Products refers to the ratio of total sales in a given period to the gross output value in the same period, which reflects the extent of industrial output sold and is calculated as follows:

Ratio of Sales to Products (%) =Total Sales (at Current Prices)/Gross Output Value (at Current Prices) ×100%

Ratio of Profits to Sales refers to the ratio of total profits to the sales revenue in a given period and is calculated as follows: *Ratio of Profits to Sales (%) =Total Profits /Sales Revenue×100%*

Ratio of Accumulated Capital to Original Capital refers to the ratio of the increased volume of creditors' equity to the creditors' equity at the year's beginning. The formula used is:

Ratio of Accumulated Capital to Original Capital (%) = Increased Volume of Creditors' Equity / Creditors' Equity at Year's Beginning×100%

Circulating Rate refers to the rate of the circulating funds to the circulating liabilities. It shows the enterprise's guaranteed solvency that the cash changed from circulating funds in a short time to pay for circulating liabilities. The formula is: *Circulating Rate = Circulating Funds / Circulating Liabilities*

Speed Rate refers to the rate of the speed funds to the circulating liabilities. The formula is:

Speed Rate = Speed Funds / Circulating Liabilities

Ratio of Equity to Production refers to the ratio of total liabilities to creditors' equity. It is the sign of financial stability of the enterprises, and also called ratio of total liabilities to total capital. The formula is:

Ratio of Equity to Production = Total Liabilities / Creditors' Equity

十二 建筑业

CONSTRUCTION

简要说明 Brief Introduction

本章资料包括我市建筑业基本情况、建筑企业房屋施工及竣工面积和劳务分包建筑业企业主要指标、建筑业企业主要经济和经济效益指标，由市统计局固定资产投资处提供。

Data in this chapter show the general situation of the construction, floor space of buildings under construction and completed, and main indicators of construction enterprises of work subcontractors, main economic indicators and efficiency indicators of construction. Data in this chapter are provided by Division of Statistics of Investment in Fixed Assets, Municipal Bureau of Statistics.

12－1 建筑业基本情况（1985－2004年）
Basic Statistics on Construction (1985-2004)

年　份 Year	企业数（个） Number of Enterprises (unit)	年末从业人数（万人） Number of Employment (10 000 persons)	建筑业总产值（万元） Gross Output Value of Construction (10 000 yuan)	建筑业增加值（万元） Value-added of Construction (10 000 yuan)	房屋建筑施工面积（万平方米） Floor Space under Construction (10 000 sq.m)	房屋建筑竣工面积（万平方米） Floor Space Completed (10 000 sq.m)
1985	298	14.12	96201	20517	684.85	340.18
1986	291	17.12	112719	26225	674.54	345.37
1987	303	18.08	138515	35738	740.55	350.79
1988	399	20.71	183070	39989	866.76	372.69
1989	400	20.60	196510	50763	853.54	391.35
1990	445	20.89	220685	69913	905.58	450.19
1991	465	21.50	262155	84556	915.31	458.23
1992	482	23.58	340256	109961	1015.59	490.88
1993	607	22.47	426228	124993	1238.22	537.78
1994	561	26.61	656959	203632	1456.78	577.22
1995	556	28.24	810548	261437	1678.02	656.38
1996	1473	64.43	2052964	564293	4065.24	2276.97
1997	1501	68.98	2440552	688463	4451.06	2562.73
1998	1655	80.46	2896198	783225	5275.68	2837.02
1999	1735	75.49	3175927	871003	5481.86	2974.82
2000	1785	73.37	3486579	945158	6088.49	3083.72
2001	1721	83.99	4368064	1208296	7962.27	4341.38
2002	1778	82.05	5015839	1353087	8707.39	4711.06
2003	1760	81.80	5862095	1287202	9754.10	4939.62
2004	2442	86.91	6902774	1519837	10184.46	5167.65

注：1）1993年实行一套表制度，附营建筑企业有所增加；1996年以前口径范围包括全民、城镇集体建筑安装企业，1996年以后为资质等级四级以上的建筑安装企业（下表同）。

2）2002年起建筑业执行新建筑资质，2002年房屋建筑施工、竣工面积和2003年起所有数据不含劳务分包企业（下表同）。

3）建筑业增加值2003年前按工程结算利润计算，2003年起按营业利润计算（下表同）。

Note: a) The system of one suit of tables was implemented in 1993, affiliated construction enterprises increased. The statistics before 1996 included whole people-owned, collective-owned construction and installation enterprises. Statistics after 1996 included construction and installation enterprises of grade 4 and above (the same below).

b) New grade system has been carried out in construction since 2002. Data floor space under construction and completed in 2002, and all data since 2003 exclude construction enterprises of work subcontractors (the same below).

c) Value-added of construction is calculated in terms of profits of project settled accounts before 2003, whereas in terms of business profits since 2003 (the same below).

12－2 建筑业企业房屋施工及竣工面积（2003－2004年）
Floor Space of Buildings under Construction and Completed by Construction Enterprises (2003-2004)

指　标	Item	2003	2004
房屋建筑施工面积（万平方米）	**Floor Space of Buildings under Construction (10 000 sq.m)**	**9754.10**	**10184.46**
其中：本年新开工面积	Of Which: New Floor Space of Buildings in Current Year	5321.84	5876.04
其中：实行投标承包面积	Of Which: Contracted Bidding Floor Space	7182.80	7429.01
其中：本年新开工	Of Which: New Floor Space of Buildings in Current Year	4248.17	4859.78
房屋建筑竣工面积（万平方米）	**Floor Space of Buildings Completed (10 000 sq.m)**	**4939.62**	**5167.65**
厂房、仓库	Works and Warehouses	378.24	484.44
住　宅	Residential Buildings	3449.40	3522.55
办公用房	Office Buildings	309.41	351.38
批发和零售用房	Wholesale and Retail Trade Buildings	174.29	203.24
住宿和餐饮用房	Hotels and Restaurants	55.12	66.31
居民服务业用房	Residential Service Buildings	109.97	71.27
教育用房	Educational Buildings	223.70	222.14
文化、体育和娱乐用房	Cultural, Sports and Entertainment Buildings	39.04	67.23
卫生医疗用房	Health Care and Medical Buildings	29.44	20.31
科研用房	Scientific and Research Buildings	2.49	18.43
其他用房	Other Buildings	168.52	140.35

12－3 劳务分包建筑业企业主要指标（2003－2004年）
Main Indicators of Construction Enterprises of Work Subcontractors (2003-2004)

单位：万元　　(10 000 yuan)

指　标	Item	2003	2004
企业个数（个）	Number of Enterprises (unit)	29	83
从业人数（人）	Number of Persons Employed (person)	29299	33420
企业总收入	Total Revenue	35782	53803
#劳务收入	Work Revenue	29612	53719
税　金	Taxes	762	1245
利润总额	Total Profits	2052	1334
从业人员劳动报酬	Earnings of Employed Persons	21757	34432

12－4 建筑施工企业主要经济指标（2003－2004年）
Main Economic Indicators of Construction Enterprises (2003-2004)

指标	Type	2003	2004
企业数(个)	**Number of Enterprises (unit)**	**1760**	**2442**
#国有及国有控股	State-owned and State-holding	183	213
年末从业人员(万人)	**Number of Employment (10 000 persons)**	**81.80**	**86.91**
#国有及国有控股	State-owned and State-holding	13.87	14.38
建筑业总产值（万元）	**Output Value of Construction (10 000 yuan)**	**5862095**	**6902774**
按登记注册类型分	By Registration		
内资企业	Domestic-Funded Enterprises	5836081	6879904
#国　有	State-owned	827443	963778
集　体	Collective-owned	644453	490334
港澳台商投资企业	Enterprises Funded by Hong Kong, Macau and Taiwan	19358	21304
外商投资企业	Foreign-funded Enterprises	6656	1566
按构成分	By Constitution		
#建筑工程	Construction	5268331	6018257
安装工程	Installation	421868	608842
按行业分	By Sector		
#房屋和土木工程建筑业	Construction of Buildings and Civil Engineering	5382569	6062521
#房屋工程建筑业	Buildings	4778661	5178146
建筑安装业	Construction Installation	291620	477965
建筑装饰业	Construction Decoration	144872	239481
按资质等级分	By Grade		
施工总承包	General Contractors of Construction	5365296	6104106
#一　级	Class I	1457974	2072887
二　级	Class II	2410977	2604562
专业承包	Professional Contractors of Construction	496799	798668
#一　级	Class I	141637	212585
二　级	Class II	195189	283028
竣工产值(万元)	**Output Value of Completed Construction (10 000 yuan)**	**4175994**	**4683281**
按登记注册类型分	By Registration		
内资企业	Domestic-Funded Enterprises	4164262	4674951
#国　有	State-owned	600106	545715
集　体	Collective-owned	492826	374453
港澳台商投资企业	Enterprises Funded by Hong Kong, Macau and Taiwan	5548	7774
外商投资企业	Foreign-funded Enterprises	6184	556
按行业分	By Sector		
#房屋和土木工程建筑业	Construction of Buildings and Civil Engineering	3907868	4240078
#房屋工程建筑业	Buildings	3497874	3803392
建筑安装业	Construction Installation	182693	295334
建筑装饰业	Construction Decoration	57855	98655
按资质等级分	By Grade		
施工总承包	General Contractors of Construction	3902331	4219313
#一　级	Class I	987077	1276820
二　级	Class II	1787886	1841211
专业承包	Professional Contractors of Construction	273663	463968
#一　级	Class I	63322	77153
二　级	Class II	104737	169227
房屋建筑施工面积(万平方米)	**Floor Space of Building under Construction (10 000 sq.m)**	**9754.10**	**10184.46**
房屋建筑竣工面积(万平方米)	**Floor Space of Building Completed (10 000 sq.m)**	**4939.62**	**5167.65**
年末自有机械设备台数(万台)	**Number of Machines Self-owned (year-end)(10 000 units)**	**20.16**	**20.28**
年末自有机械设备总功率(万千瓦)	**Power of Machines Self-owned (year-end)(10 000 kw)**	**276.84**	**286.32**

12－5 建筑施工企业主要财务和经济效益指标（2004年）

单位：万元

指标	Item	合计 Total	内资企业 Domestic -funded Enterprises
施工企业个数(个)	Construction Enterprises (unit)	2442	2429
年平均人数(万人)	Annual Persons Engaged (10 000 persons)	82.15	81.98
自有固定资产原价	Original Value of Fixed Assets Owned	1741087	1736071
自有固定资产净价	Net Value of Fixed Assets Owned	1254033	1250486
自有机械设备年末台数(万台)	Number of Machinery and Equipment Self-owned (10 000 sets)	20.28	20.08
自有机械设备年末净值	Net Value of Machinery and Equipment Self-owned	637282	635889
自有机械设备年末总功率(万千瓦)	Total Power of Machinery and Equipment Self-owned (10 000kw)	286.32	286.11
总产值	Gross Output Value	6902774	6879903
增加值	Value-added	1519837	1517336
实收资本	Total Capital	2572902	2563666
资产合计	Total Assets	6247197	6232064
流动资产	Circulating Funds	4354811	4343325
固定资产	Fixed Assets	1457317	1453769
无形及递延资产	Intangible and Deferred Assets	154997	154997
负债合计	Total Liabilities	3212487	3205136
流动负债	Circulating Liabilities	3005307	2997956
长期负债	Long-term Liabilities	207180	207180
所有者权益	Creditors' Equity	3034709	3026927
利税总额	Total Pre-tax Profits	401386	401043
#利润总额	Total Profits	180271	180446
企业总收入	Total Income of Enterprises	6426173	6412025
工程结算收入	Revenue of Project Settled Accounts	6302859	6288777
其他业务收入	Other Revenue from Business	123314	123248
施工面积(万平方米)	Floor Space of Buildings Under Construction (10 000 sq.m)	10184.46	10183.29
竣工面积(万平方米)	Floor Space of Buildings Completed (10 000 sq.m)	5167.65	5166.63
全员劳动生产率：	Overall Labor Productivity		
按总产值计算(元/人)	In Terms of Gross Output Value (yuan/person)	84026	83912
按增加值计算(元/人)	In Terms of Value-added (yuan/person)	18501	18506
技术装备率(元/人)	Value of Machines Per Laborer (yuan/person)	7758	7756
动力装备率(千瓦/人)	Power of Machines Per Laborer (kw/person)	3	3
房屋建筑面积竣工率(%)	Rate of Floor Space of Buildings Completed (%)	50.7	50.7
资产负债率(%)	Ratio of Liabilities to Assets (%)	51.4	51.4

Financial Indicators and Economic Efficiency Indicators of Construction Enterprises (2004)

(10 000 yuan)

#国有经济 State- owned Enterprises	#集体经济 Collective -owned Enterprises	#联营企业 Joint-owned Enterprises	#股份合作企业 Share Holding Enterprises	#私营企业 Private Enterprises	港澳台投资企业 Enterprises Funded by Hong Kong, Macao and Taiwan	外商投资企业 Foreign-funded Enterprises
117	234	10	71	1121	8	5
8.33	7.16	0.28	2.06	26.49	0.15	0.02
260970	153270	8596	39207	518149	1954	3062
166798	103306	7639	28521	392641	1598	1949
1.83	2.01	0.06	0.53	6.52	0.10	0.10
62514	54817	3864	15844	223336	630	763
36.61	29.39	0.82	8.84	86.45	0.11	0.10
963778	490334	17982	173589	1968983	21304	1567
168668	113912	4197	35445	459072	2223	278
268710	167409	13204	65499	921641	6057	3179
932242	413861	14670	176278	1745616	9546	5587
661064	268191	5371	138170	1200268	7874	3612
195671	132217	7731	29236	448294	1599	1949
25114	3959	1020	3752	41663		...
666087	218157	6361	93182	664072	3598	3753
650747	193331	6220	87870	624606	3598	3753
15340	24826	141	5312	39466		
266155	195704	8309	83096	1081544	5948	1834
48849	24463	1010	8167	122207	473	-130
17668	7967	344	2658	60666	73	-248
980151	449829	18121	130990	1689714	12911	1237
950164	435132	18093	130037	1675634	12846	1236
29987	14697	28	953	14080	65	1
739.21	822.67	37.45	201.74	3168.86		1.17
294.96	466.98	33.83	149.33	1675.71		1.02
115700	68482	64221	84267	74329	142027	78350
20248	15909	14989	17206	17330	14820	13900
7505	7656	13800	7691	8431	4200	38150
4	4	3	4	3	1	5
39.9	56.8	90.3	74.0	52.9		87.2
71.5	52.7	43.4	52.9	38.0	37.7	67.2

主要统计指标解释

建筑业统计单位 指从事房屋、构筑物建造和设备安装活动及装饰装修的法人企业。建筑业法人企业应同时具备的条件是：①依法成立，有自己的名称、组织机构和场所，能够承担民事责任；②独立拥有和使用资产，承担负债，有权与其他单位签订合同；③独立核算盈亏，能够编制资产负债表。

建筑业总产值（即自行完成施工产值） 是以货币表现的建筑安装企业在一定时期内生产的建筑业产品的总和。建筑业产值包括：

①建筑工程产值：指列入建筑工程预算内的各种工程价值。

②设备安装工程产值：指设备安装工程价值，不包括被安装设备本身价值。

③其他产值：指建筑业总产值中除建筑工程、安装工程以外的产值。包括房屋构筑物修理产值、非标准设备制造产值、总包企业向分包企业收取的管理费以及不能明确划分的施工活动所完成的产值。

a. 房屋构筑物修理产值：指房屋和构筑物修理所完成的产值，但不包括被修理房屋、构筑物本身价值和生产设备的修理产值。

b. 非标准设备制造产值：指加工制造没有定型的非标准生产设备的加工费和原材料价值（如化工厂、炼油厂用的各种罐、槽，矿井生产统一使用的各种漏斗、三角槽、阀门等）以及附属加工厂为本企业承建工程制作的非标准设备的价值。

建筑业增加值 指建筑业企业以货币表现的建筑业生产经营活动的最终成果。目前建筑业增加值采用分配法（收入法）计算，即从收入的角度出发，根据生产要素在生产过程中应得的收入份额计算。具体计算公式为：

建筑业增加值＝本年计提的固定资产折旧＋应付工资＋应付福利费＋管理费用中的劳动待业保险金、税金＋工程结算税金及附加＋营业利润

房屋建筑施工面积 指在报告期内施工的全部房屋建筑面积。包括本期内新开工的房屋面积、上期施工跨入本期继续施工的房屋面积、上期停缓建在本期恢复施工的房屋面积、本期竣工的房屋面积及本期施工后又停缓建的房屋面积。

房屋建筑竣工面积 指在报告期内房屋建筑按照设计要求全部完工，达到了住人和使用条件，经验收鉴定合格，正式移交使用单位的房屋建筑面积。

自有机械设备年末总台数 指归本企业所有，属于本企业固定资产的生产性机械设备年末总台数。包括施工机械、生产设备、运输设备以及其他设备。

自有机械设备年末总功率 指本企业自有施工机械、生产设备、运输设备以及其他设备列为在册固定资产的生产性机械设备年末总功率，按设定能力或查定能力计算。包括机械本身的动力和为该机械服务的单独动力设备，如电动机等。计算单位用千瓦，动力换算可按 1 马力＝0.735 千瓦折合成千瓦数。电焊机、变压器、锅炉不计算动力。

工程结算收入 指企业承包工程实现的工程价款结算收入，以及向发包单位收取的除工程价款以外的按规定列作营业收入的各种款项，如临时设施费、劳动保险费、施工机械调迁费等以及向发包单位收取的各种索赔款。

工程结算利润　指已结算工程实现的利润。如为亏损以“－”号表示。计算公式为：

工程结算利润＝工程结算收入－工程结算成本－经营费用－工程结算税金及附加

营业利润：指企业生产经营活动所实现的利润。分为主营业务利润和其他利润。计算公式为：

营业利润＝工程结算利润+其他业务利润－管理费用－财务费用

企业总收入　指与企业生产经营直接有关的各项收入，包括工程结算收入和其他业务收入。计算公式为：

企业总收入＝工程结算收入＋其他业务收入

Explanatory Notes on Main Statistical Indicators

Statistical Unit in Construction refers to the corporate enterprises engaged in the construction of buildings and structures， in the installation of equipment and in the decoration activities. A corporate construction enterprise should meet the following 3 requirements: (a) being set up in line with relevant legal basis, having its full name, organization and location, and capable of taking civil liabilities; (b) independently possessing and using its assets and assuming its liabilities, and entitled to sign contracts with other institutions; and (c) making independent accounts of its profits and losses, and capable of compiling its own balance sheet.

Gross Output Value of Construction refers to total of construction products and services, expressed in money terms, produced or rendered by construction and installation enterprises during a given period of time. It includes:

(1) Output value of construction projects, that is the value of projects covered by the project budgets;

(2) Output value of installation projects, that is the value of the installation of equipment, (excluding the value of the equipment to be installed);

(3) Output value of others, which is the output value of construction industry excluding that of construction projects and installation projects. It includes: output value of repair of buildings and structures; output value of non-standard equipment manufacturing; overhead expenses received by contracted enterprises to the sub-contracted enterprises and the completed output value of construction activities that have no clear definition.

a. Output value of repair of buildings and structures, that is the value created through the repairs of buildings or structures, but does not include the value of buildings or structures being repaired and the value of the repair of production equipment;

b. Output value of manufactured non-standard equipment, that is the value of non-standard production equipment including raw materials and manufacturing cost made for the construction project (i.e., chemical plant; kettles or tanks used by refineries; various fillers, triangle tanks, valves used by mines), and the output value of equipment manufactured by subsidiary workshops.

Value Added of Construction refers to the final result of the activities of production and management of construction in monetary terms in the reference period. At present, the value added of construction is calculated with the method of distribution. In other words, it is the sum of incomes of various production factors in the production process. The formula is as follows:

Value Added of Construction=Depreciation of Fixed Assets in the Year + Wages Payable + Welfare Expenses Payable + Insurance Premium and Tax for Waiting for Employment in the Administrative Expenses + Taxes and Surcharges on Project Settlement + Profit Gained from Project Settlement

Floor space of Buildings under Construction refers to floor space of buildings under construction during the reference period, including newly started buildings, buildings started earlier and continued during the reference period, and buildings suspended earlier but restarted during the reference period, buildings completed during the reference period, and buildings under construction and then suspended during the period.

Floor Space of Buildings Completed refers to the floor space of buildings that are completed in the reference period in accordance with the requirements of the design, up to the standard for putting them into use, and have been checked and accepted by concerned departments as qualified ones.

Total Number of Machinery and Equipment Owned by the Construction Enterprises by the End of Year refers to the number of machines and equipment owned by the enterprises, and listed as the fixed assets of the enterprises (or units) by the end of the year, including machinery and equipment for construction, production and transportation.

Total Power of Machinery and Equipment Owned by the Construction Enterprises by the End of Year refers to the total power of machinery and equipment owned by the enterprises, and listed as the fixed assets of the enterprises (or units) by the end of the year, including machinery and equipment for construction, production and transportation. The power of the machinery is calculated on basis of the designed or verified capacity, covering the power of the machinery/equipment and the separate power equipment serving the machinery/equipment (such as electric motors), but excluding welders, transformers and boilers. The unit used for the calculation of power is kilowatt, with horsepower converted to kilowatt by 1 horsepower= 0.735 kilowatt.

Income from Settlement of Projects refers to the income received by the construction enterprise unit from the completed portion of the project through settlement procedures with the contracted during the reference period, and other charges to the contracted as operational costs, such as facility fee, labor insurance premium, moving cost of construction unit, as well as various types of claims to the contracted.

Profit from Settlement of Projects refers to profit realized through settled projects. It is calculated with the following formula:

Profit from Settlement of Projects = Income from Settlement of Projects – Settled Cost – Operation Cost – Settled Taxes and Other Cost

Business Profit refers to profit realized through production and performance of enterprises. It can be divided into two classifications, that is, major business profit and other profit. It is calculated with the following formula:

Business Profit = Profit from Settlement of Projects + Other Business Profit – Administrative Expenses – Financial Expenses

Total Revenue of Enterprises refers to the sum of income from production and operation of enterprises, including income from settlement of projects and other operational income, namely:

Total Revenue of Enterprises = Income from Settlement of Projects +Other Operational Income [illegible] departments [illegible].

Total Number of Machinery and Equipment Owned by the Construction Enterprises by the End of Year refers to the number of machinery and equipment owned by the enterprises and listed as the fixed assets of the enterprises (or units) by the end of the year, including machinery and equipment for construction, production and transportation.

Total Power of Machinery and Equipment Owned by the Construction Enterprises by the End of Year refers to total power of machinery and equipment owned by the enterprises and listed as the fixed assets of the enterprises (or units) by the end of the year, including machinery and equipment for construction, production and transportation. The power of the machinery is calculated in terms of the designed or verified capacity, covering the power of the machinery (equipment) [illegible] motors, [illegible] transformers and [illegible] horsepower converted to kilowatt by [illegible] (1 horsepower = 0.735 kilowatt).

Revenue from Settlement of Projects refers to the income received by the construction enterprise [illegible] from the completed portion of the project through settlement [illegible] during the reference period, and other [illegible].

Revenue from Settlement of Projects [illegible] it is calculated with the following formula:

[illegible] = Revenue from Settlement of Projects [illegible] Cost

Business Profit [illegible]. It can be divided into [illegible] and is calculated on the following formula:

Business Profit = [illegible]

Total Amount of [illegible] including [illegible].

[illegible]

十三　运输和邮电

TRANSPORTATION, POSTAL AND TELECOMMUNICATION SERVICES

简要说明　Brief Introduction

本章反映我市交通运输业和邮电通信业情况，主要包括货物和旅客运输量、港口吞吐量、交通基础设施和运输营运工具、民用车辆和船舶、主要港口码头泊位和仓库、邮电业务、电信主要通信能力和邮电通信水平。本章资料由市统计局工业交通处负责整理编辑。

交通运输有关资料来源于市交通委员会、市公安局、原重庆铁路分局、民航重庆管理局、港口管理部门和市统计局。邮电通信业资料来源于市邮政局、市电信公司、移动通信公司、联通公司、网通公司和铁通公司等电信企业。

Data in this chapter shows the conditions of transportation, postal and telecommunication services, mainly covering freight and passenger traffic, freight handled at ports, transportation infrastructure and machinery, civil motor vehicles and transport vessels, berths and warehouses at major ports, business volume of postal and telecommunication services, main communication capacity of telecommunication services, and level of postal and telecommunication services. Data in this chapter are prepared and edited by Division of Industry and Transport Statistics, Municipal Bureau of Statistics.

Data on transportation come from Municipal Committee of Communications, Municipal Bureau of Public Security, former Chongqing Railway Ministry Branch, Civil Aviation Administration of Chongqing, administrative departments of ports and Municipal Bureau of Statistics. Data of postal and telecommunication services come from Municipal Administration of Posts and from telecommunication enterprises such as China Telecom, China Mobile, China Unicom, China Netcom and China Railcom.

13－1 主要年份客货运输量
Volume of Freight Traffic and Passenger Traffic in Major Years

年 份 Year	客运量(万人) Passenger Traffic (10 000 persons)	旅客周转量(万人公里) Passenger-kilometers (10 000 person-km)	货运量(万吨) Freight Traffic (10 000 tons)	货物周转量(万吨公里) Freight ton-kilometers (10 000 ton-km)
1952	82		134	31531
1957	121		842	132103
1962	965	12619	808	147390
1965	1707	23268	2365	141406
1970	2136	27461	2536	111415
1975	3602	40180	3226	276337
1978	5294	293741	4816	1189803
1980	7846	417025	4469	1106294
1985	16923	975571	13513	2004938
1986	18308	1119673	14860	2184266
1987	21002	1160714	15618	2296505
1988	21119	1206942	22881	2470614
1989	22692	1185786	20764	2676052
1990	20332	1068775	15546	2452448
1991	26598	1176783	16186	2702591
1992	32924	1543492	17419	3005694
1993	34025	1724473	18841	3282548
1994	36340	1890785	21130	3077590
1995	39731	2104270	22796	3359847
1996	43123	2272533	25818	3900452
1997	46999	2388433	25293	3605254
1998	49772	2476181	26494	3291566
1999	53290	2558000	26390	3379000
2000	57852	2704859	28022	3713900
2001	60087	2792000	29469	3888700
2002	62853	2925400	31177	4008200
2003	59170	2678700	34113	4467500
2004	64675	3209500	38168	7211500

13－2 主要年份港口吞吐量和公路线路里程
Freight Handled at Ports and Length of Highways in Major Years

年 份 Year	港口货物吞吐量（万吨） Freight Handled at Ports (10 000 tons)	进 口 Handled in	出 口 Handled out	公路线路里程（公里） Length of Highways (km)
1952	61.80	26.60	35.20	743
1957	356.10	73.10	283.00	1021
1962	173.50	93.40	80.10	6044
1965	217.10	115.70	101.40	7221
1970	267.00	161.00	106.00	7538
1975	228.90	108.90	120.00	9753
1978	369.80	184.10	185.70	15421
1980	378.20	194.10	184.10	16811
1985	438.30	195.40	242.90	19377
1986	532.70	303.40	229.30	19666
1987	553.70	292.30	261.42	19942
1988	570.30	296.10	274.16	20609
1989	651.93	330.74	321.19	20944
1990	572.50	275.70	296.80	21162
1991	566.10	262.77	303.33	21474
1992	664.90	326.80	338.10	21804
1993	687.70	299.50	388.20	21990
1994	665.65	289.26	376.39	22148
1995	853.00	390.00	463.00	22556
1996	1076.00	492.00	584.00	26892
1997	2548.70	977.20	1571.50	27045
1998	2477.30	1186.60	1290.70	27210
1999	2599.80	1297.30	1302.50	28086
2000	2448.00	1148.10	1299.90	30354
2001	2839.87	1690.39	1149.48	30654
2002	3004.00	1803.53	1200.47	31060
2003	3243.76	1796.24	1447.52	31407
2004	4539.00	2337.09	2201.91	32344

13－3 主要年份邮电通信指标
Indicators of Postal and Telecommunication Services in Major Years

年 份 Year	邮政局、所(个) Number of Postal Offices (unit)	邮电业务总量(万元) Total Business Volume from Postal and Telecommunication Services (10 000 yuan)	#电 信 Telecommunication Service	邮电业务收入(万元) Business Revenue from Postal and Telecommunication Services (10 000 yuan)	#电 信 Telecommunication Service
1952	1023	12		133	
1957	1846	33		874	
1962	1747	102		1000	
1965	1751	245		1461	
1970	2166	267		1371	
1975	1933	2190		1726	
1978	1925	2650		2103	
1980	1917	5071		2650	
1985	1853	7268		5796	
1986	1862	8264		6840	
1987	1896	9719		7675	
1988	1918	11853		10120	
1989	2025	14351		11734	
1990	2056	18999		14222	
1991	2047	23708		20585	
1992	2075	31305		27608	
1993	2041	47627		41653	
1994	1957	70543		71212	
1995	2220	109627		157568	
1996	2314	159929		167313	
1997	1821	233471	211458	223052	184899
1998	1958	345932	319375	264846	219493
1999	1958	519537	490494	401767	349001
2000	2018	858200	822824	544369	482075
2001	2154	706000	635041	663200	593050
2002	2202	867600	791573	770500	695409
2003	2218	1213062	1128172	870787	788000
2004	2121	1686491	1592416	1006050	918555

注：1996年前邮政电信合营，1996年前电信数据包含在邮电通信指标中；邮电业务总量2001年前为1990年不变价，2001年及以后为2000年不变价口径。

Note: Before 1996, postal services and telecommunication services are managed together. So data on telecommunication service before 1996 is included in postal and telecommunication services. Data on total business volume from postal and telecommunication services before 2001 were in terms of 1990 constant price, and since 2001 were in terms of 2000 constant price.

13－4 邮电业务主要指标（1985－2004年）
Main Indicators of Postal and Telecommunication Services (1985-2004)

年 份 Year	函件(万件) Letters (10 000 pcs)	特快专递（万件） Express Mail Services (10 000 pcs)	邮政部门报刊累计数（万份） Accumulated Newspapers and Magazines from Postal Departments (10 000 copies)	长途电话（万次） Long-distance Calls (10 000 times)	移动电话用户（万户） Mobile Telephone Subscribers (10 000 subscribers)	国际互联网络用户（万户） Subscribers of Internet Services (10 000 subscribers)	本地电话年末用户（万户） Subscribers of Local Telephone at Year-end (10 000 subscribers)	#城市电话用户 Urban Telephone Subscribers
1985	8961		32750	477			3.80	3.10
1986	10210		34696	515			4.83	3.42
1987	11755	1	36902	595			5.39	3.93
1988	12432	1	40591	707			6.07	4.58
1989	11609	2	16162	724			6.62	5.17
1990	11544	2	16037	873	0.08		7.25	5.70
1991	11539	3	17540	1227	0.09		8.87	7.15
1992	13618	7	18216	2132	0.15		12.63	10.69
1993	16013	22	18464	3519	0.59		18.53	16.30
1994	16519	40	15491	7022	1.73		29.00	25.39
1995	14633	52	16453	11650	3.62		37.24	32.10
1996	14100	63	15572	18288	9.00	0.03	66.50	56.33
1997	12159	68	28025	23527	19.15	0.20	126.25	108.91
1998	12715	97	30922	23912	40.73	0.76	156.28	123.52
1999	13266	145	33532	22210	79.90	2.49	197.88	148.22
2000	11542	210	31232	23424	160.00	10.00	268.43	186.93
2001	13561	260	27506	22555	245.80	28.60	337.70	221.40
2002	18038	235	27177	23607	424.70	55.60	413.63	262.34
2003	20497	272	25945	23408	619.40	88.65	533.40	343.80
2004	18426	334	19833	26115	811.61	122.16	642.39	425.49

13－5 交通基础设施和交通运输营运工具（2003－2004年）
Transportation Infrastructure and Transportation Machinery (2003-2004)

指　　标	Item	2003	2004
交通基础设施	**Transportation Infrastructure**		
公路里程（公里）	Total Length of Highways (km)	31407	32344
按行政等级分	By Administrative Level		
#国　道	National	1915	1861
省　道	Provincial	3850	4039
按技术等级分	By Technical Level		
等级公路	Expressway and Class I-IV Highways	22562	24046
#高速公路	Expressway	580	714
一级公路	First Class	168	187
二级公路	Second Class	3624	4166
等外公路	Highways Below Class IV	8845	8298
公路桥梁数量（座）	Number of Highway-bridges (unit)	4649	4931
公路桥梁总延米（延米）	Extended Length of Highway-bridges (extended meter)	210699	248278
铁路营运里程（公里）	Length of Railways in Operation (km)	632	632
内河航道里程（公里）	Length of Navigable Inland Waterways (km)	4086	4222
#等级航道	Standard Waterways	1773	1819
重庆机场出港航线（条）	Number of Civil Aviation Routes from Chongqing (line)	130	103
国　内	Domestic Routes	123	99
国　际（地区）	International (regional) Routes	7	4
交通运输营运工具	**Transportation Machinery**		
公路营运载货汽车（辆）	Business Trucks (vehicle)	119956	124225
公路营运载客汽车（辆）	Business Buses and Cars (vehicle)	37473	37364
运输船舶实有数（艘）	Transportation Vessels (vessel)	3986	4002
#交通部门	Transportation Department	1857	2017
机动船	Motor Vessels	1108	1344
驳　船	Barges	749	673
重庆机场飞行起降架次（万架次）	Times of Ascend and Descend of Civil Aircrafts in Chongqing Airport (10 000 times)	5.61	6.47

13－6 民用车辆、船舶拥有量（2003－2004年）
Civil Motor Vehicles and Civil Transport Vessels (2003-2004)

指　　标	Item	2003	2004
民用车辆拥有量(辆)	**Total Civil Motor Vehicles (vehicle)**	**781250**	**839352**
其中：私人民用车辆拥有量	Of Which: Private Owned	549179	621790
#载客汽车	Buses and Cars	79919	95008
载货汽车	Trucks	48677	48138
#汽　车	Motor Vehicles	342483	348419
#载客汽车	Buses and Cars	179961	193787
载货汽车	Trucks	153625	146150
摩托车	Motorcycle	363356	428784
农用运输车	Farming Wheels for Transportation	42012	31917
民用船舶拥有量(艘)	**Civil Transport Vessels (vessel)**	**3986**	**4002**
其中：私人船舶拥有量	Of which: Private Owned	2129	1985
#机动船	Motor Transport Vessels	1825	1704
#客　船	For Passengers	305	393
货　船	For Cargo	1252	1106
驳　船	Barges	38	53
#机动船	Motor Vessels	2933	3048
#客　船	For Passengers	704	744
货　船	For Cargo	1728	1921
驳　船	Barges	787	726

13－7 客货运输量及港口吞吐量（2003－2004年）
Freight Traffic, Passenger Traffic and Freight Handled at Ports (2003-2004)

指　　标	Item	2003	2004
客运量总计（万人）	**Total Passenger Traffic (10 000 persons)**	**59170**	**64675**
铁　路	Railway	1949	2346
公　路	Highway	55673	60833
水　路	Waterway	1417	1304
民　航	Civil Aviation	131	192
旅客周转量总计（亿人公里）	**Total Passenger-kilometers (100 million person-km)**	**267.87**	**320.95**
铁　路	Railway	50.06	59.63
公　路	Highway	187.51	226.08
水　路	Waterway	13.46	11.52
民　航	Civil Aviation	16.84	23.72
货运量总计（万吨）	**Total Freight Traffic (10 000 tons)**	**34113.20**	**38168.37**
铁　路	Railway	3491.00	3730.81
公　路	Highway	28406.00	31515.00
水　路	Waterway	2214.00	2917.92
民　航	Civil Aviation	2.20	2.64
管　道	Pipeline		2.00
货物周转量总计（亿吨公里）	**Total Freight Ton-kilometers (100 million ton-km)**	**446.75**	**721.15**
铁　路	Railway	181.42	196.23
公　路	Highway	107.33	128.28
水　路	Waterway	157.70	284.30
民　航	Civil Aviation	0.30	0.34
管　道	Pipeline		112.00
港口货物吞吐量（万吨）	**Total Cargo Handled at Ports (10 000 tons)**	**3243.76**	**4539.00**
其中：集装箱	Of Which: Containers	100.73	176.29
进口量	Handled in	1796.24	2337.09
出口量	Handled out	1447.52	2201.91
空港吞吐量	**Handled at Airports**		
旅　客（万人）	Civil Aviation Passenger Traffic (10 000 persons)	428.80	530.41
货　物（万吨）	Civil Aviation Freight Traffic (10 000 tons)	7.70	8.80

注：从2000年起民航货运量、货运周转量数据按新制度统计，旅客行李不再计入货运。

Note: Freight traffic, freight ton-kilometers of civil aviation since 2000 are in accordance with new statistical system. Baggages are not accounted into freight.

13－8 主要港口码头泊位数（2003－2004年）
Number of Berths at Major Ports (2003-2004)

指 标	Item	2003	2004
码头岸线长度（米）	**Length of Quay Line (m)**	**14116**	**16177**
生产用	For Productive Use	11032	13373
非生产用	For Non-Productive Use	3084	2804
泊位个数（个）	**Number of Berths (unit)**	**162**	**171**
生产用	For Productive Use	129	141
非生产用	For Non-Productive Use	33	30

13－9 主要港口码头仓库（2003－2004年）
Warehouses at Major Ports (2003-2004)

指 标	Item	2003	2004
年末职工人数（人）	Year-end Staff and Workers (person)	6023	5587
仓库总面积（平方米）	Total Area of Warehouses (sq.m)	64418	46464
堆场总面积（平方米）	Total Area of Stacking Yard (sq.m)	361921	368696
集装箱吞吐量合计（吨）	Containers Handled at Ports (ton)	1007276	1762942
国际集装箱总量	International Containers	655216	1079447
国内集装箱总量	Domestic Containers	352060	683495
集装箱吞吐量合计(TEU)	Containers Handled at Ports (TEU)	98642	159452
国际集装箱	International Containers	78139	122896
国内集装箱	Domestic Containers	20503	36556

注：1）TEU是“折合20英尺标准箱”的英文缩写。

2）重庆三峡库区的码头仓库因三峡工程蓄水，2004年面积有所减少。

Note: a) TEU is the abbreviation of " Twenty-foot Equivalent Unit".

b) As the reason of impound of Three Gorges Project, area of warehouses reduce in 2004.

13－10 邮电业务基本情况（2003－2004年）
Statistics on Postal and Telecommunication Services (2003-2004)

指　　标	Item	2003	2004
邮政局(所)总数(处)	Number of Postal Offices (unit)	2218	2121
邮路总长度(公里)	Total Length of Postal Routes (km)	83392	85909
#农村投递线路(公里)	Rural Delivery Routes (km)	66607	63469
邮电业务总量(万元)	Business Volume of Postal and Telecommunication Services (10 000 yuan)	1213062	1686491
邮　政	Postal Services	84890	94075
电　信	Telecommunication Services	1128172	1592416
函件(万件)	Number of Letters (10 000 pcs)	20497	18426
包件(万件)	Number of Parcels (10 000 pcs)	150	142
特快专递(万件)	Pieces of Express Mail Services (10 000 pcs)	272	334
邮政部门报刊累计数(万份)	Number of Newspapers and Magazines Circulation from Postal Departments (10 000 copies)	25945	19833
集邮业务（万枚）	Philately Business (10000 pcs)	1842	2169
电报(万份)	Number of Telegrams (10 000 copies)	15	11
长途电话(万次)	Number of Long-distance Calls (10 000 times)	23408	26115
本地电话年末用户合计(万户)	Year-end Local Telephone Subscribers (10 000 subscribes)	533.40	642.39
城市电话用户	Urban Telephone Subscribers	343.80	425.49
#住宅电话	Residential Telephones	249.84	308.48
乡村电话用户	Rural Telephone Subscribers	189.60	216.90
#住宅电话	Residential Telephones	176.75	203.60
公用电话（万户）	Public Telephone (10 000 subscribers)	30.50	36.42
年末移动电话用户(万户)	Year-end Mobile Telephone Subscribers (10 000 subscribes)	619.40	811.61
年末国际互联网络用户（万户）	Year-end Internet Subscribers (10 000 subscribers)	88.65	122.16

13－11 电信主要通信能力（年底数）（2003－2004年）
Main Communication Capacity of Telecommunication Services (Year-end) (2003-2004)

项　目	Item	2003	2004
长话业务电路（2M）	Number of Long Distance Telephone Lines (2M)	2754	4862
本地局用交换机容量（万门）	Capacity of Local Telephone Exchanges (10 000 gates)	752	918
移动用户交换机容量（万户）	Capacity of Mobile Telephone Exchanges (10 000 subscribers)	686	875
移动电话基站数（个）	Number of Base Stations of Mobile Telephones (unit)	6471	9112
移动电话信道数（万个）	Number of Signal Channels of Mobile Telephones (10 000 lines)	28	37
短信息中心容量（万条）	Capacity of Short Messages (10 000 times)	864	864
长途光缆线路长度（万公里）	Length of Long Distance Optical Cable Lines (10 000 km)	5.94	7.70
长途微波线路长度（公里）	Length of Long Distance Microwave Lines (km)	739	522

13－12 邮电通信水平（2003－2004年）
Level of Postal and Telecommunication Services (2003-2004)

项　目	Item	2003	2004
平均每一邮政局所服务面积（平方公里）	Average Area Served by Every Post Office (sq.m)	37.15	38.85
平均每一邮政局所服务人口（万人）	Average Persons Served by Every Post Office (10 000 persons)	0.80	0.77
平均每百人邮电业务总量(元)	Total Revenue from Postal and Telecommunication Services Per 100 Persons (yuan)	43669	60863
平均每人每年发函件数(件)	Annual Average Number of Letters Mailed Per Capita (piece)	7.38	6.65
平均每人每年自邮政部门订报刊数(份)	Annual Average Number of Newspapers and Magazines Subscribed from Postal Departments Per Capita (piece)	9.34	7.16
平均每百人拥有电话机（含移动）(部)	Number of Telephone Sets Owned Per 100 Persons (unit)	41.51	52.47
平均每百人拥有移动电话(部)	Number of Mobile Telephones Owned Per 100 Persons (unit)	22.30	29.29

注：人均指标按年末常住人口计算。

Note: The average persons refer to resident population at year-end.

主要统计指标解释

货（客）运量 指在一定时期内，各种运输工具实际运送的货物（旅客）数量。是反映运输业为国民经济和人民生活服务的数量指标，也是制定和检查运输生产计划，研究运输发展规模和速度的重要指标。货运按吨计算，客运按人计算。货物不论运输距离长短，货物类别，均按实际重量统计；旅客不论行程远近或票价多少，均按一人一次作为客运量统计。半价票，小孩票也按一人统计。

货物（旅客）周转量 指在一定时期内，由各种运输工具运送的货物（旅客）数量与其相应运输距离的乘积之总和。是反映运输业生产总成果的重要指标，也是编制和检查运输生产计划，计算运输效率、劳动生产率以及核算运输单位成本的主要基础资料。通常以吨公里和人公里为计算单位。计算货物周转量通常按发出站与到达站之间的最短距离，也就是计费距离计算。计算公式为：

货物（旅客）周转量=Σ货物（旅客）运输量×运输距离

公路里程 指在一定时期内实际达到《公路工程[WTBZ]技术标准 JTJ01-88》规定的等级公路，并经公路主管部门正式验收交付使用的公路里程数。包括大中城市的郊区公路以及通过小城镇街道部分的公路里程和桥梁、渡口的长度，不包括大中城市的街道、厂矿、林区生产用道和农业生产用道的里程。两条或多条公路共同经由同一路段，只计算一次，不得重复计算里程长度。它是反映公路建设发展规模的重要指标，也是计算运输网密度等指标的基础资料。

内河航道里程 也称内河通航里程，指在一定时期内，能通航运输船舶及排筏的天然河流、湖泊水库、运河及通航渠道的长度。包括全年季节性通航累计三个月以上的航道，不包括仅供零散流放竹、木排的河道。它是反映内河水运网规模、水平和发展情况的主要指标。

民用汽车拥有量 指报告期末，在公安交通管理部门按照《机动车注册登记工作规范》，已注册登记领有民用车辆牌照的全部汽车数量。汽车拥有量统计的主要分类：根据汽车结构分为载客汽车、载货汽车及其他汽车；根据汽车所有者不同分为个人(私人)汽车、单位汽车；根据汽车的使用性质分为营运汽车、非营运汽车和特种汽车；根据汽车大小规格不同载客汽车分为大型、中型、小型和微型，载货汽车分为重型、中型、轻型和微型。

邮电业务总量 指以货币表现的邮电通信企业为社会提供各类邮电通信服务的总数量。邮电业务量按专业分类包括函件、包件、汇票、报刊发行、邮政快件、特快专递、邮政储蓄、集邮、公众电报、用户电报、传真、长途电话、出租电路、无线寻呼、移动电话、分组交换数据通信、出租代维等。计算方法为各类产品乘以相应的平均单价（不变价）之和，再加上出租电路和设备、代用户维护电话交换机和线路等的服务收入。它综合反映了一定时期邮电业务发展的总成果，是研究邮电业务量构成和发展趋势的重要指标。计算公式为：

邮电业务总量=Σ（各类邮电业务量×不变单价）+出租代维及其他业务收入=邮电业务总量+电信业务总量

本地电话用户 指接入本地电信运营商固定电话网上的电话用户。包括：住宅用户、单位用户、公用电话用户等。按电话用户位置又分为市内电话用户和农村电话用户。1997 年以前，“市内电话用户”是指接入县城及县以上城市的电话网上的电话用户；“农村电话用户”是指接入县邮电局农话台及县以下农村电话交换点，以县城为中心(除市话用户外)联通县、乡(镇)、行政村、村民小组的用户。从 1997 年起，电话用户数分组调整为以用户所在区域划分为“城市电话用户”和“乡村电话用户”，与过去的按市内电话和农村电话划分方法不同。而电话用户总数、电话机总部数统计范围不变。

城市电话用户 指直辖市、省辖市、地级市、县级市的市区、市郊区及县城（包括县人民政府所在地的县城关区或行政建制相当于县人民政府所在地的镇）范围内接入局用交换机的电话用户数，包括分布在农村地区的独立工矿区、林区、驻军等接入局用交换机的电话用户数。

乡村电话用户 指县城关区以下的集镇和农村接入局用交换机的电话用户数。

住宅电话用户 指安装在居民住宅或农民家里并按照住宅电话用户登记注册和收费的电话用户。包括私人付费、单位付费和按规定免费的住宅电话用户。

移动电话用户 指通过移动电话交换机进入移动电话网、占用移动电话号码的各类电话用户。包括签约用户和智能网预付费用户。一个移动电话号码统计为一户。

局用交换机容量 是指安装在本地电信运营商内用于接续本地固定电话的电话交换机容量、有倍增设备按倍增后的数量计数。包括现用和备用的人工或自动交换机的全部容量。

移动电话交换机容量 指移动电话交换机根据一定话务模型和交换机处理能力计算出来的最大同时服务用户的数量。

Explanatory Notes on Main Statistical Indicators

Freight (Passenger) Traffic refers to the volume of freight (passenger) transported with various means. Freight transport is calculated in tons and passenger traffic is calculated in the number of persons. Despite the type of freight and traveling distance, the freight transport is calculated in the actual weight of the goods: and despite the traveling distance and ticket price, the passenger traffic is calculated by the principle that one person can be counted only once in one travel. The passenger who travels with a half-price ticket or a child ticket is also calculated as one person. The freight (passenger) traffic provides a quantitative measure to show how the transport industry serves the national economy and people, and is also and important indicator for planning the transport industry and for studying the development scale and speed of the transport industry.

Freight Ton-kilometers (Passenger-kilometers) refer to the sum of the products of the volume of transported cargo (passengers) multiplying by the transport distance, usually using ton-kilometer and passenger-kilometer as units for measurement. Normally, the shortest distance between the departure station and the destination station (i.e., the payable distance) is the basis to calculate the freight ton-kilometers. This is an important indicator to show the total results of the transport industry, to prepare and examine the transport plan and to measure the efficiency, the labor productivity and the unit cost of transport. The formula is as follows:

Freight Ton-kilometers (Passenger-kilometers) $=\sum$ *[Freight (Passenger) Traffic × distance of transportation]*

Measuring Unit: ton-kilometer (person-kilometer)

Length of Highways refers to the length of highways which are built in conformity with the grades specified by the highway engineering standard formulated by the Ministry of Communications, and have been formally checked and accepted by the departments of highways and put into use. The length of highways includes that of the suburb highways at large and medium-sized cities, highways passing through streets at small cities and towns, and also the length of bridge and ferries. It does not include the length of streets in big and medium-sized cities and highways built for the production purpose at factories, mines, forest areas and agricultural areas. If two more highways go the same section of the way, the length of the section is only calculated for once and no duplication is allowed. The length of highways is an important indicator to show the development of the highway construction and to provide essential information to calculate the transport network density.

Length of Navigable Inland Waterways an indicator reflecting the size and development of inland water network, it refers to the length of the natural rivers, lakes, reservoirs, canals, and ditches open to navigation during a given period, which enables the transport by ships and rafts. It includes the channels open to navigation for over an accumulative 3 months in a year, yet this does not include the river courses which are only used to float odd logs and bamboo rafts.

Possession of Civil Motor Vehicles refer to the total numbers of vehicles that are registered and received vehicles' license tags according to the Work Standard for Motor Vehicles Registration formulated by transport management office under department of public security at the end of reference period. They are divided into following categories according to the structure of motor vehicles: passenger vehicles, trucks and others; and private vehicles and vehicles for units use according to ownerships; working vehicles, non-working vehicles and special motor vehicles according to kind of usage; large passenger vehicles, medium passenger vehicles and small passenger vehicles, heavy trucks, light-heavy trucks and light trucks according to sizes of vehicles.

Business Volume of Postal and Telecommunication Services refers to the total amount of post and telecommunications services, expressed in value terms, provided by the post and telecommunications departments for the society. Postal and telecommunication services can be classified as letters, parcels, remittance, issue of newspapers and magazines, fast mail service, express mail service, saving deposits, stamps for collection, public and individual telegraph service, facsimiles, long-distance telephone service, leasing of telephone lines, urban paging service, mobile telephone service, data transfer and transmission, etc.. The accounting approach is to multiply the service products of all types with their average unit price (constant price) to get sum of business value, plus income from other services such as leasing of telephone lines and equipment, maintenance of telephone switchboards and lines on behalf of customers. This indicator reflects the overall results of post and telecommunications service during a given period, and is important to study the composition of business service and the development of post and telecommunications service. The formula is as follows:

Business Volume of Postal and Telecommunication Services = ∑ (Transaction of Post and Telecommunication Services × Constant Price) + Income from Leasing, Maintenance and other Services = Business Volume of Postal Services + Business Volume of Telecommunication Services

Local Telephone Subscribers refer to subscribers that are connected to the local telecommunication service provider through fix line network, including household subscribers, institutional subscribers and public telephones. They are also classified as city subscribers and rural subscribers according to locations. Before 1997, city subscribers referred to those connected to city telephone networks in county towns and cities, while village subscribers referred to those connected to village telephone stations at and below counties. Since 1997, the classification of telephone subscribers was modified on the basis of physical location of the subscribers as urban telephone subscribers and rural telephone subscribers, which is different from the previous classification of categorizing local telephones and rural telephones, while the definition of total subscribers and total number of telephones remain unchanged.

Urban Telephone Subscribers refer to subscribers telephone subscribers, located at municipalities, cities under the jurisdiction of province, cities at prefectural level, downtown and suburb of city at county level town and county towns (including country towns where county government located, and towns of county level according to the administrative organizational system), that are connected to the public line telephone network, including rural mineral area, forest area, military area.

Rural Telephone Subscribers refer to telephone subscribers, located at towns under county town and country, which are connected to the public line telephone network.

Household Telephone Subscribers refer to telephone sets installed in resident dwellings, including those with telephone charges paid by individuals, by public units and free of charge.

Mobile Telephone Subscribers refer to the persons who own mobile telephone numbers and are connected with the mobile telephone communication network through the mobile telephone switchboards, including contracted subscribers and pre-paid subscribers for intelligent network. One mobile telephone is taken as a subscriber.

Capacity of Office Telephone Exchanges refers to the capacity (measured in gate) of telephone exchanges installed in the offices of local telecommunication service providers for communication between fixed telephones. It includes the capacity of both manual and automatic exchanges in use and for stand-by purpose. Equipment with expansion function is to be counted by the expanded capacity.

Capacity of Mobile Telephone Exchanges refers to the capacity of the maximum services provided to subscribers at one time basing on a certain model and transacting capacity of the mobile telephone exchanges.

十四 国内贸易
DOMESTIC TRADE

简要说明 Brief Introduction

本章主要内容有社会消费品零售总额，限额以上住宿餐饮业经营情况，批发零售贸易业商品销售总额，限额以上批发零售贸易业主要商品销售金额和数量，以及限额以上批发零售贸易和餐饮企业财务状况和经济效益，限额以上连锁零售业和餐饮业经营情况。本章资料由市统计局贸易外经处提供。

The data in this chapter cover the total sales of the consumer goods, operation of hotels and catering trade above designated size, total sales of commodities of wholesale and retail trade, sales revenue and volume of major commodities of wholesale and retail trade above designated size, the financial conditions and efficiency of the wholesale & retail and catering trade above designated size, operation of chains in retail and catering trade above designated size. All data in this chapter come from Division of Trade and External Economic Relations Statistics, Municipal Bureau of Statistics.

14－1 主要年份社会消费品零售总额
Total Retail Sales of Consumer Goods in Major Years

单位：万元 (10 000 yuan)

年 份 Year	社会消费品零售总额 Total Retail Sales	国有经济 State-owned	集体经济 Collective -owned	个体及私营经济 Individual and Private	"三资"经济 Funded by Hong Kong,Macao, Taiwan & Foreign Entrepreneurs	其 他 Others
1952	61973	19332	9941	32009		691
1957	108061	55533	43171	4458		4899
1962	124248	87477	27335	6987		2449
1965	134722	94009	35935	2318		2460
1970	163612	118044	40460	2120		2988
1975	217537	148811	53318	11876		3532
1978	250188	126981	112537	6599		4071
1980	366349	178516	162400	17649		7784
1985	690779	256981	261103	155266		17429
1986	780787	290656	260816	207041		22274
1987	926227	343448	302177	253031		27571
1988	1191747	430347	372593	350032		38775
1989	1332450	445314	380342	344338		162456
1990	1371244	464257	370361	352587		184039
1991	1569138	524150	448634	359098		237256
1992	1814799	591361	495045	441651		286742
1993	2299631	834440	629276	439849	2119	393947
1994	2987218	964128	593826	786936	2829	639499
1995	3718064	897174	672140	1093289	21200	1034261
1996	4454766	988817	707589	1385643	22535	1350182
1997	5079315	1016771	762904	1367594	31211	1900835
1998	5536962	920192	635189	1880210	73728	2027643
1999	5962570	1010078	575537	2290662	102916	1983377
2000	6435817	961728	603653	2552919	146116	2171401
2001	6993273	1064023	566989	2899248	183834	2279179
2002	7630506	1042743	486734	3323611	186592	2590826
2003	8355254	998663	363783	3977293	198197	2817318
2004	10614852	858674	200188	7356814	209281	1989895

14－2 社会消费品零售总额（2003－2004年）
Total Retail Sales of Consumer Goods (2003-2004)

单位：万元 (10 000 yuan)

指　　标	Item	2003	2004
总　　计	**Total**	**8355254**	**10614852**
按地区分	**By Region**		
市	City	4823056	6532316
县	County	1127143	1201346
县以下	Below County Level	2405055	2881190
按登记注册类型分	**By Registration**		
国有经济	State-owned	998663	858674
集体经济	Collective-owned	363783	200188
个体及私营经济	Individual and Private	3977293	7356814
外资及港澳台经济	Funded by Hong Kong, Macao, Taiwan & Foreign Entrepreneurs	198197	209281
其他经济	Others	2817318	1989895
按行业分	**By Sector**		
批发零售贸易业	Wholesale and Retail Trade	7191345	9023003
餐饮业	Catering Trade	1073179	1442859
其　他	Others	90730	148990

14－3 限额以上住宿餐饮业经营情况（2004年）
Operation of Hotels and Catering Trade above Designated Size (2004)

单位：万元 (10 000 yuan)

指　　标	Item	2004
营业收入（万元）	Business Revenue (10 000 yuan)	363943
客房收入	Income from Guest Rooms	93670
餐费收入	Catering Income	241700
商品销售收入	Commodity Sales Revenue	5910
其他收入	Other Income	22663
住宿餐饮设施	Infrastructure of Hotels and Catering Trade	
客房数（间）	Guest Rooms (unit)	64022
床位数（个）	Resting Beds (unit)	124058
餐位数（位）	Catering Seats (unit)	457487
利润总额	Total Profits	-14679
资产总计	Total Assets	864817
负债总计	Total Liabilities	602878

14－4 批发零售贸易业商品销售总额（2004年）
Total Sales of Commodities of Wholesale and Retail Trade (2004)

单位：万元 (10 000 yuan)

指　　标	Item	销售总额 Total Sales	批　发 Wholesale	零　售 Retail
总　计	**Total**	**22075728**	**12844992**	**9230736**
限额以上批发零售贸易业商品销售额	**Sales of Commodities of Wholesales and Retail Trade above Designated Size**	**9796782**	**6861469**	**2935313**
按登记注册类型分	**By Registration**			
内资企业	Domestic-funded Enterprises	9551187	6788947	2762240
#国有企业	State-owned	2625599	2035484	590115
集体企业	Collective-owned	219476	192138	27338
股份合作企业	Cooperative Share Holding	64762	41813	22949
联营企业	Joint-owned	13751	13031	720
有限责任公司	Limited-liability Companies	3073138	2139771	933367
股份有限公司	Share Holding Limited Companies	1807753	1115619	692134
私营企业	Private	1598630	1115710	482920
港澳台商投资企业	Enterprises Funded by Hong Kong, Macao and Taiwan	11646	7624	4022
外商投资企业	Foreign-funded Enterprises	233949	64898	169051
按行业分	**By Sector**			
农畜产品批发业	Wholesale of Agricultural and Animal Products	61169	58370	2799
食品、饮料及烟草制品批发业	Wholesale of Food, Beverages & Tobacco Products	1451104	1428134	22970
纺织、服装及日用品批发业	Wholesale of Textiles, Garments and Daily Goods	142198	140165	2033
文化、体育用品及器材批发业	Wholesale of Cultural and Sports Articles	144765	125900	18865
医药及医疗器材批发业	Wholesale of Medicines and Medical Appliances	1034951	798095	236856
矿产品、建材及化工产品批发业	Wholesale of Mineral, Building and Chemical Products	2647681	2416995	230686
机械设备、五金交电及电子产品批发业	Wholesale of Machinery, Hardware and Electronic Products	1395114	1292119	102995
贸易经纪与代理业	Trade Agencies	19149	19149	
其他批发业	Other Wholesales	106963	104050	2913
综合零售业	Comprehensive Retails	1362307	183509	1178798
食品、饮料及烟草制品专门零售业	Special Retail of Food, Beverages and Tobacco Products	36144	11999	24145
纺织、服装及日用品专门零售业	Special Retail of Textile, Garments and Daily Goods	52011	2837	49174
文化、体育用品及器材专门零售业	Special Retail of Cultural and Sports Articles	87241	5203	82038
医药及医疗器材专门零售业	Special Retail of Medicine and Medical Appliances	109347	35196	74151
汽车、摩托车、燃料及零配件专门零售业	Special Retail of Motor Vehicles, Motorcycles, Fuel and Related Parts	764159	195299	568860
家用电器及电子产品专门零售业	Special Retail of Household Electric Equipment and Electronic Products	358932	44449	314483
五金、家具及室内装修材料专门零售业	Special Retail of Hardware, Furniture and Indoor Decoration	19823		19823
无店铺及其他零售业	Non-shops and Other Retails	3724		3724
限额以下批发零售贸易业商品销售额	**Sales of Commodities of Wholesales and Retail Trade below Designated Size**	**12278946**	**5983523**	**6295423**

14－5 限额以上批发零售贸易业主要商品分类销售额（2003－2004年）
Sales of Main Commodities of Wholesale and Retail Trade above Designated Size by Category (2003-2004)

单位：亿元 (100 million yuan)

指标	Item	销售合计 Total Sales		批发 Wholesale Trade		零售 Retail Trade	
		2003	2004	2003	2004	2003	2004
食品、饮料、烟酒类	Food, Beverages, Tobacco and Liquor	193.36	187.60	162.18	148.82	31.18	38.78
肉禽蛋类	Meat, Poultry and Eggs	6.20	4.43	2.85	0.75	3.35	3.68
其他食品类	Other Food	43.03	59.50	22.42	34.17	20.61	25.33
饮料类	Beverages	4.17	4.15	1.13	0.36	3.04	3.79
烟酒类	Tobacco and Liquor	139.96	119.52	135.78	113.54	4.18	5.98
服装鞋帽、针、纺织品类	Clothing, Shoes, Hats and Textiles	35.94	49.36	6.26	8.90	29.68	40.46
服装类	Clothing	20.64	27.16	2.06	2.87	18.58	24.29
鞋帽类	Shoes and Hats	6.89	9.26	1.34	0.49	5.55	8.77
针、纺织品类	Knitwear and Textiles	8.41	12.94	2.86	5.54	5.55	7.40
化妆品类	Cosmetics	5.93	8.98	1.48	1.89	4.45	7.09
金银珠宝类	Gold, Silver and Jewelry	3.35	5.82	0.56	1.76	2.79	4.06
日用品类	Articles for Daily Use	21.66	24.14	8.83	9.05	12.83	15.09
#洗涤用品类	Washing Articles	7.31	7.88	4.34	3.79	2.97	4.09
儿童玩具类	Children Toys	0.56	0.94	0.18	0.13	0.38	0.81
五金、电料类	Hardware and Electrical Materials	3.79	5.73	3.04	3.49	0.75	2.24
体育、娱乐用品类	Sports and Recreation Articles	1.95	3.45	0.31	0.55	1.64	2.90
书报杂志类	Newspapers and Magazines	15.52	17.04	8.45	9.02	7.07	8.02
电子出版物及音像制品类	E-journal and Video Products	0.71	2.00	0.32	1.11	0.39	0.89
家用电器和音像器材类	Household Appliances and Video Appliances	62.52	75.89	29.49	37.32	33.03	38.57
中西药品类	Traditional Chinese and Western Medicines	87.68	113.76	60.89	82.92	26.79	30.84
#西　药	Western Medicines	53.03	92.28	34.00	65.42	19.03	26.86
中草药及中成药	Traditional Chinese Medicines	26.79	19.73	21.09	16.28	5.70	3.45
文化办公用品类	Cultural and Official Goods	2.37	6.12	0.54	2.55	1.83	3.57
家具类	Furniture	1.02	1.35			1.02	1.35
通讯器材类	Communication Appliances	24.24	19.25	17.76	11.88	6.48	7.37
煤炭及制品类	Coal and Related Products	2.60	19.55	2.57	19.54	0.03	0.01
木材及制品类	Wood and Wooden Products	0.19	0.15	0.19	0.12		0.03
石油及制品类	Petroleum and Related Products	63.20	77.31	53.43	51.19	9.77	26.12
化工材料及制品类	Raw Chemical Materials	39.77	58.60	39.14	58.05	0.63	0.55
#化肥类	Fertilizer	26.83	32.84	26.37	32.82	0.46	0.02
金属材料类	Metal Materials	40.32	97.21	39.97	95.09	0.35	2.12
建筑及装潢材料类	Building and Decoration Materials	2.81	14.83	1.74	13.60	1.07	1.23
机电产品设备类	Mechanical and Electrical Products	27.10	59.73	26.22	58.07	0.88	1.66
#农机类	Agricultural Machinery	0.82	1.93	0.63	1.85	0.19	0.08
汽车类	Automobile	70.66	102.97	30.73	47.14	39.93	55.83
种子饲料类	Seed and Feedstuff	0.04	0.90	0.01	0.88	0.03	0.02
棉麻类	Cotton, Hemp	0.75	1.12	0.69	1.02	0.06	0.10
其他类	Others	22.67	26.82	18.28	22.19	4.39	4.63

14－6 限额以上批发零售业主要商品销售数量（2003－2004年）
Sales Volume of Major Commodities of Wholesale and Retail Trade above Designated Size (2003-2004)

指　　标	Item	销售总量 Total Amount		批　发 Wholesale Trade		零　售 Retail Trade	
		2003	2004	2003	2004	2003	2004
粮　食（吨）	Grain (ton)	559566	393487	449165	303308	110401	90179
食用植物油（吨）	Edible Vegetable Oil (ton)	164986	118703	132482	87321	32504	31382
摩托车（辆）	Motorcycles (vehicle)	458888	1125693	445081	989573	13807	136120
汽　车（辆）	Motor Vehicles (vehicle)	53677	153265	25880	117994	27797	35271
#轿　车	Cars	32716	45144	14993	20521	17723	24623
电视机（台）	Television Sets (unit)	502707	540810	159794	124175	342913	416635
组合音响（台）	Hi-Fi Component System (unit)	49866	46680	6013	783	43853	45897
摄像机（台）	Pickup Cameras (unit)	7837	14059	78		7759	14059
影碟机（台）	Video Disc Projectors (unit)	261180	284171	79736	55430	181444	228741
家用洗衣机（台）	Household Washing Machines (unit)	274829	351762	128695	142298	146134	209464
家用电冰箱（台）	Household Refrigerators (unit)	441463	502109	264724	271273	176739	230836
房间空调器（台）	Room Air-conditioners (unit)	797026	1453092	482557	919839	314469	533253
微波炉（台）	Microwave Ovens (unit)	308003	389706	155555	188678	152448	201028
微型计算机（台）	Personal Computers (unit)	23670	45489	6522	5858	17148	39631
普通电话机（台）	Telephones (unit)	177683	189948	43011	44370	134672	145578
移动电话机（台）	Mobile Telephones (unit)	2138952	1812279	1301284	1224483	837668	587796
化学肥料（吨）	Chemical Fertilizer (ton)	2603054	2510771	2603054	2510771		
化学农药（吨）	Chemical Pesticides (ton)	12367	38121	12367	38121		
农用塑料薄膜（吨）	Farm-use Plastic Membrane (ton)	1639	8887	1639	8887		
煤　炭（吨）	Coal (ton)	1557296	1938958	1556089	1927348	1207	11610
汽　油（吨）	Gasoline (ton)	587139	745360	477499	584815	109640	160545
柴　油（吨）	Diesel Oil (ton)	1116409	1390122	936506	1081475	179903	308647
钢　材（吨）	Rolled Steel (ton)	779272	1473808	770017	1473288	9255	520
铜（吨）	Copper (ton)	562	1703	562	1703		
铝（吨）	Aluminum (ton)	32237	30158	32237	30158		

14—7 限额以上批发贸易业财务状况和经济效益（2004年）

单位：万元

指　　标	Item	企业数（个）Number of Enterprises (unit)	流动资产合计 Total Circulating Assets	固定资产原价 Original Value of Fixed Assets
总　　计	**Total**	**502**	**2338165**	**715661**
#国有及国有控股	State-owned and State Holding	159	1561385	612443
按登记注册类型分组	**By Registration**			
内资企业	Domestic-funded Enterprises	493	2319095	712270
国有企业	State-owned Enterprises	85	765800	238096
集体企业	Collective-owned Enterprises	15	86424	9192
股份合作企业	Cooperative Share Holding Enterprises	11	14882	2223
联营企业	Joint-owned Enterprises	2	12678	1488
国有与集体联营企业	Joint State-collective Enterprises	1	11992	1453
其他联营企业	Other Joint-owned Enterprises	1	687	35
有限责任公司	Limited-liability Corporations	186	708801	179966
国有独资公司	State Sole Funded	13	216154	110355
其他有限责任公司	Other Limited-liability Corporations	173	492647	69611
股份有限公司	Share Holding Limited Companies	44	365863	255012
私营企业	Private Enterprises	146	302538	24407
私营独资企业	Private-funded Enterprises	2	4235	445
私营合伙企业	Private Partnership Enterprises	4	5357	913
私营有限责任公司	Private Limited Liability Corporations	128	281881	22223
私营股份有限公司	Private Share Holding Limited Companies	12	11066	825
其他企业	Other Enterprises	4	62109	1888
港澳台商投资企业	Enterprises Funded by Hong Kong, Macao and Taiwan	2	1274	719
合资经营企业(港或澳、台资)	Joint-venture Enterprises	2	1274	719
外商投资企业	Foreign-funded Enterprises	7	17795	2672
中外合资经营企业	Joint-venture Enterprises	4	10313	2413
中外合作经营企业	Cooperative Enterprises	1	2561	140
外资企业	Enterprises with Sole Foreign Funds	1	1074	67
外商投资股份有限公司	Share Holding Limited Companies with foreign Funds	1	3847	53
按批发行业小类分组	**By Wholesale Sector**			
农畜产品批发	Wholesale of Agricultural and Animal Products	14	51154	21271
谷物、豆及薯类批发	Wholesale of Cereal, Bean and Tuber	4	39401	13751
种子、饲料批发	Wholesale of Seed and Feed	2	6880	1784
棉、麻批发	Wholesale of Cotton and Fiber Crops	4	3494	3611
其他农畜产品批发	Other Wholesale of Agricultural and Animal Products	4	1379	2125
食品、饮料及烟草制品批发	Wholesale of Food, Beverages & Tobacco Products	51	489262	168775
米、面制品及食用油批发	Wholesale of Rice, Noodle Products and Edible Oil	8	47231	22917
糕点、糖果及糖批发	Wholesale of Cake, Candy and Sugar	2	6872	4047
果品、蔬菜批发	Wholesale of Fruit Products and Vegetables	1	147	111
肉、禽、蛋及水产品批发	Wholesale of Meat, Poultry, Eggs and Aquatic Products	2	1860	1670
盐及调味品批发	Wholesale of Salts and Condiments	4	19937	13510

Financial Indicators and Economic Efficiency of Wholesale Trade above Designated Size (2004)

(10 000 yuan)

累计折旧 Total Depreciation	资产总计 Total Assets	负债合计 Total Liabilities	实收资本 Capital Obtained	主营业务收入 Revenue of Major Business	主营业务成本 Cost of Major Business	主营业务税金及附加 Tax and Extra of Major Business	主营业务利润 Profits of Major Business
163696	**3334595**	**2541462**	**533719**	**6373214**	**5735568**	**11265**	**525793**
140412	2380181	1774769	399058	3716486	3232817	7493	395144
162840	3311496	2513172	531618	6324332	5690526	11256	522387
72940	1016574	768928	133615	1821935	1573217	4230	202565
2450	99751	86085	8731	171209	165939	134	5064
700	20043	15543	4256	41930	39137	64	2369
52	14146	4114	10100	9178	8913	4	260
31	13444	3435	10000	3830	3762	3	65
20	702	680	100	5348	5151	1	195
33655	1034010	810712	137464	2012905	1817964	2883	148361
18970	408662	333406	50603	328005	280034	1000	17328
14685	625348	477306	86862	1684900	1537930	1883	131033
47827	720544	487037	185472	1131513	1020230	2407	103923
4628	342307	281612	48386	1009303	941563	1497	57142
173	4609	3448	900	24978	23584	35	258
137	6191	4064	750	17537	15972	522	757
4206	319223	265405	43135	889207	830079	830	51162
112	12284	8695	3601	77580	71929	109	4964
589	64122	59143	3595	126361	123564	38	2704
226	1768	1565	300	6049	5745	3	301
226	1768	1565	300	6049	5745	3	301
631	21331	26725	1800	42833	39298	6	3105
521	12716	12638	1286	11904	11369	6	105
42	3233	3656	415	3178	2123		1055
35	1516	1063	50	9288	8018		1270
33	3867	9368	50	18464	17787		676
6663	67602	74416	12300	58562	53520	649	2375
5259	48272	58672	6469	28889	28394	1	-969
476	9559	6211	865	5921	4173		1240
178	7016	4915	3301	12433	10399	621	1413
749	2755	4617	1665	11319	10553	27	691
51112	672952	492139	83779	1284039	1081921	3646	170116
5520	69603	79128	11782	176523	167496	116	6470
1564	9934	6614	3245	23856	22736	28	1092
15	243	203	50	2103	1765	3	334
416	3208	3485	566	7386	7036	8	342
4077	36929	15221	3722	38688	23030	451	13915

14-7 续表1

单位：万元

指标	Item	企业数（个） Number of Enterprises (unit)	流动资产合计 Total Circulating Assets	固定资产原价 Original Value of Fixed Assets
饮料及茶叶批发	Wholesale of Beverages and Tea	8	6121	6641
烟草制品批发	Wholesale of Tobacco Products	21	390730	118077
其他食品批发	Wholesale of other Food	5	16365	1802
纺织、服装及日用品批发	Wholesale of Textiles, Garments and Daily Goods	16	30720	2938
纺织品、针织品及原料批发	Wholesale of Textiles Goods, Knit Goods and Material	7	12213	738
服装批发	Wholesale of Garments	2	3525	144
厨房、卫生间用具及日用杂货批发	Wholesale of Utensils for kitchen, Toilet and Daily Sundry Goods	3	5709	551
化妆品及卫生用品批发	Wholesale of Cosmetics and Healthy Goods	2	3117	404
其他日用品批发	Wholesale of Other Daily Goods	2	6156	1100
文化、体育用品及器材批发	Wholesale of Cultural and Sports Articles	10	59798	30704
文具用品批发	Wholesale of Cultural Goods	1	315	19
体育用品批发	Wholesale of Sports Goods	1	133	2
图书批发	Wholesale of Books	2	49707	28257
首饰、工艺品及收藏品批发	Wholesale of Ornaments, Handicrafts and Collections	1	1165	27
其他文化用品批发	Wholesale of Other Cultural Goods	5	8479	2399
医药及医疗器材批发	Wholesale of Medicines and Medical Appliances	59	395800	60395
西药批发业	Wholesale of Western Medicine	49	295859	38653
中药材及中成药批发	Wholesale of Traditional Chinese Medicine	8	98778	21625
医疗用品及器材批发	Wholesale of Medical Articles and Appliances	2	1162	118
矿产品、建材及化工产品批发	Wholesale of Mineral, Building and Chemical Products	220	666996	332373
煤炭及制品批发	Wholesale of Coal and Related Products	16	33865	10334
石油及制品批发	Wholesale of Petroleum and Related Products	37	136984	262947
非金属矿及制品批发	Wholesale of Nonmetal Mineral and Related Products	2	1230	816
金属及金属矿批发	Wholesale of Metal and Metal Mineral	84	323312	37893
建材批发	Wholesale of Building Materials	20	15250	995
化肥批发	Wholesale of Fertilizers	22	98209	7345
其他化工产品批发	Wholesale of Other Chemical Products	39	58146	12043
机械设备、五金交电及电子产品批发	Wholesale of Machinery, Hardware and Electronic Products	117	621627	97108
汽车、摩托车及零配件批发	Wholesale of Motor Vehicles, Motorcycles and Related Parts	56	428063	24654
五金、交电批发	Wholesale of Hardware and Transport	8	6573	855
家用电器批发	Wholesale of Household Electric Equipment	16	122315	60638
计算机、软件及辅助设备批发	Wholesale of Computers, Softwares and Assistant Equipment	2	1309	25
通讯及广播电视设备批发	Wholesale of Communication, Broadcast and TV Equipment	17	32007	8449
其他机械设备及电子产品批发	Other Wholesale of Machinery and Electronic Products	18	31361	2488
贸易经纪与代理	Trade Agencies	1	5470	8
贸易经纪与代理	Trade Agencies	1	5470	8
其他批发业	Other Wholesales	14	17338	2090
再生物资回收与批发	Wholesale of Recycled Materials	8	6210	1775
其他未列明的批发	Other Wholesale not listed here	6	11128	315

14-7 CONTINUED-1

(10 000 yuan)

累计折旧 Total Depreciation	资产总计 Total Assets	负债合计 Total Liabilities	实收资本 Capital Obtained	主营业务收入 Revenue of Major Business	主营业务成本 Cost of Major Business	主营业务税金及附加 Tax and Extra of Major Business	主营业务利润 Profits of Major Business
1303	14134	11812	2243	38460	35132	194	2126
37446	520197	360159	59903	947180	776970	2832	143905
771	18704	15519	2269	49844	47756	13	1932
811	34486	26111	7903	139712	132211	547	6491
75	13509	9107	2860	55807	52280	441	2625
45	4199	3970	715	7169	6080	1	1088
284	5984	5702	364	27227	25779	9	1439
132	3479	3177	420	28675	27722	9	943
274	7314	4155	3545	20834	20351	88	395
7821	106371	82374	7785	132069	89542	345	13505
3	332	233	109	2259	2115	3	141
2	133	38	100	1081	1065	1	15
7579	93214	72901	5243	98466	57383	314	12196
4	1188	1120	80	2025	1908	2	115
234	11504	8082	2253	28238	27072	25	1038
12340	496174	413135	51426	908267	870777	665	33834
9478	342962	296059	31462	771500	739416	570	29593
2840	145882	109798	19114	131114	126211	86	4240
22	7330	7279	850	5653	5150	9	2
66929	1094727	745164	266249	2467809	2268755	3274	178733
1926	51881	27202	14409	228657	202739	512	21960
47193	467752	260125	173649	594934	501126	1538	83645
184	1893	1443	330	4783	3849	15	872
11847	369905	295832	49069	1032257	988209	861	40252
290	17864	18528	3048	97016	93248	68	3091
2322	109908	88297	9733	277914	258929	47	18755
3167	75525	53737	16012	232249	220656	233	10160
17292	834088	685302	100156	1260899	1130674	2055	107166
6348	506785	407544	69274	754359	648526	1351	85651
134	7430	5008	1195	58205	55406	55	2436
6904	228959	198897	15291	219839	211594	191	6849
4	1331	1210	150	9446	9204	5	179
3147	50685	39944	8117	120676	112845	318	7406
756	38898	32700	6130	98374	93100	136	4644
	5508	5528	500	19126	9947	10	9168
	5508	5528	500	19126	9947	10	9168
729	22688	17292	3621	102731	98221	73	4404
653	9902	7398	1953	79684	76761	38	2885
76	12786	9894	1668	23047	21460	35	1519

14-7 续表2

单位：万元

指　　标	Item	其他业务利润 Profits of Other Business	营业费用 Business Cost	管理费用 Management Cost
总　　计	**Total**	**-31732**	**227607**	**169388**
#国有及国有控股	State-owned and State Holding	-37346	134200	132689
按登记注册类型分组	**By Registration**			
内资企业	Domestic-funded Enterprises	-31877	224542	168147
国有企业	State-owned Enterprises	11927	69863	96544
集体企业	Collective-owned Enterprises	657	2951	1375
股份合作企业	Cooperative Share Holding Enterprises	118	1509	1060
联营企业	Joint-owned Enterprises	10	184	106
国有与集体联营企业	Joint State-collective Enterprises	10	9	88
其他联营企业	Other Joint-owned Enterprises		175	18
有限责任公司	Limited-liability Corporations	-50629	58227	41082
国有独资公司	State Sole Funded	2016	10183	14302
其他有限责任公司	Other Limited-liability Corporations	-52645	48044	26780
股份有限公司	Share Holding Limited Companies	4785	46000	16475
私营企业	Private Enterprises	1231	44252	10673
私营独资企业	Private-funded Enterprises		1155	154
私营合伙企业	Private Partnership Enterprises	8	490	393
私营有限责任公司	Private Limited Liability Corporations	1185	40818	9638
私营股份有限公司	Private Share Holding Limited Companies	38	1789	488
其他企业	Other Enterprises	25	1555	832
港澳台商投资企业	Enterprises Funded by Hong Kong, Macao and Taiwan	125	7	474
合资经营企业(港或澳、台资)	Joint-venture Enterprises	125	7	474
外商投资企业	Foreign-funded Enterprises	21	3058	768
中外合资经营企业	Joint-venture Enterprises	18	358	414
中外合作经营企业	Cooperative Enterprises		1165	287
外资企业	Enterprises with Sole Foreign Funds		836	
外商投资股份有限公司	Share Holding Limited Companies with foreign Funds	3	700	67
按批发行业小类分组	**By Wholesale Sector**			
农畜产品批发	Wholesale of Agricultural and Animal Products	37	3177	3601
谷物、豆及薯类批发	Wholesale of Cereal, Bean and Tuber	265	1666	2423
种子、饲料批发	Wholesale of Seed and Feed		721	705
棉、麻批发	Wholesale of Cotton and Fiber Crops	1	594	316
其他农畜产品批发	Other Wholesale of Agricultural and Animal Products	-229	195	156
食品、饮料及烟草制品批发	Wholesale of Food, Beverages & Tobacco Products	9769	46439	86942
米、面制品及食用油批发	Wholesale of Rice, Noodle Products and Edible Oil	3228	4844	5429
糕点、糖果及糖批发	Wholesale of Cake, Candy and Sugar	369	799	740
果品、蔬菜批发	Wholesale of Fruit Products and Vegetables		330	4
肉、禽、蛋及水产品批发	Wholesale of Meat, Poultry, Eggs and Aquatic Products	25	249	181
盐及调味品批发	Wholesale of Salts and Condiments	2133	5883	7389

14-7 CONTINUED-2

(10 000 yuan)

营业利润 Business Profit	利润总额 Total Profits	应交所得税 Payable Income Tax	劳动、失业保险费 Insurance of Labour and Unemployment	应付工资 Payable Wages	应付福利费 Payable Welfare Funds	本年应交增值税 Payable Value-added Tax	全部从业人员年平均人数（人） Average Employment (person)
91913	**144892**	**39400**	**13667**	**97181**	**12215**	**79429**	**48012**
82792	135017	35640	11826	76349	9383	62799	26863
92753	145509	39400	13627	96593	12183	79561	47487
48822	87197	22403	8642	51900	6362	34764	14538
956	971	185	255	1317	274	626	1108
-97	52	43	79	782	99	246	1075
14	14	4		29	1	9	30
11	11	4		19			20
3	3			10	1	9	10
-4957	2119	2754	2230	22326	3017	19823	16489
-10240	-7491	736	778	8248	1060	11418	2663
5284	9610	2018	1452	14078	1957	8404	13826
41635	49693	12214	2262	13294	1600	16496	7009
6098	5045	1691	149	6191	719	7246	6611
68	68	20		202	28	222	185
98	152	6		130	16	74	142
2825	4654	1604	149	5517	639	6607	6002
3108	171	60		343	36	343	282
282	418	107	10	755	111	352	627
-79	-79		17	83		24	63
-79	-79		17	83		24	63
-761	-538		23	505	32	-155	462
-709	-454		14	145	9	76	97
-399	-400		8	139	23		250
434	402		1	29		117	20
-87	-87			192		-348	95
-5596	1094	42	397	1874	479	293	2094
-6319	299		288	967	388		1010
283	250		7	280	35		233
399	505	39	63	249	9		213
41	39	3	39	378	47	293	638
49203	82382	21947	7425	45741	4816	31611	11708
-2446	1311	205	830	1783	270	761	2159
-198	-152	4	57	359	41	184	301
				62		21	60
-118	-29	20	49	92	12	3	147
4223	4367	1375	865	3097	389	3172	1202

14-7 续表3

单位：万元

指标	Item	其他业务利润 Profits of Other Business	营业费用 Business Cost	管理费用 Management Cost
饮料及茶叶批发	Wholesale of Beverages and Tea	-366	951	1895
烟草制品批发	Wholesale of Tobacco Products	4186	31949	70836
其他食品批发	Wholesale of other Food	193	1433	469
纺织、服装及日用品批发	Wholesale of Textiles, Garments and Daily Goods	182	4201	2229
纺织品、针织品及原料批发	Wholesale of Textiles Goods, Knit Goods and Material	8	1496	667
服装批发	Wholesale of Garments		1165	314
厨房、卫生间用具及日用杂货批发	Wholesale of Utensils for kitchen, Toilet and Daily Sundry Goods	28	949	558
化妆品及卫生用品批发	Wholesale of Cosmetics and Healthy Goods	31	481	533
其他日用品批发	Wholesale of Other Daily Goods	115	110	157
文化、体育用品及器材批发	Wholesale of Cultural and Sports Articles	721	7398	4569
文具用品批发	Wholesale of Cultural Goods		119	29
体育用品批发	Wholesale of Sports Goods		8	3
图书批发	Wholesale of Books	390	6363	3937
首饰、工艺品及收藏品批发	Wholesale of Ornaments, Handicrafts and Collections		63	54
其他文化用品批发	Wholesale of Other Cultural Goods	331	845	545
医药及医疗器材批发	Wholesale of Medicines and Medical Appliances	1920	16690	14811
西药批发业	Wholesale of Western Medicine	1068	14430	11100
中药材及中成药批发	Wholesale of Traditional Chinese Medicine	852	1747	3684
医疗用品及器材批发	Wholesale of Medical Articles and Appliances		513	27
矿产品、建材及化工产品批发	Wholesale of Mineral, Building and Chemical Products	5305	100029	32067
煤炭及制品批发	Wholesale of Coal and Related Products	292	14619	2144
石油及制品批发	Wholesale of Petroleum and Related Products	1371	42805	8781
非金属矿及制品批发	Wholesale of Nonmetal Mineral and Related Products	133	54	537
金属及金属矿批发	Wholesale of Metal and Metal Mineral	2294	23028	12035
建材批发	Wholesale of Building Materials	202	3160	1175
化肥批发	Wholesale of Fertilizers	324	10028	2615
其他化工产品批发	Wholesale of Other Chemical Products	688	6335	4781
机械设备、五金交电及电子产品批发	Wholesale of Machinery, Hardware and Electronic Products	-49938	38416	23683
汽车、摩托车及零配件批发	Wholesale of Motor Vehicles, Motorcycles and Related Parts	-52289	23709	8565
五金、交电批发	Wholesale of Hardware and Transport	72	1609	681
家用电器批发	Wholesale of Household Electric Equipment	798	7287	8352
计算机、软件及辅助设备批发	Wholesale of Computers, Softwares and Assistant Equipment		114	141
通讯及广播电视设备批发	Wholesale of Communication, Broadcast and TV Equipment	91	2448	3880
其他机械设备及电子产品批发	Other Wholesale of Machinery and Electronic Products	1390	3249	2063
贸易经纪与代理	Trade Agencies	157	9379	422
贸易经纪与代理	Trade Agencies	157	9379	422
其他批发业	Other Wholesales	117	1880	1063
再生物资回收与批发	Wholesale of Recycled Materials	37	1434	699
其他未列明的批发	Other Wholesale not listed here	80	446	364

14-7 CONTINUED-3

(10 000 yuan)

营业利润 Business Profit	利润总额 Total Profits	应交所得税 Payable Income Tax	劳动、失业保险费 Insurance of Labour and Unemployment	应付工资 Payable Wages	应付福利费 Payable Welfare Funds	本年应交增值税 Payable Value-added Tax	全部从业人员年平均人数（人） Average Employment (person)
-594	-462	19	101	566	62	918	655
48495	77254	20324	5507	39470	4011	26525	6883
-161	93	1	16	312	31	28	301
-207	334	279	178	1156	157	441	1227
282	793	225	50	416	54	166	326
-393	-366		8	152	23		258
-66	-63	11	61	277	33	94	334
-96	-100	3	31	162	16	76	141
66	71	40	28	149	31	105	168
1153	2081	333	687	4777	578	1567	1721
-8	-8			42	6	23	35
4	4			6	1	2	8
1086	2015	307	580	4302	513	1372	1403
-2	-2			17	2	10	15
73	72	26	107	410	55	161	260
128	1872	730	918	8203	980	4372	7650
2381	2502	651	656	6406	799	3924	6566
-1714	-632	80	227	1719	175	449	1046
-539	2		36	77	6		38
51019	59460	14619	3272	21482	3017	25855	12993
5552	3836	1047	104	862	134	3369	645
34449	40460	10249	1976	11632	1517	7833	5714
432	428	131	9	202	23	114	65
6533	8193	1956	653	4112	746	12551	2554
-642	-659	33	13	683	67	438	653
5745	6030	887	176	1840	262	55	1974
-1050	1173	317	340	2150	269	1496	1388
-4571	-2970	1041	713	13164	2117	14620	10083
5449	6447	576	258	5844	760	12389	4334
243	110	50	42	479	64	323	420
-11791	-11416	51	224	3621	451	653	2089
-25	-30	5	2	62	9	31	60
680	1216	297	169	2438	743	636	2213
872	704	63	19	719	90	588	967
-537	-521			54	11		24
-537	-521			54	11		24
1321	1158	409	76	731	61	671	512
683	558	251	67	504	37	492	406
638	601	158	9	228	24	179	106

14－8 限额以上零售贸易业财务状况和经济效益（2004年）

单位：万元

指　　标	Item	企业数（个） Number of Enterprises (unit)	流动资产合计 Total Circulating Assets	固定资产原价 Original Value of Fixed Assets
总　计	**Total**	**403**	**813936**	**382080**
#国有及国有控股	State-owned and State Holding	101	385102	204866
按登记注册类型分	**By Registration**			
内资企业	Domestic-funded Enterprises	395	753828	347775
国有企业	State-owned Enterprises	62	203349	52777
集体企业	Collective-owned Enterprises	21	8478	5200
股份合作企业	Cooperative Share Holding Enterprises	12	2787	2568
联营企业	Joint-owned Enterprises	1	301	200
国有与集体联营企业	Joint State-collective Enterprises	1	301	200
有限责任公司	Limited-liability Corporations	128	295736	83859
国有独资公司	State Sole Funded	3	39483	1736
其他有限责任公司	Other Limited-liability Corporations	125	256253	82124
股份有限公司	Share Holding Limited Companies	27	88491	141246
私营企业	Private Enterprises	144	154686	61925
私营独资企业	Private-funded Enterprises	10	2275	1543
私营合伙企业	Private Partnership Enterprises	2	903	1957
私营有限责任公司	Private Limited Liability Corporations	124	139870	53221
私营股份有限公司	Private Share Holding Limited Companies	8	11638	5204
港澳台商投资企业	Enterprises Funded by Hong Kong, Macao and Taiwan	2	2045	402
合资经营企业(港或澳、台资)	Joint-venture Enterprises	1	977	4
港、澳、台商独资经营企业	Enterprises with Sole Funded from Hong Kong, Macao and Taiwan	1	1068	398
外商投资企业	Foreign-funded Enterprises	6	58064	33902
中外合资经营企业	Joint-venture Enterprises	3	11065	8460
中外合作经营企业	Cooperative Enterprises	3	46999	25443
按零售行业小类分	**By Retail Sector**			
综合零售	Comprehensive Retails	102	348486	222294
百货零售	Department Stores	49	291804	176471
超级市场零售	Supermarkets	34	49843	43372
其他综合零售	Other Comprehensive Retails	19	6840	2452
食品、饮料及烟草制品专门零售	Special Retail of Food, Beverages and Tobacco Products	19	16020	11207
粮油零售	Retail of Grains and Edible Oil	8	9711	4405
肉、禽、蛋及水产品零售	Retail of Meat, Poultry, Eggs and Water Products	4	2350	3436
饮料及茶叶零售	Retail of Beverages and Tea	2	2667	468
烟草制品零售	Retail of Tobacco Products	3	626	705
其他食品零售	Retail of other Food	2	666	2193

Financial Indicators and Economic Efficiency of Retail Trade above Designated Size (2004)

(10 000 yuan)

累计折旧 Total Depreciation	资产总计 Total Assets	负债合计 Total Liabilities	实收资本 Capital Obtained	主营业务收入 Revenue of Major Business	主营业务成本 Cost of Major Business	主营业务税金及附加 Tax and Extra of Major Business	主营业务利润 Profits of Major Business
77010	**1265688**	**888273**	**280035**	**2369248**	**2088856**	**8336**	**219804**
39260	621942	434371	104588	1155954	1009453	4790	122310
65431	1174206	842257	246118	2198621	1946585	8232	191551
14802	282870	219783	26365	515035	448163	2401	56557
1098	13643	11145	2483	28381	26241	132	1571
476	5416	4153	1684	19055	17592	37	1031
156	345	133	162	3076	2873	3	144
156	345	133	162	3076	2873	3	144
15417	404448	305166	93966	768607	693124	1805	43443
238	45012	38492	5000	74440	64051	204	1649
15179	359436	266674	88966	694167	629073	1601	41794
22765	228179	136737	55259	392699	333804	1954	55447
10718	239304	165141	66199	471768	424789	1901	33359
188	4107	1408	2287	9787	5732	194	675
171	2689	404	2285	2717	1845	7	641
8631	216428	155399	60427	421942	383335	1647	28798
1728	16079	7930	1200	37323	33877	54	3244
119	2328	1120	1523	4138	2875	17	1246
	981	85	923	1661	1495	17	149
119	1347	1035	600	2477	1380		1097
11461	89154	44896	32394	166490	139396	87	27007
1032	23144	15734	4627	25806	19754	30	6022
10428	66011	29162	27767	140684	119641	58	20985
43125	590634	426057	109697	1074751	915239	5423	141623
27687	490843	374432	68076	858241	732480	4622	118101
14905	88284	42235	38928	189493	157786	682	21745
534	11507	9390	2693	27016	24974	120	1778
3755	29503	22461	9129	32238	29783	49	1744
1498	13495	11714	3455	10517	9612	20	475
1264	6479	5464	1801	6521	5989	10	400
300	2950	2738	207	9268	8890	1	377
235	1258	881	145	3009	2579	9	304
459	5321	1665	3522	2924	2714	8	187

14-8 续表1

单位：万元

指　　标	Item	企业数（个） Number of Enterprises (unit)	流动资产合计 Total Circulating Assets	固定资产原价 Original Value of Fixed Assets
纺织、服装及日用品专门零售	Special Retail of Textile, Garments and Daily Goods	19	16061	17544
服装零售	Retail of Garments	9	10124	9260
鞋帽零售	Retail of Shoes and Hats	2	243	
钟表、眼镜零售	Retail of Clocks and Glasses	3	4602	4586
化妆品及卫生用品零售	Retail of Cosmetics and Healthy Goods	1	192	50
其他日用品零售	Retail of Other Daily Goods	4	900	3649
文化、体育用品及器材专门零售	Special Retail of Cultural and Sports Articles	41	39420	22878
文具用品零售	Retail of Cultural Goods	1	128	5
体育用品零售	Retail of Sports Goods	1	3104	166
图书零售	Retail of Books	35	34814	22557
珠宝首饰零售	Retail of Jewellery and Ornaments	1	120	15
工艺美术品及收藏品零售	Retail of Handicrafts and Collections	1	715	6
其他文化用品零售	Retail of Other Cultural Goods	2	540	129
医药及医疗器材专门零售	Special Retail of Medicine and Medical Appliances	39	50063	16894
药品零售	Retail of Medicine	37	48955	16859
医疗用品及器材零售	Retail of Medical Articles and Appliances	2	1108	35
汽车、摩托车、燃料及零配件专门零售	Special Retail of Motor Vehicles, Motorcycles, Fuel and Related Spares	106	224833	76844
汽车零售	Retail of Motor Vehicles	81	209810	55956
汽车零配件零售	Retail of Motor Vehicles Related Parts	2	2961	78
摩托车及零配件零售业	Retail of Motorcycles and Related Parts	7	836	606
机动车燃料零售	Retail of Motor Fuel	16	11225	20205
家用电器及电子产品专门零售	Special Retail of Household Electric Equipment and Electronic Products	67	112670	9468
家用电器零售业	Retail of Household Electric Equipment	45	100834	8560
计算机、软件及辅助设备零售	Retail of Computers, Softwares and Assistant Equipment	8	3874	431
通信设备零售	Retail of Communication Equipment	10	6678	323
其他电子产品零售	Other Retail of Electronic Products	4	1284	155
五金、家具及室内装修材料专门零售	Special Retail of Hardware, Furniture and Indoor Decoration	7	5490	4302
五金零售	Retail of Hardware	1	108	612
家具零售	Retail of Furnitures	2	2901	1405
其他室内装修材料零售	Other Retail of Indoor Decoration	4	2481	2285
无店铺及其他零售业	Non-shops and Other Retails	3	894	649
生活用燃料零售	Retail of Living Fuel	2	607	649
其他未列明的零售	Other Retail not listed here	1	287	1

14-8 CONTINUED-1

(10 000 yuan)

累计折旧 Total Depreciation	资产总计 Total Assets	负债合计 Total Liabilities	实收资本 Capital Obtained	主营业务收入 Revenue of Major Business	主营业务成本 Cost of Major Business	主营业务税金及附加 Tax and Extra of Major Business	主营业务利润 Profits of Major Business
6017	30508	20597	7071	34409	24678	133	7825
3315	16590	12929	2493	23217	18365	86	3071
	243	114	69	473	421	2	49
709	9209	5341	2277	9634	5448	14	4137
	242	100	5	485	360		126
1993	4223	2113	2226	601	85	30	443
7459	63929	24235	8247	82463	57993	1010	16753
2	132	89	50	547	496		51
16	3722	3535	100	5948	4830	9	1109
7362	58511	19444	7842	73704	50763	971	15262
2	250	50	100	600	500	18	82
3	720	695	50	520	410	1	109
75	594	422	105	1145	994	10	140
3857	70987	56636	15486	97283	86980	230	7033
3840	69656	55617	15365	93785	83762	223	6895
18	1331	1019	122	3498	3218	7	138
10066	344041	227957	106847	702441	658603	750	32037
6570	295431	213487	74508	584224	563459	400	18052
38	3012	2181	1050	3708	3571	5	132
69	4165	3061	1358	13165	12275	21	565
3389	41434	9228	29931	101345	79298	323	13289
1984	124689	102247	20066	325545	298861	669	9743
1676	112046	93233	15468	271287	247930	578	7434
167	4158	1993	2000	23205	21331	46	1344
70	7112	5700	2100	26046	25077	22	507
71	1373	1322	498	5006	4523	24	459
480	9896	7073	3146	16641	13685	66	2855
141	737	872	96	190	163	5	22
251	4442	3739	400	7210	5051	43	2116
88	4717	2462	2650	9242	8471	18	717
268	1502	1010	345	3477	3034	6	192
267	1215	804	257	2660	2344	5	66
	287	206	88	817	690	1	126

14-8 续表2

单位：万元

指标	Item	其他业务利润 Profits of Other Business	营业费用 Business Cost	管理费用 Management Cost
总计	**Total**	**27775**	**125988**	**106154**
#国有及国有控股	State-owned and State Holding	4988	54141	51403
按登记注册类型分	**By Registration**			
内资企业	Domestic-funded Enterprises	19677	112196	93117
国有企业	State-owned Enterprises	3237	20170	28001
集体企业	Collective-owned Enterprises	239	574	1266
股份合作企业	Cooperative Share Holding Enterprises	226	380	1431
联营企业	Joint-owned Enterprises		57	88
国有与集体联营企业	Joint State-collective Enterprises		57	88
有限责任公司	Limited-liability Corporations	8550	36405	27722
国有独资公司	State Sole Funded	6	969	441
其他有限责任公司	Other Limited-liability Corporations	8544	35437	27281
股份有限公司	Share Holding Limited Companies	1768	27670	20687
私营企业	Private Enterprises	5656	26940	13922
私营独资企业	Private-funded Enterprises	27	265	380
私营合伙企业	Private Partnership Enterprises		322	206
私营有限责任公司	Private Limited Liability Corporations	3519	22011	12619
私营股份有限公司	Private Share Holding Limited Companies	2110	4343	716
港澳台商投资企业	Enterprises Funded by Hong Kong, Macao and Taiwan	5	1149	201
合资经营企业(港或澳、台资)	Joint-venture Enterprises	5	41	127
港、澳、台商独资经营企业	Enterprises with Sole Funded from Hong Kong, Macao and Taiwan		1108	74
外商投资企业	Foreign-funded Enterprises	8093	12643	12836
中外合资经营企业	Joint-venture Enterprises	514	3801	1620
中外合作经营企业	Cooperative Enterprises	7579	8842	11217
按零售行业小类分	**By Retail Sector**			
综合零售	Comprehensive Retails	17554	71744	67426
百货零售	Department Stores	7738	52775	52796
超级市场零售	Supermarkets	9762	18004	14279
其他综合零售	Other Comprehensive Retails	53	966	352
食品、饮料及烟草制品专门零售	Special Retail of Food, Beverages and Tobacco Products	731	1760	3205
粮油零售	Retail of Grains and Edible Oil	285	807	853
肉、禽、蛋及水产品零售	Retail of Meat, Poultry, Eggs and Water Products	220	459	1426
饮料及茶叶零售	Retail of Beverages and Tea	34	226	364
烟草制品零售	Retail of Tobacco Products	78	141	167
其他食品零售	Retail of other Food	114	128	395

14-8 CONTINUED-2

(10 000 yuan)

营业利润 Business Profit	利润总额 Total Profits	应交所得税 Payable Income Tax	劳动、失业保险费 Insurance of Labour and Unemployment	应付工资 Payable Wages	应付福利费 Payable Welfare Funds	本年应交增值税 Payable Value-added Tax	全部从业人员年平均人数（人） Average Employment (person)
24069	**30784**	**8908**	**5458**	**45738**	**15250**	**26831**	**124923**
24773	27764	4644	4099	17407	12394	13945	92086
14286	20887	5639	5335	41089	15181	22673	121925
14101	14709	2044	1916	12227	2076	9444	8936
-9	-101	27	88	641	174	102	829
-499	-446	3	66	612	72	58	954
52	52	17		33	5	14	24
52	52	17		33	5	14	24
-5806	-2280	1546	834	13084	1656	6941	15100
1242	1483		60	630	82	631	791
-7048	-3763	1546	774	12453	1574	6311	14309
7865	9859	1832	2071	2610	9942	2216	81555
-1418	-905	171	360	11883	1257	3898	14527
62	363			277	23	52	515
222	198	5	3	103	14	154	117
-1995	-1773	158	358	10076	1035	3497	11640
293	308	8		1428	186	195	2255
-106	-106		35	214	5	78	228
-13	-13			46	5	10	56
-93	-93		35	167		69	172
9889	10002	3269	88	4436	64	4080	2770
1147	1144	386	43	935	40	1211	1113
8742	8858	2884	46	3501	24	2869	1657
20298	22539	5703	3310	21966	11905	15943	104618
18378	20356	4862	3003	15366	11359	13740	95247
1453	2012	836	233	6031	497	2175	8124
468	170	5	74	569	48	29	1247
-2267	-436	44	546	1554	474	158	1356
-765	-192	18	123	652	81	79	489
-1097	-271	8	369	551	345	14	520
-195	26	9	21	61	9	13	74
62	60	10	2	159	23	45	87
-271	-58		32	131	16	6	186

14-8 续表3

单位：万元

指 标	Item	其他业务利润 Profits of Other Business	营业费用 Business Cost	管理费用 Management Cost
纺织、服装及日用品专门零售	Special Retail of Textile, Garments and Daily Goods	605	6390	3655
服装零售	Retail of Garments	216	3543	1797
鞋帽零售	Retail of Shoes and Hats	263	8	105
钟表、眼镜零售	Retail of Clocks and Glasses	28	2736	1358
化妆品及卫生用品零售	Retail of Cosmetics and Healthy Goods		10	5
其他日用品零售	Retail of Other Daily Goods	99	93	391
文化、体育用品及器材专门零售	Special Retail of Cultural and Sports Articles	1003	7004	8215
文具用品零售	Retail of Cultural Goods		38	23
体育用品零售	Retail of Sports Goods		651	356
图书零售	Retail of Books	1003	6164	7749
珠宝首饰零售	Retail of Jewellery and Ornaments		3	10
工艺美术品及收藏品零售	Retail of Handicrafts and Collections		76	18
其他文化用品零售	Retail of Other Cultural Goods		72	60
医药及医疗器材专门零售	Special Retail of Medicine and Medical Appliances	376	5322	4732
药品零售	Retail of Medicine	376	5186	4616
医疗用品及器材零售	Retail of Medical Articles and Appliances		137	116
汽车、摩托车、燃料及零配件专门零售	Special Retail of Motor Vehicles, Motorcycles, Fuel and Related Spares	1518	17925	12269
汽车零售	Retail of Motor Vehicles	1451	10356	9665
汽车零配件零售	Retail of Motor Vehicles Related Parts	14	96	97
摩托车及零配件零售业	Retail of Motorcycles and Related Parts	18	217	66
机动车燃料零售	Retail of Motor Fuel	36	7256	2441
家用电器及电子产品专门零售	Special Retail of Household Electric Equipment and Electronic Products	5690	13168	5571
家用电器零售业	Retail of Household Electric Equipment	5600	11803	4463
计算机、软件及辅助设备零售	Retail of Computers, Softwares and Assistant Equipment	1	672	650
通信设备零售	Retail of Communication Equipment	77	328	314
其他电子产品零售	Other Retail of Electronic Products	12	364	144
五金、家具及室内装修材料专门零售	Special Retail of Hardware, Furniture and Indoor Decoration	295	2347	899
五金零售	Retail of Hardware	74	37	82
家具零售	Retail of Furnitures	2	1630	196
其他室内装修材料零售	Other Retail of Indoor Decoration	219	680	621
无店铺及其他零售业	Non-shops and Other Retails	4	329	183
生活用燃料零售	Retail of Living Fuel	4	245	141
其他未列明的零售	Other Retail not listed here		83	42

14-8 CONTINUED-3

(10 000 yuan)

营业利润 Business Profit	利润总额 Total Profits	应交所得税 Payable Income Tax	劳动、失业保险费 Insurance of Labour and Unemployment	应付工资 Payable Wages	应付福利费 Payable Welfare Funds	本年应交增值税 Payable Value-added Tax	全部从业人员年平均人数（人） Average Employment (person)
-1032	-572	53	107	2322	167	870	2698
-1335	-1014	12	45	1282	137	264	1677
199	199	2		112	2	18	169
33	27	40	40	812	12	576	705
101	56		3	20		9	30
-30	160		19	97	16	4	117
4575	3449	579	596	4443	736	2629	2824
-10	-10			17	2	2	22
88	87		40	424	57	58	392
4413	3283	578	556	3943	673	2560	2322
66	70			7			6
9	9			3			22
9	9	1		51	3	8	60
-1862	-1565	69	268	3262	384	1254	3371
-1738	-1575	67	254	3183	373	1210	3322
-124	11	3	14	79	11	44	49
2125	3311	1868	319	7142	782	4385	4881
-1833	-1324	417	122	5287	498	2329	3448
-121	-121	5		68	9	355	66
235	169	3	3	54	7	24	127
3844	4586	1444	194	1734	268	1678	1240
2569	4383	538	244	4133	686	1208	4275
2628	4430	494	185	3279	568	977	3363
63	48	33	41	485	68	85	407
-70	-39	5	11	306	34	120	366
-52	-55	5	7	63	15	25	139
-257	-247	54	55	773	96	342	740
-60	-63		4	17	2	3	17
167	177	54		223	31	288	354
-364	-360		52	532	63	51	369
-79	-79		13	144	20	42	160
-80	-80		13	84	12	34	97
1	1			60	8	9	63

14—9 限额以上餐饮业财务状况和经济效益（2004年）

单位：万元

指　　标	Item	企业数（个） Number of Enterprises (unit)	流动资产合计 Total Circulating Assets	固定资产原价 Original Value of Fixed Assets
总　计	**Total**	**239**	**68205**	**162951**
#国有及国有控股	State-owned and State Holding	14	11347	19947
按登记注册类型分组	**By Registration**			
内资企业	Domestic-funded Enterprises	235	62151	119089
国有企业	State-owned Enterprises	8	1348	7407
集体企业	Collective-owned Enterprises	8	4513	8198
股份合作企业	Cooperative Share Holding Enterprises	10	858	5612
有限责任公司	Limited-liability Corporations	45	20145	40449
其他有限责任公司	Other Limited-liability Corporations	45	20145	40449
股份有限公司	Share Holding Limited Companies	6	2256	5422
私营企业	Private Enterprises	153	31518	48226
私营独资企业	Private-funded Enterprises	55	5908	13869
私营合伙企业	Private Partnership Enterprises	9	341	1571
私营有限责任公司	Private Limited Liability Corporations	81	23734	32369
私营股份有限公司	Private Share Holding Limited Companies	8	1535	417
其他企业	Other Enterprises	5	1513	3776
港澳台商投资企业	Enterprises Funded by Hong Kong, Macao and Taiwan	2	3422	41447
合资经营企业(港或澳、台资)	Joint-venture Enterprises	1	2694	39997
港、澳、台商独资经营企业	Enterprises with Sole Funded from Hong Kong, Macao and Taiwan	1	728	1450
外商投资企业	Foreign-funded Enterprises	2	2632	2414
外资企业	Foreign-funded Enterprises	2	2632	2414
按餐饮行业中类分组	**By Sector**			
正餐服务	Dinner Services	231	64784	158501
快餐服务	Fast Food Services	4	3286	4021
其他餐饮服务	Other Catering Services	4	135	429

Financial Indicators and Economic Efficiency of Catering Trade above Designated Size (2004)

(10 000 yuan)

累计折旧 Total Depreciation	本年折旧 Depreciation in 2004	资产总计 Total Assets	负债合计 Total Liabilities	实收资本 Capital Obtained	主营业务收入 Revenue of Major Business	主营业务成本 Cost of Major Business	主营业务税金及附加 Tax and Extra of Major Business
31315	**7025**	**240746**	**155546**	**91627**	**177554**	**92450**	**10758**
8415	549	29307	13514	13347	15395	5772	989
28065	5380	182426	111252	75962	161135	86956	9910
3015	289	5944	2661	3910	3791	1947	371
593	112	12220	15168	598	2232	1675	81
932	54	9060	4078	1686	5266	2855	316
10012	2051	59811	39194	22428	44914	21038	2534
10012	2051	59811	39194	22428	44914	21038	2534
2860	11	8807	2795	4166	6030	2494	340
10238	2741	81537	45111	40692	96696	55754	6152
2975	741	20448	9684	11786	21908	14251	1414
480	138	1564	1007	833	6690	3954	516
6668	1839	57523	34161	27246	65922	36168	4108
115	22	2002	260	828	2177	1382	114
416	123	5048	2244	2481	2207	1192	116
2316	1425	52045	43113	11951	6573	1988	355
1392	1293	49863	40634	9884	4990	1481	286
924	132	2182	2480	2068	1582	507	69
934	220	6275	1181	3714	9847	3507	492
934	220	6275	1181	3714	9847	3507	492
29207	6615	231594	151224	85906	164968	87298	10172
1980	379	8417	3770	5561	11252	4425	514
128	32	736	553	160	1335	727	72

14-9 续表

单位：万元

指　　标	Item	主营业务利润 Profits of Major Business	其他业务利润 Profits of Other Business	营业费用 Business Cost
总　计	**Total**	**62565**	**1585**	**49274**
#国有及国有控股	State-owned and State Holding	6910	439	6348
按登记注册类型分组	**By Registration**			
内资企业	Domestic-funded Enterprises	52488	887	41981
国有企业	State-owned Enterprises	875	213	1498
集体企业	Collective-owned Enterprises	455	17	309
股份合作企业	Cooperative Share Holding Enterprises	1563	1	1589
有限责任公司	Limited-liability Corporations	16182	53	13659
其他有限责任公司	Other Limited-liability Corporations	16182	53	13659
股份有限公司	Share Holding Limited Companies	3147	218	2211
私营企业	Private Enterprises	29368	382	22218
私营独资企业	Private-funded Enterprises	5272	-30	2670
私营合伙企业	Private Partnership Enterprises	1914	3	1070
私营有限责任公司	Private Limited Liability Corporations	21824	93	18018
私营股份有限公司	Private Share Holding Limited Companies	358	316	459
其他企业	Other Enterprises	898	3	497
港澳台商投资企业	Enterprises Funded by Hong Kong, Macao and Taiwan	4230	634	3584
合资经营企业(港或澳、台资)	Joint-venture Enterprises	3224		2543
港、澳、台商独资经营企业	Enterprises with Sole Funded from Hong Kong, Macao and Taiwan	1006	634	1040
外商投资企业	Foreign-funded Enterprises	5847	64	3709
外资企业	Foreign-funded Enterprises	5847	64	3709
按餐饮行业中类分组	**By Sector**			
正餐服务	Dinner Services	55718	887	44375
快餐服务	Fast Food Services	6313	698	4594
其他餐饮服务	Other Catering Services	535		306

14-9 CONTINUED

(10 000 yuan)

管理费用 Management Cost	营业利润 Business Profit	利润总额 Total Profits	应交所得税 Payable Income Tax	劳动、失业保险费 Insurance of Labour and Unemployment	应付工资 Payable Wages	应付福利费 Payable Welfare Funds	全部从业人员年平均人数（人） Average Employment (person)
22663	**-208**	**2205**	**1104**	**517**	**23002**	**2168**	**35446**
3783	-1169	-412	3	337	2799	410	2583
19495	-532	1669	728	452	20368	1979	33106
733	-561	-542	3	57	708	120	1014
119	75	21	10	3	308	46	277
696	-458	-465	27		399	35	874
6998	-549	-150	287	294	5684	689	7207
6998	-549	-150	287	294	5684	689	7207
1868	-745	41	1	48	1052	23	678
8942	1460	2629	374	50	11964	1040	22728
1607	1714	1750	194	21	2405	183	3366
1173	-219	341	9	2	747	23	742
6004	-272	142	170	27	8510	794	18022
158	237	396			303	40	598
138	247	135	26		253	26	328
1996	-750	-402		37	1644	126	1654
1693	-1050	-654		17	1356	126	1357
303	300	252		20	288		297
1173	1074	938	376	28	991	63	686
1173	1074	938	376	28	991	63	686
21363	-1608	1001	732	475	21697	2095	34139
1009	1465	1281	372	32	1110	66	1023
292	-65	-77		10	195	6	284

14－10 限额以上连锁零售业和餐饮业经营情况（2003－2004年）
Operation of Chains in Retail and Catering Trade above Designated Size (2003-2004)

单位：万元 (10 000 yuan)

指　　标	Item	合　计 Total		#直营店 Direct Management	
		2003	2004	2003	2004
门店总数（个）	Total Number of Chains (unit)	5187	6245	1994	2125
#百货店	Department Stores	88	92	88	92
超级市场	Supermarkets	59	62	59	62
营业面积（平方米）	Business Areas (sq.m)	2470717	2797639	1787671	1967626
#百货店	Department Stores	330776	413761	330776	413761
超级市场	Supermarkets	65732	82039	65732	82039
从业人数（人）	Employment (person)	88007	94684	36932	37839
#百货店	Department Stores	9066	10373	9066	10373
超级市场	Supermarkets	3847	4153	3847	4153
销售总额（营业总收入）	Total Sales	1435921	1842744	1203973	1484345
#百货店	Department Stores	522773	551965	522773	551965
超级市场	Supermarkets	23882	46326	23882	46326
零售额	Retail Trade	1259437	1623197	1031279	1267577
#百货店	Department Stores	436218	509625	436218	509625
超级市场	Supermarkets	23882	46326	23882	46326
利润总额	Total Profits	16388	58572	16388	58572
#百货店	Department Stores	5156	14979	5156	14979
超级市场	Supermarkets	-1853	-863	-1853	-863
资产总计	Total Assets	643777	709712	643777	709712
#百货店	Department Stores	257266	291069	257266	291069
超级市场	Supermarkets	17203	20200	17203	20200
负债总计	Total Liabilities	430165	460084	430165	460084
#百货店	Department Stores	194924	224464	194924	224464
超级市场	Supermarkets	7884	8628	7884	8628
统一配送比重（%）	Proportion of Unified Delivery (%)	74.2	75.1	74.9	75.3
#百货店	Department Stores	79.2	84.0	79.2	84.0
超级市场	Supermarkets	66.7	55.1	66.7	55.1
自有配送中心配送比重（%）	Proportion of Own Delivery Center (%)	67.9	68.9	70.6	71.1
#百货店	Department Stores	67.5	70.4	67.5	70.4
超级市场	Supermarkets	46.0	38.7	46.0	38.7

主要统计指标解释

社会消费品零售额 指批发和零售业、餐饮业、新闻出版业、邮政业和其他服务业等，售予城乡居民用于生活消费的商品和社会集团用于公共消费的商品之总量。社会消费品零售总额包括：

一、批发和零售业企业：

1. 售予城乡居民的各种生活消费品。

2. 售予入境旅游的外国人、华侨、港澳台同胞的各类商品。

3. 售予行政事业单位、社会团体、军队和武警等机构的商品，以及以零售方式售予各类企业的商品。具体包括：用于非生产和社会交往的办公用品，如通讯设备、计算器具和设备、电讯网络设备、文印设备、音像视听器材和设备、纸张、本册、文具及装订文印材料、家具、日用电器、针纺织品、清洁卫生用品、文体用品、奖品、纪念品、礼品等；供内部人员乘坐的交通工具和燃料；用于办公设施修缮的各类配件、材料、工具等；用于取暖和防暑降温的设备、燃料、材料及食品等；专用于教学的用品和设备；非营利医疗机构的中、西药品、中药材和医疗设备器材；非专用的劳动保护用品；不对外营业的内部食堂用的餐具、炊具、设备、清洁卫生工具和食品、燃料等；军队、武警用于其人员生活的衣着品和个人用品；其他各类非生产性设备和用品。

二、餐饮业出售的主食、菜肴、烟酒饮料和其他商品。

三、新闻出版业、邮政业售予城乡居民、企事业单位、军队和武警等机构的书报杂志、音像制品、邮品等。

四、其他服务业出售的食品、烟酒饮料、服装鞋帽、日常生活用品、医药保健用品、艺术品、工艺美术品、玩具、殡葬用品以及其他消费品。

商品销售总额 指对本企业（单位）以外的单位和个人出售（包括对境外直接出口）的商品总额。这个指标反映批发零售贸易业在国内市场上销售商品以及出口商品的总量。商品销售总额包括：（1）售给城乡居民和社会集团消费用的商品；（2）售给工业、农业、建筑业、运输邮电业、批发零售贸易业、餐饮业、服务业等作为生产，经营使用的商品；（3）售给批发零售贸易业作为转卖或加工后转卖的商品；（4）对国（境）外直接出口的商品。不包括出售本企业（单位）自用的废旧包装用品；未通过买卖行为付出的商品；经本单位介绍，由买卖双方直接结算，本单位只收取手续费的业务，购货退出的商品以及商品损耗和损失等。

住宿和餐饮业经营情况

1. 营业额：指住宿和餐饮业法人企业、产业活动单位在经营活动中的因提供服务或销售商品等取得的收入。包括：客房收入、餐费收入、商品销售收入和其他收入。

2. 客房收入：指住宿和餐饮法人企业、产业活动单位在经营活动中因提供住宿服务取得的客房收入。

3. 餐费收入：指住宿和餐饮法人企业、产业活动单位因为顾客提供就餐服务取得的餐费收入。包括：经烹饪、调制加工后出售的各种食品，如主食、炒菜、凉拌菜等的收入。

4. 商品销售收入：指住宿和餐饮法人企业、产业活动单位伴随服务而出售商品所取得的收入。

5. 其他收入：指营业收入中除客房收入、餐费收入、商品销售收入以外的其他收入。包括娱乐、健身和商务服务等。

连锁企业（或称连锁店、连锁公司） 指在核心企业或总店的领导下，由分散的、经营同类商品或服务的企业或活动单位，采取共同方针，实行集中采购和分散销售的有机结合，通过规范化经营，实现规模效益的经济联合组织形式。一般连锁店应由若干个分店组成。其经营特征：（1）经营同类商品；（2）使用统一商号；（3）

统一采购配送，采购与销售相分离（部分商品可根据物流合理和保质保鲜原则，由供应商直接送货到门店，其余均由总部统一配送）。

连锁门店包括下列两种形式：

直营连锁：指正规连锁。连锁门店均由总部独资或控股开设，在总部的直接领导下统一经营。

加盟连锁：指特许连锁。各连锁门店（被特许人）通过合同形式，取得使用总部（特许人）商标、商号、经营技术和销售总部开发的商品的特许权，各加盟连锁门店为独立法人，在总部指导下统一经营。

Explanatory Notes on Main Statistical Indicators

Total Retail Sales of Consumer Goods refer to the sum of retail sales of commodities sold by wholesale, retail, catering, publishing, post and telecommunications and other service industries to urban and rural households for private consumption and to social institutions for public consumption. Retail sales of consumer goods include:

(1) Sales by wholesale and retail units:

(a) of consumer goods sold to urban and rural households.

(b) of commodities sold to foreigners, overseas Chinese and Chinese compatriots from Hong Kong, Macau and Taiwan visiting in China.

(c) of commodities sold to government agencies, institutions, social organizations, military and armed police units, and commodities sold to enterprises in the form of retail sales. More specifically, they include: office facilities and articles for non-production purposes such as communications equipment, computing equipment and instruments, TV and network equipment, printing and copying equipment, audio-visual equipment and instruments, paper, notebooks, stationeries, furniture, electric appliances, knitwear, sanitation and cleaning articles, cultural and sport articles, articles for prizes, souvenirs, etc.; transport vehicles and fuels for employees; materials, spare parts and tools for the maintenance of office facilities; equipment, fuels, materials and food for winter heating or summer cooling purposes; articles and equipment for teaching purpose; Chinese and western medicines and medical equipment and facilities purchased by non profit-making medical institutes; non-specialized work safety articles; cooking utensils, tableware, equipment, cleaning articles, food and fuels purchased by internal cafeterias; clothes and personal articles purchased by military or armed police units for their officials and soldiers; and other equipment and articles for non-production purposes.

(2) Sales of stable food, cooked dishes, beverages, tobaccos and other articles by catering units.

(3) Sales of books, newspapers, magazines, audio-visual products and post products by publishing, post and telecommunications departments to urban and rural households and to enterprises, institutions, military and armed police units.

(4) Sales of food, beverages, tobaccos, clothing, hats, footwear, articles for daily use, medicines, medical and health articles, work of art, handicrafts, toys, funeral articles and other articles by other service industries.

Total Sales of Commodities refer to selling of commodities by the establishments and individuals (including direct export). This indicator is used to show the total value of sales of commodities at domestic markets and export. The total sales include: (1) commodities sold to urban and rural residents and social groups for their consumption; (2) commodities sold to establishments in industry, agriculture, construction, transportation, post and telecommunications, wholesale and retail trades, catering trade and public utility for their production and operation; (3) commodities sold to wholesale and retail establishments for re-selling, with or without further processing; and (4) commodities for direct export to other countries. Excluded are selling of waste packaging materials used by the establishments (units) themselves, commodities transferred without buying or selling procedures, commission income from brokerage in transactions whose settlement is directly handled by buyers and sellers, rejected commodities in the purchase, loss in commodities, etc.

Operation of Hotels and Catering Trade

1. Business income: refer to the total turnover of hotels and restaurants that obtain by service offering or commodity sales. It includes room income, catering service income, commodity sales and other income.

2. Room income: refer to the turnover of hotels and restaurants that obtain by offering accommodation service.

3. Catering service income: refer to the turnover of hotels and restaurants that obtain by offering catering service for customers, including sales of various foods which are sold after cooking and processing, such as staple food, cooked dishes, cold and dressed dishes and so on.

4. Commodity sales: refer to the turnover of hotels and restaurants that obtain by selling commodities.

5. Other income: refer to the part of business income except for room income, catering service income and commodity sales, such as entertainment, exercise and commercial service and so on.

Chain Enterprises (also called chain stores or chain corporations) refer to a form of joint economic entities under which scattered enterprises or establishments engaged in providing homogeneous commodities or services, with the central leadership of core enterprise or headquarters and guided by common policies, conduct centralized purchase and distributed selling of commodities, in order to gain better efficiency through standardized operation. Consisting of a number of branch stores, the chain stores have in general following features: 1) homogeneous commodities, 2) unique name of stores, 3) centralized purchase and delivery which is separated from distributed selling operation (most commodities are delivered from the headquarters except some items which, from logistics, quality or freshness considerations, might be delivered by the suppliers directly).

Chain stores have two categories:

a) Chain stores under direct management: These are formal chain stores invested or controlled by the headquarters. They operate under the direct and unified management from the headquarters.

b) Chain stores through license arrangement: Through contracts, chain stores (their owners) obtain licenses from the headquarters to use designated trade marks, names, operation know-how, and to sell the commodity developed by the headquarters. Under this arrangement, each store in the chain is an independent legal entity and operates under the guidance from the headquarters.

十五　对外经济贸易和旅游业

FOREIGN ECONOMIC RELATIONS, TRADE AND TOURISM

重庆统计年鉴 • CHONGQING STATISTICAL YEARBOOK 2005

简要说明　Brief Introduction

本章内容包括我市海关进出口、利用外资、对外承包工程和劳务合作、旅游情况，以及利用内资方面的资料。海关进出口、利用外资、国外友好城市交流和旅游资料由市统计局贸易外经处分别根据重庆海关、市对外贸易经济委员会、市政府外事办公室和市旅游局的有关资料加工整理，利用内资数据由市统计局贸易外经处提供，外商投资企业生产经营和财务情况由市企业调查队提供，风景名胜区和重点文物由市统计局社会科技处根据市园林局和市文化局的资料整理编辑。

Data in this chapter includes the detailed data of imports & exports, utilization of foreign capital, contracted projects and labor cooperation with the foreign countries (territories), tourism and utilization of domestic capital. Data on imports & exports, utilization of foreign capital, communications with foreign friendly cities and tourism is provided by Division of Trade and External Economic Relations Statistics, Municipal Bureau of Statistics according to data from Chongqing Customs of PRC, Municipal Committee of Foreign Trade and Economics, Foreign Affairs Office of Municipal Government and Municipal Tourism Administration. Data on utilization of domestic capital are provided by Division of Trade and External Economic Relations Statistics, Municipal Bureau of Statistics. Statistics on production, business and finance of foreign-funded enterprises are provided by Municipal Enterprises Survey Organization. Scenic spots and main cultural relics are edited by Division of Social and Technology Statistics, Municipal Bureau of Statistics with data from Municipal Afforestation Bureau and from Municipal Cultural Bureau.

15－1 海关进出口总值（1987－2004年）
Total Imports and Exports (Customs Statistics) (1987-2004)

单位：万美元 (USD 10 000)

年 份 Year	进出口总值 Total Imports and Exports	进口总值 Total Imports	出口总值 Total Exports	进出口差额 Balance of Imports and Exports
1987	29681	12235	17446	5211
1988	41078	18907	22171	3264
1989	60299	31247	29052	-2195
1990	68095	35366	32729	-2637
1991	61950	22701	39249	16548
1992	74244	33377	40867	7490
1993	85470	44310	41160	-3150
1994	123957	52430	71527	19097
1995	141859	57126	84733	27607
1996	158543	99178	59365	-39813
1997	167843	89828	78015	-11813
1998	103386	51975	51411	-564
1999	121044	72005	49039	-22966
2000	178547	79025	99522	20497
2001	183384	73136	110248	37112
2002	179401	70282	109119	38837
2003	259488	100979	158509	57530
2004	385735	176616	209119	32503

15－2 利用外资基本情况（1985－2004年）
Basic Statistics on Utilization of Foreign Capital (1985-2004)

单位：个、万美元 (unit, USD 10 000)

年份 Year	新签利用外资协议(合同)数 New Signed Agreements (Contracts) on Foreign Capital to be Utilized	协议合同金额 Total Amount of Agreements and Contracts	实际利用外资额 Total Amount of Foreign Capital Actually Utilized	#对外借款 Foreign Loans	#外商直接投资 Foreign Direct investment
1985	28	3991	2499	736	427
1986	21	2957	3596	1464	790
1987	31	3320	4509	2451	1924
1988	72	54862	13153	10574	2069
1989	39	3887	22479	20427	756
1990	81	19133	14489	13187	332
1991	110	12074	16143	12340	977
1992	516	59665	29745	14359	10247
1993	795	106629	41970	14895	25915
1994	453	65266	65644	17376	44953
1995	341	112473	61554	20436	37926
1996	233	35873	44151	20772	21878
1997	289	77109	98208	36391	38466
1998	263	75099	55163	10484	43107
1999	199	70115	32699	8564	23893
2000	237	86888	34532	9953	24436
2001	191	71884	42442	16662	25649
2002	169	64824	45034	16817	28089
2003	218	71397	56654	25381	31112
2004	281	66621	68214	27462	40508

注：2004年新签利用外资协议(合同)数、协议合同金额数均不含对外借款。

Note: The indices of new signed agreements (contracts) on foreign capital to be utilized and total amount of agreements & contracts exclude foreign loans.

15－3 国际旅游人数和外汇收入（1985－2004年）
Number of International Tourists and Foreign Exchange Earnings (1985-2004)

年 份 Year	接待旅游人数(人次) Number of Tourists (person-time)	#外国人 Foreigners	#港澳台同胞 Compatriots from Hong Kong, Macao and Taiwan	旅游外汇收入(万美元) Foreign Exchange Earnings from Tourism (USD 10 000)	平均每人逗留天数(天) Average Staying Period Per Capita (day)
1985	49508	40460	8370	527	2.1
1986	55152	44290	8904	860	1.7
1987	60894	52177	8253	1063	1.5
1988	64181	45193	18711	1281	1.5
1989	41248	21454	19595	1027	1.6
1990	69609	19913	49570	1823	1.3
1991	81745	29625	51950	2354	1.6
1992	141165	52949	88050	3997	1.3
1993	135596	59140	76025	4819	1.4
1994	138593	93408	44180	5432	1.5
1995	142892	93625	48942	6333	2.0
1996	161761	108163	53238	7090	2.3
1997	259414	154919	103720	10548	2.7
1998	163738	116288	47211	8837	3.2
1999	184936	133629	51173	9726	3.2
2000	266081	192863	73218	13837	3.2
2001	313254	219214	94040	16341	3.1
2002	461484	310934	150550	21802	2.7
2003	234521	181744	52777	11323	2.8
2004	434423	338892	95531	20308	2.7

15－4 对外承包工程和劳务合作（1985－2004年）
Contracted Projects and Labor Cooperation With Foreign Countries and Territories (1985-2004)

单位：万美元 (USD 10 000)

年份 Year	签订合同数(个) Number of Contracts (unit)	合同金额 Value of Contracts	实际完成营业额 Value of Business Fulfilled
1985	9	2109	572
1986	18	1571	337
1987	15	1540	572
1988	13	2640	2683
1989	27	2605	2574
1990	14	2971	2189
1991	16	4329	2436
1992	19	3765	2896
1993	13	9440	2704
1994	45	4106	4132
1995	33	4032	3757
1996	35	6654	3160
1997	22	2607	2725
1998	24	1969	3203
1999	235	4591	3842
2000	231	9232	5806
2001	232	11590	6700
2002	117	12200	7959
2003	94	13450	8810
2004	81	14805	10078

15－5 按商品类别分的海关进出口总值（2003－2004年）
Total Imports and Exports by Commodity Category (Customs Statistics) (2003-2004)

单位：万美元 (USD 10 000)

商品类别	Categories of Commodities	进口 Import		出口 Exports	
		2003	2004	2003	2004
总　值	**Total Value**	**100979**	**176616**	**158509**	**209119**
活动物、动物产品	Live Animals and Animal Products	83	68	2916	3332
植物产品	Vegetables Fruits and Cereals	90	2947	1829	2082
动植物油脂及分解产品、精制食用油脂	Animal and Vegetable Oils Refined Edible Oils and Fats	211	597	195	152
食品、饮料、酒及醋；烟草及代用品的制品	Food, Beverage, Liquor and Vinegar; Tobacco and Tobacco Substitutes	79	45	1716	2309
矿产品	Minerals	8755	22921	2628	2280
化学工业及其相关工业的产品	Chemicals and Related Products	4843	5707	20873	26705
塑料及其制品、橡胶及其制品	Plastic and Related Products, Rubber and Related Products	3006	4029	2334	3710
生皮、皮革、毛皮及制品	Leather, Furs and Related Products; Cases and Bags, Handbags and Similar Containers	117	9	606	829
木及制品、木炭、软木、编制品	Wood and Wooden Products, Charcoal, Cork, Weave Works	30	79	347	270
木浆等、废纸、纸、纸板及其制品	Paper Pulp, Paper Waste, Paper, Paperboard and Related Products	607	911	66	105
纺织原料及纺织制品	Textile Materials and Products	269	478	10036	14144
鞋、帽、伞	Shoes, Hats and Umbrellas; Feather Products, Artificial Furs, Wigs	1	1	2050	1276
石料、石膏、水泥	Mineral Material Products, Ceramics Glass and Related Products	211	309	8055	11119
天然或养殖珍珠	Jewelry, Precious Metals and Related Products, Artificial Jewelry, Coins	4	6	13	34
贱金属及其制品	Base Metals and Related Products	7313	10640	14684	21858
机器、机械器具	Mechanical and Electrical Equipment Recorders, Video recorders and Accessories	46976	81084	35027	48699
车辆、航空器、船舶及运输设备	Vehicles, Aircraft, Ships and Related Transportation Equipment	17146	32586	51632	64905
光学、医疗等仪器；钟表、乐器	Optical and Medical Instruments, Clocks, Musical Instruments	11030	13466	2719	3819
杂项制品	Miscellaneous Products				2
艺术品	Art Works	206	731	781	1487
其　他	Others		1	2	4

15－6 按贸易方式分的海关进出口总值（2003－2004年）
Total Imports and Exports by Trade Pattern (Customs Statistics) (2003-2004)

单位：万美元 (USD 10 000)

指标	Item	进出口总值 Total Imports and Exports		进口 Imports		出口 Exports	
		2003	2004	2003	2004	2003	2004
全市总计	**Total**	**259488**	**385735**	**100979**	**176616**	**158509**	**209119**
一般贸易	General Trade	228541	332498	85517	146229	143024	186269
国家间国际组织无偿援助、赠送	Donation of International Associations	117	100	10		107	100
其他境外捐赠物资	Other Donation Abroad	30	53	30	53		
来料加工装配贸易	Processing and Assembly with Imported Material	310	593	132	236	178	357
进料加工贸易	Processing Trade with Imported Material	19651	29299	5536	7317	14115	21982
边境小额贸易	Frontier Petty Trade		34				34
对外承包工程出口货物	Exported Goods on Contracted Projects with Foreign Countries	1045	251			1045	251
外商投资企业作为投资进口的设备物品	Imported Equipment and Materials as Investment of Foreign Funded Investment Enterprises for Processing and Sold Inside Country	7210	19699	7210	19699		
保税仓库进出境货物	Import and Export Goods from Bonded Warehouse	2075	2587	2065	2586	10	1
出口加工区进口设备	Imported Equipment for Manufacture and Export Zone	306	263	306	263		
其　他	Others	203	358	173	233	30	125

15－7 按国别（地区）分的海关进出口总值（2003－2004年）
Imports and Exports by Region (Customs Statistics) (2003-2004)

单位：万美元 (USD 10 000)

国别（地区）	Region	进出口总额 Total Imports and Exports		进口总额 Imports		出口总额 Exports	
		2003	2004	2003	2004	2003	2004
总计	**Total**	**259488**	**385735**	**100979**	**176616**	**158509**	**209119**
亚洲	**Asia**						
#阿富汗	Afghanistan	574	543			574	543
孟加拉国	Bangladesh	846	766	1	2	845	764
缅甸	Burma	9594	7222	38		9556	7222
香港	Hong Kong	7166	10174	1317	562	5849	9612
印度	India	9889	16862	5024	9136	4865	7726
印度尼西亚	Indonesia	7939	10825	103	647	7836	10178
伊朗	Iran	15555	8264	237	251	15318	8013
以色列	Israel	394	329	163	56	231	273
日本	Japan	54534	76752	42784	59090	11750	17662
老挝	Laos	2977	1028			2977	1028
澳门	Macao	37	287			37	287
马来西亚	Malaysia	4053	4959	1227	1444	2826	3515
巴基斯坦	Pakistan	5097	6283	…	…	5097	6283
菲律宾	The Philippines	5262	6055	160	118	5102	5937
卡塔尔	Qatar	177	104	63	100	114	4
沙特阿拉伯	Saudi Arabia	1294	1407	126	73	1168	1334
新加坡	Singapore	1671	1775	654	445	1017	1330
韩国	South Korea	10037	14403	3527	6751	6510	7652
斯里兰卡	Sri Lanka	582	842	…		582	842
叙利亚	Syria	717	1102			717	1102
泰国	Thailand	3920	4790	837	792	3083	3998
土耳其	Turkey	1638	3756	334	1588	1304	2168
阿拉伯酋长国	United Arab Emirates	1620	1860		…	1620	1860
越南	Vietnam	5586	12575		2	5586	12573
中国	People's Republic of China	843	1842	843	1842		
中国台湾	Taiwan, China	10813	11610	9515	10104	1298	1506
非洲	**Africa**						
#阿尔及利亚	Algeria	409	270			409	270
吉布提	Djibouti	262	232			262	232
埃及	Egypt	165	800	…	1	165	799
加纳	Ghana	228	498	28	249	200	249
几内亚	Guinea-Bissau	208	255			208	255
摩洛哥	Morocco	151	125			151	125
尼日利亚	Nigeria	7336	8775		…	7336	8775
南非	South Africa	1449	2039	663	545	786	1494
苏丹	Sudan	98	314			98	314

15-7 续表 CONTINUED

单位：万美元 (USD 10 000)

国别（地区）	Region	进出口总额 Total Imports and Exports		进口总额 Imports		出口总额 Exports	
		2003	2004	2003	2004	2003	2004
坦桑尼亚	Tanzania	246	100			246	100
多哥	Togo	513	1153			513	1153
布基纳法索	Burkina Faso	216	169	…		216	169
欧洲	**Europe**						
#比利时	Belgium	1177	2184	107	662	1070	1522
丹麦	Denmark	778	726	283	109	495	617
英国	UK	3911	7892	1953	4606	1958	3286
德意志联邦共和国	Germany	18269	37523	9799	24537	8470	12986
法国	France	1458	3383	494	1942	964	1441
爱尔兰	Ireland	58	71	18	28	40	43
意大利	Italy	4251	6326	2025	2764	2226	3562
荷兰	Netherlands	3661	6323	347	866	3314	5457
希腊	Greece	727	1258			727	1258
葡萄牙	Portugal	220	472	1	28	219	444
西班牙	Spain	2206	7211	340	5011	1866	2200
奥地利	Austria	619	734	557	593	62	141
芬兰	Finland	362	1126	121	495	241	631
匈牙利	Hungary	52	155	24	16	28	139
挪威	Norway	307	1029	23	426	284	603
波兰	Poland	1098	1462	86	155	1012	1307
瑞典	Sweden	3587	4380	3222	3384	365	996
瑞士	Switzerland	1255	1516	888	995	367	521
白俄罗斯	Belorussia	36	79		54	36	25
俄罗斯	Russia	1551	2739	394	1175	1157	1564
拉丁美洲	**Latin America**						
#阿根廷	Argentina	552	1627	8	3	544	1624
巴西	Brazil	1618	3472	1006	3044	612	428
智利	Chile	898	1293	657	842	241	451
哥伦比亚	Colombia	460	613			460	613
古巴	Cuba	20	12			20	12
墨西哥	Mexico	1801	2250	1	50	1800	2200
秘鲁	Peru	1064	6349	446	5257	618	1092
北美洲	**North America**						
#加拿大	Canada	2523	5971	848	3851	1675	2120
美国	USA	21708	39446	7573	18787	14135	20659
大洋洲	**Oceania**						
#澳大利亚	Australia	2957	5150	1850	2941	1107	2209
新西兰	New Zealand	346	677	17	148	329	529

15－8 海关出口主要商品数量和金额（2003－2004年）
Main Exported Commodities in Volume and Value (Custom Statistics) (2003-2004)

单位：万美元 (USD 10 000)

品名	Name	数量 Volume		金额 Value	
		2003	2004	2003	2004
鲜冻猪肉（吨）	Fresh Frozen Pork (ton)	1744	4666	216	708
蔬菜（吨）	Vegetables (ton)	7313	7648	925	1058
干豆（吨）	Dried Pulse (ton)	159		8	
茶叶（吨）	Tea (ton)	10590	12354	644	760
猪肉罐头（吨）	Canned Pork (ton)	3478	5072	399	569
蘑菇罐头（吨）	Canned Mushroom (ton)	4480	4671	328	366
啤酒（升）	Beer (liter)	26712		1	
猪鬃（吨）	Bristle (ton)	1682	1467	1035	940
肠衣（吨）	Casings (ton)	3029	2223	1272	1333
填衣用羽毛、羽绒（吨）	Feathers and Dawn for Stuffing (ton)	620	834	383	310
药材（吨）	Medical Materials (ton)	656	640	128	109
生丝（吨）	Raw Silk (ton)	1167	922	1643	1705
黏土及其他耐火矿物（吨）	Clay and Other Refractory Minerals (ton)	228578	149234	2011	1656
重晶石（吨）	Barite (ton)	20457	27261	162	220
合成有机染料（吨）	Synthetic Organic Dyestuffs (ton)	610	263	137	131
医药品（吨）	Medical and Pharmaceutical Products (ton)	3111	2578	3704	4248
家用或装饰用木制品（吨）	Wood Products for Household Use and Decoration (ton)	93	499	18	76
纸及纸板（未切成形的）（吨）	Paper and Paperboard in Rolls (ton)	160	182	17	12
纺织纱线、织物及制品	Textile Yarn Woven Fabrics and Related Products (value)			9187	12966
水泥（吨）	Cement (ton)	4315	6036	51	58
玻璃制品	Glass Products (value)			774	1090
家用陶瓷器（吨）	Porcelain and Pottery Ware for Household Use (ton)	4044	6851	601	1117
硅铁（吨）	Ferrosilicon (ton)	20031	4000	982	317
钢胚及精锻件（吨）	Steel Embryo and Refined Casted Elements (ton)	109	28666	37	1275
钢材（吨）	Rolled Steel (ton)	1234	2817	92	266
铜（吨）	Copper (ton)	53	16	41	35
未锻造的铝及铝材（吨）	Unwrought Aluminum and Rolled Aluminum (ton)	33522	28827	6274	6518
未锻造的锌及锌合金（吨）	Unwrought Zinc and Zinc Alloys (ton)	20336	6901	1767	760
未锻造的锰（吨）	Unwrought Manganese (ton)	7692	18330	790	2575
钢铁或铜制标准紧固件（吨）	Standard Fastener Made of Steel Iron or Copper (ton)	174	397	33	57
不锈钢厨具、餐具等家用电器（吨）	Steel Kitchen wares and Dish wares (ton)	214	291	91	134
手用或机用工具（吨）	Hand Tools and Tools for Machines (ton)	5382	7181	784	1127
锁（吨）	Locks (ton)	286	333	66	85
纺织机械	Textile Machinery (value)			48	86
金属加工机床（台）	Metal Processing Machine Tools (set)	139350	174196	327	400
自动数据处理设备及其部件（万个）	Auto Data Processors and Assemblies (10 000 units)	12	2	57	18

15-8 续表 CONTINUED

单位：万美元 (USD 10 000)

品名	Name	数量 Volume 2003	数量 Volume 2004	金额 Value 2003	金额 Value 2004
自动数据处理设备的零件（吨）	Parts of Auto Data Processors (ton)	27	36	8	20
轴承(万个)	Bearings (10 000 units)	141	241	81	98
电动机及发电机(万个)	Electric Motors and Power Generators (10 000 units)	110	216	240	142
静止式变流器（万个）	Immobile Transducers (10 000 units)	44	193	273	386
原电池(万个)	Primary Batteries (10 000 units)	23673	27457	1265	1311
蓄电池（万个）	Electric Calculator (10 000 units)	4	2	30	16
扬声器(万个)	Loudspeakers (10 000 units)	17	1	63	2
录音机及收录(放)音组合机(万个)	Tape Recorders and Sound Recording Apparatus (10 000 sets)	25		29	
收音机(万个)	Radios (10 000 sets)	28	14	17	7
录放机、像机及唱机的零件（吨）	Parts of Video and Sound Apparatus (ton)			789	2872
电视、收音机及无线电讯设备零附件(吨)	Accessories of TV Sets Radios and Radio Communication (ton)	132	571	213	563
电容器(吨)	Electrical Capacitors (ton)	57	17	90	25
印刷电路（万个）	Printing Circuits (10 000 units)	83	89	58	59
二极管、晶体管及类半导体器件(万个)	Diodes Transistors and Semiconductor Devices (10 000 units)	37546	43787	142	202
集成电路及微电子组（万个）	IC and Microcircuits (10 000 units)	41	26	29	20
电线和电缆(吨)	Insulated Wires and Cables (ton)	357	586	88	155
汽车和汽车底盘(万个)	Motor Vehicles and Chassis (10 000 units)	1	7	1407	6010
汽车零件	Parts of Motor Vehicles (value)			998	1706
摩托车（个）	Motorcycles (unit)	1370085	1447889	43937	49609
自行车（个）	Bicycles(unit)	79960	62161	106	84
摩托车及自行车零件	Parts of Motorcycles and Bicycles(value)			4534	6869
船舶（个）	Ships (vehecle)	4	3	199	243
医疗仪器及器械	Medical Instruments and Appliances(value)			165	368
日用钟(万个)	Clocks (10 000 units)	44	96	58	224
家具	Furnitures (value)			11	321
床垫、寝具及类似品	Mattress Mattess and Related Products (value)			101	104
灯具、照明及类似品	Lighting Apparatus and Related Products (value)			113	143
旅行用品及箱包	Travelling Articles and Cases (value)			241	385
服装及衣着附件	Clothing and Accessories (value)			2723	4371
鞋类	Shoes (value)			1832	1165
塑料制品(吨)	Plastic Products (ton)	1775	2280	293	364
玩具	Toys (value)			208	255
圣诞用品（吨）	Christmas Articles (ton)	66	132	22	22
贵金属或包贵金属的首饰（克）	Jewelry Made of Noble Metal (g)	33740	409500	1	…
伞(万个)	Umbrellas (10 000 units)	177	39	168	23
鬃刷(万个)	Bristle Brushes (10 000 units)	1490	1512	150	157
机电产品	Mechanical and Electrical Products (value)			92675	122540

15－9 海关进口主要商品数量和金额（2003－2004年）
Main Imported Commodities in Volume and Value (Custom Statistics) (2003-2004)

单位：万美元 (USD 10 000)

品名	Name	数量 Volume 2003	数量 Volume 2004	金额 Value 2003	金额 Value 2004
食用植物油（吨）	Edible Vegetable Oil (ton)	4905	13022	201	589
天然橡胶（包括胶乳）（吨）	Natural Rubber (including Latex) (ton)	2879	2419	204	317
合成橡胶(吨)	Synthetic Rubber (including Latex) (ton)	495	1121	159	329
铁矿砂及其精矿（吨）	Iron Ore and Refined Ore (ton)	1443507	1889977	5036	15606
锰矿砂及其精矿（吨）	Manganese Ore and Refined Ore (ton)	16063	43230	116	502
铬矿砂及其精矿（吨）	Chromium Ore and Refined Ore (ton)	136978	159281	1331	3167
氧化铝（吨）	Aluminum Oxide (ton)	10500		173	
成品油（吨）	Petroleum Products Refined (ton)	460	4063	170	384
乙二醇（吨）	Ethylene Glycol (ton)	1998	5102	93	432
医药品（吨）	Pharmaceutical Products (ton)	12	3	396	259
合成有机染料（吨）	Synthetic Organic Dyestuffs (ton)	134	121	109	123
钛白粉（吨）	Titanium White (ton)	528	516	101	99
聚合物油漆及清漆（吨）	Polymer Paint (ton)	556	136	201	83
感光材料	Sensitive Material			22	0.03
初级形状的塑料（吨）	Plastic in Primary Shape (ton)	16648	10450	1414	1456
非泡沫塑料的板、片、膜、箔（吨）	Sheet, Film and Foil Made of Foam Plastic (ton)	456	201	262	118
农药（吨）	Pesticides (ton)	13	0.2	11	0.08
纸及纸板（未切成形的）（吨）	Paper and Paperboard Unchopped (ton)	3247	3426	490	636
废钢（吨）	Waste Steel (ton)	309	725	6	14
钢材（吨）	Rolled Steel (ton)	48242	41853	3283	2944
钢铁制标准坚固件（吨）	Standard Fastener Made of Steel (ton)	1367	2850	1207	2402
未锻造的铜及铜材（吨）	Unforged Copper and Rolled Copper (ton)	563	112	113	54
废铜（吨）	Waste Copper (ton)	6300	1381	235	75
未锻造的铝及铝材（吨）	Unforged Aluminum and Rolled Aluminum (ton)	7681	15018	1278	3072
废铝（吨）	Waste Aluminum (ton)	388	949	12	42
钢铁或铝制结构体及其部件（吨）	Structure and Relative Parts Made of Steel or Aluminum (ton)	112	56	27	18
钢铁或铝制绞股线、缆及类似品(吨)	Wires and Relative Products Made of Steel or Aluminum (ton)	271	200	125	133
活塞式内燃机的零件（吨）	Parts of Piston Combustion Engines (ton)	7843	11249	8964	12988
液泵及液体提升机（个）	Liquid Pumps and Elevators (set)	132841	261209	651	3064
制冷设备用压缩机（个）	Compressors for Refrigerating Equipment (set)	1131	42907	67	508
冷冻机及制冷设备	Refrigerators and Refrigerating Equipment			87	40

15-9 续表 CONTINUED

单位：万美元 (USD 10 000)

品名	Name	数量 Volume		金额 Value	
		2003	2004	2003	2004
机械提升搬运装设备及零件	Mechanical Elevators for Transport and Relative Parts			351	510
建筑及采矿用机械	Machinery for Construction and Mining			394	140
食品加工机械	Machinery for Food Processing			262	559
印刷装订机械	Machinery for Printing and Binding			441	623
纺织机械	Textile Machinery			178	104
金属加工机床（个）	Machine Tools (set)	309	448	4925	6165
金属冶炼锻造设备及零件	Metal Smelting and Forging Equipment and Relative Parts			131	645
金属轧机及零件	Metal Mills and Relative Parts			194	239
玻璃热加工机械	Machinery for Glass Hot Processing			807	804
橡胶或塑料加工机械	Machinery for Rubber or Plastic Processing			495	707
型模及金属铸造用型箱	Casting Molds for Metal Forging			1559	2847
阀门（个）	Valves (unit)	175511	680678	283	602
自动数据处理及其部件（个）	Automatic Data Processing Machines and Components (set)	9651	8200	829	1670
自动数据处理设备的零件	Parts of Data Processing Machines			485	1032
电动机及发电机（台）	Electric Motors and Generators (set)	3524749	5267708	337	631
变压、整流、电感器及零件	Transformers, Rectifiers, Inductancers and Relative Parts			243	293
焊接机器及零件	Welders and Relative Parts			249	982
手持或车载无线电话机（个）	Hand or Car Wireless Telephones (unit)	1530		34	
录放机、像机及唱机的零附件（吨）	Parts of Video and Sound Apparatus (ton)	36	81	582	1158
电视收音机及无线电讯设备的零附件（吨）	Accessories of TV Sets, Radios and Radio Communication (ton)	24	26	763	678
电容器（吨）	Electrical Capacitors (ton)	15	19	149	145
印刷电路（个）	Printing Circuits (unit)	756178	1023610	147	309
通断及保护电路装置	Breaking-off and Safety Circuit Sets			491	1243
二极管晶体管及类似半导体器件（个）	Diodes Transistors and Semiconductor Devices (unit)	138221638	161120222	290	317
集成电路及微电子组件（个）	IC and Microcircuits (unit)	9195227	11728512	502	621
电线和电缆（吨）	Insulated Wires and Cables	448	315	347	317
汽车和汽车底盘（个）	Motor Vehicles and Chassis (unit)	3871	260	6169	1396
汽车零件	Parts of Motor Vehicles			10913	31046
医疗仪器及器械	Medical Instruments and Appliances			2702	2468
计量检测分析自控仪器及器具	Measuring, Checking and Analyzing Auto-controlling Apparatus			7768	10337
塑料制品（吨）	Plastic Products (ton)	330	536	247	465
机电产品	Mechanical and Electrical Products			77728	131620
高新技术产品	High-tech Products			19679	24459

15－10 利用外资情况（2003－2004年）
Utilization of Foreign Capital (2003-2004)

指　　标	Item	2003	2004
新签利用外资协议（合同）数（个）	**Number of New Signed Agreements and Contracts on Foreign Capital to Be Utilized (unit)**	**218**	**281**
#外商直接投资	Foreign Direct Investment	187	258
外商其他投资	Other Foreign Investment	23	23
协议（合同）额（万美元）	**Total Amount of Agreements and Contracts (USD 10 000)**	**71397**	**66621**
#外商直接投资	Foreign Direct Investment	55301	66315
外商其他投资	Other Foreign Investment	353	306
实际利用外资额（万美元）	**Total Amount of Foreign Capital Actually Utilized (USD 10 000)**	**56654**	**68214**
对外借款	Foreign Loans	25381	27462
外商直接投资	Foreign Direct Investment	31112	40508
外商其他投资	Other Foreign Investment	161	244

15－11 对外承包工程、劳务合作和设计咨询（2003－2004年）
Contracted Projects, Labor Cooperations and Design & Consultation with Foreign Countries and Territories (2003-2004)

指　　标	Item	2003	2004
签订合同数（个）	**Number of Contracts (unit)**	**94**	**81**
对外承包工程	Contracted Projects	8	11
对外劳务合作	Labor Cooperation	85	67
设计咨询	Design and Consultation	1	3
合同金额（万美元）	**Value of Contract (USD 10 000)**	**13450**	**14805**
对外承包工程	Contracted Projects	11747	11961
对外劳务合作	Labor Cooperation	1678	1586
设计咨询	Design and Consultation	25	1258
实际完成营业额（万美元）	**Value of Business Fulfilled (USD 10 000)**	**8810**	**10078**
对外承包工程	Contracted Projects	6514	8045
对外劳务合作	Labor Cooperation	2287	1983
设计咨询	Design and Consultation	9	50
劳务输出（人）	**Labor Exported (person)**	**2608**	**2751**
#技术人员	Technicians	550	800

15－12 外商直接投资项目(企业)数和投资额（2003－2004年）

单位：个、万美元

指 标	Item	签定项目(合同)数 Number of Projects with Contracts Signed		
		2003	2004	至当年底累计 Year-end Accumulation
全市总计	**Total**	**187**	**258**	**3748**
按投资方式分	**By Investment Mode**			
合资经营	Joint Venture	80	109	2045
合作经营	Cooperative Operation	14	13	240
独资经营	Foreign Enterprises	92	135	1461
股份制	Share Holding	1	1	2
其 他	Others			
按行业分	**By Sector**			
第一产业	Primary Industry	8	3	54
第二产业	Secondary Industry	103	155	2463
工 业	Industry	97	145	2267
建筑业	Construction	2	10	196
第三产业	Tertiary Industry	76	100	1231
交通运输、仓储及邮电通讯业	Transportation, Storage, Postal and Telecommunication Services	4	8	68
批发零售贸易及餐饮业	Wholesale Retail Trade and Catering Trade	17	21	180
金融保险业	Finance and Insurance			
房地产业	Real Estate	22	37	462
社会服务业	Social Services	28		483
卫生体育和社会福利业	Health Care, Sports and Social Welfare			1
教育文化艺术和广播电影电视业	Education, Culture & Arts, Radio, Film and Television	3	2	14
其他行业	Other Sectors	2		23
按主要国别(地区)分	**By Country (Region)**			
澳门	Macao	3	2	38
台湾	Taiwan	26	32	691
日本	Japan	2	14	185
美国	United States	23	32	423
加拿大	Canada	3	5	72
香港	Hong Kong	79	90	1691
新西兰	New Zealand	1		11
新加坡	Singapore	4	15	123
马来西亚	Malaysia	1	3	37
澳大利亚	Australia	6	6	44
法国	France	1		24
英国	United Kingdom	3	2	42
瑞典	Sweden			6
韩国	Korea Rep	6	9	54
印度尼西亚	Indonesia		2	13
泰国	Thailand	2	3	44
比利时	Belgium			3
瑞士	Switzerland		1	4

注：本表当年底累计数据均为1998年开始的累计数。

Number and Value of Foreign Direct Investment (2003-2004)

(unit, USD 10 000)

外商协议投资额 Foreign Investment Through Agreements			实际利用外资额 Foreign Capital Actually Utilized		
2003	2004	至当年底累计 Year-end Accumulation	2003	2004	至当年底累计 Year-end Accumulation
55301	**66315**	**684091**	**31112**	**40508**	**368655**
22814	23280	317535	17398	25315	228998
13021	2331	105143	3951	3842	54228
19315	36346	253734	6727	10032	80930
151	658	3979	151	495	646
	3700	3700		824	3853
1096	118	6590	55	67	1554
25279	42751	407304	13897	22424	126035
23408	39690	367288	12305	22379	123737
1076	3061	40016	31	45	2298
28926	23446	270197	17160	18017	89205
2942	1502	20091	461	142	5577
1083	-714	17406	936	166	166
	250	250	3385		3385
20304	18917	158422	9659	14591	52348
4145	1082	50821	1879		12466
	43	58			54
422		1359	799	111	2103
30	2366	21790	41	3007	13106
840	235	5223	68	233	690
838	1672	35013	833	501	10029
110	2638	65145	1030	2112	29687
6208	9563	71098	4378	2269	19656
24	483	5281	117	29	1726
25842	26337	313906	11227	13401	75498
38		148			126
4019	2069	26624	895	3514	11499
78	123	6173	23	1318	1531
2184	1351	6495	397	427	2104
207	306	4040	75	87	2039
2257	729	19835	403	539	11596
		2268	7		1451
321	2710	7340	235	91	1209
30	296	1366			75
977	-138	6622	752	123	1049
		167			104
622	6	3099	622	6	4033

Note: All data of year-end accumulation are summed from 1998.

15－13 外商投资企业生产经营和财务情况（2003－2004年）
Statistics on Production, Business and Finance of Foreign-Funded Enterprises (2003-2004)

单位：万元 (10 000 yuan)

指　　标	Item	2003	2004
调查企业数（个）	Number of Surveyed Enterprises (unit)	905	929
#第一产业	Primary Industry	5	2
第二产业	Secondary Industry	517	515
第三产业	Tertiary Industry	383	412
#港澳台商投资企业	Enterprises with Funds from Hong Kong, Macao and Taiwan	447	437
协议总投资额（万美元）	Total Investment on Contracts (USD 10 000)	739758	791125
#协议外商总投资额	Total Foreign Investment on Contracts	386009	406848
当年外商实际投资额（万美元）	Actual Foreign Investment in Current Year (USD 10 000)	31112	28069
实际现金投资	Cash Investment	29592	27239
实际实物投资	Available Objects as Investment	574	636
无形资产作价投资	Intangible Assets as Investment	946	194
注册资本金总额（万美元）	Total Registered Capital (USD 10 000)	428624	497839
中　方	Chinese Participant	189575	214561
外　方	Foreign Participant	239049	283278
工业总产值（现价）	Gross Output Value of Industry (current prices)	3509214	4970253
主营业务收入	Major Business Revenue	3847232	5738241
销售（营业）成本	Business Cost	3026739	4462820
销售（营业）税金及附加	Business Tax and Extra Charges	61262	103427
其他业务收入	Other Business Revenue	51256	59546
利润总额	Total After-tax Profits	275735	457143
资产总计	Total Assets	7587154	9737129
负债总计	Total Liabilities	4620336	5768496
#流动负债	Circulating Liabilities	3050454	4177934
长期负债	Long Term Liabilities	1430995	1528837

15－14 旅游事业发展情况（2003－2004年）
Statistics on Tourism (2003-2004)

指　　标	Item	2003	2004
国际旅游者人数（人次）	**International Tourists (person-time)**	**234521**	**434423**
外国人	Foreigners	181744	338892
#日本	Japan	36152	60153
新加坡	Singapore	3827	8505
泰国	Thailand	2321	4251
美国	United States	38905	91903
加拿大	Canada	4681	6384
法国	France	4262	11820
英国	United Kingdom	18186	20302
德国	Germany	16639	18315
意大利	Italy	1179	2611
澳大利亚	Australia	5398	9141
港澳同胞	Compatriots from Hong Kong and Macao	27418	56899
台湾同胞	Compatriots from Taiwan	25359	38632
来渝旅游者平均逗留天数(天)	Average Period Tourists Staying in Chongqing (day)	2.8	2.7
外国人	Foreigners	2.9	2.8
港澳同胞	Compatriots from Hong Kong and Macao	2.6	2.4
台湾同胞	Compatriots from Taiwan	2.4	2.4
旅行社组织国内居民出境旅游人数（万人次）	**Outbound Tourism of Domestic Residents through Travel Agencies (10 000 person-times)**	**27.40**	**40.26**
国内旅游者人数（万人次）	**Domestic Tourists (10 000 person-times)**	**4262.80**	**5235.60**
旅游收入	**Earnings from Tourism**		
国际旅游外汇收入(万美元)	Foreign Exchange Earnings from Tourism (USD 10 000)	11323	20308
国内旅游收入(亿元)	Income from Domestic Tourism (100 million yuan)	194.52	242.92
星级饭店数(个)	**Number of Tourist Hotel (unit)**	**148**	**168**
年末旅行社数（个）	**Number of Travel Agencies at Year-end (unit)**	**203**	**212**
国际旅行社	International Travel Agencies	23	23
国内旅行社	Domestic Travel Agencies	180	189
年末旅行社职工人数（人）	**Number of Staff and Workers of Travel Agencies at Year-end (person)**	**4250**	**4083**
国际旅行社	International Travel Agencies	1514	1803
国内旅行社	Domestic Travel Agencies	2736	2280

15－15 星级饭店基本情况（2003－2004年）
Basic Statistics on Tourist Hotels (2003-2004)

指　　标	Item	2003	2004
星级饭店数（个）	**Number of Tourist Hotels (unit)**	**148**	**168**
按星级分	By Star Level		
#五星级	5-star	2	4
四星级	4-star	17	23
三星级	3-star	54	64
按注册类型分	By Registration		
内　资	Domestic Funded	139	158
#国　有	State-owned	74	72
集　体	Collective-owned	19	21
私　营	Private	31	41
股份制	Share-holding	11	16
外商及港澳台投资	Foreign-funded and Funded from Hong Kong, Macao and Taiwan	9	10
按饭店客房规模分	By Capacity		
#300间以上	With 300 Rooms and Over	5	33
200-299间	With 200-299 Rooms	14	33
100-199间	With 100-199 Rooms	45	67
99间以下	With Less Than 100 Rooms	84	35
星级饭店客房数（间）	**Number of Rooms in Tourist Hotels (unit)**	**16615**	**18878**
#五星级	5-star	907	1746
四星级	4-star	3587	4499
三星级	3-star	6544	7265
星级饭店床位数（张）	**Number of Beds in Tourist Hotels (unit)**	**30497**	**33948**
#五星级	5-star	1428	2627
四星级	4-star	5945	7568
三星级	3-star	12185	13416

15－16 重庆与国外友好城市交流（2003－2004年）
Communications with Foreign Sister Cities (2003-2004)

指　　标	Item	2003	2004
与国外结成友好城市累计数（个）	**Total Number of Foreign Sister Cities with Chongqing (unit)**	**11**	**14**
出访交流考查	**People Sent for Study Tour**		
批　数	Lots	11	11
人　次	Person-time	127	167
派出进修生	**Sent Abroad to Engage in Advanced Studies**		
批　数	Lots		2
人　次	Person-time		32
接待来访团组	**Foreign Institutions Visiting Chongqing**		
批　数	Lots	7	8
人　次	Person-time	83	49

15－17 风景名胜区（2004年）
Scenic Spots (2004)

名称 Name	级别 Grade	主要特点 Main Characteristics	面积 (平方公里) Area (sq.km)	#林地 Forest	#中心游览区 Central Sight-seeing	#水面 Water Area	地址 Address
长江三峡	国家级	江峡景观、文化遗址	480				奉节县、巫山县
缙云山	国家级	森林自然景观	14	13	1		北碚区
北温泉	国家级	山水泉洞	0.568	0.471	0.094	0.003	北碚区
钓鱼城	国家级	宋古战场遗址	2.5	0.367	0.444	0.02	合川市
四面山	国家级	林湖石瀑	213.37	86.4	86	41	江津市
金佛山	国家级	原始珍稀森林	441				南川市
芙蓉江	国家级	溶洞溪河	100.35	61	23.92	11.1	武隆县
天坑地缝	省级	地缝式峡谷漏斗奇观	340				奉节县
张关溶洞	省级		49.14				渝北区
巫山小三峡	省级	山水峡谷	370				巫山县
南山、南泉	省级	林泉、抗战遗址	92.5				南岸区、巴南区
大足石刻	省级	石刻艺术文化	84				大足县
红池坝	省级	高山草场	358	317.8	30	10	巫溪县
百里竹海	省级	竹海景观	92.44	66.64		2	梁平县
青龙瀑布	省级	高位瀑布	60.13	25.2	8.31		万州区
小南海	省级	地震遗址湖泊	30	15.2	12	2.8	黔江区
小溪	省级	巴文化、天生桥	25	2	19	4	涪陵区
渝北统景	省级	温泉峡猿	14.5	6	4	1	渝北区
黑山-石林	省级	石林溪河	60		21.4	0.04	万盛区
黑石山-滚子坪	省级	石瀑山水林	125	100	65	10	江津市
巴岳山-西温泉	省级	森林温泉	51	26	15	10	铜梁县
长寿湖	省级	湖泊	58.7	3	2.25	53.45	长寿县
定明山-运河	省级	民居寺庙、人造运河	65	9.3	2	0.9	潼南县
歌乐山	省级	森林、历史纪念地	51	12.2	2	0.1	沙坪坝区
东温泉	省级	温泉溪河	58.7		1		巴南区
龙泉	省级		74				万州区
井沟	省级		191		12.3		忠县
青龙湖	省级	山林湖泊	55		5		璧山县
黄水	省级		117.5				石柱县
涞滩-双龙湖	县级	古镇寺庙、湖泊	16				合川市
金刀峡－胜天湖	县级	峡谷湖泊	50		1	0.6	北碚区
古剑山-清溪河	县级	山林溪河	50		5	2	綦江县
神田	县级		64				城口县
青龙峡	县级		45				城口县
方斗坪	县级		37				城口县
龙潭河	县级		34				城口县
崩溪河	县级		35				城口县
温泉	县级		52				开县
凤凰山	县级		4.1				开县
桃花源	县级		5		0.5		酉阳县
万寿山	县级		5				石柱县
官渡峡	县级		20				黔江区
骆来山	县级						江津市
碑槽山	县级						江津市

15－18 重点文物保护单位（2004年）
Main Cultural Relics（2004）

名　　称　　Name	时　代　　Era	地　址　　Address
古遗址		
龙骨坡遗址	更新世	巫山县庙宇镇
高家镇遗址	旧石器	丰都县高家镇
烟墩堡遗址	旧石器	丰都县汇集乡
玉溪遗址	新石器	丰都县高镇乡
大溪遗址	新石器	巫山县大溪镇
杠（音）洽井口遗址群	新石器至汉	忠县忠州镇
中坝遗址	新石器至汉	忠县杠（音）井镇
李家坝遗址	商周至汉	云阳县高阳镇
双堰塘遗址	商周至汉	巫山县大昌镇
涂山窑遗址	宋	南岸区黄桷垭镇新力村
古墓葬		
小田溪墓群	战国	涪陵区白涛镇
巴蔓子墓	战国至清	渝中区莲花池
荆竹坝岩棺群	汉	巫溪县荆竹坝
汇南墓群	汉、南北朝	丰都县汇南乡
石坎崖墓群	东汉	江津市凤场乡
雷劈石崖墓群	东汉	南川市太平场乡
双墙崖墓群	东汉	大足县邮亭镇
柏树林崖墓群	东汉	綦江县中峰镇
七拱嘴崖墓群	东汉	綦江县文龙乡
长沟崖墓群	东汉	江津市柏林镇
南屏墓群	东汉	合川市城南南津街
长孙无忌墓	唐	武隆县江口镇
沙坝子墓	宋	荣昌县许溪乡
高洞子墓群	南宋	永川市板桥镇
清溪苗王墓	明	秀山县清溪场镇
明玉珍睿陵	元、明	江北区洗布堂街
秦良玉陵园	清	石柱县大河乡
古建筑		
盘溪无铭阙	汉	江北区石马河镇
丁房阙	汉	忠县忠州镇
佑溪无铭阙	汉	忠县杠（音）井镇
白帝城	汉至清	奉节县草塘区
碑记桥	宋	涪陵区马武镇
岩溪桥	宋	合川市城北高石坎办事处
河包报恩寺塔	宋	荣昌县河包镇
钓鱼城	南宋、元	合川市城东钓鱼山上
龙崖城	南宋、元	南川市马嘴乡

15-18 续表1 CONTINUED-1

名　　称 Name	时　代 Era	地　　址 Address
磐石城	南宋、元	云阳县双江镇
多功城	南宋、元	渝北县鸳鸯镇
天生城	南宋、元	万州区周家坝
塔坪寺塔	宋、清	北碚区静观镇
独柏寺正殿	元	潼南县上和镇
净果寺	明	合川市古楼镇
龙兴寺正殿	明	潼南县小渡镇
宝轮寺正殿	明	沙坪坝区磁器口
铜梁武庙	明	铜梁县巴川镇
朝元寺牌坊	明	璧山县梅江乡
东华观藏经楼	明	渝中区凯旋路
江公享堂	明、清	江津市几江镇
缙云寺	明、清	北碚区缙云山
宝城寺	明、清	荣昌县昌元镇
铁佛寺	明、清	铜梁县巴川镇
板桥寺	明、清	合川市九岭乡
温泉寺	明、清	北碚区澄江镇
东水门及城墙	明、清	渝中区东水门段
通道门及城墙	明、清	渝中区七星岗
梁平文峰塔	明	梁平县梁山镇
湖广会馆	清	渝中区芭蕉园
张桓侯庙	清	云阳县水磨乡
石宝寨	清	忠县石宝镇
双桂堂	清	梁平县金带镇
大成殿	清	璧山县璧城镇
彭氏宗祠	清	云阳县里市乡
利济桥	清	江津市朱杨镇
彭氏民居	清	巴南区南泉镇
涂山寺	清	南岸区黄桷垭镇
合川文峰塔	清	合川市合阳镇
黄桷垭文峰塔	清	南岸区黄桷垭镇
塔子山文峰塔	清	江北区寸滩
觉林寺报恩塔	清	南岸区下浩觉林寺街
华岩寺	清	九龙坡区华岩镇
何氏百岁坊	清	璧山县青杠乡
石窟寺及石刻		
灰千岩崖画	汉以前	江津市四面山镇
潼南大佛寺摩崖造像	隋至宋	潼南县梓潼镇
临江岩摩崖造像	唐	忠县忠州镇

15-18 续表2 CONTINUED-2

名　　称 Name	时　代 Era	地　址 Address
尖子山摩崖造像	唐至宋	大足县宝山乡
北山摩崖造像	唐至宋	大足县龙岗镇、城东乡、石桌乡
白鹤梁题刻	唐至清	涪陵区崇义办事处
五硐岩摩崖造像	唐至清	潼南县塘坝镇
宝顶山摩崖造像	宋	大足县宝顶镇、石马镇
涞滩二佛寺摩崖造像	宋	合川市涞滩镇
舒成岩摩崖造像	宋	大足县中敖镇
妙高山摩崖造像	宋	大足县季家镇
西山碑	宋	万州区太白岩下高笋塘
罗汉寺古佛崖摩崖造像	宋	渝中区小什字
莲花石题刻	宋至清	江津市几江镇
弹子石摩崖造像	元	南岸区弹子石
石门大佛寺摩崖造像	明	江津市石门镇
朝源观道教造像	明	江津市四面山镇
大足千佛岩摩崖造像	明	大足县三驱镇千佛村
马龙山摩崖造像	民国	潼南县卧佛镇
近现代重要史迹		
杨沧白故居及墓	清（故居）、1984（墓）	巴南区木洞镇(故居)、东泉镇(墓)
法国水师兵营	1902年	南岸区弹子石
马跑教堂	1909年	大足县石马镇
余栋臣故居及墓	清	双桥区通桥镇
刘伯承故居	清	开县赵家镇
聂荣臻故居	清	江津市吴滩镇
赵世炎故居	清	酉阳县龙潭镇
杨闇公故居及墓	清（故居）、1987（墓）	潼南县双江镇(故居)、梓潼镇(墓)
张培爵烈士纪念碑及墓	1946年（碑）、1934年（墓）	渝中区沧白路(碑) 荣昌昌元镇公园(墓)
重庆“三・三一”惨案烈士墓	1927年	江北区五里店（群葬墓地）
国民党左派四川省党部暨重庆高中旧址	1927-1929年	渝中区解放东巷6号
桂园	1931年	渝中区上清寺
南腰界红三军司令部旧址	1934年	酉阳县李溪区南腰界乡
石壕红军烈士墓	1935年	綦江县石壕镇
中国西部科学院旧址	1935-1949年	北碚区朝阳街道
八路军重庆办事处旧址	1938-1946年	渝中区红岩村
黄山、南山陪都遗迹	1938-1946年	南岸区黄山干部疗养院内
林园	1938-1946年	沙坪坝区山洞街道
重庆郭沫若旧居既国民政府军事委员会政治部第三厅旧址	1938-1946年	渝中区天官府、沙坪坝区赖家桥
国民参政会旧址	1938-1946年	渝中区中华路
重庆大韩民国临时政府旧址	1938-1946年	渝中区莲花池

15-18 续表3 CONTINUED-3

名　　称 Name	时　代 Era	地　　址 Address
中苏文协旧址	1938-1947年	渝中区中山一路
重庆冯玉祥旧居	1939-1945年	九龙坡区后工、沙坪坝区陈家桥镇
育才学校旧址	1939-1945年	合川市草街镇
重庆美国大使馆旧址	1938-1946年	渝中区王家坡
重庆苏联大使馆旧址	1938-1946年	渝中区枇杷山
重庆陈独秀旧居	1939-1942年	江津市几江镇
《新华日报》馆及营业部旧址	1939-1947年	渝中区化龙桥（报馆）、民生路（营业部）
重庆沈钧儒旧居	1939-1949年	渝中区枣子岚垭
张自忠墓	1940年	北碚区北温泉镇
“六．五”隧道惨案旧址	1941年	渝中区磁器街、十八梯、石灰市隧道
重庆宋庆龄旧居	1942-1945年	渝中区两路口
重庆史迪威旧居	1942-1945年	渝中区嘉陵新村
重庆徐悲鸿旧居	1942-1946年	江北区大石坝
重庆老舍旧居	1943-1946年	北碚区天生街道
“中美合作所”集中营旧址	1943-1949年	沙坪坝区童家桥街道
重庆谈判旧址	1945年	渝中区中四路
中共代表团驻地旧址	1946年	渝中区中三路305号
四川革命先烈纪念碑	1946年	渝中区人民公园
邹容烈士纪念碑	1946年	渝中区南区公园
中国人民解放军第二野战军司令部旧址	1949年	秀山县中和镇
南泉革命烈士陵园	1953年	巴南区南泉镇西
人民解放纪念碑	1950年	渝区中解放碑地区
库里申科烈士墓	1958年	万州区西山公园
苏军烈士墓	1959年	渝中区鹅岭公园
邱少云烈士纪念碑	1962年	铜梁县巴川镇
近现代代表性建筑		
大昌民居	清	巫山县大昌镇
杨氏民居	清	潼南县双江镇
聚奎书院	清	江津市白沙镇
客寨桥	清	秀山县龙凤乡
江津中学	1906年	江津市几江镇
慈云寺	1927年	南岸区玄坛庙
菩提金刚塔	1930年	渝中区观音岩金刚塔
万县钟楼	1931年	万州区西山公园
交通银行旧址	1936年	渝中区打铜街
跳伞塔	1942年	渝中区大田湾体育场
若瑟堂	1946年	渝中区民生路
重庆人民大礼堂	1953年	渝中区人民路

15－19 全社会实际利用内资（2003－2004年）
Total Actual Utilization of Domestic Capital (2003-2004)

单位：万元 (10 000 yuan)

项　目	Item	2003	2004
总计	**Total**	**572766**	**868731**
按重庆市行政区划分	**By District (county)**		
万州区	Wanzhou District	10301	83292
涪陵区	Fuling District	26385	43794
渝中区	Yuzhong District	45827	76265
大渡口区	Dadukou District	306	5508
江北区	Jiangbei District	30994	35966
沙坪坝区	Shapingba District	18061	27064
九龙坡区	Jiulongpo District	58575	81319
南岸区	Nan'an District	31418	67830
北碚区	Beibei District	24956	25803
万盛区	Wansheng District	2176	4888
双桥区	Shuangqiao District	27500	380
渝北区	Yubei District	11634	28567
巴南区	Ba'nan District	11808	12187
黔江区	Qianjiang District	4165	8774
长寿区	Changshou District	4505	9650
綦江县	Qijiang County	11280	19475
潼南县	Tongnan County	2481	4140
铜梁县	Tongliang County	17855	16468
大足县	Dazu County	5151	12316
荣昌县	Rongchang County	10130	19980
璧山县	Bishan County	14840	46115
梁平县	Liangping County	3224	6590
城口县	Chengkou County	1652	4450
丰都县	Fengdu County	13526	7688
垫江县	Dianjiang County	11167	10454
武隆县	Wulong County	3043	1597
忠　县	Zhongxian County	9339	10585
开　县	Kaixian County	15778	16442
云阳县	Yunyang County	16278	15420
奉节县	Fengjie County	3825	3529
巫山县	Wushan County	150	425
巫溪县	Wuxi County	671	3952
石柱土家族自治县	Shizhu County	91	226
秀山土家族苗族自治县	Xiushan County	17188	13933
酉阳土家族苗族自治县	Youyang County	640	860
彭水苗族土家族自治县	Pengshui County	16064	60711
江津市	Jiangjin City	42984	22848
合川市	Hechuan City	22648	12097
永川市	Yongchuan City	15865	43603
南川市	Nanchuan City	4880	3540
不分区县	Transregional	3405	
按重庆三大经济区分组	**By Three Economic Spheres**		
都市发达经济圈	Advanced Economic Sphere	233579	360509
渝西经济走廊	Economic Corridor in West Chongqing	177790	205850
三峡库区生态经济区	Ecological Economic Zone in Three Gorges Reservoir Area	157992	302372
不分区县	Transregional	3405	

15-19 续表 CONTINUED

单位：万元 (10 000 yuan)

项　　目	Item	2003	2004
按内资来源分	**By Source of Domestic Capital**		
北　京	Beijing	74913	136726
天　津	Tianjin	1231	2918
河　北	Hebei	12897	9656
山　西	Shanxi	1307	5501
内蒙古	Inner Mongolia	32	152
辽　宁	Liaoning	4254	1173
吉　林	Jilin	2608	315
黑龙江	Heilongjiang	522	6053
上　海	Shanghai	45750	80758
江　苏	Jiangsu	18541	30591
浙　江	Zhejiang	98358	187869
安　徽	Anhui	2162	5234
福　建	Fujian	36450	69766
江　西	Jiangxi	5583	8447
山　东	Shandong	9041	19014
河　南	Henan	2434	16971
湖　北	Hubei	11940	23521
湖　南	Hunan	52208	19248
广　东	Guangdong	51049	61155
广　西	Guangxi	966	2405
海　南	Hainan	5385	807
四　川	Sichuan	112058	149949
贵　州	Guizhou	8166	6105
云　南	Yunnan	7860	12132
西　藏	Tibet	260	4
陕　西	Shaanxi	2212	6630
甘　肃	Gansu	262	730
青　海	Qinghai	100	37
宁　夏	Ningxia	200	250
新　疆	Xinjiang	4017	4614
按东、中、西部地区分	**By Eastern, Middle and Western Region**		
东部地区	Eastern Region	357869	600433
中部地区	Middle Region	78764	85290
西部地区	Western Region	136133	183008
按行业分	**By Sector**		
第一产业	Primary Industry	15393	18667
第二产业	Secondary Industry	261593	471589
采矿业	Mining and Quarrying	10927	26748
制造业	Manufacturing	210466	332037
电力、燃气及水的生产和供应业	Electricity, Gas & Water Production and Supply	22195	72883
建筑业	Construction	18005	39921
第三产业	Tertiary Industry	295780	378475
交通运输、仓储及邮政业	Transportation, Storage, Postal Services	21961	10580
信息传输、计算机服务和软件业	Information Transmission, Computer Service and Soft wares	4555	10658
批发与零售业	Wholesale and Retail Trade	89807	90569
住宿和餐饮业	Hotels and Restaurants	6596	4468
金融业	Financing	900	6679
房地产业	Real Estate	117425	205479
租赁与商务服务业	Renting and Business Activities	18198	7190
科学研究、技术服务与地质勘查业	Scientific Research, Technology Services and Geological Prospecting	4849	4075
水利、环境和公共设施管理业	Administration of Water Conservancy, Environment and Public Facilities	10846	11804
居民服务和其他服务业	Household Services and Other Services	1090	12291
教育	Education	8474	3945
卫生、社会保障和社会福利业	Health, Social Security and Social Welfare	2533	3073
文化、体育与娱乐业	Culture, Sports and Entertainment	7093	7014
公共管理与社会组织	Public Administration and Social Organizations	1453	650

15－20 利用内资（100万元以上项目）（2003－2004年）

单位：万元 (10 000 yuan)

项 目	Item	2003		
		项目合同（协议、计划）总资金 Total Capital on Agreements and Contracts	#外省投入 From Outside Chongqing	实际利用内资 Domestic Capital Actually Utilized
总 计	**Total**	**3434272**	**2633470**	**487207**
#固定资产投资	Investment in Fixed Assets	2745262	2013437	263248
按内资来源分	**By Source of Domestic Capital**			
北 京	Beijing	1168470	793199	70459
天 津	Tianjin	56200	56200	729
河 北	Hebei	16620	15971	10994
山 西	Shanxi	2000	955	955
内蒙古	Inner Mongolia			
辽 宁	Liaoning	4201	4201	3496
吉 林	Jilin	5000	5000	2400
黑龙江	Heilongjiang	100	40	40
上 海	Shanghai	557688	476177	39400
江 苏	Jiangsu	44165	37149	14295
浙 江	Zhejiang	406271	320043	85506
安 徽	Anhui	3100	3050	1080
福 建	Fujian	201472	179704	29399
江 西	Jiangxi	8850	8150	4650
山 东	Shandong	17477	17477	7635
河 南	Henan	2050	1000	322
湖 北	Hubei	39329	38745	5975
湖 南	Hunan	98205	75675	49893
广 东	Guangdong	83888	70625	43456
广 西	Guangxi	1100	1100	500
海 南	Hainan	5850	5772	5102
四 川	Sichuan	450756	362752	91841
贵 州	Guizhou	198450	103255	6620
云 南	Yunnan	11270	10420	6390
西 藏	Tibet	260	150	260
陕 西	Shaanxi	18800	18720	1120
甘 肃	Gansu			
青 海	Qinghai	100	40	100
宁 夏	Ningxia	7000	6400	200
新 疆	Xinjiang	9200	9200	3790
按东、中、西部地区分	**By Eastern, Middle and Western Region**			
东部地区	Eastern Region	2562302	1976518	310471
中部地区	Middle Region	158634	132615	65315
西部地区	Western Region	696936	512037	110821

Utilization of Domestic Capital (Project above 1 Million Yuan) (2003-2004)

单位：万元 (10 000 yuan)

项目	Item	2004 项目合同（协议、计划）总资金 Total Capital on Agreements and Contracts	#外省投入 From Outside Chongqing	实际利用内资 Domestic Capital Actually Utilized
总计	**Total**	**5480492**	**4603295**	**776839**
#固定资产投资	Investment in Fixed Assets	4072962	3548792	542079
按内资来源分	**By Source of Domestic Capital**			
北京	Beijing	1973071	1568702	134283
天津	Tianjin	57300	56900	2468
河北	Hebei	26598	23618	8498
山西	Shanxi	10162	8874	5021
内蒙古	Inner Mongolia			
辽宁	Liaoning	2560	2510	764
吉林	Jilin	200	200	200
黑龙江	Heilongjiang	18100	18100	5600
上海	Shanghai	366408	339578	78434
江苏	Jiangsu	88396	85708	26737
浙江	Zhejiang	1316343	1161962	173439
安徽	Anhui	22900	22900	4600
福建	Fujian	500387	321529	62452
江西	Jiangxi	28988	26512	6478
山东	Shandong	237600	237580	17767
河南	Henan	30910	21350	14710
湖北	Hubei	30215	27892	18535
湖南	Hunan	46550	42083	16495
广东	Guangdong	188105	147147	55460
广西	Guangxi	2600	2600	1985
海南	Hainan	100	100	100
四川	Sichuan	469309	429350	118927
贵州	Guizhou	7090	6600	4630
云南	Yunnan	34067	29567	9127
西藏	Tibet	393	393	1
陕西	Shaanxi	7750	7750	5588
甘肃	Gansu			
青海	Qinghai			
宁夏	Ningxia	7000	6400	200
新疆	Xinjiang	7390	7390	4340
按东、中、西部地区分	**By Eastern, Middle and Western Region**			
东部地区	Eastern Region	4756868	3945334	560402
中部地区	Middle Region	188025	167911	71639
西部地区	Western Region	535599	490050	144798

15-20 续表1

单位：万元 (10 000 yuan)

项　　目	Item	2003 项目合同（协议、计划）总资金 Total Capital on Agreements and Contracts	#外省投入 From Outside Chongqing	实际利用内资 Domestic Capital Actually Utilized
按行业分	**By Sector**			
第一产业	Primary Industry	77284	75394	9317
第二产业	Secondary Industry	1674948	1225587	239181
采矿业	Mining and Quarrying	17631	17631	8578
制造业	Manufacturing	606452	509385	196274
电力、燃气及水的生产和供应业	Electricity, Gas & Water Production and Supply	983795	633751	21879
建筑业	Construction	67070	64820	12450
第三产业	Tertiary Industry	1682040	1332489	349551
交通运输、仓储及邮政业	Transportation, Storage, Postal Services	257000	152000	19574
信息传输、计算机服务和软件业	Information Transmission, Computer Service and Soft wares	10400	9150	4555
批发与零售业	Wholesale and Retail Trade	88029	80065	52718
住宿和餐饮业	Hotels and Restaurants	27997	27403	6596
金融业	Financing			
房地产业	Real Estate	1156283	935685	112390
租赁与商务服务业	Renting and Business Activities	17300	15385	10065
科学研究、技术服务与地质勘查业	Scientific Research, Technology Services and Geological Prospecting	11562	6091	4536
水利、环境和公共设施管理业	Administration of Water Conservancy, Environment and Public Facilities	78120	73740	10821
居民服务和其他服务业	Household Services and Other Services	1940	1850	1090
教　育	Education	15404	13766	8474
卫生、社会保障和社会福利业	Health, Social Security and Social Welfare	9450	8850	2250
文化、体育与娱乐业	Culture, Sports and Entertainment	8055	8004	5142
公共管理与社会组织	Public Administration and Social Organizations	500	500	498
按登记注册类型分	**By Registration**			
国有企业	State-owned	339226	240426	27989
集体企业	Collective-owned	24909	24909	2476
股份合作企业	Cooperative Share Holding	980051	630007	17976
联营企业	Joint Ownership	1500	1500	850
有限责任公司	Limited Liabilities	1504812	1248055	235431
股份有限公司	Share-holding Ltd.	261085	230853	72171
私营企业	Private	173881	137662	82749
其他企业	Others	43000	30100	300
港、澳、台商投资企业	Funded by Hong Kong, Macao and Taiwan	1760	1760	900
外商投资企业	Foreign-funded			
个　人	Individual	95310	80283	45695
其　他	Others			
按合作方式分	**By Means of Co-operation**			
独资经营	Sole Investment	954959	946088	256444
合作投资	Cooperative Investment	2443675	1656594	222172
资产重组	Asset Recombination	15600	11800	400
经营权完全转让	Entire Transformation of Operation Right	5438	5438	5438
经营权部份转让	Part Transformation of Operation Right			
其　他	Others	14600	13550	2753

15-20 CONTINUED-1

单位：万元 (10 000 yuan)

项目	Item	2004 项目合同（协议、计划）总资金 Total Capital on Agreements and Contracts	#外省投入 From Outside Chongqing	实际利用内资 Domestic Capital Actually Utilized
按行业分	**By Sector**			
第一产业	Primary Industry	153903	151087	14446
第二产业	Secondary Industry	2493190	2073282	450656
采矿业	Mining and Quarrying	46765	44345	24766
制造业	Manufacturing	1123178	978161	318951
电力、燃气及水的生产和供应业	Electricity, Gas & Water Production and Supply	1201370	931370	71832
建筑业	Construction	121877	119406	35107
第三产业	Tertiary Industry	2833399	2378926	311737
交通运输、仓储及邮政业	Transportation, Storage, Postal Services	25902	25802	8986
信息传输、计算机服务和软件业	Information Transmission, Computer Service and Soft wares	17413	17413	2321
批发与零售业	Wholesale and Retail Trade	115301	98761	58046
住宿和餐饮业	Hotels and Restaurants	1390	1330	1330
金融业	Financing	28100	28030	6630
房地产业	Real Estate	2309603	1910222	197498
租赁与商务服务业	Renting and Business Activities	27497	6477	2745
科学研究、技术服务与地质勘查业	Scientific Research, Technology Services and Geological Prospecting	3500	2722	2995
水利、环境和公共设施管理业	Administration of Water Conservancy, Environment and Public Facilities	99934	84850	11364
居民服务和其他服务业	Household Services and Other Services	81183	81093	7783
教　育	Education	34420	34220	2720
卫生、社会保障和社会福利业	Health, Social Security and Social Welfare	9540	8940	2440
文化、体育与娱乐业	Culture, Sports and Entertainment	40616	40066	6229
公共管理与社会组织	Public Administration and Social Organizations	39000	39000	650
按登记注册类型分	**By Registration**			
国有企业	State-owned	329366	290986	56275
集体企业	Collective-owned	4048	3500	760
股份合作企业	Cooperative Share Holding	1255578	980710	77321
联营企业	Joint Ownership	3250	2025	1600
有限责任公司	Limited Liabilities	2244735	1845634	238746
股份有限公司	Share-holding Ltd.	851614	751103	163882
私营企业	Private	349898	307283	121131
其他企业	Others	43000	30100	4000
港、澳、台商投资企业	Funded by Hong Kong, Macao and Taiwan	1760	1760	330
外商投资企业	Foreign-funded			
个　人	Individual	394189	387363	112489
其　他	Others	3054	2831	305
按合作方式分	**By Means of Co-operation**			
独资经营	Sole Investment	2493458	2472093	486638
合作投资	Cooperative Investment	1743766	1159834	220077
资产重组	Asset Recombination	3400	3400	10
经营权完全转让	Entire Transformation of Operation Right	10188	8288	4308
经营权部份转让	Part Transformation of Operation Right			
其　他	Others	1229680	959680	65806

15-20 续表2

单位：万元 (10 000 yuan)

项目	Item	2003 项目合同（协议、计划）总资金 Total Capital on Agreements and Contracts	#外省投入 From Outside Chongqing	实际利用内资 Domestic Capital Actually Utilized
按重庆市行政区划分	**By District (county)**			
万州区	Wanzhou District	23429	23429	6151
涪陵区	Fuling District	49653	29620	19315
渝中区	Yuzhong District	71225	65437	31498
大渡口区	Dadukou District			
江北区	Jiangbei District	77390	76342	21811
沙坪坝区	Shapingba District	62802	62757	16423
九龙坡区	Jiulongpo District	350899	227049	54262
南岸区	Nan'an District	601200	521200	25950
北碚区	Beibei District	85346	72096	23096
万盛区	Wansheng District	3880	3880	1960
双桥区	Shuangqiao District	50000	27500	27500
渝北区	Yubei District	9043	6743	2703
巴南区	Ba'nan District	59431	55331	11454
黔江区	Qianjiang District	13560	13560	3641
长寿区	Changshou District	34350	18650	4200
綦江县	Qijiang County	12950	12950	10170
潼南县	Tongnan County	5500	5500	1695
铜梁县	Tongliang County	23930	23780	16430
大足县	Dazu County	11860	11300	4721
荣昌县	Rongchang County	15830	13760	8330
璧山县	Bishan County	103050	103050	14410
梁平县	Liangping County	13580	13440	2940
城口县	Chengkou County	5105	3805	1605
丰都县	Fengdu County	23338	18638	11648
垫江县	Dianjiang County	19344	16165	10403
武隆县	Wulong County	5096	4200	1485
忠县	Zhongxian County	57450	57450	8934
开县	Kaixian County	24560	23160	13735
云阳县	Yunyang County	50715	49565	15948
奉节县	Fengjie County	69460	69460	3068
巫山县	Wushan County			
巫溪县	Wuxi County	650	460	660
石柱县	Shizhu County			
秀山县	Xiushan County	40775	40775	16678
酉阳县	Youyang County	193	193	140
彭水县	Pengshui County	976725	626681	15800
江津市	Jiangjin City	154996	107172	41670
合川市	Hechuan City	100286	98101	15173
永川市	Yongchuan City	29891	29891	13315
南川市	Nanchuan City	6780	5380	4880
跨区县(不便于区分区县的)	Transregional	190000	95000	3405
按重庆三大经济区分	**By Three Economic Spheres**			
都市发达经济圈	Advanced Economic Sphere	1317336	1086955	187197
渝西经济走廊	Economic Corridor in West Chongqing	518953	442264	160254
三峡库区生态经济区	Ecological Economic Zone in Three Gorges Reservoir Area	1407983	1009251	136351
跨区县(不便于区分区县的)	Transregional	190000	95000	3405

15-20 CONTINUED-2

单位：万元 (10 000 yuan)

项目	Item	2004 项目合同（协议、计划）总资金 Total Capital on Agreements and Contracts	#外省投入 From Outside Chongqing	实际利用内资 Domestic Capital Actually Utilized
按重庆市行政划分	**By District (county)**			
万州区	Wanzhou District	457427	451545	78042
涪陵区	Fuling District	90850	85398	38456
渝中区	Yuzhong District	175337	160720	64972
大渡口区	Dadukou District	47500	7000	5250
江北区	Jiangbei District	83960	75067	29709
沙坪坝区	Shapingba District	34448	34360	25269
九龙坡区	Jiulongpo District	340466	251736	58265
南岸区	Nan'an District	836355	571875	67400
北碚区	Beibei District	406100	391400	23675
万盛区	Wansheng District	33700	33700	4534
双桥区	Shuangqiao District	800	800	380
渝北区	Yubei District	436300	419020	22982
巴南区	Ba'nan District	43700	42460	12127
黔江区	Qianjiang District	38160	23060	8265
长寿区	Changshou District	49750	34750	9170
綦江县	Qijiang County	70603	68564	19111
潼南县	Tongnan County	5600	5600	3288
铜梁县	Tongliang County	40418	40168	14818
大足县	Dazu County	27220	27070	11356
荣昌县	Rongchang County	33340	28050	16840
璧山县	Bishan County	141370	140195	45505
梁平县	Liangping County	32007	31687	6255
城口县	Chengkou County	5300	4000	4450
丰都县	Fengdu County	18228	9676	6558
垫江县	Dianjiang County	33124	30014	5632
武隆县	Wulong County	2948	2400	300
忠　县	Zhongxian County	65309	65309	10107
开　县	Kaixian County	20000	19510	13500
云阳县	Yunyang County	135320	120170	15189
奉节县	Fengjie County	69120	68910	3390
巫山县	Wushan County	26487	5889	275
巫溪县	Wuxi County	3990	3800	3940
石柱县	Shizhu County	500	500	76
秀山县	Xiushan County	38680	38680	13676
酉阳县	Youyang County			
彭水县	Pengshui County	1180000	910000	60530
江津市	Jiangjin City	175644	126186	22100
合川市	Hechuan City	73716	73716	6051
永川市	Yongchuan City	202990	196610	41856
南川市	Nanchuan City	3725	3700	3540
跨区县(不便于区分区县的)	Transregional			
按重庆三大经济区分	**By Three Economic Spheres**			
都市发达经济圈	Advanced Economic Sphere	2404166	1953638	309649
渝西经济走廊	Economic Corridor in West Chongqing	809126	744359	189379
三峡库区生态经济区	Ecological Economic Zone in Three Gorges Reservoir Area	2267200	1905298	277811
跨区县(不便于区分区县的)	Transregional			

主要统计指标解释

进出口总额 海关进出口总额指实际进出我国国境的货物总金额，进出我国关境并列入海关统计的货物包括：我国境内法人和其他组织以一般贸易、易货贸易、加工贸易、补偿贸易、寄售代销贸易等方式进出口的货物，保税区和保税仓库进出境货物，租赁期一年以上的租赁进出口货物，边境小额贸易货物，国际援助物资及捐赠品，溢卸货物，无进出口经营权的单位经批准临时进出口的货品等。进出口总额用以观察一个国家在对外贸易方面的总规模。我国规定出口货物按FOB型价值统计，进口货物按CIF型价值统计。

利用外资 指我国各级政府、部门、企业和其他经济组织通过对外借款、吸收外商直接投资以及用其他方式筹措的境外现汇、设备、技术等。

对外借款 指通过对外正式签订借款协议，从境外筹措的资金，包括外国政府贷款、国际金融组织贷款、外国商业银行贷款、出口信贷以及对外发行债券等。1996年及以前还包括对外发行股票。

外商直接投资 指外国企业、经济组织或个人(包括华侨、港澳台胞以及我国在境外注册的企业)按我国有关政策、法规，用现汇、实物、技术等在我国境内开办外商独资企业、与我国境内的企业或经济组织共同举办中外合资经营企业、合作经营企业或合作开发资源的投资（包括外商投资收益的再投资），以及经政府有关部门批准的项目投资总额内企业从境外借入的资金。

外商其他投资 指除对外借款和外商直接投资以外的各种利用外资的形式。包括企业在境内外股票市场公开发行的以外币计价的股票（目前主要是在香港证券市场发行的H股和在境内证券市场发行的B股）发行价总额，国际租赁进口设备的应付款，补偿贸易中外商提供的进口设备、技术、物料的价款，加工装配贸易中外商提供的进口设备、物料的价款。

对外承包工程 指我国境内企业法人或者其他经济组织按照国际通行做法，在过及港澳台地区承揽、实施工程建设项目的勘察、设计、施工、监理、设备材料采购、安装调试、工程咨询、工程管理等经营活动。

对外劳务合作 指我国境内企业法人与国（境）外允许招收或雇佣外籍劳务人员的公司、中介机构或私人雇主签定合同，并按合同约定的条件有组织地招聘、选拔、派遣我国公民到国（境）外为外方雇主提供劳务服务并进行管理的经济活动。

对外设计咨询 指我国境内企业法人或者其他经济组织在国外及港澳台地区承担地形地貌测绘，地质资源普查与勘探，建设区域规划，工程设计、生产工艺、技术资料和工程技术咨询，工程项目的可行性考察、研究和评估，工程监理，技术指导等经济活动。

国际旅游人数 指来我国参观、访问、旅行、探亲、访友、休养、考察、参加会议和从事经济、科技、文化、教育、体育、宗教等活动的外国人、华侨、港澳和台湾同胞的人数。不包括外国在我国的常住机构，如使领馆、通讯社、企业办事处的工作人员；来我国常驻的外国专家、留学生以及在岸逗留不过夜人员。

国内旅游者人数 指我国大陆居民和在我国常住1年以上的外国人、华侨、港澳台同胞离开常住地在境内其他地方的旅游设施内至少停留一夜，最长不超过12个月的人数。

国际旅游（外汇）收入 指入境游客在中国（大陆）境内旅行、游览过程中由于交通、参观游览、住宿、餐饮、购物、娱乐等全部花费。

国际旅行社 指经营对外招徕并接待外国人、华侨、港澳同胞和台湾同胞来中国、归国或回内地的旅游业务的旅行社。

国内旅行社 指负责经营招徕、组团、接待国内旅客的旅游业务，以及不对外招徕，负责经营接待国际旅行社或其它涉外部门组织的外国人、华侨、港澳同胞和台湾同胞来中国、归国或回内地的旅游业务的旅行社。

星级饭店 指设备、设施、服务符合《旅游饭店星级的划分与评定》（中华人民共和国国家标准），通过相关旅游管理部门评定，并取得星级饭店称号的饭店（含预备星级饭店）。

内资 指重庆市外中华人民共和国境内（不包括港、澳、台地区）的企、事业单位、社会团体及其他投资者，来渝以从事经济社会活动为主要目的，遵循市场机制法则，本着互利互惠的原则进行的独资、合资、参股合作等而流入的资金。它不包括中央和各级政府无偿捐赠及公益性捐赠。

Explanatory Notes on Main Statistical Indicators

Total Imports and Exports at Customs refer to the value of commodities imported into and exported from the boundary of China. That commodities which are listed into the customs statistic either include: imported and exported goods of corporations or other Organizations in China by ordinary trade, commodity exchanged trade, processing trade, compensated trade, proxy sale trade, and so on; imported and exported goods from bonded districts and warehouses; leasing imported and exported commodities whose leasing period is one year and above; frontier petty trading commodities; contributions or supplies donated by International; spilled and unloaded goods; temporary approved imported and exported goods of corporations without imported and exported running right. The indicator of the total imports and exports at customs can be used to observe the total size of external trade in a country. In accordance with the stipulation of the Chinese government, imports are calculated at CIF, while exports are calculated at FOB.

Utilization of Foreign Capital refers to remittance, equipment and technology financed from abroad, by loans, foreign direct investment and other forms undertaken by the Chins governments at all levels, by various departments, enterprises and other economic units.

Foreign Loans refer to funds borrowed from abroad through formal signing of borrowing agreements with foreign institutions, including loans of foreign governments, loans of international financial institutions, commercial loans of foreign banks, export credit, and funds raised by Chinese bonds (and shares before 1996) issued abroad.

Foreign Direct Investment refers to the investments inside China by foreign enterprises and economic organizations or individuals (including overseas Chinese, compatriots from Hong Kong and Macao, and Chinese enterprises registered abroad), following the relevant policies and laws of China, for the establishment of ventures exclusively with foreign own investment, Sino-foreign joint ventures and cooperative enterprises or for co-operative exploration of resources with enterprises or economic organizations in China. It includes the re-investment of the foreign entrepreneurs with the profits gained from the investment and the funds that enterprises borrow from abroad in the total investment of projects which are approved by the relevant department of the government.

Other Foreign Investment refers to all forms of utilization of foreign capitals other than foreign borrowings and foreign direct investment. It includes the total value of stock shares in foreign currencies issued by enterprises at domestic or foreign stock exchanges (now mainly consisting of K shares issued at Hong Kong Security Market and B shares issued at domestic security markets), rent payable for the imported equipment through international leasing arrangement, cost of imported equipment, technology and materials provided by foreign counterparts in compensation trade and processing and assembly trade.

Contracted Projects with Foreign Countries refer to projects' administrations, including exploration, designing, construction, supervision, procurement of material, installment and adjustment, projects' consultation and management, which are undertaken abroad and in Hong Kong, Macao, Taiwan by corporations or other Economic organizations in China according to international traditional.

Service Co-operation with Foreign Countries refers to the activities of providing labor services and management to employers abroad by recruiting, selecting and dispatching Chinese citizens according to the contracts which are signed between corporations in China and foreign companies, mediate agencies or personal employers allowed recruiting and employing outlanders.

Overseas Design and Consultation Service refers to the economic activities, including geographic and topographic mapping, geological resource prospecting and survey, planning of construction areas, consultation of engineering designing, manufacturing techniques, technologic information and engineering techniques, as well as feasibility study research, evaluation and supervision, which are undertaken abroad and in Hong Kong, Macao, Taiwan by corporations or other Economic organizations in China.

International Tourists refer to foreigners, overseas Chinese, Chinese compatriots from Hong Kong, Macao and Taiwan coming to China for sight-seeing, visits, tours, family reunions, vacations, study tours, conferences and other activities of a business, scientific and technological, cultural, educational and religious nature. It does not include representatives and employees of resident institutions of foreign countries in China such as embassies, consulates, news agencies and offices of foreign companies and organizations, nor does it include long-term foreign experts or students residing in China, or persons in transition without spending a night in China.

Domestic Tourists refer to residents of the mainland of China who stay for one night at least but no more than 12 months at tourist facilities in other places than their permanent residence within the territory of the mainland China, including foreigners, overseas Chinese and Chinese compatriots from Hong Kong, Macao and Taiwan who have resided in China for over one year.

Foreign Exchange Earnings from International Tourism refer to the total expenditures cost in the process of foreigners' tourism in the mainland of China, including traffic, visit, accommodation, table, shopping and amusement expenditures.

International Travel Agencies refer to travel agencies engaged in the promotion, solicitation, organization and reception of tours to the mainland of china by foreigners, overseas Chinese, Chinese compatriots from Hong Kong, Macao and Taiwan.

Domestic Travel Agencies refer to travel agencies engaged tin the promotion, solicitation, organization and reception of domestic tourists, and in the reception of foreigners, overseas Chinese, Chinese compatriots from Hong Kong, Macao and Taiwan organized by international travel agencies or other departments concerned, without their own promotion and solicitation programs.

Star-Hotels refer to hotels whose facilities, installments and services are consistent with *Stars Distinction and Estimate of Hotels* (standards of PRC) and have passed the estimate of travel management department and gained the title.

Domestic Capital refers to capital inpoured by the way of sole investment, joint venture and cooperative operation from the corporations, social unions and other investors within China boundaries but outside Chongqing municipality (excluding Hong Kong, Macao, Taiwan) who consider engaging economic and social activities as their main destination in Chongqing, and follow the market system on behalf of equality. It excludes the subscription for no payment of central and local governments.

十六　金融业

FINANCIAL STATISTICS

简要说明 Brief Introduction

本章资料包括我市金融机构信贷收支、证券和保险业情况，由市统计局综合处根据有关部门资料整理编辑。资料分别来源于中国人民银行重庆营业部、重庆市发展和改革委员会、重庆证监局、重庆保监局和重庆保险行业协会。

The data in this chapter includes credit funds balance of financial institutions, securities and insurance. All information is prepared by Division of Comprehensive Statistics, Municipal Bureau of Statistics. The data come from Chongqing Operations Office of the People's Bank of China, Chongqing Municipal Development and Reform Commission, China Securities Regulatory Commission Chongqing Bureau, China Insurance Regulatory Commission Chongqing Bureau and Chongqing Insurance Association.

16－1 金融机构（含外资）人民币存贷款年末余额（1980－2004年）
Year-end Deposit and Loan Balances of RMB of Financial Institutions (Including Foreign-funded) (1980-2004)

单位：亿元 (100 million yuan)

年 份 Year	存款余额 Total Deposit Balance	#企业存款 Enterprise Deposits	#储蓄存款 Urban and Rural Saving Deposits	贷款余额 Total Loan Balance	#短期贷款 Short-term Loans	#中长期贷款 Medium & Long-term Loans
1980	29.15	11.32	6.22	42.19	40.96	1.23
1981	33.98	11.86	8.35	50.29	47.69	2.21
1982	38.66	12.44	10.56	55.30	51.50	3.05
1983	45.22	15.29	13.34	63.25	58.14	4.32
1984	70.86	25.40	18.39	84.53	70.42	11.76
1985	62.38	22.87	25.41	101.56	84.85	14.89
1986	84.57	27.94	34.79	131.70	110.61	18.86
1987	110.37	31.84	44.46	163.63	125.85	22.99
1988	123.47	38.22	50.50	183.32	141.01	25.90
1989	146.71	39.27	68.17	214.41	167.66	29.65
1990	198.00	48.51	92.17	268.40	205.63	38.30
1991	253.57	63.76	121.95	336.85	249.51	58.82
1992	315.70	83.75	154.45	408.64	294.63	78.75
1993	386.86	89.57	198.05	495.71	357.59	98.88
1994	518.27	143.26	285.40	596.96	409.16	136.46
1995	676.70	193.38	401.45	755.39	501.66	185.89
1996	846.43	266.42	500.71	913.93	601.10	219.05
1997	1098.67	429.42	580.67	1156.13	873.14	248.06
1998	1306.04	483.80	724.54	1358.61	978.51	299.59
1999	1580.80	544.00	909.10	1611.68	1093.09	398.22
2000	1904.71	645.54	1085.36	1881.29	1246.81	470.70
2001	2294.05	750.81	1317.17	1871.98	1043.84	631.26
2002	2821.04	909.43	1595.01	2244.72	1191.70	754.57
2003	3438.61	1098.15	1896.56	2774.81	1378.85	1010.69
2004	4039.61	1230.85	2189.73	3246.28	1362.75	1346.91

16－2 人民币对主要外币年平均汇价（中间价）（1985－2004年）
RMB Annual Average Rate of Exchange for Major Foreign Currencies (Middle Rates) (1985-2004)

单位:人民币元 (RMB yuan)

年 份 Year	美元（100） USD 100	日元（100） JPY 100	港元（100） HKD 100	欧元（100） EUR 100
1985	293.66	1.2457	37.57	
1986	345.28	2.0694	44.22	
1987	372.21	2.5799	47.74	
1988	372.21	2.9082	47.70	
1989	376.51	2.7360	48.28	
1990	478.32	3.3233	61.39	
1991	532.33	3.9602	68.45	
1992	551.46	4.3608	71.24	
1993	576.20	5.2020	74.41	
1994	861.87	8.4370	111.53	
1995	835.10	8.9225	107.96	
1996	831.42	7.6352	107.51	
1997	828.98	6.8600	107.09	
1998	827.91	6.3488	106.88	
1999	827.83	7.2932	106.66	
2000	827.84	7.6864	106.18	
2001	827.70	6.8075	106.08	
2002	827.70	6.6237	106.07	800.58
2003	827.70	7.1466	106.24	936.13
2004	827.68	7.6552	106.23	1029.00

注：2002年欧元汇价为4－12月的平均汇价。
Note: Rate of EUR in 2002 refers to the average rate from April to December.

16－3 金融机构（含外资）本外币信贷资金平衡表(2003－2004年)
Credit Funds Balance of RMB and Foreign Currencies of Financial Institutions (Including Foreign-funded) (2003-2004)

单位:亿元 (100 million yuan)

项 目	Item	2003	2004
资金来源总计	**All Sources**	**3126.91**	**3463.50**
#各项存款余额	Total Deposit Balance	3512.82	4105.01
#企事业单位存款	Deposits of Enterprises and Undertakings	1120.36	1251.75
活期存款	Demand	906.61	1036.52
定期存款	Time	213.75	215.23
储蓄存款	Urban and Rural Saving Deposits	1941.36	2227.92
活期存款	Demand	637.08	729.38
定期存款	Time	1304.28	1498.54
资金运用总计	**All Uses**	**3126.91**	**3463.50**
各项贷款余额	Total Loan Balance	2976.67	3309.13
#短期贷款	Short-term Loans	1393.52	1378.42
中长期贷款	Medium & Long-term Loans	1276.14	1552.93
有价证券及投资	Securities and Investment	150.24	154.37

注：外币折本币所用汇率为当年最后一个交易日的中间汇率。
Note: The exchange rates of foreign currencies for RMB are the middle rates of exchange on the last market day in current year.

16－4 金融机构（含外资）人民币信贷资金平衡表（2003-2004年）
Credit Funds Balance of RMB of Financial Institutions (Including Foreign-funded) (2003-2004)

单位：亿元　　　　(100 million yuan)

项　目	Item	2003	2004
资金来源总计	**All Sources**	**3092.49**	**3553.91**
#各项存款余额	Total Deposit Balance	3438.61	4039.61
#企业存款	Enterprise Deposits	1098.15	1230.85
#定期存款	Time	201.16	206.69
财政存款	Treasury Deposits	44.41	87.99
机关团体存款	Deposits of Government Agencies and Organizations	90.61	141.42
储蓄存款	Urban and Rural Saving Deposits	1896.56	2189.73
#定期储蓄	Time	1265.52	1469.99
农业存款	Agricultural Deposits	62.76	74.09
信托及委托存款	Trusted Deposits	0.02	0.01
金融债券	Bonds	-47.99	-72.17
同业往来	Interbank Deposits	52.04	37.64
各项准备	Various Reserves	18.07	32.63
#贷款损失准备金	Reserve for Loan Losses	17.56	29.43
资金运用总计	**All Uses**	**3092.49**	**3553.91**
#各项贷款余额	Total Loan Balance	2774.81	3246.28
#短期贷款	Short-term Loans	1378.85	1362.75
#工业贷款	Industrial Loans	342.95	333.80
商业贷款	Commercial Loans	221.04	194.45
农业贷款	Agricultural Loans	158.14	170.98
个人短期消费贷款	Personal Short-term Consumer Loans	10.22	26.92
中期流动资金贷款	Medium-term Circulating Asset Loans	183.02	195.16
中长期贷款	Medium & Long-term Loans	1010.69	1346.91
#基本建设贷款	Loans to Capital Construction	521.16	718.63
技术改造贷款	Loans to Technique Innovation	21.15	32.58
个人中长期消费贷款	Personal Medium & Long-term Consumer Loans	250.03	319.72
委托贷款	Trusted Loans	4.82	3.71
票据融资	Bills for Financing	187.81	331.80
#贴现	Discount	187.81	331.80
有价证券及投资	Securities and Investment	145.92	151.28
同业往来	Interbank Loans	10.47	0.70
外汇占款	Purchase of Foreign Exchanges	-0.25	1.23
固定资产	Fixed Assets	86.21	86.96
库存现金	Cash on Hand	35.33	37.36

16－5 金融机构人民币现金收入和支出（2003－2004年）
Cash Income and Expenditures of RMB of Financial Institutions (2003-2004)

单位：亿元 (100 million yuan)

项　目	Item	2003	2004
现金收入合计	**Total Cash Income**	**8957.72**	**10576.23**
商品销售收入	Income from Commodity Sales	861.22	961.08
服务事业收入	Income from Services	419.11	446.46
税款收入	Income from Taxes	54.63	54.32
城乡个体经营收入	Income from Individual Business	224.47	263.52
储蓄存款收入	Income from Saving Deposits	6116.68	7467.96
其他金融机构收入	Income from Other Financial Institutions	48.14	37.88
居民归还贷款收入	Income from Household Loan Recovery	125.38	143.05
汇兑收入	Income from Remittances	84.07	71.86
有价证券收入	Income from Securities	13.83	13.76
其他收入	Other Income	1010.19	1116.34
#兑换外币收入	Income from Foreign Currency Exchanges	0.56	0.36
现金回笼	**Cash Withdrawn**	**15.23**	**24.36**
现金支出合计	**Total Cash Expenditures**	**8942.49**	**10551.87**
工资性支出	Wages	752.39	876.76
#国家工资及奖金支出	Expenditures for Wages and Bonus from Government	382.75	422.00
国家对个人其他支出	Other Payments to Individuals from Government	114.00	120.82
其他单位工资性支出	Expenditures for Wages of Other Units	240.40	310.13
农副产品采购支出	Purchases of Agricultural and Sideline Products	122.69	153.67
工矿及其他产品采购支出	Purchases of Industrial & Mineral Products and Other Products	98.34	124.22
行政事业管理费支出	Government and Enterprise Overhead	480.80	466.51
城乡个体经营支出	Expenditure for Individual Business	293.60	333.22
储蓄存款支出	Expenditure for Saving Deposits	5901.05	7243.85
其他金融机构支出	Expenditure for Other Financial Institutions	32.95	36.51
居民提取贷款支出	Expenditure for Household Loan Drawn	120.64	122.57
汇兑支出	Expenditure for Remittances	111.89	101.71
有价证券支出	Expenditure for Securities	12.21	8.40
其他支出	Other Expenditure	1015.93	1085.46
#兑换外币支出	Expenditure for Foreign Currency Exchanges	0.91	1.34
现金投放	**Currency Issuance**		

16－6 金融机构（含外资）本外币贷款结构（2003－2004年）
Loan Composition of RMB and Foreign Currency of Financial Institutions (Including Foreign-funded) (2003-2004)

单位：亿元 (100 million yuan)

项　　目	Item	2003	2004
贷款总计	**Total Loans**	**2824.30**	**3115.50**
按贷款对象分	By Loanee		
内资企业贷款	Loans to Domestic-funded Enterprises	2286.98	2566.82
#国有企业	State-owned	905.44	955.92
港澳台商投资企业贷款	Loans to Funded by Hong Kong, Macao and Taiwan	37.42	44.76
外商投资企业贷款	Loans to Foreign-funded Enterprises	111.91	83.71
个人贷款	Individual Loans	387.99	420.21
#个人消费	Personal Expenditure	274.05	346.64
境外贷款	Loans Abroad		
按信用方式分	By Form of Credit		
#信用贷款及透支	Credit Loan and Related Overdraft	605.70	676.85
保证贷款	Secured Loan	351.18	413.11
#国家大型或特大型企业担保	By State-owned (Over) Large-sized Enterprises	143.24	173.31
质押贷款	Pledge Loan	344.36	486.80
抵押贷款	Mortgage Loan	1095.45	1107.57
#土地房产权转让抵押	Mortgage on Transferring Rights of Land & Real Estate	603.33	594.37
按行业分	By Sector		
#农林牧渔业	Primary Industry	155.86	146.15
制造业	Manufacturing	648.26	665.71
交通运输、仓储和邮政业	Transportation, Storage, Postal Services	258.56	277.06
批发和零售业	Wholesale and Retail Trade	224.52	261.59
房地产业	Real Estate	358.01	396.06
水利、环境和公共设施管理业	Water Conservancy, Environment & Public Utility Administration	207.53	262.42

注：本表数据不含商业银行在人民银行的再贴现。
Note: Data excludes the rediscount.

16－7 上市公司情况（1993－2004年）
Number of Listed Companies (1993-2004)

单位：个 (unit)

年份 Year	全市总计 Total	上交所 Shanghai Stock Exchange	深交所 Shenzhen Stock Exchange	仅发A股公司 A Share Only	发A、B股公司 A&B Share	仅发B股公司 B Share Only
1993	3	1	2	3		
1994	5	2	3	5		
1995	7	3	4	6		1
1996	11	4	7	10		1
1997	19	8	11	17	1	1
1998	19	8	11	17	1	1
1999	22	9	13	20	1	1
2000	25	11	14	23	1	1
2001	26	12	14	24	1	1
2002	27	13	14	25	1	1
2003	27	13	14	25	1	1
2004	29	14	15	27	1	1

注：本表不包括重庆钢铁和庆铃汽车两家仅发H股的公司。
Note: Two listed companies of Chongqing Steel and Qingling Motor, which issue H share only are not included in this tables.

16－8 有价证券发行情况（1981－2004年）
Issuance of Securities (1981-2004)

单位：亿元 (100 million yuan)

年 份 Year	国债发行额 Issued Value of National Debt	企业债券发行额 Issued Value of Corporate Bonds	股票发行量（万股） Amount of Issued Shares（10 000 shares）	A 股 A Shares	B 股 B Shares	股票筹资额 Raised Capital of Shares	A 股 A Shares	B 股 B Shares
1981	0.57							
1982	0.53							
1983	0.53							
1984	0.54							
1985	0.83							
1986	0.84	1.50						
1987	0.83	0.59						
1988	0.66	1.85						
1989	3.09	0.39						
1990	1.84	1.95						
1991	1.88	3.90						
1992	5.81	5.45						
1993	3.94	4.18	7220	7220		2.08	2.08	
1994	8.29	1.17	3000	3000		1.13	1.13	
1995	12.96		17200	5200	12000	5.30	0.52	4.78
1996	2.06	3.60	50610	15610	35000	10.41	4.56	5.85
1997	13.31	4.85	42039	42039		26.76	26.76	
1998	23.62	3.40	5000	5000		3.75	3.75	
1999	12.10	4.10	10000	10000		7.21	7.21	
2000	23.46		29600	29600		22.63	22.63	
2001	20.20		3108	3108		4.73	4.73	
2002	20.77	15.00	2000	2000		3.16	3.16	
2003	34.12		3275	3275		3.74	3.74	
2004	19.67		22285	22285		15.65	15.65	

注：股票发行量和筹资额均不含H股。

Note: Amount of issued shares and raised capital of shares don't include H share.

16－9 保险业务基本情况（1996－2004年）
Basic Statistics on Insurance Business (1996-2004)

单位：亿元 (100 million yuan)

年 份 Year	保费收入 Premium	财产保险 Property Insurance	人身保险 Life Insurance	赔款及给付 Claim and Payments	财产保险 Property Insurance	人身保险 Life Insurance
1996	12.82	8.05	4.77	6.48	4.44	2.04
1997	19.52	9.03	10.49	7.18	4.39	2.79
1998	22.77	9.31	13.46	10.64	6.55	4.09
1999	25.39	10.04	15.35	8.91	4.96	3.95
2000	27.71	10.72	16.99	8.27	5.28	2.99
2001	33.72	11.32	22.40	11.25	5.91	5.34
2002	46.17	13.31	32.86	14.20	7.57	6.63
2003	57.93	15.24	42.69	14.53	8.56	5.97
2004	66.51	17.45	49.06	16.25	9.43	6.82

16－10 按险种分的保险业务指标（2003－2004年）
Statistics on Insurance Business by Classification (2003-2004)

单位：万元 (10 000 yuan)

项 目	Item	保 费 Premium 2003	保 费 Premium 2004	赔款及给付 Claim and Payment 2003	赔款及给付 Claim and Payment 2004
合 计	**Total**	**579369**	**665118**	**145266**	**162538**
财产保险	**Property Insurance**	**152441**	**174465**	**85592**	**94273**
企业财产保险	Enterprise Property Insurance	14181	15732	4353	4976
家庭财产保险	Family Property Insurance	3051	3555	246	329
机动车辆保险	Motor Vehicle Insurance	111704	128239	71098	78856
船舶保险	Ship Insurance	3905	5331	2810	3000
货物运输保险	Freight Transport Insurance	6928	8771	2772	3129
卫星及核能险	Satellite and Nuclear Energy Insurance	74	512	11	40
建筑、安装工程保险及责任保险	Construction and installation Projects Insurance and Related Liability Insurance	1973	3556	633	572
责任保险	Liability Insurance	4509	4195	3300	2509
保证保险	Guarantee Insurance	21	692	7	356
信用保险	Export Credit Insurance		669		198
农业保险	Agriculture Insurance	76	34	37	1
其他保险	Other Insurances	6020	3180	327	306
人寿保险	**Life Insurance**	**426928**	**490653**	**59674**	**68266**
寿 险	Life Insurance	361291	414585	38107	39964
健康险	Health Insurance	43498	49644	13386	18920
人身意外伤害险	Unforeseen Human Injury Insurance	22139	26425	8181	9382

16－11 主要金融机构数（2003－2004年）
Number of Main Financial Institutions (2003-2004)

单位：个 (unit)

指　　标	Item	2003	2004
银行机构	**Banks**		
内资银行	Dometic-funded Banks		
省（市）级分行/市联社会	Sivisions /Rural Credit Cooperative at Provincial Level	21	21
一级支行/地（区）级联合社	Divisions at 1st Level /Rural Credit Cooperative at District Level	58	23
二级支行/信用社	Divisions at 2nd Level /Credit Cooperative	1159	502
分理处（分社）	Small Local Branch	2397	1585
储蓄所	Saving Offices	498	1517
中外合资、外资银行分行	Bank Branches of Joint-venture with Foreign Investment and Sole Foreign Investment	2	2
保险机构	**Insurance Companies**		
其中：专业保险中介机构	Of Which: Professional Insurance Intermediary Institutions		
保险代理公司	Insurance Agent Companies	7	12
保险公估公司	Insurance Assessment Companies	5	8
保险经纪公司	Insurance Broker Companies	1	2
内资保险公司	Dometic-funded Insurance Companies		
省（市）级分公司	Divisions at Provincial Level	12	14
中心支公司	Center Sub-divisions	16	17
支公司	Sub-divisions	155	157
营销服务部	Operating & Service Offices	668	731
中外合资、外资保险公司	Insurance Company Branches of Joint-venture with Foreign Investment and Sole Foreign Investment	1	1
外资保险公司代表处	Agencies of Foreign-funded Insurance Companies	3	1
证券机构	**Security Companies**		
内资证券公司	Dometic-funded Security Companies		
法人机构	Corporate Entity	2	2
营业部	Operating Offices	63	65
服务部	Service Offices	26	26
中外合资、外资证券公司分公司	Security Company Branches of Joint-venture with Foreign Investment and Sole Foreign Investment		

注：1）中外合资、外资金融机构数只统计到省（市）级。

2）内资银行机构数因2004年撤、并等机构调整，比2003年下降；保险机构数不含中国出口信用保险公司重庆营业管理部。

Note: a) Financial Institutions of Joint-venture with foreign investment and sole foreign investment at provincial level are only accounted.

b) Data on domestic-funded banks in 2004 is less than that in 2003 for the adjustment of organnizational structure. Data on domestic-funded insurance companies excludes Chongqing Operation Office of China Export & Credit Insurance Corporation.

主要统计指标解释

信贷资金 指金融机构以信用方式积聚和分配的货币资金。金融机构信贷资金的来源有各项贷款、对国际金融机构负债、流通中货币、银行自有资金及当年结益等；信贷资金的运用有各项贷款、黄金占款、外汇占款、财政借款及在国际金融机构中的资产等。

存款 指金融机构接受客户存入的货币款项，存款人可随时或按约定时间支取款项的信用业务。包括活期存款、定期存款、住户储蓄存款、财政存款、外汇存款和其他存款等。

贷款 指金融机构接受客户存入的货币款项，存款人可随时或按约定时间支取款项的信用业务。包括活期存款、定期存款、住户储蓄存款、财政存款、外汇存款和其他存款等。

金融机构往来 指各金融机构之间的资金往来，包括同业存放款和同业拆借款。

准备金 指各金融机构在中央银行的存款及缴存中央银行的法定准备金。

保险公司 在中国境内的、经过保险监督部门批准设立，并依法登记注册的各类商业保险公司。

保费 指投保人为取得保险人在约定范围内所承担赔偿责任而支付给保险人的费用。

赔款 指保险人根据保险合同的规定，向被保险人支付的赔偿保险责任损失的金额。

给付 包括死伤医疗给付和满期给付。死伤医疗给付是指保险人根据人寿保险及长期健康保险合同的规定，因被保险人在保险期内发生保险责任范围内的保险事故支付给被保险人(或受益人)的金额。满期给付是指被保险人生存期满，保险人按人寿保险合同规定支付给被保险人的满期保险金额。

证券 由债券购买者承购的或因销售产品而拥有的，可在金融市场上交易并代表一定债权的书面证明。包括政府债券、金融债券、企业债券、商业票据、股票、支付固定收入但不提供法人企业残余价值分享权的优先股等。

股票 指股票购买者及直接投资者对其投资企业净资产所拥有的权益。股票是股份公司签发的证明股东投资并按其所持股份享有权益和承担义务的权益性证券。

Explanatory Notes on Main Statistical Indicators

Credit Funds refer to the funds issued as loans by banking institutions. The sources of credit funds of the banking institutions included deposits, liabilities to international financial institutions, currency in circulation, self-owned funds and current retained profits, etc. The credit funds can be used in forms of loans, gold, foreign exchange, government debt and assets in the international financial institutions.

Deposit refers to credit transactions by which financial institutions accept deposits from clients who could withdraw their deposit at any time or by agreed time frame. They include current deposit, fixed deposit, household savings deposit, government deposit, foreign exchange deposit and other deposits.

Loan refers to credit transactions by which financial institutions lend their capital to clients at certain level of interest rates, which the latter will repay by agreed time frame. They include short-term loans, medium and long-term loans, government loans, foreign exchange loans and other loans.

Transactions between Financial Institutions refer to flow of capital between financial institutions, including inter-bank deposits and loans.

Reserve Funds refer to savings of financial institutions in the central bank and designated reserves to the central bank.

Insurance Companies refer to commercial insurance companies of various forms registered by law and established in China with the approval of insurance regulatory agencies.

Premium is the fee paid by the insurant based on a proportion of the benefit he or she may get from the insurance plus the insurance value. It includes the income from the deposit of property insurance and personal insurance.

Settled Claim is the compensation paid by the insurer to the insurant in accordance with the insurance contract.

Payment includes payment for death, injury or medical treatment and mature payment. Payment for death, injury or medical treatment refers to the money paid to the insurant (of the beneficiary) in accordance with the life of health insurance contract when the insurant encounters accidents within the insured period covered in the contract. Mature payment refers to the mature payment to the insurant in accordance with the life insurance contract at the end of the insured period for the loss which has been checked and found to be in the range of liability of the insurance after an accident has happened to the insured property or to a person who has insured his life. It is further divided into settled and unsettled claim.

Securities refer to written certificates representing creditors' rights, purchased by bond holders or owned by selling products, which can be transacted at the financial markets. They include government bonds, financial bonds, corporation bonds, commercial drafts, stocks, preferential stocks that provide fixed income without the right to share the residual value of corporations, etc.

Stocks refer to the rights by stockholders and direct investors on the net assets of corporations they invested in. Stocks refer to negotiable securities on creditor's rights, issued by stock companies certifying the investment by stockholders and their rights and duties depending on their stocks.

十七　教育、科技和文化业

EDUCATION, SCIENCE, TECHNOLOGY AND CULTURE

简要说明　Brief Introduction

本章资料主要包括我市教育事业、科学技术活动和文化事业的基本情况，由市统计局社会科技处根据有关部门资料整理编辑。

教育部分包括各类教育的学校、教师和学生情况，由市教育委员会提供；科学技术部分主要包括科技机构、大中型工业企业和高等学校的科技活动情况，以及2000年R&D资源清查主要数据，由市科学技术委员会、市教育委员会和市统计局社会科技处提供；专利资料由市知识产权局提供；商标申请注册来源于市工商行政管理局；产品商品质量监督检查资料由市质量技术监督局提供；文化部分主要包括图书馆、文物、群众艺术文化、广播电视、新闻出版等情况，资料主要来自市文化局、市广播电视局、市新闻出版局。

The data in this chapter show the basic statistics on education, scientific & technological activities and culture undertakings. All data are edited by Division of Social and Technology Statistics, Municipal Bureau of Statistics according to data from related departments.

Education covers the data on schools, teachers and students of various kinds, rooting from Municipal Education Committee. The data on science and technology mainly include scientific and technological activities in scientific & technological institutions, large and medium-sized industrial enterprises, universities and colleges, and survey of R&D resources in 2000, being provided by Municipal Scientific and Technological Committee, Municipal Education Committee and Division of Social and Technology Statistics, Municipal Bureau of Statistics. The data on patent are provided by Municipal Bureau of Intellectual Properties. Applications for registration of trade marks come from Municipal Administration for Industry and Commerce. The data on results of sampling supervision & check on product and commodity quality are from Municipal Bureau of Quality and Technical Supervision. Data on culture includes libraries, cultural relics, mass arts & culture, broadcasting, televisions, news and publication from Municipal Culture Bureau, Municipal Administration of Broadcasting and Television, Municipal Bureau of News and Publication.

17－1 主要年份各级各类学校数
Number of Various Schools in Major Years

单位：所 (unit)

年 份 Year	普通高等学校 Regular Institutions of Higher Education	普通中等专业学校 Specialized Secondary Schools	普通中学 Regular Secondary Schools	小 学 Primary Schools	特殊教育学校 Schools for the Blind, Deaf and Deaf-mute	幼 儿 园 Kindergartens
1952	7	50	128	12920		
1957	9	43	249	16201		
1962	10	14	402	14148		
1965	11	52	696	31503		
1970	11	22	1700	21253		
1975	8	72	1366	25465		
1978	13	76	2948	25002		
1980	16	73	1989	25120		
1985	18	74	1788	22793	7	5800
1986	19	77	1739	22486	19	5230
1987	19	81	1759	22094	18	5542
1988	20	82	1753	21629	20	5009
1989	20	82	1751	20972	23	4726
1990	20	82	1753	20248	24	5232
1991	20	82	1762	19829	29	4486
1992	20	82	1766	19496	32	4814
1993	20	82	1746	18849	30	4061
1994	20	83	1725	18175	31	4094
1995	22	83	1638	19637	30	6046
1996	22	81	1651	16779	36	5538
1997	22	81	1606	16261	37	5741
1998	22	81	1555	15737	37	5412
1999	23	78	1552	15223	42	6007
2000	22	62	1568	14730	42	6659
2001	29	52	1607	13076	44	3726
2002	29	47	1574	12031	38	3477
2003	33	39	1564	10966	41	3093
2004	34	38	1511	10409	43	3408

注：2001年起幼儿园资料按教育部对幼儿园数的认定标准统计，与以往年数不可比（下表同）。

Note: The Data of kindergartens are in accordance with the definition by Ministry of Education since 2001, so it is not comparable with previous years (the same below).

17－2 主要年份各级各类学校在校学生数
Number of Student Enrollment in Various Schools in Major Years

单位：人 (person)

年 份 Year	普通高等学校 Regular Institutions of Higher Education	普通中等专业学校 Specialized Secondary Schools	普通中学 Regular Secondary Schools	小 学 Primary Schools	特殊教育学校 Schools for the Blind, Deaf and Deaf-mute	幼儿园 Kindergartens
1952	6437	20712	61345	1524145		
1957	15211	29238	181423	1539805		
1962	21173		163628	1640036		
1965	17408	19715	266504	1967997		
1970	4235		651232	2130534		
1975	10194	18901	963304	3415196		
1978	16357	25626	1631581	4035934		
1980	25349	33954	1323181	4316902		
1985	39871	31952	1102702	3857331	418	296336
1986	44454	34591	1107545	3610433	543	306591
1987	47644	36894	1122462	3279059	571	409209
1988	49981	38580	1124510	2858642	669	389185
1989	48449	40719	1111706	2581889	831	351175
1990	49331	40820	1080755	2393235	803	413552
1991	49964	41100	978204	2314986	1179	505799
1992	54121	44023	868431	2361261	1966	549271
1993	63795	53031	790396	2500362	1850	445940
1994	71118	52795	876008	2595400	1415	534177
1995	73398	62734	977079	2638555	1783	577162
1996	79929	69491	1012654	2737051	1832	588854
1997	80565	78800	1002915	2854307	1706	590464
1998	83187	91479	1083691	2884385	2325	613298
1999	101601	91954	1282599	2802741	9007	625666
2000	132512	84524	1477861	2761308	21160	640804
2001	170006	77056	1540317	2777859	18383	599282
2002	211221	86046	1574357	2797557	17199	587645
2003	255266	95057	1663728	2779441	14483	572538
2004	303913	99541	1707489	2718999	15973	544759

注：高等学校在校学生含研究生。

Note: Student enrollment in regular institutions of higher education includes postgraduates.

17－3 主要年份各级各类学校专任教师数
Number of Full-time Teachers in Various Schools in Major Years

单位：人 (person)

年 份 Year	普通高等学校 Regular Institutions of Higher Education	普通中等专业学校 Specialized Secondary Schools	普通中学 Regular Secondary Schools	小 学 Primary Schools	特殊教育学校 Schools for the Blind, Deaf and Deaf-mute	幼儿园 Kindergartens
1952	839	1090	3385	41698		
1957	2193	2446	7940	52530		
1962	3297			55213		
1965	3336	2336		78503		
1970	3177		24970	73695		
1975	3574	2659	42893			
1978	3914					
1980	5025	3944	60953	125304		
1985	8061	4443	58886	119119	74	11937
1986	8236		55071	113724	101	12054
1987	8622		57044	112163	113	15090
1988	8823	4665	60450	111596	145	15873
1989	8726	4745	61938	109691	186	15898
1990	8677	4726	64056	110580	186	17443
1991	8596	4786	64934	111305	277	19313
1992	8696	4502	65030	111667	321	19244
1993	8777	4663	63555	113834	326	18388
1994	9186	4664	65316	116603	360	19729
1995	9409	4542	67498	117497	353	19948
1996	9400	4505	69503	117711	383	20111
1997	9432	4538	70661	119881	411	20665
1998	9498	4615	72333	121062	400	20962
1999	9987	4791	76158	120229	469	21088
2000	10449	4125	81766	119014	569	22598
2001	12125	3248	85030	118623	474	12067
2002	13954	2953	87427	117543	510	11666
2003	16013	2656	89560	115212	543	12141
2004	18214	2821	92051	114007	541	12351

17－4 主要年份文化事业机构数
Number of Cultural Institutions in Major Years

单位：个 (unit)

年 份 Year	专业剧团 Specialized Dramatic Groups	文化馆、艺术馆 Cultural Centers and Art Centers	图书馆 Libraries
1975	54	33	10
1978	54	36	10
1980	55	35	21
1985	54	35	25
1986	52	35	26
1987	51	35	26
1988	45	35	27
1989	44	35	35
1990	42	39	36
1991	42	39	38
1992	42	39	38
1993	41	39	41
1994	36	40	41
1995	36	40	42
1996	39	46	42
1997	39	43	42
1998	39	43	42
1999	36	42	42
2000	35	44	42
2001	36	44	42
2002	32	44	43
2003	32	44	44
2004	29	44	44

17－5 教育事业基本情况（2003－2004年）
Basic Statistics on Education (2003-2004)

指　　标	Item	2003	2004
学校数(所)	**Number of Schools (unit)**		
普通高等学校	Regular Institutions of Higher Education	33	34
普通中等学校	Secondary Schools	1771	1728
普通中等专业学校	Specialized Secondary Schools	39	38
＃中等技术学校	Technical Training Schools	28	27
中等师范学校	Teacher Training Schools	11	11
普通中学	Regular Secondary Schools	1564	1511
＃高　中	Senior	293	291
初　中	Junior	1271	1220
职业中学	Vocational Secondary Schools	168	179
小　学	Primary Schools	10966	10409
幼儿园	Kindergartens	3093	3408
特殊教育学校	Schools for the Blind Deaf and Deaf-mute	41	43
专任教师(人)	**Number of Full-time Teachers (person)**		
普通高等学校	Regular Institutions of Higher Education	16013	18214
普通中等学校	Secondary Schools	99217	102429
普通中等专业学校	Specialized Secondary Schools	2656	2821
＃中等技术学校	Technical Training Schools	1881	2094
中等师范学校	Teacher Training Schools	775	727
普通中学	Regular Secondary Schools	89560	92051
＃高　中	Senior	21561	24067
初　中	Junior	67999	67984
职业中学	Vocational Secondary Schools	7001	7557
小　学	Primary Schools	115212	114007
幼儿园	Kindergartens	12141	12351
特殊教育学校	Schools for the Blind Deaf and Deaf-mute	543	541
招生数(人)	**New Student Enrollment (person)**		
普通高等学校	Regular Institutions of Higher Education	91866	108094
普通中等学校	Secondary Schools	701010	691910
普通中等专业学校	Specialized Secondary Schools	34621	33616
＃中等技术学校	Technical Training Schools	30822	30516
中等师范学校	Teacher Training Schools	3799	3100
普通中学	Regular Secondary Schools	603658	590263
＃高　中	Senior	157825	162613
初　中	Junior	445833	427650
职业中学	Vocational Secondary Schools	62731	68031
小　学	Primary Schools	444276	410479
幼儿园	Kindergartens	407641	377174

17-5 续表 CONTINUED

指　　标	Item	2003	2004
特殊教育学校	Schools for the Blind Deaf and Deaf-mute	1513	2044
在校学生数(人)	**Student Enrollment (person)**		
普通高等学校	Regular Institutions of Higher Education	255266	303913
普通中等学校	Secondary Schools	1894446	1965082
普通中等专业学校	Specialized Secondary Schools	95057	99541
#中等技术学校	Technical Training Schools	80491	87691
中等师范学校	Teacher Training Schools	14566	11850
普通中学	Regular Secondary Schools	1663728	1707489
#高　中	Senior	407905	452705
初　中	Junior	1255823	1254784
职业中学	Vocational Secondary Schools	135661	158052
小　学	Primary Schools	2779441	2718999
幼儿园	Kindergartens	572538	544759
特殊教育学校	Schools for the Blind Deaf and Deaf-mute	14483	15973
毕业生数(人)	**Graduates (person)**		
普通高等学校	Regular Institutions of Higher Education	45368	54025
中等学校	Secondary Schools	528545	540203
普通中等专业学校	Specialized Secondary Schools	23414	24610
#中等技术学校	Technical Training Schools	18245	19145
中等师范学校	Teacher Training Schools	5169	5465
普通中学	Regular Secondary Schools	475066	476561
#高　中	Senior	74895	102356
初　中	Junior	400171	374205
职业中学	Vocational Secondary Schools	30065	39032
小　学	Primary Schools	456848	446095
幼儿园	Kindergartens	313689	295635
特殊教育学校	Schools for the Blind Deaf and Deaf-mute	1891	2326
每一教师负担学生数（人）	**Student-teacher Ratio (person)**		
普通高等学校	Regular Institutions of Higher Education	15	17
普通中等学校	Secondary Schools	19	19
小　学	Primary Schools	24	24
平均每万人在校学生数（人）	**Student Enrollment per 10 000 persons (person)**		
大学生	University and College Students	82	97
中专生	Specialized Secondary School Students	30	32
中学生	Secondary School Students	575	593
小学生	Primary School Students	888	865
各级各类在校学生数占全市人口(%)	**Student Enrollment as Percentage of Total Population (%)**	**17.8**	**17.8**

注：1）本表未含技工校、工读校数据。

2）普通高校招生数、在校学生数、毕业生数均包括研究生。

Note: a) Basic statistics excluded data of skilled workers' schools and reformatory schools.

b) Number of new student enrollment, student enrollment and graduates in regular institutions of higher education all includes postgraduates.

17－6 高等学校（含机构）基本情况（2004年）
Basic Statistics on Institutions of Higher Education (Including Agencies) (2004)

单位：人 (person)

指标	Item	学校数（个） Number of Institutions	招生数 New Student Enrollment	#研究生 Postgraduates	毕业生数 Graduates	#研究生 Postgraduates
全市总计	**Total**	**34**	**108094**	**8202**	**54025**	**3426**
部属学校	Colleges Affiliated to Ministries	2	17398	4590	11394	1956
本科院校	Senior Colleges	2	17398	4590	11394	1956
市属学校	Colleges Affiliated to Municipality	32	90696	3612	42631	1470
本科院校	Senior Colleges	14	56809	3612	33162	1470
专科学校	Junior Colleges	18	18302		5219	
独立学院	Self-governing Colleges		11150		1356	
成人高校	Adult Education Schools		4435		2894	

指标	Item	在校学生数 Student Enrollment	#研究生 Postgraduates	专任教师数 Full-time Teachers	#教授、副教授 Professors and Associate Professors	专任教师平均负担学生数 Ratio of Student to Full-time Teacher
全市总计	**Total**	**303913**	**19367**	**18214**	**7036**	**20**
部属学校	Colleges Affiliated to Ministries	58158	11149	3796	1762	24
本科院校	Senior Colleges	58158	11149	3796	1762	24
市属学校	Colleges Affiliated to Municipality	245755	8218	14418	5274	19
本科院校	Senior Colleges	175452	8218	10214	4014	20
专科学校	Junior Colleges	37708		3083	844	12
独立学院	Self-governing Colleges	22064		1121	416	20
成人高校	Adult Education Schools	10531				

注：1）根据教育部规定，计算专任教师平均负担学生数时，学生数中的研究生按1比3折算。
2）独立学院和成人高校不计入学校数。

Note: a) According to regulations of Education Ministry, postgraduates are accounted for 1:3 while calculating ratio of student to full-time teacher.
b) The number of institutions excludes self-governing colleges and adult education schools.

17－7 研究生基本情况（1996－2004年）
Basic Statistics on Postgraduates (1996-2004)

单位：人 (person)

年 份 Year	在学人数 Student Enrollment	招 生 数 New Student Enrollment	毕业生数 Graduates
1996	2953	1052	762
1997	3199	1108	847
1998	3726	1389	862
1999	5032	2132	991
2000	6233	2686	1084
2001	8358	3410	1401
2002	11110	4423	1616
2003	14763	6392	2715
2004	19367	8202	3426

17－8 普通高等学校分科学生数（2004年）
Student Enrollment in Regular Institutions of Higher Education by Field of Study (2004)

单位：人 (person)

项 目	Item	在校学生数 Student Enrollment	#本科 Regular College Course	招生数 New Student Enrollment	#本科 Regular College Course	毕业生数 Graduates	#本科 Regular College Course
总 计	**Total**	**303913**	**178622**	**108094**	**53770**	**54025**	**27692**
哲 学	Philosophy	233	39	95		24	
经济学	Economics	14204	10509	4781	2955	2537	1727
法 学	Law	21698	13690	7216	4071	3829	2485
教育学	Education	13245	5073	5488	1539	2301	610
文 学	Literature	57470	39314	21591	13671	10151	5002
历史学	History	1208	951	472	392	235	119
理 学	Science	25387	19439	8481	5939	3915	2450
工 学	Engineering	95679	49374	33361	13382	17072	8383
农 学	Agriculture	7932	5294	2751	1412	1587	1231
医 学	Medicine	13745	5907	4990	1487	2256	720
管理学	Administration	53112	29032	18868	8922	10118	4965

注：本表数据含研究生数。

Note: Data in this table includes postgraduates.

17－9 普通中等专业学校分类情况（2004年）
Regular Specialized Secondary Schools by Type (2004)

单位：人 (person)

项　目	Item	毕业生数 Graduates	招生数 New Student Enrollment	在校学生数 Student Enrollment
全市总计	**Total**	**24610**	**33616**	**99541**
农林类	Agriculture and Forestry	760	243	1397
资源与环境类	Resources and Environment	66	89	344
能源类	Energy	269	1122	2519
土木水利工程类	Civil Engineering and water Conservancy	736	1572	4107
加工制造类	Processing and Manufacture	2673	6161	15908
交通运输类	Transportation	100	216	538
信息技术类	Information and Technology	5236	5842	19217
医药卫生类	Medicine and Health Care	6188	10583	29812
商贸与旅游类	Trade and Tourism	1282	1375	4593
财经类	Finance and Economics	1202	1917	5444
文化艺术与体育类	Culture, Art and Sports	1442	1766	5158
社会公共事务类	Social Public Affairs	535	431	1667
师范类	Teacher Training	4080	2299	8802
其　他	Others	41		35

17－10 成人教育基本情况（2004年）
Basic Statistics on Adult Education (2004)

单位：人 (person)

项　目	Item	学校数（所） Schools (unit)	毕业生数 Graduates	招生数 New Student Enrollment	在校学生数 Student Enrollment	教职工数 Teachers and Staff	#专任教师 Full-time Teachers
总　计	**Total**	**1598**	**103959**	**79051**	**222665**	**11366**	**5811**
成人高等学校	**Adult Higher Education Schools**	**11**	**38342**	**54178**	**95870**	**3272**	**2018**
#广播电视大学	Radio and TV Universities	1	7519	9187	14956	1487	899
职工、农民高等学院	Schools of Higher Education for Staff, Workers and Peasants	8	1636	3490	4271	1172	642
管理干部学院	Colleges for Management Cadres	1	236	81	81	64	52
教育学院	Pedagogical Colleges	1	2119	3084	5624	549	425
成人中等专业学校	**Specialized Secondary Schools for Adults**	**91**	**12130**	**24873**	**64505**	**4435**	**2569**
#教师进修学校	Teacher Training Schools	35	1204	481	2124	1361	876
成人中学	**Secondary Schools for Adults**	**75**	**3923**		**4199**	**259**	**133**
职工中学	Secondary Schools for Staff and Workers	3	120		118	16	14
农民中学	Secondary Schools for Peasants	72	3803		4081	243	119
成人初等学校	**Primary Schools for Adults**	**1421**	**49564**		**58091**	**3400**	**1091**
职工初等学校	Primary Schools for Staff and Workers	100	1908		1880	14	9
农民初等学校	Primary Schools for Peasants	1321	47656		56211	3386	1082
#扫盲班	Literacy Courses	791	12623		16587	2640	661

17－11 初中毕业生和小学生毕业生升学率及小学学龄儿童入学率（2003－2004年）
Percentage of Graduates of Junior Secondary Schools and Primary Schools Entering Higher Level Schools, Percentage of School-aged Children Enrolled (2003-2004)

指　　标	Item	2003	2004
初中毕业生数（万人）	Graduates of Junior Secondary Schools (10 000 persons)	40.02	37.42
高中阶段学校招生数（万人）	Students entering Senior Secondary Schools (10 000 persons)	30.80	31.52
初中毕业生升学率（%）	Percentage of Graduates of Junior Secondary Schools Entering Senior Secondary Schools (%)	76.4	80.7
小学毕业生数（万人）	Graduates of Primary Schools (10 000 persons)	45.68	44.61
初中学校招生数（万人）	Students entering Junior Secondary Schools (10 000 persons)	44.58	42.77
小学毕业生升学率（%）	Percentage of Graduates of Primary Schools Entering Junior Secondary Schools (%)	97.9	95.9
学龄儿童数（万人）	School-aged Children (10 000 persons)	251.73	247.22
已入学学龄儿童数（万人）	School-aged Children Enrolled in Schools (10 000 persons)	251.39	246.98
小学学龄儿童入学率（%）	Percentage of School-aged Children Enrolled (%)	99.9	99.9

17－12 幼儿园基本情况（2003－2004年）
Basic Statistics on Kindergartens (2003-2004)

指　　标	Item	2003	2004
园数（所）	Number of Kindergartens (unit)	3093	3408
班数（个）	Number of Classes (unit)	18840	19809
在园幼儿数（人）	Student Enrollment (person)	572538	544759
教职工数（人）	Number of Staff and Teachers (person)	19013	19801
#教师	Teachers	12141	12351

17－13 各级学校女学生和女教师数（2003－2004年）
Number of Female Students and Teachers by School Level (2003-2004)

单位：人 (person)

项目	Item	2003	2004
女学生数	**Number of Female Students**		
普通高等学校	Institutions of Higher Education	107268	131566
普通中等专业学校	Specialized Secondary Schools	53499	55860
普通中学	Regular Secondary Schools	778388	801521
职业中学	Vocational Secondary Schools	66213	75653
小　学	Primary Schools	1325437	1296860
女学生占学生总数的百分比(%)	**Percentage of Female Students to Total Students (%)**		
普通高等学校	Institutions of Higher Education	44.6	46.2
普通中等专业学校	Specialized Secondary Schools	56.3	56.1
普通中学	Regular Secondary Schools	46.8	46.9
职业中学	Vocational Secondary Schools	48.8	47.9
小　学	Primary Schools	47.7	47.7
女教职工数	**Number of Female Teachers**		
普通高等学校	Institutions of Higher Education	12514	14673
普通中等专业学校	Specialized Secondary Schools	2051	1858
普通中学	Regular Secondary Schools	39794	41209
职业中学	Vocational Secondary Schools	4137	3799
小　学	Primary Schools	60578	60318
女教职工占教师总数的百分比(%)	**Percentage of Female Teachers to Total Teachers (%)**		
普通高等学校	Institutions of Higher Education	40.3	40.0
普通中等专业学校	Specialized Secondary Schools	40.8	42.6
普通中学	Regular Secondary Schools	36.1	37.0
职业中学	Vocational Secondary Schools	42.2	40.3
小　学	Primary Schools	46.9	47.4

17－14 科技经费、科技奖励情况（2003－2004年）
Funds and Rewards for Science and Technology (2003-2004)

指　标	Item	2003	2004
国家科技部计划拨款（万元）	**Appropriate Funds by Ministry of Science and Technology in Plan (10 000 yuan)**	**12529**	**14501**
重庆市财政科技拨款（万元）	**Appropriate Funds of Science and Technology by Municipal Finance (10 000 yuan)**	**36890**	**50063**
科学事业费	Funds for Science	8666	10172
科技三项费	Funds for Science and Technology Innovation	27969	39668
科技基建费	Capital Construction of Science and Technology	255	223
科技奖励情况（项）	**Rewards of Science and Technology (item)**		
科技进步奖	Advanced Rewards of Science and Technology		
国家级	National Rewards	7	11
一等奖	1st Prize	1	1
二等奖	2nd Prize	6	10
三等奖	3rd Prize		
重庆市级	Municipal Rewards	85	80
一等奖	1st Prize	2	4
二等奖	2nd Prize	16	11
三等奖	3rd Prize	67	65
自然科学奖	Rewards of Natural Science		
重庆市级	Municipal Rewards	6	8
一等奖	1st Prize		
二等奖	2nd Prize	1	3
三等奖	3rd Prize	5	5
技术发明奖	Rewards of Technological Invents		
重庆市级	Municipal Rewards	3	3
一等奖	1st Prize	1	
二等奖	2nd Prize		2
三等奖	3rd Prize	2	1

注：重庆市级自然科学奖和技术发明奖从2002年起开始评定。

Note: Municipal rewards of natural science and technological invents were assessed since 2002.

17－15 科学协会活动情况（2004年）
Activities of Science and Technology Associations (2004)

指　　标	Item	合　计 Total	＃市级科协 Science and Technology Associations at Municipal Level	＃市级学会 Learned Societies at Municipal Level
国内学术会议	**Domestic Academic Meetings**			
举办次数（次）	Holding Number (time)	357	3	328
参加人数（人次）	Number of Participants (person-time)	35667	710	31592
交流论文数（篇）	Number of Papers Presented (piece)	11734	230	6504
国际学术会议	**International Academic Meetings**			
在国内举行的国际学术会议（次）	Held in China Number (time)	16	2	14
中方参加人数（人次）	Number of Chinese Participants (person-time)	2673	1100	1573
中方交流论文（篇）	Number of Chinese Papers Presented (piece)	1050	450	600
外方参加人数（人次）	Number of Foreign Participants (person-time)	321	40	281
外方交流论文（篇）	Number of Foreign Papers Presented (piece)	168	12	156
科学考察	**Scientific Study Tour**			
外派科技团组个数（个）	Number of Scientific Groups Sent Abroad (unit)	60	3	51
外派总人次（人次）	Number of Person-times Sent Abroad (person-time)	192	10	138
科普活动	**Activities for Popular Science**			
科普讲座次数（次）	Number of Lectures (time)	1189	39	297
科普讲座参加人数（人次）	Number of Participants (person-time)	758311	118500	63638
科普展览次数（次）	Number of Exhibitions (time)	832	80	81
科普展览参加人数（人次）	Number of Participants (person-time)	2000856	219500	71455
科技夏（冬）令营（次）	Technical Summer (winter) Camp (time)	137	95	9
青年科技竞赛次数（次）	Number of Teenagers Participating in Science-technology Competitions (time)	827	264	435
科技培训	**Training Program**			
院校培训结业学员数（人）	Number of Persons Trained by Universities and Colleges (person)	1636	1	
培训班培训人次（人次）	Number of Persons Trained by Training Classes (person-time)	774062	60	
外派研修生人数（人次）	Number of Trainees Sent Abroad (person-time)	15	10	
咨　询	**Consultative Activities**			
无偿咨询项目数（项）	Number of Non-payable Consultative Projects (item)	4315	5	2273
完成技术合同数（项）	Number of Consultative Contracts Completed (item)	603	98	218
咨询合同实现金额（万元）	Revenue from Fulfillment of Consultative Contracts (10 000 yuan)	1163	920	163
＃技术交易额（万元）	Technology Business Value (10 000 yuan)	993	920	42
科技建议被采纳项数（项）	Technological Suggestions Adopted (item)	481	5	159
向市人大、政协提案被采纳（项）	Suggestions Adopted by Chongqing People's Congress and People's Political Consultative Conference (item)	70	4	

17－16 重庆市科技活动基本情况（2000年）
Basic Statistics on Scientific and Technological Activities in Chongqing (2000)

指　　标	Item	合　计 Total	科研机构 Research Institutes	高等院校 Colleges & Universities	#附属医院 Attached Hospitals
有科技活动的单位数（个）	Units Engaged in Scientific and Technological Activities (unit)	958	86	23	3
科技活动人员（人）	Personnel Engaged in Scientific and Technological Activities (person)	66094	6720	14008	1903
#科学家和工程师	Scientists and Engineers	41955	4017	10829	1772
科技活动经费筹集总额（万元）	Total Funds Raised for Scientific and Technological Activities (10 000 yuan)	335115	56738	25834	2082
政府资金	Funds from Government	79095	37940	15000	1527
企业资金	Funds from Enterprises	177709	2148	9117	62
事业单位资金	Funds from Institutions	14564	9145	1237	343
金融机构贷款	Funds from Financial Institutions	42533	914	164	150
国外资金	Foreign Funds	1302		19	
其他资金	Others	19912	6592	298	
科技活动经费内部支出（万元）	Inner Expenditure of Funds for Scientific and Technological Activities (10 000 yuan)	301964	58230	22500	1937
人员劳务费	Remuneration for Personnel	72455	16370	4875	666
固定资产购建	Purchases of Fixed Assets	88788	12018	4780	463
#设备购置	Facilities	72819	8043	4754	463
其　他	Others	140721	29842	12845	808
科技活动经费外部支出（万元）	Outside Expenditure of Funds for Scientific and Technological Activities (10 000 yuan)	21969	138	201	
全部科技项目(课题)数（项）	Total Scientific and Technological Projects (item)	7410	727	2819	213
科技项目(课题)参加人员全时当量（人年）	Full-time Converted Personnel Engaged in Scientific and Technological Projects (person-year)	27738	3937	5510	469
#科学家和工程师	Scientists and Engineers	16421	2230	2937	225
科技项目(课题)经费内部支出（万元）	Inner Expenditure of Funds for Scientific and Technological Projects (10 000 yuan)	199966	29254	11319	290
专利申请数（件）	Patents Applied (pcs)	636	4	25	1
#发明专利申请数	Invents	123	2	16	1
拥有发明专利（件）	Patents Owned (pcs)	225	8		
发表科技论文（篇）	Scientific and Technological Papers Issued (unit)	10245	830	7857	723
出版科技著作（种）	Scientific and Technological Works Issued (sort)	483	30	443	24
研究与技术开发机构数（个）	Institutes of Research and Technological Development (unit)	622	89	206	
#法人机构	Juridical	89	89		
机构从事科技活动人员（人）	Personnel of Institutes Engaged in Scientific and Technological Activities (person)	21475	6720	3393	
#全时人员	Full-time Personnel	19999	6518	2119	
#科学家和工程师	Scientists and Engineers	13346	4017	2293	
机构科技经费内部支出（万元）	Inner Expenditure of Scientific and Technological Funds of Institutes (10 000 yuan)	144597	58230	8566	
机构年末固定资产原价（万元）	Year-end Net Value of Fixed Assets of Institutes (10 000 yuan)	361918	97681	24265	
#仪器设备	Apparatus and Facilities	128005	44798	16961	

注：本表17-16与17-17表为重庆市2000年R&D资源清查数据。R&D资源每五年清查一次。

Note: Tables of 17-16 and 17-17 were the data on R&D resource survey in Chongqing in 2000. R&D resource survey is carried out every 5 years.

17-16 续表 CONTINUED

指　　标	Item	企　业 Enterprises	#工业企业 Industrial Enterprises	其　他 Others
有科技活动的单位数（个）	Units Engaged in Scientific and Technological Activities (unit)	637	569	212
科技活动人员（人）	Personnel Engaged in Scientific and Technological Activities (person)	39997	37125	5369
#科学家和工程师	Scientists and Engineers	23233	20835	3876
科技活动经费筹集总额（万元）	Total Funds Raised for Scientific and Technological Activities (10 000 yuan)	242405	216073	10138
政府资金	Funds from Government	21703	18227	4452
企业资金	Funds from Enterprises	164949	152804	1496
事业单位资金	Funds from Institutions	317	317	3866
金融机构贷款	Funds from Financial Institutions	41203	39926	253
国外资金	Foreign Funds	1252	1252	32
其他资金	Others	12982	3548	40
科技活动经费内部支出（万元）	Inner Expenditure of Funds for Scientific and Technological Activities (10 000 yuan)	208960	192900	12274
人员劳务费	Remuneration for Personnel	46318	42981	4893
固定资产购建	Purchases of Fixed Assets	66867	60301	5123
#设备购置	Facilities	56623	52577	3399
其他	Others	95776	89618	2258
科技活动经费外部支出（万元）	Outside Expenditure of Funds for Scientific and Technological Activities (10 000 yuan)	21021	20402	609
全部科技项目(课题)数（项）	Total Scientific and Technological Projects (item)	3204	2935	660
科技项目(课题)参加人员全时当量（人年）	Full-time Converted Personnel Engaged in Scientific and Technological Projects (person-year)	16506	15647	1786
#科学家和工程师	Scientists and Engineers	9944	9190	1310
科技项目(课题)经费内部支出（万元）	Inner Expenditure of Funds for Scientific and Technological Projects (10 000 yuan)	152132	146672	7261
专利申请数（件）	Patents Applied (pcs)	582	394	25
#发明专利申请数	Invents	102	99	3
拥有发明专利（件）	Patents Owned (pcs)	213	190	4
发表科技论文（篇）	Scientific and Technological Papers Issued (unit)	243	126	1315
出版科技著作（种）	Scientific and Technological Works Issued (sort)	2		8
研究与技术开发机构数（个）	Institutes of Research and Technological Development (unit)	294	271	33
#法人机构	Juridical			
机构从事科技活动人员（人）	Personnel of Institutes Engaged in Scientific and Technological Activities (person)	10899	10393	463
#全时人员	Full-time Personnel	10899	10393	463
#科学家和工程师	Scientists and Engineers	6686	6298	350
机构科技经费内部支出（万元）	Inner Expenditure of Scientific and Technological Funds of Institutes (10 000 yuan)	76825	75467	977
机构年末固定资产原价（万元）	Year-end Net Value of Fixed Assets of Institutes (10 000 yuan)	233037	230020	6936
#仪器设备	Apparatus and Facilities	62648	60739	3598

17－17 重庆市研究与试验发展（R&D）活动基本情况（2000年）
Basic Statistics on R&D Activities in Chongqing (2000)

指　　标	Item	合　计 Total	科研机构 Research Institutes	高等院校 Colleges & Universities	#附属医院 Attached Hospitals
有R&D活动的单位数（个）	Units Engaged in R&D Activities (unit)	525	28	23	3
R&D人员全时当量（人年）	Full-time Converted R&D Personnel (person-year)	16115	2864	4250	672
#科学家和工程师	Scientists and Engineers	12311	1453	4013	648
#全时人员	Full-time Personnel	10321	1658	1592	371
#基础研究人员	Personnel of Basic Research	1063		1035	316
应用研究人员	Personnel of Application Research	3963	716	2431	244
试验发展人员	Personnel of Testing Development	11089	2148	784	112
R&D经费内部支出（万元）	Inner Expenditure of R&D Funds (10 000 yuan)	101294	22353	14939	397
#基础研究	Basic Research	1442		1384	173
应用研究	Application Research	20572	5045	10018	156
试验发展	Testing Development	79280	17309	3537	68
#人员劳务费	Remuneration for Personnel	24592	3906	2974	133
固定资产购置	Purchases of Fixed Assets	23443	7570	2910	98
#设备购置费	Facilities	19967	4528	2910	98
其　他	Others	53259	10878	9054	165
#政府资金	Funds from Government	34256	20980	8214	290
企业资金	Funds from Enterprises	54836	39	6005	13
国外资金	Foreign Funds	292	54	10	
其　他	Others	11910	1280	710	94
R&D资金外部支出（万元）	Outside Expenditure of R&D Funds (10 000 yuan)	8707	81	144	
R&D项目（课题）数（项）	R&D Projects (item)	4041	337	2311	223
基础研究	Basic Research	675		672	83
应用研究	Application Research	1617	52	1370	101
试验发展	Testing Development	1749	285	269	39
R&D项目（课题）参加人员全时当量（人年）	Full-time Converted Personnel Engaged in R&D Projects (person-year)	12298	1871	3501	509
基础研究	Basic Research	908		893	231
应用研究	Application Research	2962	378	2069	195
试验发展	Testing Development	8429	1493	539	83
R&D项目（课题）经费内部支出（万元）	Inner Expenditure of R&D Projects (10 000 yuan)	67879	2929	6447	379
基础研究	Basic Research	800		746	139
应用研究	Application Research	9277	134	4536	174
试验发展	Testing Development	57802	2795	1166	66
有R&D活动的研究与技术开发机构（个）	Institutes of R&D Research and Technological Development (unit)	445	29	187	
机构中R&D人员折合全时当量（人年）	Converted Full-time Personnel of Institutes Engaged in R&D Activities (person-year)	10338	2864	1734	
#科学家和工程师	Scientists and Engineers	6766	1453	1633	
机构R&D经费内部支出（万元）	Inner R&D Expenditure of Institutes (10 000 yuan)	58765	22353	7025	

注：本表R&D经费内部支出的"基础研究、应用研究、试验发展"数据是按R&D经费支出中"基础研究、应用研究、试验发展"的比例折算的，与2001年10月发布的《重庆市全社会R&D资源清查主要数据统计公报》有差异的原因是分摊方法不同，本表是每个调查单位的实际比例分摊折算后的汇总数据；《公报》是全部调查单位汇总后的综合比例分摊折算的数据。

Note: Data of basic research, application research and testing development of inner expenditure of R&D funds is converted with proportion of current expenditure of R&D funds. So it is different from that of *Statistical Communique on Major Figures of R&D Resource Check of Chongqing Municipality* issued in October, 2001.

17-17 续表 CONTINUED

指　　标	Item	企　业 Enterprises	#工业企业 Industrial Enterprises	其　他 Others
有R&D活动的单位数（个）	Units Engaged in R&D Activities (unit)	389	350	85
R&D人员全时当量（人年）	Full-time Converted R&D Personnel (person-year)	8376	7691	626
#科学家和工程师	Scientists and Engineers	6329	5754	517
#全时人员	Full-time Personnel	6702	6225	369
#基础研究人员	Personnel of Basic Research	18	18	10
应用研究人员	Personnel of Application Research	537	470	279
试验发展人员	Personnel of Testing Development	7820	7203	337
R&D经费内部支出（万元）	Inner Expenditure of R&D Funds (10 000 yuan)	61449	58424	2553
#基础研究	Basic Research	47	47	11
应用研究	Application Research	4717	4127	792
试验发展	Testing Development	56685	54250	1750
#人员劳务费	Remuneration for Personnel	16599	15341	1113
固定资产购置	Purchases of Fixed Assets	12182	11265	781
#设备购置费	Facilities	11822	10915	707
其　他	Others	32668	31819	659
#政府资金	Funds from Government	4144	3623	918
企业资金	Funds from Enterprises	47383	45303	1409
国外资金	Foreign Funds	228	223	
其　他	Others	9694	9275	226
R&D资金外部支出（万元）	Outside Expenditure of R&D Funds (10 000 yuan)	8330	7989	153
R&D项目（课题）数（项）	R&D Projects (item)	1145	1021	248
基础研究	Basic Research	1	1	2
应用研究	Application Research	69	35	126
试验发展	Testing Development	1075	985	120
R&D项目（课题）参加人员全时当量（人年）	Full-time Converted Personnel Engaged in R&D Projects (person-year)	6390	5924	536
基础研究	Basic Research	5	5	10
应用研究	Application Research	283	226	232
试验发展	Testing Development	6102	5693	295
R&D项目（课题）经费内部支出（万元）	Inner Expenditure of R&D Projects (10 000 yuan)	56473	53702	2029
基础研究	Basic Research	44	44	11
应用研究	Application Research	3977	3498	629
试验发展	Testing Development	52452	50160	1389
有R&D活动的研究与技术开发机构（个）	Institutes of R&D Research and Technological Development (unit)	208	191	21
机构中R&D人员折合全时当量（人年）	Converted Full-time Personnel of Institutes Engaged in R&D Activities (person-year)	5544	5269	196
#科学家和工程师	Scientists and Engineers	3531	3308	149
机构R&D经费内部支出（万元）	Inner R&D Expenditure of Institutes (10 000 yuan)	28690	27756	698

17－18 普通高等学校教学和科研人员（2004年）
Personnel of Teaching and Research in Regular Institutions of Higher Education (2004)

单位：人 (person)

项　目	Item	合　计 Total	自然科学 Natural Sciences	工程与技术 Engineering and Technology	医学科学 Medical Sciences	农业科学 Agricultural Sciences	社会和人文科学 Social Sciences and Humanities	其 他 Other
总　计	**Total**	**18328**	**1949**	**5195**	**2707**	**596**	**7540**	**341**
按职称分	**By Title**							
#高　级	Senior	6923	926	1914	933	268	2882	
中　级	Medium	7091	741	2269	1147	258	2676	
初　级	Junior	3811	282	1012	627	70	1820	
按技术等级分	**By Technical Grade**							
#科学家和工程师	Scientists and Engineers	10478	315	1114	1467	123	7459	
技术员	Technical Personnel	1046	61	338	529	37	81	

17－19 普通高等学校科技项目情况（2004年）
Scientific and Technological Projects of Regular Institutions of Higher Education (2004)

项　目	Item	课题数（项） Number of Projects (unit)	当年投入经费（万元） Funds of Projects (10 000 yuan)	当年支出经费（万元） Expenditures for Projects (10 000 yuan)	当年投入人员（人年） Personnel Engaged in Projects (person-year)	#科学家和工程师（理工农医类项目） Scientists and Engineers (Science, Industry, Agriculture and Medical Fields)
总　计	**Total**	**7054**	**45016**	**41215**	**6198**	**5647**
R&D项目	R&D Projects	5385	22289	19562	4286	4045
基础研究	Basic Research	1604	5082	3778	1312	1244
应用研究	Application Research	2497	13953	11594	2071	1936
试验发展	Testing Development	1284	3254	4190	903	865
非R&D项目	Non-R&D Projects	1669	22727	21653	1912	1602
R&D成果应用	Application of R&D Achievements	982	15227	14620	1185	980
科技服务	Technological Services	687	7500	7033	727	622

17－20 大中型工业企业科技机构情况（2004年）
Scientific and Technological Institutions of Large & Medium-sized Industrial Enterprises (2004)

单位：人、万元 (person, 10 000 yuan)

项　目	Item	科技机构数（个） Number of Institutions (unit)	科技机构科技活动人数 Personnel of Institutions	科技机构经费内部支出 Inner Expenditures for Science and Technology
总　计	**Total**	**183**	**11255**	**130800**
按隶属关系分	**By Relationship**			
中　央	Central	43	4163	31302
地　方	Local	140	7092	99498
按登记注册类型分	**By Registration**			
国有企业	State-owned	34	1423	16536
集体企业	Collective-owned	3	33	253
股份合作企业	Cooperative Enterprises			
联营企业	Joint Ownership Enterprises			
有限责任公司	Limited Liability Corporations	77	5015	44238
#国有独资公司	Sole State-funded	20	2336	21609
股份有限公司	Share Holding Corporations Limited	27	2425	25832
私营企业	Private Enterprises	26	1538	26304
#私营独资企业	Private-funded			
其他企业	Other Domestic-funded Enterprises			
港、澳、台商投资企业	Enterprises Funded by Hong Kong, Macao and Taiwan	6	219	1664
外商投资企业	Shareholding Corporations Ltd. With Foreign Investment	10	602	15973
按工业行业分	**By Industrial Sector**			
采矿业	Mining and Quarrying	1	16	96
煤炭开采和洗选业	Coal Mining and Dressing			
石油和天然气开采业	Petroleum and Natural Gas Extraction			
黑色金属矿采选业	Ferrous Metals Mining and Dressing			
有色金属矿采选业	Nonferrous Metals Mining and Dressing			
非金属矿采选业	Nonmetal Minerals Mining and Dressing	1	16	96
其他采矿业	Other Minerals Mining			
制造业	Manufacturing	179	11039	129189
农副食品加工业	Farm Products and By-food Processing	3	161	1127
食品制造业	Food Production	3	122	543
饮料制造业	Beverage Production	2	130	1287

17-20 续表 CONTINUED

单位：人、万元 (person, 10 000 yuan)

项　目	Item	科技机构数（个） Number of Institutions (unit)	科技机构科技活动人数 Personnel of Institutions	科技机构经费内部支出 Inner Expenditures for Science and Technology
烟草制品业	Tobacco Products	3	86	1088
纺织业	Textile Industry	5	191	1172
纺织服装、鞋、帽制造业	Garments, Shoes and Hats Production			
皮革、毛皮、羽毛（绒）及其制品业	Leather, Furs, Down and Related Products			
木材加工及木竹藤棕草制品业	Timber Processing,Bamboo,Cane,Palm, Straw Products			
家具制造业	Furniture Manufacturing	1	162	839
造纸及纸制品业	Papermaking and Paper Products	1	11	20
印刷业、记录媒介的复制	Printing and Record Medium Reproduction	1	56	25
文教体育用品制造业	Cultural Educational and Sports Goods			
石油加工、炼焦及核燃料加工业	Petroleum, Coking and Nuclear Fuel Processing	1	140	1431
化学原料及化学制品制造业	Raw Chemical Materials and Chemical Products	16	589	9186
医药制造业	Medical and Pharmaceutical Products	13	454	6808
化学纤维制造业	Chemical Fiber	1	48	327
橡胶制品业	Rubber Products	3	39	67
塑料制品业	Plastic Products	1	37	127
非金属矿物制品业	Nonmetal Mineral Products	11	505	3126
黑色金属冶炼及压延加工业	Smelting and Pressing of Ferrous Metals	3	202	998
有色金属冶炼及压延加工业	Smelting and Pressing of Nonferrous Metals	2	316	2244
金属制品业	Metal Products	3	75	360
通用设备制造业	Ordinary Equipment	18	1043	14981
专用设备制造业	Special Equipment	7	960	3816
交通运输设备制造业	Transportation Equipment	46	4296	69425
电气机械及器材制造业	Electric Equipment and Machinery	7	140	1111
通信设备、计算机及其他电子设备制造业	Communication, Computers and Other Electronic Equipment	11	522	4068
仪器仪表及文化、办公用机械制造业	Instruments, Meters,Cultural and Office Machinery	17	754	5013
工艺品及其他制造业	Handicraft and Other Production			
废弃资源和废旧材料回收加工业	Recovery and Processing of Waste Resources and Materials			
电力、燃气及水的生产和供应业	Electricpower, Gas & Water Production and Supply	3	200	1515
电力、热力的生产和供应业	Electricpower and Hot Power Production and Supply	3	200	1515
燃气生产和供应业	Gas Production and Supply			
水的生产和供应业	Water Production and Supply			

17－21 大中型工业企业科技活动人员与经费筹集情况（2004年）
Personnel in Scientific and Technological Activities and Funds of Large & Medium-Sized Industrial Enterprises (2004)

项　目	Item	从事科技活动人员数(人) Personnel in Scientific and Technological Activities (person)	#科学家和工程师 Scientists and Engineers	当年筹集额(万元) Funds of Current Year (10 000 yuan)	#政府部门资金 Funds from Government	#金融机构贷款 Loans of Financial Institutions	#企业自筹 Funds Self-raised by Enterprises
总　计	**Total**	**31021**	**20291**	**360950**	**19795**	**23060**	**312909**
按隶属关系分	**By Relationship**						
中　央	Central	9941	7286	125308	11088	1700	110935
地　方	Local	21080	13005	235642	8706	21360	201974
按登记注册类型分	**By Registration**						
国有企业	State-owned	5227	3126	52308	6053	1440	44242
集体企业	Collective-owned	234	55	622	3		619
股份合作企业	Cooperative Enterprises	104	5	444			444
联营企业	Joint Ownership Enterprises						
有限责任公司	Limited Liability Corporations	13949	9181	113700	9345	6994	94956
#国有独资公司	Sole State-funded	5087	4111	50884	6059	1620	41619
股份有限公司	Share Holding Corporations Limited	4858	3148	83660	2574	3650	77396
私营企业	Private Enterprises	4170	3061	58415	1420	8526	46302
#私营独资企业	Private-funded						
其他企业	Other Domestic-funded Enterprises						
港、澳、台商投资企业	Enterprises Funded by Hong Kong, Macao and Taiwan	1291	921	23973	100	2300	21573
外商投资企业	Shareholding Corporations Ltd. With Foreign Investment	1188	794	27828	300	150	27378
按工业行业分	**By Industrial Sector**						
采矿业	Mining and Quarrying	1085	570	4138	25		4113
煤炭开采和洗选业	Coal Mining and Dressing	900	480	2028			2028
石油和天然气开采业	Petroleum and Natural Gas Extraction	80	15	1550			1550
黑色金属矿采选业	Ferrous Metals Mining and Dressing						
有色金属矿采选业	Nonferrous Metals Mining and Dressing						
非金属矿采选业	Nonmetal Minerals Mining and Dressing	105	75	560	25		535
其他采矿业	Other Minerals Mining						
制造业	Manufacturing	29176	19146	354650	19770	23060	306634
农副食品加工业	Farm Products and By-food Processing	275	146	1400	105	48	1247
食品制造业	Food Production	282	225	642	130		512
饮料制造业	Beverage Production	255	131	2700	532		2168
烟草制品业	Tobacco Products	105	67	1088			1088

17-21 续表 CONTINUED

项　　目	Item	从事科技活动人员数(人) Personnel in Scientific and Techonlo-gical Activities (person)	#科学家和工程师 Scientists and Engineers	当年筹集额(万元) Funds of Current Year (10 000 yuan)	#政府部门资金 Funds from Govern-ment	#金融机构贷款 Loans of Financial Institutions	#企业自筹 Funds Self-raised by Enterprises
纺织业	Textile Industry	451	178	2483	57	800	1626
纺织服装、鞋、帽制造业	Garments, Shoes and Hats Production						
皮革毛皮羽毛（绒）及其制品业	Leather, Furs, Down and Related Products						
木材加工及木竹藤棕草制品业	Timber Processing,Bamboo, Cane,Palm,Straw Products						
家具制造业	Furniture Manufacturing	162	91	839			839
造纸及纸制品业	Papermaking and Paper Products	142	54	4537		980	3557
印刷业、记录媒介的复制	Printing and Record Medium Reproduction	56	10	1000		600	400
文教体育用品制造业	Cultural Educational and Sports Goods						
石油加工、炼焦及核燃料加工业	Petroleum, Coking and Nuclear Fuel Processing	228	127	1492			1492
化学原料及化学制品制造业	Raw Chemical Materials and Chemical Products	1722	980	32588	1200	5150	26198
医药制造业	Medical and Pharmaceutical Products	1314	1028	15952	1854	2460	11638
化学纤维制造业	Chemical Fiber	48	21	467			467
橡胶制品业	Rubber Products	144	76	179			179
塑料制品业	Plastic Products	40	20	806	10		796
非金属矿物制品业	Nonmetal Mineral Products	994	481	7789	300	129	7360
黑色金属冶炼及压延加工业	Smelting and Pressing of Ferrous Metals	1387	897	31054	33	2000	29021
有色金属冶炼及压延加工业	Smelting and Pressing of Nonferrous Metals	1473	508	6825	437		6288
金属制品业	Metal Products	1049	874	3192		106	3082
通用设备制造业	Ordinary Equipment	3063	1754	29423	1193	1360	26317
专用设备制造业	Special Equipment	3252	2836	32029	7926		23959
交通运输设备制造业	Transportation Equipment	9889	6751	157546	4212	7683	142550
电气机械及器材制造业	Electric Equipment and Machinery	500	294	3696	1	900	2795
通信设备、计算机及其他电子设备制造业	Communication, Computers and Other Electronic Equipment	791	598	6494	1717	600	3768
仪器仪表及文化、办公用机械制造业	Instruments, Meters,Cultural and Office Machinery	1534	982	10117	62	94	9126
工艺品及其他制造业	Handicraft and Other Production	20	17	313		150	163
废弃资源和废旧材料回收加工业	Recovery and Processing of Waste Resources and Materials						
电力、燃气及水的生产和供应业	Electricpower, Gas & Water Production and Supply	760	575	2162			2162
电力、热力的生产和供应业	Electricpower and Hot Power Production and Supply	725	560	2072.1			2072.1
燃气生产和供应业	Gas Production and Supply	35	15	89.8			89.8
水的生产和供应业	Water Production and Supply						

17－22 大中型工业企业科技活动经费支出与项目情况（2004年）
Expenditures and Projects of Scientific & Technological Activities of Large & Medium-sized Industrial Enterprises (2004)

单位：项、万元 (unit, 10 000 yuan)

项　目	Item	项目数 Projects	科技活动经费支出 Expenditures for Scientific and Technological Activities	#用于开发新产品 For New Product Development	技术改造经费支出 Expenditures for Technical Transformation	技术引进经费支出 Expenditures for Technical Recommendation	购买国内技术用款 Purchases of Civil Technology	研究与发展经费内部支出 Internal Expenses for R&D
总　计	**Total**	**2260**	**444598**	**163480**	**622896**	**253162**	**36568**	**146463**
按隶属关系分	**By Relationship**							
中　央	Central	693	197730	58824	339063	146459	24696	54261
地　方	Local	1567	246869	104656	283833	106703	11873	92203
按登记注册类型分	**By Registration**							
国有企业	State-owned	354	58899	27457	42722	2237	499	21473
集体企业	Collective-owned	34	600	227	228		12	68
股份合作企业	Cooperative Enterprises	4	544	51	19		12	513
联营企业	Joint Ownership Enterprises							
有限责任公司	Limited Liability Corporations	1039	177820	62299	195274	141421	9833	60192
#国有独资公司	Sole State-funded	326	55542	33155	55248	3884	102	32476
股份有限公司	Share Holding Corporations Limited	323	95656	33129	163840	14566	21751	29361
私营企业	Private Enterprises	319	59810	29931	18880	467	1874	24845
#私营独资企业	Private-funded	11	60					32
其他企业	Other Domestic-funded Enterprises							
港、澳、台商投资企业	Enterprises Funded by Hong Kong, Macao and Taiwan	111	24156	1729	28311	6457	519	2398
外商投资企业	Shareholding Corporations Ltd. With Foreign Investment	76	27113	8658	173623	88015	2069	7614
按工业行业分	**By Industrial Sector**							
采矿业	Mining and Quarrying	85	4742	507	9842		15	1042
煤炭开采和洗选业	Coal Mining and Dressing	79	2512	500	5279		15	290
石油和天然气开采业	Petroleum and Natural Gas Extraction	1	1550					180
黑色金属矿采选业	Ferrous Metals Mining and Dressing				4171			
有色金属矿采选业	Nonferrous Metals Mining and Dressing							
非金属矿采选业	Nonmetal Minerals Mining and Dressing	5	680	7	393			572
其他采矿业	Other Minerals Mining							
制造业	Manufacturing	2117	436075	162966	593506	253162	36254	145045
农副食品加工业	Farm Products and By-food Processing	16	2152	947	638	1800		976
食品制造业	Food Production	11	757	390	435	29		46
饮料制造业	Beverage Production	12	2472	1643	1465			863
烟草制品业	Tobacco Products	7	1088	348	2200			539

17-22 续表 CONTINUED

单位：项、万元 (unit, 10 000 yuan)

项　　目	Item	项目数 Projects	科技活动经费支出 Expenditures for Scientific and Technological Activities	#用于开发新产品 For New Product Development	技术改造经费支出 Expenditures for Technical Transformation	技术引进经费支出 Expenditures for Technical Recommendation	购买国内技术用款 Purchases of Civil Technology	研究与发展经费内部支出 Internal Expenses for R&D
纺织业	Textile Industry	28	4963	1585	7991	2900	3339	2855
纺织服装、鞋、帽制造业	Garments, Shoes and Hats Production							
皮革毛皮羽毛（绒）及其制品业	Leather, Furs, Down and Related Products							
木材加工及木竹藤棕草制品业	Timber Processing, Bamboo, Cane, Palm, Straw Products							
家具制造业	Furniture Manufacturing	7	839	839				
造纸及纸制品业	Papermaking and Paper Products	6	2896	847	90		200	1142
印刷业、记录媒介的复制	Printing and Record Medium Reproduction	1	524	395	82			
文教体育用品制造业	Cultural Educational and Sports Goods							
石油加工、炼焦及核燃料加工业	Petroleum, Coking and Nuclear Fuel Processing	8	1708	358	120	100		1442
化学原料及化学制品制造业	Raw Chemical Materials and Chemical Products	147	34087	5173	33312	4117	324	10370
医药制造业	Medical and Pharmaceutical Products	130	19275	6995	32184	2646	3378	7016
化学纤维制造业	Chemical Fiber	2	467	214	467			
橡胶制品业	Rubber Products	17	172	125	31			92
塑料制品业	Plastic Products	3	796	426				426
非金属矿物制品业	Nonmetal Mineral Products	47	9812	4484	2506	116		5232
黑色金属冶炼及压延加工业	Smelting and Pressing of Ferrous Metals	99	31714	7922	26939	6456	683	9084
有色金属冶炼及压延加工业	Smelting and Pressing of Nonferrous Metals	70	63935	4838	72169	130023	3500	8337
金属制品业	Metal Products	21	3112	918	2321			97
通用设备制造业	Ordinary Equipment	243	30296	16852	19915	310	1311	9427
专用设备制造业	Special Equipment	131	32490	17445	8866	619	90	17341
交通运输设备制造业	Transportation Equipment	852	170400	74281	371941	102433	23160	55407
电气机械及器材制造业	Electric Equipment and Machinery	45	3544	1909	636	1430	210	1792
通信设备、计算机及其他电子设备制造业	Communication, Computers and Other Electronic Equipment	33	6155	4882	5330	9		2637
仪器仪表及文化、办公用机械制造业	Instruments, Meters, Cultural and Office Machinery	180	11839	9153	3556	174	59	9625
工艺品及其他制造业	Handicraft and Other Production	1	583		313			301
废弃资源和废旧材料回收加工业	Recovery and Processing of Waste Resources and Materials							
电力、燃气及水的生产和供应业	Electricpower, Gas & Water Production and Supply	58	3781	7	19548		300	376
电力、热力的生产和供应业	Electricpower and Hot Power Production and Supply	55	3692		19548		300	370
燃气生产和供应业	Gas Production and Supply	3	90	7				7
水的生产和供应业	Water Production and Supply							

17－23 大中型工业企业新产品开发情况（2004年） New Products Development of Large & Medium-sized Industrial Enterprises (2004)

单位：项、万元 (unit, 10 000 yuan)

项目	Item	新产品项目数 Projects of New Products	新产品销售收入 Sales Revenue of New Products	#新产品出口 Exports of New Products
总　计	**Total**	**1780**	**4883322**	**329110**
按隶属关系分	**By Relationship**			
中　央	Central	518	1586550	73588
地　方	Local	1262	3296772	255522
按登记注册类型分	**By Registration**			
国有企业	State-owned	300	269122	30924
集体企业	Collective-owned	33	5171	987
股份合作企业	Cooperative Enterprises	2	1823	
联营企业	Joint Ownership Enterprises			
有限责任公司	Limited Liability Corporations	811	1378136	54335
#国有独资公司	Sole State-funded	273	459872	2223
股份有限公司	Share Holding Corporations Limited	262	868116	70683
私营企业	Private Enterprises	265	824005	128377
#私营独资企业	Private-funded	11		
其他企业	Other Domestic-funded Enterprises			
港、澳、台商投资企业	Shareholding Corporations Ltd. With Investment from Hong Kong, Macao and Taiwan	50	230782	7064
外商投资企业	Shareholding Corporations Ltd. With Foreign Investment	57	1306168	36739
按工业行业分	**By Industrial Sector**			
煤炭开采和洗选业	Coal Mining and Dressing	15		
石油和天然气开采业	Petroleum and Natural Gas Extraction			
黑色金属矿采选业	Ferrous Metals Mining and Dressing			
有色金属矿采选业	Nonferrous Metals Mining and Dressing			
非金属矿采选业	Nonmetal Minerals Mining and Dressing	1	2522	
其他矿采选业	Other Minerals Mining and Dressing			
木材及竹材采运业	Logging and Transport of Timber and Bamboo			
农副食品加工业	Farm Products and By-food Processing	15	23379	1388
食品制造业	Food Production	7	3877	

17-23 续表 CONTINUED

单位：项、万元 (unit, 10 000 yuan)

项目	Item	新产品项目数 Projects of New Products	新产品销售收入 Sales Revenue of New Products	#新产品出口 Exports of New Products
饮料制造业	Beverage Production	5	31788	
烟草加工业	Tobacco Processing	4	98543	
纺织业	Textile Industry	25	51804	26419
服装及其他纤维制品制造业	Garments and other Fiber Products			
皮革、毛皮、羽绒及其制品业	Leather, Furs, Down and Related Products			
木材加工及竹、藤、棕、草制品业	Timber Processing, Bamboo, Cane, Palm Fiber and Straw Products			
家具制造业	Furniture Manufacturing	7		
造纸及纸制品业	Papermaking and Paper Products	5	25689	
印刷业、记录媒介的复制	Printing and Record Medium Reproduction	1	5099	
文教体育用品制造业	Cultural Educational and Sports Goods			
石油加工及炼焦业	Petroleum Refining and Coking	8	1300	
化学原料及化学制品制造业	Raw Chemical Materials and Chemical Products	94	198385	33907
医药制造业	Medical and Pharmaceutical Products	124	135432	312
化学纤维制造业	Chemical Fiber	2	4076	16
橡胶制品业	Rubber Products	13	3394	10
塑料制品业	Plastic Products	3	3292	
非金属矿物制品业	Nonmetal Mineral Products	27	237563	64606
黑色金属冶炼及压延加工业	Smelting and Pressing of Ferrous Metals	38	196241	100
有色金属冶炼及压延加工业	Smelting and Pressing of Nonferrous Metals	16	71840	2207
金属制品业	Metal Products	19	41836	2842
通用设备制造业	Odinary Equipment	214	218528	19524
专用设备制造业	Special Purpose Equipment	115	97874	
交通运输设备制造业	Transport Equipment	772	3265702	170040
电气机械及器材制造业	Electric Equipment and Machinery	42	39880	344
电子及通信设备制造业	Electronic and Telecommunication Equipment	29	68854	1169
仪器仪表及文化、办公用机械制造业	Instruments Meters Cultural and Clerical Machinery	173	56426	6226
其他制造业	Other Manufacturing			
电力、蒸汽、热水的生产和供应业	Electricity Steam & Hot Water Production and Supply	6		
煤气生产和供应业	Gas Production and Supply			
自来水的生产和供应业	Tap Water Production and Supply			

17－24 专利申请受理量及专利授权量（2003－2004年）
Patent Applications Examined and Authorized (2003-2004)

单位：件 (item)

项　目	Item	申请受理量 Applications Examined		专利授权量 Applications Authorized	
		2003	2004	2003	2004
总　计	**Total**	**4595**	**5171**	**2873**	**3601**
按种类分	**By Type**				
发　明	Creations and Inventions	559	562	126	147
实用新型	Utility Models	1842	1910	1085	1247
外观设计	Designs	2194	2699	1662	2207
按对象分	**By Object**				
个　人	Individuals	2119	2088	1364	1351
大专院校	Universities and Colleges	194	201	43	102
科研单位	Research Institutions	31	42	24	22
工矿企业	Industrial and Mineral Enterprises	2241	2821	1421	2117
机关团体	Government Agencies and Organizations	10	19	21	9

17－25 商标申请注册情况（2003－2004年）
Application for Registration of Trade Marks (2003-2004)

指　标	Item	2003	2004	到2004年底累计 Total at 2004's End
商标申请注册数（件）	Number of Application for Registration of Trade Marks (pcs)	2380	2357	19653
#著名商标	Well-known Trade Marks	34	9	245
驰名商标	Famous Trade Marks		4	9

17－26 各类技术合同签定及执行情况（2004年）
Signed and Implemented Technical Contracts by Type (2004)

项　目	Item	合同数 (项) Number of Contracts (item)	合同成交金额 (万元) Value of Contracts (10 000 yuan)	#技术交易额 (万元) Revenue from Fulfillment of Consultative Contracts (10 000 yuan)	技术交易额比重 (%) As Percentage of Contract Value (%)
总　计	**Total**	**1768**	**596186**	**427281**	**71.7**
技术开发	Technical Development	366	406165	246724	60.7
技术转让	Technical Transfer	185	75893	70982	93.0
技术咨询	Technical Consultation	243	16717	15729	94.1
技术服务	Technical Services	974	97411	93846	96.3

17－27 产品质量监督检查情况（2004年）
Results of Sampling Supervision & Check on Product Quality (2004)

产品名称	Name of Product	监督检验企业数（个）Number of Enterprises Supervised & Checked (unit)	检验批次（批次）Number of Batch-time Checked (batch-time)	合格批次（批次）Number of Batch-time Qualified (batch-time)	批次合格率（%）Rate of Batch-time Qualified (%)
总　　计	**Total**	**21822**	**28042**	**22766**	**81.19**
农用产品	**Chemical Production**	**754**	**991**	**820**	**82.74**
拖拉机	Tractor	3	3	3	100.00
农业用运输车	Chemical Transport Car	14	19	14	73.68
农用配件	Chemical Accessory	20	23	20	86.96
农用化肥	Chemical Fertilizers	518	670	554	82.69
化学农药	Chemical Pesticides	15	22	17	77.27
饲料	Forages	55	84	52	61.90
农用薄膜	Chemical Film	11	15	10	66.67
其它	Others	118	155	150	96.77
加工食品和饮料	**Processing Foods and Drinks**	**9013**	**11693**	**9146**	**78.22**
小麦粉、大米	Wheat Powder and Rice	1241	1409	1232	87.44
肉制品	Meat Products	215	405	335	82.72
食用盐	Edible Salts	17	18	16	88.89
调味品	Condiments	719	1380	1136	82.32
保健食品	Hygienic Food	92	194	140	72.16
白酒	Distilled Spirit	2385	2671	2050	76.75
啤酒	Beer	28	119	118	99.16
黄酒、果酒	Millet Wine and Fruit Wine	14	17	16	94.12
食用植物油	Edible Vegetable Oil	1087	1196	963	80.52
罐头	Canned Food	116	157	75	47.77
糕点、糖果	Cake and Sugar	1838	2464	1885	76.50
非酒精液体饮料	Non-alcoholic Beverage	255	349	242	69.34
冷冻饮品	Frozen Beverage	178	193	146	75.65
方便主食品	Instant Staple Food	101	112	100	89.29
乳制品	Dairy Products	169	231	149	64.50
其它	Others	558	778	543	69.79
家用电器	**Household Appliances**	**69**	**139**	**115**	**82.73**
收录机、音响设备	Radio and Cassette Players, Hi-fi Stereo Component Systems	12	13	11	84.62
电视机、录象机	TV Sets, Videocorders	2	2	2	100.00
洗衣机	Washing Machines	4	4		0.00
电风扇	Electric Fans	13	44	36	81.82
吸油烟机	Smoke Absorbers	3	5	3	60.00
厨房电器具	Electric Cooking Utensils	3	5	5	100.00
电热器具	Electric Heating Appliances	4	6	6	100.00
计算机	Computers	1	1	1	100.00
电话机	Telephone Sets	9	9	7	77.78
其它	Others	18	50	44	88.00
轻工产品	**Light Industry Products**	**1504**	**2225**	**1723**	**77.44**
纸	Paper	92	99	58	58.59
纸制品	Paper Products	119	177	106	59.89
玩具	Toys	9	25	18	72.00
家具	Furniture	465	530	316	59.62
眼镜（架、片）	Spectacles (glass & frame)	155	165	124	75.15
灯泡、灯管	Electric Bulbs & Fluorescence Tubes	30	72	70	97.22
镇流器	Ballast	9	14	12	85.71
电热燃气淋浴器	Water Heaters	18	18	18	100.00
铝制品、压力锅	Aluminum Products and Pressure Cooker	23	25	25	100.00
玻璃制品	Glass Products	39	69	61	88.41
日用五金	Daily Metals	132	146	124	84.93
燃气灶具	Gas Stoves	31	31	29	93.55
金银首饰	Gold and Silver Ornaments	1	30	30	100.00
合成洗涤剂	Synthetic Detergent	19	24	16	66.67
化妆品	Cosmetics	42	142	118	83.10
橡胶、塑料制品	Rubber and Plastic Products	272	588	529	89.97
其它	Others	48	70	69	98.57

17-27 续表 CONTINUED

产品名称	Name of Product	监督检验企业数（个）Number of Enterprises Supervised & Checked (unit)	检验批次（批次）Number of Batch-time Checked (batch-time)	合格批次（批次）Number of Batch-time Qualified (batch-time)	批次合格率（%）Rate of Batch-time Qualified (%)
纺织、鞋类产品	**Textile and Shoes Product**	**1234**	**1532**	**1325**	**86.49**
布(印染、色织、坯布)	Cloth	8	26	26	100.00
服装	Clothes	65	69	40	57.97
棉纺织	Cottony Textile	8	13	6	46.15
毛织品	Wool Fabric	2	2	1	50.00
针织品	Knit Goods	34	34	18	52.94
皮革及制品	Leather and Leather Products	206	219	171	78.08
鞋	Shoes	799	997	946	94.88
丝麻织品	Silk and Linen Fabrics	3	3	2	66.67
其它	Others	109	169	115	68.05
化工产品	**Chemical Products**	**368**	**619**	**469**	**75.77**
涂料、油漆	Paints	195	315	261	82.86
化学试剂	Chemical Reagent	68	136	89	65.44
其它	Others	105	168	119	70.83
建材产品	**Building Materials Products**	**5999**	**6615**	**5718**	**86.44**
水泥	Cement	839	1030	993	96.41
水泥预制构件	Cement Prefabricated Components	2367	2463	2229	90.50
砖、瓦	Bricks & Tiles	1904	2013	1671	83.01
油毡、油纸	Asphalt Felt and Oilpaper	7	7	1	14.29
平板玻璃	Plate Glass	20	35	29	82.86
水暖管件	Waterpipe	57	73	49	67.12
卫生建筑陶瓷	Toilet Architectural Poppery	56	73	64	87.67
装饰材料	Decoration Materials	125	145	63	43.45
石棉制品	Asbestos Products	31	31	15	48.39
人造板	Artificial Board	169	211	111	52.61
其它	Others	424	534	493	92.32
机电产品	**Medical Electric Products**	**509**	**854**	**750**	**87.82**
轴承	Bearings	6	7	6	85.71
阀类、泵	Valves	31	50	42	84.00
电线、电缆	Electric Wires	140	269	261	97.03
通用设备	Universal Equipment	14	33	21	63.64
电动工具	Electric Tools	16	34	28	82.35
工业专用设备	Industry Special Equipment	14	23	8	34.78
电工仪器仪表	Electrical Instrument	17	26	26	100.00
低压电器及元件	Low-voltage Electric Elements	13	24	23	95.83
消防器材	Fire-fighting Equipment & Materials	1	1		
安全防范设备	Safety	36	44	37	84.09
电动机、柴油机	Electric and Diesel Engines	81	120	111	92.50
汽车、摩托车	Motor Vehicles and Motorcycles	43	80	78	97.50
自行车	Bicycles	4	7	5	71.43
其它	Others	93	136	104	76.47
冶金产品及金属制品	**Metal Products**	**503**	**812**	**587**	**72.29**
线材	Wire Rods	172	270	194	71.85
型材	Section Steel	216	301	210	69.77
其它	Others	115	241	183	75.93
能源产品	**Power Products**	**1325**	**1571**	**1330**	**84.66**
原煤	Coal	878	1046	903	86.33
焦炭	Coke	5	12	12	100.00
汽油、柴油	Gasoline and Diesel	137	193	181	93.78
其它	Others	305	320	234	73.13
医疗器械	**Medicine Appliance**	**143**	**257**	**193**	**75.10**
普通医疗器械	Ordinary Medicine Appliance	1	1	1	100.00
其它	Others	142	256	192	75.00
其它	**Others**	**401**	**734**	**590**	**80.38**

17－28 商品质量监督检查情况（2004年）
Results of Sampling Supervision & Check on Commodity Quality (2004)

商品名称	Name of Commodity	检查商业企业数（个） Number of Commercial Enterprises Supervised & Checked (unit)	检查商品（批次） Number of Batch-time Checked (batch-time)	合格批次（批次） Number of Batch-time Qualified (batch-time)	批次合格率（%） Rate of Batch-time Qualified (%)
总计	**Total**	**10829**	**15419**	**10302**	**66.81**
农用产品	**Chemical Pesticides**	**1260**	**1634**	**1216**	**74.42**
农用配件	Chemical Fittings	24	30	4	13.33
农用化肥	Chemical Fertilizers	1070	1293	972	75.17
化学农药	Chemical Pesticides	52	135	114	84.44
饲料	Forages	22	25	14	56.00
种子	Seeds	45	93	89	95.70
农用薄膜	Chemical Film	19	24	6	25.00
其它	Others	28	34	17	50.00
加工食品和饮料	**Artificial Foods and Drinks**	**2154**	**2863**	**2213**	**77.30**
小麦粉、大米	Wheat Powder and Rice	314	380	318	83.68
肉制品	Meat Products	73	106	87	82.08
食用盐	Edible Salts	5	7	4	57.14
调味品	Condiments	158	211	157	74.41
保健食品	Hygienic Food	2	2	1	50.00
白酒	Distilled Spirit	573	705	536	76.03
啤酒	Beer	88	110	79	71.82
黄酒、果酒	Millet Wine and Fruit Wine	12	12	1	8.33
食用植物油	Edible Vegetable Oil	269	329	248	75.38
罐头	Canned Food	1	1		
糕点、糖果	Cake and Sugar	206	279	218	78.14
非酒精液体饮料	Non-alcoholic Beverage	98	116	86	74.14
冷冻饮品	Frozen Beverage	21	34	34	100.00
方便主食品	Instant Staple Food	36	164	143	87.20
乳制品	Dairy Products	79	102	82	80.39
其它	Others	219	305	219	71.80
家用电器	**Household Appliances**	**436**	**823**	**500**	**60.75**
收录机、音响设备	Radio and Cassette Players, Hi-fi Stereo Component Systems	8	8	2	25.00
电视机、录像机	TV Sets, Videocorders	4	9	8	88.89
洗衣机	Washing Machines	23	52	22	42.31
电风扇	Electric Fans	95	268	189	70.52
吸油烟器	Smoke Absorbers	34	45	27	60.00
空调器	Air Conditioners	13	24	3	12.50
厨房电器具	Cooker Electric Appliances	14	19	18	94.74
电热器具	Electric Heating Appliances	117	204	148	72.55
计算机	Computer	12	25	17	68.00
电话机	Telephone Sets	10	11	7	63.64
其它	Others	106	158	59	37.34
轻工产品	**Light Industry Products**	**1486**	**2574**	**1881**	**73.08**
纸	Paper	16	16	11	68.75
纸制品	Paper Products	80	167	105	62.87
玩具	Toys	7	45	15	33.33
家具	Furniture	41	62	53	85.48
眼镜（架、片）	Spectacles (glass & frame)	554	730	610	83.56
灯泡、灯管	Electric Bulbs	108	195	133	68.21
镇流器	Ballast	5	5		
电热燃气淋浴器	Water Heaters	9	13	9	69.23
玻璃制品	Glass Products	78	123	24	19.51
日用五金	Daily Metals	25	44	16	36.36
燃气灶具	Gas Stoves	89	129	86	66.67
金银首饰	Gold and Silver Ornaments	125	370	340	91.89
合成洗涤剂	Synthetic Detergent	56	88	80	90.91

17-28 续表 CONTINUED

商品名称	Name of Commodity	检查商业企业数（个）Number of Commercial Enterprises Supervised & Checked (unit)	检查商品（批次）Number of Batch-time Checked (batch-time)	合格批次（批次）Number of Batch-time Qualified (batch-time)	批次合格率（%）Rate of Batch-time Qualified (%)
化妆品	Cosmetics	5	30	28	93.33
橡胶、塑料制品	Rubber and Plastic Products	274	530	350	66.04
其它	Others	14	27	21	77.78
纺织、鞋类产品	**Textile and Shoes Product**	**785**	**953**	**510**	**53.52**
服装	Clothes	196	285	76	26.67
棉纺织	Cotton Textile Fabric	26	32	2	6.25
毛织品	Wool Fabric	33	39	6	15.38
针织品	Knit Goods	96	129	63	48.84
皮革及制品	Leather and Leather Products	108	111	100	90.09
鞋	Shoes	246	261	242	92.72
丝麻织品	Silk and Linen Fabrics	23	25	17	68.00
其它	Others	57	71	4	5.63
化工产品	**Chemical Products**	**136**	**189**	**138**	**73.02**
涂料，油漆	Paints	99	124	87	70.16
化学制剂	Chemical Reagent	16	44	41	93.18
其它	Others	21	21	10	47.62
建材产品	**Building Materials Products**	**1676**	**2206**	**1294**	**58.66**
水泥	Cement	104	151	146	96.69
水泥预制构件	Cement Prefabricated Components	124	124	112	90.32
砖、瓦	Bricks & Tiles	163	236	197	83.47
油毡、油纸	Asphalt Felt and Oilpaper	4	4	2	50.00
平板玻璃	Plate Glass	13	30	25	83.33
水暖管件	Waterpipe	41	53	19	35.85
卫生建筑陶瓷	Toilet Architectural Poppery	127	208	148	71.15
装饰材料	Decoration Materials	171	227	89	39.21
石棉制品	Asbestos Products	2	11		
人造板	Artificial Board	385	415	174	41.93
其它	Others	542	747	382	51.14
机电产品	**Medical Electric Products**	**1165**	**1784**	**959**	**53.76**
轴承	Bearings	37	60	39	65.00
阀类、泵	Valves	76	98	30	30.61
电线、电缆	Electric Wires	275	432	324	75.00
通用设备	Universal Equipment	45	55	12	21.82
电动工具	Electric Tools	74	120	33	27.50
低压电器及元件	Low-voltage Electric Elements	260	449	167	37.19
消防器材	Fire-fighting Equipment & Materials	86	96	84	87.50
安全防范设备	Safety	51	78	46	58.97
电动机、柴油机	Electric and Diesel Engines	16	18	14	77.78
汽车、摩托车	Motor Vehicles and Motorcycles	182	307	183	59.61
其它	Others	63	71	27	38.03
冶金产品及金属制品	**Metallurgical and Metal Products**	**734**	**1053**	**461**	**43.78**
线材	Wire Rod	157	279	155	55.56
型材	Section Steel	375	497	224	45.07
其它	Others	202	277	82	29.60
能源产品	**Power Products**	**689**	**848**	**753**	**88.80**
原煤	Coal	261	290	239	82.41
焦炭	Coke	14	14	10	71.43
汽油、柴油	Gasoline	400	522	491	94.06
其它	Others	14	22	13	59.09
医疗器械	**Medicine Appliance**	**23**	**23**	**22**	95.65
普通医疗器械	Ordinary Medicine Appliance	10	10	10	100.00
其它	Others	13	13	12	92.31
其它	**Others**	**285**	**469**	**355**	**75.69**

17－29 文化事业机构和人员数（2003－2004年）
Cultural Institutions and Personnel (2003-2004)

项　目	Item	2003	2004
机构数总计(个)	**Total Institutions (unit)**	**1384**	**1317**
艺术事业	Art Institutions	65	53
#艺术表演团体	Art Performance Troupes	32	29
艺术表演场所	Art Centers	25	20
文物事业	Cultural Institutions	63	64
图书馆事业	Libraries	44	44
群众文化事业	Mass Culture Institutions	1193	1135
艺术教育事业	Art Education Institutions	1	2
文艺科研	Art Research Institutions	1	1
其　他	Others	17	18
从业人员数总计(人)	**Total Personnel (person)**	**7190**	**6757**
艺术事业	Art Institutions	1793	1573
#艺术表演团体	Art Performance Troupes	1525	1411
艺术表演场所	Art Centers	207	136
文物事业	Cultural Institutions	1191	1059
图书馆事业	Libraries	737	754
群众文化事业	Mass Culture Institutions	2705	2607
艺术教育事业	Art Education Institutions	143	77
文艺科研	Art Research Institutions	15	18
其　他	Others	606	669

17－30 公共图书馆情况（2003－2004年）
Public Libraries (2003-2004)

项　　目	Item	总　计 Total		#省　级 At Provincial Level	
		2003	2004	2003	2004
总藏量(万册、件)	Total Collections (10 000 volumes)	701	736	263	272
书架总长度(万米)	Total Length of Bookshelves (10 000 meters)	17.0	11.8	4.0	4.0
发放借书证数(万个)	Number of Library Cards Distributed (10 000 units)	12	12	3	6
图书流通情况	Circulation of Books				
总流通人次(万人次)	Total Number of Circulation (10 000 person-times)	1279	557	207	86
书刊外借册次(万册次)	Number of Books Borrowed by Readers (10 000 volume-times)	1402	689	248	160
为读者举办各种活动服务次数(次)	Number of Service Activities Provided for Readers (time)	887	504	105	82
总支出(万元)	Total Expenditures (10 000 yuan)	3010	3166	1330	1074
#藏量购置费	Purchase Expenses	420	434	155	198
本年新购藏量(万册)	Number of Books Purchased During Current Year (10 000 volumes)	22	16	9	7
公用房屋建筑面积(万平方米)	Floor Space of Public Buildings (10 000 sq.m)	12	12	3	3
#书库	Stack Rooms	3	3	1	1
阅览室座席(个)	Seating Capacity of Reading Rooms (seat)	7641	7808	822	822

注：2004年主城区部分图书馆拆建，某些活动比2003年减少。

Note: Some libraries in downtown have been demolished in 2004, which make some data of activities less than that of 2003.

17－31 文物机构情况（2004年）
Cultural Relic Agencies (2004)

项　　目	Item	文物机构 Cultural Relic Agencies	#博物馆 Museums	#文物保护管理机构 Protection and Management Agencies
藏　品(件)	Number of Collections (piece)	499121	282688	75738
#一级品	Grade One	806	715	91
经费支出(万元)	Total Expenditure (10 000 yuan)	8745	5438	3199
维修费（万元）	Maintenance Expenses (10 000 yuan)	242	82	149

17－32 群众艺术馆和文化馆（站）情况（2004年）
Mass Art Centers and Cultural Centers (2004)

项目	Item	合计 Total	群众艺术馆 Mass Art Centers	文化馆 Cultural Centers	文化站 Cultural Stations
单位数（个）	Number of Units (unit)	1135	1	43	1091
举办展览个数（个）	Conducting Exhibitions (unit)	2280	5	304	1971
组织文艺活动次数（次）	Organizing Art Performances (time)	7386	10	1374	6002
举办培训班	Training Courses				
班次（次）	Classes (time)	2414	30	707	1677
结业人数（万人次）	Persons Completed Courses (10 000 person-times)	8.32	0.06	1.60	6.66

17－33 艺术表演团体演出情况（2004年）
Basic Statistics on Performance of Art Troupes (2004)

种类	Item	演出场数（千场） Number of Performances (1000 shows)	观众人数（万人次） Number of Spectators (10 000 person)
总计	**Total**	**3.2**	**435.5**
#国有剧团	Troupes Sponsored by State-owned Units	3.1	392.2
集体经营剧团	Troupes Sponsored by Collective Units	0.1	43.3
按剧种分:	Art Troupes		
话剧、儿童剧、滑稽剧团	Drama, Children's Play and Comedy Troupes	0.3	30.6
歌舞剧团	Song and Dance Drama Troupes	0.3	63.8
歌舞团、轻音乐团	Song and Dance, Light Music	0.3	166.5
文工团、宣传队、乌兰牧骑	Cultural and Performance Troupes and Ulanmuchi (equestrian art troupes)	0.1	42.5
乐团、合唱团	Philharmonic and Chorus Troupes		
戏曲剧团	Local Opera Troupes	0.5	33.5
#京剧	Local Beijing Opera Troupes	0.3	16.3
川剧	Local Sichuan Opera Troupes	0.2	17.2
曲艺、杂技、木偶、皮影团	Recitation and Ballad Troupes, Acrobatics and Circus Troupes, Puppet Show Troupes, and Shadow Play Troupes	1.5	98.6

注：歌舞剧团包括歌剧、舞剧、歌舞剧团。

Note: Song and dance drama troupes include opera, dance and light music troupes.

17－34 广播电台、电视台情况（2004年）
Statistics on Broadcasting and TV Stations (2004)

项　　目	Item	2004
广播电台情况	**Statistics on Broadcasting Stations**	
广播电台(座)	Broadcasting Stations (unit)	1
广播节目套数(套)	Number of Programs (set)	31
广播人口覆盖率(%)	Listener Rating (%)	92.26
中短波转播发射台(座)	Transmission and Relaying Stations of MW & SW (unit)	5
中短波广播发射功率(千瓦)	Power of MW & SW Transmitters (kw)	137
调频转播发射台(座)	FM Transmission and Relaying Stations (unit)	52
调频发射功率(千瓦)	Power of FM Transmitters (kw)	113
全年公共广播节目播出时间（小时）	Public Program Hours in Whole Year (hour)	97170
#新闻资讯	News Programs	24871
专题服务	Special Subject Service	19809
综　艺	Programs of Performance	26169
广播剧	Radio Plays	3896
广　告	Advertisement	8322
电视台情况	**Statistics on TV Stations**	
电视台(座)	TV Stations (unit)	1
电视节目套数(套)	Number of Programs (unit)	31
电视人口覆盖率(%)	Viewer Rating (%)	95.73
电视转播发射台(座)	TV Transmission Stations and Relaying Stations (unit)	53
电视发射功率(千瓦)	Power of TV Transmitters (kw)	72
全年公共电视节目播出时间(小时)	Public Program Hours in Whole Year (hour)	168438
#新闻资讯	News Programs	20544
专题服务	Special Subject Service	19005
综艺益智	Programs of Performance and Intelligence	16658
影视剧	Films and Teleplays	76947
广　告	Advertisement	18894

注：1）按国家广播电视总局规定，从2002年起省级以上广播电台电视台记入台数，地县级台记入节目套数。

2）2001年有线电视台与无线电视台合并。

Note: a) According to regulations of State Administration of Broadcasting, Film and Television in 2002, the number of stations only at provincial level and above is counted, whereas the stations at county level is counted as programs.

b) In 2001, CNT and TV stations were merged together.

17－35 新闻出版事业机构和人员数（2003－2004年）
Number of Institutions and Persons Engaged in News and Publishing Undertakings (2003-2004)

指　　标	Item	2003	2004
书刊出版社	**Publishing Houses**		
机构数（个）	Institutions (unit)	3	3
从业人员（人）	Personnel (person)	670	728
国家定点书刊印刷厂	**Printing Houses**		
机构数（个）	Institutions (unit)	2	2
从业人员（人）	Personnel (person)	999	917
国有书店	**State-owned Book Stores**		
机构数（个）	Institutions (unit)	591	320
从业人员（人）	Personnel (person)	4259	3824

17－36 图书、杂志和报纸出版情况（2003－2004年）
Publication of Books, Magazines and Newspapers (2003-2004)

指　　标	Item	2003	2004
图　书	**Books Published**		
种　数（种）	Number of Publications (kind)	1764	2127
#新出版	New Publications	795	1157
总印数（万册、万张）	Printed Copies (10 000 copies)	11175	11164
总印张数（万印张）	Printed Sheets (10 000 sheets)	64063	69428
期　刊	**Magazines Published**		
种　数（种）	Number of Publications (kind)	130	133
每期平均印数(万册)	Average Printed Copies Per Issue (10 000 copies)	286	281
总印数（万册）	Printed Copies (10 000 copies)	4191	4397
总印张数（万印张）	Printed Sheets (10 000 sheets)	20340	23456
报　纸	**Newspapers Published**		
种　数（种）	Number of Publications (kind)	46	45
每期平均印数（万份）	Average Printed Copies Per Issue (10 000 copies)	259.20	293.02
总印数（万份）	Printed Copies (10 000 copies)	47420	47575
总印张数（万印张）	Printed Sheets (10 000 sheets)	257720	263979

17—37 图书分类出版数量（2004年）
Books Published by Category (2004)

项　目	Item	本版图书种数(种) Number of Publications (unit)	#新出版 New Publications	种型种数（种） Number of Publication from Renting (unit)	总印数(万册) Total Printed Copies (10 000 copies)	总印张(万印张) Printed Sheets (10 000 sheets)
总　计	**Total**	**2127**	**1157**	**501**	**11164**	**694280**
哲学、社会科学总论	Philosophy and General Social Sciences	57	44		49	6496
政治、法律	Politics and Law	73	47		141	6490
军　事	Military Affairs	2	1		2	75
经　济	Economics	127	87		50	8893
文化、科学、教育、体育	Culture, Science, Education and Sports	1027	507	439	10043	574276
语言、文字	Languages	121	48		122	15197
文　学	Literature	76	67		37	4005
艺　术	Art	180	66	62	360	23238
历史、地理	History and Geography	59	46		52	4708
数理科学、化学	Mathematics and Chemistry	41	22		16	2333
生物科学、医药、卫生	Biology	22	18		10	1566
农业科学	Agricultural Science	5	4		2	149
工业技术	Industrial Technology	323	190		275	46273
交通运输	Transportation	9	5		3	464
航空、航天	Aeronautics and Aerospace					
环境科学	Environmental Science	3	3		1	107
综合性图书	General Books					
其　他	Others	2	2		1	10
在总计中：	**Of Total:**					
课　本	**Textbooks**	**1553**	**418**	**487**	**8007**	**535525**
#大专及以上课本	Textbooks for Colleges and Universities	769	339		497	72726
中专、技校课本	Textbooks for Secondary Technical Schools	34	6		41	5249
中学课本	Textbooks for Secondary Schools	275	9	218	2538	228098
小学课本	Textbooks for Primary Schools	366	27	224	4776	138567
业余教育课本	Textbooks for Spare-time Education	3	2		59	14047
教学用书	Teaching Materials	106	35	45	96	7838
儿童读物	**Children's Reading Materials**	**128**	**72**		**231**	**4847**

17－38 录像制品和录音制品出版情况（2003－2004年）
Publication of Video Products (2003-2004)

项　　目	Item	2003	2004
数码激光视盘	VCD		
种数（种）	Kind	85	180
数量（万张）	Volume (10 000 disks)	40.47	196.00
高密度激光视盘	DVD		
种数（种）	Kind	13	87
数量（万张）	Volume (10 000 disks)	10.00	138.00
录音带	Audio-tapes		
种数（种）	Kind	81	83
数量（万盒）	Volume (10 000 cassettes)	24.56	62.00
激光唱盘	CDs		
种数（种）	Kind	87	56
数量（万张）	Volume (10 000 disks)	16.40	21.00
高密度激光唱盘	DVD-A		
种数（种）	Kind		
数量（万张）	Volume (10 000 disks)		

17－39 图书发行流转及纯销售情况（2003－2004年）
Statistics on Distribution, Circulation and Net Sales of Books (2003-2004)

项　　目	Item	册 数（万册） Copies (10 000 copies)		金 额（万元） Value (10 000 yuan)	
		2003	2004	2003	2004
图书购进	**Purchases**	**32755**	**30461**	**199263**	**206082**
图书销售	**Sales**	**32864**	**31593**	**189679**	**207722**
＃纯销售合计	Net Sales			87489	90003
＃对居民和社会集团零售小计	Retail Sales to Households and Institutions	12263	12208	76674	81548
市及县	Cities and Counties		10106	64105	68896
县以下	Below Counties		2102	12569	12652
批发合计	Total Wholesale		19385	10815	126174
＃供销社	Supply & Marketing Coops		592	5573	3617
集体和个体	Collectives and Individuals		934	5242	4838
图书库存	**Stock**	**6125**	**5636**	**42307**	**41503**

主要统计指标解释

普通高等学校 指按照国家规定的设置标准和审批程序批准举办的，通过全国普通高等学校统一招生考试，招收高中毕业生为主要培养对象，实施高等教育的全日制大学、独立设置的学院和高等专科学校、高等职业学校和其他机构。

大学、独立设置的学院主要实施本科层次以上教育，高等专科学校、高等职业学校实施专科层次教育，其他机构是承担国家普通招生计划任务不计校数的机构。包括普通高等学校分校和批准筹建的普通高等学校等。

成人高等学校 指按照国家规定的设置标准和审批程序批准举办的，通过全国成人高等学校统一招生考试，招收具有高中毕业或同等学历的在职从业人员为主要培养对象，利用函授、业余、脱产等多种形式对其实施高等学历教育的学校。包括职工高等学校、农民高等学校、管理干部学院、教育学院、独立函授学院、广播电视大学、其他机构等。其他机构是承担国家成人招生计划任务不计校数的机构。

小学学龄儿童入学率 指调查范围内已入小学学习的学龄儿童占校内外学龄儿童总数（包括弱智儿童在内，但不包括盲聋哑儿童）的比重。计算公式：

小学学龄儿童入学率＝已入学的小学学龄儿童数/校内外小学学龄儿童总数×100％

科技活动 指在自然科学、农业科学、医药科学、工程与技术科学、人文与社会科学领域(简称科学技术领域)中，与科技知识的产生、发展、传播和应用密切相关的有组织的活动。可分为研究与试验发展(R&D)、研究与试验发展成果应用及相关的科技服务三类活动。该定义是联合国教科文组织考虑成员国特别是发展中国家开展科技统计工作的需要，而对科技活动所作的统计界定。

科技活动人员 指直接从事科技活动、以及专门从事科技活动管理和为科技活动提供直接服务的人员。累计从事科技活动的实际工作时间占全年制度工作时间 10%以上的人员。（1）直接从事（或参与）科技活动的人员包括：在独立核算的科学研究与技术开发机构、高等学校、各类企业及其他事业单位内设的研究室、实验室、技术开发中心及中试车间（基地）等机构中从事科技活动的研究人员、工程技术人员、技术工人及其它辅助人员；虽不在上述机构工作，但编入科技活动项目（课题）组的人员；科技信息与文献机构中的专业技术人员；从事论文设计的研究生等。（2）专门从事科技活动管理和为科技活动提供直接服务的人员包括：独立核算的科学研究与技术开发机构、科技信息与文献机构、高等学校、各类企业及其他事业单位主管科技工作的负责人，专门从事科技活动的计划、行政、人事、财务、物资供应、设备维护、图书资料管理等工作的各类人员。不包括保卫、医疗保健人员、司机、食堂人员、茶炉工、水暖工、清洁工等为科技活动提供间接服务的人员。

科学家和工程师 指科技活动人员中具有高、中级技术职称(职务)的人员和不具有高、中级技术职称(职务)的大学本科及以上学历人员。该指标用来反映投入科技活动人力的素质。

研究与试验发展（R&D） 指在科学技术领域，为增加知识总量，以及运用这些知识去创造新的应用而进行的系统的创造性的活动，包括基础研究、应用研究、试验发展三类活动。国际上通常采用 R&D 活动的规模和强度指标反映一国的科技实力和核心竞争力。

基础研究 指为了获得关于现象和可观察事实的基本原理的新知识（揭示客观事物的本质、运动规律，获得新发现、新学说）而进行的实验性或理论性研究，它不以任何专门或特定的应用或使用为目的。其成果以科学论文和科学著作为主要形式。用来反映知识的原始创新能力。

应用研究 指为获得新知识而进行的创造性研究，主要针对某一特定的目的或目标。应用研究是为了确定基础成果可能的用途，或是为达到预定的目标探索应采取的新方法（原理性）或新途径。其成果形式以科学论文、专著、原理性模型或发明专利为主。用来反映对基础研究成果应用途径的探索。

试验发展 指利用从基础研究、应用研究和实际经验所获得的现有知识，为产生新的产品、材料和装置，建立新的工艺、系统和服务，以及对已产生和建立的上述各项作实质性的改进而进行的系统性工作。其成果形式主要是专利、专有技术、具有新产品基本特征的产品原型或具有新装置基本特征的原始样机等。在社会科学领域，试验发展是指把通过基础研究、应用研究获得的知识转变成可以实施的计划(包括为进行检验和评估实施示范项目)的过程。人文科学领域没有对应的试验发展活动。主要反映将科研成果转化为技术和产品的能力，是科技推动经济社会发展的物化成果。

研究与试验发展人员 指参与研究与试验发展项目局研究、管理和辅助工作的人员， 包括项目（课题）组人员，企业科技行政管理人员和直接为项目（课题）活动提供服务的辅助人员。反映投入从事拥有自主知识产权的研究开发活动的人力规模。

研究与试验发展人员全时当量 指全时人员数加非全时人员按工作量折算为全时人员数的总和。例如：有两个全时人员和三个非全时人员（工作时间分别为 20%、30%和 70%），则全时当量为 2+0.2+0.3+0.7=3.2 人年。为国际上比较科技人力投入而制定的可比指标。

科技活动经费筹集 指从各种渠道筹集到的计划用于科技活动的经费，包括政府资金、企业资金、事业单位资金、金融机构贷款、国外资金和其他资金等。

研究与开发机构 指有明确的任务和研究方向，有一定学术水平的业务骨干和一定数量的研究人员，具有研究、开发、开展学术工作的基本条件，主要进行科学研究与技术开发活动，并且在行政上有独立的组织形式，财务上独立核算盈亏，有权与其他单位签订合同，在银行有单独户头的单位。包括国务院各部门、中国科学院、中国社会科学院和各省、自治区、直辖市以及地(市)以上［含地(市)］各部门所属的国有独立的科学研究与技术开发机构。

研究与开发机构职工 指在科学研究与技术开发机构工作，并由其支付工资的各种人员。包括长期职工和临时职工，不包括编制以外的离休，退休人员和停薪留职人员，但包括招聘人员。

研究与发展经费支出 指报告期内用于研究与实验发展课题活动(基础研究、应用研究、实验发展)的全部实际支出。包括用于研究与发展课题活动的直接支出，还包括间接用于研究与发展活动的一切支出(院、所管理费、维持院、所正常运转的必需费用和与研究发展有关的基本建设支出)。

新产品 指采用新技术原理、新设计构思研制、生产的全新产品，或在结构、材质、工艺等某一方面比原有产品有明显改进，从而显著提高了产品性能或扩大了使用功能的产品。既包括政府有关部门认定并在有效期内的新产品，也包括企业自行研制开发，未经政府有关部门认定，从投产之日起一年之内的新产品。用来反映科技产出及对经济增长的直接贡献。

专利 是专利权的简称，是对发明人的发明创造经审查合格后，由专利局依据专利法授予发明人和设计人对该项发明创造享有的专有权。包括发明、实用新型和外观设计。反映拥有自主知识产权的科技和设计成果情况。

发明 指对产品、方法或其改进所提出的新的技术方案。是国际通行的反映拥有自主知识产权技术的核心指标。

实用新型 指对产品的形状、构造或者其结合所提出的适于实用的新的技术方案。反映具有一定技术含量的技术成果情况。

外观设计 指对产品的形状、图案、色彩或者其结合所做出的富有美感并适于工业上应用的新设计。反映拥有自主知识产权的外观设计成果情况。

驰名商标 是指在市场上享有较高声誉并为相关公众所熟知的注册商标，也是一种法律保护手段。

著名商标 著名商标的知名度介于驰名商标和普通商标之间的商标群落，是驰名商标坚实的后备力量。

文化事业机构 指从事专业文化工作和为专业文化工作服务的独立建制的单位。不包括这些单位另外举办独立核算的其他机构和各部门的业余文化组织。

艺术表演团体 指从事戏曲、音乐、舞蹈、杂技等专业艺术表演，有独立帐户。不包括半工半艺、半农半艺和民间职业剧团。

艺术表演观众人数（人次） 指售票、包场演出或民族地区免费演出的艺术表演观众人次数，不包括彩排审查和内部观摩演出的观看人次数。

Explanatory Notes on Main Statistical Indicators

Regular Institutions of Higher Education refer to educational establishments set up according to the government evaluation and approval procedures, enrolling graduates from senior secondary schools and providing higher education courses and training for senior professionals. They include full-time universities, colleges, high professional schools, high professional vocational schools and others.

Universities and colleges are mainly providing undergraduate courses; those high professional schools and high professional vocational schools are mainly providing professional trainings; and others refer to educational establishments, which are responsible for enrolling students but not covered in the total number of schools, including: branch schools of universities and colleges, and universities and colleges that have been proved and prepared to construct.

Institutions of Higher Learning for Adults refer to educational establishments, set up in line with relevant rules approved by the government, enrolling staff and workers with senior secondary school or equivalent education, and providing higher education courses in many forms of correspondence, spare time, or full time for adults. Professionals thus trained receive a qualification equivalent to graduates studying regular courses at regular universities, colleges and professional colleges. Institutions of higher learning for adults include schools of high education for staff and workers, schools of high education for peasants, colleges for management cadres, pedagogical colleges, independent correspondence colleges, Radio and TV universities and other educational establishments. Other educational establishments are responsible for enrolling adult students but not covered in the number of schools.

Enrollment Rate of Primary School-aged Children refers to the proportion of school-aged children enrolled at schools to the total number of school-age children both in and outside schools (including retarded children, but excluding blind, deaf and mute children). The formula is:

Enrollment Rate of Primary School-aged Children =Total Primary School-aged Children at Schools/Total Primary School-age Children Both at and Outside Schools×100%

Scientific and Technological Activities (S&T Activities) refer to organized activities which are closely related with the creation, development, dissemination and application of the scientific and technical knowledge in the fields of natural sciences, agricultural science, medical science, engineering and technological science, humanities and social sciences (referred to as scientific and technological fields). S&T activities can be classified in to 3 categories: research and development (R&D) activities, application of R&D results, and related S&T services. This statistical definition is made by UNICHIEF for scientific and technological activities to meet the need of carrying out statistical work in this field for its member countries in particular those developing countries.

Personnel Engaged in S&T Activities refer to personnel directly engaged in S&T activities, in the management of S&T activities, who spend over 10% of the total working hours in a year in S&T activities. (1) Personnel directly engaged in S&T activities include researchers, engineers, technicians and other related personnel engaged in SUT activities in independent-accounting R&D institutions, institutions of higher learning, and in research institutes, laboratories, technology development centers and central experiment workshops under enterprises and institutions. Also included are people working in S&T research project team, professional and technical personnel working in S&T information archiving institutes, and graduate students working on the design of their thesis. (2) Personnel engaged in the management of S&T activities and in providing direct service to S&T activities include senior management people responsible for S&T activities in independent-accounting R&D institutions, S&T information archiving institutes, institutions of higher learning, and in enterprises and institutions where S&T activities are undertaken. Also included are people responsible for the planning, administration, personnel management, financial management, logistics supply, equipment maintenance, information and library management that are related with S&T activities. People providing indirect services are excluded, such as security, medical service, drivers, plumbers, cleaners and those providing catering and related service.

Scientists and Engineers refer to persons engaged in S&T activities that have obtained titles of senior and middle level professional positions, and those without such position but have completed university or higher education. This indicator reflects the quality of personnel engaged in S&T activities.

Research and Development (R&D) refers to systematic and creative activities in the field of science and technology aiming at increasing the knowledge and using the knowledge for new application. R&D includes 3 categories of activities: basic research, applied research and experiments and development. The scale and intensity of R&D are widely used internationally to reflect the strength of S&T and the core competitiveness of a country in the world.

Basic Research refers to empirical or theoretical research aiming at obtaining new knowledge on the fundamental principles of phenomena of observable facts to reveal the nature and law of movement of objects and to acquire new discoveries or new theories. Basic research takes no specific or designated application as the aim of the research. Results of basic research are mainly released or disseminated in the form of scientific papers or monographs. This indicator reflects the original innovation capacity of knowledge.

Applied Research refers to creative research aiming at obtaining new knowledge on a specific objective or target. Purpose of the applied research is to identify the possible use of results from basic research, or to explore new (fundamental) methods or new approaches. Results of applied research are expressed in the form of scientific papers, monographs, fundamental models or invention patents. This indicator reflects the exploration of ways to apply the results of basic research.

Experiments and Development refer to systematic activities aiming at using the knowledge from basic and applied researches or from practical experience to develop new products, materials and equipment, to establish new production process, systems and services, or to make substantial improvement on the existing products, process or services. Results of experiment and development activities are embodied in patents, exclusive technology, and monotype of new products or equipment. In social sciences, experiment and development activities refer to the process of converting the knowledge from basic or applied researches into feasible programs (including conduct of demonstration projects for assessment and evaluation). There are no experiment and development activities in the science of humanities. This indicator reflects the capability of transferring the results of S&T into technique and products, which is the materialized measurement of S&T pushing forward the economic and social development.

R&D Personnel refer to persons engaged in research, management and supporting activities of R&D, including persons in the project teams, persons engaged in the management of S&T activities of enterprises and supporting staff providing direct service to the research projects. This indicator reflects the size of personnel engaged in R&D activities with independent intellectual property.

Full-time Equivalent of R&D Personnel refers to the sum of the full-time persons and the full-time equivalent of part-time persons converted by workload. For instance, if there are 2 full-time persons and 3 part-time workers (20%, 30% and 70% of working hours respectively on R&D activities), the full-time equivalent is 2+0.2+0.3+0.7=3.2 person-years. This is an internationally comparable indicator of input of personnel in S&T activities.

Funding for S&T Activities refers to funds obtained from various sources for S&T activities including government funds, self-raised funds by enterprises, self-raised funds by institutions, loans from financial institution, foreign funds and other funds.

Research and Development Institutions refer to the state-owned institutions which have direct mission and research purpose, a certain number of core member with higher research level and a certain number of research personnel, favorable conditions for R & D and engaging in scientific research and technological development. The institutions also have their own independent organization and finance, authority to sign contracts with other units, with their own accounts in banks. Independent research and development institutions include the institutions attached to central government agencies, Chinese Academy of Sciences. Chinese Academy of Social and the institutions attached to local governments.

Personnel of Research and Development Institutions refers to the persons who work and receive payment in research and development institutions. It includes regular full-time and temporary staff and workers, but excludes retirees and persons who leave their work temporarily without payment but still retain their posts.

Total Expenditure on Research and Development refers to all actual expenditure made for R&D (basic research, applied research and experimental development) in reference period. It included direct expenditure on R&D and indirect expenditure on R&D (including management expenses, administrative expense and investment in capital construction relating to R&D.

New Products refer to new products produced with new technology and new design, or products that represent noticeable improvement in terms of structure, material, or production process so as to improve significantly the character or function of the older versions. They include new products certified by relevant government agencies within the period of certification, as well as new products designed and produced by enterprises within a year without certification by government agencies. This indictor reflects the direct contribution of S&T output to economic growth.

Patent is an abbreviation for the patent right and refers to the exclusive right of ownership by the inventors or designers for the creation or inventions, given from the patent offices after due process of assessment and approval in accordance with the Patent Law. Patents are granted for inventions, utility models and designs. This indicator reflects the achievements of S&T and design with independent intellectual property.

Inventions refer to the new technical proposals to the products or methods or their modifications. This is universal core indicator reflecting the technologies with independent intellectual property.

Utility Models refer to the practical and new technical proposals on the shape and structure of the product or the combination of both. This indicator reflects the condition of technological results with certain technical content.

Designs refer to the aesthetics and industrially applicable new designs for the shape, pattern and color of the product, or their combinations. This indicator reflects the appearance design achievements with independent intellectual property.

Famous Trade Marks refer to trade marks publicly known with higher honors. It is also a legal protection.

Well-known Trade Marks their fames are between famous trade marks and ordinary trade marks. And they are tough reserve force of famous trade marks.

Cultural Institutions refer to units which have their own organizational system and independent accounting system and specialize in or serve cultural development. They exclude other establishments run by these cultural institutions and amateur cultural groups established by various departments.

Art Troupe refers to the troupe who is engaged in drama, opera, music, dance, acrobatics or other art performance, opens independent accounts with banks and has self-supporting accounting system; excluding the troupes who are engaged partly in industrial or agricultural activities, partly in art performance and the professional troupes organized by the people.

Number of Spectators at Art Performance refers to the number of attendants at commercial shows, completely booked shows of free shows given in minority national areas, and does not include the number of spectators at rehearsals for examination and internal shows for study.

十八　卫生、体育和其他社会活动

PUBLIC HEALTH, SPORTS AND OTHER SOCIAL ACTIVITIES

简要说明　Brief Introduction

本章资料主要包括卫生事业、体育事业、民政事业、劳动和社会保障事业、公检法司情况、道路交通事故和火灾事故等内容，由市统计局社会科技处根据有关部门资料整理提供。

卫生资料来自市卫生局，体育资料来源于市体育局，民政和劳动社会保障有关资料分别由市民政局、市劳动和社会保障局提供，公检法司资料分别由市公安局、市人民检察院、市高级人民法院和市司法局提供，道路交通事故和火灾事故分别由市公安交通管理局和市消防总队提供。

Data in this chapter mainly cover public health, sports, civil affairs, labor & social securities, public security, procuratorial, legal & judicial affairs, and highway traffic & fire accidents. Data are edited and provided by Division of Social and Technology Statistics, Municipal Bureau of Statistics.

Data on public health come from Municipal Bureau of Public Health. Data on sports are from Municipal Sports Administration. Data on civil affairs and labor & social securities are provided by Municipal Bureau of Civil Affairs and Municipal Bureau of Labor and Social Security. And Data on public security, procuratorial and legal affairs are provided by Municipal Bureau of Public Security, Municipal People’s Procuratorate, Higher People’s Court and Municipal Bureau of Justice. Data on highway traffic & fire accidents root from Municipal Bureau of Traffic Administration and Municipal Fire Brigade.

18－1 主要年份卫生事业情况
Statistics on Public Health in Major Years

年 份 Year	机构数（个） Number of Institutions (unit)	#医院、卫生院 Hospitals	床位数（张） Number of Hospital Beds (bed)	卫生技术人员（人） Medical Technical Personnel (person)	#执 业（助理）医师 Certified (Assistant) Doctors	#注册护士 Registration Nurses
1952	742		5031	19807		
1957	2185		10255	30290		
1962	3591		22971	35681		
1965	3938		20314	36762	10234	
1970	3579	2183	25038	39813	10475	
1975	4221	2286	37300	51536	12442	
1978	4789	2294	48948	59934	12870	
1980	4686	2316	51194	65441	12806	
1985	4796	2170	54054	76486	12577	11724
1986	5095	2140	54801	77437	12895	11921
1987	5136	2136	57178	78382	13201	12156
1988	5148	2151	59514	80153	21004	13688
1989	5229	2152	61912	81219	27789	16027
1990	5248	2154	62568	82690	28824	16929
1991	5326	2153	64057	83973	28652	17163
1992	5328	2160	64978	85204	28643	17557
1993	4807	2114	65859	84125	29516	17714
1994	4795	2590	66891	85586	30915	18298
1995	4801	2505	67243	86041	31169	18692
1996	4777	2567	66339	87542	30733	19289
1997	4743	2553	69591	88423	43178	19593
1998	4643	2438	65934	83696	43423	19804
1999	4552	2351	66003	88569	44453	20263
2000	4382	2250	65666	88619	44940	20773
2001	4151	2020	64981	86430	44666	20533
2002	2725	1717	61875	79850	37873	20729
2003	2705	1682	63287	78628	37122	20629
2004	2539	1574	63899	77516	36603	20249

注：1）本表机构数不含个体办诊所。
2）卫生技术人员数不含离退休人员(表18-1至18-5同)。
3）2002年起卫生统计制度变更，其指标名称和统计口径变化，与往年不可比：从2002年起卫生机构、床位、卫生技术人员统计范围均不含"医学院校"、"卫生学校"和"计生站"。卫生技术人员中，2002年前为医生和护师（士），2002年后改为执业(助理)医师和注册护士(表18-1至18-5同)。

Note: a) Number of institutions in this table exclude individual-run medical units.
b) The number of medical technical personnel exclude retired persons (the same from 18-1 to 18-5).
c) Indices of health care has been changed since 2002, and their range are not comparable with previous years. Since 2002, institutes, hospital beds and medical technical personnel have not covered medical colleges, medical schools and family planning centers. The statistical range of doctors and junior & senior nurses is from 1952 to 2001, whereas of certified (assistant) doctors and registration nurses since 2002 (the same from 18-1 to 18-5).

18－2 卫生事业情况（2003－2004年） Statistics on Public Health (2003-2004)

指　　标	Item	2003	2004
执业（助理）医师数（人）	Certified (Assistant) Doctors (person)	37122	36603
#市医院	City Hospitals	11866	11363
县医院	County Hospitals	3919	3798
医院床位数（张）	Beds in Hospitals (bed)	43775	43784
市医院	City Hospitals	33460	33157
县医院	County Hospitals	10315	10627
孕产妇死亡率（1/10万）	Mortality Rate of Pregnant Women (per 100 000 persons)	80.9	79.3
新生儿死亡率（‰）	Mortality Rate of New Infants (‰)	9.5	9.3
急性传染病发病率（1/10万）	Incidence Disease Rate of Acute Infections Diseases (per 100 000 persons)	232.4	318.9
农村饮用自来水人口比重（%）	Percentage of Rural Population Using Tap Water (%)	63.5	65.9

18－3 医院、卫生院诊疗情况（2004年） Number of Hospital Patients (2004)

机构类别	Type of Institution	诊疗人次（万人次） Number of Hospital Patients (10 000 person -times)	#门诊急诊 Out-patients	健康检查人数（万人） Health Examining (10 000 patients)	住院人数（万人） Hospital Admission (10 000 patients)	每百门急诊次的入院人数（人） Hospital Admissions Per 100 Patients (person)	治愈率（%） Rate of Fully Recovery (%)	好转率（%） Rate of Taking a Turn for the Better (%)	病死率（%） Mortality Rate by Disease Patients (%)
医　院	**Total Hospitals**	**2364**	**2271**	**80**	**82.39**	**3.63**	**56.0**	**39.4**	**1.4**
#综合医院	General Hospitals	1778	1701	66	64.50	3.79	55.8	39.4	1.6
中医医院	Hospitals of Chinese Medicine	289	283	8	8.59	3.04	49.3	46.9	0.9
中西医结合医院	Hospitals Combining Chinese and Western Medicine	47	46	1	1.47	3.16	62.6	33.7	1.6
口腔医院	Hospitals for Mouth Cavity Disease Care	19	19		0.07	0.39	88.2	10.5	0.1
肿瘤医院	Tumor Hospitals	8	8	1	0.84	10.41	32.5	54.9	3.0
胸科医院	Breast Hospitals	5	5		0.22	4.68	10.3	78.4	2.2
妇产(科)医院	Hospitals for Maternity and Child Care	32	32	1	0.77	2.42	90.8	8.9	
儿科医院	Hospitals for Children	84	84		2.61	3.11	75.6	23.1	0.2
精神病院	Mental Hospitals	41	37	2	1.74	4.76	59.2	37.6	0.3
传染病院	Hospitals for Infectious Diseases	3	3		0.04	1.63	13.4	64.8	3.4
卫生院	**Township Hospitals**	**2359**	**2309**	**52**	**46.87**	**2.03**	**78.3**	**19.4**	**0.2**
#乡镇卫生院	Rural Township Hospitals	2276	2230	50	45.75	2.05	78.1	19.6	0.2

18－4 卫生机构、床位、人员数（2004年）
Number of Health Institutions, Beds and Engaged Personnel (2004)

机构类别	Type of Institutions	机构数（个） Health Institutions (unit)	床位数（张） Hospital Beds (bed)	人员合计（人） Total Personnel (person)	卫生技术人员 Medical Technical Personnel	其他技术人员 Other Technical Personnel	管理人员 Management Personnel	工勤人员 Logistics Workers
总计	**Total**	**6539**	**63899**	**93485**	**77516**	**2858**	**6078**	**7033**
一、医院、卫生院合计	Total Number of Hospitals	1574	60565	75088	61170	2415	5139	6364
1、县及县以上医院小计	Hospitals at County Level and above	364	43784	48434	38191	1719	3713	4811
＃综合医院	Comprehensive Hospitals	266	32115	35935	28394	1318	2603	3620
中医医院	Hospitals of Chinese Medicine	44	4969	6337	5207	154	509	467
中西医结合医院	Hospitals Combining Chinese and Western Medicine	9	667	994	777	14	80	123
口腔医院	Hospitals for Mouth Cavity Disease Care	1	40	180	139	10	13	18
肿瘤医院	Tumor Hospitals	1	437	529	397	18	67	47
胸科医院	Breast Hospitals	2	450	384	253	11	53	67
妇产(科)医院	Hospitals for Maternity and Child Care	1	200	365	274	8	39	44
儿科医院	Hospitals for Children	1	511	720	512	24	97	87
精神病院	Mental Hospitals	19	3028	1772	1364	50	163	195
传染病院	Hospitals for Infectious Diseases	1	103	142	95	10	14	23
疗养院	Sanatoriums	5	1200	226	158	3	25	40
2、卫生院小计	Total Hospital Centers	1210	16781	26654	22979	696	1426	1553
城市街道卫生院	Urban Subdistrict Hospital Centers	25	642	905	758	18	54	75
乡镇卫生院	Rural Township Hospital Centers	1185	16139	25749	22221	678	1372	1478
二、门诊部	Clinics	49	149	639	529	8	47	55
三、采供血机构	Blood Centers	13		412	292	23	54	43
四、妇幼保健院(所、站)	Maternity and Child Care Centers	44	1159	2074	1626	53	252	143
五、专科疾病防治院(所)	Specialized Prevention & Treatment Stations	14	123	232	185	8	25	14
六、疾病预防控制中心	CDC (Epidemic Preventation Stations)	46	30	2417	1819	124	287	187
七、医学科学研究机构	Research Institutes of Medical Sciences	3	261	314	109	150	29	26
八、医学在职培训机构	Training Institutes for Medical Staff and Workers	5		65	39	6	16	4
九、健康教育所(中心)	Health Care Training Centers	2		11			11	
十、诊所、卫生保健所、室	Clinics、 Hygienic Centers	4734		10454	10454			
十一、其他卫生机构	Other Health Care Institutions	55	1612	1779	1293	71	218	197

18－5 卫生机构各类人员数（2003－2004年）
Personnel Engaged in Public Health Institutions (2003-2004)

人员分类	Type of Personnel	人数（人） Personnel (person)		构成 Composition（%）	
		2003	2004	2003	2004
全市总计	**Total**	**94157**	**93485**	**100.0**	**100.0**
卫生技术人员	Medical Technical Personnel	78628	77516	83.5	82.9
执业医师	Certified Doctors	27194	26598	34.6	34.3
执业助理医师	Certified Assistant Doctors	9928	10005	12.6	12.9
注册护士	Registration Nurses	20629	20249	26.2	26.1
药剂人员	Pharmacists	6457	6264	8.2	8.1
检验人员	Laboratory Technicians	3335	3257	4.2	4.2
其他人员	Others	11085	11143	14.2	14.4
其他技术人员	Other Technical Personnel	2686	2858	2.9	3.1
管理人员	Management Personnel	5707	6078	6.1	6.5
工勤人员	Logistics Workers	7136	7033	7.5	7.5
每万人口拥有卫生技术人员	**Number of Medical Technical Personnel Per 10 000 Population**	**25.2**	**24.6**		
#执业（助理）医师	Certified (Assistant) Doctors	11.9	11.6		

18－6 结婚登记和离婚登记情况（2003－2004年）
Registered Marriages and Divorces (2003-2004)

单位：对 (couple)

项目	Item	2003	2004
结婚登记数	Registered Marriages	180496	190290
内地居民	Inland Residents	178842	188705
初婚	First Marriages	153866	153321
再婚	Remarriages	24976	35384
涉外及华侨、港澳台居民	Foreign Marriages	1654	1585
离婚登记数	Registered Divorces	31418	48352
#内地居民	Inland Residents	31341	48229
离婚率（‰）	Divorce Rate (‰)	2.0	3.1

18－7 民政事业情况（2003－2004年）
Statistics on Civil Affairs (2003-2004)

指　　标	Item	2003	2004
民政经费支出（万元）	Funds for Civil Affairs (10 000 yuan)	125114	145713
社会救济对象人数（万人）	Persons Receiving Social Relieves (10 000 persons)	168.33	207.99
#城镇居民最低生活保障人数	Number of Persons Receiving Lowest Cost-of-living in Urban Areas	70.21	69.92
#农村居民最低生活保障人数	Number of Persons Receiving Lowest Cost-of-living in Rural Areas	0.19	0.49
#城镇临时救济人次数	Number of Poor Persons Receiving Temporary Almsgiving in Urban Area	3.03	2.46
#农村临时救济人数	Number of Poor Persons Receiving Temporary Almsgiving in Rural Area	74.35	85.31
享受城镇居民最低生活保障人数占非农业人口比重（%）	Coverage Rate of Urban Residents Receiving Lowest Cost-of-living to Non-agricultural Population (%)	9.3	8.9
各种社会福利收养性单位床位数（张）	Beds in Various Adopting Social Welfare Institutions (bed)	43797	43200
各种社会福利院床位数（张）	Beds in Various Social Welfare Institutions (bed)	43228	42853
福利企业职工人数（人）	Staff and Workers in Welfare Enterprises (person)	31134	35831
#残疾职工	Disabled Staff and Workers	14122	16763
城镇社区服务设施数（个）	Number of Urban Welfare Facilities (unit)	1305	1349
城镇便民、利民服务网点（个）	Number of Urban Service Points for Civilian (unit)	5175	6641
福利彩票销售额（万元）	Issue of Welfare Lotteries (10 000 yuan)	4349	6012

18－8 优抚对象基本情况（2003－2004年）
Statistics on Residents Receiving Special Cares (2003-2004)

项　　目	Item	2003	2004
优抚对象（人）	**Residents Receiving Special Cares (person)**	**133892**	**137705**
革命伤残人员	Revolutionary Disabled Persons	21467	21323
享受定期抚恤金人数	Persons Receiving Regular Pensions	7859	7433
在乡退伍红军老战士	Red Army Veterans in the Countryside	25	14
在乡复员军人	Demobilized Soldiers in the Countryside	63248	59779
在乡退伍军人	Veterans in the Country	41200	49087
红军失散人员	Scattered Red Army Soldiers	93	69

18－9 社会福利事业、企业单位数和工作人员数（2003－2004年）
Number of Social Welfare Institutions & Enterprises and Personnel Engaged (2003-2004)

项　目	Item	机　构（个） Number of Institutions and Enterprises (unit)		工作人员（人） Number of Personnel (person)	
		2003	2004	2003	2004
全市总计	**Total**	**2167**	**2231**	**37885**	**42983**
收养性福利事业单位	Adopting Social Welfare Institutions	1084	1061	3451	3610
国家办	Run by Governments	65	94	1263	1495
集体办	Run by Collective Units	1010	946	2137	1923
民　办	Run by Private Units	9	21	51	192
社会福利企业单位	Social Welfare Enterprises	831	889	31134	35831
国家办	Run by Governments	9	8	1186	751
集体办	Run by Collective Units	568	322	22035	13017
民　办	Run by Private Units	254	559	7913	22063
优抚事业单位	Administration Agencies for Martyrs	64	64	394	422
救助管理站	Relief Management Stations	30	34	289	314
殡葬事业单位	Funeral and Interment Institutions	85	102	2058	2237
福利彩票发行单位	Welfare Lottery Issuing Units	1	1	95	95
募捐单位	Collecting Purse Units	1	2	9	10
社区服务单位	Community Service Institutions	71	78	455	464

18－10 收养性福利事业单位基本情况（2004年）
Basic Statistics on Welfare Institutions (2004)

项　目	Item	院数(个) Number of Homes (unit)	工作人员(人) Number of Staff and Workers (person)	床位数(张) Number of Beds (bed)	年末收养人数(人) Year-end Persons Adopted (person)
收养性福利事业单位	**Adopting Social Welfare Institutions**	**1061**	**3610**	**43200**	**31215**
国家办	Run by Governments	94	1495	8817	7125
集体办	Run by Collective Units	946	1923	32957	23225
民　办	Run by Private Units	21	192	1426	865
优抚休、疗养院	Convalescent Homes	1	72	180	102
光荣院	Homes for Disabled Veterans	9	45	375	251
社会福利院	Social Welfare Homes	19	546	4267	3495
儿童福利院	Baby Welfare Homes	3	169	968	778
精神病福利院	Psychopathic Welfare Homes	7	386	930	810
城镇老年性福利机构	Urban Elderly Welfare Units	53	253	2630	1815
农村老年性福利机构	Rural Elderly Welfare Units	969	2139	33850	23964

18－11 社会活动参与情况（2003－2004年）
Participation in Social Activities (2003-2004)

单位：人 (person)

指　标	Item	2003	2004
省级人大代表人数	Number of Municipal Deputies of People's Congress	870	853
#女　性	Female	186	186
省级政协委员人数	Number of Municipal Deputies of People's Political Consultative Conferences	821	816
#女　性	Female	145	148
基层地方妇联组织数（个）	Number of Local Women's Federation Unions (unit)	17551	17552
工会基层组织数（个）	Number of Grassroots Unions (unit)	15857	16448
工会会员人数	Membership of Grassroots Unions	1795710	2152073

18－12 基本养老保险情况（2003－2004年）
Conditions of Basic Endowment Insurance (2003-2004)

单位：万元 (10 000 yuan)

指　标	Item	2003	2004
年末参加城镇基本养老保险的人数（万人）	Year-end Contributors of Urban Basic Endowment Insurance (10 000 persons)	278.08	282.13
#参保职工	Staff and Workers	186.06	185.67
#企　业	Enterprises	147.68	138.23
养老保险当年实际缴纳保险金	Actual Revenue of Urban Basic Endowment Insurance in Current Year	390109	445200
养老保险实际支付人数（万人）	Actual Payees of Urban Basic Endowment Insurance (10 000 persons)	92.02	96.46
养老保险基金当年支出额	Expenses of Urban Basic Endowment Insurance in Current Year	533551	604013
养老保险基金当年末结余额	Balance of Urban Basic Endowment Insurance in Current Year	138354	182269
应发养老金额	Retirement Pension Supposed to Provide	528824	587600
实发养老金额	Retirement Pension Actually Provided	528824	587600
社会化发放人数（万人）	Persons Receiving Retirement Pension	92.02	96.46
社会化发放养老金额	Retirement Pension	528824	587600
离休、退休、退职人员年末人数（万人）	Year-end Retirees (10 000 persons)	92.02	96.46

18－13 失业保险基本情况（2003－2004年）
Basic Conditions of Unemployment Insurance (2003-2004)

单位：万元 (10 000 yuan)

指 标	Item	2003	2004
年末失业保险参保人数(万人)	Year-end Active Contributors (10 000 persons)	199.47	193.45
企 业	Enterprises	164.82	154.37
#国有企业	State-owned	121.97	114.32
集体企业	Collective-owned	29.67	28.09
事业单位	Institutions	33.15	36.41
其 他	Others	1.50	2.67
失业保险当年实际缴纳保险金	Actual Revenue of Unemployment Insurance in Current Year	26509.00	31161.60
失业保险实际支付人数（万人）	Actual Payees of Unemployment Insurance (10 000 persons)	14.17	13.57
失业保险基金当年支出额	Expenses of Unemployment Insurance in Current Year	20221.69	24791.23
失业保险基金当年末结余额	Balance of Unemployment Insurance in Current Year	14658.68	23068.84
年末城镇登记失业人员数（人）	Year-end Urban Registered Unemployees (person)	161583	167620
年末企业实有下岗职工人数（人）	Year-end Laid-off Staff and Workers of Enterprises (person)	61565	50837
城镇登记失业人员就业人数（人）	Employment of Urban Registered Unemployees (person)	109942	121007
本年企业下岗职工再就业人数（人）	Reemployment of Laid-off Staff and Workers of Enterprises in Current Year (person)	68130	14213
本年领取失业保险金人月数（万人月）	Beneficiaries of Unemployment Insurance Per Month in Current Year (10 000 person-month)	102.71	120.16
领取失业保险金人数（万人）	Beneficiaries of Unemployment Insurance in Current Year (10 000 persons)	14.17	13.57
#下岗转失业人数	Laid-off Workers	1.87	2.73
#当年再就业人数	Re-employed in Current Year	0.85	0.57

18－14 基本医疗保险情况（2003－2004年）
Conditions of Basic Medical Insurance (2003-2004)

单位：万元 (10 000 yuan)

指 标	Item	2003	2004
年末参保人数（万人）	Year-end Contributors (10 000 persons)	121.77	206.34
职 工	Staff and Workers	80.04	130.17
离休、退休、退职人员	Retirees	41.73	76.17
参加大病统筹的职工人数（万人）	Staff and Workers Participating in Disease System (10 000 persons)	2.98	2.43
基本医疗保险当年实际缴纳保险金	Actual Revenue of Basic Medical Insurance in Current Year	55219.12	156062.47
基本医疗保险基金当年支出额	Expenses of Basic Medical Insurance in Current Year	38564.07	75569.49
基本医疗保险基金当年末结余额	Balance of Basic Medical Insurance in Current Year	16655.05	80492.98

18－15 体育事业基本情况（2003－2004年）
Stadiums & Gymnasiums and Activities of Mass Sports (2003-2004)

项　　目	Item	2003	2004
体育经费（万元）	Sports Expenditures (10 000 yuan)	15237	17698
体育彩票销售额（万元）	Sales Value of Sports Lotteries (10 000 yuan)	19333	14522
体育场地数（个）	Stadiums and Gymnasiums (unit)	17351	17351
#体育场	Stadiums	65	65
体育馆	Gymnasiums	31	31
游泳馆	Natatoriums	4	4
室内外游泳池	Indoor and Outdoor Swimming Pools	120	120
有固定看台的灯光球场	Illuminated Fields with Fixed Seating	70	70
《国家体育锻炼标准》达标人数(万人)	Number of Persons Come up to State Physical Training Standards (10 000 persons)	316	331
县以上体委举办运动会次数(次)	Times of Sports Meets Held by Sports Commissions at and above County Level (time)	209	128
等级运动员（人）	Number of Athletes in Grade (person)		
国际级运动健将	International Master Athletes	5	5
运动健将	Master Athletes	78	105
一级运动员	First Grade Sportsman	56	30
二级运动员	Second Grade Sportsman	697	1185
等级裁判员（人）	Number of Referees in Grade (person)		
国际裁判	International Referees	12	13
国家级裁判	National Referees	173	192
一级裁判	First Grade Referees	153	159
二级裁判	Second Grade Referees	1038	1384

注：1）体育经费包括体育事业费和体育基建支出。

2）体育场地数为2003年普查数。

3）国际级健将、运动健将、国际裁判、国家级裁判均为累计数，其它指标为当年发展数。

Note: a) Sports Expenditures include sports funds and expenditure for sports capital construction.

b) Number of stadiums and gyms refers to general survey in 2003.

c) Data on international master athletes, master athletes, international referees and national referees were accumulative numbers, whereas other items were data of current year.

18－16 律师、公证、调解工作基本情况（2003－2004年）
Lawyers, Notarization and Mediation (2003-2004)

项　　目	Item	2003	2004
律师工作	**Lawyers**		
律师事务所（所）	Number of Law Offices (unit)	292	323
律师工作者（人）	Number of Lawyers (person)	4161	4564
#专　职	Full-time Lawyers	2588	3300
聘请担任法律顾问单位（处）	Number of Units with Permanent Legal Advisors (unit)	3956	6336
民事诉讼代理（件）	Agent of Civil Cases (case)	17268	19705
经济诉讼代理（件）	Agent of Economic Cases (case)	5543	4950
刑事辩护（件）	Defender of Criminal Cases (case)	5716	5523
行政诉讼代理（件）	Agent of Administrative Action (case)	1012	1106
非诉讼法律事务（件）	Cases of Non-litigious Legal Affairs (case)	10370	7950
涉外及涉港澳台法律事务（件）	Agent of Foreign-related, Hong Kong, Macao & Taiwan Legal Affairs (case)	159	172
解答法律询问（件）	Advisory Services of Legal Affairs (case)	112304	128327
代写法律事务文书（件）	Legal Documents Written on Behalf of Clients (case)	26690	38621
公证工作	**Notarization**		
公证处（个）	Number of Notarial Offices (unit)	45	45
公证员（人）	Public Notaries (person)	203	205
办理公证书（件）	Notarized Documents (case)	163738	144031
人民调解工作	**Number of People's Mediation**		
专职司法助理员（人）	Number of Full-time Judicial Assistants (person)	1035	1806
人民调解委员会（个）	Number of People's Mediation Committees (unit)	17874	15794
调解员（人）	Number of Mediators (person)	114264	89205
调解纠纷（件）	Number of Disputes Mediated (case)	137860	143918
婚姻家庭	Family Disputes	44933	38235
房屋、宅基地	Housing and Housing Sites	11288	10978
债　务	Debt	16309	
生产经营	Business	14038	
邻　里	Neighbor Disputes	17584	23765
损害赔偿	Compensation for Damages	11734	14380
其　他	Others	21974	56560

18－17 国内外公证文书（2003－2004年）
Domestic and Foreign Related Notarial Documents (2003-2004)

单位：件 (case)

项 目	Item	国内公证文书 Domestic Notarial Documents 办证件数 Number of Notarial Documents Issued 2003	2004	比 重（%） Proportion 2003	2004
经济公证合计	**Total Notarized Documents on Economic Affairs**	**82124**	**51465**	**100.0**	**100.0**
#购 销	Purchases and Sales of Products	1235	346	1.5	0.7
建筑工程承包	Construction Project Contracts	798	478	1.0	0.9
农林牧渔承包	Farming, Forestry, Animal Husbandry and Fishery Contracts	733	186	1.0	0.4
财产租赁	Property Leasing	242	49	0.3	0.1
劳务合同	Labor Contracts	3761	86	4.6	0.2
贷款合同	Loan Contracts	24694	23995	30.1	46.6
民事公证合计	**Total Notarized Documents on Civil Affairs**	**58363**	**69003**	**100.0**	**100.0**
#收 养	Child Adoption	296	74	0.5	0.1
继承权	Right of Inheritance	5914	5752	10.1	8.3
遗 嘱	Testament	1153	938	2.0	1.4
房屋买卖	Purchases and Sales of Houses	4882	2758	8.4	4.0
产 权	Property Right	323	4121	0.6	6.0
民事协议	Agreement Documents	11125	21829	19.1	31.6

项 目	Item	涉外公证文书 Foreign-related Notarial Documents 办证件数 Number of Notarial Documents Issued 2003	2004	比 重（%） Proportion 2003	2004
合 计	**Total**	**21026**	**19915**	**100.0**	**100.0**
#出 生	Birth	2774	3708	13.2	18.6
学 历	Schooling	3395	2857	16.1	14.3
死 亡	Death	155	18	0.7	0.1
婚姻状况	Marital Status	1898	1291	9.0	6.5
亲属关系	Kinship Confirmation	1797	1398	8.5	7.0
受刑事处分	Criminal Records	4801	1994	22.8	10.0
委托书	Trust Deeds	365	80	1.7	0.4
声明书	Declaration	212	301	1.0	1.5
经 历	Personal Histories	531	234	2.5	1.2
副本与原本相符	Conformation of Copies and Photo-offset Copies to Originals	2202	4367	10.5	21.9
商标注册	Trademark Registrations	7		...	
其他经济合同	Other Business Contracts	16	1305	0.1	6.6

18－18 公安机关受理查处治安案件情况（2003－2004年） Offense Cases against Public Order Handled by Public Security Organs (2003-2004)

单位：起 (case)

案件类别	Category of Cases	受理 Number of Cases Accepted to be Treated		查处 Number of Cases Investigated and Treated	
		2003	2004	2003	2004
合　计	**Total**	**113334**	**106888**	**102950**	**95651**
扰乱工作、公共秩序	Disturbing Work or Public Order	3249	3252	3130	3214
结伙斗殴、寻衅滋事	Gang Fighting or Picking Quarrels and Making Troubles	1286	1024	1127	888
侮辱妇女及其他流氓活动	Acting Indecently towards Women	246	143	235	133
阻碍国家工作人员执行职务	Obstruction the Government Workers to Perform Their Duty	934	543	907	519
违反枪支管理规定	Violating Regulations on Management of Firearms	195	149	187	140
违反爆炸物品管理规定	Violating Regulations on Management of Explosives	2680	1694	2692	1653
殴打他人	Beating Other Body	25121	24421	21411	20792
偷窃财物	Robbing Other People of Their Valuables	13863	14235	9537	9586
骗取、抢夺、敲诈勒索财物	Defrauding, Snatching or Extorting and Racketeering Valuables	3028	3148	2119	2058
哄抢公私财物	Making Stirs and Robbing Public or Private Valuables	98	98	74	82
故意损坏公私财物	Intentionally Damaging Public or Private Valuables	1900	1721	1595	1436
伪造倒卖票卷、证件	Forging and Fraudulently Selling Bills or Certificates	63	53	61	46
利用迷信扰乱秩序或骗财	Disturbing Public Order of Defrauding People of Their Superstition	307	199	312	194
卖淫、嫖娼	Prostitution or Going Whoring	4369	2899	4367	2886
赌　博	Gambling	3910	2913	3869	2880
违反户口、居民身份证管理	Violating Regulations on Management of Residence or Identity Cards	19344	19427	19294	19419
其　他	Others	32741	30969	32033	29725

18－19 公安机关立案的刑事案件情况（2003－2004年）
Criminal Cases Registered in Public Security Organs (2003-2004)

指　　标	Item	2003	2004
人民警察数（人）	**Number of Police (person)**	**25211**	**25881**
刑事案件立案数（起）	**Total Registered Criminal Cases (case)**	**101145**	**97280**
杀　人	Homicide	532	463
伤　害	Injury	2286	2273
抢　劫	Robbery	9549	8410
强　奸	Rape	1080	800
拐卖妇女儿童	Abducting Women or Children	99	46
盗　窃	Larceny	61491	60775
诈　骗	Fraud	5763	5602
走　私	Smuggling		
伪造、变造货币，出售、购买、运输、持有、使用假币	Forging Coin, and Selling, Buying, Transporting, Using False Coin	75	38
其　他	Others	20270	18873
刑事案件破案率（%）	**Detection Rate of Criminal Cases (%)**	**52.9**	**52.9**

18－20 检察机关直接立案侦查案件情况（2004年）
Cases under Direct Investigation by Procurator's Offices (2004)

案件分类	Category of Cases	受案（件） Cases Accepted (case)	立案件数（件） Registered Cases (case)	#大案 Large Cases	#要案 Key Cases	立案人数（人） Person of Cases Registered (person)	结案合计 Total Settled Cases 件 (case)	人 (person)
合　计	**Total**	**1543**	**680**	**413**	**147**	**780**	**681**	**775**
贪污贿赂案件小计	**Sub-total of Cases on Corruption and Bribery**	**1345**	**587**	**373**	**128**	**680**	**597**	**685**
贪　污	Corruption	611	195	128	30	264	206	269
贿　赂	Bribery	597	320	195	84	333	317	329
挪用公款	Misappropriation of Public Funds	88	58	45	7	66	58	67
集体私分	Collective Illegal Possession of Public Funds	39	12	4	6	15	14	18
巨额财产来源不明	Unstated Source of Large Properties	10	2	1	1	2	2	2
其　他	Others							
渎职案件小计	**Sub-total of Cases on Abuse and Dereliction of Duty**	**198**	**93**	**40**	**19**	**100**	**84**	**90**
滥用职权	Abuse of Power	47	20	8	9	21	17	18
玩忽职守	Dereliction of Duty	57	37	25	5	37	31	31
徇私舞弊	Fraudulent Practice	63	30	6	5	36	30	35
其　他	Others	31	6	1		6	6	6

18－21 检察机关审查批准、决定逮捕犯罪嫌疑人和提起公诉被告人情况（2004年）
Arrests of Criminal Suspects and Defendants under Public Prosecution Approved by Procurator's Offices (2004)

案件类别	Category of Cases	批捕、决定逮捕合计 Total Arrests		决定起诉合计 Total Public Prosecutions	
		件 (case)	人 (person)	件 (case)	人 (person)
合　计	**Total**	**12233**	**17348**	**14786**	**21161**
公安、安全、监狱机关提请小计	**Sub-total of Requests by Departments of State and Public Security and Prisons**	**11878**	**16963**	**14308**	**20606**
危害国家安全案	Offences Against State Security	2	2	3	3
危害公共安全案	Offences Against Public Security	696	843	1409	1560
破坏社会主义市场经济秩序案	Offences Against Socialist Economic Order	181	257	216	328
侵犯公民人身、民主权利案	Offences Against Citizens' Personal and Democratic Rights	2076	2664	2556	3202
侵犯财产案	Offences Against Properties	6898	10311	7736	11881
妨害社会管理秩序案	Offences Against Social Management of Order	2024	2885	2386	3630
危害国防利益案	Offences Against National Defense	1	1	2	2
军人违反职责案	Offences on Dereliction of Duty by Servicemen				
检察机关直接立案侦查案件小计	**Sub-total of Cases Handled by Procuratorates**	**355**	**385**	**478**	**555**
贪污贿赂案	Offences on Corruption and Bribery	329	356	432	501
渎职案	Offences on Abuse and Dereliction of Duty	26	29	46	54

18－22 人民法院刑事一审案件收结案情况（2003－2004年）
First Trial Criminal Cases Accepted and Settled by Courts (2003-2004)

单位：件　　(case)

类　别	Category of Cases	收　案 Accepted Cases		结　案 Settled Cases	
		2003	2004	2003	2004
合　计	**Total**	**16333**	**15880**	**15734**	**15230**
#自诉案件	Private Prosecution	1148	902	966	740
危害公共安全罪	Offences against Public Security	1342	1415	1298	1366
破坏社会主义市场经济秩序罪	Offences against Socialist Economic Order	222	205	205	194
侵犯公民人身权利、民主权利罪	Offences against Citizens' Personal and Democratic Rights	4009	3588	3691	3290
侵犯财产罪	Offences against Properties	7719	7760	7599	7587
妨害社会管理秩序罪	Offences against social Management of Order	2559	2410	2498	2344
危害国防利益罪	Offences against National Defense	2	1	2	1
贪污贿赂罪	Offences on Corruption and Bribery	445	453	413	408
渎职罪	Offences on Dereliction of Duty	31	41	24	33
其　他	Others	4	7	4	7

注：收结案中含上年旧存。

Note: Accepted and settled cases include turned over from the previous year.

18－23 人民法院民事、行政一审案件收结案情况（2003－2004年）
First Trial Civil and Administrative Cases Accepted and Settled by Courts (2003-2004)

单位：件 (case)

类别	Category of Cases	收案 Accepted Cases		结案 Settled Cases	
		2003	2004	2003	2004
民事一审案件	**First Trial of Civil Cases**	**95558**	**89624**	**89788**	**83210**
婚姻家庭纠纷案件	Disputes of Marriages and Family Affairs	37691	31671	36193	30124
继承纠纷案件	Disputes of Inheritance	453	475	395	436
合同纠纷案件	Disputes of Contracts	37408	38252	34957	35503
权属、侵权纠纷案件	Disputes of Ownership and Torts	14005	14173	12568	12417
其他民事案件	Other Civil Cases	6001	5053	5675	4730
行政一审案件	**First Trial of Administrative Cases**	**2334**	**2858**	**2182**	**2634**
公　安	Public Security	278	283	270	261
资　源	Resources	328	233	321	212
城　建	City Construction	609	659	572	613
工　商	Industry and Commerce	80	84	57	73
交　通	Traffic	111	154	106	148
环　保	Environmental Protection	22	9	19	6
劳动和社会保障	Labor and Social Security	176	273	165	259
其　他	Others	730	1163	672	1062

注：收案中含上年旧存。
Note: Accepted cases include turned over from the previous year.

18－24 人民法院合同纠纷一审案件收结案情况（2003－2004年）
First Trial Cases of Contract Disputes Accepted and Settled by Courts (2003-2004)

单位：件 (case)

类别	Category of Cases	收案 Accepted Cases		结案 Settled Cases	
		2003	2004	2003	2004
合　计	**Total**	**37408**	**38252**	**34957**	**35503**
#买卖合同	Contracts of Business	9039	7780	8553	7236
房地产开发经营合同	Contracts of Real Estate Development and Operation	3879	4925	3572	4653
赠与合同	Contracts of Gift	22	13	18	12
借款合同	Contracts of Loans	13959	12500	13286	11674
租赁合同	Contracts of Leasing	1770	1555	1656	1425
建设工程合同	Contracts of Construction Projects	2003	2056	1740	1787
运输合同	Contracts of Transportation	379	445	349	393
技术合同	Contracts of Technique	3		3	
知识产权合同	Contracts of Intellectual Property	5	8	3	8
劳动争议	Labor Disputes	777	2875	666	2711

注：收案中含上年旧存。
Note: Accepted cases include turned over from the previous year.

18－25 人民法院权属、侵权纠纷一审案件收结案情况（2003－2004年）
First Trial Cases of Ownership & Tort Disputes Accepted and Settled by Courts (2003-2004)

单位：件　(case)

类　别	Category of Cases	收案 Accepted Cases 2003	收案 Accepted Cases 2004	结案 Settled Cases 2003	结案 Settled Cases 2004
合　计	**Total**	**20006**	**19226**	**18243**	**17147**
#所有权及与所有权相关权利纠纷	Ownership and Relative Disputes	4616	4663	4221	4181
票据、证券权益纠纷	Disputes of Bill & Security Rights and Interests	36	45	32	35
股东权纠纷	Disputes of Stock-holders' Rights	102	307	87	154
知识产权纠纷	Disputes of Intellectual Property	122	129	95	85
不正当竞争纠纷	Disputes of Illicit Competitions	31	21	26	14
人身权纠纷	Disputes of Personal Rights	8605	8469	7608	7470
特殊侵权纠纷	Disputes of Special Torts	409	426	344	386

注：收案中含上年旧存。
Note: Accepted cases include turned over from the previous year.

18－26 人民法院审理婚姻家庭、继承一审案件收结案情况（2003－2004年）
First Trial Civil Cases of Marriages, Family Affairs and Inheritance Accepted and Settled by Courts (2003-2004)

单位：件　(case)

类　别	Category of Cases	收案 Accepted Cases 2003	收案 Accepted Cases 2004	结案 Settled Cases 2003	结案 Settled Cases 2004
合　计	**Total**	**38144**	**32146**	**36588**	**30560**
其中：离　婚	Of Which: Divorce	33230	27775	31918	26381
解除非法同居关系	Relieving the Relation of Lawless Cohahit	887	380	850	375
赡养纠纷	Suppport Disputes	1185	1054	1139	1020
抚养关系纠纷	Upbringing Disputes	148	1089	136	1043
抚育费纠纷	Upbringing Fee Disputes	751	677	729	648
法定继承	Legal Inheritance	269	271	235	244
遗嘱继承	Testament Inheritance	23	20	21	18
其　他	Other	151	202	127	185
婚姻家庭	Marrigaes and Family Affairs	37691	31671	36193	30124
继　承	Inhertance	453	475	395	436

注：收案中含上年旧存。
Note: Accepted cases include turned over from the previous year.

18－27 道路交通事故情况（2004年）
Basic Statistics on Highway Traffic Accidents (2004)

类别	Type	发生数（起） Number of Traffic Accidents (case)	死亡人数（人） Number of Deaths (person)	受伤人数（人） Number of Injuries (person)	损失折款（万元） Losses Converted into Cash (10 000 yuan)
总计	**Total**	**12246**	**932**	**10090**	**3494.00**
其中：重大事故	Of Which: Extraordinarily Serious	876	842	570	277.56
特大事故	Serious	18	90	132	30.92
#机动车	Motor-driven Vehicles	11677	875	9714	3465.00
#汽　车	Automobiles	8816	584	7116	3112.18
摩托车	Motorcycles	2346	206	2188	248.05
拖拉机	Tractors	189	49	166	39.48
非机动车	Non-motor-driven Vehicles	99	7	87	6.29
#自行车	Bicycles	58	5	48	3.84
行人乘车人	Pedestrians and Passengers	427	42	264	18.87

注：1）本表数据不含高速公路交通事故。
2）损失折款指直接经济损失。

Note: a) Data in this table exclude traffic accidents on expressway.
b) Losses converted into cash refer to direct losses.

18－28 火灾事故情况（2004年）
Basic Statistics on Fires (2004)

项目	Item	合计 Total	按事故发生程度分 By Serious Degree of Fires	
			#特大 Extra-ordinarily Serious	#重大 Serious
发生（起）	Fires (case)	7391		4
死亡（人）	Deaths (person)	63		7
受伤（人）	Injuries (person)	97		1
损失折款（万元）	Losses Converted into Cash (10 000 yuan)	1602.15		163.21
平均每起事故损失（万元）	Average Loss per Fire (10 000 yuan)	0.22		40.80

注：损失折款指直接经济损失。

Note: Losses converted into cash refer to direct losses.

主要统计指标解释

等级运动员人数 指经考核正式批准授予等级运动员称号的人数。运动员等级分为国际级运动健将、运动健将、一级运动员、二级运动员、三级运动员、少年级运动员。

等级裁判员人数 指经考核正式批准授予等级裁判员称号的人数。裁判员等级分为国际裁判、国家级裁判、一级裁判、二级裁判、三级裁判。

体育场 指有400米跑道（中心含足球场），有固定道牙，跑道6条以上，并有固定看台的室外田径场地。体育场按看台容纳观众人数分为：甲级25000人以上，乙级15000-25000人，、丙级5000-15000人，丁级5000人以下。

体育馆 指有固定看台，可供篮球、排球、羽毛球、乒乓球、体操等项目训练比赛活动用的室内运动场地。体育馆按看台容纳观众人数分为：甲级6000人以上，乙级4000-6000人，丙级2000-4000人，丁级2000人以下。

卫生机构 包括医疗机构、疾病预防控制中心(防疫站)、采供血机构、卫生监督及监测(检验)机构、医学科研和在职培训机构、健康教育所等。

医疗机构 包括医院、社区卫生服务中心(站)、疗养院、卫生院、门诊部、诊所(卫生所、医务室)、妇幼保健院(所、站)、专科疾病防治院(所、站)、急救中心(站)和临床检验中心。医疗机构分为非赢利性医疗机构和赢利性医疗机构。

医院 包括综合医院、中医医院、中西医结合医院、民族医院、各类专科医院和护理院。

卫生技术人员 指卫生机构中医生、护理人员 、药剂人员、检验人员等卫生技术人员。

医生 指在医疗、预防保健机构工作且取得《执业医师证书》的执业医师和执业助理医师。

社会福利事业单位 指集中收养社会孤老、残、幼的机构，包括由民政部门管理的社会福利院、儿童福利院、精神病人福利院和城镇集体举办的福利院及农村集体举办的敬老院以及优抚医院和具有收养能力的社区服务中心等。

社会福利事业单位收养人数 包括民政部门管理的和城镇及农村集体举办的社会福利事业单位中收养的老人、少年儿童、缺乏生活自理能力的残疾人员和精神病人。

社会福利企业单位 指以安置城镇有一定劳动能力的盲、聋、哑和肢体残疾人员就业为目的，享受国家减免税待遇的国有或集体企业。包括福利工厂、福利商业和服务业、假肢厂和安置农场等单位。该指标主要反映我国对残疾人照顾的特殊政策。

基本养老保险

1. 参加保险人数：指报告期末按照国家法律、法规和有关政策规定参加基本养老保险的职工人数。包括不能正常缴费、已中断缴费但未终止保险关系的职工人数。

2. 社会统筹基金收入：指根据国家规定，由纳入基本养老保险范围的单位，按照国家规定的缴费基数和缴费比例缴纳的社会统筹基金，以及通过其他方式取得的形成基金来源的收入，包括：单位缴纳的社会统筹基金收入、财政补贴收入、利息收入、其他收入。

3. 社会统筹基金支出：指按照国家政策规定的开支范围和开支标准从社会统筹基金中支付给参加基本养老保险的离休、退休、退职人员个人的养老金、丧葬抚恤补助，以及由于保险关系转移、上下级之间调剂资金等原因而发生的支出。包括：基础性养老金、过渡性养老金、离休金、退休金、退职金、补贴、丧葬抚恤补助、其他支出。

4. 社会统筹基金结余：指截止报告期末基本养老保险的社会统筹基金结余金额。包括银行存款、财政专户、债券投资和其他。

离休、退休、退职人员　指正式办理了离休、退休、退职手续，并享受相应的离休、退休、退职待遇的人员。

失业保险

1. 参加保险人数：指报告期末按照国家法律、法规和有关政策规定参加了失业保险的城镇企业事业单位的职工及地方政府规定参加失业保险的其他人员的人数。

2. 失业保险金：指为保障失业人员的基本生活而按规定支付的失业保险金金额。

基本医疗保险

1. 参加保险人数：指报告期末按国家有关规定参加基本医疗保险的人数。包括参加保险的职工人数和退休人员人数。

2. 社会统筹基金收入：指根据国家有关规定，由纳入基本医疗保险范围的缴费单位，按国家规定的缴费基数和缴费比例缴纳的社会统筹基金，以及通过其他方式取得的形成基金来源的款项，包括：单位缴纳的社会统筹基金收入、财政补贴收入、利息收入、其他收入。

3. 社会统筹基金支出：指按照国家政策规定的开支范围和开支标准从社会统筹基金中支付给参加基本医疗保险的职工和退休人员的医疗保险待遇支出及其他支出。包括：住院医疗费用支出、门急诊医疗费用支出、其他支出。

4. 社会统筹基金结余：指截止报告期末基本医疗保险的社会统筹基金结余金额。包括银行存款、财政专户、债券投资和其他。

律师　指依法取得律师执业证书，担任法律顾问，民事(刑事、行政)案件代理人、刑事案件辩护人、办理非诉讼业务，解答法律询问，代写法律事务文书等，为社会提供法律服务的人员。

公证人员　指在公证处工作的人员总称，包括公证处主任、副主任、公证员、公证员助理(助理公证员)和其他从事辅助性工作的人员。

公证文书　指公证处根据当事人申请，依照事实和法律，按照法定程序制作的，具有法律效力的司法证明文书。根据公证书用途和使用地，公证书分为国内公证书、国内经济公证书、涉外民事公证书、涉外经济公证书四类。

调解员　指在人民调解委员会担负调解民间纠纷工作的人员，包括调解委员会的委员和调解小组的调解员。

调解民间纠纷　指调解委员会按照法律规定，根据自愿原则，用说服教育的方法调解民间发生的有关民事权利和义务争执的件数，包括调解成功数和调解未成功数。

立案　指人民检察院对受理的报案、控告、举报或自首及自行发现的犯罪线索、犯罪嫌疑人进行初步调查后，认为存在职务犯罪事实和应追究刑事责任，并决定作为刑事案件进行侦查的诉讼活动，是追究犯罪的开始。该指标主要反映人民检察院依法将职务犯罪线索作为刑事案件进行侦查的诉讼活动。

大案 指贪污、贿赂案数额在5万元以上，挪用公款案数额在10万元以上，集体私分、巨额财产来源不明、隐瞒境外存款案数额在50万元以上以及按照《人民检察院直接受理的渎职、侵权重、特大案件标准(试行)》认定的案件。该指标主要反映人民检察院立案查办的职务犯罪案件中经济损失大、社会危害严重的案件。

要案 指县、处级以上干部的犯罪案件。该指标主要反映国家工作人员中县、处级以上干部因职务犯罪被人民检察院依法立案侦查的情况。

决定逮捕 指人民检察机关对直接受理、自行侦查的案件，认为需要逮捕犯罪嫌疑人时，依据法律作出的逮捕决定。

批准逮捕 指人民检察机关对公安机关、国家安全机关、监狱管理机关提出逮捕的犯罪嫌疑人进行审查，根据事实，依法作出逮捕决定。

决定起诉 指人民检察机关对公安机关、国家安全机关、监狱管理机关和检察机关内设机构反贪污贿赂部门移送起诉的刑事犯罪嫌疑人进行审查，根据事实，依法向人民法院提起公诉。

Explanatory Notes on Main Statistical Indicators

Number of Athletes in Grades refers to the number of athletes who have been given titles through examination. The titles of athletes include international masters of sports, masters of sports, first-grade, second-grade and third-grade sportsmen and young athletes.

Number of Referees in Grades refers to the number of referees who have been given titles after examination. They are classified as international referees, national referees and referees of the first, second and third grades.

Stadiums refer to stadiums for track and field events with six lane 400-meter tracks around soccer fields, permanent track marks and permanent bleachers. Stadiums are classified according to seating capacity. They include: Class A stadiums seating 25000 people each, Class B stadiums seating 15000 to 25000 people each, Class C stadiums seating 5000 to 15000 people each, and Class D stadiums seating fewer than 5000 people.

Gymnasiums refer to indoor sports grounds with permanent seats in which basketball, volleyball, badminton, table tennis and gymnastics competitions can be held. Gymnasiums are classified according to seating capacity. They include Class A gymnasiums seating over 6000 people, Class B gymnasiums seating 4000 to 6000 people, Class C gymnasiums seating 2000 to 4000 people, and Class D gymnasiums seating fewer than 2000 people.

Health Care Institutions include medical institutions, disease prevention and control centers (epidemic prevention stations), blood gathering and supplying institutions, health supervision and inspection (check up) institutions, medicinal scientific research and on-job training institutions, health education and so on.

Medical Organizations include hospitals, health service centers (stations) of communities, nursing homes, health centers, clinics, clinics (health stations and infirmaries), maternity and child care agencies (centers and stations), special disease prevention and curing agencies (centers and stations), first aid centers (stations) and clinical inspection centers. Medical organizations are grouped by two types: profit-making and non-profit-making medical organizations.

Hospitals include polyclinics, traditional Chinese medical hospitals, hospitals integrated with traditional Chinese therapeutics and western therapeutics, ethical hospitals, various specialties hospitals and nursing hospitals.

Medical Technical Personnel refers to doctors, assistant nurses, pharmacists, and laboratory technicians working in medical institutions.

Doctors refer to certified physicians and certified assistant physicians with certifications working in medical and health care and prevention agencies.

Social Welfare Institutions refer to institutions taking care of old people without children, handicapped people and orphans. They include social welfare institutions run by civil affairs departments, children welfare institutions, social welfare institutions for mental patients, collective-owned old peoples homes in rural areas, convalescent homes and community service centers with the capacity of receiving those people.

Number of People Taken in by Social Welfare Institutions refers to the number of old people, children, totally dependent handicapped people and mental patients taken in by social welfare institutions run by civil affairs departments and those run by collective units in urban and rural areas.

Social Welfare Enterprises are collective owned enterprises which employ the blind, deaf-mute, and other handicapped people who are able to work in cities and towns and enjoy exemption from state taxes, including welfare plants, welfare commercial services, artificial limb plants and farms, etc. This indicator reflects the preferential policies toward disabled persons.

Basic Endowment Insurance

1. Number of people participating in the insurance program: by the end of reference period, number of staff and workers participating in the insurance program in line with national laws, regulations and related policies, including those who can not make regular payment or interrupt payment but not terminate the insurance program.

2. Revenue of social comprehensive funds: according to national provision, payments made by units covered in basic endowment insurance program, and income from other resources, including: income of social comprehensive funds paid by unites, financial subsidies, interest income and others.

3. Expenditure of social comprehensive funds: refer to payment made to those retired and resigned people covered in endowment insurance program in terms of pension or compensation within the expenditure scope and standards according to related national policies, and the expenditure occurred due to shift of the insurance relationship or adjustment funds among agencies, including: basic pension, transitional pension, pension for resigned people, pension for retired people, pension for people quitting jobs, subsidies, funeral subsidies and other expenditure.

4. Balance of social comprehensive funds: refer to the balance of basic endowment insurance of social comprehensive funds at the end of the reference period, including: bank savings, special fiscal account, investment in bonds and others.

Retired or Resigned Personnel refers to people who have formally gone through the formalities for their retirement or quitting work and enjoy the corresponding treatments.

Unemployment Insurance

1. Number of people participated in unemployment insurance program: number of staff and workers in urban enterprises or institutions and other people according to local government regulations participated in unemployment insurance program in line with national law, regulations and related policies by the end of the reference period.

2. Sum of Unemployment Insurance: refer to total amount of insurance paid to un-employees to guarantee their basic lives according to related regulations.

Basic Medical Care Insurance

1. Number of people participated in the insurance program: refer to number of people participated in the basic medical care insurance program according to related regulation by the end of reference period, including: number of staff and workers and retired persons participated in this insurance program.

2. Revenue of social comprehensive funds: according to national provision, payments made by units covered in basic medical care insurance program, and income from other resources, including: income of social comprehensive funds paid by unites, financial subsidies, interest income and others.

3. Expenditure of social comprehensive funds: refer to payment made to those retired and resigned people covered in basic medical care insurance within the expenditure scope and standards according to related national policies, including: expenditure on fee-for-service in hospital, expenditure on fee-for-service in clinic and other expenditure.

4. Balance of social comprehensive funds: refer to the balance of medical care insurance of social comprehensive funds at the end of the reference period, including: bank savings, special fiscal account, investment in bonds and others.

Lawyers are certified legal workers according to law, and who are employed by legal counseling firms to act as legal advisers, agents in criminal or civil lawsuits, or defenders in criminal lawsuits, or to handle non-litigious legal affairs, to advise on matters of law or to write legal papers for others, and provide service to the public.

Notary Personnel refers to people working for notary offices including: directors, deputy director, notaries, assistant notaries, and other people providing assistance.

Notary Documents refer to the judicatory notary documents drawn up by the request of the party and are in accordance with facts and laws and following certain legal proceedings. According to usage and locality, the notary documents are divided into following 4 types: domestic notary documents, domestic economic notary documents, foreign-related civil notary documents and foreign-related economic notary documents.

Mediators refer to workers on people mediation committees responsible for mediating in civil disputes and cases of slight infraction of the law. They include members of the mediation committees and mediators of mediation groups.

Mediation of Civil Disputes refers to number of cases made by mediation committees in mediating in civil disputes concerning civil rights and duties through persuasion and education in accordance with the provisions of law on a voluntary basis, so as to solve disputes by helping the parties involved come to an agreement and understanding, including those unsuccessful ones.

Acceptance of Case refers to the decision made by the people's procuratorate office on reported cases, prosecution, impeachment, surrender, self-found criminal clues or suspects after initial investigation to confirm the act of crime and to start legal proceedings of the case as criminal case.

Large Cases refer to cases involving a corruption or bribery of over 50,000 yuan, or a misappropriation of over 100,000 yuan, Cases of collectively illegal possession of public funds, unstated sources of large properties, or disguised overseas savings deposits involving 500,000 yuan, or a case that has been defined by the *Standard on Serious and Large Cases of Misconduct and Tortious that Directly Accepted by People's Procurators Office (trial).* This indicator mainly reflects number of accepted cases of job-related criminals that caused serious economic losses or extremely harmful to the society.

Key Cases refer to cases committed by government officials with a ranking of division director or county administrator. This indicator mainly reflects the recorded and spied on cases by the people's procurators offices toward government official with a ranking of division director or county administrator.

Decision of Arrest refers to decision made by procurators office, in accordance with laws, to arrest the suspect(s) in the cases that are accepted and to be investigated by procurators office.

Approval for Arrest refers to the decision made by procurators office, in accordance with laws and relevant facts, to approve the arrest of the suspect(s) that is proposed by the public security departments, state security departments or authority of prisons.

Decision on Prosecution refers to the decision made by procurators office, in accordance with laws and relevant facts, to institute proceedings to the people court against the suspect(s) of criminal cases handed over by the public security departments, state security departments or authority of prisons, or by the anti-corruption departments within the procurators office.

十九　区县（自治县、市）和开发区

DISTRICTS (COUNTIES) AND DEVELOPMENT ZONE

简要说明　Brief Introduction

本章资料包括2004年按三大经济区分组的全市40个区县（自治县、市）的主要经济社会统计资料，以及重庆市开发区、经济技术开发区和高新技术产业开发区的主要统计资料。

三大经济区的多数统计数据经过评估和测算而取得，其合计数不等于各区县数据直接相加数。

本章资料分别由市统计局人口就业处、核算处、工业交通处、固定资产投资处、贸易外经处、社会科技处、综合处和市农村社会经济调查队根据有关专业统计资料、各区县统计局资料和市级有关部门的区县资料整理编辑。

Data in this chapter include main economic and social indicators of 40 districts (counties) by region of three economic zones in 2004, as well as main economic indicators of development zones, Economic & Technology Development Zone and High-tech Development Zone in Chongqing.

Most data of three economic zones are assessed and examined. The data of three economic zones are not equal to the sums of districts (counties).

Data in this chapter are prepared and edited by Division of Population and Employment Statistics, Division of National Economic Accounting, Division of Industry and Transport Statistics, Division of Statistics of Investment in Fixed Assets, Division of Trade and External Economic Relations Statistics, Division of Social and Technology Statistics, Division of Comprehensive Statistics of Municipal Bureau of Statistics and Municipal Rural Socio-economic Survey Organization, on basis of data from related divisions of Municipal Bureau of Statistics, statistical bureaus of districts (counties) and from related municipal departments.

19－1 各区县（自治县、市）人口（2004年）
Population by Region (2004)

区 县	Region	年末总户数（户籍统计）（万户）Year-end Households (registration statistics) (10 000 households)	年末总人口（户籍统计）（万人）Year-end Population (registration statistics) (10 000 persons)	#非农业人口 Non-agricultural	#女 性 Female
都市发达经济圈	**Metropolitan Advanced Economic Sphere**	**191.93**	**567.17**	**344.70**	**278.12**
渝中区	Yuzhong District	19.44	59.92	59.92	29.97
大渡口区	Dadukou District	7.69	21.30	15.40	10.62
江北区	Jiangbei District	16.47	48.87	39.49	24.01
沙坪坝区	Shapingba District	22.92	72.67	51.67	35.90
九龙坡区	Jiulongpo District	26.22	76.15	53.12	37.33
南岸区	Nan'an District	17.62	52.68	40.69	25.87
北碚区	Beibei District	21.42	65.05	29.80	31.91
渝北区	Yubei District	30.51	84.78	29.29	41.17
巴南区	Ba'nan District	29.64	85.75	25.32	41.34
渝西经济走廊	**West Chongqing Economic Corridor**	**316.23**	**998.78**	**203.23**	**478.78**
万盛区	Wansheng District	8.04	26.68	12.08	13.30
双桥区	Shuangqiao District	1.55	4.71	2.25	2.29
綦江县	Qijiang County	29.36	94.66	20.41	45.55
潼南县	Tongnan County	25.38	90.40	10.61	42.47
铜梁县	Tongliang County	26.10	80.40	13.14	38.56
大足县	Dazu County	26.32	92.48	15.27	43.43
荣昌县	Rongchang County	25.43	81.36	15.84	39.47
璧山县	Bishan County	20.72	61.17	13.97	29.70
江津市	Jiangjin City	51.63	145.48	36.80	69.37
合川市	Hechuan City	48.07	149.94	27.05	71.67
永川市	Yongchuan City	33.50	107.20	26.51	51.65
南川市	Nanchuan City	20.13	64.30	9.30	31.32
三峡库区生态经济区	**Ecological Economic Zone in Three Gorges Reservoir Area**	**480.43**	**1578.28**	**237.90**	**750.15**
万州区	Wanzhou District	55.41	169.70	45.58	82.36
涪陵区	Fuling District	37.23	111.57	30.47	54.28
黔江区	Qianjiang District	14.99	50.24	7.35	23.67
长寿区	Changshou District	28.68	87.49	17.76	42.33
梁平县	Liangping County	27.60	88.31	10.68	41.88
城口县	Chengkou County	6.80	23.07	2.55	10.63
丰都县	Fengdu County	24.60	78.67	11.88	37.38
垫江县	Dianjiang County	27.05	90.11	12.63	42.57
武隆县	Wulong County	11.48	39.84	5.22	18.75
忠 县	Zhongxian County	29.00	96.25	13.36	46.26
开 县	Kaixian County	46.65	152.95	16.15	71.74
云阳县	Yunyang County	34.92	128.75	14.85	60.86
奉节县	Fengjie County	30.30	100.20	10.10	47.45
巫山县	Wushan County	18.25	59.45	6.80	28.03
巫溪县	Wuxi County	16.05	51.95	5.14	24.54
石柱县	Shizhu County	14.82	51.45	7.25	24.81
秀山县	Xiushan County	16.50	61.19	7.44	29.14
酉阳县	Youyang County	21.69	74.99	7.03	34.75
彭水县	Pengshui County	18.41	62.10	5.66	28.72

19-1 续表 CONTINUED

区　县	Region	人口自然增长（户籍统计） Natural Growth of Population (registration statistics)		常住人口（万人） Resident Popolation (10 000 persons)	城镇化率（%） Urban Rate (%)
		人数（万人） Population (10 000 persons)	自然增长率（‰） Natural Growth Rate (‰)		
都市发达经济圈	**Metropolitan Advanced Economic Sphere**	**-0.22**	**-0.39**	**627.16**	**85.05**
渝中区	Yuzhong District	-0.19	-3.20	68.63	100.00
大渡口区	Dadukou District	…	-0.22	25.70	100.00
江北区	Jiangbei District	-0.03	-0.71	63.51	100.00
沙坪坝区	Shapingba District	-0.03	-0.39	84.09	100.00
九龙坡区	Jiulongpo District	0.03	0.40	92.22	100.00
南岸区	Nan'an District	0.03	0.64	65.13	100.00
北碚区	Beibei District	-0.17	-2.63	66.20	63.60
渝北区	Yubei District	0.18	2.14	81.88	54.46
巴南区	Ba'nan District	-0.04	-0.42	79.80	59.41
渝西经济走廊	**West Chongqing Economic Corridor**	**0.85**	**0.86**	**835.40**	**37.75**
万盛区	Wansheng District	0.04	1.37	24.86	64.72
双桥区	Shuangqiao District	0.02	4.94	4.64	86.42
綦江县	Qijiang County	0.17	1.78	83.32	30.70
潼南县	Tongnan County	0.50	5.61	70.68	22.07
铜梁县	Tongliang County	-0.11	-1.37	61.52	29.84
大足县	Dazu County	-0.05	-0.54	75.77	27.52
荣昌县	Rongchang County	0.29	3.63	64.74	29.80
璧山县	Bishan County	…	-0.02	50.94	31.10
江津市	Jiangjin City	-0.03	-0.22	125.87	47.00
合川市	Hechuan City	-0.20	-1.35	126.90	44.00
永川市	Yongchuan City	0.18	1.71	91.98	47.80
南川市	Nanchuan City	0.04	0.57	54.18	38.34
三峡库区生态经济区	**Ecological Economic Zone in Three Gorges Reservoir Area**	**9.65**	**6.13**	**1308.42**	**27.28**
万州区	Wanzhou District	0.60	3.57	150.67	44.48
涪陵区	Fuling District	0.13	1.16	100.67	47.45
黔江区	Qianjiang District	0.04	0.84	43.99	26.44
长寿区	Changshou District	0.18	2.03	74.69	42.05
梁平县	Liangping County	0.13	1.50	71.28	25.58
城口县	Chengkou County	0.10	4.38	19.15	14.62
丰都县	Fengdu County	1.15	14.72	64.32	22.62
垫江县	Dianjiang County	0.50	5.56	72.71	24.58
武隆县	Wulong County	0.25	6.40	34.63	24.11
忠　县	Zhongxian County	0.21	2.15	74.21	23.03
开　县	Kaixian County	1.69	11.11	116.10	25.42
云阳县	Yunyang County	1.62	12.63	101.21	22.51
奉节县	Fengjie County	1.19	11.97	85.78	22.32
巫山县	Wushan County	0.41	6.85	49.85	19.70
巫溪县	Wuxi County	0.35	6.66	44.25	14.31
石柱县	Shizhu County	0.37	7.25	43.36	17.23
秀山县	Xiushan County	0.25	4.12	50.12	17.32
酉阳县	Youyang County	0.41	5.49	57.38	14.33
彭水县	Pengshui County	0.07	1.14	54.05	15.32

19－2 各区县（自治县、市）就业（2004年）
Employment by Region (2004)

区 县	Region	年末全部就业人员数（万人） Year-end Employment (10 000 persons)	第一产业 Primary Industry	第二产业 Secondary Industry	第三产业 Tertiary Industry	城镇就业人员（万人） Urban Registered Unemployment (10 000 persons)
都市发达经济圈	**Metropolitan Advanced Economic Sphere**	**329.19**	**81.27**	**93.78**	**154.14**	**265.39**
渝中区	Yuzhong District	34.31		7.67	26.64	34.31
大渡口区	Dadukou District	14.56	2.37	6.56	5.63	10.94
江北区	Jiangbei District	28.21	3.28	11.84	13.09	22.63
沙坪坝区	Shapingba District	39.27	5.27	17.08	16.92	27.60
九龙坡区	Jiulongpo District	55.27	7.54	27.18	20.55	35.23
南岸区	Nan'an District	24.19	3.78	11.25	9.16	17.86
北碚区	Beibei District	32.63	12.29	13.00	7.34	10.97
渝北区	Yubei District	51.71	20.75	11.52	19.44	22.16
巴南区	Ba'nan District	50.59	19.08	20.03	11.48	14.97
渝西经济走廊	**West Chongqing Economic Corridor**	**549.37**	**268.93**	**99.18**	**181.26**	**129.51**
万盛区	Wansheng District	12.62	5.12	4.48	3.02	4.59
双桥区	Shuangqiao District	3.03	0.51	1.52	1.00	1.54
綦江县	Qijiang County	54.60	23.71	15.07	15.82	9.11
潼南县	Tongnan County	57.76	39.34	9.78	8.64	5.27
铜梁县	Tongliang County	48.89	19.38	14.83	14.68	6.40
大足县	Dazu County	53.10	26.81	7.59	18.70	4.00
荣昌县	Rongchang County	39.92	24.18	7.41	8.33	7.78
璧山县	Bishan County	38.25	11.16	15.16	11.93	8.78
江津市	Jiangjin City	74.49	28.26	22.97	23.26	16.81
合川市	Hechuan City	89.87	44.71	15.49	29.67	13.19
永川市	Yongchuan City	44.20	15.11	13.29	15.80	13.03
南川市	Nanchuan City	35.22	18.04	10.03	7.15	5.47
三峡库区生态经济区	**Ecological Economic Zone in Three Gorges Reservoir Area**	**837.06**	**519.10**	**108.46**	**209.50**	**187.89**
万州区	Wanzhou District	73.35	29.14	19.13	25.08	25.35
涪陵区	Fuling District	64.84	33.62	12.42	18.80	16.31
黔江区	Qianjiang District	24.68	17.64	2.38	4.66	5.88
长寿区	Changshou District	54.61	30.15	12.27	12.19	11.99
梁平县	Liangping County	36.34	14.76	10.31	11.27	9.21
城口县	Chengkou County	11.61	5.74	3.66	2.21	1.49
丰都县	Fengdu County	47.34	34.98	5.05	7.31	5.10
垫江县	Dianjiang County	45.70	29.00	11.90	4.80	3.73
武隆县	Wulong County	25.56	14.98	5.03	5.55	4.53
忠 县	Zhongxian County	54.14	27.02	7.58	19.54	4.52
开 县	Kaixian County	77.80	44.60	10.60	22.60	6.90
云阳县	Yunyang County	66.00	37.54	12.63	15.83	9.99
奉节县	Fengjie County	49.00	33.19	6.76	9.05	12.44
巫山县	Wushan County	33.95	24.39	3.62	5.94	5.67
巫溪县	Wuxi County	28.38	22.17	1.92	4.29	3.26
石柱县	Shizhu County	32.53	23.27	5.39	3.87	3.81
秀山县	Xiushan County	30.23	20.07	6.34	3.82	3.13
酉阳县	Youyang County	45.85	30.06	11.99	3.80	2.31
彭水县	Pengshui County	39.08	30.71	3.70	4.67	3.62

19-2 续表 CONTINUED

区 县	Region	职 工（万人） Staff and Workers (10 000 persons)	#国 有 Primary Industry	#集 体 Secondary Industry	城镇经济单位专业技术人员（人） Specialized Technicians in Urban Economic Units (person)	年末失业人员登记数（人） Urban Registered Unemployment (person)
都市发达经济圈	**Metropolitan Advanced Economic Sphere**	**99.49**	**55.79**	**6.79**	**258844**	**80300**
渝中区	Yuzhong District	23.71	16.19	1.16	58765	15437
大渡口区	Dadukou District	5.28	3.79	0.55	11551	3510
江北区	Jiangbei District	11.62	5.79	0.82	27438	9324
沙坪坝区	Shapingba District	10.71	5.20	0.82	28368	13858
九龙坡区	Jiulongpo District	20.79	8.23	1.35	51690	16360
南岸区	Nan'an District	9.44	5.62	0.78	27681	8599
北碚区	Beibei District	5.70	3.21	0.31	17787	4453
渝北区	Yubei District	5.74	3.50	0.30	17886	4633
巴南区	Ba'nan District	6.50	4.26	0.70	17678	4126
渝西经济走廊	**West Chongqing Economic Corridor**	**46.40**	**26.07**	**4.24**	**145075**	**36581**
万盛区	Wansheng District	2.41	1.89	0.18	5372	3628
双桥区	Shuangqiao District	0.86	0.18	0.10	2259	314
綦江县	Qijiang County	5.42	3.55	0.66	16159	3380
潼南县	Tongnan County	1.88	1.59	0.08	9158	1710
铜梁县	Tongliang County	2.36	1.53	0.30	10332	1917
大足县	Dazu County	2.92	1.87	0.24	10773	1598
荣昌县	Rongchang County	4.07	2.82	0.65	13698	3162
璧山县	Bishan County	3.16	1.23	0.28	9307	1882
江津市	Jiangjin City	9.76	3.88	0.84	27243	6485
合川市	Hechuan City	5.54	2.64	0.44	18516	4214
永川市	Yongchuan City	4.98	3.29	0.19	16791	4688
南川市	Nanchuan City	3.04	1.60	0.28	5467	3603
三峡库区生态经济区	**Ecological Economic Zone in Three Gorges Reservoir Area**	**62.15**	**38.99**	**5.82**	**212685**	**50739**
万州区	Wanzhou District	12.34	5.98	1.17	34055	7970
涪陵区	Fuling District	9.09	4.63	1.20	27638	5270
黔江区	Qianjiang District	2.14	1.83	0.13	8111	2271
长寿区	Changshou District	4.08	2.44	0.67	12959	3896
梁平县	Liangping County	3.13	1.73	0.27	10275	2055
城口县	Chengkou County	0.87	0.74	0.08	2977	384
丰都县	Fengdu County	2.30	1.39	0.12	7307	1864
垫江县	Dianjiang County	2.41	1.59	0.12	10391	2231
武隆县	Wulong County	1.95	1.17	0.15	6123	1897
忠 县	Zhongxian County	2.47	2.03	0.20	12473	3430
开 县	Kaixian County	3.57	2.68	0.39	16003	3220
云阳县	Yunyang County	3.78	2.15	0.25	15097	3495
奉节县	Fengjie County	2.72	1.80	0.12	9747	2729
巫山县	Wushan County	1.90	1.52	0.33	2121	1902
巫溪县	Wuxi County	1.59	1.20	0.13	7168	1039
石柱县	Shizhu County	1.92	1.34	0.19	7468	2776
秀山县	Xiushan County	1.95	1.47	0.12	6810	1377
酉阳县	Youyang County	2.09	1.88	0.10	8624	1128
彭水县	Pengshui County	1.85	1.42	0.08	7338	1805

19－3 各区县（自治县、市）生产总值（2004年）
Gross Domestic Product by Region (2004)

区 县	Region	地区生产总值（现价）（万元）Gross Domestic Product (current prices) (10000 yuan)	第一产业 Primary Industry	第二产业 Secondary Industry	#工 业 Industry	第三产业 Tertiary Industry	人均地区生产总值（元）Per Capita GDP (yuan)
都市发达经济圈	**Metropolitan Advanced Economic Sphere**	**10419800**	**564200**	**5329300**	**4498000**	**4526300**	**16703**
渝中区	Yuzhong District	1761728		342294	148436	1419434	25764
大渡口区	Dadukou District	571577	14427	454465	417663	102685	22358
江北区	Jiangbei District	949312	15549	632103	533996	301660	15066
沙坪坝区	Shapingba District	1387067	49698	780178	607092	557191	16608
九龙坡区	Jiulongpo District	1855323	66815	1130115	924416	658393	20272
南岸区	Nan'an District	948011	33486	627709	480224	286816	14666
北碚区	Beibei District	809671	56534	428764	357990	324373	12307
渝北区	Yubei District	950951	115279	571940	372276	263732	11815
巴南区	Ba'nan District	823715	184665	410004	340105	229046	10349
渝西经济走廊	**West Chongqing Economic Corridor**	**8219300**	**1777100**	**3277500**	**2558300**	**3164700**	**9821**
万盛区	Wansheng District	200692	29357	79309	51937	92026	8119
双桥区	Shuangqiao District	88334	2304	70531	65537	15499	19120
綦江县	Qijiang County	717983	191457	322457	196810	204069	8605
潼南县	Tongnan County	541540	156190	151100	85010	234250	7608
铜梁县	Tongliang County	652232	129332	284840	205890	238060	10590
大足县	Dazu County	611451	130392	244668	185871	236391	8027
荣昌县	Rongchang County	498914	140667	187006	141606	171241	7661
璧山县	Bishan County	581294	71731	325716	277292	183847	11409
江津市	Jiangjin City	1297420	278431	510566	372625	508423	10274
合川市	Hechuan City	1235254	257160	503450	348228	474644	9705
永川市	Yongchuan City	941372	177772	375980	258821	387620	10228
南川市	Nanchuan City	527251	124825	251544	189038	150882	9687
三峡库区生态经济区	**Ecological Economic Zone in Three Gorges Reservoir Area**	**8014800**	**1895700**	**3205600**	**2218800**	**2913500**	**6110**
万州区	Wanzhou District	1092902	145717	542390	308888	404795	7234
涪陵区	Fuling District	1129193	142056	601639	498546	385498	11205
黔江区	Qianjiang District	289038	61107	143985	115467	83946	6605
长寿区	Changshou District	778018	141816	383636	264350	252566	10431
梁平县	Liangping County	426140	108996	182152	111876	134992	5945
城口县	Chengkou County	78787	23493	31717	22220	23577	4067
丰都县	Fengdu County	339573	86878	127782	66786	124913	5248
垫江县	Dianjiang County	443271	99359	194684	136284	149228	6059
武隆县	Wulong County	256694	65388	104345	55189	86961	7357
忠 县	Zhongxian County	381454	121514	109294	48611	150646	5114
开 县	Kaixian County	610789	169978	224004	122991	216807	5261
云阳县	Yunyang County	373036	126589	144413	56991	102034	3666
奉节县	Fengjie County	339415	105886	83059	40515	150470	3934
巫山县	Wushan County	193055	58547	44491	15713	90017	3848
巫溪县	Wuxi County	127644	53706	32545	21161	41393	2862
石柱县	Shizhu County	203712	63148	69983	43947	70581	4670
秀山县	Xiushan County	233121	69120	94840	73193	69161	4642
酉阳县	Youyang County	175319	74800	42170	26870	58349	3023
彭水县	Pengshui County	232999	84324	77564	33438	71111	4270

注：人均地区生产总值按常住人口计算。

Note: Per capita GDP is calculated by resident population.

19-3 续表 CONTINUED

区 县	Region	地区生产总值指数（可比价）（上年=100） Indices of GDP (comparable prices) (preceding year=100)	第一产业 Primary Industry	第二产业 Secondary Industry	#工 业 Industry	第三产业 Tertiary Industry
都市发达经济圈	**Metropolitan Advanced Economic Sphere**	**113.4**	**101.2**	**117.4**	**117.0**	**110.0**
渝中区	Yuzhong District	111.5	100.0	107.9	105.0	112.4
大渡口区	Dadukou District	112.0	90.7	116.0	116.0	99.2
江北区	Jiangbei District	112.5	100.0	112.6	112.1	113.1
沙坪坝区	Shapingba District	113.5	98.3	113.2	114.2	115.1
九龙坡区	Jiulongpo District	116.2	100.1	119.6	120.8	112.4
南岸区	Nan'an District	113.0	96.6	114.5	112.2	111.7
北碚区	Beibei District	112.0	105.2	113.9	114.1	110.4
渝北区	Yubei District	133.9	101.0	154.4	176.4	116.3
巴南区	Ba'nan District	115.0	104.6	120.3	119.2	114.6
渝西经济走廊	**West Chongqing Economic Corridor**	**111.3**	**105.0**	**115.2**	**115.5**	**110.6**
万盛区	Wansheng District	114.9	104.0	124.9	128.7	111.0
双桥区	Shuangqiao District	112.1	106.7	112.5	112.6	110.8
綦江县	Qijiang County	113.3	104.6	119.7	119.2	111.9
潼南县	Tongnan County	113.2	106.0	119.9	117.0	113.9
铜梁县	Tongliang County	113.6	106.6	117.4	125.3	112.8
大足县	Dazu County	112.3	105.2	117.8	118.2	111.2
荣昌县	Rongchang County	112.3	106.1	115.1	117.2	113.6
璧山县	Bishan County	113.8	106.0	115.3	115.6	114.6
江津市	Jiangjin City	111.2	105.8	112.8	114.6	112.4
合川市	Hechuan City	112.5	102.8	114.9	116.0	115.8
永川市	Yongchuan City	113.0	108.1	115.5	115.6	112.8
南川市	Nanchuan City	113.0	106.5	116.8	118.1	112.4
三峡库区生态经济区	**Ecological Economic Zone in Three Gorges Reservoir Area**	**111.5**	**105.5**	**115.3**	**118.2**	**110.6**
万州区	Wanzhou District	114.2	106.0	117.1	118.5	113.1
涪陵区	Fuling District	113.0	106.9	114.3	117.7	112.8
黔江区	Qianjiang District	109.3	107.1	107.7	114.5	113.5
长寿区	Changshou District	113.3	105.5	118.7	123.4	109.3
梁平县	Liangping County	112.6	108.2	113.8	112.4	114.2
城口县	Chengkou County	124.0	103.9	165.8	202.6	107.6
丰都县	Fengdu County	111.7	106.0	113.9	114.8	113.5
垫江县	Dianjiang County	112.7	105.1	118.3	120.6	110.7
武隆县	Wulong County	114.9	106.1	124.4	156.3	111.9
忠 县	Zhongxian County	112.1	106.1	118.3	122.9	112.3
开 县	Kaixian County	112.1	104.0	116.8	114.8	114.3
云阳县	Yunyang County	111.1	104.7	113.5	114.9	115.8
奉节县	Fengjie County	111.1	105.4	105.3	139.9	119.7
巫山县	Wushan County	109.2	107.2	100.2	116.9	115.7
巫溪县	Wuxi County	110.4	106.0	112.2	115.7	114.7
石柱县	Shizhu County	112.8	106.5	116.5	109.5	114.5
秀山县	Xiushan County	118.3	106.8	133.8	145.3	112.8
酉阳县	Youyang County	109.6	110.3	105.0	120.1	112.2
彭水县	Pengshui County	113.6	106.9	121.6	108.0	112.8

19－4 各区县（自治县、市）农业和农村经济（2004年）
Agriculture and Rural Economy by Region (2004)

区 县	Region	农林牧渔业总产值(现价)(万元) Gross Output Value of Farming, Forestry, Animal Husbandry and Fishery (current prices) (10 000 yuan)	农业 Farming	林业 Forestry	牧业 Animal Husbandry	渔业 Fishery	农林牧渔服务业 Farming, Forestry, Animal Husbandry and Fishery Services	农林牧渔业总产值指数(可比价)(上年=100) Indices of Gross Output Value of Farming, Forestry, Animal Husbandry and Fishery (comparable prices) (preceding year=100)
都市发达经济圈	**Metropolitan Advanced Economic Sphere**	**700754**	**441696**	**10123**	**203535**	**36924**	**8477**	**104.0**
渝中区	Yuzhong District							
大渡口区	Dadukou District	22741	11110	485	8267	1981	898	93.9
江北区	Jiangbei District	23896	10241	688	11640	1158	169	110.4
沙坪坝区	Shapingba District	73378	41072	585	24876	3230	3615	97.8
九龙坡区	Jiulongpo District	92963	55362	1623	27849	4367	3762	100.4
南岸区	Nan'an District	47425	35942	655	8471	2254	103	83.4
北碚区	Beibei District	88687	48567	897	33589	4552	1082	105.6
渝北区	Yubei District	168345	96592	6421	58815	4708	1809	102.6
巴南区	Ba'nan District	283318	158866	3822	102006	13879	4745	106.1
渝西经济走廊	**West Chongqing Economic Corridor**	**2400360**	**1299643**	**69637**	**917007**	**87547**	**26525**	**106.3**
万盛区	Wansheng District	50136	31324	4185	12705	1509	413	103.6
双桥区	Shuangqiao District	3659	1415	88	1783	253	120	111.7
綦江县	Qijiang County	237367	119012	1670	106758	8131	1796	105.3
潼南县	Tongnan County	208779	115162	7375	72602	11769	1871	105.8
铜梁县	Tongliang County	209611	89198	3040	101895	11484	3994	106.9
大足县	Dazu County	184085	103006	6873	63694	8177	2335	105.1
荣昌县	Rongchang County	200990	88887	8668	94353	6867	2215	105.0
璧山县	Bishan County	118165	63976	865	45964	6193	1167	108.7
江津市	Jiangjin City	427538	229668	34021	140337	15266	8246	104.9
合川市	Hechuan City	320595	183321	1855	121279	11127	3013	107.2
永川市	Yongchuan City	266649	150194	4417	100069	8446	3523	106.6
南川市	Nanchuan City	183651	87784	12639	75854	4823	2551	106.5
三峡库区生态经济区	**Ecological Economic Zone in Three Gorges Reservoir Area**	**3026609**	**1588177**	**105055**	**1188832**	**87993**	**56553**	**106.2**
万州区	Wanzhou District	265572	123564	9092	120385	9962	2569	103.4
涪陵区	Fuling District	222896	116299	2189	92143	6392	5873	107.1
黔江区	Qianjiang District	112981	60355	7752	42193	1365	1316	107.4
长寿区	Changshou District	209737	107474	3883	82811	10755	4814	104.3
梁平县	Liangping County	177368	103476	1747	65621	4485	2039	104.2
城口县	Chengkou County	37286	16416	4237	15683	502	448	103.1
丰都县	Fengdu County	137357	61655	3428	66822	3727	1725	107.1
垫江县	Dianjiang County	174714	80526	2651	78472	5431	7634	105.3
武隆县	Wulong County	102678	52868	3812	44023	1502	473	108.0
忠 县	Zhongxian County	228772	110577	5146	96450	3486	13113	107.2
开 县	Kaixian County	283255	136182	12786	120476	5390	8421	105.1
云阳县	Yunyang County	199404	89335	8178	96901	3650	1340	104.8
奉节县	Fengjie County	182901	102926	5274	69603	3600	1498	107.2
巫山县	Wushan County	98507	51518	7516	37014	986	1473	107.2
巫溪县	Wuxi County	84454	36915	7245	38541	364	1389	106.1
石柱县	Shizhu County	111789	62055	4735	43149	893	957	102.9
秀山县	Xiushan County	112499	73091	2551	32584	1001	3271	104.1
酉阳县	Youyang County	139336	77939	4533	55609	756	499	106.4
彭水县	Pengshui County	140800	82449	7435	49521	707	688	106.9

19-4 续表1 CONTINUED-1

区 县	Region	农业商品产值（万元） Output Value of Agricultural Commodities (10 000 yuan)	农业商品率（%） Commodity Rate (%)	乡村从业人员（万人） Rural Employment (10 000 persons)	年末常用耕地面积（公顷） Year-end Common Cultivated Area (hectare)	农作物播种面积（公顷） Sown Areas of Farm Crops (hectare)	#粮食 Grain	农用化肥施用量(折纯)（吨） Consumption of Chemical Fertilizer (net)(tons)
都市发达经济圈	**Metropolitan Advanced Economic Sphere**	**512191**	**74.0**	**136.3**	**116890**	**292496**	**191392**	**65451**
渝中区	Yuzhong District							
大渡口区	Dadukou District	20466	93.7	3.6	1593	4021	1347	3830
江北区	Jiangbei District	14928	62.9	5.6	3902	7306	4601	5268
沙坪坝区	Shapingba District	44384	63.6	11.7	10313	20418	10363	8168
九龙坡区	Jiulongpo District	73350	82.2	13.9	9987	20712	10844	5028
南岸区	Nan'an District	36188	76.5	9.5	4640	11364	5416	1916
北碚区	Beibei District	45181	51.6	22.2	15930	34901	22718	9009
渝北区	Yubei District	77979	46.8	35.2	29335	76043	52924	14519
巴南区	Ba'nan District	155676	55.9	34.6	41190	113990	79836	17713
渝西经济走廊	**West Chongqing Economic Corridor**	**1373319**	**57.9**	**469.8**	**485765**	**1049583**	**767311**	**273572**
万盛区	Wansheng District	19177	38.6	9.1	5877	20384	13042	5890
双桥区	Shuangqiao District	1716	48.5	1.3	780	1729	1360	348
綦江县	Qijiang County	117719	50.0	38.9	50456	108948	80756	27070
潼南县	Tongnan County	136511	66.0	43.1	53670	109590	75614	29400
铜梁县	Tongliang County	130547	63.5	38.2	42430	79338	64221	27866
大足县	Dazu County	110808	61.0	41.2	42488	77907	58271	21582
荣昌县	Rongchang County	75633	38.0	38.6	31655	79396	52652	20127
璧山县	Bishan County	69993	59.8	33.4	26118	51304	34371	7190
江津市	Jiangjin City	283142	67.5	75.3	68478	153837	109447	30174
合川市	Hechuan City	159602	50.3	74.1	74479	167990	129562	28195
永川市	Yongchuan City	99423	37.8	44.0	50249	96679	69885	45030
南川市	Nanchuan City	108322	59.8	32.6	39085	89055	64729	30700
三峡库区生态经济区	**Ecological Economic Zone in Three Gorges Reservoir Area**	**1541333**	**51.9**	**755.3**	**797935**	**2093878**	**1557804**	**431160**
万州区	Wanzhou District	152363	57.9	74.9	57743	158927	117187	36133
涪陵区	Fuling District	129483	59.7	47.9	67241	148398	99812	36096
黔江区	Qianjiang District	55827	49.4	28.4	28580	89105	61740	20173
长寿区	Changshou District	114266	55.8	41.2	37497	91136	75026	22462
梁平县	Liangping County	96059	54.8	47.0	42048	96364	77601	19761
城口县	Chengkou County	12542	34.0	10.6	19669	42216	32646	6062
丰都县	Fengdu County	75545	55.7	40.9	36943	116044	85175	17482
垫江县	Dianjiang County	80841	48.4	42.9	38981	81913	66897	26914
武隆县	Wulong County	43527	42.6	21.0	29646	74074	51890	16818
忠 县	Zhongxian County	133986	62.1	44.3	55382	115134	89758	28999
开 县	Kaixian County	145082	52.8	70.5	66212	178986	135927	42249
云阳县	Yunyang County	88237	44.5	54.3	48787	147739	113781	23812
奉节县	Fengjie County	91231	50.3	44.4	49387	135203	99785	19167
巫山县	Wushan County	40669	41.9	25.5	33515	88417	66350	17384
巫溪县	Wuxi County	32708	39.4	22.5	31433	79590	66511	14250
石柱县	Shizhu County	54721	49.4	28.2	29348	79717	57231	20346
秀山县	Xiushan County	59962	54.9	35.0	30141	95774	58101	19004
酉阳县	Youyang County	64043	46.1	43.5	46927	137193	94927	22219
彭水县	Pengshui County	70755	50.5	32.3	48455	111163	80251	21831

19-4 续表2 CONTINUED-2

区 县	Region	农村用电量（万千瓦时） Electricity Consumption in Rural Areas (10 000 kwh)	农药使用量（吨） Consumption of Chemical Pesticides (ton)	粮食产量（吨） Output of Grain (ton)	油料产量（吨） Output of Oil-bearing Crops (ton)	糖料产量（吨） Output of Sugar (ton)	烟叶产量（吨） Output of Tobacco (ton)	茶叶产量（吨） Output of Tea (ton)
都市发达经济圈	**Metropolitan Advanced Economic Sphere**	**105603**	**1605**	**913364**	**9224**	**1337**	**769**	**1799**
渝中区	Yuzhong District							
大渡口区	Dadukou District	7058	61	6300				5
江北区	Jiangbei District	5891	69	20431	180	75		4
沙坪坝区	Shapingba District	27529	218	62778	274	18		86
九龙坡区	Jiulongpo District	10772	225	59000	582	870		1
南岸区	Nan'an District	6665	58	26500	403	24	4	
北碚区	Beibei District	33936	322	110028	1273	74	45	69
渝北区	Yubei District	5455	186	257666	2752	172	113	20
巴南区	Ba'nan District	8297	466	398500	2961	104	607	1614
渝西经济走廊	**West Chongqing Economic Corridor**	**134719**	**7964**	**4298990**	**129830**	**96425**	**6073**	**9764**
万盛区	Wansheng District	4756	129	54300	1446		93	622
双桥区	Shuangqiao District	120	14	8604	106			
綦江县	Qijiang County	7980	479	392846	8474	217	1183	970
潼南县	Tongnan County	7924	440	405955	30021	6642	36	200
铜梁县	Tongliang County	8266	615	361345	3855	660	2	157
大足县	Dazu County	10100	961	468643	11117	2058	220	500
荣昌县	Rongchang County	6257	540	304900	12015	7726	4	3004
璧山县	Bishan County	38708	1078	197414	1781	898	4	340
江津市	Jiangjin City	15392	739	680551	10543	72708	1105	968
合川市	Hechuan City	10698	655	729135	13005	756	130	81
永川市	Yongchuan City	6878	1929	486221	9107	4760	16	722
南川市	Nanchuan City	17640	385	337128	17108		3280	2200
三峡库区生态经济区	**Ecological Economic Zone in Three Gorges Reservoir Area**	**144305**	**9897**	**6233307**	**278447**	**19972**	**78194**	**4501**
万州区	Wanzhou District	10859	1155	513580	13515	650	2592	101
涪陵区	Fuling District	22413	828	438630	7108	140	1258	640
黔江区	Qianjiang District	2282	560	252540	13868		9863	540
长寿区	Changshou District	6650	464	386482	6964	1112	168	48
梁平县	Liangping County	5368	627	370519	10683	4461	53	96
城口县	Chengkou County	1048	21	84500	1141		427	353
丰都县	Fengdu County	8729	346	328840	15056	75	2260	8
垫江县	Dianjiang County	7601	564	373734	10616	1180	396	110
武隆县	Wulong County	6513	136	169763	5487		9613	32
忠 县	Zhongxian County	3811	695	425135	28300	2029	773	12
开 县	Kaixian County	10952	842	556931	23756	2898	930	671
云阳县	Yunyang County	6715	445	438818	14356	430	1750	270
奉节县	Fengjie County	16301	636	429100	21405		4788	198
巫山县	Wushan County	4353	135	225000	7922		9015	135
巫溪县	Wuxi County	4780	181	198800	4340		2159	327
石柱县	Shizhu County	6337	469	255911	11041	309	4703	195
秀山县	Xiushan County	12559	864	310172	25889	6286	2895	192
酉阳县	Youyang County	4024	552	360303	19410		10881	420
彭水县	Pengshui County	3010	377	300215	13456	402	13670	153

19-4 续表3 CONTINUED-3

区 县	Region	水果产量（吨） Output of Fruit (ton)	蔬菜产量（吨） Output of Vegetable (ton)	肉类总产量（吨） Output of Meat (ton)	#猪 肉 Output of Pork	#牛 肉 Output of Beef	水产品产量（吨） Output of Aquatic Products (ton)
都市发达经济圈	**Metropolitan Advanced Economic Sphere**	**109100**	**1587419**	**167162**	**129585**	**666**	**75500**
渝中区	Yuzhong District						44822
大渡口区	Dadukou District	826	90115	6951	6122	11	1945
江北区	Jiangbei District	4529	36086	7600	6457	15	1402
沙坪坝区	Shapingba District	5667	215486	17020	7019	6	4080
九龙坡区	Jiulongpo District	18668	202144	20424	13867	14	5021
南岸区	Nan'an District	2652	99724	3769	3008	30	2662
北碚区	Beibei District	12034	151470	22450	18279	81	5057
渝北区	Yubei District	31654	328266	45466	35521	216	7100
巴南区	Ba'nan District	33070	464128	71379	54907	316	17555
渝西经济走廊	**West Chongqing Economic Corridor**	**435981**	**3729236**	**620648**	**494124**	**8528**	**92937**
万盛区	Wansheng District	3066	133772	12624	11074	123	1709
双桥区	Shuangqiao District	547	3812	2009	1742		341
綦江县	Qijiang County	21024	354238	73133	56267	3115	9500
潼南县	Tongnan County	45514	319040	52835	48327	338	11804
铜梁县	Tongliang County	22928	233500	63497	43577	112	11216
大足县	Dazu County	18321	230625	56073	44534	302	9129
荣昌县	Rongchang County	12853	292728	64891	46060	766	6611
璧山县	Bishan County	54375	221582	43997	21029	51	11257
江津市	Jiangjin City	116980	738349	103609	80919	640	16733
合川市	Hechuan City	25593	656718	104356	91278	121	14258
永川市	Yongchuan City	86321	425098	90463	66759	112	12065
南川市	Nanchuan City	28459	205350	56738	42024	3137	5725
三峡库区生态经济区	**Ecological Economic Zone in Three Gorges Reservoir Area**	**827166**	**3318996**	**882254**	**740626**	**49898**	**70818**
万州区	Wanzhou District	104122	389493	97050	82453	3256	12028
涪陵区	Fuling District	51969	255675	73515	58773	1520	8812
黔江区	Qianjiang District	27484	95940	38923	34250	2757	1220
长寿区	Changshou District	76971	220225	69194	61180	717	14040
梁平县	Liangping County	44961	283504	57277	43503	1043	5240
城口县	Chengkou County	1886	29006	16319	13068	701	380
丰都县	Fengdu County	23250	127727	55728	33803	9362	5375
垫江县	Dianjiang County	33200	202767	58176	46440	1500	6000
武隆县	Wulong County	6357	89447	36160	29531	2712	2000
忠 县	Zhongxian County	31589	169080	53283	39849	2813	5000
开 县	Kaixian County	160169	252957	96195	74045	2997	6716
云阳县	Yunyang County	56393	236950	77911	60505	5132	4473
奉节县	Fengjie County	147473	164267	64152	54041	2606	2933
巫山县	Wushan County	19206	125572	40534	35562	403	850
巫溪县	Wuxi County	4619	102500	36743	31399	784	580
石柱县	Shizhu County	9972	80295	26257	19654	3350	6410
秀山县	Xiushan County	19405	192883	40323	35854	1853	978
酉阳县	Youyang County	4001	124507	47343	38747	3800	820
彭水县	Pengshui County	4139	186201	44405	37100	4080	230

19－5 各区县（自治县、市）工业（2004年）
Industry by Region (2004)

区　县	Region	工业总产值（现价）（万元） Gross Output Value of Industry (current prices) (10 000 yuan)	工业总产值指数（上年=100） Index of Gross Output Value of Industry (preceding year=100)	工业企业资产合计（万元） Total Property of Industrial Enterprises (10 000 yuan)	主营业务收入（万元） Revenue of Major Business (10 000 yuan)	利润总额（万元） Total Profits (10 000 yuan)
都市发达经济圈	**Metropolitan Advanced Economic Sphere**	**14805331**	**128.7**	**17945058**	**14614509**	**769198**
渝中区	Yuzhong District	1046206	125.4	2418935	1145485	30592
大渡口区	Dadukou District	1374983	138.6	1315968	1374479	117229
江北区	Jiangbei District	2192883	110.8	3392406	2165491	216780
沙坪坝区	Shapingba District	1949244	121.6	1929779	1939773	40352
九龙坡区	Jiulongpo District	3093693	130.3	4154569	2982282	82791
南岸区	Nan'an District	1631100	128.4	1717869	1608051	75121
北碚区	Beibei District	731536	117.6	863020	690577	27353
渝北区	Yubei District	1508733	196.9	1056669	1443318	120869
巴南区	Ba'nan District	1276953	119.1	1095843	1265053	58111
渝西经济走廊	**West Chongqing Economic Corridor**	**3626932**	**129.5**	**4096786**	**3611983**	**203125**
万盛区	Wansheng District	111410	148.9	159240	108953	7734
双桥区	Shuangqiao District	395070	97.2	258469	396143	-201
綦江县	Qijiang County	391746	138.7	441548	397848	13879
潼南县	Tongnan County	76171	112.4	92532	73729	2894
铜梁县	Tongliang County	195262	146.2	206073	185831	11544
大足县	Dazu County	135734	148.0	127592	140356	14802
荣昌县	Rongchang County	224273	137.5	243011	216376	-12924
璧山县	Bishan County	498817	138.1	434524	502184	19560
江津市	Jiangjin City	742018	126.8	1159774	743731	67003
合川市	Hechuan City	183744	122.2	282124	170750	6430
永川市	Yongchuan City	405402	145.8	325299	397644	51238
南川市	Nanchuan City	267285	131.1	366600	278438	21166
三峡库区生态经济区	**Ecological Economic Zone in Three Gorges Reservoir Area**	**2994997**	**137.0**	**5140661**	**2861941**	**183575**
万州区	Wanzhou District	473544	129.9	697098	454174	15107
涪陵区	Fuling District	909851	130.4	1589045	809861	33948
黔江区	Qianjiang District	209164	117.0	463544	197856	8621
长寿区	Changshou District	504537	134.8	762642	506013	78081
梁平县	Liangping County	50254	112.1	45546	49800	344
城口县	Chengkou County	57604	242.8	55840	57441	5565
丰都县	Fengdu County	57370	127.8	83608	46130	737
垫江县	Dianjiang County	149041	146.5	147341	147872	7991
武隆县	Wulong County	77169	273.5	337513	71974	15285
忠　县	Zhongxian County	37813	129.2	82226	40082	-989
开　县	Kaixian County	110089	143.9	310878	112364	1179
云阳县	Yunyang County	33487	108.6	91873	33782	574
奉节县	Fengjie County	22361	103.2	53496	29878	395
巫山县	Wushan County	13064	108.9	51194	13609	-176
巫溪县	Wuxi County	13160	143.3	46617	12341	-2143
石柱县	Shizhu County	55392	120.8	81954	60784	3558
秀山县	Xiushan County	158935	248.4	139089	156356	8498
酉阳县	Youyang County	35671	180.0	38560	33648	5677
彭水县	Pengshui County	26491	116.8	62597	27976	1323

注：本页为全部国有和规模以上非国有工业企业统计数。

Note: Data of industry in this table refer to state-owned industrial enterprises and non-state-owned industrial enterprises above designated size.

19-5 续表 CONTINUED

区 县	Region	经济效益综合指数 Comprehensive Index of Economic Efficiency	总资产贡献率（%） Ratio of Total Assets to Industrial Output Value (%)	资产负债率（%） Ratio of Liabilities to Assets (%)	产品销售率（%） Ratio of Sales to Products (%)	全员劳动生产率（元/人年） Overall Labor Productivity (yuan/person-year)
都市发达经济圈	**Metropolitan Advanced Economic Sphere**	**141.6**	**9.9**	**61.4**	**99.6**	**71954**
渝中区	Yuzhong District	145.7	6.2	67.0	100.7	105697
大渡口区	Dadukou District	185.6	14.5	55.8	100.0	95238
江北区	Jiangbei District	159.3	11.5	55.3	100.2	66263
沙坪坝区	Shapingba District	116.7	6.6	72.7	99.9	56094
九龙坡区	Jiulongpo District	118.5	6.5	59.2	99.9	73129
南岸区	Nan'an District	154.7	12.6	62.3	99.6	81748
北碚区	Beibei District	114.3	8.1	62.3	99.3	42592
渝北区	Yubei District	215.6	23.6	63.6	96.1	110723
巴南区	Ba'nan District	136.8	11.9	58.3	100.2	59039
渝西经济走廊	**West Chongqing Economic Corridor**	**142.5**	**12.0**	**60.4**	**100.8**	**52917**
万盛区	Wansheng District	134.5	17.5	53.8	98.7	25243
双桥区	Shuangqiao District	116.9	5.3	73.9	107.0	74744
綦江县	Qijiang County	108.6	8.4	49.4	100.2	38942
潼南县	Tongnan County	140.6	6.9	49.5	98.4	59977
铜梁县	Tongliang County	155.2	12.9	49.6	96.4	59563
大足县	Dazu County	187.7	21.2	37.2	103.6	50414
荣昌县	Rongchang County	77.1	7.7	76.0	99.6	29721
璧山县	Bishan County	139.9	10.5	63.7	101.3	56181
江津市	Jiangjin City	179.3	13.2	65.8	98.2	96191
合川市	Hechuan City	124.3	11.1	63.7	96.0	43254
永川市	Yongchuan City	201.2	17.6	51.6	101.2	52760
南川市	Nanchuan City	177.1	13.8	57.6	106.1	56535
三峡库区生态经济区	**Ecological Economic Zone in Three Gorges Reservoir Area**	**144.2**	**11.7**	**59.3**	**100.1**	**61569**
万州区	Wanzhou District	110.3	7.6	56.6	98.6	46973
涪陵区	Fuling District	134.3	11.5	60.3	99.5	65428
黔江区	Qianjiang District	252.1	18.0	68.6	97.9	235212
长寿区	Changshou District	217.3	16.2	44.9	101.1	98000
梁平县	Liangping County	94.9	7.9	79.0	103.0	16276
城口县	Chengkou County	212.4	33.8	46.8	101.0	65335
丰都县	Fengdu County	122.6	5.8	56.8	90.7	63249
垫江县	Dianjiang County	159.9	11.9	57.0	100.4	73585
武隆县	Wulong County	276.6	10.5	70.3	98.2	95637
忠 县	Zhongxian County	70.0	4.4	57.6	107.9	24609
开 县	Kaixian County	117.1	5.4	69.9	102.7	38375
云阳县	Yunyang County	92.4	6.1	57.8	110.4	21258
奉节县	Fengjie County	93.0	6.3	79.0	106.0	23047
巫山县	Wushan County	59.3	3.3	57.1	104.9	15283
巫溪县	Wuxi County	11.2	-1.1	49.8	101.7	23525
石柱县	Shizhu County	124.2	9.7	45.5	103.1	33815
秀山县	Xiushan County	174.6	21.0	69.5	101.2	56268
酉阳县	Youyang County	286.0	23.2	65.9	97.6	142076
彭水县	Pengshui County	124.6	9.4	50.0	107.4	41872

注：本页为全部国有和规模以上非国有工业企业统计数。

Note: Data of industry in this table refer to state-owned industrial enterprises and non-state-owned industrial enterprises above designated size.

19-6 各区县（自治县、市）建筑业（2004年）
Construction by Region (2004)

区 县	Region	建筑企业单位数（个） Number of Construction Enterprises (unit)	建筑企业从业人员（人） Employment of Construction Enterprises (person)	建筑业总产值（万元） Gross Output Value of Construction (10 000 yuan)	房屋建筑施工面积（万平方米） Space Floor under Construction (10 000 sq.m)	房屋建筑竣工面积（万平方米） Space Floor Completed (10 000 sq.m)	#住 宅 Residential Buildings
都市发达经济圈	**Metropolitan Advanced Economic Sphere**	**1371**	**411434**	**4026471**	**4770.96**	**2158.38**	**1460.40**
渝中区	Yuzhong District	332	50411	669380	745.30	260.06	148.87
大渡口区	Dadukou District	67	17565	177088	115.96	60.35	36.83
江北区	Jiangbei District	118	42087	304018	349.49	157.35	99.07
沙坪坝区	Shapingba District	140	40343	347097	357.09	158.12	96.85
九龙坡区	Jiulongpo District	215	82788	939812	1436.06	562.08	351.72
南岸区	Nan'an District	126	39811	408149	192.32	110.36	62.26
北碚区	Beibei District	42	18370	140549	247.85	99.70	71.14
渝北区	Yubei District	233	75186	693758	806.17	431.98	360.55
巴南区	Ba'nan District	98	44873	346619	520.72	318.37	233.10
渝西经济走廊	**West Chongqing Economic Corridor**	**491**	**207514**	**1401486**	**2488.47**	**1343.92**	**960.40**
万盛区	Wansheng District	20	4602	19037	110.46	23.07	20.11
双桥区	Shuangqiao District	4	207	2744	3.90	1.37	0.96
綦江县	Qijiang County	33	13792	53578	135.73	73.91	49.02
潼南县	Tongnan County	37	25565	173420	251.38	200.13	138.48
铜梁县	Tongliang County	28	11693	76707	183.91	143.81	114.32
大足县	Dazu County	35	9702	53039	106.91	57.94	43.63
荣昌县	Rongchang County	29	14040	64275	133.81	73.75	49.44
璧山县	Bishan County	42	16722	94328	196.88	127.59	93.36
江津市	Jiangjin City	74	39421	273501	474.41	221.76	157.64
合川市	Hechuan City	85	21566	165880	293.10	198.73	139.79
永川市	Yongchuan City	69	41383	391039	539.52	187.28	135.00
南川市	Nanchuan City	35	8821	33939	58.47	34.59	18.64
三峡库区生态经济区	**Ecological Economic Zone in Three Gorges Reservoir Area**	**580**	**250155**	**1474817**	**2925.02**	**1665.36**	**1101.75**
万州区	Wanzhou District	153	59702	346366	648.97	369.64	251.92
涪陵区	Fuling District	88	34973	276052	573.72	265.84	209.75
黔江区	Qianjiang District	20	4198	50956	101.41	64.76	32.15
长寿区	Changshou District	50	33606	214962	403.20	192.51	133.34
梁平县	Liangping County	15	4259	20894	45.62	32.31	16.38
城口县	Chengkou County	5	955	2346	3.02	2.62	0.10
丰都县	Fengdu County	18	10104	47287	127.05	83.36	64.88
垫江县	Dianjiang County	32	19148	71041	122.35	84.22	60.79
武隆县	Wulong County	17	5036	28640	40.06	31.06	13.76
忠 县	Zhongxian County	23	19090	110450	205.99	136.74	85.56
开 县	Kaixian County	43	27746	142838	226.51	178.50	113.47
云阳县	Yunyang County	34	11014	55686	144.41	70.10	52.29
奉节县	Fengjie County	26	4647	31252	75.11	48.17	21.89
巫山县	Wushan County	15	2730	13493	22.61	20.35	12.73
巫溪县	Wuxi County	8	2712	7365	13.62	10.70	9.39
石柱县	Shizhu County	8	1828	13716	29.29	21.12	11.08
秀山县	Xiushan County	7	3857	20834	99.18	31.95	5.34
酉阳县	Youyang County	7	3072	8614	21.83	10.69	2.61
彭水县	Pengshui County	11	1478	12027	21.08	10.71	4.33

注：本表数据不包括劳务分包企业情况。

Note: Data in this table exclude construction enterprises of work subcontractors.

19—7 各区县（自治县、市）公路交通运输业（2004年） Highway Transportation by Region (2004)

区 县	Region	公路里程（公里） Length of Highways (km)	#等级公路 Expressway and Class I-IV Highways	公路客运量（万人） Passenger Traffic by Highways (10 000 persons)	公路货运量（万吨） Freight Traffic by Highways (10 000 tons)
都市发达经济圈	**Metropolitan Advanced Economic Sphere**	**2941**	**2750**	**9403**	**9309**
渝中区	Yuzhong District			151	690
大渡口区	Dadukou District	87	87	580	1732
江北区	Jiangbei District	121	121	422	476
沙坪坝区	Shapingba District	104	91	615	662
九龙坡区	Jiulongpo District	445	445	1311	1526
南岸区	Nan'an District	275	169	2252	934
北碚区	Beibei District	385	383	758	865
渝北区	Yubei District	648	633	468	1593
巴南区	Ba'nan District	876	821	2846	831
渝西经济走廊	**West Chongqing Economic Corridor**	**8081**	**6516**	**16073**	**4900**
万盛区	Wansheng District	317	295	265	210
双桥区	Shuangqiao District	35	35	108	151
綦江县	Qijiang County	958	892	1016	698
潼南县	Tongnan County	493	493	537	240
铜梁县	Tongliang County	748	712	766	150
大足县	Dazu County	555	186	2307	629
荣昌县	Rongchang County	430	417	1267	163
璧山县	Bishan County	403	403	1596	527
江津市	Jiangjin City	1661	1352	2616	597
合川市	Hechuan City	871	671	1546	728
永川市	Yongchuan City	839	422	2861	643
南川市	Nanchuan City	771	638	1188	164
三峡库区生态经济区	**Ecological Economic Zone in Three Gorges Reservoir Area**	**20337**	**13802**	**17992**	**7006**
万州区	Wanzhou District	1434	1294	4588	861
涪陵区	Fuling District	1392	624	1361	661
黔江区	Qianjiang District	1178	991	1196	272
长寿区	Changshou District	582	404	1000	761
梁平县	Liangping County	835	619	969	529
城口县	Chengkou County	621	413	92	56
丰都县	Fengdu County	1067	523	1499	319
垫江县	Dianjiang County	649	649	1340	1146
武隆县	Wulong County	1152	837	300	217
忠 县	Zhongxian County	878	878	871	98
开 县	Kaixian County	1565	1465	1033	707
云阳县	Yunyang County	1448	1228	1022	186
奉节县	Fengjie County	1386	1059	231	137
巫山县	Wushan County	1087	274	311	338
巫溪县	Wuxi County	963	775	277	143
石柱县	Shizhu County	1127	718	328	142
秀山县	Xiushan County	697	222	403	155
酉阳县	Youyang County	1170	186	482	190
彭水县	Pengshui County	1106	643	689	88
其 他	**Others**	**985**	**978**	**17365**	**10300**

注：1）指标"其他"为市级交通单位数据，其中公路里程和等级公路为2家单位合计数；公路客和货运量为5家单位合计数。
2）渝中区公路归为市政道路，不属于本表统计范围。

Note: a) "others" are data of municipal transportation units. Data of length of highways and expressway and class I-IV highways are total of 2 units, while data of passenger traffic by highways and freight traffic by highways are total of 5 units.
b) Highways in Yuzhong District are civil roads, which don't belong to the statistic range of this table.

19－8 各区县（自治县、市）固定资产投资（2004年）
Investment in Fixed Assets by Region (2004)

区 县	Region	全社会固定资产投资（万元） Total Investment in Fixed Assets (10 000 yuan)	#建设与改造投资 Construction and Innovation	#工 业 Industry	#房地产开发 Real Estate Development	全社会固定资产投资指数（上年=100） Index of Total Investment in Fixed Assets (preceding year=100)
都市发达经济圈	**Metropolitan Advanced Economic Sphere**	**8023515**	**4777191**	**1376295**	**3164478**	**138.9**
渝中区	Yuzhong District	891292	555812	54667	335438	125.9
大渡口区	Dadukou District	313088	229238	150596	80582	132.4
江北区	Jiangbei District	947102	487354	110575	456188	122.9
沙坪坝区	Shapingba District	861856	501081	99341	353221	130.1
九龙坡区	Jiulongpo District	1126505	627996	278052	488097	135.6
南岸区	Nan'an District	1203181	594053	171114	604143	135.0
北碚区	Beibei District	378648	256309	57804	114238	132.1
渝北区	Yubei District	1758180	1182553	310843	563113	173.7
巴南区	Ba'nan District	543663	342795	143303	169458	143.1
渝西经济走廊	**West Chongqing Economic Corridor**	**3574820**	**2736617**	**1241462**	**480028**	**129.8**
万盛区	Wansheng District	109647	78537	47214	19785	150.3
双桥区	Shuangqiao District	34417	24408	14445	9402	113.0
綦江县	Qijiang County	339902	282325	79646	34617	130.2
潼南县	Tongnan County	215767	166587	58546	17892	127.1
铜梁县	Tongliang County	302748	221387	140015	16892	128.7
大足县	Dazu County	220150	166513	57070	24475	125.2
荣昌县	Rongchang County	195856	147820	70964	28959	132.1
璧山县	Bishan County	263858	204350	153170	49922	146.1
江津市	Jiangjin City	485148	378810	187679	76340	110.4
合川市	Hechuan City	498454	409583	162319	59891	145.3
永川市	Yongchuan City	626316	429111	143610	122008	133.2
南川市	Nanchuan City	282557	227186	126784	19845	123.9
三峡库区生态经济区	**Ecological Economic Zone in Three Gorges Reservoir Area**	**4620868**	**3852330**	**1380268**	**406285**	**111.1**
万州区	Wanzhou District	806688	678495	148039	93331	128.7
涪陵区	Fuling District	466028	388411	132782	59877	94.9
黔江区	Qianjiang District	182148	144533	44029	29392	90.6
长寿区	Changshou District	407521	346645	185679	42367	125.0
梁平县	Liangping County	213870	163975	45387	25882	90.3
城口县	Chengkou County	51948	47339	15645	774	136.5
丰都县	Fengdu County	212826	168088	51078	24312	102.4
垫江县	Dianjiang County	195139	152688	49394	19562	105.6
武隆县	Wulong County	202670	171298	84155	1334	118.9
忠 县	Zhongxian County	216534	154191	57741	30295	125.1
开 县	Kaixian County	340123	275365	89473	21984	138.5
云阳县	Yunyang County	268328	218986	33800	13312	111.1
奉节县	Fengjie County	200085	173194	47079	15619	79.0
巫山县	Wushan County	104663	83284	14995	8957	69.0
巫溪县	Wuxi County	60004	49574	11601	2489	126.2
石柱县	Shizhu County	152869	140368	62239	6352	148.2
秀山县	Xiushan County	119582	110741	47534	5432	88.5
酉阳县	Youyang County	101916	93145	27354	1941	80.2
彭水县	Pengshui County	317926	292010	232264	12030	159.3

注：建设与改造投资不包括城镇工矿区私人建房投资及农村私人投资。

Note: Data on construction and innovation exclude housing construction by individuals in cities and rural individual investment.

19-8 续表 CONTINUED

区 县	Region	商品房竣工面积（平方米） Floor Space Completed of Commercial Buildings (sq.m)	#住 宅 Residential Buildings	商品房销售面积（平方米） Floor Space Sold of Commercial Buildings (sq.m)	#住 宅 Residential Buildings	商品房销售额（万元） Sales Revenue of Commercial Buildings (sq.m)	#住 宅 Residential Buildings
都市发达经济圈	**Metropolitan Advanced Economic Sphere**	**9990132**	**7757044**	**8316787**	**7511944**	**1799212**	**1508295**
渝中区	Yuzhong District	619669	329843	418407	320336	111282	83747
大渡口区	Dadukou District	471983	394042	474643	406429	96752	76274
江北区	Jiangbei District	1512468	1103087	1165478	1080343	235649	200913
沙坪坝区	Shapingba District	1280703	1008323	1064024	952596	224588	182245
九龙坡区	Jiulongpo District	1533603	1142732	1072826	902189	240084	191957
南岸区	Nan'an District	1850139	1575123	1462709	1374590	338791	293738
北碚区	Beibei District	359116	312927	374507	331494	72498	60142
渝北区	Yubei District	1764883	1421156	1737393	1634850	391591	353168
巴南区	Ba'nan District	597568	469811	546800	509117	87977	66111
渝西经济走廊	**West Chongqing Economic Corridor**	**2937325**	**2294402**	**2475645**	**2038126**	**260455**	**156073**
万盛区	Wansheng District	68272	60518	61546	54843	6047	3971
双桥区	Shuangqiao District	64700	50972	59660	47672	4877	2605
綦江县	Qijiang County	166565	117150	185205	162031	18220	10959
潼南县	Tongnan County	127472	97195	136707	106999	12945	5227
铜梁县	Tongliang County	246028	228990	151561	141326	13327	10380
大足县	Dazu County	210861	166292	203584	181999	18505	11773
荣昌县	Rongchang County	196899	155711	128833	118248	12146	8887
璧山县	Bishan County	331789	236373	229109	142985	22602	10897
江津市	Jiangjin City	473240	363545	420518	332124	49242	28606
合川市	Hechuan City	452170	400267	371241	335029	36330	27058
永川市	Yongchuan City	522783	353172	479215	369073	62641	32935
南川市	Nanchuan City	76546	64217	48466	45797	3573	2775
三峡库区生态经济区	**Ecological Economic Zone in Three Gorges Reservoir Area**	**2932389**	**2225188**	**2500732**	**2029401**	**268311**	**152912**
万州区	Wanzhou District	586669	394110	624299	433572	85677	37535
涪陵区	Fuling District	443769	288795	196869	154832	35220	15529
黔江区	Qianjiang District	51309	46005	53297	51397	4820	4593
长寿区	Changshou District	388184	342425	421246	384819	38424	29970
梁平县	Liangping County	257111	197724	198910	154126	22252	10257
城口县	Chengkou County	3487		3487		370	
丰都县	Fengdu County	420408	300577	291938	243521	23632	11817
垫江县	Dianjiang County	91850	75433	153619	142035	12029	11133
武隆县	Wulong County						
忠 县	Zhongxian County	123834	103986	137940	119741	13425	9145
开 县	Kaixian County	323192	275091	235326	205491	16221	12463
云阳县	Yunyang County	22886	19386	19288		1377	
奉节县	Fengjie County	124728	100367	36789	34066	4080	2884
巫山县	Wushan County						
巫溪县	Wuxi County						
石柱县	Shizhu County	36870	32520	40008	32520	3930	1879
秀山县	Xiushan County	19017	16433	9215	6433	804	316
酉阳县	Youyang County	30075	23636	23297	17722	1154	793
彭水县	Pengshui County	9000	8700	55204	49126	4896	4598

19—9 各区县（自治县、市）社会消费品零售总额（2004年）
Total Retail Sales of Consumer Goods by Region (2004)

区 县	Region	社会消费品零售总额（万元） Total Retail Sales of Consumer Goods (10 000 yuan)	批发零售贸易业 Wholesale and Retail Trade	餐饮业 Catering Trade	其他行业 Others	社会消费品零售总额指数（上年=100） Index of Total Retail Sales of Consumer Goods (preceding year=100)
都市发达经济圈	**Metropolitan Advanced Economic Sphere**	**5281116**	**4482705**	**729901**	**68510**	**115.4**
渝中区	Yuzhong District	1427390	1282995	132694	11701	113.3
大渡口区	Dadukou District	93404	75211	17802	390	111.7
江北区	Jiangbei District	530738	443510	82244	4984	118.1
沙坪坝区	Shapingba District	747698	645662	87375	14661	119.2
九龙坡区	Jiulongpo District	920909	822865	87937	10107	116.1
南岸区	Nan'an District	595521	494062	101459		118.1
北碚区	Beibei District	266812	233930	30535	2347	115.8
渝北区	Yubei District	298006	236519	59667	1820	131.4
巴南区	Ba'nan District	261062	226040	34572	450	119.2
渝西经济走廊	**West Chongqing Economic Corridor**	**2477077**	**2107879**	**329829**	**39369**	**113.5**
万盛区	Wansheng District	73485	61137	11460	888	114.6
双桥区	Shuangqiao District	14829	11669	2860	300	112.2
綦江县	Qijiang County	210980	161693	44306	4981	114.8
潼南县	Tongnan County	154836	129171	21949	3716	115.0
铜梁县	Tongliang County	191450	155524	30326	5600	115.5
大足县	Dazu County	173951	142501	27680	3770	114.5
荣昌县	Rongchang County	165676	128469	32522	4685	114.3
璧山县	Bishan County	184944	157198	25599	2147	115.5
江津市	Jiangjin City	370158	315058	46248	8852	114.6
合川市	Hechuan City	346705	296958	49448	300	115.4
永川市	Yongchuan City	379190	322552	54735	1902	115.1
南川市	Nanchuan City	151475	133820	17355	300	114.3
三峡库区生态经济区	**Ecological Economic Zone in Three Gorges Reservoir Area**	**2856659**	**2432419**	**383129**	**41111**	**113.1**
万州区	Wanzhou District	423669	350530	59078	14061	116.1
涪陵区	Fuling District	349907	301478	47534	895	116.5
黔江区	Qianjiang District	129076	115252	13824		115.3
长寿区	Changshou District	204939	158311	40828	5800	110.9
梁平县	Liangping County	141493	119741	20329	1424	114.0
城口县	Chengkou County	25918	21936	3427	556	112.6
丰都县	Fengdu County	116331	99670	14521	2140	113.4
垫江县	Dianjiang County	158224	126678	24011	7534	112.5
武隆县	Wulong County	84872	66751	15505	2616	114.2
忠 县	Zhongxian County	140558	117981	18519	4058	114.8
开 县	Kaixian County	248081	208342	31162	8578	114.6
云阳县	Yunyang County	158383	133593	20245	4546	115.0
奉节县	Fengjie County	113779	96615	13756	3408	113.6
巫山县	Wushan County	72057	61813	7502	2742	113.9
巫溪县	Wuxi County	51559	45147	5696	716	114.0
石柱县	Shizhu County	89427	72676	14161	2590	115.0
秀山县	Xiushan County	98432	87318	9814	1300	115.3
酉阳县	Youyang County	69897	59702	7315	2879	114.3
彭水县	Pengshui County	113314	97962	13392	1960	115.2

19－10 各区县（自治县、市）财政收支（2004年）
Financial Budgetary Revenue and Expenditures by Region (2004)

单位：万元 (10 000 yuan)

区　县	Region	区县级财政预算内收入 Financial Budgetary Revenue at District (county) Level	#一般预算收入 General Budgetary Revenue	#增值税 Value-added Tax	#营业税 Business Tax	#企业所得税 Enterprises Income Tax	#个人所得税 Personal Income Tax
都市发达经济圈	**Metropolitan Advanced Economic Sphere**	**789830**	**528482**	**54276**	**155748**	**29094**	**21287**
渝中区	Yuzhong District	90098	86361	6863	38677	5530	6310
大渡口区	Dadukou District	24613	22729	6844	4741	592	531
江北区	Jiangbei District	72298	70121	7360	19115	5343	2286
沙坪坝区	Shapingba District	86552	72936	4451	14343	2041	1893
九龙坡区	Jiulongpo District	60275	45475	5415	11770	2489	1765
南岸区	Nan'an District	45404	40320	3194	9479	1643	1400
北碚区	Beibei District	20758	20324	2825	4425	872	1041
渝北区	Yubei District	52980	50999	1762	18405	1654	2005
巴南区	Ba'nan District	34549	29044	4194	4732	1404	756
渝西经济走廊	**West Chongqing Economic Corridor**	**282373**	**241649**	**46004**	**32288**	**10882**	**8575**
万盛区	Wansheng District	8277	7702	2396	1249	401	442
双桥区	Shuangqiao District	5739	5733	2179	588	413	122
綦江县	Qijiang County	27373	20378	5434	3321	1101	759
潼南县	Tongnan County	15349	14893	1115	1303	189	335
铜梁县	Tongliang County	26826	25368	2379	1954	1238	696
大足县	Dazu County	16137	14864	2215	2460	1652	540
荣昌县	Rongchang County	17481	16523	2708	1825	487	590
璧山县	Bishan County	30459	24574	4412	2946	830	885
江津市	Jiangjin City	49983	38597	11246	5881	1494	1450
合川市	Hechuan City	37684	32036	4036	4969	1401	1235
永川市	Yongchuan City	30196	25189	4405	3928	772	963
南川市	Nanchuan City	16869	15792	3479	1864	904	558
三峡库区生态经济区	**Ecological Economic Zone in Three Gorges Reservoir Area**	**365627**	**335603**	**54278**	**66898**	**14655**	**13987**
万州区	Wanzhou District	63653	55361	6702	14029	2724	2013
涪陵区	Fuling District	64086	60933	12841	11414	4364	1999
黔江区	Qianjiang District	21950	21246	4713	4569	631	822
长寿区	Changshou District	33214	25580	6889	4346	1706	1324
梁平县	Liangping County	16397	15521	2113	2178	250	788
城口县	Chengkou County	6209	6193	1634	606	127	139
丰都县	Fengdu County	14604	12302	780	2474	160	524
垫江县	Dianjiang County	19445	18956	2297	2336	1123	778
武隆县	Wulong County	12163	11416	2400	1953	402	278
忠　县	Zhongxian County	15291	12848	1274	2945	511	611
开　县	Kaixian County	20755	19670	2698	2786	366	767
云阳县	Yunyang County	12223	12161	1559	2810	321	665
奉节县	Fengjie County	13933	13703	2025	1744	154	528
巫山县	Wushan County	8643	8581	1206	2039	431	311
巫溪县	Wuxi County	4859	4480	543	674	86	159
石柱县	Shizhu County	9020	8106	695	2688	115	624
秀山县	Xiushan County	11032	10916	3013	2577	479	1003
酉阳县	Youyang County	5261	5004	-34	1343	190	307
彭水县	Pengshui County	12889	12626	930	3387	515	347

注：1）都市发达经济圈的财政收支数据包括经开区和高新区，九龙坡、南岸、渝北区数据不含高新区和经开区。

2）酉阳县由于出口退税的原因，其增值税为负数。

Note: a) Data of Metropolitan Advanced Economic Sphere include Chongqing High-tech and Economic & Technology Development Zones. Data of High-Tech and Economic & Technology Development Zones are exclude from districts of Jiulongpo, Nan'an and Yubei.

b) Data of value-added tax of Youyang County is negative because of export rebate.

19-10 续表 CONTINUED

单位：万元 (10 000 yuan)

区 县	Region	区县级财政预算内支出 Local Budgetary Financial Expenditures at District (county) Level	# 一 般 预算支出 General Budgetary Expenditures	#基本建设支 出 Expenditure of Capital Construction	#教育支出 Expenditure of Education	#卫生支出 Expenditure of Public Health	#社会保障补助支出 Social Security Subsidies
都市发达经济圈	**Metropolitan Advanced Economic Sphere**	**1370167**	**1035710**	**189222**	**89107**	**28230**	**111495**
渝中区	Yuzhong District	168876	148849	10629	12389	4998	12400
大渡口区	Dadukou District	38715	37000	2831	3509	1144	4473
江北区	Jiangbei District	123631	108442	10388	8076	2767	15188
沙坪坝区	Shapingba District	149160	127603	15492	11015	3703	24344
九龙坡区	Jiulongpo District	123643	97826	6990	8523	3150	15335
南岸区	Nan'an District	118061	105305	12855	9242	2295	14266
北碚区	Beibei District	60565	58821	2844	7288	2069	8411
渝北区	Yubei District	122420	101553	11849	12148	4992	1610
巴南区	Ba'nan District	95438	86418	8171	13748	2333	12162
渝西经济走廊	**West Chongqing Economic Corridor**	**638289**	**596136**	**44875**	**108452**	**21627**	**39399**
万盛区	Wansheng District	27996	26993	1615	3504	811	2021
双桥区	Shuangqiao District	8904	8762	208	966	243	522
綦江县	Qijiang County	66617	59055	2348	13171	2208	6876
潼南县	Tongnan County	43492	42906	2182	10318	1518	3101
铜梁县	Tongliang County	53555	51165	6420	8904	1799	1623
大足县	Dazu County	45356	43360	2401	9357	1012	2095
荣昌县	Rongchang County	52772	52050	8945	8547	1409	3207
璧山县	Bishan County	50856	44577	2980	6415	1703	1283
江津市	Jiangjin City	103006	91808	5721	15542	3546	5996
合川市	Hechuan City	74402	70197	4666	12983	2939	5005
永川市	Yongchuan City	64437	59321	2588	11357	3244	5317
南川市	Nanchuan City	46896	45942	4801	7388	1195	2353
三峡库区生态经济区	**Ecological Economic Zone in Three Gorges Reservoir Area**	**1173884**	**1111205**	**107206**	**188358**	**39802**	**47329**
万州区	Wanzhou District	163393	149773	9421	23672	6068	11275
涪陵区	Fuling District	143488	137452	14874	15446	5406	5383
黔江区	Qianjiang District	79201	78584	12951	8398	2406	1607
长寿区	Changshou District	71899	61442	3795	10835	3086	5601
梁平县	Liangping County	41668	40584	1405	9250	1478	1452
城口县	Chengkou County	29698	29518	3366	4575	809	569
丰都县	Fengdu County	43364	40398	3160	8308	1377	1461
垫江县	Dianjiang County	48600	47666	3803	9627	1772	1612
武隆县	Wulong County	39921	38725	2126	5204	1136	1986
忠 县	Zhongxian County	56437	51841	5253	9424	1928	1763
开 县	Kaixian County	78920	77558	4068	15171	1921	3617
云阳县	Yunyang County	64730	60077	8572	10132	2506	1696
奉节县	Fengjie County	53093	52209	4482	10380	1540	3073
巫山县	Wushan County	49718	39016	5099	7953	1304	978
巫溪县	Wuxi County	35451	34890	4780	7240	1265	816
石柱县	Shizhu County	39489	37986	5257	6848	1594	1224
秀山县	Xiushan County	42234	41615	3884	6704	1376	1075
酉阳县	Youyang County	53676	53277	8288	11305	1623	1024
彭水县	Pengshui County	38904	38594	2622	7886	1207	1117

19－11 各区县（自治县、市）金融机构存贷款、人民生活和社会福利（2004年）

Deposit and Loan of Financial Institutions, People's Livelihood and Social Welfare by Region (2004)

区 县	Region	年末金融机构存款余额（万元） Year-end Deposit Balance of Financial Institutions (10 000 yuan)	#城乡居民储蓄 Saving Deposits of Urban and Rural Residents	年末金融机构贷款余额（万元） Year-end Loan Balance of Financial Institutions (10 000 yuan)	在岗职工年平均工资（元） Average Wages of Staff and Workers at Post (yuan)	农村居民人均纯收入（元） Per Capita Net Income of Rural Residents (yuan)
都市发达经济圈	**Metropolitan Advanced Economic Sphere**	**25760810**	**10431798**	**24164568**	**17059**	**3401**
渝中区	Yuzhong District	10186054	2056536	12441959	19263	
大渡口区	Dadukou District	590052	371444	351762	19513	3812
江北区	Jiangbei District	2639674	1112025	1619275	17388	3748
沙坪坝区	Shapingba District	2752562	1596902	1777643	17981	3814
九龙坡区	Jiulongpo District	3909127	1715122	2746657	15580	3760
南岸区	Nan'an District	2013282	1100189	1534330	16514	3965
北碚区	Beibei District	1001681	710731	507801	15148	3280
渝北区	Yubei District	1788872	975385	1068318	16357	3168
巴南区	Ba'nan District	970154	689075	609181	12838	3124
渝西经济走廊	**West Chongqing Economic Corridor**	**6099364**	**5163562**	**3035625**	**12041**	**3087**
万盛区	Wansheng District	214500	166600	75800	12230	2998
双桥区	Shuangqiao District	82755	56860	40470	16661	3275
綦江县	Qijiang County	530822	434584	259600	11923	3031
潼南县	Tongnan County	356832	319553	142766	12240	2805
铜梁县	Tongliang County	549499	482428	227836	10356	3271
大足县	Dazu County	356019	293122	153019	11973	3118
荣昌县	Rongchang County	427213	346954	178424	10892	3048
璧山县	Bishan County	534536	444722	223545	13339	3285
江津市	Jiangjin City	982538	814483	490533	12602	3234
合川市	Hechuan City	979576	845704	498114	11290	3150
永川市	Yongchuan City	755649	629379	350049	13013	3234
南川市	Nanchuan City	350888	277502	206075	10355	2717
三峡库区生态经济区	**Ecological Economic Zone in Three Gorges Reservoir Area**	**8535887**	**6301985**	**5262634**	**11784**	**2147**
万州区	Wanzhou District	1664714	1200054	910479	11132	2287
涪陵区	Fuling District	1184619	694735	1087455	12932	2529
黔江区	Qianjiang District	248814	147093	309999	15420	1968
长寿区	Changshou District	831135	634284	313809	14289	3034
梁平县	Liangping County	478247	414043	168581	12026	2521
城口县	Chengkou County	87821	60125	63887	11200	1831
丰都县	Fengdu County	363492	298297	207241	11627	2193
垫江县	Dianjiang County	422848	355003	181117	12556	2614
武隆县	Wulong County	169714	118881	178350	9585	2203
忠 县	Zhongxian County	555165	450570	222755	11695	2282
开 县	Kaixian County	752320	567268	223572	10906	2186
云阳县	Yunyang County	421596	321472	163512	10594	1974
奉节县	Fengjie County	287984	200118	163677	11019	1886
巫山县	Wushan County	242123	137583	128986	10916	1834
巫溪县	Wuxi County	130848	92844	90754	9890	1703
石柱县	Shizhu County	233609	179076	128090	11024	1882
秀山县	Xiushan County	161832	128008	98168	11457	1837
酉阳县	Youyang County	185440	137665	115539	10912	1745
彭水县	Pengshui County	143602	101804	178324	11967	1962

19-11 续表1 CONTINUED-1

区 县	Region	农村居民人均生活消费支出（元） Per Capita Living Consumption of Rural Residents (yuan)	#食品支出 Expenditure of Food	农村居民人均住房面积（平方米） Per Capita Rural Residential Area (sq.m)	社会福利收养单位（个） Adopting Social Welfare Institutions (unit)	社会福利收养单位床位数（张） Beds in Adopting Social Welfare Institutions (bed)
都市发达经济圈	**Metropolitan Advanced Economic Sphere**	**2697**	**1458**	**37.44**	**176**	**8133**
渝中区	Yuzhong District				16	456
大渡口区	Dadukou District	2704	1284	42.50	4	204
江北区	Jiangbei District	2890	1402	31.38	10	482
沙坪坝区	Shapingba District	2972	1471	36.44	21	1392
九龙坡区	Jiulongpo District	3144	1662	43.73	14	609
南岸区	Nan'an District	3092	1302	39.00	14	775
北碚区	Beibei District	3009	1536	34.60	23	1263
渝北区	Yubei District	2557	1331	38.97	37	1490
巴南区	Ba'nan District	2319	1275	34.00	37	1462
渝西经济走廊	**West Chongqing Economic Corridor**	**2264**	**1245**	**34.19**	**345**	**13645**
万盛区	Wansheng District	2490	1210	41.84	8	195
双桥区	Shuangqiao District	2751	1326	37.00	3	58
綦江县	Qijiang County	2461	1408	31.41	23	564
潼南县	Tongnan County	1961	1144	29.52	30	770
铜梁县	Tongliang County	2465	1223	38.40	35	1141
大足县	Dazu County	2174	1108	34.41	30	1056
荣昌县	Rongchang County	1724	969	30.65	24	1100
璧山县	Bishan County	2365	1235	38.00	39	1441
江津市	Jiangjin City	2350	1300	36.12	45	1811
合川市	Hechuan City	2372	1305	31.54	48	1800
永川市	Yongchuan City	2401	1437	37.00	23	2959
南川市	Nanchuan City	2208	1175	36.90	37	750
三峡库区生态经济区	**Ecological Economic Zone in Three Gorges Reservoir Area**	**1771**	**961**	**32.88**	**533**	**18384**
万州区	Wanzhou District	1713	962	32.34	74	3264
涪陵区	Fuling District	1773	998	35.24	48	2254
黔江区	Qianjiang District	1964	959	29.31	13	547
长寿区	Changshou District	2071	1100	39.18	27	1042
梁平县	Liangping County	2118	1165	39.28	28	765
城口县	Chengkou County	1617	863	26.40	13	355
丰都县	Fengdu County	1680	860	32.00	27	818
垫江县	Dianjiang County	2197	1177	37.84	32	1386
武隆县	Wulong County	1549	858	33.18	18	671
忠 县	Zhongxian County	1757	928	31.02	29	1056
开 县	Kaixian County	1561	797	35.60	47	1100
云阳县	Yunyang County	1579	815	33.45	55	2412
奉节县	Fengjie County	1369	819	26.53	30	735
巫山县	Wushan County	1562	824	29.63	12	305
巫溪县	Wuxi County	1879	960	30.90	19	680
石柱县	Shizhu County	1984	1140	32.87	15	290
秀山县	Xiushan County	1586	809	26.42	11	150
酉阳县	Youyang County	1889	950	30.10	24	332
彭水县	Pengshui County	1756	946	28.20	11	222

注：本表社会福利收养单位及床位数未含重庆市本级7个单位和2738张床位。

Note: Number of adopting social welfare institutions exclude 7 institutions at municipal level and that of beds exclude 2738 beds at municipal level.

· 19-11 续表2 CONTINUED-2

区 县	Region	城镇居民最低生活保障人数（人） Number of Urban Residents Receiving Lowest-living--security (person)	城镇社区服务设施数（个） Number of Urban Welfare Facilities (unit)	#社区服务单位数 Number of Community Service	城镇便民利民服务网点（个） Number of Urban Service Points for Civilian (unit)
都市发达经济圈	**Metropolitan Advanced Economic Sphere**	**230691**	**655**	**38**	**1719**
渝中区	Yuzhong District	25366	112	10	279
大渡口区	Dadukou District	10155	29	3	15
江北区	Jiangbei District	20556	134	5	206
沙坪坝区	Shapingba District	34128	57	7	69
九龙坡区	Jiulongpo District	31564	62	2	453
南岸区	Nan'an District	30203	110	4	251
北碚区	Beibei District	15703	60	1	240
渝北区	Yubei District	27598	52	3	152
巴南区	Ba'nan District	35418	39	3	54
渝西经济走廊	**West Chongqing Economic Corridor**	**185367**	**266**	**9**	**810**
万盛区	Wansheng District	24587	16	1	41
双桥区	Shuangqiao District	1060	5	1	4
綦江县	Qijiang County	27075	7		27
潼南县	Tongnan County	11764	12		35
铜梁县	Tongliang County	9638	21		48
大足县	Dazu County	8155	45		4
荣昌县	Rongchang County	14963	75	2	47
璧山县	Bishan County	8618	19		86
江津市	Jiangjin City	30912	17		120
合川市	Hechuan City	23908	15	3	236
永川市	Yongchuan City	12454	20		128
南川市	Nanchuan City	12233	14	2	34
三峡库区生态经济区	**Ecological Economic Zone in Three Gorges Reservoir Area**	**283131**	**428**	**31**	**4112**
万州区	Wanzhou District	60767	46	9	153
涪陵区	Fuling District	22188	58	4	2768
黔江区	Qianjiang District	11625	19		247
长寿区	Changshou District	14052	10		125
梁平县	Liangping County	4376	10	1	100
城口县	Chengkou County	2483	6	1	150
丰都县	Fengdu County	9733	12		26
垫江县	Dianjiang County	7508	31	1	60
武隆县	Wulong County	5686	12		60
忠 县	Zhongxian County	12270	12	1	81
开 县	Kaixian County	17965	56	1	135
云阳县	Yunyang County	23681	63		
奉节县	Fengjie County	18238	10	2	
巫山县	Wushan County	10877	5	1	60
巫溪县	Wuxi County	11920	5	5	
石柱县	Shizhu County	10240	5		10
秀山县	Xiushan County	9162	55		110
酉阳县	Youyang County	17947	5	5	4
彭水县	Pengshui County	12413	8		23

19－12 各区县（自治县、市）教育和文化（2004年）
Education and Culture by Region (2004)

区县	Region	学校数（所） Number of Schools (unit)	#普通中学 Regular Secondary Schools	#小学 Primary Schools	专任教师数（人） Full-time Teachers (person)	#普通中学 Regular Secondary Schools	#小学 Primary Schools
都市发达经济圈	**Metropolitan Advanced Economic Sphere**	**2093**	**287**	**860**	**61749**	**19576**	**18742**
渝中区	Yuzhong District	138	19	39	7214	2211	2221
大渡口区	Dadukou District	85	9	30	2039	789	797
江北区	Jiangbei District	181	18	62	4654	1474	1858
沙坪坝区	Shapingba District	251	38	82	11311	2958	2080
九龙坡区	Jiulongpo District	312	36	100	7995	2612	2426
南岸区	Nan'an District	212	25	61	7101	1692	1524
北碚区	Beibei District	193	29	109	7108	2142	1957
渝北区	Yubei District	440	57	263	8207	3189	3140
巴南区	Ba'nan District	281	56	114	6120	2509	2739
渝西经济走廊	**West Chongqing Economic Corridor**	**5215**	**523**	**3004**	**71140**	**29514**	**33254**
万盛区	Wansheng District	150	16	86	2249	885	1148
双桥区	Shuangqiao District	23	3	12	499	188	266
綦江县	Qijiang County	464	61	362	7419	2940	4024
潼南县	Tongnan County	447	59	339	5887	2740	2789
铜梁县	Tongliang County	257	26	178	5823	2569	2837
大足县	Dazu County	547	54	326	6703	2899	3331
荣昌县	Rongchang County	348	41	227	5685	2456	2797
璧山县	Bishan County	218	33	106	4369	1844	1984
江津市	Jiangjin City	764	65	488	9525	3857	4136
合川市	Hechuan City	850	47	312	9154	3874	3966
永川市	Yongchuan City	751	63	322	9039	3454	3493
南川市	Nanchuan City	396	55	246	4788	1808	2483
三峡库区生态经济区	**Ecological Economic Zone in Three Gorges Reservoir Area**	**8318**	**701**	**6545**	**114677**	**42961**	**62011**
万州区	Wanzhou District	780	84	526	13415	4925	5889
涪陵区	Fuling District	421	63	231	10206	3927	4631
黔江区	Qianjiang District	278	22	236	3947	1514	2157
长寿区	Changshou District	296	38	173	6621	2851	3398
梁平县	Liangping County	415	44	320	5900	2241	3049
城口县	Chengkou County	267	7	252	1746	530	1115
丰都县	Fengdu County	344	56	197	5136	1981	2822
垫江县	Dianjiang County	301	45	194	6377	2525	3491
武隆县	Wulong County	179	14	128	3223	1056	1968
忠县	Zhongxian County	729	33	566	6505	2917	3206
开县	Kaixian County	944	66	826	10665	4042	5848
云阳县	Yunyang County	531	55	449	7588	2522	4754
奉节县	Fengjie County	652	30	561	6340	2355	3649
巫山县	Wushan County	393	18	339	4065	1638	2182
巫溪县	Wuxi County	409	19	374	3696	1371	2117
石柱县	Shizhu County	280	20	243	4443	1345	2791
秀山县	Xiushan County	386	31	322	4659	1712	2747
酉阳县	Youyang County	418	42	357	5625	1945	3401
彭水县	Pengshui County	295	14	251	4520	1564	2796

注：本表学校数包括普通高校、中专、职中、普通中学、小学和特殊教育及工读学校。

Note: Data on schools included institutions of higher education, specialized secondary schools, vocational secondary schools, regular secondary schools, primary schools, schools of special educations and reformatory schools.

19-12 续表 CONTINUED

区 县	Region	在校学生数（人） Student Enrollment (person)	#普通中学 Regular Secondary Schools	#小 学 Primary Schools	广播覆盖率（%） Listener Rating of Broadcasting (%)	电视覆盖率（%） Viewer Rating of Television (%)	公共图书馆（个） Number of Public Libraries (unit)	公共图书馆藏书（万册） Book Collection in Public Libraries (10 000 volumes)
都市发达经济圈	**Metropolitan Advanced Economic Sphere**	**1101568**	**294473**	**346723**			**11**	**474.99**
渝中区	Yuzhong District	117779	31479	32893	100.00	100.00	3	316.36
大渡口区	Dadukou District	39019	12258	15231	100.00	100.00	1	4.71
江北区	Jiangbei District	71050	19166	28201	100.00	100.00	1	11.72
沙坪坝区	Shapingba District	199640	46635	43268	100.00	100.00	1	18.48
九龙坡区	Jiulongpo District	158051	40412	48623	100.00	100.00	1	5.76
南岸区	Nan'an District	130072	24912	30214	100.00	100.00	1	9.66
北碚区	Beibei District	125109	32226	35595	99.20	98.21	1	82.49
渝北区	Yubei District	136864	43511	57550	99.20	99.20	1	16.12
巴南区	Ba'nan District	123984	43874	55148	95.00	97.99	1	9.69
渝西经济走廊	**West Chongqing Economic Corridor**	**1567187**	**534187**	**774814**			**12**	**102.38**
万盛区	Wansheng District	39169	13569	21400	94.41	96.86	1	4.48
双桥区	Shuangqiao District	8769	2568	4618	100.00	100.00	1	
綦江县	Qijiang County	153288	46226	84241	94.50	89.72	1	7.20
潼南县	Tongnan County	161045	61049	85425	96.42	98.23	1	9.30
铜梁县	Tongliang County	125269	48532	62358	100.00	98.00	1	6.50
大足县	Dazu County	156607	59085	81750	96.00	95.00	1	8.91
荣昌县	Rongchang County	115091	42288	57449	100.00	100.00	1	8.53
璧山县	Bishan County	92111	30302	44724	98.98	93.00	1	6.18
江津市	Jiangjin City	208994	68218	101565	98.95	99.13	1	18.92
合川市	Hechuan City	223648	76322	106263	95.00	95.00	1	17.80
永川市	Yongchuan City	178378	53468	70655	96.00	96.10	1	8.00
南川市	Nanchuan City	104818	32560	54366	95.26	90.51	1	6.56
三峡库区生态经济区	**Ecological Economic Zone in Three Gorges Reservoir Area**	**2860434**	**878829**	**1597462**			**21**	**158.79**
万州区	Wanzhou District	302471	96727	129820	93.16	95.16	2	18.99
涪陵区	Fuling District	189698	59619	92202	98.48	96.50	2	53.52
黔江区	Qianjiang District	98810	28402	58647	94.50	95.10	1	10.00
长寿区	Changshou District	123064	44257	67747	95.58	96.88	1	10.00
梁平县	Liangping County	146065	48134	75580	95.00	90.00	1	1.20
城口县	Chengkou County	35770	9891	22734	68.00	92.20	1	0.70
丰都县	Fengdu County	120393	38641	68232	91.40	95.50	1	4.50
垫江县	Dianjiang County	175795	63710	82235	100.00	98.00	1	3.42
武隆县	Wulong County	64960	19156	36760	87.10	93.68	1	6.67
忠 县	Zhongxian County	150927	53960	78467	97.90	98.31	1	3.00
开 县	Kaixian County	301982	100623	170708	95.09	96.05	1	18.29
云阳县	Yunyang County	244431	70026	147102	95.30	98.00	1	2.36
奉节县	Fengjie County	206144	56693	127481	89.18	97.00	1	5.50
巫山县	Wushan County	106163	32969	63972	82.89	94.73	1	0.90
巫溪县	Wuxi County	89199	26659	54288	87.01	94.21	1	2.15
石柱县	Shizhu County	97183	28566	56136	92.29	79.50	1	5.07
秀山县	Xiushan County	122592	31347	80917	24.74	85.59	1	4.49
酉阳县	Youyang County	154224	38957	98303	60.51	88.58	1	5.43
彭水县	Pengshui County	130563	30492	86131	58.20	90.85	1	2.60

注：本表数据包括普通高校、中专、职中、普通中学、小学和特殊教育及工读学校。

Note: Data in this table included institutions of higher education, specialized secondary schools, vocational secondary schools, regular secondary schools, primary schools, schools of special educations and reformatory schools.

19－13 各区县（自治县、市）卫生（2004年）
Public Health by Region (2004)

区 县	Region	卫生机构数（个） Number of Health Institutions (unit)	#医院、卫生院 Number of Hospitals and Health Centers	卫生机构床位数（张） Hospital Beds in Health Institutions (bed)	卫生技术人员（人） Medical Technical Personnel (person)	#执业(助理)医师 Certified (Assistant) Doctors	#注册护士 Registration Nurses
都市发达经济圈	**Metropolitan Advanced Economic Sphere**	**1993**	**262**	**25073**	**28307**	**12759**	**9154**
渝中区	Yuzhong District	362	25	6452	7728	3348	2733
大渡口区	Dadukou District	111	10	906	1155	522	367
江北区	Jiangbei District	373	33	3515	3528	1454	1260
沙坪坝区	Shapingba District	219	35	2879	3086	1394	948
九龙坡区	Jiulongpo District	293	35	3315	3995	1900	1271
南岸区	Nan'an District	178	28	2448	2572	1251	781
北碚区	Beibei District	107	29	2604	2081	1005	577
渝北区	Yubei District	130	37	913	1635	730	367
巴南区	Ba'nan District	220	30	2041	2527	1155	850
渝西经济走廊	**West Chongqing Economic Corridor**	**1543**	**420**	**17396**	**20495**	**9673**	**5121**
万盛区	Wansheng District	43	13	1059	1037	389	373
双桥区	Shuangqiao District	16	4	179	154	64	50
綦江县	Qijiang County	147	35	2019	2084	927	678
潼南县	Tongnan County	167	37	953	1403	690	399
铜梁县	Tongliang County	141	37	1330	1789	1026	410
大足县	Dazu County	122	42	1280	1678	685	268
荣昌县	Rongchang County	153	25	1263	1800	870	396
璧山县	Bishan County	134	37	1124	1560	639	311
江津市	Jiangjin City	174	41	2318	2655	1318	545
合川市	Hechuan City	212	61	2162	2372	1143	592
永川市	Yongchuan City	135	46	2495	2510	1271	766
南川市	Nanchuan City	99	42	1214	1453	651	333
三峡库区生态经济区	**Ecological Economic Zone in Three Gorges Reservoir Area**	**3003**	**892**	**21430**	**28714**	**14171**	**5974**
万州区	Wanzhou District	816	105	3569	4737	2540	1282
涪陵区	Fuling District	249	60	2375	3015	1463	617
黔江区	Qianjiang District	69	30	811	1073	428	206
长寿区	Changshou District	193	54	1886	1878	882	499
梁平县	Liangping County	106	37	970	1254	646	287
城口县	Chengkou County	115	27	309	472	228	65
丰都县	Fengdu County	149	37	1045	1216	569	212
垫江县	Dianjiang County	49	28	1009	1402	723	289
武隆县	Wulong County	102	30	572	744	396	133
忠 县	Zhongxian County	167	46	1340	1840	777	443
开 县	Kaixian County	150	60	1190	2232	1309	413
云阳县	Yunyang County	117	91	1252	2113	1006	284
奉节县	Fengjie County	95	31	1088	1160	605	227
巫山县	Wushan County	84	43	684	699	340	130
巫溪县	Wuxi County	127	60	522	909	327	115
石柱县	Shizhu County	70	34	766	1096	512	215
秀山县	Xiushan County	78	34	603	822	373	154
酉阳县	Youyang County	191	42	706	1325	665	228
彭水县	Pengshui County	76	43	733	727	382	175

注：本页卫生机构含个体诊所。

Note: Data on health institutions included individual-run medical units.

19－14 重庆市开发区主要统计指标（2004年）
Main Indicators of Development Zones in Chongqing (2004)

单位：万元 (10 000 yuan)

指标	Item	北部新区和两区合计 Total	经开区 Economic & Technology Development Zone	高新区 High-tech Development Zone
开发区生产总值	Gross Domestic Product	1458763	771321	687442
工业总产值	Gross Output Value of Industry	5153326	2104246	3049080
工业增加值	Value-added of Industry	1578936	619375	959561
固定资产投资完成额	Completed Investment in Fixed Assets	1789194	922683	866511
#基础设施建设	Infrastructure Construction	702577	339343	363234
入库税金	Laid-up Taxes	339639	161004	178635
开发区财政收入	Financial Revenues Preserved	302303	191969	110334
进出口总额（万美元）	Total Imports and Exports (USD 10 000)	77274	64187	13087
#出　口	Total Imports	16852	8020	8832
招商引资签约合同投资总额	Absorbed Capitals on Contract	1498512	971317	527195
#合同外资（万美元）	Foreign Capitals on Contract (USD 10 000)	19694	11216	8478
招商引资到位资金	Absorbed Capitals Utilized	617967	280172	337795
#外资到位（万美元）	Foreign Capitals Utilized (USD 10 000)	13633	5028	8605

指标	Item	#北部新区 Northern New Development Zone	经开园 Economic & Technology Development Garden	高新园 High-tech Development Garden
开发区生产总值	Gross Domestic Product	301458	214991	86467
工业总产值	Gross Output Value of Industry	1056589	873556	183033
工业增加值	Value-added of Industry	229993	198291	31702
固定资产投资完成额	Completed Investment in Fixed Assets	1193776	685048	508728
#基础设施建设投资完成额	Completed Investment in Infrastructure Construction	572378	320537	251841
入库税金	Laid-up Taxes	126047	101010	25037
开发区财政收入	Financial Revenues Preserved	183090	137722	45368
进出口总额（万美元）	Total Imports and Exports (USD 10 000)	47050	47050	
#出　口	Total Imports	1918	1918	
招商引资签约合同投资总额	Absorbed Capitals on Contract	1311830	890409	421421
#合同外资（万美元）	Foreign Capitals on Contract (USD 10 000)	11383	9883	1500
招商引资到位资金	Absorbed Capitals Utilized	404277	157245	247032
#外资到位（万美元）	Foreign Capitals Utilized (USD 10 000)	8561	4711	3850

注：1）本表包括重庆市北部新区、经济技术开发区、高新技术产业开发区的数据。
2）经开区入库税金已扣除烟草数据。

Note: a) Statistics in this table are on basis of region, including Northern New Development Zone, Economic & Technology Development Zone and High-tech Development Zone.
b) Laid-up taxes of Economic & Technology Development Zone excludes data of tobacco.

19－15 重庆市经济技术开发区主要统计指标（2003－2004年）
Main Indicators of Chongqing Economic and Technology Development Zone (2003-2004)

项　目	Item	2003	2004
占地面积（平方公里）	Land Area Used (sq.km)	93.30	93.30
企业累计数（个）	Number of Enterprises (unit)	2109	2794
总收入（亿元）	Total Revenue (100 million yuan)	240.09	272.37
经开区生产总值（万元）	GDP (10 000 yuan)	724849	771321
＃第二产业	Secondary Industry	645574	664486
＃工　业	Industry	627580	619375
第三产业	Tertiary Industry	79275	101232
工业总产值（现价）（万元）	Gross Output Value of Industry (current prices) (10 000 yuan)	1911438	2104246
税金总额（万元）	Total Profits and Taxes (10 000 yuan)	152066	161004
预算内财政收入（万元）	Financial Budgetary Revenue (10 000 yuan)	35100	65049
进出口总额（万美元）	Total Exports and Imports (USD 10 000)	29406	64187
＃出　口	Exports	3389	8020
当年批准外商投资企业（户）	Foreign-funded Enterprises Authorized (household)	21	33
＃投资额在1000万美元以上	With Investment over USD 10 million	3	10
外商投资企业投资总额（万美元）	Contracted Capital of Foreign-funded Enterprises (USD 10 000)	26347	27621
实际到位资金（万美元）	Actual Executed Fund (USD 10 000)	4656	6103
＃实际到位外资	Executed Value of Foreign Fund	3465	5028
全区年末累计高新技术企业户数（户）	Year-end Total High-tech Enterprises (household)	46	70
高新技术企业产值（万元）	Output Value of High-tech Enterprises (10 000 yuan)	1226108	1395351
占工业总产值比重（%）	As Percentage of Gross Output Value of Industry (%)	64.1	66.3
技术合同登记项目（项）	Registered Projects of Technological Contracts (unit)	28	25
成交金额（万元）	Business Volume (10 000 yuan)	6295	2876
全社会固定资产投资额（万元）	Investment in Fixed Assets (10 000 yuan)	514178	922683
＃基础设施建设	Infrastructure Construction	249739	339343
社会从业人员人数（万人）	Employment (10 000 persons)	5.98	7.83
人均经开区生产总值（万元）	Per Capita GDP (10 000 yuan)	12.12	9.85
人均工业总产值（万元）	Per Capita Gross Output Value of Industry (10 000 yuan)	31.96	26.88
人均总收入（万元）	Per Capita Income (10 000 yuan)	40.15	34.79
人均创税（万元）	Per Capita Taxes Created (10 000 yuan)	2.54	2.06

19－16 重庆市高新技术产业开发区主要统计指标（2003－2004年）
Main Indicators of Chongqing High-tech Development Zone (2003-2004)

项　　目	Item	2003	2004
占地面积（平方公里）	Land Area (sq.km)	20	20
开发区基建投资总额（万元）	Investment in Capital Construction (10 000 yuan)	200245	363234
区级财政收入（万元）	Financial Revenue (10 000 yuan)	56158	110334
企业数（个）	Number of Enterprises (unit)	11255	10891
工业增加值（万元）	Industrial Value-added (10 000 yuan)	632199	959561
工业总产值（现价）（万元）	Gross Output Value of Industry (current prices) (10 000 yuan)	2401312	3049080
总收入（万元）	Total Revenue (10 000 yuan)	2753955	3335217
＃技术收入	Technical Revenue	317264	431282
产品销售收入	Product Sales Revenue	2297735	2840965
净利润（万元）	Net Profits (10 000 yuan)	125962	163939
实际上缴税额（万元）	Total Taxes (10 000 yuan)	152399	165415
注册企业进出口总额（万美元）	Total Exports and Imports of Registered Enterprises (USD 10 000)	39032	47626
＃出　口	Exports	37157	43447
年末从业人员（万人）	Total Employment (10 000 persons)	10.84	10.53
人均总产值（万元）	Gross Output Value Per Capita (10 000 yuan)	23.58	31.07
人均总收入（万元）	Total Income Per Capita (10 000 yuan)	27.04	33.98
人均创利润（万元）	Per Capita Profits (10 000 yuan)	1.24	1.67
人均创税（万元）	Per Capita Taxes (10 000 yuan)	1.50	1.69
人均出口额（万美元）	Per Capita Exports (USD 10 000)	0.36	0.44

注：本表前四项指标按地域统计，其余指标均为国家科委火炬计划值。

Note: The first four indices in this table are on basis of region, and others refer to *Torch Plan* of State Scientific and Technological Committee.

二十 各类企业资料

VARIOUS ENTERPRISES

简要说明　Brief Introduction

本章资料主要包括工业企业、建筑业企业、房地产开发业企业、高新技术产品生产企业、企业集团和亿元以上商品交易市场按各类分组的排序，工业企业50强名单，大中型工业企业、重点建筑企业、重点房地产开发企业、重点批发零售贸易企业、企业集团目录，以及企业法人知名字号。

本章资料分别由市统计局工业交通处、社会科技处、固定资产投资处、贸易外经处和市企业调查队根据有关资料整理提供，其中企业法人知名字号来自市工商行政管理局。

This chapter covers industrial, construction, real estate development, high-tech product enterprises, and business groups, commodity markets in various kinds of orders. And it also includes lists of top 50 industrial enterprises, large & medium sized industrial enterprises, major construction enterprises, major real estate development enterprises, major wholesale & retail trade enterprises, business groups and noted titles of legal enterprises.

Data in this chapter are provided by Division of Industry and Transport Statistics, Division of Social and Technology Statistics, Division of Statistics of Investment in Fixed Assets, Division of Trade and External Economic Relations Statistics, and Enterprises Survey Organization of Municipal Bureau of Statistics using related data, of which list of noted titles of legal enterprises is from Municipal Administration for Industry and Commerce.

20－1 重庆工业企业五十强名单（2003－2004年）
List of Top 50 Industrial Enterprises (2003-2004)

序号 Order	2003	序号 Order	2004
1	重庆长安汽车股份有限公司	1	重庆长安汽车股份有限公司
2	重庆烟草工业有限责任公司	2	重庆烟草工业有限责任公司
3	重庆钢铁股份有限公司	3	重庆钢铁股份有限公司
4	庆铃汽车（集团）有限公司	4	中国石化集团四川维尼纶厂
5	黔江卷烟厂	5	重庆太极实业（集团）股份有限公司
6	扬子江乙酰化工有限公司	6	黔江卷烟厂
7	重庆啤酒股份有限公司	7	重庆力帆实业（集团）有限公司
8	重庆力帆实业（集团）有限公司	8	重庆啤酒股份有限公司
9	宗申产业集团有限公司	9	庆铃汽车（集团）有限公司
10	重庆隆鑫工业（集团）有限公司	10	扬子江乙酰化工有限公司
11	重庆太极实业（集团）股份有限公司	11	宗申产业集团有限公司
12	重庆药友制药有限责任公司	12	重庆隆鑫工业（集团）有限公司
13	重庆华邦制药股份有限公司	13	重庆康明斯发动机有限公司
14	重庆市迪马实业股份有限公司	14	重庆药友制药有限责任公司
15	重庆康明斯发动机有限公司	15	重庆国际复合材料有限公司
16	中国石化集团四川维尼纶厂	16	重庆市博赛矿业（集团）有限公司
17	重庆华立控股股份有限公司	17	重庆川仪总厂有限公司
18	重庆川仪总厂有限公司	18	重庆潍柴发动机厂
19	重庆长江轴承工业有限公司	19	重庆齿轮箱有限责任公司
20	重庆大足红蝶锶业有限公司	20	重庆顶益食品有限公司
21	重庆银钢科技（集团）有限公司	21	綦江齿轮传动有限公司
22	重庆市博赛矿业（集团）有限公司	22	中化重庆涪陵化工有限公司
23	重庆国际复合材料有限公司	23	西南铝业（集团）有限责任公司
24	重庆腾辉地维水泥有限公司	24	重庆美心（集团）有限公司
25	重庆红岩汽车有限责任公司	25	重庆紫光化工有限责任公司
26	中国嘉陵工业股份有限公司（集团）	26	重庆ABB变压器有限公司
27	重庆清华紫光英力天然气化工有限责任公司	27	重庆李尔长安汽车内饰件有限责任公司
28	重庆顶益食品有限公司	28	重庆宇通客车有限公司
29	重庆科瑞制药有限责任公司	29	重庆红宇精密工业有限责任公司
30	重庆鼎发实业股份有限公司	30	重庆建设摩托车股份有限公司
31	重庆登康口腔护理用品股份有限公司	31	中国核工业建峰化工总厂
32	重庆潍柴发动机厂	32	重庆市迪马实业股份有限公司
33	西南药业股份有限公司	33	重庆泰山电线电缆有限责任公司
34	重庆齿轮箱有限责任公司	34	重庆华立控股股份有限公司
35	西南铝业（集团）有限责任公司	35	西南药业股份有限公司
36	重庆四维瓷业（集团）股份有限公司	36	嘉陵－本田发动机有限公司
37	重庆市江津酒厂有限责任公司	37	格力电器（重庆）有限公司
38	重庆美心（集团）有限公司	38	中国嘉陵工业股份有限公司（集团）
39	中国核工业建峰化工总厂	39	重庆红岩汽车有限责任公司
40	重庆市渝江压铸有限公司	40	重庆市天友乳业股份有限公司
41	涪陵化工股份有限公司	41	重庆赛力盟电机有限责任公司
42	重庆机床厂	42	国营重庆重型铸锻厂
43	国营重庆重型铸锻厂	43	重庆青山工业有限责任公司
44	重庆泰山电线电缆有限责任公司	44	双赢集团有限公司
45	重庆青山工业有限责任公司	45	重庆渝江压铸有限公司
46	重庆市太白酒厂	46	重庆腾辉地维水泥有限公司
47	重庆市东升铝业股份有限公司	47	重庆四维瓷业（集团）股份有限公司
48	重庆市天友乳业股份有限公司	48	重庆市东升铝业股份有限公司
49	重庆索特盐化股份有限公司	49	重庆鸽牌电线电缆有限公司
50	江津增压器厂	50	重庆四钢钢业有限责任公司

20－2 工业企业按销售产值排序（2004年）
Industrial Enterprises in Order of Sales Value (2004)

序号 Order	企业名称 Name of Enterprises	序号 Order	企业名称 Name of Enterprises
1	重庆长安汽车股份有限公司	51	重庆松藻煤电有限责任公司
2	重庆钢铁股份有限公司	52	重庆宇通客车有限公司
3	重庆市电力公司	53	重庆南桐矿业有限责任公司
4	长安福特汽车有限公司	54	重庆银翔摩托车集团有限公司
5	重庆力帆实业（集团）有限公司	55	重庆长寿化工有限责任公司
6	重庆长安铃木汽车有限公司	56	UT斯达康（重庆）通讯有限公司
7	庆铃汽车（集团）有限公司	57	重庆市东华特殊钢有限责任公司
8	西南铝业（集团）有限责任公司	58	重庆永荣矿业有限公司
9	重庆红岩汽车有限责任公司	59	重庆钢铁集团矿业有限公司
10	重庆烟草工业有限责任公司	60	重庆李尔长安汽车内饰件有限责任公司
11	中国嘉陵工业股份有限公司（集团）	61	重庆腾辉地维水泥有限公司
12	重庆隆鑫工业（集团）有限公司	62	重庆力之星机车制造有限责任公司
13	重庆建设工业有限责任公司	63	重庆乌江电力（集团）有限公司
14	格力电器（重庆）有限公司	64	西南合成制药股份有限公司
15	重庆建设摩托车股份有限公司	65	重庆市自来水公司
16	中国石化集团四川维尼纶厂	66	西南药业股份有限公司
17	华能重庆珞璜发电有限责任公司	67	重庆市东升铝业股份有限公司
18	重庆宗申发动机制造有限公司	68	綦江齿轮传动有限公司
19	太极集团涪陵制药厂	69	双赢集团有限公司
20	重庆川仪总厂有限公司	70	重庆市赛力盟电机有限责任公司
21	重庆市博赛矿业（集团）有限公司	71	重庆鼎泰铝业有限公司
22	重庆信威通信技术有限责任公司	72	重庆新涪食品有限公司
23	长安汽车（集团）有限责任公司	73	国营重庆重型铸锻厂
24	黔江卷烟厂	74	重庆银钢科技集团有限公司
25	扬子江乙酰化工有限公司	75	重庆精通工业集团有限公司
26	重庆劲隆科技集团有限公司	76	重庆检测仪表厂
27	重庆潍柴发动机厂	77	重庆大江摩托车发动机制造有限公司
28	中化重庆涪陵化工有限公司	78	重庆华邦制药股份有限公司
29	中国核工业建峰化工总厂	79	重庆药友制药有限责任公司
30	重庆燃气（集团）有限责任公司	80	重庆鸽牌电线电缆有限公司
31	重庆美心（集团）有限公司	81	重庆紫光化工有限责任公司
32	重庆大江信达车辆股份有限公司	82	重庆跨越（集团）股份有限公司
33	重庆宗申机车工业制造有限公司	83	重庆银鸿铝业有限公司
34	重庆四钢钢业有限责任公司	84	重庆长江电工(集团)有限公司
35	重庆康明斯发动机有限公司	85	重庆福雷德化工有限公司
36	重庆渝江压铸有限公司	86	重庆长江轴承有限公司
37	重庆市涪陵水利电力投资集团有限责任公司	87	重庆长安汽车电器股份有限公司
38	重庆顶益食品有限公司	88	重庆环松工业集团有限公司
39	重庆泰山电线电缆有线责任公司	89	重庆世纪精信实业有限公司
40	重庆啤酒股份有限公司	90	重庆钢铁集团铁业有限责任公司
41	重庆ABB变压器有限公司	91	重庆嘉鹏摩托车制造有限公司
42	重庆望江工业有限公司	92	重庆重型汽车集团专用汽车有限责任公司
43	重庆齿轮箱有限责任公司	93	重庆市涪陵金帝工业集团有限公司
44	重庆铁马工业集团有限公司	94	重庆市迪马实业股份有限公司
45	重庆红宇精密工业有限责任公司	95	重庆市志成机械厂
46	重庆国际复合材料有限公司	96	重庆市太白酒厂
47	重庆正大有限公司	97	重庆市三峡牧业集团有限公司
48	嘉陵－本田发动机有限公司	98	重庆恒胜集团有限公司
49	重庆青山工业有限责任公司	99	重庆江口水电有限责任公司
50	重庆长安金陵汽车零部件有限公司	100	重庆鑫腾冶金炉料有限责任公司

20－3 工业企业按主营业务收入排序（2004年）
Industrial Enterprises in Order of Major Business Revenue (2004)

序号 Order	企业名称 Name of Enterprises	序号 Order	企业名称 Name of Enterprises
1	重庆长安汽车股份有限公司	51	重庆青山工业有限责任公司
2	重庆市电力公司	52	重庆宇通客车有限公司
3	重庆钢铁股份有限公司	53	重庆南桐矿业有限责任公司
4	长安福特汽车有限公司	54	重庆银翔摩托车集团有限公司
5	重庆力帆实业（集团）有限公司	55	重庆长寿化工有限责任公司
6	重庆长安铃木汽车有限公司	56	UT斯达康（重庆）通讯有限公司
7	庆铃汽车（集团）有限公司	57	重庆永荣矿业有限公司
8	西南铝业（集团）有限责任公司	58	重庆市东华特殊钢有限责任公司
9	重庆红岩汽车有限责任公司	59	重庆钢铁集团矿业有限公司
10	重庆烟草工业有限责任公司	60	重庆李尔长安汽车内饰件有限责任公司
11	中国嘉陵工业股份有限公司（集团）	61	重庆长江电工(集团)有限公司
12	重庆隆鑫工业（集团）有限公司	62	重庆腾辉地维水泥有限公司
13	重庆建设工业有限责任公司	63	重庆力之星机车制造有限责任公司
14	格力电器（重庆）有限公司	64	重庆乌江电力（集团）有限公司
15	中国石化集团四川维尼纶厂	65	西南合成制药股份有限公司
16	重庆建设摩托车股份有限公司	66	重庆市自来水公司
17	华能重庆珞璜发电有限责任公司	67	西南药业股份有限公司
18	重庆宗申发动机制造有限公司	68	重庆市东升铝业股份有限公司
19	重庆川仪总厂有限公司	69	双赢集团有限公司
20	重庆市博赛矿业（集团）有限公司	70	重庆市赛力盟电机有限责任公司
21	黔江卷烟厂	71	中国嘉陵工业有限公司
22	扬子江乙酰化工有限公司	72	綦江齿轮传动有限公司
23	重庆劲隆科技集团有限公司	73	重庆新涪食品有限公司
24	长安汽车（集团）有限责任公司	74	重庆银钢科技集团有限公司
25	重庆潍柴发动机厂	75	国营重庆重型铸锻厂
26	中化重庆涪陵化工有限公司	76	重庆市天友乳业股份有限公司
27	太极集团涪陵制药厂	77	重庆精通工业集团有限公司
28	中国核工业建峰化工总厂	78	重庆检测仪表厂
29	重庆燃气（集团）有限责任公司	79	重庆大江摩托车发动机制造有限公司
30	重庆四钢钢业有限责任公司	80	重庆四维瓷业（集团）股份有限公司
31	重庆美心（集团）有限公司	81	重庆药友制药有限责任公司
32	重庆大江信达车辆股份有限公司	82	重庆紫光化工有限责任公司
33	重庆宗申机车工业制造有限公司	83	重庆鼎泰铝业有限公司
34	重庆康明斯发动机有限公司	84	重庆跨越（集团）股份有限公司
35	重庆泰山电线电缆有限责任公司	85	重庆福雷德化工有限公司
36	重庆渝江压铸有限公司	86	重庆银鸿铝业有限公司
37	重庆ABB变压器有限公司	87	重庆长安汽车电器股份有限公司
38	重庆啤酒股份有限公司	88	重庆环松工业集团有限公司
39	重庆市涪陵水利电力投资集团有限责任公司	89	重庆嘉鹏摩托车制造有限公司
40	重庆顶益食品有限公司	90	重庆钢铁集团铁业有限责任公司
41	重庆齿轮箱有限责任公司	91	重庆市涪陵金帝工业集团有限公司
42	重庆红宇精密工业有限责任公司	92	重庆市迪马实业股份有限公司
43	重庆信威通信技术有限责任公司	93	重庆市志成机械厂
44	重庆望江工业有限公司	94	重庆市三峡牧业集团有限公司
45	重庆铁马工业集团有限公司	95	重庆恒胜集团有限公司
46	重庆正大有限公司	96	重庆索特盐化股份有限公司
47	重庆国际复合材料有限公司	97	重庆江口水电有限责任公司
48	重庆松藻煤电有限责任公司	98	重庆鑫腾冶金炉料有限责任公司
49	嘉陵－本田发动机有限公司	99	重庆浙中铝合金有限公司
50	重庆长安金陵汽车零部件有限公司	100	重庆凯源石油天然气有限责任公司

20－4 工业企业按利税总额排序（2004年）
Industrial Enterprises in Order of Per-tax Profits (2004)

序号 Order	企业名称 Name of Enterprises	序号 Order	企业名称 Name of Enterprises
1	重庆长安汽车股份有限公司	51	重庆鼎发实业股份有限公司
2	重庆烟草工业有限责任公司	52	重庆红宇精密工业有限责任公司
3	长安福特汽车有限公司	53	煤炭科学研究总院重庆分院
4	重庆钢铁股份有限公司	54	重庆索特盐化股份有限公司
5	重庆市电力公司	55	重庆机床厂
6	重庆长安铃木汽车有限公司	56	重庆泰山电线电缆有限责任公司
7	黔江卷烟厂	57	重庆宗申机车工业制造有限公司
8	华能重庆珞璜发电有限责任公司	58	重庆拓源实业有限公司
9	重庆市博赛矿业（集团）有限公司	59	重庆朝阳气体有限公司
10	扬子江乙酰化工有限公司	60	重庆松藻煤电有限责任公司
11	中国石化集团四川维尼纶厂	61	重庆齿轮箱有限责任公司
12	庆铃汽车(集团)有限公司	62	攀钢集团重庆钛业股份有限公司
13	长安汽车（集团）有限责任公司	63	重庆燃气（集团）有限责任公司
14	重庆力帆实业（集团）有限公司	64	城口县矿产资源开发有限责任公司
15	重庆啤酒股份有限公司	65	涪陵宏声(集团)有限责任公司
16	太极集团涪陵制药厂	66	重庆天雄锰业有限公司
17	重庆江口水电有限责任公司	67	重庆大江渝强塑料制品有限公司
18	西南铝业（集团）有限责任公司	68	重庆油泵油咀厂
19	重庆川仪总厂有限公司	69	重庆顺博铝合金有限公司
20	重庆国际复合材料有限公司	70	重庆建设工业有限责任公司
21	重庆潍柴发动机厂	71	重庆老山沟锰业有限责任公司
22	重庆康明斯发动机有限公司	72	重庆中法供水有限公司
23	重庆宗申发动机制造有限公司	73	重庆四钢钢业有限责任公司
24	重庆隆鑫工业（集团）有限公司	74	重庆登康口腔护理用品股份有限公司
25	重庆药友制药有限责任公司	75	重庆永荣矿业有限公司
26	中国核工业建峰化工总厂	76	重庆长江轴承有限公司
27	格力电器（重庆）有限公司	77	西南药业股份有限公司
28	中国嘉陵工业股份有限公司（集团）	78	重庆龙珠电力股份有限公司
29	重庆美心（集团）有限公司	79	重庆市太白酒厂
30	重庆九龙电力股份有限公司	80	重庆市大足县天青石矿业公司
31	綦江齿轮传动有限公司	81	重庆市赛力盟电机有限责任公司
32	重庆市大足红蝶锶业有限公司	82	重庆利时德拉索系统有限公司
33	重庆华立控股股份有限公司	83	重庆秦川工贸有限公司
34	重庆市自来水公司	84	重庆市富皇水泥集团有限公司
35	重庆钢铁集团矿业有限公司	85	重庆川东化工集团有限公司
36	重庆建设摩托车股份有限公司	86	重庆市涪陵榨菜[集团]有限公司
37	重庆华邦制药股份有限公司	87	重庆四维瓷业（集团）股份有限公司
38	重庆乌江电力（集团）有限公司	88	重庆拉法基水泥有限公司
39	重庆顶益食品有限公司	89	重庆科瑞制药有限责任公司
40	福耀玻璃(重庆)配件有限公司	90	太极集团重庆桐君阁药厂
41	重庆市涪陵水利电力投资集团有限责任公司	91	重庆通盛机械工业有限公司
42	重庆ABB变压器有限公司	92	重庆凯源石油天然气有限责任公司
43	重庆劲隆科技集团有限公司	93	重庆市仁和压铸有限公司
44	重庆李尔长安汽车内饰件有限责任公司	94	重庆市天友乳业股份有限公司
45	中化重庆涪陵化工有限公司	95	重庆世纪精信实业有限公司
46	江津市禾丰化工有限责任公司	96	重庆市富丰水泥集团有限责任公司
47	重庆渝江压铸有限公司	97	嘉陵－本田发动机有限公司
48	双赢集团有限公司	98	重庆钢铁集团铁业有限责任公司
49	重庆宇通客车有限公司	99	重庆华孚工业股份有限公司
50	重庆三峡水利电力(集团)股份有限公司	100	重庆合川市供电有限责任公司

20－5 工业企业按资产总计排序（2004年）
Industrial Enterprises in Order of Total Property (2004)

序号 Order	企业名称 Name of Enterprises	序号 Order	企业名称 Name of Enterprises
1	重庆市电力公司	51	重庆青山工业有限责任公司
2	庆铃汽车（集团）有限公司	52	西南合成制药股份有限公司
3	重庆长安汽车股份有限公司	53	重庆拉法基水泥有限公司
4	长安汽车（集团）有限责任公司	54	重庆天府矿业有限责任公司
5	重庆钢铁股份有限公司	55	重庆康明斯发动机有限公司
6	西南铝业（集团）有限责任公司	56	重庆永荣矿业有限公司
7	华能重庆珞璜发电有限责任公司	57	重庆美心（集团）有限公司
8	长安福特汽车有限公司	58	西南药业股份有限公司
9	中国嘉陵工业股份有限公司（集团）	59	重庆腾辉特种水泥有限公司
10	重庆烟草工业有限责任公司	60	西南计算机有限责任公司
11	重庆市涪陵水利电力投资集团有限责任公司	61	重庆望江工业有限公司
12	重庆力帆实业（集团）有限公司	62	攀钢集团重庆钛业股份有限公司
13	中国石化集团四川维尼纶厂	63	重庆信威通信技术有限责任公司
14	太极集团涪陵制药厂	64	重庆民丰农化股份有限公司
15	重庆建设工业有限责任公司	65	中国嘉陵工业有限公司
16	重庆长安铃木汽车有限公司	66	重庆市迪马实业股份有限公司
17	重庆建设摩托车股份有限公司	67	重庆泰山电线电缆有限责任公司
18	重庆江口水电有限责任公司	68	重庆索特盐化股份有限公司
19	扬子江乙酰化工有限公司	69	重庆三爱海陵实业有限责任公司
20	重庆乌江电力（集团）有限公司	70	重庆通用工业（集团）有限责任公司
21	重庆红岩汽车有限责任公司	71	重庆普天通信设备有限公司
22	格力电器（重庆）有限公司	72	重庆钢铁集团矿业有限公司
23	重庆松藻煤电有限责任公司	73	重庆拓源实业有限公司
24	重庆大江信达车辆股份有限公司	74	重庆佳通轮胎有限公司
25	重庆白鹤电力有限责任公司	75	长寿化工总厂
26	重庆国际复合材料有限公司	76	海康纺织(集团)有限公司
27	重庆啤酒股份有限公司	77	重庆渝江压铸有限公司
28	中国核工业建峰化工总厂	78	重庆四钢钢业有限责任公司
29	重庆市自来水公司	79	重庆市涪陵金帝工业集团有限公司
30	重庆川仪总厂有限公司	80	重庆市东升铝业股份有限公司
31	重庆燃气（集团）有限责任公司	81	国营重庆重型铸锻厂
32	黔江卷烟厂	82	重庆宗申发动机制造有限公司
33	重庆铁马工业集团有限公司	83	綦江齿轮传动有限公司
34	重庆长江电工(集团)有限公司	84	重庆三峡油漆股份有限公司
35	重庆隆鑫工业（集团）有限公司	85	重庆新涪食品有限公司
36	重庆华立控股股份有限公司	86	双赢集团有限公司
37	重庆九龙电力股份有限公司	87	重庆大川门业集团有限公司
38	重庆三峡水利电力(集团)股份有限公司	88	望江机器制造总厂
39	重庆市博赛矿业（集团）有限公司	89	重庆长寿化工有限责任公司
40	中化重庆涪陵化工有限公司	90	重庆天泰铝业有限公司
41	重庆西南合成制药有限公司	91	重庆市开县供电有限责任公司
42	重庆四维瓷业（集团）股份有限公司	92	嘉陵－本田发动机有限公司
43	重庆潍柴发动机厂	93	重庆华陶瓷业有限公司
44	重庆齿轮箱有限责任公司	94	重庆水轮机厂有限责任公司
45	重庆中法供水有限公司	95	重庆大溪河水电开发有限公司
46	重庆红宇精密工业有限责任公司	96	重庆药友制药有限责任公司
47	重庆ABB变压器有限公司	97	重庆朝华晶化石有限公司
48	重庆南桐矿业有限责任公司	98	重庆顶益食品有限公司
49	重庆市涪陵建筑陶瓷集团有限公司	99	重庆市富丰水泥集团有限责任公司
50	重庆腾辉地维水泥有限公司	100	重庆华邦制药股份有限公司

20－6 建筑企业按增加值排序（2004年）
Construction Enterprises in Order of Value-added (2004)

序号 Order	企业名称 Name of Enterprises	序号 Order	企业名称 Name of Enterprises
1	广厦重庆第一建筑集团有限公司	26	重庆市渝万建设集团有限公司
2	中国十八冶金建设公司	27	重庆伟太建筑工程有限公司
3	重庆第二建设有限公司	28	重庆北部双龙建设(集团)有限公司
4	中铁八局集团第一工程有限公司	29	江津市第十建筑工程有限公司
5	重庆市第七建筑工程有限责任公司	30	重庆巴洲建筑安装工程有限公司
6	重庆市一品建设集团有限公司	31	中铁十一局集团第五工程有限公司
7	重庆长安建设工程有限公司	32	重庆市巴南建设（集团）有限公司
8	重庆市渝通公路工程总公司	33	重庆隆西建设集团有限公司
9	重庆第九建设有限公司	34	重庆中发建筑工程有限公司
10	重庆工业设备安装集团有限公司	35	九龙坡区金凤建筑（集团）有限公司
11	重钢集团建设工程有限公司	36	重庆第六建设有限责任公司
12	重庆住宅建设有限公司	37	重庆南电实业集团有限公司
13	重庆第三建设有限责任公司	38	重庆移通实业总公司
14	重庆渝发建设公司	39	重庆永和建筑工程有限公司
15	重庆电力建设总公司	40	重庆市亚龙建筑工程公司
16	重庆江电实业有限公司	41	重庆覃家岗建筑工程有限公司
17	重庆九龙建设（集团）有限公司	42	重庆市华升建筑工程集团有限公司
18	重庆渝康建筑工程有限公司	43	重庆市江龙建设工程有限公司
19	重庆合营建筑工程有限公司	44	重庆市涪陵建设工程公司
20	重庆市公路工程股份有限公司	45	重庆市渝集建筑工程有限公司
21	重庆市庆华建筑工程有限公司	46	重庆市渝达公路桥梁有限责任公司
22	重庆北部新城建设集团有限公司	47	重庆商社中天物业发展有限公司
23	重庆花溪建设(集团)有限公司	48	长江重庆航道工程局
24	重庆恒滨建设（集团）有限公司	49	重庆渝风建筑工程有限公司
25	重庆市德感建筑安装工程有限公司	50	重庆广信电力建设有限责任公司

20－7 建筑企业按生产用固定资产原值排序（2004年）
Construction Enterprises in Order of Original Value of Productive Fixed Assets (2004)

序号 Order	企业名称 Name of Enterprises	序号 Order	企业名称 Name of Enterprises
1	长江重庆航道工程局	26	重庆市第一市政工程公司
2	重庆移通实业总公司	27	重庆隆西建设集团有限公司
3	中国十八冶金建设公司	28	合川市云门建筑安装工程公司
4	中铁八局集团第一工程有限公司	29	重庆第四建筑工程公司
5	重庆市公路工程股份有限公司	30	重庆市涪陵建设工程公司
6	重庆市渝通公路工程总公司	31	重庆市庆华建筑工程有限公司
7	万州区万河水电配送实业公司	32	重庆市涪陵路桥工程有限公司
8	重钢集团建设工程有限公司	33	重庆市万州区建筑工程总公司
9	重庆电力建设总公司	34	重庆第三建设有限责任公司
10	重庆桥梁工程总公司	35	重庆工业设备安装集团有限公司
11	中铁十一局集团第五工程有限公司	36	重庆荣华建筑集团有限公司
12	重庆市华升建筑工程集团有限公司	37	重庆建筑机械化工程总公司
13	广厦重庆第一建筑集团有限公司	38	重庆南川市公路路桥有限责任公司
14	中电投远达环保工程有限公司	39	重庆九龙建设（集团）有限公司
15	重庆市渝达公路桥梁有限责任公司	40	重庆市涪陵第二建筑总公司
16	重庆市智翔铺道技术工程有限公司	41	重庆市德感建筑安装工程有限公司
17	重庆煤矿建设第十工程处	42	重庆山峡建设工程总公司
18	重庆广信电力建设有限责任公司	43	重庆煤炭第二建筑安装工程公司
19	重庆住宅建设有限公司	44	重庆新市建设有限公司
20	重庆建工集团有限责任公司	45	中国四海工程公司重庆有限公司
21	重庆市金科建筑工程有限公司	46	重庆市银鹰实业集团有限公司
22	重庆市一品建设集团有限公司	47	重庆花溪建设(集团)有限公司
23	重庆第二建设有限公司	48	重庆立信建筑安装工程有限公司
24	重庆市巴南建设（集团）有限公司	49	重庆黄金建设集团有限公司
25	重庆川维建安工程有限公司	50	重庆第六建设有限责任公司

20－8 建筑企业按利税总额排序（2004年）
Construction Enterprises in Order of Pre-tax Profits (2004)

序号 Order	企业名称 Name of Enterprises	序号 Order	企业名称 Name of Enterprises
1	中铁八局集团第一工程有限公司	26	重庆俊鼎建设（集团）有限公司
2	广厦重庆第一建筑集团有限公司	27	重庆工业设备安装集团有限公司
3	重庆市渝通公路工程总公司	28	重庆市庆华建筑工程有限公司
4	重庆江电实业有限公司	29	江津市第十建筑工程有限公司
5	中国十八冶金建设公司	30	中铁十一局集团第五工程有限公司
6	重庆市公路工程股份有限公司	31	重庆移通实业总公司
7	重庆市一品建设集团有限公司	32	秀山县教育建筑有限公司
8	重庆九龙建设（集团）有限公司	33	重庆市渝万建设集团有限公司
9	重庆第三建设有限责任公司	34	重庆元方实业有限公司
10	重庆永和建筑工程有限公司	35	重庆市兴达实业(集团)有限公司
11	重庆恒滨建设（集团）有限公司	36	重庆北部双龙建设(集团)有限公司
12	重庆合营建筑工程有限公司	37	重庆煤矿建设第五工程处
13	重庆住宅建设有限公司	38	重庆隆西建设集团有限公司
14	重钢集团建设工程有限公司	39	重庆市黔江振兴实业集团有限公司
15	重庆第二建设有限公司	40	重庆市华升建筑工程集团有限公司
16	重庆长安建设工程有限公司	41	重庆市智翔铺道技术工程有限公司
17	重庆市渝达公路桥梁有限责任公司	42	重庆深港机电消防工程有限公司
18	重庆商社中天物业发展有限公司	43	重庆伟太建筑工程有限公司
19	重庆电力建设总公司	44	重庆市博海集团建筑工程有限公司
20	重庆渝发建设公司	45	重庆花溪建设(集团)有限公司
21	重庆渝康建筑工程有限公司	46	九龙坡区金凤建筑（集团）有限公司
22	重庆南电实业集团有限公司	47	重庆明华建筑安装有限责任公司
23	中电投远达环保工程有限公司	48	重庆渝堰土木建筑工程有限公司
24	重庆友诚水电建设有限公司	49	重庆先华建设集团有限公司
25	重庆第九建设有限公司	50	重庆新力时代建筑工程有限公司

20—9 房地产开发企业按投资额排序（2004年）
Real Estate Development Enterprises in Order of Investment (2004)

序号 Order	企业名称 Name of Enterprises	序号 Order	企业名称 Name of Enterprises
1	重庆华宇物业（集团）有限公司	26	重庆东原房地产开发有限公司
2	重庆佳辰经济发展有限公司	27	重庆鲁能开发（集团）有限公司
3	融侨长江（重庆）房地产有限公司	28	重庆鑫隆达房地产开发有限公司
4	和记黄埔地产（重庆南岸）有限公司	29	重庆洋世达房地产开发有限公司
5	重庆南方集团有限公司	30	永川市名豪物业发展有限公司
6	重庆隆鑫置业有限责任公司	31	重庆嘉发实业有限公司
7	重庆光华房地产开发有限公司	32	重庆珠江实业有限公司
8	重庆渝高科技产业（集团）股份有限公司	33	重庆建工集团有限责任公司
9	重庆业瑞房地产开发有限公司	34	重庆宏源房地产开发公司
10	重庆同创置业集团有限公司	35	重庆弘景房地产开发有限公司
11	重庆龙湖地产发展有限公司	36	重庆斌鑫物业（集团）有限公司
12	重庆天人房地产开发有限公司	37	金融街重庆置业有限公司
13	重庆汇金置业有限公司	38	重庆丹龙实业（集团）有限公司
14	重庆协信城市建设发展有限公司	39	重庆市明瑜实业有限公司
15	重庆建工集团房地产开发有限公司	40	重庆渝能置业发展有限公司
16	重庆世家地产发展有限公司	41	融侨锦江（重庆）房地产有限公司
17	重庆聚富房地产开发有限公司	42	重庆宏帆实业有限公司
18	重庆正升置业有限公司	43	重庆庆隆屋业发展有限公司
19	重庆市鸿程房地产发展公司	44	重庆康田置业有限公司
20	重庆黑格实业(集团)有限公司	45	重庆升伟房地产集团有限公司
21	重庆钢铁集团朵力房地产股份有限公司	46	重庆交院江南大学城置业有限公司
22	重庆海宇置业（集团）有限公司	47	重庆锦天置业（集团）有限公司
23	重庆浦辉房地产开发有限公司	48	广厦重庆置业发展有限公司
24	龙庆物业发展（重庆）有限公司	49	重庆嘉华建设开发有限公司
25	重庆贝迪房地产开发有限公司	50	重庆春风实业有限公司

20－10 房地产开发企业按销售额排序（2004年）
Real Estate Development Enterprises in Order of Sales (2004)

序号 Order	企业名称 Name of Enterprises	序号 Order	企业名称 Name of Enterprises
1	重庆华宇物业（集团）有限公司	26	重庆商社中天物业开发有限公司
2	重庆弘景房地产开发有限公司	27	重庆市康德实业(集团)有限公司
3	重庆市鸿程房地产发展公司	28	重庆升伟房地产集团有限公司
4	重庆竟地实业有限公司	29	重庆隆鑫置业有限责任公司
5	重庆通亚房地产开发有限公司	30	重庆钰茂地产有限责任公司
6	融侨长江（重庆）房地产有限公司	31	重庆市兴茂房地产开发有限公司
7	重庆汇金置业有限公司	32	重庆重点工程建设拆迁开发公司
8	重庆港城房地产（集团）有限公司	33	重庆中城置业发展有限公司
9	重庆宏源房地产开发公司	34	重庆天龙房地产开发有限公司
10	重庆康居物业发展有限公司	35	重庆财信江景物业发展有限公司
11	重庆嘉发实业有限公司	36	重庆新原兴企业集团有限公司
12	重庆香江高科地产发展有限公司	37	和记黄埔地产（重庆江北）有限公司
13	重庆庆丰实业有限公司	38	重庆南方集团有限公司
14	龙庆物业发展（重庆）有限公司	39	重庆东海房地产开发有限公司
15	重庆钢铁集团朵力房地产股份有限公司	40	重庆泰正（集团）有限公司
16	重庆天合物业发展有限责任公司	41	重庆市华南房地产开发有限公司
17	重庆晋愉地产（集团）股份有限公司	42	永川市名豪物业发展有限公司
18	重庆中渝物业发展有限公司	43	重庆斌鑫物业（集团）有限公司
19	重庆中安房地产开发有限公司	44	重庆光华房地产开发有限公司
20	重庆金鹏物业（集团）有限公司	45	重庆锦辉物业发展有限公司
21	重庆建工集团有限责任公司	46	重庆金阳房地产开发有限公司
22	重庆旭庆房地产开发有限公司	47	重庆皇冠建设开发有限公司
23	重庆名豪实业（集团）股份有限公司	48	重庆长寿光宇开发有限公司
24	重庆市新城开发建设股份有限公司	49	重庆长安房地产开发有限公司
25	重庆顺祥房地产开发有限公司	50	重庆浦辉房地产开发有限公司

20－11 房地产开发企业按销售面积排序（2004年）
Real Estate Development Enterprises in Order of Floor Space of Sales (2004)

序号 Order	企业名称 Name of Enterprises	序号 Order	企业名称 Name of Enterprises
1	重庆华宇物业（集团）有限公司	26	重庆渝复房地产开发有限公司
2	重庆市鸿程房地产发展公司	27	重庆重点工程建设拆迁开发公司
3	重庆天合物业发展有限责任公司	28	重庆升伟房地产集团有限公司
4	重庆康居物业发展有限公司	29	重庆东海房地产开发有限公司
5	重庆汇金置业有限公司	30	重庆隆鑫置业有限责任公司
6	重庆市兴茂房地产开发有限公司	31	重庆市万州海托房地产开发有限公司
7	重庆市新城开发建设股份有限公司	32	重庆南岸长生开发实业有限公司
8	重庆中渝物业发展有限公司	33	重庆国闳置业(集团)有限公司
9	融侨长江（重庆）房地产有限公司	34	重庆锦辉物业发展有限公司
10	重庆竟地实业有限公司	35	大足县华丰有限责任公司
11	重庆名豪实业（集团）股份有限公司	36	重庆香江高科地产发展有限公司
12	重庆旭庆房地产开发有限公司	37	重庆黄阁堡房地产开发有限公司
13	重庆嘉发实业有限公司	38	重庆斌鑫物业（集团）有限公司
14	重庆钢铁集团朵力房地产股份有限公司	39	重庆开宇房地产开发有限公司
15	重庆正华物业发展有限公司	40	重庆天龙房地产开发有限公司
16	重庆庆丰实业有限公司	41	重庆新原兴企业集团有限公司
17	重庆钰茂地产有限责任公司	42	重庆银建房地产开发有限公司
18	重庆宏源房地产开发公司	43	重庆商社中天物业开发有限公司
19	重庆建工集团有限责任公司	44	江津市建宇房地产开发有限责任公司
20	重庆晋愉地产（集团）股份有限公司	45	重庆武城房地产开发有限公司
21	永川市名豪物业发展有限公司	46	重庆泰正（集团）有限公司
22	重庆长安房地产开发有限公司	47	重庆市静观房地产开发有限公司
23	重庆弘景房地产开发有限公司	48	重庆市正德房地产开发有限公司
24	重庆长寿光宇开发有限公司	49	重庆南方集团有限公司
25	重庆通亚房地产开发有限公司	50	重庆金鹏物业（集团）有限公司

20－12 高新技术产品销售收入超亿元企业排序（2004年）
Enterprises in Order of Sales of High-tech Products over 100 Million Yuan (2004)

序号 Order	企业名称 Name of Enterprises	序号 Order	企业名称 Name of Enterprises
1	重庆长安汽车股份有限公司	38	重庆朝阳气体有限公司
2	长安福特汽车有限公司	39	重庆市三峡牧业集团有限公司
3	重庆长安铃木汽车有限公司	40	重庆超力电器有限责任公司
4	重庆力帆实业（集团）有限公司	41	重庆长安跨越车辆有限公司
5	重庆隆鑫汽油机公司	42	重庆普天通信设备有限公司
6	建设工业（集团）有限责任公司	43	重庆涪陵金帝集团
7	格力电器（重庆）有限公司	44	重庆徐巷电子有限公司
8	中国嘉陵工业股份有限公司（集团 ）	45	重庆爱立信通讯有限公司
9	西南铝业（集团）有限责任公司	46	重庆长丰宽带通信技术产业有限公司
10	重庆信威通信技术有限责任公司	47	重庆宗申机车工业制造有限公司
11	重庆ABB变压器有限公司	48	重庆飞亚实业公司
12	太极集团涪陵制药厂	49	重庆世纪精信实业有限公司
13	重庆宗申发动机制造有限公司	50	西南药业股份有限公司
14	重庆国际复合材料有限公司	51	重庆宝井钢材加工配送有限公司
15	重庆青山工业责任有限公司	52	重庆市涪陵榨菜（集团）有限公司
16	UT斯达康(重庆)通讯有限公司	53	重庆拓源华冠碳素有限公司
17	中国石化集团四川维尼纶厂	54	重庆四维瓷业（集团）股份有限公司
18	重庆美心（集团）有限公司	55	百力通(重庆)发动机有限公司
19	重庆银钢科技(集团)有限公司	56	重庆华立控股股份有限公司
20	重庆精通工业集团有限公司	57	西南计算机有限责任公司
21	重庆清华紫光英力天然气化工有责任限公司	58	重庆海特实业有限公司
22	重庆市迪马特种汽车制造有限公司	59	重庆华洋电器有限公司
23	重庆齿轮箱有限责任公司	60	重庆金美通讯有限责任公司
24	重庆大足红蝶锶业有限公司	61	重庆市巴南区吉力电装品厂
25	嘉陵本田发动机有限公司	62	四川固体电路研究所
26	中国石化股份重庆一坪润滑油分公司	63	重庆涪陵三海兰陵有限责任公司
27	攀钢集团重庆钛业股份有限公司	64	江津增压器厂
28	重庆捷力轮毂制造有限公司	65	重庆嘉陵化学制品有限公司
29	重庆药友制药有限责任公司	66	重庆汽车空调器有限责任公司
30	重庆长江轴承工业有限公司	67	重庆东软金算盘软件有限公司
31	扬子乙酰化工有限公司	68	和记奥普泰通信技术有限公司
32	国营重型铸锻厂	69	重庆华孚工业股份有限公司
33	重庆三峡油漆股份有限公司	70	重庆博联变压器有限公司
34	重庆佳辰经济发展有限公司	71	重庆耐德工业股份有限公司
35	重庆中电投远达环保工程有限公司	72	太极集团重庆桐君阁药厂
36	重庆天友乳业股份有限公司	73	重庆宗申汽车发动机制造有限公司
37	重庆华邦制药股份有限公司	74	重庆庆佳电子有限公司

20－13 高新技术产品实现利税上千万元企业排序（2004年）
Enterprises in Order of Pre-tax Profits of High-tech Products over 10 Million Yuan (2004)

序号 Order	企业名称 Name of Enterprises	序号 Order	企业名称 Name of Enterprises
1	重庆长安汽车股份有限公司	47	重庆中电投远达环保工程有限公司
2	长安福特汽车有限公司	48	重庆华立控股股份有限公司
3	重庆长安铃木汽车有限公司	49	重庆金美通讯有限责任公司
4	太极集团涪陵制药厂	50	重庆三峡油漆股份有限公司
5	重庆佳辰经济发展有限公司	51	UT斯达康(重庆)通讯有限公司
6	重庆国际复合材料有限公司	52	江津增压器厂
7	扬子乙酰化工有限公司	53	重庆华陶瓷业有限公司
8	重庆药友制药有限责任公司	54	煤炭科学研究总院重庆分院
9	中国石化集团四川维尼纶厂	55	重庆汉光电子工程有限责任公司
10	重庆大足红蝶锶业有限公司	56	重庆集诚汽车电子有限责任公司
11	重庆龙湖地产发展有限公司	57	中国石化股份重庆一坪润滑油分公司
12	西南药业股份有限公司	58	重庆机床厂
13	重庆ABB变压器有限公司	59	重庆川仪总厂有限公司重庆川仪十八厂
14	重庆宗申发动机制造有限公司	60	重庆西源凸轮轴有限公司
15	中国嘉陵工业股份有限公司（集团）	61	重庆大桥化工有限公司
16	重庆隆鑫汽油机公司	62	重庆飞亚实业公司
17	西南铝业（集团）有限责任公司	63	重庆红江机械厂
18	重庆美心（集团）有限公司	64	重庆捷力轮毂制造有限公司
19	攀钢集团重庆钛业股份有限公司	65	重庆新华多媒体发展有限公司
20	重庆市迪马特种汽车制造有限公司	66	重庆华森制药有限公司
21	重庆徐巷电子有限公司	67	重庆八菱汽车配件有限责任公司
22	重庆长江轴承工业有限公司	68	重庆葛洲坝易普力化工有限公司
23	重庆四维瓷业（集团）股份有限公司	69	林同炎国际（重庆）工程咨询有限公司
24	重庆汽车研究所	70	重庆三峡光盘发展有限责任公司
25	重庆华邦制药股份有限公司	71	重庆宝井钢材加工配送有限公司
26	重庆青山工业责任有限公司	72	重庆博联变压器有限公司
27	重庆力帆实业（集团）有限公司	73	重庆市玻璃纤维厂
28	重庆华孚工业股份有限公司	74	重庆新泰机械制造有限责任公司
29	重庆大新药业股份有限公司	75	重庆宗申机车工业制造有限公司
30	重庆清华紫光英力天然气化工有责任限公司	76	重庆市涪陵建筑陶瓷集团有限公司
31	嘉陵本田发动机有限公司	77	重庆庆佳电子有限公司
32	重庆长风机器有限责任公司	78	重庆耐德工业股份有限公司
33	重庆齿轮箱有限责任公司	79	重庆赛迪工业炉有限公司
34	重庆李尔长安汽车内饰件有限公司	80	重庆市三峡牧业集团有限公司
35	重庆东方药业股份有限公司	81	重庆水泵厂有限责任公司
36	重庆海特实业有限公司	82	重庆市电信规划设计院有限公司
37	重庆信威通信技术有限责任公司	83	重庆宗申汽车发动机制造有限公司
38	百力通(重庆)发动机有限公司	84	重庆美联制药有限公司
39	重庆天友乳业股份有限公司	85	重庆力宏精细化工有限公司
40	建设工业（集团）有限责任公司	86	重庆市天友乳业股份有限公司乳品二厂
41	重庆超力电器有限责任公司	87	重庆长安跨越车辆有限公司
42	重庆博恩科技有限公司	88	重庆市涪陵榨菜（集团）有限公司
43	重庆广播电视网络传输有限责任公司	89	重庆合盛工业有限公司
44	太极集团重庆桐君阁药厂	90	重庆莱美药业有限公司
45	重庆东软金算盘软件有限公司	91	重庆川仪十一厂有限公司
46	重庆赛力盟电机有限责任公司	92	重庆涪陵金帝集团

20－14 大中型工业企业按科技活动人员数排序（2004年）
Large & Medium-sized Industrial Enterprises in Order of Personnel in Scientific and Technological Activities (2004)

序号 Order	企业名称 Name of Enterprises	序号 Order	企业名称 Name of Enterprises
1	重庆市红岩汽车有限责任公司	26	重庆宇通客车有限公司
2	西南铝业（集团）有限责任公司	27	重庆长江电工(集团)有限公司
3	长安汽车（集团）有限责任公司	28	重庆鼎泰铝业有限公司
4	重庆钢铁股份有限公司	29	重庆市三峡牧业集团有限公司
5	重庆美心（集团）有限公司	30	重庆四钢钢业有限责任公司
6	重庆长安汽车股份有限公司	31	綦江齿轮传动有限公司
7	重庆川仪总厂有限公司	32	中石化股份有限公司重庆一坪润滑油分公司
8	重庆建设工业有限责任公司	33	太极集团涪陵制药厂
9	重庆力帆实业（集团）有限公司	34	重庆齿轮箱有限责任公司
10	重庆潍柴发动机厂	35	重庆市博赛矿业集团有限公司
11	重庆望江工业有限公司	36	重庆市涪陵水利电力投资集团有限责任公司
12	重庆大江信达车辆股份有限公司	37	重庆红宇精密工业有限责任公司
13	庆铃汽车集团有限公司	38	中国核工业建峰化工总厂
14	重庆市电力公司	39	重庆水轮机厂有限责任公司
15	西南计算机有限责任公司	40	重庆红岩长力汽车弹簧有限公司
16	西南合成制药股份有限公司	41	中国石化集团四川维尼纶厂
17	重庆建设摩托车股份有限公司	42	重庆红江机械厂
18	重庆机床厂	43	长安福特汽车有限公司
19	重庆四维瓷业（集团）股份有限公司	44	重庆长风机器有限责任公司
20	国营重庆重型铸锻厂	45	重庆啤酒股份有限公司
21	中国嘉陵工业股份有限公司（集团）	46	重庆起重机厂
22	重庆力之星机车制造有限责任公司	47	重庆市涪陵榨菜(集团)有限公司
23	重庆松藻煤电有限责任公司	48	重庆重大高科技股份有限公司
24	重庆南桐矿业有限责任公司	49	重庆金美通信有限责任公司
25	重庆巴山仪器厂	50	重庆耐德工业股份有限公司

20－15 大中型工业企业按科技活动经费支出排序（2004年）
Large & Medium-sized Industrial Enterprises in Order of Funds Expenditure for Scientific and Technological Activities (2004)

序号 Order	企业名称 Name of Enterprises	序号 Order	企业名称 Name of Enterprises
1	重庆力帆实业（集团）有限公司	26	重庆大江信达车辆股份有限公司
2	重庆钢铁股份有限公司	27	重庆长安铃木汽车有限公司
3	长安福特汽车有限公司	28	重庆华诚四棉纺织有限公司
4	庆铃汽车集团有限公司	29	重庆望江工业有限公司
5	重庆建设工业有限责任公司	30	重庆市万利来化工股份有限公司
6	重庆长安汽车股份有限公司	31	重庆华帮制药股份有限公司
7	重庆机床厂	32	太极集团涪陵制药厂
8	西南铝业（集团）有限责任公司	33	重庆华强化肥有限公司
9	重庆重钢集团钢管有限公司	34	重庆美心（集团）有限公司
10	重庆建设摩托车股份有限公司	35	重庆银翔摩托车集团有限公司
11	中国嘉陵工业股份有限公司（集团）	36	西南计算机有限责任公司
12	重庆长风机器有限责任公司	37	重庆隆鑫工业集团有限公司
13	重庆川仪总厂有限公司	38	重庆起重机厂
14	中国石化集团四川维尼纶厂	39	重庆通用工业（集团）有阴责任公司
15	长安汽车（集团）有限责任公司	40	重庆清华紫光英力天然气化工有限责任公司
16	中化重庆涪陵化工有限公司	41	重庆江北化肥有限公司
17	重庆市富源化工有限责任公司	42	重庆劲隆科技集团有限公司
18	重庆红宇精密工业有限责任公司	43	重庆检测仪表厂
19	重庆齿轮箱有限责任公司	44	重庆青山工业有限责任公司
20	重庆力之星机车制造有限责任公司	45	中国核工业建峰化工总厂
21	重庆市电力公司	46	重庆康明斯发动机有限公司
22	重庆精通工业集团有限公司	47	重庆鼎发实业股份有限公司
23	重庆巴山仪器厂	48	中石化股份有限公司重庆一坪润滑油分公司
24	嘉陵本田发动机有限公司	49	重庆长安跨越车辆有限公司
25	重庆潍柴发动机厂	50	西南合成制药股份有限公司

20－16 大中型工业企业按科技活动经费支出占产品销售收入比重排序（2004年）

Large & Medium-sized Industrial Enterprises in Order of Expenditure of Funds for Scientific and Technological Activities as Percentage of Sales Revenue (2004)

序号 Order	企业名称 Name of Enterprises
1	重庆巴山仪器厂
2	重庆机床厂
3	重庆长风机器有限责任公司
4	重庆重钢集团钢管有限公司
5	重庆市万利来化工股份有限公司
6	重庆重大高科技股份有限公司
7	重庆市富源化工有限责任公司
8	重庆起重机厂
9	重庆龙章铜版纸厂
10	重庆红江机械厂
11	重庆华诚四棉纺织有限公司
12	重庆华森万元纸业有限责任公司
13	重庆华强化肥有限公司
14	重庆海通机械制造集团
15	西南计算机有限责任公司
16	重庆朝华晶化石有限公司
17	重庆锦晖陶瓷有限公司
18	重庆虎溪电机厂
19	重庆通用工业（集团）有阴责任公司
20	重庆工具厂
21	重庆綦江汽车半轴厂
22	重庆江北化肥有限公司
23	重庆华江印务有限责任公司
24	重庆特种电机厂
25	重庆正川玻璃有限公司
26	重庆华伟工业集团有限责任公司
27	重庆精通工业集团有限公司
28	重庆金美通信有限责任公司
29	重庆三五三三印染服装总厂
30	重庆红岩长力汽车弹簧有限公司
31	重庆驰骋轻型汽车部件股份有限公司
32	重庆市江东机械有限责任公司
33	重庆力之星机车制造有限责任公司
34	重庆耐德工业股份有限公司
35	重庆华帮制药股份有限公司
36	重庆市海伦地毯有限公司
37	重庆市涪陵建筑陶瓷集团有限公司
38	重庆长安跨越车辆有限公司
39	重庆气体压缩机厂有限责任公司
40	重庆利时德拉索系统有限公司
41	重庆市传动轴股份有限公司
42	重庆华陶瓷业有限公司
43	重庆鼎发实业股份有限公司
44	国营建安仪器厂
45	重庆大川门业集团有限公司
46	重庆市长河煤矿
47	中石化股份有限公司重庆一坪润滑油分公司
48	重庆华孚工业股份有限公司
49	嘉陵本田发动机有限公司
50	重庆清华紫光英力天然气化工有限责任公司

20－17 大中型工业企业按研究与试验发展经费支出占产品销售收入比重排序（2004年）

Large & Medium-sized Industrial Enterprises in Order of R&D Expenditure as Percentage of Sales Revenue (2004)

序号 Order	企业名称 Name of Enterprises	序号 Order	企业名称 Name of Enterprises
1	重庆重钢集团钢管有限公司	26	长安汽车（集团）有限责任公司
2	重庆龙章铜版纸厂	27	重庆齿轮箱有限责任公司
3	重庆华强化肥有限公司	28	西南计算机有限责任公司
4	重庆朝华晶化石有限公司	29	重庆市传动轴股份有限公司
5	重庆通用工业（集团）有阴责任公司	30	重庆华森制药有限公司
6	重庆华诚四棉纺织有限公司	31	重庆四维瓷业（集团）股份有限公司
7	重庆綦江汽车半轴厂	32	重庆建设工业有限责任公司
8	重庆华伟工业集团有限责任公司	33	重庆华渝电气仪表总厂
9	重庆特种电机厂	34	重庆庆佳电子有限公司
10	重庆三五三三印染服装总厂	35	重庆市江津酒厂（集团）有限公司
11	重庆重大高科技股份有限公司	36	重庆川仪总厂有限公司
12	重庆耐德工业股份有限公司	37	重庆银钢科技集团有限公司
13	重庆华帮制药股份有限公司	38	重庆工具厂
14	重庆市涪陵建筑陶瓷集团有限公司	39	重庆江北机械有限责任公司
15	重庆市江东机械有限责任公司	40	重庆长江涂装机械厂
16	重庆利时德拉索系统有限公司	41	重庆新时代摩托车有限责任公司
17	重庆力之星机车制造有限责任公司	42	重庆民丰农化股份有限公司
18	重庆华陶瓷业有限公司	43	綦江齿轮传动有限公司
19	中石化股份有限公司重庆一坪润滑油分公司	44	重庆川仪有限公司
20	重庆古华畜产有限公司	45	重庆市博联变压器有限公司
21	重庆检测仪表厂	46	重庆药友制药有限责任公司
22	国营建安仪器厂	47	重庆云河实业（集团）有限公司忠州水轮机厂
23	中化重庆涪陵化工有限公司	48	重庆潍柴发动机厂
24	煤炭科学研究总院重庆分院	49	重庆三爱海陵实业有限责任公司
25	重庆市水泵厂有限责任公司	50	重庆顾地塑胶电器有限公司

20－18 大中型工业企业目录（2004年）
List of Large & Medium-sized Industrial Enterprises (2004)

企业名称 Name of Enterprises	企业详细地址 Address	电话号码 Tel.
重庆清平机械厂	重庆市万州区高梁镇新店子	67659230
重庆市太白酒厂	重庆市万州区天城镇塘坊	58415004
重庆长江涂装机械厂	重庆市万州区天城大道123号	58325456
重庆飞亚实业公司(重庆昊元集团)	重庆市万州区黄泥包8号	58355366
白猫(重庆)有限公司	重庆市万州区万忠路191号	58800850
重庆谭木匠工艺品有限公司	重庆市万州区双河口	58830950
重庆市江东机械有限责任公司	重庆市万州区五桥百安大道1008号	58555111
万州环球陶瓷有限公司	重庆市万州区天城镇	58412207
重庆东方药业股份有限公司	重庆市万州区王牌路1378号	58981677
重庆市三峡牧业集团有限公司	重庆市万州区沙龙路三段218号	58965575
重庆迪康长江制药有限公司	重庆市万州区五桥街道民安社区	87502888
海康纺织(集团)有限公司	重庆市万州区王牌路698号	58115392
重庆三峡水利电力(集团)股份有限公司	重庆市万州区鸽子沟72号	58251834
重庆万州鱼泉榨菜有限公司	重庆市万州区外贸路98号	58967099
重庆万光电源股份有限公司	重庆市万州区观音岩万丰路299号	58965872
重庆三峡果业集团有限公司	重庆市万州区申明凤仙路466号	58367102
重庆万兴烟叶有限责任公司	重庆市万州区申明大道248号	58367199
重庆索特盐化股份有限公司	重庆市万州区观音岩1号	58960318
重庆华森万元纸业有限责任公司	重庆市万州区南山社区	58529421
中国核工业建峰化工总厂	重庆市涪陵区白涛镇麦子坪	72591442
国营川东造船厂	重庆市涪陵区李渡镇双河口	72145129
太极集团涪陵制药厂	重庆市涪陵区百花路8号	72800440
重庆市博联变压器有限公司	重庆市涪陵区乌江路21号	72230220
重庆涪陵安成燃气有限责任公司	重庆市涪陵区涪陵广场环路14号	72244394
重庆市涪陵金帝工业集团有限公司	重庆市涪陵区涪清路233号	72280008
涪陵宏声(集团)有限责任公司	重庆市涪陵区兴华路中段8号	62906948
重庆市涪陵榨菜(集团)有限公司	重庆市涪陵区体育南路29号	72234067
重庆市涪陵区自来水公司	重庆市涪陵区涪陵新华中路39号	72862447
重庆市涪陵娃哈哈饮料有限公司	重庆市涪陵区涪陵兴华西路58号	72802580
重庆市东升铝业股份有限公司	重庆市涪陵区清溪镇四合村	64669080
重庆市涪陵建筑陶瓷集团有限公司	重庆市涪陵区江东涪清路31号	72374058
中化重庆涪陵化工有限公司	重庆市涪陵区黎明路二号	72884093
重庆三爱海陵实业有限责任公司	重庆市涪陵区人民东路50号	85686680
重庆市涪陵闽发金属制造有限公司	重庆市涪陵区义和镇大鹅村	72109017
重庆朝华晶化石有限公司	重庆市涪陵区李渡镇大石庙	72100789
重庆市涪陵水利电力投资集团有限责任公司	重庆市涪陵区望州路5号	72286171
重庆市自来水公司	重庆市渝中区金汤街81号	63835624
重庆海浪科技实业集团有限公司	重庆市渝中区虎头岩1号	68591512
重庆市电力公司	重庆市渝中区中山三路21号	63682063
重庆新华化工厂	重庆市渝中区平安街174号	68811039
重庆电池总厂	重庆市渝中区平安街175号	68813004
重庆特种电机厂	重庆市渝中区龙隐路48号	63312701
重庆市天友乳业股份有限公司	重庆市渝中区中山三路121号中山大厦7楼	63871568

20-18 续表1 CONTINUED-1

企业名称 Name of Enterprises	企业详细地址 Address	电话号码 Tel.
重庆红岩长力汽车弹簧有限公司	重庆市渝中区龙隐路2号	63310245
重庆卡福汽车制动转向系统有限公司	重庆市渝中区红岩村91号	89053637
重庆中南橡胶有限公司	重庆市渝中区化龙桥正街48号	63310055
国营重庆重型铸锻厂	重庆市大渡口区长征村	68541510
重庆钢铁股份有限公司	重庆市大渡口区钢铁路30号	68845566
重钢产业公司	重庆市大渡口区大堰三村路口	68845262
重庆三钢钢业有限责任公司	重庆市大渡口区茄子溪刘家坝	61584019
重庆大正肉类食品有限公司	重庆市大渡口区陈家坝15号	68554938
重庆嘉威啤酒有限公司	重庆市大渡口区八桥镇建桥工业园金桥路17号	68910338
重庆大渡口区利德工业制造有限公司	重庆市大渡口区八桥镇双山村156号	68910107
重庆钢铁集团产业有限公司	重庆市大渡口区大堰三村路口	68842979
重庆钢铁集团矿业有限公司	重庆市大渡口区大堰一村	68846964
重庆市玻璃纤维厂	重庆市大渡口区庹家坳	68908148
重庆钢铁集团机械制造有限责任公司	重庆市大渡口区石槽门	68846762
重庆小南海水泥厂	重庆市大渡口区跳磴镇白沙沱	68530688
重庆钢铁集团电子有限责任公司	重庆市大渡口区钢花路5号	68846178
重庆国际复合材料有限公司	重庆市大渡口区建胜镇建胜正街118号	89090568
重庆朝阳气体有限公司	重庆市大渡口区钢铁路1号	68423643
重庆秋田齿轮有限责任公司	重庆市大渡口区八桥镇双山村168号	68908542
重庆精通工业集团有限公司	重庆市大渡口区八桥镇建桥工业园金桥路8号	68903999
重庆沪渝塑料五金有限公司	重庆市大渡口区八桥镇桥梓塘村7社	68900686
重庆今普食品有限公司	重庆市大渡口区八桥镇建桥工业园区	61589166
重庆前卫仪表厂	重庆市江北区大石坝三村	67076391
重庆光电仪器有限公司	重庆市江北区电测村252号一楼	67507333
重庆东风船舶工业公司	重庆市江北区唐家沱东风一村1号	67780390
长安汽车（集团）有限责任公司	重庆市江北区建新东路260号	67590114
重庆燃气（集团）有限责任公司	重庆市江北区嘉陵四村1号	67850685
重庆通用工业（集团）有限责任公司	重庆市江北区石马河玉带山1号	67658834
重庆长安汽车股份有限公司	重庆市江北区建新东路260号	67590114
重庆长安跨越车辆有限公司	重庆市江北区鲤鱼池三村44号	67865139
重庆天人汽车车身制造有限公司	重庆市江北区唐家沱太平冲村	67783888
重庆通用机械工业公司	重庆市江北区观音桥建新北路一支路58号	67850693
重庆天原化工总厂	重庆市江北区建新西路34号	67771956
重庆登康口腔护理用品股份有限公司	重庆市江北区兴隆桥正街57号	67015858
重庆江利机器厂	重庆市江北区大石坝	67936354
江川机械厂	重庆市江北区大石坝五村88-1号	67932448
重庆必扬企业（集团）有限公司	重庆市江北区石马河南桥寺必扬工业园	67653204
重庆龙章铜版纸厂	重庆市江北区建新西路52号	67772693
重庆耐德工业股份有限公司	重庆市江北区电仪村49号	67855563
重庆长安汽车配件总厂	重庆市江北区雨花村174号	67592297
白猫（重庆）日化有限公司	重庆市江北区建新西路17号	67855722
重庆茂源实业公司	重庆市江北区寸滩茅溪白云村30号	67121172
西南合成制药股份有限公司	重庆市江北区寸滩水口	67505609
重庆长安汽车电器股份有限公司	重庆市江北区长安厂建国村58号	67870987

20-18 续表2 CONTINUED-2

企业名称 Name of Enterprises	企业详细地址 Address	电话号码 Tel.
重庆李尔长安汽车内饰件有限责任公司	重庆市江北区鲤鱼池三村42号	67738818
奥妮化妆品有限公司	重庆市江北区建新西路11号	67703751
重庆利时德拉索系统有限公司	重庆市江北区电测村4号	67515414
重庆中法供水有限公司	重庆市江北区石马河河嘴1号	67651404
望江铃木发动机有限责任公司	重庆市江北区铁山村	67110810
重庆康佳电子有限公司	重庆市江北区下石门1号	67516164
重庆庆佳电子有限公司	重庆市江北区电测村1号	67520531
重庆检测仪表厂	重庆市江北区电测村4号	67505292
重庆前卫克罗姆表业有限责任公司	重庆市江北区大石坝三村	67075720
重庆好媳妇食品研究所	重庆市江北区唐家沱马鞍村大塘口	67781385
重庆市山城燃气设备有限公司	重庆市江北区石马河南桥寺	67654656
重庆凯源石油天然气有限责任公司	重庆市江北区大庆村	67311155
重庆秦川工贸有限公司	重庆市江北区建新东路260号	67668251
重庆长安金陵汽车零部件有限公司	重庆市江北区鲤鱼池世纪中环大厦四楼	67591613
重庆望江工业有限公司	重庆市江北区郭家沱	67110021
中国嘉陵工业股份有限公司（集团）	重庆市沙坪坝区自由村100号	65190114
重庆轴承工业公司	重庆市沙坪坝区石小路60号	65317987
西南药业股份有限公司	重庆市沙坪坝区天星桥21号	89855366
重庆跨越（集团）股份有限公司	重庆市沙坪坝区沙坪公园58号	65300180
中国嘉陵工业有限公司	重庆市沙坪坝区自由村100号	65190114
重庆金美通信有限责任公司	重庆市沙坪坝区童家桥街小杨公桥51号	61705322
重庆虎溪电机厂	重庆市沙坪坝区陈家桥镇陈电路1号	65625226
重庆市水泵厂有限责任公司	重庆市沙坪坝区小正街340号	65312261
重庆铝制品加工厂	重庆市沙坪坝区新桥石梯沟20号	65210813
重庆华孚工业股份有限公司	重庆市沙坪坝区凤天大道18号	65225669
重庆气体压缩机厂有限责任公司	重庆市沙坪坝区上桥东风新4村1号	65237534
重庆锻造厂	重庆市沙坪坝区上桥五星村1号	65209400
重庆华诚第一棉纺织厂	重庆市沙坪坝区土湾胜利村100号	65400500
重庆市爱华机电有限公司	重庆市沙坪坝区杨梨路160号	65409904
重庆华洋电器有限公司	重庆市沙坪坝区井口镇南溪经济园57号	65156457
重庆康达机械（集团）有限责任公司	重庆市沙坪坝区井口镇井口工业园	65370744
重庆金仑机械制造有限责任公司	重庆市沙坪坝区新桥朝阳山22号	89851308
重庆新世纪电气有限公司	重庆市沙坪坝区渝碚路39号	65317819
重庆嘉华摩托车曲轴工业有限公司	重庆市沙坪坝区井口镇二塘村杨家滩社	65183731
重庆民丰农化股份有限公司	重庆市沙坪坝区井口经济桥30号	65180568
重庆市青木关煤矿	重庆市沙坪坝区青木关镇关口20号	65603778
重庆飞达表面处理中心	重庆市沙坪坝区青木关镇青木湖	65601188
重庆长安减震器有限公司	重庆市沙坪坝区凤凰镇杨家庙	89095666
煤炭科学研究总院重庆分院	重庆市沙坪坝区上桥三村55号	65239218
重庆重大高科技股份有限公司	重庆市沙坪坝区沙正街174号	65121947
重庆市传动轴股份有限公司	重庆市沙坪坝区陈电路97号	63633201
重庆大川门业集团有限公司	重庆市沙坪坝区童家桥正街	89053041
重庆油泵油咀厂	重庆市沙坪坝区先锋街瓦窑沟78号	65294499
重庆新汇源高压开关有限公司	重庆市沙坪坝区磁建村1号	65474835

20-18 续表3 CONTINUED-3

企业名称 Name of Enterprises	企业详细地址 Address	电话号码 Tel.
重庆长江轴承有限公司	重庆市沙坪坝区联芳经济园区联芳桥5号	68616550
重庆康明斯发动机有限公司	重庆市沙坪坝区壮志路100号	65335888
重庆智能实业有限公司	重庆市沙坪坝区井口镇南溪经济园42号	65170021
重庆探矿机械厂	重庆市沙坪坝区快乐里1号	65404314
重庆市旺成汽车配件制造有限责任公司	重庆市沙坪坝区井口镇工业园	65184179
重庆雁山机械制造（集团）有限公司	重庆市沙坪坝区中梁镇新兴路1号	65540709
重庆力帆实业（集团）有限公司	重庆市沙坪坝区覃家岗镇上桥张家湾60号	61663017
重庆九方铸造有限公司	重庆市沙坪坝区双碑自由村100号	65194254
重庆渝安创新科技（集团）有限公司	重庆市沙坪坝区覃家岗镇上桥金桥路61-3号	89095666
重庆嘉鹏摩托车制造有限公司	重庆市沙坪坝区井口镇大兴村50号	65189871
重庆华岗机械制造有限公司	重庆市沙坪坝区青木关镇青木湖	65601362
重庆渝安弹簧制造有限公司	重庆市沙坪坝区凤凰镇杨家庙村	89095666
重庆市东华特殊钢有限责任公司	重庆市沙坪坝区团结坝155号	65138989
重庆胜利工业（集团）有限公司	重庆市沙坪坝区虎溪镇石牛岗村	65631228
重庆市志成机械厂	重庆市九龙坡区九龙镇盘龙四村22号	68653366
重庆建设摩托车股份有限公司	重庆市九龙坡区谢正街47号	68810556
重庆普天通信设备有限公司	重庆市九龙坡区石桥铺二郎科技城69号	68466098
重庆巴山仪器厂	重庆市九龙坡区石新路83号	68462037
西南铝业（集团）有限责任公司	重庆市九龙坡区西彭镇	65809118
重庆铁马工业集团有限公司	重庆市九龙坡区杨家坪正街43号	68423523
重庆标准件工业公司	重庆市九龙坡区石新路12号	68610317
重庆啤酒股份有限公司	重庆市九龙坡区石杨路16号	68624393
庆铃汽车(集团)有限公司	重庆市九龙坡区协兴村1号	65262233
重庆建设工业有限责任公司	重庆市九龙坡区谢正街47号	68813741
重庆华邦制药股份有限公司	重庆市九龙坡区科园四街55号	68030903
中国石化集团重庆一坪高级润滑油公司	重庆市九龙坡区渝洲路62号	68799380
重庆新华印刷厂	重庆市九龙坡区兴胜路7号	68825323
重庆建锋摩托配件总厂	重庆市九龙坡区谢家湾谢正街25幢	89127329
重庆长兴工业有限公司	重庆市九龙坡区九龙镇九龙园区火炬大道18号	68881711
重庆环松工业集团有限公司	重庆市九龙坡区华岩镇石堰村七社	65270508
重庆三峡油漆股份有限公司	重庆市九龙坡区石坪桥正街119号	68823076
捷力轮毂制造有限公司	重庆市九龙坡区九龙镇盘龙8村	68821589
重庆聚兴交通工业（集团）有限公司	重庆市九龙坡区玉灵洞208号	68619137
重庆耀勇减震器有限公司	重庆市九龙坡区九龙镇朵力名都8号	68901454
重庆和邦碱胺实业总公司	重庆市九龙坡区铜罐驿镇二居委会	65902713
重庆起重机厂	重庆市九龙坡区起重新村1号	65267774
重庆蓝天工业集团有限公司	重庆市九龙坡区白市驿镇白华西街1号	65702751
重庆中梁山煤电气有限公司	重庆市九龙坡区中梁山田坝二村18栋	65263436
重庆百事天府饮料有限公司	重庆市九龙坡区石坪桥横街7号	68828688
重庆宗申机车工业制造有限公司	重庆市九龙坡区二郎路25号	68460323
重庆秦安机电制造有限公司	重庆市九龙坡区二郎科技园兰美大道701号	61711105
重庆ABB变压器有限公司	重庆市九龙坡区中梁山玉清寺华岩南村1号	65093688
重庆市智能水表有限责任公司	重庆市九龙坡区华岩镇华岩村四社	89809018
重庆三信电子有限公司	重庆市九龙坡区科园四路168号C3楼	68608886

20-18 续表4 CONTINUED-4

企业名称 Name of Enterprises	企业详细地址 Address	电话号码 Tel.
重庆润通工业有限公司	重庆市九龙坡区华岩镇新政村	89805533
重庆华龙制造有限公司	重庆市九龙坡区华岩镇中梁山人和社	65259588
重庆市九龙橡胶制品有限公司	重庆市九龙坡区石坪桥矿机村85号	68825891
重庆恒胜集团有限公司	重庆市九龙坡区九龙镇	68929915
重庆富川电装品有限公司	重庆市九龙坡区白市驿镇牟家十四社	65704113
重庆赛力盟电机有限责任公司	重庆市九龙坡区中梁山半山一村128号	89093049
重庆新时代摩托车有限责任公司	重庆市九龙坡区华岩镇石堰村七社	65270502
重庆世纪精信实业有限公司	重庆市九龙坡区二郎火炬大道96号	68889999
重庆银角制动器有限公司	重庆市九龙坡区含谷镇含盛路	65731473
格力电器（重庆）有限公司	重庆市九龙坡区二郎创业大道98号	68465333
重庆万丰新锐车轮有限公司	重庆市九龙坡区九龙镇大堰工业园区	68446918
重庆佳通轮胎有限公司	重庆市九龙坡区华玉路888号	65266100
重庆劲隆科技集团有限公司	重庆市九龙坡区九龙镇九龙园区火炬大厦10号	89067620
重庆隆创动力有限公司	重庆市九龙坡区九龙镇盘龙四社69-2号	89805406
重庆天泰铝业有限公司	重庆市九龙坡区陶家镇锣鼓村	89803009
包头北方奔驰重型汽车有限责任公司重庆公司	重庆市九龙坡区杨家坪正街43号	89803242
包头北方奔驰重型汽车有限责任公司重庆变速器分公司	重庆市九龙坡区杨家坪正街43号	89803156
重庆新生机电有限责任公司	重庆市南岸区弹子石群慧路94号	62507734
西南计算机有限责任公司	重庆市南岸区光电路	62928200
国营建安仪器厂	重庆市南岸区南坪西路168号	62805374
重庆烟草工业有限责任公司	重庆市南岸区南城大道197号	62916176
重庆美心（集团）有限公司	重庆市南岸区南坪白鹤路51号	62762516
重庆阿波罗机电技术开发公司	重庆市南岸区窍角沱正街1号	89022705
重庆制钳厂	重庆市南岸区广黔路70号	62750343
重庆三棉纺织厂	重庆市南岸区窍角沱正街14号	62505362
重庆第二机床厂	重庆市南岸区南坪村191号	62801210
重庆长江橡胶厂	重庆市南岸区四公里	62758506
重庆广益摩托车厂	重庆市南岸区南坪西路63号	62927044
重庆科瑞制药有限责任公司	重庆市南岸区经济技术开发区大石支路二号	62765066
重庆川东化工集团有限公司	重庆市南岸区鸡冠石镇白沙沱中窑街20号	62950880
重庆市健力鞋业有限责任公司	重庆市南岸区涂山镇玄坛庙由于里22号	62968519
重庆零一精密机械有限公司	重庆市南岸区上新街桂花新村249号	62870306
重庆宏林建筑装饰材料有限公司	重庆市南岸区鸡冠石镇盘龙村山王坡91号	62502233
重庆两江机械制造有限责任公司	重庆市南岸区南坪镇白鹤路130号	62753700
重庆长丰麻纺织厂	重庆市南岸区苗背沱1号	62503080
重庆长江电工(集团)有限公司	重庆市南岸区长生桥镇茶园新城区长电路1号	62489152
太极集团重庆桐君阁药厂	重庆市南岸区敦厚街50号	89881060
重庆市迪马实业股份有限公司	重庆市南岸区南坪镇白鹤路108号	89021551
嘉陵一本田发动机有限公司	重庆市南岸区白鹤路45号	62793100
重庆四方制装有限公司	重庆市南岸区南城大道445号	62801822
重庆顶益食品有限公司	重庆市南岸区丹龙路77号	62826999
爱思帝（重庆）驱动系统有限公司	重庆市南岸区桃源路	62762702
重庆顶津食品有限公司	重庆市南岸区丹龙路77号	62826999
重庆通盛机械工业有限公司	重庆市南岸区长生桥镇玉马池工业园区2号	89023606

20-18 续表5 CONTINUED-5

企业名称 Name of Enterprises	企业详细地址 Address	电话号码 Tel.
重庆江南化工有限责任公司	重庆市南岸区弹子石新街75号	62504656
重庆昊晟玻璃晶品有限公司	重庆市南岸区长生桥镇茶园新城区玉马池工业园15号	61920995
重庆力帆重柴动力有限公司	重庆市南岸区长生桥镇茶园新区世纪大道64号	62873804
重庆华福卷烟配套材料有限责任公司	重庆市南岸区南坪南路323号B栋4楼	62967982
重庆力宏精细化工有限公司	重庆市南岸区鸡冠石镇白沙沱正街155号	62809367
重庆隆鑫工业（集团）有限公司	重庆市南岸区南坪镇白鹤工业园	89026165
重庆拉法基水泥有限公司	重庆市南岸区黄桷垭镇泉山村	62496666
重庆雅戈尔服饰有限公司	重庆市南岸区长生桥镇茶园新城区玉马池工业园68号	62763995
重庆华立控股股份有限公司	重庆市北碚区龙凤桥258号	67750888
重庆川仪有限公司	重庆市北碚区天生街道人民村	68862766
重庆银钢科技集团有限公司	重庆市北碚区童家溪镇同兴南路71号	68327809
重庆北碚玻璃仪器总厂	重庆市北碚区树人路34号	68272301
重庆大新药业股份有限公司	重庆市北碚区创造路20号	68328153
重庆市八四五化工有限责任公司	重庆市北碚区蔡家岗镇灯塔街148号	68304028
重庆华伟工业集团有限责任公司	重庆市北碚区歇马镇盐井湾1号	68243987
重庆歇马机械曲轴有限公司	重庆市北碚区歇马镇农荣村曹家坝	68242488
重庆市富丰水泥集团富华水泥有限公司	重庆市北碚区天府镇代家村青新桥	68320212
重庆宏大纸业集团有限公司	重庆市北碚区天生街道月兴村	68865617
重庆新兴齿轮有限公司	重庆市北碚区龙凤一村195号	68262013
重庆江北机械有限责任公司	重庆市北碚区水土镇解放路50号	68230481
重庆川仪总厂有限公司	重庆市北碚区天生街道人民村	68862766
重庆永发摩托车配件有限公司	重庆市北碚区龙凤一村66号	68265156
重庆正川玻璃有限公司	重庆市北碚区联龙	68349808
重庆市富皇水泥集团有限公司	重庆市北碚区水土镇屋基村江家院	68348928
重庆江北特种建材有限公司	重庆市北碚区三圣镇三圣街119号	68234288
重庆天府矿业有限责任公司	重庆市北碚区天府镇后丰岩	68301271
重庆力帆汽车有限公司	重庆市北碚区梨园村72号	68295153
福耀玻璃(重庆)配件有限公司	重庆市万盛区清溪桥21号	48290777
重庆南桐矿业有限责任公司	重庆市万盛区清溪桥87号	48340304
重庆红岩汽车有限责任公司	重庆市双桥区双龙东路建设新村1号	49639888
重庆泰山电线电缆有限责任公司	重庆市渝北区松牌路99号	67914835
重庆华渝电气仪表总厂	重庆市渝北区龙山村	67660402
重庆华江印务有限责任公司	重庆市渝北区安家嘴1号	63670095
重庆江北化肥有限公司	重庆市渝北区悦来镇清溪口清南村1号	67483625
重庆江合煤化（集团）有限公司	重庆市渝北区双凤路273号	67815038
重庆驰骋轻型汽车部件股份有限公司	重庆市渝北区科园产业园兴科大道2号地块	67457398
重庆市仁和压铸有限公司	重庆市渝北区大竹林镇凤栖沱居委会	67682368
重庆秦川实业(集团)有限公司	重庆市渝北区鸳鸯街道凉井村	67196688
重庆川庆化工厂	重庆市渝北区洛碛镇药川路37号	86003008
重庆药友制药有限责任公司	重庆市渝北区人和镇星光大道100号	67527018
重庆信威通信技术有限责任公司	重庆市渝北区北部新区高新园星光大道62号海王星科技大厦	86076738
马勒发动机零部件(重庆)有限公司	重庆市渝北区汉渝路125号	67837840
重庆超力高科技有限责任公司	重庆市渝北区鸳鸯街道经开大道2001号	89110289
重庆希望饲料有限公司	重庆市渝北区人和镇万平路555号	67644787

20-18 续表6 CONTINUED-6

企业名称 Name of Enterprises	企业详细地址 Address	电话号码 Tel.
重庆市渝帆机械有限公司	重庆市渝北区空港工业园区	67456566
重庆渝江压铸有限公司	重庆市渝北区大竹林镇石粱桥	67682938
重庆鸽牌电线电缆有限公司	重庆市渝北区松牌路99号	67602014
长安福特汽车有限公司	重庆市渝北区长福西路1号	67458322
延锋伟世通（重庆）汽车饰件系统有限公司	重庆市渝北区北部新区金开大道1999号	67457213
重庆银翔摩托车集团有限公司	重庆市渝北区科技产业园	67459328
重庆宇通客车有限公司	重庆市渝北区松牌路109号	67630072
重庆延锋江森座椅有限公司	重庆市渝北区长福西路4号	89185771
重庆万里蓄电池股份有限公司	重庆市巴南区花溪镇苦竹坝31号	62594921
重庆工具厂	重庆市巴南区花溪镇道角二村七号	62556151
重庆机床厂	重庆市巴南区花溪镇道角莲花一村1号	62555283
重庆水轮机厂有限责任公司	重庆市巴南区李家沱马正街10号	62858148
重庆前进化工有限公司	重庆市巴南区鱼洞镇吊耳嘴13号	68546491
重庆力之星机车制造有限责任公司	重庆市巴南区花溪镇炒油场宗申工业园	66372903
重庆重钢集团钢管有限公司	重庆市巴南区花溪镇王家坝土桥新溪村1号	62590870
重庆弘愿气动工具厂	重庆市巴南区界石镇界南街107号	66419598
重庆长安铃木汽车有限公司	重庆市巴南区鱼洞镇大江厂内	66283285
攀钢集团重庆钛业股份有限公司	重庆市巴南区花溪镇走马二村51号	62555499
重庆华陶瓷业有限公司	重庆市巴南区陈家湾	62570900
重庆大江渝强塑料制品有限公司	重庆市巴南区鱼洞街道办事处万泉街	66288821
重庆平山泰凯化油器有限公司	重庆市巴南区鱼洞街道大同工业园	89088631
重庆宗申通用动力机械有限公司	重庆市巴南区花溪镇宗申工业园区	66372532
重庆文辉摩托车制造有限公司	重庆市巴南区南泉镇虎啸村二社	62849013
重庆耐德山花特种车有限责任公司	重庆市巴南区花溪镇王家坝路100号	62596324
重庆大江美利信压铸有限责任公司	重庆市巴南区鱼洞镇大江厂内	66286673
重庆大江信达车辆股份有限公司	重庆市巴南区鱼洞镇大江厂内	66285404
重庆川渝精工机械配件开发有限公司	重庆市巴南区花溪镇民主新街168号	62581270
重庆宗申发动机制造有限公司	重庆市巴南区花溪镇炒油场宗申工业园	66372608
重庆锦晖陶瓷有限公司	重庆市巴南区陈家湾2村20号	62571229
重庆市巴南区吉力电装品厂	重庆市巴南区花溪镇先锋村八社	62570560
重庆市黔江区供电有限公司	重庆市黔江区杨柳街215号	79225192
重庆弘扬建材集团	重庆市黔江区杉木	79250998
黔江卷烟厂	重庆市黔江区长征南路88号	79222497
重庆市黔龙印务集团	重庆市黔江区解放路	79235109
重庆乌江电力（集团）有限公司	重庆市黔江区城西路118号	79235086
中国石化集团四川维尼纶厂	重庆市长寿区查家湾	68974465
长寿化工总厂	重庆市长寿区梅村	40262549
重庆鑫腾冶金炉料有限责任公司	重庆市长寿区梅村	40514581
重庆长风化工厂	重庆市长寿区长风村	40450100
中国长江航运集团川江船厂	重庆市长寿区朱家岩	40721207
重庆金盘山水泥有限公司	重庆市长寿区葛兰镇	40814891
扬子江乙酰化工有限公司	重庆市长寿区查家湾	68974765
重庆长寿化工有限责任公司	重庆市长寿区梅村	40262651

20-18 续表7 CONTINUED-7

企业名称 Name of Enterprises	企业详细地址 Address	电话号码 Tel.
重庆泰丰泰兴化工有限责任公司	重庆市长寿区轻化路	40613354
重庆市綦齿汽车零部件有限责任公司	重庆市綦江县古南镇桥河	48641918
綦江长风齿轮有限公司	重庆市綦江县古南镇新山村48号	48662888
重庆綦江汽车半轴厂	重庆市綦江县古南镇桥河独石沱	48642179
重庆鼎泰铝业有限公司	重庆市綦江县古南镇新山村8号	48660727
重庆古华畜产有限公司	重庆市綦江县古南镇上升街187号	48655834
綦江齿轮传动有限公司	重庆市綦江县古南镇桥河	48609442
重庆松藻煤电有限责任公司	重庆市綦江县打通镇红星二村	48731116
重庆四钢钢业有限责任公司	重庆市綦江县三江镇	48249572
重庆华强化肥有限公司	重庆市綦江县古南镇玉龙村	85899168
重庆市万利来化工股份有限公司	重庆市潼南县梓潼镇中间坡2号	44551839
重庆市潼南简氏纸业包装有限公司	重庆市潼南县双江镇金龙寺65号	44860558
重庆市潼南电熔耐火材料有限公司	重庆市潼南县梓潼镇东安大道218号	44550377
重庆市潼南供电有限责任公司	重庆市潼南县梓潼镇石院街38号	44560688
重庆天青锶化股份有限公司	重庆市铜梁县巴川镇中兴路185号	45682840
重庆龙珠电力股份有限公司	重庆市铜梁县巴川镇滨河东路35号	45643825
重庆铜梁红蝶锶业有限公司	重庆市铜梁县安居镇油房街214号	45855073
重庆拓源华冠碳素有限公司	重庆市铜梁县西河镇农森村	62984081
重庆庆龙精细盐化工有限公司	重庆市铜梁县华兴镇白水村七社	45363638
重庆市铜梁县供电有限责任公司	重庆市铜梁县巴川镇滨河东路34号	45632783
重庆市长河煤矿	重庆市大足县邮亭镇长河居委会	43387012
重庆市大足县天青石矿业公司	重庆市大足县古龙乡古龙村新街	43451525
重庆市大足红碟锶业有限公司	重庆市大足县龙水镇下河坝	43624218
重庆市大足县供电有限责任公司	重庆市大足县龙岗街道办事处北环西路1号	43733871
重庆嘉陵化学制品有限公司	重庆市荣昌县昌元镇王家坪四组	46796873
重庆益民机械厂	重庆荣昌县双河镇益民机械厂居委会	46287371
重庆华森制药有限公司	重庆市荣昌县昌元镇板桥工业园区	46785738
重庆力帆摩托车制造有限公司	重庆市荣昌县昌元镇板桥工业园区	46781751
重庆益峰高压容器有限责任公司	重庆市荣昌县双河镇益民厂内	46287027
重庆永荣矿业有限公司	重庆市荣昌县广顺镇	46384506
重庆青山工业有限责任公司	重庆市璧山县团结村	41819333
重庆市璧山大兴金属厂	重庆市璧山县大兴镇交通街101号	41550036
重庆川东减震制造有限公司	重庆市璧山县璧城镇璧兴路67-1号	41426397
重庆顾地塑胶电器有限公司	重庆市璧山县工贸区	41781268
重庆市蓝黛实业有限公司	重庆市璧山县璧城金剑路	41410186
重庆南雁实业集团有限公司	重庆市璧山县皂角路51号	41432411
重庆大江摩托车发动机制造有限公司	重庆市璧山县青杠石河村	87382809
重庆市璧山县顺山机械有限公司	重庆市璧山县青杠白云大道	41782118
重庆金冠汽车制造有限公司	重庆市璧山县璧城红宇大道	41412933
重庆红旗缸盖制造有限公司	重庆市璧山县璧城镇牛角湾	87382616
重庆华陵工业有限公司	重庆市璧山县丁家镇回龙路55号	41783957
重庆红宇精密工业有限责任公司	重庆市璧山县红宇大道九号	45585987
重庆市鞍子水泥有限责任公司	重庆市璧山县大路镇龙泉村	41520141

20-18 续表8 CONTINUED-8

企业名称 Name of Enterprises	企业详细地址 Address	电话号码 Tel.
梁平县国营邵新煤矿	重庆市梁平县袁驿镇邵新村	53635586
重庆市城口县百步梯锰业有限公司	重庆市城口县葛城镇柳杨村	59222136
城口县矿产资源开发有限责任公司	重庆市城口县高燕乡大园村	59501191
重庆市丰都供电有限责任公司	重庆市丰都县三合镇新湾路一号	70715189
重庆市富源化工有限责任公司	重庆市垫江县砚台镇砚台村4社	74588705
重庆鼎发实业股份有限公司	重庆市垫江县桂溪镇工农路296号	74515491
重庆市垫江县供电有限责任公司	重庆市垫江县桂溪镇过境中路	74512409
重庆市赛德化工有限公司	重庆市垫江县桂溪镇南阳居委南阳小区	74635403
重庆市武隆县供电有限责任公司	重庆市武隆县巷口镇建设街中路23号	77722310
重庆云河实业（集团）有限公司忠州水轮机厂	重庆市忠县忠州镇忠州大道云河工业园	54401888
重庆市清溪丝绸厂	重庆市忠县汝溪镇丝绸路29号	54729454
重庆市忠县供电有限责任公司	重庆市忠县忠州镇健康路35号	54235224
重庆市建忠发电有限责任公司	重庆市忠县忠州镇苏家社区	54400456
重庆德泉电力股份有限公司	重庆市开县汉丰镇内西街76号	52222244
重庆市钱江食品有限责任公司	重庆市开县铁桥镇铁桥村	52700788
佛山新美陶瓷有限公司	重庆市开县汉丰镇富厚居委会新城建材路1号	52264371
白鹤发电厂	重庆市开县白鹤镇	52177011
重庆星星套装门有限责任公司	重庆市开县温泉镇金玉街3号	52412022
重庆市开县供电有限责任公司	重庆市开县汉丰镇富厚居委农行办公楼	52280020
重庆市云阳县曲轴厂	重庆市云阳县双江镇道湾	55159050
云阳县供电有限责任公司	重庆市云阳县双江镇枣花路	55166695
奉节县三峡水利电力有限责任公司	重庆市奉节县永安镇夔州路306号	56558501
重庆市巫山县供电有限责任公司	重庆市巫山县巫峡镇广东中路78号	57682530
巫溪县供电有限责任公司	重庆市巫溪县城厢镇人民街26号	51522525
重庆市石柱县供电有限责任公司	重庆市石柱县南宾镇正街73号	73336006
重庆东田药业有限公司	重庆市石柱县南宾镇城南路20号	73327767
石柱土家族自治县方斗山水泥有限公司	重庆市石柱县万朝乡	73369031
秀山土家族苗族自治县石耶水泥厂	重庆市秀山县石耶镇西大居委会	76624650
重庆市秀山县鑫发电解锰厂	重庆市秀山县清溪场镇	76603568
重庆市乌江三角滩锰业有限责任公司	重庆市秀山县石堤镇石堤村	76863622
重庆老山沟锰业有限责任公司	重庆市秀山县孝溪乡细沙村	76665121
重庆市秀山县供电有限责任公司	重庆市秀山县中和镇构皮社区居委会	76863690
重庆天雄锰业有限公司	重庆市酉阳县龙潭镇五育村	75310325
重庆金益烟草有限责任公司	重庆市彭水县汉葭镇河堡	78841245
重庆市彭水县供电有限责任公司	重庆市彭水县汉葭镇鼓楼	78443021
江津增压器厂	重庆市江津市东方红	47221101
重庆长风机器有限责任公司	重庆市江津市长风路88号	47512540
重庆潍柴发动机厂	重庆市江津市	47858815
重庆三五三九鞋业总厂	重庆市江津市	47556008
重庆齿轮箱有限责任公司	重庆市江津市东方红	47211043
重庆钢铁集团铁业有限责任公司	重庆市江津市夏坝镇江钢街	47681712
重庆三五三三印染服装总厂	重庆市江津市中渡	47848600
重庆四维瓷业（集团）股份有限公司	重庆市江津市油溪镇迎宾路145号四维公司	61088699

20-18 续表9 CONTINUED-9

企业名称 Name of Enterprises	企业详细地址 Address	电话号码 Tel.
重庆市川江车辆制造有限公司	重庆市江津市白沙镇东山村川江路1号	47332186
重庆华能石粉有限责任公司	重庆市江津市珞璜镇矿山村	47601250
重庆市江津酒厂（集团）有限公司	重庆市江津市牌坊	47838347
重庆市江津夏强实业有限公司	重庆市江津市夏坝镇余粮	47681781
重庆江洲粉末冶金科技有限公司	重庆市江津市正街339号	47833472
重庆腾辉地维水泥有限公司	重庆市江津市珞璜镇矿山村	47600098
重庆市海伦地毯有限公司	重庆市江津市环城南路119号	47521255
江津市禾丰化工有限责任公司	重庆市江津市几江街道办事处	47581166
重庆柏衫丝绸有限公司	重庆市江津市白沙镇滩盘村	61171858
重庆市江津市供电有限责任公司	重庆市江津市南郊路9号	47546955
江津市水力发电有限公司	重庆市江津市通泰码头滨江大厦	85568835
华能重庆珞璜发电有限责任公司	重庆市江津市珞璜镇通江	66221647
重庆华诚四棉纺织有限公司	重庆市合川市合川工业园区东津沱上予丰3号	42723421
重庆合川盐化工业有限公司	重庆市合川市合川钓办处甘家坝	42727004
重庆希尔安药业有限公司	重庆市合川市工业园区希尔安大道168号	42741118
重庆市富丰水泥集团有限责任公司	重庆市合川市三汇镇皂角树社区居委会	42422024
重庆腾辉特种水泥有限公司	重庆市合川市草街镇高枧村六社	62767888
重庆天嘉日用品实业有限公司	重庆市合川市合阳办利川村一社	42880986
重庆金铂实业集团有限公司	重庆市合川市盐井镇回龙桥	42701474
重庆合川市供电有限责任公司	重庆市合川市瑞山路167号	42822253
重庆红江机械厂	重庆市永川市青城路190号	49893432
重庆跃进机械厂	重庆市永川市化工路1号	49803920
重庆市渝西钢铁(集团)有限公司	重庆市永川市三教镇川主街	49352168
重庆市参天水泥有限公司	重庆市永川市红炉镇新店会龙桥村	49336258
重庆金凤丝绸集团有限公司	重庆市永川市环城东路158号	49800894
重庆渝永电力股份有限责任公司	重庆市永川市箕山路25号	49835285
重庆市渝西矿业集团有限公司	重庆市永川市外环西路53号	49896212
重庆西源凸轮轴有限公司	重庆市永川市东外街233号	49835185
重庆海通机械制造集团	重庆市永川市小桥子59号	49832906
重庆紫光化工有限责任公司	重庆市永川市化工路426号	87161881
永川龙城精锻有限公司	重庆市永川市双石镇二三五库	49403032
重庆昌州茧丝绸有限公司	重庆市永川市化工路599号	49804552
中船重工重庆液压机电有限公司	重庆市永川市萱花路	49888445
南川市东胜电业有限责任公司	重庆市南川市东城大铺子	71401096
南川市供电有限责任公司	重庆市南川市渚堰塘一号	71412097
重庆市南川嘉南水泥制造有限公司	重庆市南川市西城长远居委	71645136
南川市宏原化工有限公司	重庆市南川市汇江路5号	71405752
重庆市博赛矿业(集团)有限公司	重庆市南川市	71484976
双赢集团有限公司	重庆市南川市两路永生桥	71404463
重庆市龙济化肥有限责任公司	重庆市南川市	71405248
重庆纵横纺织有限公司	重庆市南川市安平居委	71404666
南川市大兴煤化工业有限责任公司	重庆市南川市大兴居委	71484831
南川市宏能煤业有限责任公司	重庆市南川市鹰岩桂三社	71436207

20－19 重点建筑企业目录（2004年）
List of Major Construction Enterprises (2004)

企业名称 Name of Enterprises	企业详细地址 Address	电话号码 Tel.
广厦重庆第一建筑集团有限公司	九龙坡区石坪桥横街78＃	68822740
中国十八冶金建设公司	九龙坡区石坪桥正街1号	68821333
中铁八局集团第一工程有限公司	九龙坡区兴胜路8号	68826227
重庆第三建设有限责任公司	渝中区袁家岗1号	68810608
重钢集团建设工程有限公司	大渡口区三岗门	68845602
重庆第二建设有限公司	沙坪坝区天正街2号	65312451
重庆住宅建设有限公司	渝中区桂花园43号	89875082
中铁十一局集团第五工程有限公司	沙坪坝区新桥新村71号	89065297
重庆工业设备安装集团有限公司	渝中区中山二路99号	63510250
重庆第九建设有限公司	九龙坡区西郊路69号	68414144
重庆市渝通公路工程总公司	南岸区花园材街道桃源路22号	62905128
重庆电力建设总公司	南岸区花园路街道金子村101号	62607045
重庆市一品建设集团有限公司	重庆市九龙坡区高新技术开发区科园六路30号	68571578
重庆市第七建筑工程有限责任公司	江北区建新南路10号	67726724
重庆长安建设工程有限公司	江北区建新东路251#	67591624
重庆市江龙建设工程有限公司	涪陵区兴华中路55号	85663703
重庆北部新城建设集团有限公司	渝北区金龙路21号	67912006
重庆市庆华建筑工程有限公司	渝北区松牌路102＃	67528719
重庆市第八建筑工程公司	九龙坡区五一新村21号	68961398
重庆九龙建设（集团）有限公司	九龙坡区杨家坪西郊路98号	61587968
重庆渝发建设公司	长寿区轻化路	40611437
重庆伟太建筑工程有限公司	巴南区土桥正街4号3楼	61579886
重庆广信电力建设有限责任公司	沙坪坝区沙南街56号	63684015
重庆渝康建筑工程有限公司	沙坪坝区渝碚路88号	65466289
九龙坡区金凤建筑（集团）有限公司	九龙坡区金凤镇正街98号	65740168

20-19 续表 CONTINUED

企业名称 Name of Enterprises	企业详细地址 Address	电话号码 Tel.
重庆花溪建设(集团)有限公司	巴南区花溪新村15号	62858708
重庆煤矿建设第五工程处	渝北区宝圣东路291号	67136332
重庆山海建筑集团有限公司	渝中区健康路82号	63862394
重庆巴洲建筑安装工程有限公司	巴南区鱼洞街道鱼轻路45号	13983947715
重庆建工集团有限责任公司	渝中区捍卫路8#	63500756
重庆市渝万建设集团有限公司	万州区王牌路398号	58117188
重庆第十一建筑工程有限责任公司	九龙坡区石小路164#	68624634
重庆市涪陵建设工程公司	涪陵区兴华中路60号财贸大厦中楼	72226338
重庆北部双龙建设(集团)有限公司	渝北区翠湖路110号	67801638
重庆桥梁工程总公司	南岸区南坪南城大道4#	86115627
重庆中发建筑工程有限公司	渝中区枇杷山正街213#D栋703	63531754
重庆渝风建筑工程有限公司	长寿区长寿路106号	40243242
重庆市第二市政工程公司	渝中区下肖家湾107号	68890584
重庆市德感建筑安装工程有限公司	江津市德感正街339号	47835354
重庆恒滨建设（集团）有限公司	渝中区九尺坎66号泰安大厦15楼	63727420
重庆市五一实业(集团）有限公司	涪陵区兴华中路八段65号	72881248
重庆先华建设集团有限公司	南岸区惠工路196#	62834835
重庆第四建筑工程公司	江北区建东54号	67850325
重庆市万州区建筑工程总公司	万州区新城路43号	58148196
重庆博达建设集团股份有限公司	江津市大什字建宇综合楼	47538870
重庆鸡冠石建设工程有限公司	南岸区南坪东路581号	62942124
重庆机场建设有限责任公司	渝中区渝建村130号	63896717
重庆第六建设有限责任公司	九龙坡区含谷镇含盛路59号	65730712
重庆成盛建设集团有限公司	南岸区南坪丹龙路	62751418
重庆渝永建设集团有限公司	永川市玉屏路98号	49862546

20－20 重点房地产开发企业目录（2004年）
List of Major Real Estate Development Enterprises (2004)

企业名称 Name of Enterprises	企业详细地址 Address	电话号码 Tel.
重庆市万州区锦鸿综合开发公司	万州区太白路55号	64853681
重庆市万州建设开发有限公司	万州区桂花路30号	58233439
重庆市万州城市建设综合开发公司	万州区国本路106号	85782548
重庆市三信建设(集团)有限公司	万州区周家社区3-6号	58373667
重庆市兴茂房地产开发有限公司	万州区渝东大花园	58912621
重庆市荣庭房地产开发有限责任公司	涪陵区兴华中路18号	72248043
重庆市涪陵城市建设综合开发公司	涪陵区建涪路56号	72223050
重庆市华祥房地产开发有限责任公司	涪陵区中山东路102号	72281177
重庆市兴地实业有限公司	涪陵区广场路133号	66979758
重庆市嘉信实业(集团)有限公司	涪陵区兴华东路46号	67981907
重庆市涪陵华新房地产开发有限公司	涪陵区望州路25号	72301057
涪陵区城镇发展有限责任公司	涪陵区四环路建委大院	72379430
重庆市涪陵堤防工程建设开发有限责任公司	涪陵区兴华中路45号	72869170
重庆优霸房地产开发有限公司	渝中区华一路17号10楼	63510655
重庆洲际房地产开发有限公司	渝中区华一路63号3楼	63530538
重庆建工集团有限责任公司房地产开发公司	渝中区捍卫路8号	68740800
林建物业公司	渝中区中山一路181号4楼	63530001
江州实业集团开发有限公司	渝中区中山一路181号4楼	63521036
重庆巨宇实业集团有限公司	渝中区鲁祖庙79号	63819928
重庆聚富房地产开发有限公司	渝中区万豪5楼U-5	63830000
重庆中发房地产开发有限公司	渝中区中华路174号	63840585
重庆大信房地产开发有限责任公司	渝中区大同路16#	63783214
重庆住宅建设开发有限公司	渝中区民生路224号	63847629
重庆达美实业有限公司	渝中区民生巷18#B座	63725632
重庆润隆实业有限公司	渝中区民生路235号2788房	63810008
重庆海旭实业发展有限公司	渝中区宏声巷24号宏声大厦4楼	63827599
重庆渝世弟物业发展有限公司	渝中区民生路235号2588室	63705597
重庆台庆房地产综合开发有限公司	渝中区较场口88#A塔28F	63798333
重庆泰正（集团）有限公司	渝中区较场口85号9楼	63731070
重庆万兴房地产开发有限公司	渝中区较场口88#25-3	13983288888
龙庆物业发展（重庆）有限公司	渝中区邹容路100号时代豪宛	63804788
重庆名豪实业（集团）股份有限公司	渝中区都市广场9楼	63782340
重庆渝亚房地产开发建设有限公司	渝中区九尺坎66#泰安大厦13楼	63819009
重庆合景园际投资有限公司	渝中区临江支路2#7楼	63786971
重庆洲际酒店投资有限公司	渝中区邹容路68号大都会商厦B01＋12A	63739632
和记黄埔地产（重庆江北）有限公司	渝中区邹容路68号	63813800
重庆恒通房地产发展有限公司	渝中区公园路19号	66891515
重庆鸥鹏物业开发有限公司	渝中区新华路216号	63741523
重庆远鹏物业发展有限公司	渝中区新华路337#11层	63811058
重庆皇冠建设开发有限公司	渝中区107号	13320331022
重庆斌鑫物业（集团）有限公司	渝中区健康路46号2楼	63613319
重庆庆隆屋业发展有限公司	渝中区中山二路131号庆隆希尔顿商务中心36楼	89031111

20-20 续表1 CONTINUED-1

企业名称 Name of Enterprises	企业详细地址 Address	电话号码 Tel.
重庆瑞安天地房地产发展有限公司	渝中区中山二路131号庆隆希尔顿商务中心9楼	89061818
重庆谊德实业公司	渝中区中山四路1号渝中大厦12楼	13983069517
重庆太平洋屋业发展有限公司	渝中区上清寺路2#A-16	63857310
重庆万康房地产开发有限责任公司	渝中区上大田湾65号	63616696
重庆市房地综合开发公司	渝中区学田湾正街1#8楼	63854737
重庆渝开发股份有限公司	渝中区上清寺曾家岩1号	63855545
重庆中安房地产开发有限公司	渝中区中山支路168号28楼	63630808
重庆天景置业有限公司	渝中区中山支路136号19楼	63630111
重庆协信城市建设发展有限公司	渝中区新华路4号附1号时代天骄大厦5楼	63819666
重庆市新城开发建设股份有限公司	渝中区筷子街2号旅业大厦10楼	89886901
重庆斯达房屋建筑开发有限公司	渝中区新华路160号	89038455
重庆大正房地产开发有限公司	渝中区陕西路38号	63781111
重庆长航房地产开发有限公司	渝中区陕西路22号9F	63772210
重庆渝海控股（集团）有限责任公司	渝中区棉花街18号-8	63788336
重庆瑞奇物业有限公司	渝中区人和街15号星都大厦8楼	63652340
重庆顺祥房地产开发有限公司	渝中区巴教村88号	68796161
重庆聚金实业有限公司	渝中区大溪沟街73号6楼	63667618
重庆诚投房地产开发有限公司	渝中区人民路123号蒲田大厦14楼	63615860
重庆海天实业有限公司	渝中区渝建村130号	63896717
重庆乐信经济技术发展有限公司	渝中区石油路2号	68692211
重庆光华房地产开发有限公司	渝中区长江二路174号	68587872
重庆竟地实业有限公司	渝中区大黄路6号	68801318
重庆万联房地产开发有限公司	大渡口区新山村钢花路	74919811
重庆市大渡口新城建设有限责任公司	大渡口区钢花路648#	68902679
重庆嘉瑞房地产开发（集团）有限公司	大渡口区翠园村18#	68903182
重庆秋实房地产开发（集团）有限责任公司	大渡口区金华大厦4-4-12#	68838193
重庆钢铁集团朵力房地产股份有限公司	大渡口区钢花路8号钢城大厦19楼	68842351
重庆天泰房地产开发有限责任公司	大渡口区三木花园33#	68830597
重庆科而士房地产开发有限公司	大渡口区天辰华府	68927011
重庆龙厦房地产开发有限公司	大渡口区松青路1000#	61593156
重庆钰茂地产有限责任公司	大渡口区金桥路16#	68952888
重庆锦天置业（集团）有限公司	大渡口区江北区文体路128#	68908866
东宏实业（重庆）有限公司	江北区华新村360号	89078137
金诚三峡经济开发有限公司	江北区西普16-1	89072302
重庆银星经济技术发展股份有限公司	江北区华新村	89078137
重庆中农物业发展有限公司	江北区华新	65408899
重庆市宏发房地产开发公司	江北区中兴段1号	67862106
重庆市江北区滨江路房地产开发有限公司	江北区建东54号18楼	67748739
重庆鹏翔物业有限责任公司	江北区建新东路87号	63727300
重庆爱华实业发展有限公司	江北区福村1号	67618302
江苏信一房地产开发有限公司重庆分公司	江北区扬河一村1#2楼	67872992

20-20 续表2 CONTINUED-2

企业名称 Name of Enterprises	企业详细地址 Address	电话号码 Tel.
重庆银鑫房地产开发有限公司	江北区杨河一村78号	67707665
重庆洋河开发房地产公司	江北区洋河二村3#	67864673
重庆大众房地产开发公司	江北区中冶大厦19楼	67879092
重庆中渝物业发展有限公司	江北区电测村237号陈列馆	67621477
重庆东部房地产开发有限公司	江北区建东一村29号3楼	67737686
重庆敬业房地产开发有限公司	江北区建新东路一村29号	67741816
重庆新原兴经济发展有限公司	江北区建北三支路23-7	67726064
重庆邦兴物业有限责任公司	江北区观音桥街道邦渝花园	67746798
重庆市鸿程房地产发展公司	江北区望海花园1-1-1号	89185056
重庆华立地产（集团）有限公司	江北区国际商会大厦23楼	67748661
重庆东海房地产开发有限公司	江北区江北洋河路2号阳光城26楼	62982838
重庆新原兴企业集团有限公司	江北区观音桥塔坪120	67719003
重庆市金科实业（集团）有限公司	江北区金岗大厦20楼	67861688
重庆市明瑜实业有限公司	江北区嘉陵二村6#	67759334
重庆航星置业发展有限公司	江北区观音桥北岸星座7F	67726731
重庆建川房地产开发责任有限公司	江北区建新东路286号	67850979
重庆长安房地产开发有限公司	江北区长安村特1号	67591672
重庆成浩物业发展有限公司	沙坪坝区黄桷湾208	65353555
重庆欣阳房地产开发有限公司	沙坪坝区沙正街8号	89056000
重庆创豪土地整治房屋开发有限公司	沙坪坝区沙北街83号	65127230
重庆同创置业集团有限公司	沙坪坝区沙北街98号	65401890
重庆天人房地产开发有限公司	沙坪坝区沙北街98号	65401890
重庆大学房地产开发有限公司	沙坪坝区沙北街174号	89055888
重庆大川集团房地产开发有限公司	沙坪坝区大杨公桥104#	65474651
重庆市沙坪坝区房地产开发总公司	沙坪坝区沙南街43号	65314626
重庆世源房地产（集团）有限公司	沙坪坝区天陈路2号	65409823
重庆市利得尔实业有限公司	沙坪坝区渝碚路119号	65407905
重庆世家地产发展有限公司	沙坪坝区渝碚路39号	65010405
重庆业瑞房地产开发有限公司	沙坪坝区小新街29号	68857864
重庆金都实业有限公司	沙坪坝区渝碚路39号	65317819
重庆恒鑫房地产开发有限公司	沙坪坝区小新街85号	65479696
重庆特钢房地产开发有限公司	沙坪坝区窍门山120号	65139870
重庆跨越置业发展有限公司	沙坪坝区小正街333-21号	65450388
重庆洪燕物业发展有限公司	沙坪坝区天陈路44号	65310971
重庆宏华房地产开发有限公司	沙坪坝区天星桥正街121号	65411178
重庆天合物业发展有限责任公司	沙坪坝区都市花园西路99号	65461992
重庆沙坪坝区滨江建设开发有限公司	沙坪坝区天马支路27号	65465538
重庆港城房地产（集团）有限公司	沙坪坝区凤天路119号	65319816
重庆升伟房地产集团有限公司	沙坪坝区凤天大道119-8号	65338888
重庆武城房地产开发有限公司	沙坪坝区凤天路南部新城8号	65400359
重庆市君和实业有限公司	沙坪坝区凤鸣山康居苑	86339155

20-20 续表3 CONTINUED-3

企业名称 Name of Enterprises	企业详细地址 Address	电话号码 Tel.
重庆市金霸房地产开发有限公司	沙坪坝区童家桥正街175号	65475005
重庆鑫隆达房地产开发有限公司	沙坪坝区石小路153号	68606216
重庆旭庆房地产开发有限公司	沙坪坝区显丰大道8号	68790743
重庆新亚房地产开发有限公司	九龙坡区西郊路56#	68781966
重庆力扬物业发展有限公司	九龙坡区杨家坪西郊路24号	68420872
重庆祥宏物业发展有限公司	九龙坡区杨家坪西郊三村47-C-8-1	68782768
自贡市荣州房地产有限公司重庆分公司	九龙坡区杨家坪兴胜路7号	68820724
重庆金鹏物业（集团）有限公司	九龙坡区直港12号	68443849
重庆晋愉地产（集团）股份有限公司	九龙坡区西效路2号6楼	68428888
重庆志龙建设开发有限公司	九龙坡区西郊路98#	61587968
重庆珠江实业有限公司	九龙坡区直港大道19号-1	89089898
重庆五星房地产开发有限公司	九龙坡区杨家坪直港大道22号	68431809
重庆裕达房地产开发有限公司	九龙坡区直港大道天宝新城天长路	61552805
重庆荣安实业（集团）有限公司	九龙坡区九龙坡区天宝路118号2楼	68122103
重庆艾佳集团实业有限公司	九龙坡区谢正街98号	68826495
重庆佳宇房地产开发有限责任公司	九龙坡区杨家坪直巷大道17号	61580888
重庆龙九建设有限责任公司	九龙坡区直港大道15号2楼	68453885
重庆隆鑫置业有限责任公司	九龙坡区石坪桥横街特设	89805868
重庆隆鑫地产置业有限公司	九龙坡区石坪桥横街特5号	89805870
重庆建兴房地产开发建筑有限公司	九龙坡区石杨路4号	68601509
重庆渝高科技产业（集团）股份有限公司	九龙坡区科园一路166号-2#14楼	68602544
重庆春风实业有限公司(房地产)	九龙坡区科园一路渝州广场C座7-3、4号	68881166
重庆大果房地产开发有限公司	九龙坡区石桥铺科园一路（渝高广场D—12—5）	68692211
重庆南方集团有限公司	九龙坡区科园四路195#	68521194
重庆太和物业（集团）有限公司	九龙坡区石桥铺科园元路190号	68889296
重庆百康年城市建设发展有限公司	九龙坡区南方花园C区161号	68699911
重庆枫丹实业有限公司	九龙坡区科园三街78号	68609774
重庆明生实业（集团）有限公司	九龙坡区渝州路33#	68616876
重庆港龙实业有限公司	九龙坡区歇台子科园四路195号	68521194
重庆和生恒力置业有限公司	九龙坡区石杨路44号19楼	61586001
重庆一城置业有限公司	九龙坡区石杨路44号19楼	61586000
重庆华宇物业（集团）有限公司	九龙坡区朝田村118#	68857864
重庆市绅豪房地产开发有限公司	九龙坡区朝田村200号	68679898
重庆国闳置业(集团)有限公司(房地产)	九龙坡区渝州路35号	68637189
重庆石桥房地产开发总公司	九龙坡区渝州路6#	68791193
重庆泰兴科技物业发展有限公司	九龙坡区渝州路80#1楼	68614465
重庆合飞记地产开发有限公司	九龙坡区白马凼35号8楼	68628322
广厦重庆置业发展有限公司	九龙坡区九龙坡区广厦城	68600666
重庆奥林匹克（集团）公司	九龙坡区科园六路298#	68968896
重庆郡都物业发展有限公司	九龙坡区科园六路295号	68653182
重庆金谷（集团）有限公司	九龙坡区含谷镇三重村	63553795

20-20 续表4 CONTINUED-4

企业名称 Name of Enterprises	企业详细地址 Address	电话号码 Tel.
重庆全兴物业有限公司	九龙坡区含谷镇含兴路1号	66684070
重庆瀛丹物业（集团）有限公司	九龙坡区西彭镇四合院	62910088
融侨长江（重庆）房地产有限公司	南岸区明佳路33号	62928376
融侨锦江（重庆）房地产有限公司	南岸区明佳路33号	62928376
重庆贝迪房地产开发有限公司	南岸区惠工路196号	62834835
重庆帝景置业有限公司	南岸区铜元局新村1号	62983020
重庆嘉发实业有限公司	南岸区南坪西路32号	62318668
重庆丹龙实业（集团）有限公司	南岸区南坪万寿路57号	67463451
重庆市华竹房地产开发有限公司	南岸区四小区花园村湖滨路4号	62906970
重庆金阳房地产开发有限公司	南岸区南坪西路68号	62958205
重庆路桥股份有限公司	南岸区南坪经济技术开发区丹龙路1号	62802225
重庆怡丰房地产开发总公司	南岸区花园村桃源路89号	62901902
重庆天骄物业发展有限公司	南岸区南坪金山路39号	62923063
重庆洋世达房地产开发有限公司	南岸区南坪金山支路18号	62914325
重庆江山物业发展有限公司	南岸区明佳园1号	62817658
重庆浦辉房地产开发有限公司	南岸区南坪东路581号	62942103
重庆聚丰房地产开发（集团）有限公司	南岸区南路17号	62819888
重庆康庄物业发展有限公司	南岸区工贸大厦12号6-4	67725119
重庆天龙房地产开发有限公司	南岸区珊瑚村	62942966
重庆福天房地产开发有限公司	南岸区南坪西路27号	62986966
重庆昌龙实业（集团）有限公司	南岸区惠工路35号	62980008
重庆市南坪实业总公司	南岸区浪高	62959050
重庆宏声房地产开发有限责任公司	南岸区南坪南路323号	62967070
重庆市裕佳房地产开发有限公司	南岸区南坪南路9号	62962209
重庆渝能产业（集团）有限公司	南岸区金台大厦23楼	62984034
重庆正扬实业（集团）有限公司	南岸区南城大道197号	62900212
重庆市江大建设开发（集团）有限公司	南岸区金紫街216号	62923288
重庆万凯实业有限公司	南岸区南城大道199#	62988665
重庆市江南城市建设资产经营管理有限公司	南岸区南城大道199号	62988026
重庆南岸滨江路开发建设有限公司	南岸区海棠晓月B区8号	62954848
重庆重点工程建设拆迁开发公司	南岸区四公里新民园F栋	62757636
重庆交院江南大学城置业有限公司	南岸区学府大道66号	62652363
重庆大帝集团房地产开发有限公司	南岸区石牛村长房子	63848855
重庆宏声远景实业（集团）有限公司	南岸区龙洞坡70#	62466296
重庆市森林房地产开发有限公司	南岸区黄桷垭镇南山索道南山站	62873021
重庆天奇物业（集团）有限公司	北碚区胜利街81	68210767
重庆市迪鸥城市建设有限公司	北碚区天生新村18号	68216322
重庆海宇置业（集团）有限公司	北碚区北碚区碚南大道123号	68256838
重庆缙云旅游综合开发有限公司	北碚区北温泉街道团山堡	68218519
黑龙江省大庆巨豪房地产开发有限公司	北碚区同兴	13896093612
重庆华新国际实业有限公司	北碚区水天花园商业行A幢	68326001

20-20 续表5 CONTINUED-5

企业名称 Name of Enterprises	企业详细地址 Address	电话号码 Tel.
重庆龙脊置业发展有限公司	渝北区双龙大道318号	66396817
重庆长帆地产发展有限公司	渝北区银鑫路	86010636
重庆成全房地产开发(集团)有限公司	渝北区双龙湖街道双龙大道11号	67809366
重庆浩博实业(集团)有限公司	渝北区双龙大道488号	67847688
重庆佳辰经济发展有限公司	渝北区北城天街北岸星座7楼	67726731
重庆鲁能开发（集团）有限公司	渝北区五童路	67988666
重庆鸿恩寺实业发展有限公司	渝北区红石路147号	67603695
重庆时代建设集团有限公司	渝北区龙溪镇松石北路106号	67791834
重庆康居物业发展有限公司	渝北区松石支路470号-1号	67579251
重庆市琼海实业（集团）有限公司	渝北区龙溪街道黄泥磅五人支路66号	67081850
重庆申基实业（集团）有限公司	渝北区红石路147	67603695
重庆金岛置业有限公司	渝北区松石北路58#	67600766
重庆市新城房地产开发公司	渝北区龙溪街道龙脊路101号	67801638
重庆旭日房地产开发有限公司	渝北区花卉东路28号	67906120
重庆市渝北房屋开发公司	渝北区花卉东路	67906883
重庆市康德实业(集团)有限公司	渝北区红全路34号	67516004
重庆北部新城建设集团北城物业发展有限公司	渝北区金龙路	67600035
重庆富悦实业集团有限公司	渝北区金龙路240号	67080100
重庆市龙德房地产开发有限公司	渝北区金龙路75号附号	67606301
重庆燕城房地产开发有限责任公司	渝北区松石北路102号	67791917
重庆天江坤宸置业有限公司	渝北区武陵路	89038515
重庆渝安房地产开发有限公司	渝北区金龙路268号	67525336
重庆通亚房地产开发有限公司	渝北区加州花园A2栋3楼	67625793
重庆市渝北区华夏物业有限公司	渝北区新南路9号	89116000
重庆环球物业发展有限公司	渝北区双龙大道348号	67532877
重庆龙湖地产发展有限公司	渝北区新南路6号	67726731
重庆加新产业集团有限公司	渝北区新南路9号	67535612
重庆华润物业发展有限公司	渝北区五红路66号	67856658
重庆市城北房地产开发有限公司	渝北区宝圣东路299号	67457789
重庆市刘奇霖房地产开发有限公司	渝北区宝圣西路	13983453576
重庆市木鱼石物业发展有限公司	渝北区双湖路木鱼石花园	67135888
重庆聚信房地产开发(集团)有限公司	渝北区渝航路渝航市场	67608288
重庆友诚水电建设有限公司(房地产)	渝北区渝航路三巷29号	67528882
重庆金凯实业股份有限公司	渝北区白寺村	67463254
重庆华新国际城市有限公司	渝北区人和锦秀山庄	67638195
重庆香江高科地产发展有限公司	渝北区新光大道16号	67528899
重庆耀文房地产开发有限公司	渝北区万寿村8社	67915423
重庆黎强房地产开发有限公司	巴南区鱼洞街道鱼轻路48号	66212847
重庆源聚房地产开发有限公司	巴南区鱼洞街道鱼轻路50号	66224648
重庆庆丰实业有限公司	巴南区鱼洞新市街79-6	86533110
重庆宏源房地产开发公司	巴南区巴县大道35-3号	66228877

20-20 续表6 CONTINUED-6

企业名称 Name of Enterprises	企业详细地址 Address	电话号码 Tel.
重庆市巴南区建设集团有限公司	巴南区鱼洞街道建河路5-9号	66239170
重庆东南亚实业总公司	巴南区马正街12号	62865969
重庆塑皇建设（集团）有限公司	巴南区土桥正街4号	61579885
重庆凯光置业有限公司	巴南区土桥正街4号楼	62595510
重庆典雅房地产开发集团有限公司	巴南区岔路口典雅综合楼	62585186
重庆日月房地产开发有限公司	巴南区民主新街	86539766
重庆市振兴房地产开发有限公司	黔江区新华大道中段1094号	79324448
重庆黄阁堡房地产开发有限公司	长寿区向阳路社区	40244733
重庆长寿光宇开发有限公司	长寿区向阳路社区	67737213
重庆长峡物业有限公司	长寿区向阳路社区	40245656
重庆市双杰物业有限公司	长寿区凤岭路社区	40255657
重庆市宋城建设开发有限公司	长寿区望江路社区	40228058
重庆市渝鸿房地产开发有限公司	长寿区三峡路社区	40406604
重庆渝发建设房地产开发公司	长寿区轻化路社区	40461458
重庆维丰房地产开发有限公司	长寿区查家湾社区	68974377
潼南县凉风垭经济园区建设有限责任公司	潼南县凉风垭	44559968
潼南县新城开发建设有限公司	潼南县潼古路8号	44578005
重庆丰都渝丰房地产开发有限公司	丰都县滨江东路178号	70715409
重庆市奇正房地产有限公司	丰都县平都大道西路295号	70723666
重庆市垫江房地产有限责任公司	垫江县南内街31号	74513598
开县龙泰房地产开发有限责任公司	开县富厚	52253048
重庆飞洋物业（集团）有限公司	江津市夔州路320号	56552222
江津市建宇房地产开发有限责任公司	江津市大什字建宇综合楼	47552733
江津市金桥房地产开发有限公司	江津市小什字	47557954
重庆祥瑞房地产集团有限公司	江津市大同路393附2号	47522177
合川市城镇建设综合开发有限公司	合川市合办交通街6号	42821616
重庆金万科房地产开发有限公司	合川市名人街60号	42749709
重庆金九实业（集团）有限公司	合川市合办久长路社区苏家街31号	42863388
合川市堤防建设总公司	合川市苏家街195号	42748888
重庆市茂田实业集团有限公司	合川市合阳办营盘街1号（现：杨江二村3号附1号8-1.8-2）	67730528
重庆驰华实业有限公司	合川市瑞社区瑞山路141号	43827877
重庆市中人实业（集团）有限公司	合川市钓办处城北市场F幢3楼	42838650
永川市炳力实业有限公司	永川市中山路同文里1号	49867388
重庆永川成全房地产开发（集团）有限公司	永川市中山路12号	67809366
重庆市伟映实业有限公司	永川市中山路办事处中山大道东段5号	49807788
重庆渝荣房屋建设开发有限公司	永川市渝西大道中段36号	49821038
重庆市腾龙实业集团有限公司	永川市汇龙大道438号三楼	13983191795
重庆宸宙房地产开发有限公司	永川市汇龙大道105号	13908362006
重庆渝永建设集团开发公司	永川市玉屏路98号	49862546
永川市群力房地产开发有限公司	永川市泸州街37号	49847658

20－21 重点批发零售贸易企业目录（2004年）
List of Major Wholesale and Retail Trade Enterprises (2004)

企业名称 Name of Enterprises	企业详细地址 Address	电话号码 Tel.
重庆桐君阁股份有限公司	重庆市渝中区解放西路1号	89885200
中国汽车工业西南销售公司	重庆市九龙坡区石新路二郎路口	68614054
中国邮电器材重庆公司	重庆市渝中区两路口体育村44号	63600109
重庆百货大楼股份有限公司	重庆市渝中区民权路2号	63843197
重庆医药股份有限公司	重庆市渝中区民族路128号	63842684
中国石油天然气股份有限公司重庆销售分公司	重庆市渝中区五四路46号	67325508
重庆商社（集团）有限公司	重庆市渝中区青年路18号	63803262
重庆新华书店(集团)有限责任公司	重庆市渝中区民权路10号	63737412
九禾农资股份有限公司	重庆市九龙坡区杨家坪街道兴胜路68号	68966630
重庆正典汽车销售有限责任公司	重庆市渝北区新南路50号	67531788
重庆市新大兴实业（集团）有限公司	重庆市涪陵区兴华中路37号	87800032
重庆市国美电器有限公司	重庆市沙坪坝区小龙坎正街166号	89054591
重庆大都会广场太平洋百货有限公司	重庆市渝中区邹容路68号	63710088
重庆家乐福商业有限公司	重庆市渝中区民族路2号	63788560
中国石化销售有限公司川渝重庆分公司	重庆市渝中区邹容广场B座6楼	63799206
上海大众汽车重庆中汽销售服务有限公司	重庆市渝北区经开大道99号	89112005
重庆山城超市平价连锁有限公司	重庆市九龙坡区石坪桥建筑二村20号	68828988
中国汽车工业重庆销售公司	重庆市南岸区六公里正街1号	62766545
重庆家乐福连锁超市有限公司	重庆市渝中区沧白路2号	63789006
中国石化销售三川公司重庆公司	重庆市渝中区大溪沟静园4号楼1-5	63872334
重庆家乐福连锁超市有限公司金观音店	重庆市江北区建新西路金观音广场2号	67763392

20－22 企业集团目录（2004年）
List of Business Groups (2004)

企业集团名称 Name of Business Groups	母公司地址 Address of Parent Companies	电话号码 Telephone
长安汽车集团	重庆市江北区建新东路260号	67590114
朝华科技（集团）股份有限公司	重庆市涪陵区江东群沱子31号	68886881
大江工业集团	重庆市巴南区鱼洞街道办事处	66283641
海康纺织（集团）有限公司	重庆市万州区王牌路698号	58115392
华西包装（集团）有限责任公司	重庆市渝中区捍卫路6号临华大夏10楼	63506212
建设工业集团	重庆市谢家湾正街47号	68813741
隆鑫控股集团	重庆市九龙坡区石坪桥横街特5号	89062170
太极集团有限公司	重庆市涪陵区百花路8号	72800613
西南铝业集团	重庆市九龙坡区西彭镇	65809118
中国嘉陵集团	重庆市沙坪坝区双碑	65190114
中国四联仪器仪表集团有限	重庆市北碚区碚峡路人民村1号	68862766
中国天府可乐集团公司（重庆）	重庆市九龙坡区石坪桥横街7号	68822354
重庆北部双龙建设集团	重庆市渝北区双龙湖街道翠湖路110号	67812688
重庆北部新城建设集团	重庆市渝北区金龙路21号	67912006
重庆必扬企业（集团）有限公司	重庆市江北区渝北三村6号	67653204
重庆斌鑫物业集团	渝中区健康路46号花园大厦二楼	61659199
重庆博达建设集团股份有限公司	重庆江津几江大什字建宇商城9楼	47538870
重庆长江电工（集团）有限公司	重庆市南岸区茶园新城区光电路1#	62489122
重庆长途汽车运输（集团）有限公司	重庆市高新区石杨村88号	89088458
重庆城建控股集团	重庆市渝中区人民支路2号	63617226
重庆川东化工集团有限公司	重庆市南岸区白沙沱中窑街20#	62950880
重庆大帝集团	重庆市南岸区南山镇石牛村长房子	63848855
重庆涪陵宏声实业（集团）有限责任公司	重庆市涪陵区兴华中路8号	62906948
重庆富悦实业集团有限公司	重庆市渝北区龙溪街道金龙路240号	67080100
重庆钢铁集团	重庆市大渡口区大堰三村1栋1号	68843548
重庆港务（集团）有限责任公司	重庆市渝中区朝千路3号	63100216
重庆海浪科技实业集团	重庆市渝中区大坪虎头岩1号	68591512
重庆海通机械制造集团	重庆市永川市南大街小桥子59号	49832088
重庆宏大纸业集团	重庆市北碚区澄江镇烟湖滩	68865617
重庆华伟工业集团	重庆市北碚区歇马镇	68243987
重庆华夏建工集团	重庆市渝北区龙溪镇新南路9#	89116000
重庆华宇集团	重庆市九龙坡区陈家坪朝田村118号	68857864
重庆化医控股（集团）公司	重庆市渝中区五四路28号赛格尔大厦8楼	89887261
重庆机场集团	重庆江北国际机场	67152355

20-22 续表1 CONTINUNED-1

企业集团名称 Name of Business Groups	母公司地址 Address of Parent Companies	电话号码 Telephone
重庆机电控股（集团）公司	重庆市渝中区中山三路155号	63891163
重庆鸡冠石建设集团	重庆市南岸区南坪东路581#	62942110
重庆建工集团	重庆市渝中区捍卫路8号	63500756
重庆江合煤化（集团）有限公司	重庆市渝北区两路镇双凤路273号	67815038
重庆金凤丝绸（集团）有限公司	重庆市永川市环北东路158号	49800874
重庆金弓集团	重庆市渝北区新牌坊一街41号	67630679
重庆金冠科技集团	重庆市九龙坡区石桥铺科园四街6号	68622255
重庆金九实业集团	重庆市合川市合阳办苏家街31号	42863388
重庆金山科技集团	重庆市渝中区中山三路155号	63860333
重庆九龙建设集团	重庆市九龙坡区杨家坪西郊路98号	61587968
重庆聚信地产集团	重庆市渝北区两路渝航路渝航商场	67608288
重庆跨越集团	重庆市沙坪坝区沙坪公园58号	65300186
重庆力帆实业集团有限公司	重庆市沙坪坝区上桥张家湾60号	61663112
重庆隆西建设集团	重庆市永川市中山大道东段345-7#	49822490
重庆旅业（集团）有限公司	重庆市沙坪坝区小新街84号	65344532
重庆美心集团	重庆市南岸区南坪经济开发区白鹤路51#	62762516
重庆南方集团有限公司	重庆市高新区科园四路195号	68521111
重庆平伟科技集团	重庆市渝北区回兴镇科技产业园16号	67451802
重庆轻纺控股（集团）公司	重庆渝中区上清寺嘉陵桥东村56号	63861350
重庆庆铃铃汽车集团	重庆市九龙坡区中梁山协兴村1号	65262233
重庆燃气（集团）有限责任公司	重庆市江北区嘉陵四村1号	67710344
重庆日报报业集团	重庆市渝中区较场口85号	63907065
重庆荣达建设集团有限公司	重庆市渝北区龙溪镇红黄路169号	67082068
重庆三峡水利电力(集团)股份有限公司	重庆市万州区鸽子沟72号	87509600
重庆商社集团	重庆市渝中区青年路18号	63803262
重庆盛源建设集团	重庆市渝中区捍卫路32号10F	63520720
重庆食品集团公司	重庆市渝中区陕西路72号	63841360
重庆市博赛矿业集团	重庆市南川市二环路博赛矿业大厦	71484976
重庆市长江农工商控股集团	重庆市江北区华唐路2号	67765295
重庆市涪陵建筑陶瓷集团	重庆市涪陵区江东办事处涪清路31号	72374058
重庆市涪陵金帝集团	重庆市涪陵区涪清路233号	72380008
重庆市涪陵水利电力投资集团	重庆市涪陵区望州路20号	72286171
重庆市涪陵榨菜（集团）有限公司	重庆市涪陵区体育南路29号	72234067
重庆市富丰水泥集团有限公司	重庆市合川市三汇镇皂树村	68320212
重庆市公共交通控股（集团）有限公司	重庆市渝中区长江一路1号	63893167

20-22 续表2 CONTINUNED-2

企业集团名称 Name of Business Groups	母公司地址 Address of Parent Companies	电话号码 Telephone
重庆市汽车运输集团	重庆市渝中区临江路60号	63842759
重庆市水利电力产业（集团）有限责任公司	重庆市渝中区中山三路131号	89067829
重庆市水务控股集团	重庆市江北区红黄路中北大楼	67502449
重庆市万州港口（集团）有限责任公司	重庆市万州区金港路港口办公楼	58295502
重庆市万州粮油（集团）有限公司	重庆市万州区新城路20号	58151075
重庆市物资集团	重庆市渝中区领事巷15号	89037765
重庆市渝万建设集团	重庆市万州区王牌路398号	58117188
重庆四维瓷业（集团）股份有限公司	重庆市江津市油溪镇	61088699
重庆索特集团	重庆市万州区观音岩1号	58960318
重庆泰正集团	重庆市渝中区较场口85号大元广场9楼	63731070
重庆腾辉集团	重庆市经济技术开发区丹龙路18号	62767888
重庆天奇物业集团	重庆市北碚区胜利路81号	68866380
重庆铁马工业集团	重庆市九龙坡区杨家坪正街43#	68423523
重庆乌江电力集团有限公司	重庆市黔江区城西路118号	79235653
重庆小天鹅投资控股（集团）有限公司	江北区建新北路78号	67866656
重庆协信控股集团	重庆市渝中区新华路4号附1号	63819666
重庆新大兴实业集团	重庆市涪陵区兴华中路37号	87800001
重庆新华书店集团	重庆市渝中区民权路10号	63814724
重庆新原兴企业集团有限公司	重庆市江北区塔坪120号	67719003
重庆阳光旅业集团公司	重庆市渝中区民生路235号	63554192
重庆洋世达实业集团	南岸区南坪金山支路18号	62914325
重庆一品建设集团有限公司	重庆市高新区科园六路30号	68571578
重庆怡然房地产开发集团	重庆市九龙坡区石坪桥横街特16号	68668655
重庆银钢科技集团	重庆市北碚区同兴南路71号	68327809
重庆渝高科技产业（集团）股份有限公司	重庆高新区石桥铺科园一路166号2号	68602544
重庆渝能产业集团	重庆市南岸区南坪金台大厦23楼	62984034
重庆渝永建设集团	重庆市永川市玉屏路98号	49862546
重庆雨水企业（集团）有限公司	重庆市沙坪坝区汉渝路66号	68967301
重庆钰鑫实业集团有限责任公司	重庆建桥工业园(大渡口区)金桥路16号	68952888
重庆跃华（集团）有限公司	重庆市九龙坡区石桥铺石杨路9号	68609699
重庆中天环保产业（集团）有限公司	重庆市南岸区南坪白鹤路47号	62927744
宗申产业集团有限公司	重庆市巴南区花溪镇民主村宗申工业园	66372824

20－23 营业收入、总资产均上亿元的企业集团按营业收入排序（2004年）
Business Groups with Business Revenue and Total Assets Both over 100 Million Yuan in Order of Business Revenue (2004)

序号 Order	名　称 Name	序号 Order	名　称 Name
1	长安汽车集团	40	重庆一品建设集团有限公司
2	重庆钢铁集团	41	重庆跨越集团
3	重庆商社集团	42	重庆日报报业集团
4	重庆机电控股（集团）公司	43	重庆三峡水利电力(集团)股份有限公司
5	重庆化医控股（集团）公司	44	重庆北部新城建设集团
6	重庆力帆实业集团有限公司	45	重庆涪陵宏声实业（集团）有限责任公司
7	重庆建工集团	46	重庆市汽车运输集团
8	太极集团有限公司	47	重庆四维瓷业（集团）股份有限公司
9	隆鑫控股集团	48	重庆鸡冠石建设集团
10	建设工业集团	49	重庆市涪陵金帝集团
11	中国嘉陵集团	50	重庆新大兴实业集团
12	宗申产业集团有限公司	51	重庆九龙建设集团
13	重庆庆铃汽车集团	52	重庆市富丰水泥集团有限公司
14	西南铝业集团	53	重庆机场集团
15	重庆轻纺控股（集团）公司	54	重庆钰鑫实业集团有限责任公司
16	重庆市物资集团	55	海康纺织（集团）有限公司
17	中国四联仪器仪表集团有限	56	重庆市涪陵榨菜（集团）有限公司
18	重庆新华书店集团	57	重庆金冠科技集团
19	朝华科技（集团）股份有限公司	58	重庆北部双龙建设集团
20	重庆华宇集团	59	重庆渝能产业集团
21	大江工业集团	60	重庆长途汽车运输（集团）有限公司
22	重庆市博赛矿业集团	61	重庆博达建设集团股份有限公司
23	重庆城建控股集团	62	重庆泰正集团
24	重庆燃气（集团）有限责任公司	63	重庆金弓集团
25	重庆市水利电力产业（集团）有限责任公司	64	重庆渝永建设集团
26	重庆市公共交通控股（集团）有限公司	65	重庆江合煤化（集团）有限公司
27	重庆美心集团	66	重庆金凤丝绸（集团）有限公司
28	重庆腾辉集团	67	中国天府可乐集团公司（重庆）
29	重庆协信控股集团	68	重庆平伟科技集团
30	重庆乌江电力集团有限公司	69	重庆富悦实业集团有限公司
31	重庆市涪陵水利电力投资集团	70	重庆隆西建设集团
32	重庆铁马工业集团	71	华西包装（集团）有限责任公司
33	重庆银钢科技集团	72	重庆洋世达实业集团
34	重庆市水务控股集团	73	重庆华伟工业集团
35	重庆港务（集团）有限责任公司	74	重庆海浪科技实业集团
36	重庆南方集团有限公司	75	重庆荣达建设集团有限公司
37	重庆川东化工集团有限公司	76	重庆市涪陵建筑陶瓷集团
38	重庆长江电工（集团）有限公司	77	重庆市万州港口（集团）有限责任公司
39	重庆市长江农工商控股集团	78	重庆小天鹅投资控股（集团）有限公司

20－24 营业收入、总资产均上亿元的企业集团按总资产排序（2004年）
Business Groups with Business Revenue and Total Assets Both over 100 Million Yuan in Order of Total Assets (2004)

序号 Order	名称 Name	序号 Order	名称 Name
1	长安汽车集团	40	重庆四维瓷业（集团）股份有限公司
2	重庆钢铁集团	41	重庆市万州港口（集团）有限责任公司
3	重庆庆铃汽车集团	42	重庆市涪陵建筑陶瓷集团
4	重庆机电控股（集团）公司	43	重庆市汽车运输集团
5	重庆化医控股（集团）公司	44	重庆美心集团
6	重庆市水务控股集团	45	重庆鸡冠石建设集团
7	重庆轻纺控股（集团）公司	46	重庆渝能产业集团
8	西南铝业集团	47	重庆市物资集团
9	太极集团有限公司	48	海康纺织（集团）有限公司
10	建设工业集团	49	重庆市涪陵金帝集团
11	重庆商社集团	50	重庆跨越集团
12	中国嘉陵集团	51	重庆市富丰水泥集团有限公司
13	重庆建工集团	52	重庆小天鹅投资控股（集团）有限公司
14	重庆市涪陵水利电力投资集团	53	重庆博达建设集团股份有限公司
15	重庆力帆实业集团有限公司	54	重庆钰鑫实业集团有限责任公司
16	重庆市水利电力产业（集团）有限责任公司	55	华西包装（集团）有限责任公司
17	隆鑫控股集团	56	重庆银钢科技集团
18	宗申产业集团有限公司	57	重庆九龙建设集团
19	大江工业集团	58	重庆长途汽车运输（集团）有限公司
20	重庆机场集团	59	重庆市涪陵榨菜（集团）有限公司
21	中国四联仪器仪表集团有限	60	重庆川东化工集团有限公司
22	朝华科技（集团）股份有限公司	61	重庆北部新城建设集团
23	重庆乌江电力集团有限公司	62	重庆华伟工业集团
24	重庆腾辉集团	63	重庆泰正集团
25	重庆港务（集团）有限责任公司	64	重庆江合煤化（集团）有限公司
26	重庆协信控股集团	65	重庆北部双龙建设集团
27	重庆南方集团有限公司	66	重庆金弓集团
28	重庆新华书店集团	67	重庆富悦实业集团有限公司
29	重庆华宇集团	68	重庆平伟科技集团
30	重庆市公共交通控股（集团）有限公司	69	重庆荣达建设集团有限公司
31	重庆燃气（集团）有限责任公司	70	重庆洋世达实业集团
32	重庆日报报业集团	71	重庆金冠科技集团
33	重庆市长江农工商控股集团	72	重庆一品建设集团有限公司
34	重庆铁马工业集团	73	中国天府可乐集团公司（重庆）
35	重庆城建控股集团	74	重庆隆西建设集团
36	重庆长江电工（集团）有限公司	75	重庆海浪科技实业集团
37	重庆三峡水利电力(集团)股份有限公司	76	重庆新大兴实业集团
38	重庆涪陵宏声实业（集团）有限责任公司	77	重庆渝永建设集团
39	重庆市博赛矿业集团	78	重庆金凤丝绸（集团）有限公司

20－25 亿元以上商品交易市场按成交额排序（2004年）
Commodity Markets with Transaction Value over 100 Million Yuan in Order of Transaction Value (2004)

序 号 Order	市场名称 Name of Markets	序 号 Order	市场名称 Name of Markets
1	重庆朝天门综合交易市场	35	重庆全悦钢材销售有限公司
2	重庆市观音桥农贸市场	36	重庆市渝北区龙溪建材市场
3	绿云石都建材市场	37	黄水黄莲市场
4	重庆小天鹅综合批发市场	38	江津市几江农贸市场
5	重庆马家岩装饰材料批发市场	39	开县鑫新物业服务中心汉丰大市场
6	重庆金属材料现货交易市场	40	龙水废金属市场
7	重庆大渡口区鑫鹏福钢材市场	41	重庆西北建材仓储批发市场
8	重庆机动车交易市场	42	重庆联芳建材市场
9	重庆汽车配件整车交易中心	43	重庆市两路农贸市场有限公司
10	重庆龙文实业有限公司大渡口钢材市场	44	万州区银河综合市场有限公司
11	重庆高新区老顶坡汽摩综合市场	45	南川市中心市场
12	重庆西南物资交易市场	46	重庆新东方女人广场
13	重庆市家具交易市场	47	开县伟业糖酒有限公司工业品市场
14	重庆市龙水五金市场有限公司	48	重庆外滩摩配交易市场
15	西南建材中心四三六处钢材现货交易市场	49	重庆坤源物业发展有限公司
16	重庆万隆小食品批发市场	50	重庆较场口联讯五金电线市场
17	重庆市万州商贸城	51	永川玉屏农贸市场
18	重庆市旧车交易市场	52	重庆杨家坪农贸市场
19	重庆陶瓷市场	53	重庆中兴塑料市场
20	重庆市巴南区鱼洞农贸市场	54	重庆渝北区渝航百货商场有限公司
21	中国重庆畜牧科技城饲料兽药市场管理中心	55	重庆市万盛区鹏生综合市场有限公司
22	重庆得意装饰世界	56	重庆巴山陶瓷建材市场
23	南坪正扬市场	57	重庆市垫江县北门市场
24	重庆市万州区江南大市场有限公司	58	潼南县八角庙综合交易市场
25	重庆市菜园坝皮革市场	59	重庆大坪天海汽配城
26	重庆市川东农副产品批发市场	60	重庆雅兰电子城
27	重庆渝中区七星岗家具市场	61	长寿区凤城镇消费品综合市场
28	重庆大正交易城水产品批发市场	62	重庆泰兴物业发展有限公司
29	重庆渝州交易城市场	63	重庆赛博特尔数码广场有限公司
30	重庆市涪陵合智商业广场	64	丰都县平都商场
31	合川市合州市场	65	重庆市巴南区马王坪农贸市场
32	重庆市菜园坝农副产品批发市场	66	重庆市德意家具城
33	重庆渝中区中天广场装饰城	67	綦江河东市场
34	重庆市西三街农副水产品批发市场	68	重庆市涪陵南门山农贸市场

20—26 重庆市企业法人知名字号（2004年底）
Noted Titles of Legal Enterprises in Chongqing (at End of 2004)

序号 Order	企业法人名称 Legal Names of Enterprises	知名字号 Noted Titles
1	中国嘉陵工业股份有限公司（集团）	嘉陵
2	重庆建设·雅马哈摩托车有限公司	建设·雅马哈
3	长安汽车（集团）有限责任公司	长安
4	重庆太极实业（集团）股份有限公司	太极
5	中国四联仪器仪表集团有限公司	川仪
6	重庆桐君阁股份有限公司	桐君阁
7	西南铝加工厂	西南铝（西铝）
8	重庆隆鑫工业（集团）有限公司	隆鑫
9	重庆小天鹅饮食文化（集团）有限公司	小天鹅
10	重庆宗申摩托车科技（集团）有限公司	宗申
11	重庆梦柯达鞋业有限公司	梦柯达
12	重庆华宇物业（集团）有限公司	华宇
13	中国石化集团重庆一坪高级润滑油公司	一坪
14	重庆大川门业集团有限公司	大川
15	重庆显丰实业（集团）有限公司	显丰
16	重庆明月皮鞋厂有限公司	明月
17	重庆跃华（集团）有限公司	跃华
18	重庆必扬企业（集团）有限公司	必扬
19	重庆万友经济发展有限责任公司	万友
20	重庆人道美蔬菜副食品连锁公司	人道美
21	重庆百吉厨房用具有限公司	百吉
22	重庆美心（集团）有限公司	美心
23	重庆千叶实业总公司	千叶
24	重庆金联陶瓷有限公司	金联
25	重庆瀛丹物业（集团）有限公司	瀛丹
26	重庆金弓（集团）有限公司	金弓
27	重庆互邦实业发展有限公司	互邦
28	重庆天厨味精厂	天厨
29	重庆精益光学眼镜公司	精益
30	重庆涪柴工业有限责任公司	涪柴
31	重庆市新胜茶场	新胜
32	重庆晋愉地产（集团）股份有限公司	晋愉
33	重庆桃都城市酒店有限责任公司	桃都
34	重庆写真广告有限公司	写真
35	重庆劲力实业（集团）有限公司	劲力
36	重庆腾辉特种水泥有限公司	腾辉
37	重庆名豪实业（集团）有限公司	名豪
38	重庆天龙发展（集团）有限公司	天龙
39	重庆银星智业（集团）有限公司	银星
40	重庆大江工业（集团）有限责任公司	大江
41	重庆渝能产业（集团）有限公司	渝能

20-26 续表 CONTINUED

序号 Order	企业法人名称 Legal Names of Enterprises	知名字号 Noted Titles
42	重庆华林印务有限公司	华林
43	重庆诚泰贸易有限公司	诚泰
44	重庆市欣宏建筑有限责任公司	欣宏
45	重庆庆隆屋业发展有限公司	庆隆
46	重庆同创置业发展有限公司	同创
47	重庆市御临建筑工程有限公司	御临
48	重庆科而士鞋业（集团）有限公司	科而士
49	重庆市安吉尔富氧纯水厂	安吉尔
50	重庆洋世达房地产开发有限公司	洋世达
51	重庆时珍阁医药科技开发有限公司	时珍阁
52	重庆市新大兴百货集团有限责任公司	新大兴
53	重庆新原兴企业集团有限公司	新原兴
54	重庆山城超市有限公司	山城超市
55	重庆和平药房连锁有限责任公司	和平药房
56	百年光彩实业（重庆）有限公司	百年光彩
57	重庆南川金山刚玉有限公司	金山刚玉
58	重庆力帆轰达实业（集团）有限公司	力帆轰达
59	重庆朝华科技股份有限公司	朝华
60	重庆长丰通信股份有限公司	长丰
61	重庆协信控股（集团）有限公司	协信
62	重庆沁园实业有限公司	沁园
63	重庆荣华建筑（集团）有限公司	荣华
64	重庆德泉电力股份有限公司	德泉
65	重庆天青锶化股份有限公司	天青
66	重庆青山工业有限责任公司	青山
67	重庆正扬实业（集团）有限公司	正扬
68	重庆双叶药业有限公司	双叶
69	重庆泰正（集团）有限公司	泰正
70	重庆海浪科技实业（集团）有限公司	海浪
71	重庆市天友乳业有限公司	天友
72	广厦重庆第一建筑（集团）有限公司	广厦
73	重庆渝堰实业（集团）有限公司	渝堰
74	重庆洁诚洗染有限公司	洁诚
75	重庆扬子岛康乐健身有限责任公司	扬子岛
76	重庆谭木匠工艺品有限公司	谭木匠
77	重庆陈川粤实业有限公司	陈川粤
78	重庆市三利百货有限责任公司	三利百货
79	重庆万达仪器有限公司	万达仪器
80	重庆富侨保健服务有限公司	富侨保健
81	重庆清华大酒楼有限责任公司	清华大酒楼
82	重庆市永固工程拉筋带厂有限公司	永固
83	重庆贝迪房地产开发有限公司	贝迪

二十一　高新技术产业

HIGH-TECH INDUSTRY

简要说明　Brief Introduction

本章资料包括高新技术产业单位基本情况和高新技术产品主要指标，由市统计局社会科技处整理提供。

Data in this chapter cover basic statistics on high-tech enterprises and main indicators of high-tech products. The data are provided by Division of Social and Technology Statistics, Municipal Bureau of Statistics.

21－1 高新技术产业单位基本情况（2003－2004年）
Basic Statistics on High-tech Enterprises (2003-2004)

单位：万元 (10 000 yuan)

项　　目	Item	2003	2004
总产值（现价）	Gross Output Value (current price)	7705479	9735932
#高新技术及产品产值	Of Which: Output Value of High-tech and Related Products	4270127	6060801
#专利产品产值	Of Which: Output Value of Patent Products	421203	481505
增加值	Value Added	1967324	2478215
技工贸总收入	Technical Revenue, Industrial Revenue and Sales Revenue	7366373	9655155
#主营业务收入	Major Business Revenue	7154820	9025628
利润总额	Total Profits	481547	709737
产品销售税金及附加	Sales Tax and Extra Charges	116471	159683
本年应交增殖税	Value Added Tax Payable	302135	379760
高新技术产品实现利润	Profits Accomplished by High-tech Products	591050	769860
期末固定资产原价	Original Value of Fixed Assets	5711139	5909499
期末固定资产净值	Net Value of Fixed Assets	3679201	3892146
科技活动经费支出	Expenses for Scientific and Technological Activities	243549	316897
#新产品开发经费支出	Expense for New Product Development	147219	195765
科技活动项目（课题）数（项）	Number of Scientific and technological Projects (unit)	3119	2663
科技活动机构数（个）	Number of Scientific and technological Institutions (unit)	260	311
从业人员劳动报酬总额	Total Earnings of Employed Persons	383336	447805
从业人员平均人数（人）	Average Employed Persons (person)	255202	265193
享受各级政府对高新技术产品的减免税	Reduction and Free Tax Received from Various Governments for High-tech Products	23899	23066

21－2 高新技术产品主要指标（2003－2004年）
Main Indicators of High-tech Products (2003-2004)

单位：万元 (10 000 yuan)

项目	Item	现价总产值 Gross Output Value at Current Prices	
		2003	2004
总计	**Total**	**4231304**	**6023194**
按登记注册类型分	**By Registration**		
国有企业	State-owned	197687	266304
集体企业	Collective-owned	37997	8706
股份合作企业	Cooperative Enterprises	12523	9391
联营企业	Joint Ownership Enterprises	78616	58624
有限责任公司	Limited Liability Corporations	1061543	1722883
股份有限公司	Share Holding Corporations Limited	1393676	1356708
私营企业	Private Enterprises	543354	772307
其他企业	Other Domestic-funded Enterprises		
港澳台商投资企业	Shareholding Corporations Ltd. with Investment from Hong Kong Macao and Taiwan	127642	156304
外商投资企业	Shareholding Corporations Ltd. with Foreign Investment	778266	1671966
按技术领域分	**By Technology Field**		
#电子信息	Electronics and Information	224099	405238
生物、医药和医疗器械	Biology and Medical Technologies	283978	330753
新材料	New Materials	588203	763800
光机电一体化	Photoelectric Mechanical and Electrical Products	2893503	3968478
新能源与高效节能	New Energy Facilities Concentrated and Economized on Energy	111097	318461
环境保护	Environmental Protection	30862	57170
航空航天	Aviation and Aerospace Technology	5115	8836

项目	Item	产品销售收入 Sales Revenue	
		2003	2004
总计	**Total**	**3960140**	**5920894**
按登记注册类型分	**By Registration**		
国有企业	State-owned	183943	253031
集体企业	Collective-owned	33376	7538
股份合作企业	Cooperative Enterprises	11852	8336
联营企业	Joint Ownership Enterprises	71239	59237
有限责任公司	Limited Liability Corporations	977743	1540857
股份有限公司	Share Holding Corporations Limited	1288620	1335073
私营企业	Private Enterprises	568452	938184
其他企业	Other Domestic-funded Enterprises		
港澳台商投资企业	Shareholding Corporations Ltd. with Investment from Hong Kong Macao and Taiwan	102675	153536
外商投资企业	Shareholding Corporations Ltd. with Foreign Investment	722240	1625102
按技术领域分	**By Technology Field**		
#电子信息	Electronics and Information	205462	309204
生物、医药和医疗器械	Biology and Medical Technologies	241300	282341
新材料	New Materials	582068	701815
光机电一体化	Photoelectric Mechanical and Electrical Products	2704339	4103896
新能源与高效节能	New Energy Facilities Concentrated and Economized on Energy	105901	301696
环境保护	Environmental Protection	24023	46692
航空航天	Aviation and Aerospace Technology	3810	9026

二十二　企业集团、景气调查

ENTERPRISE GROUPS AND BUSINESS SURVEY

简要说明　Brief Introduction

本章资料主要包括企业集团和重点企业的主要经济指标，企业家信心指数、企业景气指数以及各行业景气指数，由市企业调查队提供。

Data of this chapter mainly include main economic indicators of business groups and key enterprises, entrepreneur expectation index, business survey index and indices of business surveys by sector. All data are from Municipal Enterprises Survey Organization.

22－1 企业集团主要经济指标（1997－2004年）
Main Economic Indicators of Business Groups (1997-2004)

单位：万元 (10 000 yuan)

指　标	Item	1997	1998	1999	2000
企业集团数（户）	Number of Groups (unit)	18	23	24	48
年末资产总计	Year-end Total Assets	4333065	5700220	6049192	7681247
#固定资产原价	Original Value of Fixed Assets			2875761	3374332
#累计折旧	Total Depreciation			838926	1037691
#存　货	Inventory			875579	1177347
流动资产年平均余额	Average Balance of Circulating Funds	2138429	2703579	2954120	3832100
年末负债总计	Year-end Total Liabilities	2667820	3571156	3849253	4841175
#流动负债	Circulating Liabilities	2080670	2942595	3099791	4108455
年末股东（所有者）权益合计	Year-end Total Shareholders' Equity	1656446	1833750	1885101	2336213
#股本（实收资本）	Capital Obtained	970264	1066258	1212303	1646857
营业收入	Business Revenue	2483707	3135743	3530817	4730462
主营业务收入	Major Business Revenue	2402541	3071598	3387727	4569428
#主营业务成本	Cost of Major Business	1951065	2504058	2821822	3747666
主营业务税金及附加	Tax and Extra Charges of Major Business	67429	503323	69845	96205
其他业务收入	Other Business Revenue	81166	64145	143090	161034
存货跌价损失及期间费用合计	Loses for Inventory Price Fall and Business Expenses	361848	490369	521858	573938
投资收益	Investment Revenue	6571	12148	11225	8191
营业外收入	Non-Business Revenue	11310	28145	36796	24015
利润总额	Total After-tax Profits	-51153	34099	2196	118492
固定资产投资完成额	Completed Investment in Fixed Assets	135093	158322	125828	202854
研究开发费用	Expenses for Research and Development	13968	31089	31418	64198
从业人员年末人数（万人）	Year-end Employees (10 000 persons)	17.95	17.56	17.97	19.07
从业人员人均劳动报酬（元）	Average Per Capita Compensation of Employees (yuan)	7150	8978	8543	11342

注：企业集团统计口径2001年以前为市政府及其主管部门以上批准的企业集团，2001年及以后统计口径扩大为资产和营业收入均在五千万元以上的企业集团。

Note: Data before 2001 are the figures of groups which were approved by municipal government and related administrative departments, since 2001 are the figures of groups with business revenue and total assets both over 50 million yuan.

22-1 续表 CONTINUED

单位：万元 (10 000 yuan)

指　　标	Item	2001	2002	2003	2004
企业集团数（户）	Number of Groups (unit)	97	95	102	101
年末资产总计	Year-end Total Assets	11093928	11982140	15617012	19279416
#固定资产原价	Original Value of Fixed Assets	5184676	5441237	6612577	8475004
#累计折旧	Total Depreciation	1617068	1764767	2017146	2778699
#存　货	Inventory	1727103	1835261	2107914	3063629
流动资产年平均余额	Average Balance of Circulating Funds	5616761	6213567	7339922	9678566
年末负债总计	Year-end Total Liabilities	6937580	7453865	9965547	12346012
#流动负债	Circulating Liabilities	5750838	6257308	7644094	9789442
年末股东（所有者）权益合计	Year-end Total Shareholders' Equity	3502122	3808217	4664654	5614583
#股本（实收资本）	Capital Obtained	2701611	3070390	3483531	4014948
营业收入	Business Revenue	6769774	7890331	10301415	14867225
主营业务收入	Major Business Revenue	6486642	7571334	9954899	14326234
#主营业务成本	Cost of Major Business	5288534	5816455	8011253	11731212
主营业务税金及附加	Tax and Extra Charges of Major Business	129120	154237	189936	256217
其他业务收入	Other Business Revenue	283132	318997	346516	540991
存货跌价损失及期间费用合计	Loses for Inventory Price Fall and Business Expenses	897420	1085816	1386827	1961892
投资收益	Investment Revenue	16071	655	29695	59345
营业外收入	Non-Business Revenue	21544	22978	32043	42240
利润总额	Total After-tax Profits	142577	204904	351967	512119
固定资产投资完成额	Completed Investment in Fixed Assets	373009	459005	986959	1281022
研究开发费用	Expenses for Research and Development	118936	125576	171361	247237
从业人员年末人数（万人）	Year-end Employees (10 000 persons)	29.86	29.51	34.45	43.69
从业人员人均劳动报酬（元）	Average Per Capita Compensation of Employees (yuan)	11207	13111	14597	16216

22－2 国有控股企业集团主要经济指标（1997－2004年）
Main Economic Indicators of State-holding Groups (1997-2004)

单位：万元 (10 000 yuan)

指　　标	Item	1997	1998	1999	2000
企业集团数（户）	Number of Groups (unit)	18	22	22	33
年末资产总计	Year-end Total Assets	4333065	5646882	5923878	6889393
#固定资产原价	Original Value of Fixed Assets			2867516	3205985
#累计折旧	Total Depreciation			837339	1016518
#存　货	Inventory			858328	971692
流动资产年平均余额	Average Balance of Circulating Funds	2318429	2662062	2854692	3448584
年末负债总计	Year-end Total Liabilities	2667820	3527779	3763905	4371095
#流动负债	Circulating Liabilities	2080670	2899617	3019588	3713077
年末股东（所有者）权益合计	Year-end Total Shareholders' Equity	1656446	1823789	1845135	2015515
#股本（实收资本）	Capital Obtained	970264	1063933	1197478	1514289
营业收入	Business Revenue	2483706	3079840	3308443	3859247
主营业务收入	Major Business Revenue	2402540	3016299	3039650	3716009
#主营业务成本	Cost of Major Business	1951065	2454359	2509937	3026461
主营业务税金及附加	Tax and Extra Charges of Major Business	67429	499273	65889	75138
其他业务收入	Other Business Revenue	81166	63541	268793	143238
存货跌价损失及期间费用合计	Loses for Inventory Price Fall and Business Expenses	361848	499917	506279	511388
投资收益	Investment Revenue	6571	12148	11670	8107
营业外收入	Non-Business Revenue	11309	27906	36412	22398
利润总额	Total After-tax Profits	-51152	33102	-11065	72620
固定资产投资完成额	Completed Investment in Fixed Assets	135093	158017	123328	162688
研究开发费用	Expenses for Research and Development	13968	31061	27407	48225
从业人员年末人数（万人）	Year-end Employees (10 000 persons)	17.95	17.43	17.62	16.82
从业人员人均劳动报酬（元）	Average Per Capita Compensation of Employees (yuan)	7150	8996	8511	11469

注：企业集团统计口径2001年以前为市政府及其主管部门以上批准的企业集团，2001年及以后统计口径扩大为资产和营业收入均在五千万元以上的企业集团。

Note: Data before 2001 are the figures of groups which were approved by municipal government and related administrative departments, since 2001 are the figures of groups with business revenue and total assets both over 50 million yuan.

22-2 续表 CONTINUED

单位：万元 (10 000 yuan)

指　　标	Item	2001	2002	2003	2004
企业集团数（户）	Number of Groups (unit)	46	46	47	45
年末资产总计	Year-end Total Assets	9454108	10026374	12384738	15516926
#固定资产原价	Original Value of Fixed Assets	4857091	5084495	5880264	7587188
#累计折旧	Total Depreciation	1544344	1685637	1809390	2552091
#存　货	Inventory	1180349	1278379	1313795	2120922
流动资产年平均余额	Average Balance of Circulating Funds	4559603	4944589	5498909	7449762
年末负债总计	Year-end Total Liabilities	5953846	6180468	7879691	9932865
#流动负债	Circulating Liabilities	4872392	5132807	5928198	7934193
年末股东（所有者）权益合计	Year-end Total Shareholders' Equity	2859440	3144746	3553786	4326572
#股本（实收资本）	Capital Obtained	2311348	2501734	2917771	3330174
营业收入	Business Revenue	5065117	5934678	7568333	11634904
主营业务收入	Major Business Revenue	4848458	5682544	7298746	11177084
#主营业务成本	Cost of Major Business	3927326	4223645	5814691	9143974
主营业务税金及附加	Tax and Extra Charges of Major Business	90631	105466	130726	191581
其他业务收入	Other Business Revenue	216659	252134	269587	457820
存货跌价损失及期间费用合计	Loses for Inventory Price Fall and Business Expenses	784220	948237	1123218	1603141
投资收益	Investment Revenue	15163	-1250	26249	47882
营业外收入	Non-Business Revenue	15620	19331	25399	33932
利润总额	Total After-tax Profits	70464	128653	252992	356969
固定资产投资完成额	Completed Investment in Fixed Assets	243558	335126	716163	1042278
研究开发费用	Expenses for Research and Development	95524	96385	137045	200135
从业人员年末人数（万人）	Year-end Employees (10 000 persons)	23.42	22.78	25.13	33.52
从业人员人均劳动报酬（元）	Average Per Capita Compensation of Employees (yuan)	11570	13504	15519	17342

22－3 企业集团主要经济指标（2004年）
Main Economic Indicators of Business Groups (2004)

单位：万元 (10 000 yuan)

指 标	Item	集团个数(个) Number of Groups (unit)	成员单位个数(个) Number of Enterprises Belonged to (unit)	资产总计 Total Funds	固定资产净值 Net Value of Fixed Assets
总 计	**Total**	**101**	**784**	**19279416**	**5696305**
按审批部门划分	**By Departments Responsible for Approval**				
国务院	The State Council	2	35	1539049	551834
国务院主管部门	Competent Authorities of the State Council	9	73	3991823	1249046
省级人民政府	Municipal Government	20	309	8484662	2738227
省级政府主管部门	Municipal Departments in Charge	33	186	2819867	669985
其 他	Others	37	181	2444015	487213
按行业划分	**By Sector**				
工 业	Industry	48	424	13898733	4457586
建筑业	Construction	15	75	934089	108224
交通运输、仓储及邮政业	Transportation, Storage, Postal Services	6	52	856268	450927
信息传输、计算机服务和软件业	Data Transmission, Computer Service and Softwares				
批发与零售业	Wholesale and Retail Trade	9	131	2050502	509627
住宿和餐饮业	Hotels and Restaurants	2	13	114278	31341
房地产业	Real Estate	18	80	1259228	86451
其他行业	Other Sectors	3	9	166318	52149
母公司注册登记类型	**Registration of Parent Company**				
国有企业	State-owned	4	18	247937	74769
国有独资公司	Exclusively State-owned	28	386	12804877	3967744
其他有限责任公司	Other Limited-Liabilities Companies	57	298	4508267	1196901
股份有限公司	Share Holding Limited Companies	8	68	1359875	362895
中外合资企业	Joint-ventures with Foreign Investment	1	4	239354	88451
港澳台合资企业	Cooperative Enterprises with Funds from Hong Kong, Macao and Taiwan	3	10	119106	5545
母公司控股情况	**Share Holding of Parent Company**				
国有绝对控股	Exclusively State Holding	43	498	15371949	4945324
国有相对控股	Relatively State Holding	2	13	144977	89773
集体绝对控股	Exclusively Collective Holding	4	24	172789	48941
其 他	Others	52	249	3589701	612267
按隶属关系划分	**By Administrative Relationship**				
中 央	Central	11	108	5530872	1800880
地 方	Local	90	676	13748544	3895425

22-3 续表1 CONTINUED-1

单位：万元 (10 000 yuan)

指 标	Item	流动资产平均余额 Average Balance of Circulating Funds	负债合计 Total Liabilities	营业收入 Business Revenue	#主营收入 Major Business Revenue
总 计	**Total**	**9678566**	**12346012**	**14867225**	**14326234**
按审批部门划分	**By Departments Responsible for Approval**				
国务院	The State Council	714915	1013330	1298717	1296544
国务院主管部门	Competent Authorities of the State Council	2017565	2773844	4197947	3964541
省级人民政府	Municipal Government	4118915	5077694	5713301	5512869
省级政府主管部门	Municipal Departments in Charge	1581764	1977280	2040080	1950321
其 他	Others	1245407	1503864	1617180	1601959
按行业划分	**By Sector**				
工 业	Industry	6517943	8705174	10683868	10240693
建筑业	Construction	572278	696814	966805	922683
交通运输、仓储及邮政业	Transportation, Storage, Postal Services	238197	415298	243461	204348
信息传输、计算机服务和软件业	Data Transmission, Computer Service and Softwares				
批发与零售业	Wholesale and Retail Trade	1216874	1403688	2411420	2399551
住宿和餐饮业	Hotels and Restaurants	45115	68546	19866	19866
房地产业	Real Estate	1020761	943084	483536	481762
其他行业	Other Sectors	67398	113408	58269	57331
母公司注册登记类型	**Registration of Parent Company**				
国有企业	State-owned	106652	174985	74583	72511
国有独资公司	Exclusively State-owned	6226146	7983895	10284233	9873886
其他有限责任公司	Other Limited-Liabilities Companies	2378182	2967601	3530515	3411239
股份有限公司	Share Holding Limited Companies	800580	958974	871512	862559
中外合资企业	Joint-ventures with Foreign Investment	66280	165119	85440	85130
港澳台合资企业	Cooperative Enterprises with Funds from Hong Kong, Macao and Taiwan	100726	95438	20942	20909
母公司控股情况	**Share Holding of Parent Company**				
国有绝对控股	Exclusively State Holding	7400794	9843205	11545050	11087644
国有相对控股	Relatively State Holding	48968	89660	89854	89440
集体绝对控股	Exclusively Collective Holding	104451	127422	75343	73155
其 他	Others	2124353	2285725	3156978	3075995
按隶属关系划分	**By Administrative Relationship**				
中 央	Central	2732480	3787174	5496664	5261085
地 方	Local	6946086	8558838	9370561	9065149

22-3 续表2 CONTINUED-2

单位：万元 (10 000 yuan)

指标	Item	利税总额 Total Pre-tax Profits	#利润总额 Total Profits	从业人员人数(人) Number of Employees (person)	从业人员报酬 Payment for Employees
总计	**Total**	**1156599**	**512119**	**436906**	**708483**
按审批部门划分	**By Departments Responsible for Approval**				
国务院	The State Council	165251	91591	35554	84315
国务院主管部门	Competent Authorities of the State Council	366813	138070	78095	165085
省级人民政府	Municipal Government	322904	111575	188222	293442
省级政府主管部门	Municipal Departments in Charge	178777	101758	68720	83876
其他	Others	122854	69125	66315	81765
按行业划分	**By Sector**				
工业	Industry	934239	390255	285078	482343
建筑业	Construction	44422	15765	46406	68476
交通运输、仓储及邮政业	Transportation, Storage, Postal Services	19146	11240	31588	46722
信息传输、计算机服务和软件业	Data Transmission, Computer Service and Softwares				
批发与零售业	Wholesale and Retail Trade	52082	19715	52333	82159
住宿和餐饮业	Hotels and Restaurants	437	-371	2853	3036
房地产业	Real Estate	101474	73695	15397	17865
其他行业	Other Sectors	4799	1820	3251	7882
母公司注册登记类型	**Registration of Parent Company**				
国有企业	State-owned	3450	-650	4430	10259
国有独资公司	Exclusively State-owned	808333	322727	284759	503564
其他有限责任公司	Other Limited-Liabilities Companies	287685	170304	118642	152334
股份有限公司	Share Holding Limited Companies	45235	14504	23392	34797
中外合资企业	Joint-ventures with Foreign Investment	3331	-2581	4458	6199
港澳台合资企业	Cooperative Enterprises with Funds from Hong Kong, Macao and Taiwan	8565	7815	1225	1330
母公司控股情况	**Share Holding of Parent Company**				
国有绝对控股	Exclusively State Holding	886042	350910	330258	575756
国有相对控股	Relatively State Holding	12004	6059	4927	5527
集体绝对控股	Exclusively Collective Holding	8036	5049	4007	4673
其他	Others	250517	150101	97714	122527
按隶属关系划分	**By Administrative Relationship**				
中央	Central	532064	229661	113649	249400
地方	Local	624535	282458	323257	459083

22－4 重点企业主要经济指标（2004年）
Main Economic Indicators of Key Enterprises (2004)

单位：万元 (10 000 yuan)

指　标	Item	单位数（个） Number of Units (unit)	资产总计 Total Funds	固定资产原价 Original Value of Fixed Assets	累计折旧 Total Depreciation
总　计	**Total**	**167**	**20863506**	**10406050**	**3825309**
按控股情况分	**By Status of Share Holding**				
国有及国有控股	State-owned and State Holding	122	17563060	9375086	3519282
国有绝对控股	Exclusively State Holding	103	16174351	8830806	3328556
国有相对控股	Relatively State Holding	19	1388709	544280	190726
集体控股	Collective Holding	3	122808	37678	9036
集体绝对控股	Exclusively Collective Holding	3	122808	37678	9036
集体相对控股	Relatively Collective Holding				
其　他	Others	42	3177638	993286	296991
按主营行业分	**By Sector of Major Business**				
工　业	Industry	124	16648142	9163277	3424634
建筑业	Construction	5	461516	54234	20632
交通运输、仓储及邮政业	Transportation, Storage, Postal Services	10	888451	622512	241216
批发与零售业	Wholesale and Retail Trade	16	1461846	393965	83445
住宿和餐饮业	Hotels and Restaurants	2	25258	20471	10313
房地产业	Real Estate	3	318801	10380	2817
其　他	Others	7	1059492	141211	42252
按登记注册类型分	**By Registration**				
国有企业	State-owned Enterprises	31	1826551	1384338	697086
公司制企业	Enterprises of Company System	136	19036955	9021712	3128223
国有独资企业	Exclusively State-owned Enterprises	36	8433890	4430387	1558874
其他有限责任公司	Other Limited-Liabilities Enterprises	42	4449567	2103530	724748
股份有限公司	Share Holding Limited Enterprises	38	4832454	1723448	540954
中外合资企业	Joint-ventures with Foreign Investment	16	1201815	673278	263662
港澳台合资企业	Cooperative Enterprises with Funds from Hong Kong, Macao and Taiwan	4	119229	91069	39985
按企业规模分	**By Size**				
大　型	Large-sized	55	15255059	8104634	2970890
中　型	Medium-sized	91	4000062	2044515	754799
小　型	Small-sized	11	230092	105310	54551
其　他	Others	10	1378293	151591	45069
附：特别分组	**Special Classification**				
国家重点企业	Key Enterprises of State Level	8	5190061	3063508	1186323
现企原试点企业	Former Experimental Enterprises with Modern Enterprises System	60	8260475	4017677	1437207

22-4 续表1 CONTINUED-1

单位：万元 (10 000 yuan)

指　　标	Item	累　计 对外投资 Total External Investment	本　年 对外投资 External Investment in Current Year	长期投资 Long-term Investment	短期投资 Short-term Investment
总　计	**Total**	**2330387**	**703219**	**2376823**	**248061**
按控股情况分	**By Status of Share Holding**				
国有及国有控股	State-owned and State Holding	1881311	604452	1918032	246960
国有绝对控股	Exclusively State Holding	1739677	587217	1782853	237014
国有相对控股	Relatively State Holding	141634	17235	135179	9946
集体控股	Collective Holding	9176	3888	9106	70
集体绝对控股	Exclusively Collective Holding	9176	3888	9106	70
集体相对控股	Relatively Collective Holding				
其　他	Others	439900	94879	449685	1031
按主营行业分	**By Sector of Major Business**				
工　业	Industry	1605996	427188	1648046	178237
建筑业	Construction	5042		66088	440
交通运输、仓储及邮政业	Transportation, Storage, Postal Services	76542	7544	42071	35438
批发与零售业	Wholesale and Retail Trade	78970	12620	82065	8420
住宿和餐饮业	Hotels and Restaurants	945		1187	
房地产业	Real Estate	7584	297	7584	
其　他	Others	555308	255570	529782	25526
按登记注册类型分	**By Registration**				
国有企业	State-owned Enterprises	126143	10636	139274	9360
公司制企业	Enterprises of Company System	2204244	692583	2237549	238701
国有独资企业	Exclusively State-owned Enterprises	1172689	450495	1204568	202462
其他有限责任公司	Other Limited-Liabilities Enterprises	191536	67183	206088	6958
股份有限公司	Share Holding Limited Enterprises	833242	174655	815848	29229
中外合资企业	Joint-ventures with Foreign Investment	4675	63	8995	
港澳台合资企业	Cooperative Enterprises with Funds from Hong Kong, Macao and Taiwan	2102	187	2050	52
按企业规模分	**By Size**				
大　型	Large-sized	1439252	397476	1503308	196247
中　型	Medium-sized	283382	46042	284090	23223
小　型	Small-sized	44861	3834	52059	3065
其　他	Others	562892	255867	537366	25526
附：特别分组	**Special Classification**				
国家重点企业	Key Enterprises of State Level	631204	26280	638372	8228
现企原试点企业	Former Experimental Enterprises with Modern Enterprises System	873607	54970	902334	11258

22-4 续表2 CONTINUED-2

单位：万元 (10 000 yuan)

指　标	Item	流动资产平均余额 Average Balance of Circulating Funds	年末负债合计 Year-end Total Liabilities	年末股东权益合计 Year-end Total Shareholders' Equity	实收资本 Capital Obtained
总　计	**Total**	**9356022**	**12517137**	**8346369**	**4221298**
按控股情况分	**By Status of Share Holding**				
国有及国有控股	State-owned and State Holding	7689332	10539948	7023112	3612528
国有绝对控股	Exclusively State Holding	6846198	9702988	6471363	3322311
国有相对控股	Relatively State Holding	843134	836960	551749	290217
集体控股	Collective Holding	79817	99669	23139	11876
集体绝对控股	Exclusively Collective Holding	79817	99669	23139	11876
集体相对控股	Relatively Collective Holding				
其　他	Others	1586873	1877520	1300118	596894
按主营行业分	**By Sector of Major Business**				
工　业	Industry	7046679	9717026	6931116	3619860
建筑业	Construction	305553	364490	97026	89217
交通运输、仓储及邮政业	Transportation, Storage, Postal Services	383012	457892	430559	207869
批发与零售业	Wholesale and Retail Trade	902912	1118291	343555	152174
住宿和餐饮业	Hotels and Restaurants	10379	11396	13862	9490
房地产业	Real Estate	336316	281310	37491	20256
其　他	Others	371171	566732	492760	122432
按登记注册类型分	**By Registration**				
国有企业	State-owned Enterprises	797092	1182204	644347	488691
公司制企业	Enterprises of Company System	8558930	11334933	7702022	3732607
国有独资企业	Exclusively State-owned Enterprises	3194213	5682727	2751163	1106653
其他有限责任公司	Other Limited-Liabilities Enterprises	2300585	2372936	2076631	1440594
股份有限公司	Share Holding Limited Enterprises	2441896	2627617	2204837	790634
中外合资企业	Joint-ventures with Foreign Investment	559754	589834	611981	362552
港澳台合资企业	Cooperative Enterprises with Funds from Hong Kong, Macao and Taiwan	62482	61819	57410	32174
按企业规模分	**By Size**				
大　型	Large-sized	6680776	9175129	6079930	2916908
中　型	Medium-sized	1867765	2357062	1643000	1094421
小　型	Small-sized	99994	136904	93188	67281
其　他	Others	707487	848042	530251	142688
附：特别分组	**Special Classification**				
国家重点企业	Key Enterprises of State Level	2114313	2951600	2238461	1325612
现企原试点企业	Former Experimental Enterprises with Modern Enterprises System	3650377	5216007	3044468	1586429

22-4 续表3 CONTINUED-3

单位：万元 (10 000 yuan)

指　标	Item	主营业务收入 Major Business Revenue	其他业务收入 Other Business Revenue	新产品销售收入 Sales Revenue of New Products	出口销售总额 Total Sales of Exports
总　计	**Total**	**14585843**	**575935**	**3988481**	**853039**
按控股情况分	**By Status of Share Holding**				
国有及国有控股	State-owned and State Holding	11624708	487992	3000972	521881
国有绝对控股	Exclusively State Holding	10754861	482085	2832312	432337
国有相对控股	Relatively State Holding	869847	5907	168660	89544
集体控股	Collective Holding	44764	803	18685	4161
集体绝对控股	Exclusively Collective Holding	44764	803	18685	4161
集体相对控股	Relatively Collective Holding				
其　他	Others	2916371	87140	968824	326997
按主营行业分	**By Sector of Major Business**				
工　业	Industry	11275307	474362	3988481	683640
建筑业	Construction	549267	23693		
交通运输、仓储及邮政业	Transportation, Storage, Postal Services	267204	47369		
批发与零售业	Wholesale and Retail Trade	2340872	18833		166249
住宿和餐饮业	Hotels and Restaurants	8525			
房地产业	Real Estate	31267	9193		
其　他	Others	113401	2485		3150
按登记注册类型分	**By Registration**				
国有企业	State-owned Enterprises	1230135	47839	212625	61165
公司制企业	Enterprises of Company System	13355708	528096	3775856	791874
国有独资企业	Exclusively State-owned Enterprises	5092321	206109	818684	75900
其他有限责任公司	Other Limited-Liabilities Enterprises	3756104	176741	1452388	429704
股份有限公司	Share Holding Limited Enterprises	3289358	132363	787921	230838
中外合资企业	Joint-ventures with Foreign Investment	1084838	5727	699797	55148
港澳台合资企业	Cooperative Enterprises with Funds from Hong Kong, Macao and Taiwan	133087	7156	17066	284
按企业规模分	**By Size**				
大　型	Large-sized	11557562	501979	3255918	574158
中　型	Medium-sized	2712373	61580	716902	202050
小　型	Small-sized	171240	698	15661	73681
其　他	Others	144668	11678		3150
附：特别分组	**Special Classification**				
国家重点企业	Key Enterprises of State Level	2937248	149689	1095593	206381
现企原试点企业	Former Experimental Enterprises with Modern Enterprises System	5129541	174843	1465487	239797

22-4 续表4 CONTINUED-4

单位：万元 (10 000 yuan)

指　　标	Item	存货跌价损失和营业管理财务等费用 Loses for Inventory Price Fall and Business Expenses	利息支出 Interest Expenses	投资收益 Investment Revenues	利润总额 Total After-tax Profits
总　计	**Total**	**1893735**	**253698**	**206048**	**709506**
按控股情况分	**By Status of Share Holding**				
国有及国有控股	State-owned and State Holding	1508389	208888	192734	537900
国有绝对控股	Exclusively State Holding	1382077	195705	187361	492503
国有相对控股	Relatively State Holding	126312	13183	5373	45397
集体控股	Collective Holding	7434	1149	428	3704
集体绝对控股	Exclusively Collective Holding	7434	1149	428	3704
集体相对控股	Relatively Collective Holding				
其　他	Others	377912	43661	12886	167902
按主营行业分	**By Sector of Major Business**				
工　业	Industry	1578022	206666	195954	690344
建筑业	Construction	15858	1781	890	5211
交通运输、仓储及邮政业	Transportation, Storage, Postal Services	61792	9053	2183	-10318
批发与零售业	Wholesale and Retail Trade	195365	21345	341	19629
住宿和餐饮业	Hotels and Restaurants	5252	384	22	-67
房地产业	Real Estate	1489	192	963	4799
其　他	Others	35957	14277	5695	-92
按登记注册类型分	**By Registration**				
国有企业	State-owned Enterprises	207905	23149	21256	62985
公司制企业	Enterprises of Company System	1685830	230549	184792	646521
国有独资企业	Exclusively State-owned Enterprises	634413	127734	107408	177898
其他有限责任公司	Other Limited-Liabilities Enterprises	432791	40808	3430	129279
股份有限公司	Share Holding Limited Enterprises	460594	50926	73718	211149
中外合资企业	Joint-ventures with Foreign Investment	131700	9670	244	118247
港澳台合资企业	Cooperative Enterprises with Funds from Hong Kong, Macao and Taiwan	26332	1411	-8	9948
按企业规模分	**By Size**				
大　型	Large-sized	1391025	189234	182847	507552
中　型	Medium-sized	439626	46002	16141	193112
小　型	Small-sized	25638	3993	402	4135
其　他	Others	37446	14469	6658	4707
附：特别分组	**Special Classification**				
国家重点企业	Key Enterprises of State Level	426312	77215	81368	162938
现企原试点企业	Former Experimental Enterprises with Modern Enterprises System	778771	127331	114602	226436

22-4 续表5 CONTINUED-5

单位：万元 (10 000 yuan)

指　　标	Item	应缴所得税 Payable Income Tax	应缴增值税 Payable Value-added Tax	固定资产投资完成额 Completed Investment in Fixed Assets	研究开发费用 Expenses for Research and Development
总　计	**Total**	**75123**	**580249**	**3079131**	**197038**
按控股情况分	**By Status of Share Holding**				
国有及国有控股	State-owned and State Holding	52861	501673	2873417	149014
国有绝对控股	Exclusively State Holding	46428	460078	2838421	142137
国有相对控股	Relatively State Holding	6433	41595	34996	6877
集体控股	Collective Holding	1203	1379	4860	80
集体绝对控股	Exclusively Collective Holding	1203	1379	4860	80
集体相对控股	Relatively Collective Holding				
其　他	Others	21059	77197	200854	47944
按主营行业分	**By Sector of Major Business**				
工　业	Industry	65027	544714	2928279	191129
建筑业	Construction	969	98	6764	19
交通运输、仓储及邮政业	Transportation, Storage, Postal Services	1652	452	51317	51
批发与零售业	Wholesale and Retail Trade	6055	34506	47421	3212
住宿和餐饮业	Hotels and Restaurants		39	115	
房地产业	Real Estate	524		9784	
其　他	Others	896	440	35451	2627
按登记注册类型分	**By Registration**				
国有企业	State-owned Enterprises	9582	55839	67792	18157
公司制企业	Enterprises of Company System	65541	524410	3011339	178881
国有独资企业	Exclusively State-owned Enterprises	19288	242697	2346600	47614
其他有限责任公司	Other Limited-Liabilities Enterprises	18987	119788	234367	61315
股份有限公司	Share Holding Limited Enterprises	15974	97068	223857	58559
中外合资企业	Joint-ventures with Foreign Investment	9763	56067	197520	10384
港澳台合资企业	Cooperative Enterprises with Funds from Hong Kong, Macao and Taiwan	1529	8790	8995	1009
按企业规模分	**By Size**				
大　型	Large-sized	48109	449104	2719497	155633
中　型	Medium-sized	23766	116815	305002	37604
小　型	Small-sized	1828	13890	9397	1174
其　他	Others	1420	440	45235	2627
附：特别分组	**Special Classification**				
国家重点企业	Key Enterprises of State Level	8587	155291	245121	59046
现企原试点企业	Former Experimental Enterprises with Modern Enterprises System	24975	251399	393894	74494

22-4 续表6 CONTINUED-6

单位：万元 (10 000 yuan)

指 标	Item	从业人员人数（人） Number of Employees (person)	#研究开发人员 Research and Development Personnel	从业人员报酬 Compensation of Employees	#研究开发人员 Research and Development Personnel
总 计	**Total**	**430753**	**20169**	**738610**	**53572**
按控股情况分	**By Status of Share Holding**				
国有及国有控股	State-owned and State Holding	357531	16370	617152	43635
国有绝对控股	Exclusively State Holding	336270	15827	578731	42265
国有相对控股	Relatively State Holding	21261	543	38421	1370
集体控股	Collective Holding	1830		2576	
集体绝对控股	Exclusively Collective Holding	1830		2576	
集体相对控股	Relatively Collective Holding				
其 他	Others	71392	3799	118882	9937
按主营行业分	**By Sector of Major Business**				
工 业	Industry	335750	19297	597504	49911
建筑业	Construction	19185	7	39408	13
交通运输、仓储及邮政业	Transportation, Storage, Postal Services	30298	21	48276	47
批发与零售业	Wholesale and Retail Trade	41887	394	45598	1704
住宿和餐饮业	Hotels and Restaurants	858		730	
房地产业	Real Estate	463		915	
其 他	Others	2312	450	6179	1897
按登记注册类型分	**By Registration**				
国有企业	State-owned Enterprises	60181	2452	107391	5871
公司制企业	Enterprises of Company System	370572	17717	631219	47701
国有独资企业	Exclusively State-owned Enterprises	164044	8911	293823	24487
其他有限责任公司	Other Limited-Liabilities Enterprises	126280	4989	186027	10065
股份有限公司	Share Holding Limited Enterprises	60351	2899	110352	10100
中外合资企业	Joint-ventures with Foreign Investment	17214	842	33537	2763
港澳台合资企业	Cooperative Enterprises with Funds from Hong Kong, Macao and Taiwan	2683	76	7480	286
按企业规模分	**By Size**				
大 型	Large-sized	320271	15339	568529	41496
中 型	Medium-sized	104078	4211	157137	9652
小 型	Small-sized	3629	169	5850	527
其 他	Others	2775	450	7094	1897
附：特别分组	**Special Classification**				
国家重点企业	Key Enterprises of State Level	74166	4526	162977	13909
现企原试点企业	Former Experimental Enterprises with Modern Enterprises System	165517	6355	298455	17937

22－5 企业家信心指数（2003－2004年）
Entrepreneur Expectation Index (2003-2004)

单位：点 (point)

指标	Item	2003 一季度 1st. Quarter	二季度 2nd. Quarter	三季度 3rd. Quarter	四季度 4th. Quarter
全　市	**Total**	**122.38**	**108.31**	**115.97**	**126.83**
按行业门类分	**By Sector**				
工　业	Industry	127.69	119.07	121.84	134.64
建筑业	Construction	127.96	124.20	123.03	126.04
交通运输、仓储及邮政业	Transportation, Storage, Postal Services	87.47	52.59	69.98	88.31
信息传输、计算机服务和软件业	Data Transmission, Computer Service and Softwares	131.56	130.26	130.51	136.22
批发与零售业	Wholesale and Retail Trade	94.78	78.12	89.38	96.00
住宿和餐饮业	Hotels and Restaurants	115.41	58.32	128.78	139.99
房地产业	Real Estate	158.13	157.66	152.63	169.14
社会服务业	Social Services	132.04	95.08	112.22	121.16
按注册类型分	**By Registration**				
国有企业	State-owned	105.19	93.53	105.52	116.58
集体企业	Collective-owned	92.32	87.04	89.05	98.38
有限责任公司	Limited-liability Companies	123.95	111.65	118.80	126.77
股份有限公司	Share Holding Ltd. Companies	142.27	108.52	126.17	141.31
港澳台外商投资	Funded by Overseas Entrepreneurs	156.47	146.94	144.67	153.24
按企业规模分	**By Size of Enterprises**				
大型企业	Large	146.28	119.68	134.31	153.06
中型企业	Medium	125.83	115.77	120.92	131.21
小型企业	Small	107.71	95.39	104.16	110.84
附：特殊分组	**Special Classification**				
上市公司	Share Listed Companies	153.90	82.07	116.93	165.17
增长点企业	Potential Enterprises	153.75	140.68	140.67	150.92
工业企业五十强	Top 50 Industrial Enterprises	155.67	135.31	134.04	151.48

22-5 续表 CONTINUED

单位：点 (point)

指标	Item	2004 一季度 1st. Quarter	二季度 2nd. Quarter	三季度 3rd. Quarter	四季度 4th. Quarter
全　市	**Total**	**125.04**	**119.61**	**119.25**	**121.05**
按行业门类分	**By Sector**				
工　业	Industry	128.26	118.04	123.68	123.20
建筑业	Construction	131.73	130.95	125.48	133.89
交通运输、仓储及邮政业	Transportation, Storage, Postal Services	98.70	93.92	93.70	98.79
信息传输、计算机服务和软件业	Data Transmission, Computer Service and Softwares	142.42	142.42	134.09	135.11
批发与零售业	Wholesale and Retail Trade	95.40	96.88	93.12	91.86
住宿和餐饮业	Hotels and Restaurants	120.59	123.75	120.68	125.23
房地产业	Real Estate	177.89	162.21	149.57	156.15
社会服务业	Social Services	114.52	122.10	109.84	111.96
按注册类型分	**By Registration**				
国有企业	State-owned	112.31	114.40	113.34	118.97
集体企业	Collective-owned	98.82	104.76	97.56	104.77
有限责任公司	Limited-liability Companies	121.88	122.96	121.02	116.47
股份有限公司	Share Holding Ltd. Companies	142.24	117.94	128.20	124.12
港澳台外商投资	Funded by Overseas Entrepreneurs	152.13	144.81	131.16	143.19
按企业规模分	**By Size of Enterprises**				
大型企业	Large	150.79	133.30	140.08	130.40
中型企业	Medium	127.94	123.52	122.72	125.86
小型企业	Small	109.88	109.73	104.04	108.74
附：特殊分组	**Special Classification**				
上市公司	Share Listed Companies	162.51	111.93	132.41	112.07
增长点企业	Potential Enterprises	153.76	124.70	144.05	139.13
工业企业五十强	Top 50 Industrial Enterprises	157.91	124.18	146.22	145.35

22－6 企业景气指数（2003－2004年）
Business Survey Index (2003-2004)

单位：点 (point)

指 标	Item	2003			
		一季度 1st. Quarter	二季度 2nd. Quarter	三季度 3rd. Quarter	四季度 4th. Quarter
全 市	**Total**	**115.64**	**103.54**	**119.84**	**125.71**
按行业门类分	**By Sector**				
工 业	Industry	119.39	118.49	126.70	132.56
建筑业	Construction	108.12	107.03	113.80	123.84
交通运输、仓储及邮政业	Transportation, Storage, Postal Services	92.14	52.46	97.68	89.02
信息传输、计算机服务和软件业	Data Transmission, Computer Service and Softwares	125.63	118.05	129.13	146.27
批发与零售业	Wholesale and Retail Trade	105.79	89.88	95.11	100.93
住宿和餐饮业	Hotels and Restaurants	119.34	39.78	128.84	130.29
房地产业	Real Estate	140.75	142.11	150.03	162.60
社会服务业	Social Services	118.77	69.60	114.75	120.42
按注册类型分	**By Registration**				
国有企业	State-owned	109.30	88.01	111.73	114.25
集体企业	Collective-owned	87.69	74.99	95.32	103.10
有限责任公司	Limited-liability Companies	117.59	105.44	119.74	124.88
股份有限公司	Share Holding Ltd. Companies	133.85	125.97	140.49	144.28
港澳台外商投资	Funded by Overseas Entrepreneurs	143.90	121.27	142.92	149.23
按企业规模分	**By Size of Enterprises**				
大型企业	Large	154.24	137.46	151.81	150.66
中型企业	Medium	116.12	104.56	120.00	128.14
小型企业	Small	99.04	86.41	105.38	112.81
附：特殊分组	**Special Classification**				
上市公司	Share Listed Companies	161.10	152.57	157.51	158.06
增长点企业	Potential Enterprises	145.75	140.15	156.46	158.43
工业企业五十强	Top 50 Industrial Enterprises	156.56	149.02	159.75	161.81

22-6 续表 CONTINUED

单位：点 (point)

指　标	Item	2004 一季度 1st. Quarter	二季度 2nd. Quarter	三季度 3rd. Quarter	四季度 4th. Quarter
全　市	**Total**	**117.48**	**119.27**	**118.87**	**124.17**
按行业门类分	**By Sector**				
工　业	Industry	118.19	119.83	122.02	129.32
建筑业	Construction	110.24	121.68	126.87	130.96
交通运输、仓储及邮政业	Transportation, Storage, Postal Services	93.76	95.96	94.11	102.10
信息传输、计算机服务和软件业	Data Transmission, Computer Service and Softwares	145.20	130.71	129.95	135.51
批发与零售业	Wholesale and Retail Trade	107.70	108.76	106.11	109.03
住宿和餐饮业	Hotels and Restaurants	118.72	114.59	102.17	128.67
房地产业	Real Estate	156.77	149.16	152.47	134.82
社会服务业	Social Services	117.74	123.71	103.28	102.13
按注册类型分	**By Registration**				
国有企业	State-owned	109.79	106.25	111.47	114.19
集体企业	Collective-owned	93.90	99.78	93.90	98.52
有限责任公司	Limited-liability Companies	118.21	123.26	121.04	125.39
股份有限公司	Share Holding Ltd. Companies	140.67	141.40	137.15	144.73
港澳台外商投资	Funded by Overseas Entrepreneurs	139.65	137.59	132.47	143.02
按企业规模分	**By Size of Enterprises**				
大型企业	Large	155.29	159.66	154.71	162.31
中型企业	Medium	120.38	120.34	118.68	121.77
小型企业	Small	100.74	99.75	102.27	108.48
附：特殊分组	**Special Classification**				
上市公司	Share Listed Companies	170.11	163.44	162.89	158.40
增长点企业	Potential Enterprises	153.71	152.37	149.72	163.18
工业企业五十强	Top 50 Industrial Enterprises	153.83	148.37	154.71	160.30

22－7 工业景气指数（2003－2004年）
Business Survey Index of Industry (2003-2004)

单位：点 (point)

指标	Item	2003 一季度 1st. Quarter	2003 二季度 2nd. Quarter	2003 三季度 3rd. Quarter	2003 四季度 4th. Quarter
综合生产经营状况	**Comprehensive Conditions of Production and Management**	**119.39**	**118.49**	**126.70**	**132.56**
生产成本	Production Cost	84.07	87.70	89.00	67.91
生产总量	Total Production Quantity	106.30	115.35	123.24	139.91
产品订货	Production Order	118.61	106.21	116.68	129.50
#国外订货	From Overseas	88.14	84.44	88.65	95.41
产品销售	Sales of Products	110.13	110.58	126.31	138.85
产品销售价格	Selling Price of Products	81.54	82.16	79.02	99.33
产成品库存	Inventory of Products	116.34	105.38	114.72	119.57
盈利（亏损）变化	Changes in Profits (loses)	107.17	118.60	127.01	136.97
流动资金	Circulating Funds	72.22	73.70	74.03	82.13
货款拖欠	Payment Delinquent	103.25	95.59	100.11	112.83
设备利用（%）	Utilization of Equipment (%)	80.28	80.32	80.19	82.22
劳动力需求	Labor Demand	96.43	96.30	104.01	109.05
固定资产投资	Investment in Fixed Assets	115.55	116.54	128.36	126.34
科技创新	Scientific and Technical Innovation	111.23	118.03	125.23	128.07
主要原材料及能源购进价格	Bid of Main Raw Materials and Energy	57.08	71.35	77.60	47.68
主要原材料及能源供应	Supply of Main Raw Materials and Energy	106.11	112.92	115.36	106.79

指标	Item	2004 一季度 1st. Quarter	2004 二季度 2nd. Quarter	2004 三季度 3rd. Quarter	2004 四季度 4th. Quarter
综合生产经营状况	**Comprehensive Conditions of Production and Management**	**118.19**	**119.83**	**122.02**	**129.32**
生产成本	Production Cost	53.86	64.65	59.28	62.25
生产总量	Total Production Quantity	113.33	121.64	112.43	130.96
产品订货	Production Order	124.63	117.93	112.02	117.97
#国外订货	From Overseas	86.14	87.60	91.43	87.69
产品销售	Sales of Products	116.26	126.16	117.98	133.91
产品销售价格	Selling Price of Products	108.05	94.06	100.24	103.52
产成品库存	Inventory of Products	112.75	101.76	105.91	113.79
盈利（亏损）变化	Changes in Profits (loses)	112.85	119.27	118.34	122.02
流动资金	Circulating Funds	79.95	80.28	69.64	68.33
企业融资	Fundraising	86.08	76.53	75.48	79.98
货款拖欠	Payment Delinquent	104.01	102.97	98.92	111.37
设备利用（%）	Utilization of Equipment (%)	82.53	83.05	83.46	85.28
劳动力需求	Labor Demand	100.95	98.21	101.80	101.55
固定资产投资	Investment in Fixed Assets	114.43	127.12	123.33	125.30
科技创新	Scientific and Technical Innovation	119.73	121.86	122.36	122.79
主要原材料及能源购进价格	Bid of Main Raw Materials and Energy	27.55	56.27	38.09	45.22
主要原材料及能源供应	Supply of Main Raw Materials and Energy	89.98	93.68	87.66	84.26

注：为了更加准确地反映企业设备利用状况，自2002年1季度起，国家统计局企业调查总队对工业设备利用率景气指数的调查及计算方法进行了修订、完善，改为以百分数表示。

Note: To show utilization of equipment more exactly, the survey and calculation of equipment utilization have been improved and the index has been presented in terms of percent.

22－8 建筑业景气指数（2003－2004年）
Business Survey Index of Construction (2003-2004)

单位：点 (point)

指　标	Item	2003			
		一季度 1st. Quarter	二季度 2nd. Quarter	三季度 3rd. Quarter	四季度 4th. Quarter
综合生产经营状况	**Comprehensive Conditions of Production and Management**	**108.12**	**107.03**	**113.80**	**123.84**
工程合同	Assignment of Project Contracts	98.38	112.52	115.38	116.98
#国（境）外的工程合同	Foreign Contracts	85.71	100.00	95.99	112.10
建筑工程量	Volume of Projects	98.19	127.93	134.50	134.13
新开工工程量	Volume of New Projects	98.66	102.97	118.68	112.22
技术设备能力	Capacity of Technique and Facilities	95.47	138.64	141.75	133.38
工程进度	Progress of Projects	66.52	105.68	122.47	125.14
工程结算收入	Income from Project Settlement	84.74	120.50	120.44	148.51
建筑材料购进价格	Bid of Construction Materials	65.20	59.12	70.45	23.88
工程结算成本	Cost of Project Settlement	88.20	68.25	79.45	42.51
盈利（亏损）变化	Changes in Profits (loses)	99.91	105.18	109.71	116.91
流动资金	Circulating Funds	56.92	62.31	59.71	59.59
工程款拖欠	Payment Delinquent	83.86	80.51	73.75	71.75
劳动力需求	Labor Demand	91.76	104.94	122.46	119.87
固定资产投资	Investment in Fixed Assets	90.62	104.71	101.17	103.14

指　标	Item	2004			
		一季度 1st. Quarter	二季度 2nd. Quarter	三季度 3rd. Quarter	四季度 4th. Quarter
综合生产经营状况	**Comprehensive Conditions of Production and Management**	**110.24**	**121.68**	**126.87**	**130.96**
工程合同	Assignment of Project Contracts	106.67	124.12	118.15	115.05
#国（境）外的工程合同	Foreign Contracts	88.11	117.98	124.32	80.44
建筑工程量	Volume of Projects	102.41	140.87	127.51	136.30
新开工工程量	Volume of New Projects	101.84	115.43	116.95	120.90
技术设备能力	Capacity of Technique and Facilities	134.61	144.54	132.25	140.50
工程进度	Progress of Projects	138.63	144.44	144.24	155.32
工程结算收入	Income from Project Settlement	91.93	118.71	124.28	140.80
建筑材料购进价格	Bid of Construction Materials	15.31	92.41	55.83	62.03
工程结算成本	Cost of Project Settlement	56.34	89.61	65.24	67.94
盈利（亏损）变化	Changes in Profits (loses)	81.97	121.46	117.10	137.86
流动资金	Circulating Funds	63.96	63.12	63.44	52.87
企业融资	Fundraising	54.89	53.50	50.65	50.00
工程款拖欠	Payment Delinquent	84.50	92.80	91.93	87.59
劳动力需求	Labor Demand	110.01	124.28	121.35	122.25
固定资产投资	Investment in Fixed Assets	93.84	101.05	99.29	111.88

22－9 交通运输、仓储和邮政业景气指数（2003－2004年）
Business Survey Index of Transportation, Storage and Postal Services (2003-2004)

单位：点　　(point)

指　标	Item	2003			
		一季度 1st. Quarter	二季度 2nd. Quarter	三季度 3rd. Quarter	四季度 4th. Quarter
综合生产经营状况	**Comprehensive Conditions of Production and Management**	**92.14**	**52.46**	**97.68**	**89.02**
业务预订	Ordered Business	111.48	62.24	120.00	93.82
业务量	Business Volume	109.56	51.30	113.28	108.87
业务收费价格	Business Charges	113.08	72.34	95.24	101.91
营业成本	Business Cost	54.95	67.67	56.90	61.54
盈利（亏损）变化	Changes in Profits (loses)	98.18	47.01	100.26	106.00
流动资金	Circulating Funds	64.91	50.77	56.48	53.13
货款拖欠	Payment Delinquent	102.96	100.70	105.93	98.66
劳动力需求	Labor Demand	77.14	68.27	91.99	82.83
固定资产投资	Investment in Fixed Assets	86.44	112.12	105.85	106.79

指　标	Item	2004			
		一季度 1st. Quarter	二季度 2nd. Quarter	三季度 3rd. Quarter	四季度 4th. Quarter
综合生产经营状况	**Comprehensive Conditions of Production and Management**	**93.76**	**95.96**	**94.11**	**102.10**
业务预订	Ordered Business	114.16	103.48	123.78	94.05
业务量	Business Volume	122.68	100.24	132.81	93.73
业务收费价格	Business Charges	119.64	95.18	102.42	91.54
营业成本	Business Cost	82.99	37.71	53.72	58.26
盈利（亏损）变化	Changes in Profits (loses)	113.39	92.87	100.51	107.56
流动资金	Circulating Funds	56.65	65.03	61.62	61.05
企业融资	Fundraising	68.83	63.35	66.57	62.56
货款拖欠	Payment Delinquent	100.43	99.20	99.20	104.72
劳动力需求	Labor Demand	84.72	96.32	98.99	104.94
固定资产投资	Investment in Fixed Assets	91.00	125.79	120.48	134.15

22－10 信息传输、计算机服务和软件业景气指数（2003－2004年）
Business Survey Index of Data Transmission, Computer Service and Software (2003-2004)

单位：点 (point)

指　　标	Item	2003			
		一季度 1st. Quarter	二季度 2nd. Quarter	三季度 3rd. Quarter	四季度 4th. Quarter
综合生产经营状况	**Comprehensive Conditions of Production and Management**	**125.63**	**118.05**	**129.13**	**146.27**
产品销售（提供服务）	Sales of Products (Service)	109.94	117.52	138.00	127.69
产品订货	Order of Products	94.25	98.60	116.52	116.26
竞争能力	Competition Abilities	154.12	129.07	141.93	141.93
销售（收费）价格	Business Charges	87.79	87.79	75.73	84.86
营业收入	Business Revenue	109.06	131.03	141.38	144.79
营业成本	Business Cost	109.47	101.36	76.25	81.96
盈利（亏损）变化	Changes in Profits (loses)	96.39	132.92	123.44	139.11
流动资金	Circulating Funds	108.92	109.45	98.56	95.70
货款拖欠	Payment Delinquent	96.81	83.78	94.29	83.41
劳动力需求	Labor Demand	108.60	102.70	122.86	125.71
固定资产投资	Investment in Fixed Assets	104.59	101.89	102.00	107.16

指　　标	Item	2004			
		一季度 1st. Quarter	二季度 2nd. Quarter	三季度 3rd. Quarter	四季度 4th. Quarter
综合生产经营状况	**Comprehensive Conditions of Production and Management**	**145.20**	**130.71**	**129.95**	**135.51**
产品销售（提供服务）	Sales of Products (Service)	136.11	128.95	147.37	127.94
产品订货	Order of Products	113.24	110.34	118.67	115.90
竞争能力	Competition Abilities	161.87	144.86	153.19	142.85
销售（收费）价格	Business Charges	100.00	81.31	86.10	75.75
营业收入	Business Revenue	136.11	140.06	139.04	138.28
营业成本	Business Cost	71.45	66.50	64.49	56.16
盈利（亏损）变化	Changes in Profits (loses)	118.01	102.76	122.21	115.90
流动资金	Circulating Funds	100.41	100.41	89.30	98.41
企业融资	Fundraising	96.35	79.41	66.67	69.70
货款拖欠	Payment Delinquent	111.10	105.56	99.23	83.33
劳动力需求	Labor Demand	119.44	111.11	115.90	100.00
固定资产投资	Investment in Fixed Assets	104.22	109.78	116.32	107.77

22－11 批发和零售业景气指数（2003－2004年）
Business Survey Index of Wholesale and Retail Trade (2003-2004)

单位：点 (point)

指标	Item	2003 一季度 1st. Quarter	2003 二季度 2nd. Quarter	2003 三季度 3rd. Quarter	2003 四季度 4th. Quarter
综合生产经营状况	**Comprehensive Conditions of Production and Management**	**105.79**	**89.88**	**95.11**	**100.93**
购货合同	Purchasing Contracts	99.36	89.37	119.26	110.73
商品购进价格	Bid of Commodities	85.62	100.90	95.00	80.25
商品销售额	Sales of Commodities	104.06	91.29	109.77	116.09
#出口	Export	106.77	121.43	100.00	109.51
商品销售价格	Selling Price of Commodities	98.37	72.52	92.09	109.47
商品库存	Inventory of Commodities	116.51	113.82	110.97	110.13
经营费用	Business Cost	95.59	93.06	84.52	72.15
盈利（亏损）变化	Changes in Profits (loses)	112.98	96.20	104.58	108.32
流动资金	Circulating Funds	70.03	72.13	74.36	78.70
货款拖欠	Payment Delinquent	119.49	105.72	102.52	110.10
劳动力需求	Labor Demand	84.10	74.83	95.51	84.43
固定资产投资	Investment in Fixed Assets	99.27	104.07	99.69	102.87

指标	Item	2004 一季度 1st. Quarter	2004 二季度 2nd. Quarter	2004 三季度 3rd. Quarter	2004 四季度 4th. Quarter
综合生产经营状况	**Comprehensive Conditions of Production and Management**	**107.70**	**108.76**	**106.11**	**109.03**
购货合同	Purchasing Contracts	91.10	78.99	90.05	86.94
商品购进价格	Bid of Commodities	75.87	94.69	88.55	86.74
商品销售额	Sales of Commodities	114.46	96.80	102.62	110.67
#出口	Export	79.58	119.79	131.54	104.45
商品销售价格	Selling Price of Commodities	100.51	84.91	98.11	89.54
商品库存	Inventory of Commodities	110.94	100.11	96.17	101.82
经营费用	Business Cost	95.24	90.98	82.44	73.02
竞争能力	Competition Abilities	110.95	108.95	106.64	106.56
盈利（亏损）变化	Changes in Profits (loses)	108.54	111.65	102.61	108.50
流动资金	Circulating Funds	87.68	80.78	75.65	71.64
企业融资	Fundraising	77.65	64.50	65.33	67.07
货款拖欠	Payment Delinquent	107.77	104.78	115.34	113.46
劳动力需求	Labor Demand	84.02	77.71	87.22	82.85
固定资产投资	Investment in Fixed Assets	98.56	90.40	102.87	101.48

22－12 住宿和餐饮业景气指数（2003－2004年）
Business Survey Index of Hotels and Restaurants (2003-2004)

单位：点 (point)

指　　标	Item	2003 一季度 1st. Quarter	二季度 2nd. Quarter	三季度 3rd. Quarter	四季度 4th. Quarter
综合生产经营状况	**Comprehensive Conditions of Production and Management**	**119.34**	**39.78**	**128.84**	**130.29**
业务量	Business Volume	87.86	24.27	156.57	139.23
竞争能力	Competition Ability	125.64	109.48	133.34	134.96
客房出租（限住宿业）	Rent of Guest Rooms (Hotels)	89.99	21.02	94.13	105.94
收费（服务）价格	Business Charge	74.16	50.35	97.92	92.75
营业收入	Business Revenue	72.69	9.00	155.29	146.08
营业成本	Business Cost	93.05	125.55	64.53	72.49
盈利（亏损）变化	Changes in Profits (loses)	80.69	11.59	128.39	134.78
流动资金	Circulating Funds	88.05	44.58	97.40	101.64
货款拖欠	Payment Delinquent	111.24	93.98	89.95	99.30
劳动力需求	Labor Demand	100.23	35.58	128.07	115.28
固定资产投资	Investment in Fixed Assets	111.74	99.88	115.40	114.39

指　　标	Item	2004 一季度 1st. Quarter	二季度 2nd. Quarter	三季度 3rd. Quarter	四季度 4th. Quarter
综合生产经营状况	**Comprehensive Conditions of Production and Management**	**118.72**	**114.59**	**102.17**	**128.67**
业务预订	Business Order	99.88	111.82	98.85	129.96
业务量	Business Volume	92.05	120.08	87.72	128.04
竞争能力	Competition Ability	127.57	114.62	125.25	128.34
客房出租（限住宿业）	Rent of Guest Rooms (Hotels)	85.71	96.43	88.44	98.08
收费（服务）价格	Business Charge	96.84	90.58	85.07	99.26
营业收入	Business Revenue	93.77	107.62	87.74	128.82
营业成本	Business Cost	76.63	65.25	76.72	83.59
盈利（亏损）变化	Changes in Profits (loses)	97.29	118.78	71.73	121.82
流动资金	Circulating Funds	93.96	100.82	96.42	102.01
企业融资	Fundraising	81.12	79.79	90.70	94.12
货款拖欠	Payment Delinquent	105.15	94.41	103.39	111.83
劳动力需求	Labor Demand	97.07	110.50	99.24	119.20
固定资产投资	Investment in Fixed Assets	111.47	121.62	106.62	107.10

22－13 房地产业景气指数（2003－2004年）
Business Survey Index of Real Estate Trade (2003-2004)

单位：点 (point)

指　　标	Item	2003 一季度 1st. Quarter	2003 二季度 2nd. Quarter	2003 三季度 3rd. Quarter	2003 四季度 4th. Quarter
综合生产经营状况	**Comprehensive Conditions of Production and Management**	**140.75**	**142.11**	**150.03**	**162.60**
土地开发面积	Floor Space of Land Development	109.27	101.29	104.14	123.24
完成投资	Completed Investment	123.52	126.78	129.69	147.65
新开工面积	Floor Space of New Buildings	110.61	110.94	105.88	123.32
房屋竣工面积	Floor Space of Completed Buildings	84.46	114.89	98.58	125.32
商品房预售面积	Floor Space of Presold Commercial Buildings	109.36	123.51	136.20	140.07
商品房销售面积	Floor Space of Sold Commercial Buildings	110.42	128.96	129.76	120.01
商品房销售价格	Selling Price of Commercial Buildings	117.90	122.21	130.92	145.56
空置商品房面积	Vacant Space of Commercial Buildings	163.27	167.52	161.34	157.06
盈利（亏损）变化	Changes in Profits (loses)	116.78	125.64	141.58	148.07
流动资金	Circulating Funds	104.61	109.61	106.67	121.19
货款拖欠	Payment Delinquent	124.11	134.01	132.57	134.75
劳动力需求	Labor Demand	114.41	112.19	113.61	122.40
固定资产投资	Investment in Fixed Assets	102.48	122.58	128.85	144.28

指　　标	Item	2004 一季度 1st. Quarter	2004 二季度 2nd. Quarter	2004 三季度 3rd. Quarter	2004 四季度 4th. Quarter
综合生产经营状况	**Comprehensive Conditions of Production and Management**	**156.77**	**149.16**	**152.47**	**134.82**
土地开发面积	Floor Space of Land Development	106.66	106.01	101.79	104.58
完成投资	Completed Investment	133.21	149.02	133.60	127.46
新开工面积	Floor Space of New Buildings	105.02	95.32	110.02	106.71
房屋竣工面积	Floor Space of Completed Buildings	103.48	110.64	112.88	109.57
商品房预售面积	Floor Space of Presold Commercial Buildings	119.37	119.69	101.21	99.70
商品房销售面积	Floor Space of Sold Commercial Buildings	117.28	110.12	86.29	104.18
商品房销售价格	Selling Price of Commercial Buildings	160.50	147.70	125.48	122.27
空置商品房面积	Vacant Space of Commercial Buildings	163.37	164.77	160.99	153.60
盈利（亏损）变化	Changes in Profits (loses)	139.12	138.62	125.15	122.59
流动资金	Circulating Funds	117.61	110.03	107.34	101.78
企业融资	Fundraising	88.83	88.64	91.76	87.18
货款拖欠	Payment Delinquent	129.04	133.37	129.98	131.59
劳动力需求	Labor Demand	120.79	113.95	115.33	101.58
固定资产投资	Investment in Fixed Assets	125.61	138.56	125.64	108.28

22－14 社会服务业景气指数（2003－2004年）
Business Survey Index of Social Services (2003-2004)

单位：点 (point)

指　标	Item	2003 一季度 1st. Quarter	二季度 2nd. Quarter	三季度 3rd. Quarter	四季度 4th. Quarter
综合生产经营状况	**Comprehensive Conditions of Production and Management**	**118.77**	**69.60**	**114.75**	**120.42**
服务预订	Service Order	114.75	53.95	123.69	98.36
竞争能力	Competition Abilities	138.45	118.03	126.97	130.41
旅游客源（限于旅游业）	Tourists (tourism)	109.09	20.00	172.00	60.61
业务收费（服务）价格	Business (services) Charges	86.30	61.40	91.80	88.52
业务量	Business Volume	107.30	49.92	115.50	106.56
营业成本	Business Cost	86.73	92.86	76.15	88.53
盈利（亏损）变化	Changes in Profits (loses)	125.49	51.72	109.25	100.90
流动资金	Circulating Funds	101.48	86.89	91.06	82.87
货款拖欠	Payment Delinquent	108.78	101.60	88.33	106.82
劳动力需求	Labor Demand	108.19	66.47	107.30	94.18
固定资产投资	Investment in Fixed Assets	113.86	86.89	102.38	110.75

指　标	Item	2004 一季度 1st. Quarter	二季度 2nd. Quarter	三季度 3rd. Quarter	四季度 4th. Quarter
综合生产经营状况	**Comprehensive Conditions of Production and Management**	**117.74**	**123.71**	**103.28**	**102.13**
服务预订	Service Order	101.61	116.13	107.04	96.23
竞争能力	Competition Abilities	129.51	135.48	127.84	123.33
旅游客源（限于旅游业）	Tourists (tourism)	94.44	155.00	130.43	60.00
业务收费（服务）价格	Business (services) Charges	81.97	86.44	96.49	81.36
业务量	Business Volume	92.41	121.31	111.17	105.58
营业成本	Business Cost	77.05	78.20	72.16	90.65
盈利（亏损）变化	Changes in Profits (loses)	98.87	116.13	96.72	112.63
流动资金	Circulating Funds	89.84	83.87	83.12	95.08
企业融资	Fundraising	83.61	77.78	81.13	73.02
货款拖欠	Payment Delinquent	91.80	95.08	100.00	112.63
劳动力需求	Labor Demand	95.64	104.84	98.85	89.68
固定资产投资	Investment in Fixed Assets	112.90	98.39	103.77	93.44

主要统计指标解释

企业集团 是以母子公司为主体，通过投资及生产经营协作等多种方式与众多的企事业单位共同组成的经济联合体。企业集团不具有企业法人资格。

景气指数 又称为景气度，它是对企业景气调查中的定性指标通过定量方法加工汇总，综合反映某一特定调查群体或某一社会经济现象所处的状态或发展趋势的一种指标。景气指数以100为临界值，范围在0—200点之间，即景气指数高于100，表明经济状态趋于上升或改善，处于景气状态；景气指数低于100，表明经济状况处于下降或恶化，处于不景气状态。

为了更好地反映不同规模企业（尤其是大型企业）在全市经济份额中的代表性差异，在编制景气指数时以反映企业综合生产经营状况的总量指标（如产品销售收入）为权数，对各企业所做结论进行了加权处理。

企业家信心指数 也称"宏观经济景气指数"是根据企业家对企业外部市场经济环境与宏观政策的认识、看法、判断与预期（通常为对"乐观"、"一般"、"不乐观"的选择）而编制的指数，用以综合反映企业家对宏观经济环境的感受与信心。日常生活中，为便于反映企业家信心指数的涵义，常表述为"反映企业家对宏观经济环境的信心与预期的企业家信心指数"。

企业景气指数 也称"企业综合生产经营景气指数"，是根据企业家对本企业综合生产经营情况的判断与预期（通常为对"好"、"一般"、"不佳"的选择）而编制的指数，用以综合反映企业的生产经营状况。为便于直观地反映企业景气指数的涵义，日常生活中，常常表述为"反映企业综合生产经营状况的企业景气指数"。

Explanatory Notes on Main Statistical Indicators

Business Groups refer to economic ally that is composed of parent company and subsidiary principally, and combined with many enterprises and institutions in the way of investment, production or cooperation. Business groups are not legal entities of corporations.

Business Survey Index is the quantitative description of the qualitative economic indicators of the business survey, which can comprehensively reflect the situation of some colony or of the economy. The business survey index is ranging from 0 to 200%. 100 is the critical value, when the index is larger than 100, it indicates that the economic performance is picking up or improving. When it is lower than 100, it shows that the economic performance is declining or worsening.

To calculate business survey index, the gross indicators showing general production and management of enterprises, such as sales revenue, are used as weight coefficients, and the results of every enterprise are specially treated, reflecting the representatives of different sized enterprises (especially large-sized) in overall economy much better.

Entrepreneur Expectation Index also called as macro-economic climate index is compiled basing on entrepreneurs judgment on development situation of the sector and their expectation for the performance (as choices of "Optimistic", "Ordinary" and "Unoptimistic").

Enterprise Business Survey Index also called as comprehensive production and management index of enterprises, is compiled basing on entrepreneurs judgment on production situation of their own enterprises and their expectation for the performance (as choices of "Good", "Ordinary" and "Bad").

二十三　三峡工程重庆库区移民情况

RESETTLEMENT OF CHONGQING RESERVOIR AREA OF THREE GORGES PROJECT

简要说明　Brief Introduction

本章资料包括三峡工程重庆库区城乡人口迁移、农村生产安置人口、移民工程投资、房屋建筑面积情况，由市统计局综合处根据市移民局资料整理编辑。

This chapter includes resettlement of urban and rural residents, resettlement of rural residents for production in Chongqing Reservoir Area of Three Gorges rojects, and completed investment and floor space of buildings of Three Gorges Resettlement Projects. Data are prepared and edited by Division of Comprehensive Statistics, Municipal Bureau of Statistics using information from Chongqing Resettlement Affairs Bureau of Three Gorges.

23－1 三峡工程重庆库区城乡人口迁移情况（2004年底止）
Resettlement of Urban and Rural Residents in Chongqing Reservoir Area of Three Gorges Project (End of 2004)

单位：人 (person)

项 目	Item	应迁人口 Residents ought to be Resettled 合计 Total	城镇 Urban	乡村 Rural	实迁人口 Actually Resettled Residents 合计 Total	城镇 Urban	乡村 Rural	县内安置 Resettled inside the County	县外安置 Resettled outside the County	#省外安置 Resettled outside Chong-qing
搬迁总人数	**Total Resettled Residents**	**951335**	**636155**	**315180**	**817929**	**558276**	**259653**	**117609**	**142044**	**117880**
1. 90米以下	Below 90m	51894	38383	13511	9124	5415	3709	3484	225	225
2. 90米-135米	90-135m	385371	268665	116706	309944	232849	77095	45115	31980	24378
3. 135米-156米	135-156m	325967	190850	135117	357133	228228	128905	52722	76183	61876
4. 156米-175米	156-175m	188103	138257	49846	141728	91784	49944	16288	33656	31401

注：本表不含生产安置人口。

Note: Resettled persons for production in this table are excluded.

23－2 三峡工程重庆库区农村生产安置人口（2004年底止）
Resettlement of Rural Residents for Production in Chongqing Reservoir Area of Three Gorges Project (End of 2004)

单位：人 (person)

项 目	Item	应迁人口 Residents ought to be Resettled	实际生产安置人口 Actually Resettled Residents	县内安置 Resettled inside the County 小计 Sub-total	农业安置 Engaged in Agriculture	二、三产业安置 Engaged in Secondary & Tertiary Industry	其他 Others	县外安置 Resettled outside the County	#省外安置 Resettled outside Chong-qing
搬迁总人数	**Total Resettled Residents**	**328932**	**321068**	**174275**	**112932**	**21103**	**40240**	**146793**	**119238**
1. 90米以下	Below 90m	33909	19052	18169	14449	1605	2115	883	674
2. 90米-135米	90-135m	132078	96403	53736	31391	5627	16718	42667	27719
3. 135米-156米	135-156m	114957	134706	64898	45091	8803	11004	69808	58638
4. 156米-175米	156-175m	47988	70907	37472	22001	5068	10403	33435	32207

23－3 三峡移民工程投资完成情况（2004年）
Completed Investment in Three Gorges Resettlement (2004)

单位：万元 (10 000 yuan)

项目	Item	工程设计总投资 Total Planned Investment	移民资金累计计划 Total Resettlement Funds on Plan	移民资金累计完成 Total Investment Completed	本年计划移民资金 Investment Planned in This Year	本年完成移民资金 Investment Completed in This Year
合　计	**Total**	**3406079**	**3326898**	**3414562**	**304454**	**323081**
农村移民安置	**Resettlement of Rural Residents**		**705733**	**745933**	**73718**	**101145**
内迁生产安置	Resettlement Inside for Production		215722	155672	7801	11662
土地开发	Land Development		186156	130686	6294	9176
小型水利设施	Mini Water Conservancies		13758	7939	129	139
过渡期生活补助	Living Subsidies During Interim		15808	17047	1378	2347
内迁生活安置	Resettlement Inside for Living		195865	200682	17779	18373
基础设施	Capital Construction		7170	24231	8	1084
农村道路	Rural Roads		8756	9621	1797	1066
农村建房	Rural Buildings		151261	119693	13181	14039
村组副业	Other Avocations Founding		2337	2873	13	457
搬迁补偿	Compensation for Resettlement		375	3864	1	111
学校搬迁补偿	Compensation for School Moving		528	580	50	50
其　他	Others		25438	39821	2729	1566
外迁生产安置	Resettlement Outside for Production		188142	286200	21710	31734
外迁生活安置	Resettlement Outside for Living		106004	103378	26429	39376
城市迁建	**Resettlement and Reconstruction of Cities**	**1323642**	**1213072**	**1295777**	**129680**	**108524**
基础设施	Capital Construction	717051	764448	827748	74338	66604
征　地	Land Requisition	131751	218791	248986	3254	12077
场地平整	Ground Grading	52115	68569	97102	8712	12960
道　路	Roads	245809	267167	260905	38673	18820
大中型桥梁	Bridges of Large & Medium-sized	33525	33351	32318	1251	1100
给排水	Water Supply and Drainage	89815	74780	83095	10424	6206
邮电通讯	Posts and Communications	5773	10708	11459	19	250
广播电视	Broadcasting and TV	5340	1985	3136	200	300
防洪护岸	Flood Prevention and Embankment	69604	29264	32862	50	200
输气管道	Gas Tubes	18159	4513	7528		1657
输变电	Transmission and Transformer Substations	19714	21032	19732	4698	1428
绿　化	Afforestations	2728	8559	9157	1642	2370
其　他	Others	42719	25729	21469	5415	9236
城市建房	Urban Buildings	606591	448624	468028	55342	41920
集镇迁建	**Resettlement and Reconstruction of Towns**	**168714**	**210224**	**208478**	**21790**	**28569**
基础设施	Capital Construction	46467	75654	76778	5663	8132
集镇建房	Buildings in Towns	100175	113037	105801	14126	17004
道　路	Roads	22072	21533	25898	2000	3433
工矿企业迁建	**Resettlement and Reconstruction of Industrial and Mineral Enterprises**	**1214963**	**670870**	**669003**	**50860**	**47582**
专项设施复建	**Reconstruction of Special Establishment**	**653476**	**435510**	**398642**	**19424**	**29480**
公　路	Highways	143114	136714	130622	5472	7350
大中型桥梁	Bridges of Large & Medium-sized	47782	48852	49114	200	-601
港口码头	Quays at Ports	137967	97351	87018	2307	6742
港　口	Ports	10355	19399	14423	145	1649
码　头	Quays	126694	77207	71795	2097	4675
停靠站	Harbours	917	744	801	65	418
水电站	Hydro-power Stations	107847	32303	27627	204	1804
抽水站	Pumping Stations	1428	2055	898	81	241
输变电	Transmission and Transformer Substations	19427	22117	25671	1289	3048
110KV变电站	110KV Substations	2434	1948	1680	101	172
110KV输电线路	110KV Transmission Circuits	6454	3310	5051	400	610
35KV及以下变电站	35KV and below Substations	3232	5790	5487		417
35KV及以下输电线	35KV and below Transmission Circuits	7307	11069	13453	789	1848

23-3 续表 CONTINUED

单位：万元 (10 000 yuan)

项　目	Item	工程设计总投资 Total Planned Investment	移民资金累计计划 Total Resettlement Funds on Plan	移民资金累计完成 Total Investment Completed	本年计划移民资金 Investment Planned in This Year	本年完成移民资金 Investment Completed in This Year
广播电视	Broadcasting and TV	7190	8715	8840	203	399
中转站	Intermediate Stations	312	704	607		36
线　路	Circuits	6878	8010	8232	203	363
输气管道	Gas Tubes	11459	9034	7877		546
汛后工程	Projects after Floodwater	100000	150	150	150	150
库底清理	Liquidation below Water Line	5485	10328	11663		387
邮政通讯	Posts and Communications	31328	20576	20487	1021	1038
文物古迹	Cultural Relics and Historic Sites	27100	39580	22968	7977	7974
水文网站	Hydrographic Stations	4105	4390	2980	520	172
汽　渡	Transilience of Cars	975	975	1093		
航道设施	Equipment of Water-routes	8270	2370	1634		230
环境保护	**Environmental Protection**	**42777**	**8983**	**8740**		**455**
水土保持	Water and Earth Maintenance	766	244	88		
城集镇迁建	Urban Resettlement	36764	3824	3806		32
污水治理	Waste Governance	25604	2423	2567		32
垃圾处理	Rubbish Management	11161	1401	1239		
其　他	Others	5247	4915	4846		423
勘测设计费	**Costs of Reconnaissance and Design**		**52483**	**56407**	**2982**	**3994**
监理费	**Costs of Monitor**		**26587**	**21985**	**6000**	**2539**
单项监理	Single Monitor		10640	8760	4110	2135
综合监理	Comprehensive Monitor		15948	13225	1890	404
滑坡治理	**Landslide Treatment**	**2505**	**3436**	**9599**		**793**

23－4 三峡移民工程房屋建筑面积情况（2004年）

Floor Space of Building Construction of Three Gorges Resettlement Project (2004)

单位：万平方米 (10 000 sq.m)

项　目	Item	设计总面积 Total Designed Area	累计竣工建筑面积 Total Space Floor Completed	本年计划竣工面积 Space Floor Planned to Complete in This Year	本年竣工面　积 Space Floor Complete in This Year	本年竣工房屋价值（万元） Value of Completed Buildings in This Year (10 000 yuan)
合　计	**Total**	**2560.07**	**3176.32**	**250.81**	**296.63**	**137960.12**
一、厂房	Factory Buildings	319.92	356.74	2.05	6.04	1890.00
二、住宅	Residential Buildings	1701.87	2263.91	234.51	257.89	104358.38
1、农村住房	Rural Areas	463.59	720.89	51.93	68.08	22285.49
2、城（集）镇住房	Urban Areas	1059.01	1274.26	164.46	168.60	73695.89
3、工矿企业住房	Industrial and Mining Enterprises	179.27	268.76	18.12	21.21	8377.00
三、办公用房	Offices	256.49	283.58	7.20	13.80	14613.24
四、商业、居民服务业用房	Buildings for Commerce and Residential Services	140.43	137.41	6.05	10.19	14495.00
五、文化教育用房	Buildings for Culture and Education	81.62	69.55	0.37	7.78	2270.00
六、医疗用房	Buildings for Medical Cares	27.35	27.87	0.30	0.62	243.50
七、科研用房	Buildings for Research	0.41	0.40			
八、其他用房	Buildings for Other Purposes	31.98	36.86	0.33	0.31	90.00

附　录
APPENDIX

重庆统计年鉴 · CHONGQING STATISTICAL YEARBOOK 2005

统计年鉴

重庆 · 2005

CHONGQING STATISTICAL YEARBOOK 2005

附录1：重庆市国民经济主要指标占全国的比重（2004年）
Appendix I: Chongqing's Main Indicators of National Economy as Percentage of Whole Nation (2004)

指　标	Item	全　国 Whole Nation	重　庆 Chongqing	重庆占全国的比重（%） Chongqing as Percentage of Whole Nation (%)
土地面积（万平方公里）	Land Area (10 000 sq.km)	960	8.24	0.86
年底总人口（万人）	Year-end Population (10 000 persons)	129988	3144.23	2.42
年底就业人员数（万人）	Year-end Employment (10 000 persons)	75200	1715.62	2.28
#年底职工人数	Year-end Staff and Workers	10576	208.04	1.97
#第一产业	Primary Industry	35269	869.30	2.46
第二产业	Secondary Industry	16920	301.42	1.78
第三产业	Tertiary Industry	23011	544.90	2.37
国内（地区）生产总值（现价）（亿元）	Gross Domestic Product (current prices) (100 million yuan)	136876	2665.39	1.95
第一产业	Primary Industry	20768	423.70	2.04
第二产业	Secondary Industry	72387	1181.24	1.63
工　业	Industry	62815	927.51	1.48
建筑业	Construction	9572	253.73	2.65
第三产业	Tertiary Industry	43721	1060.45	2.43
#交通运输仓储邮电通信业	Transportation Storage Postal and Telecommunication Services	7694	153.83	2.00
批发、零售贸易和餐饮业	Wholesale and Retail Trade Catering Trade	10099	227.51	2.25
工业总产值（现价）（亿元）	Gross Output Value of Industry (current prices) (100 million yuan)	187221	2142.73	1.14
#国有及国有控股	State-owned and State Holding	65971	1178.19	1.79
农林牧渔业总产值（现价）（亿元）	Gross Output Value of Farming Forestry Animal Husbandry and Fishery (current prices) (100 million yuan)	36239	612.77	1.69
#农　业	Farming	18138	332.95	1.84
林　业	Forestry	1327	18.48	1.39
牧　业	Animal Husbandry	12174	230.94	1.90
渔　业	Fishery	3606	21.25	0.59
货运量（万吨）	Total Freight Traffic (10 000 tons)	1706226	38168	2.24
客运量（万人次）	Total Passenger Traffic (10 000 person-times)	1767453	64675	3.66
邮电业务总量（亿元）	Total Business Revenue of Postal and Telecommunication Services (100 million yuan)	9791.2	168.65	1.72
社会消费品零售总额（亿元）	Retail Sales of Consumer Goods (100 million yuan)	53950	1061.5	1.97
全社会固定资产投资额（亿元）	Investment in Fixed Assets (100 million yuan)	70073	1621.92	2.31
#房地产开发投资	Real Estate Development	13158	405.08	3.08
地方财政预算收入（亿元）	Local Financial Budgetary Revenue (100 million yuan)	11879.8	302.44	2.55
年底城乡居民人民币储蓄存款余额（亿元）	Year-end Saving Deposits of RMB of Urban and Rural Residents (100 million yuan)	119555.4	2189.73	1.83

注：1）本表中全国数据摘自2005年《中国统计摘要》，部分数据为初步统计数，正式统计数据以《中国统计年鉴—2005》为准。
2）工业部分为国有及规模以上非国有工业企业数。

Note: a) Most of figures of whole nation in this table are primary statistics from *China Statistical Summary—2005*. The official figures are seen in *China Statistical Yearbook—2005*.

b) Data of industry refers to state-owned industrial enterprises and non-state-owned industrial enterprises above designated size.

附录2：全国国民经济与社会发展总量与速度指标
Appendix II: Principal Aggregate Indicators of National Economic and Social Development and Their Related Indices and Growth Rates of Whole Nation

指　　标	Item	1978	1989	2000	2003	2004	平均每年增长% Average Annual Growth Rate%		
							1979-2004	1990-2004	2001-2004
人　口	**Population**								
年末总人口（万人）	Year-end Population (10 000 persons)	96259	112704	126743	129227	129988	1.2	1.0	0.6
城镇人口	Urban Population	17245	29540	45906	52376	54283	4.5	4.1	4.3
乡村人口	Rural Population	79014	83164	80837	76851	75705	-0.2	-0.6	-1.6
就　业	**Employment**								
年底就业人员数（万人）	Year-end Employment (10 000 persons)	40152	55329	72085	74432	75200	2.4	2.1	1.1
#年底职工人数	Year-end Staff and Workers	9499	13742	11259	10492	10576	0.4	-1.7	-1.6
#第一产业	Primary Industry	28318	33225	36043	36546	35269	0.8	0.4	-0.5
第二产业	Secondary Industry	6945	11976	16219	16077	16920	3.5	2.3	1.1
第三产业	Tertiary Industry	4890	10129	19823	21809	23011	6.1	5.6	3.8
国民核算	**National Accounting**								
国内生产总值（亿元）	Gross Domestic Product (100 million yuan)	3624	16909	89468	117252	136876	9.4	9.3	8.7
第一产业	Primary Industry	1018	4228	14628	16928	20768	4.6	4.0	3.6
第二产业	Secondary Industry	1745	7278	44935	61274	72387	11.3	12.0	10.5
工　业	Industry	1607	6484	39047	53093	62815	11.5	12.3	10.7
建筑业	Construction	138	794	5888	8181	9572	9.8	9.3	8.9
第三产业	Tertiary Industry	861	5403	29904	39188	43721	10.0	8.4	8.3
#交通运输仓储邮电通信业	Transportation Storage Postal and Telecommunication Services	173	786	5409	6644	7694	10.1	10.5	9.6
批发、零售贸易和餐饮业	Wholesale and Retail Trade Catering Trade	266	1687	7316	9238	10099	9.1	6.7	7.7
固定资产投资	**Investment in Fixed Assets**								
全社会固定资产投资总额（亿元）	Total Investment in Fixed Assets (100 million yuan)		4410.4	32917.7	55566.6	70072.7		20.9	18.8
国有及其他经济	State-owned and Other Units		2808.1	23406.9	39837.0	50250.7		22.1	19.1
集体经济	Collective-owned Units		570.0	4801.5	8009.5	9886.9		22.3	17.4
个体经济	Individuals Economy		1032.3	4709.4	7720.1	9935.1		15.4	18.9

注：1）本表数据摘自2005年《中国统计摘要》，2004年部分数据为初步统计数，正式统计数据以《中国统计年鉴—2005》为准。

2）本表国内生产总值、农林牧渔业总产值、邮电业务总量和平均工资增长按可比价格计算，其他按当年价格计算。

3）平均每年增长速度除固定资产投资按累计法计算外，其他均按水平法计算。

4）从1997年起固定资产投资的部分统计起点调整；增长速度按可比口径计算(下表同)。

Note: a) Figures in this table are from *China Statistical Summary—2005* . Some figures in 2004 are preliminary statistics. The official figures are seen in *China Statistical Yearbook—2005* .

b) The growth rate of follow indicators are calculated at comparable prices: GDP, gross output value of farming, forestry, animal husbandry and fishery, business volume of postal and telecommunication services and average wages in value terms.

c) Average annual growth rates are calculated by level approach except that of investment in fixed assets is by accumulative approach.

d) The starting-point of some data on investment in fixed assets has been ajusted since 1997. The growth rate is calculated at comparable terms (the same below).

附录2 续表1 APPENDIX II CONTINUED-1

指 标	Item	1978	1989	2000	2003	2004	平均每年增长% Average Annual Growth Rate% 1979-2004	1990-2004	2001-2004
财 政	**Public Finance**								
国家财政收入（亿元）	Government Finance Revenue (100 million yuan)	1132.3	2664.9	13395.2	21715.3	26355.9	12.9	16.5	18.4
#地 方	Local Government Finance Revenue	956.5	1842.4	6406.1	9850.0	11879.8	10.2	13.2	16.7
国家财政支出（亿元）	Government Finance Expenditures (100 million yuan)	1122.1	2823.8	15886.5	24650.0	28360.8	13.2	16.6	15.6
#地 方	Local Government Financial Expenditures	590.0	1935.0	10366.7	17230.0	20465.2	14.6	17.0	18.5
农 业	**Agriculture**								
农林牧渔业总产值（亿元）	Gross Output Value of Farming, Forestry, Animal Husbandry and	1397.0	6534.7	24915.8	29691.8	36239.0	6.2	6.4	5.1
主要农产品产量	Output of Major Farm Products								
粮 食（万吨）	Grain (10 000 tons)	30477	40755	46218	43070	46947	1.7	0.9	0.4
油 料（万吨）	Oil-bearing Crops (10 000 tons)	522	1295	2955	2811	3066	7.0	5.9	0.9
肉 类（万吨）	Meat (10 000 tons)			6125	6933	7245			4.3
#猪牛羊肉	Pork, Beef and Mutton			4838	5506	5777			4.5
水产品（万吨）	Aquatic Products (10 000 tons)	465	1152	4278.5	4705	4902	9.5	10.1	3.5
工 业	**Industry**								
规模以上工业总产值（亿元）	Gross Output Value of Industry above Designated Size (100 million yuan)			85674	142271	187221			21.6
#国有及国有控股	State-owned and State Holding			40554	53408	65971			12.9
主要工业产品产量	Output of Major Industrial Products								
化学纤维（万吨）	Chemical Fiber (10 000 tons)	28.5	148.1	694.0	1181.1	1424.5	16.2	16.3	19.7
机制纸及纸板（万吨）	Machine-made Paper and Paperboards (10 000 tons)	439	1333	2487	4849	4863	9.7	9.0	18.3
原 煤（亿吨）	Coal (100 million tons)	6.2	10.5	10.0	16.7	19.6	4.5	4.2	18.3
发电量（亿千瓦小时）	Electricity (100 million kwh)	2566	5848	13556	19106	21870	8.6	9.2	12.7
成品钢材（万吨）	Steel Products (10 000 tons)	2208	6159	13146	24108	29723	10.5	11.1	22.6
水 泥（万吨）	Cement (10 000 tons)	6524	21029	59700	86208	97000	10.9	10.7	12.9
汽 车（万辆）	Motor Vehicles (10 000 vehicles)	14.9	58.4	207.0	444.4	507.4	14.5	15.5	25.1
建筑业	**Construction**								
建筑企业总产值（亿元）	Gross Output Value of Construction (100 million yuan)		1283.0	12497.6	23083.9	27745.4			
建筑企业房屋施工面积（万平方米）	Floor Space of Buildings under Construction (10 000 sq.m)		40650	160141	259377	291939			
建筑企业房屋竣工面积（万平方米）	Floor Space of Buildings Completed (10 000 sq.m)		19723	80715	122828	128163			

注：从2002年起建筑业统计口径变更，数据与往年不可比。

Note: The data on construction has been modified since 2002.The figures are not comparable with previous years.

附录2 续表2 APPENDIX II CONTINUED-2

指 标	Item	1978	1989	2000	2003	2004	平均每年增长% Average Annual Growth Rate%		
							1979-2004	1990-2004	2001-2004
交通运输	**Transportation**								
货物量（亿吨）	Freight Traffic (100 million tons)	24.89	98.84	135.87	156.14	170.62	7.7	3.7	5.9
货运周转量（亿吨公里）	Freight Ton-kilometers (100 million ton-km)	9829	25591	44321	53859	69442	7.8	6.9	11.9
客运量（亿人）	Passenger Traffic (100 million persons)	25.40	79.14	147.86	158.75	176.75	7.7	5.5	4.6
旅客周转量（亿人公里）	Passenger-kilometers (100 million passenger-km)	1743	6075	12261	13811	16309	9.0	6.8	7.4
沿海主要港口货物吞吐量（万吨）	Cargo Handled at Major Coastal Ports (10 000 tons)	19834	49025	125603	201126	246074	10.2	11.4	18.3
邮电通信业	**Postal and Telecommunications Services**								
邮电业务总量（亿元）	Total Business Volume (100 million yuan)	34.1	123.5	4792.7	7019.8	9791.2	26.0	37.0	19.6
本地电话年末用户（万户）	Capacity of Telephone Exchanges at Year-end (10 000 subscribers)	193	568	14483	26275	31244	21.6	30.6	21.2
移动电话用户（万户）	Mobile Telephone Subscribers (10 000 subscribers)		1	8453	26995	33482		100.3	41.1
国内贸易	**Domestic Trade**								
社会消费品零售总额（亿元）	Retail Sales of Consumer Goods (100 million yuan)	1559	8101	34153	45842	53950	14.6	13.5	12.1
市	City	505	3667	21110	29777	35573	17.8	16.4	13.9
县	County	381	1329	4217	5248	6161	11.3	10.8	9.9
县以下	Below County Level	673	3105	8825	10817	12216	11.8	9.6	8.5
对外经济贸易和国际旅游	**Foreign Trade and International Tourism**								
进出口总额（亿美元）	Total Imports and Exports (USD 100 million)	206.4	1116.8	4742.9	8509.9	11547.9	16.7	16.9	24.9
出口额	Exports	97.5	525.4	2492.0	4382.3	5933.7	17.1	17.5	24.2
进口额	Imports	108.9	591.4	2250.9	4127.6	5614.2	16.4	16.2	25.7
实际利用外资额（亿美元）	Amount of Foreign Capital Actually Utilized (USD 100 million)		100.6	593.6	561.4	640.7		13.1	1.9
#外商直接投资	Foreign Direct Investment		33.9	407.2	535.1	606.3		21.2	10.5
入境过夜旅游者人数（万人次）	Inbound Overnight Tourists (10 000 person-times)	72	936	3123	3297	4176	16.9	10.5	7.5
国际旅游收入（亿美元）	Foreign Exchange Earnings from Tourism (USD 100 million)	2.6	18.6	162.2	174.1	257.4	19.3	19.1	12.2

注：1）邮电业务总量指标2000年及以前按1990年不变价格计算，2001年及以后按2000年不变价格计算。

2）社会消费品零售总额1989年及以前为社会商品零售总额，即包括农业生产资料零售额在内。

Note: a) Total business volume of postal services is at 1990 constant prices before 2000 and at 2000 constant prices since 2001.

b) Retail sales of consumer goods before and in 1989 refer to commodity sales revenue, which include retail sales of agricultural means of production.

附录2 续表3 APPENDIX II CONTINUED-3

指 标	Item	1978	1989	2000	2003	2004	平均每年增长% Average Annual Growth Rate% 1979-2004	1990-2004	2001-2004
金 融	**Finance**								
金融机构人民币各项存款余额（亿元）	Deposit Balance of Financial Institutions (100 million yuan)	1134.5	10786.2	123804.4	208055.6	240525.1	22.9	23.0	18.1
金融机构人民币各项贷款余额（亿元）	Loan Balance of Financial Institutions (100 million yuan)	1850.0	14360.1	99371.1	158996.2	177363.5	19.2	18.2	15.6
教 育	**Education**								
学校数（所）	Number of Schools (unit)								
#普通高等学校	Regular Institutions of Higher Education	598	1075	1041	1552	1731	4.2	3.2	13.6
普通中等学校	Secondary Schools	165105	102732	93935	92450	91543	-2.2	-0.8	-0.6
小 学	Primary Schools	949323	777244	553622	425846	394183	-3.3	-4.4	-8.1
专任教师数（万人）	Full-time Teachers (10 000 persons)								
#普通高等学校	Regular Institutions of Higher Education	20.6	39.7	46.3	72.5	85.8	5.6	5.3	16.7
普通中等学校	Secondary Schools	328.1	342.3	473.4	518.4	535.3	1.9	3.0	3.1
小 学	Primary Schools	522.6	554.4	586.0	570.3	562.9	0.3	0.1	-1.0
在校学生数（万人）	Student Enrollment (10 000 persons)								
#普通高等学校	Regular Institutions of Higher Education	85.6	208.2	556.1	1108.6	1333.5	11.1	13.2	24.4
普通中等学校	Secondary Schools	6637.2	5054.0	8518.4	9807.6	10054.6	1.6	4.7	4.2
小 学	Primary Schools	14624.0	12373.1	13013.3	11689.7	11246.2	-1.0	-0.6	-3.6
卫 生	**Public Health**								
医院卫生院（个）	Number of Hospitals (unit)	64311	61613	66095	62968	60867			
医院卫生院床位数（万张）	Hospitals Beds (10 000 units)	184.7	253.8	290.8	295.5	304.7			
卫生技术人员数（万人）	Medical Technical Personnel (10 000 persons)	246.4	380.9	449.1	430.6	439.0			
#医 生（万人）	Doctors (10 000 persons)	103.3	171.8	207.6	186.8	190.5			
人民生活	**People's Livelihood**								
职工工资总额（亿元）	Total Wages of worker Staff and Worker (100 million yuan)	568.9	2618.5	10656.2	14743.5	16900.2	13.9	13.2	12.2
职工平均工资（元）	Average Annual Wages of Staff and Workers (yuan)	615	1935	9371	14040	16024	6.3	8.5	14.4
城镇居民人均可支配收入（元）	Per Capita Disposable Income of Urban Residents (yuan)	343	1374	6280	8472	9422	13.6	13.7	10.7
农村居民人均纯收入（元）	Per Capita Net Income of Rural Residents (yuan)	134	602	2253	2622	2936	12.6	11.1	6.8
城乡居民储蓄存款余额（亿元）	Saving Deposits of Urban and Rural Residents (100 million yuan)	211	5196	64332	103617	119555	27.6	23.3	16.8

注：2002年起卫生统计制度变更，与往年不可比；2002年及以后的医生数据实为执业（助理）医师。

Note: Health care system has been changed since 2002. The figures are not comparable with previous years. The data of doctors refer to certified (assistant) doctors since 2002.

附录3：全国各省、市、自治区国民经济主要指标及排位（2004年）

Appendix III: Main Indicators and Order of National Economy by Province, Municipality and Autonomous Region (2004)

地区	Region	土地面积（万平方公里） Land Area (10 000 sq.km) 绝对数 Value	位次 Order	年底总人口（万人） Year-end Population (10 000 persons) 绝对数 Value	位次 Order	年底就业人员数（万人） Year-end Employment (10 000 persons) 绝对数 Value	位次 Order	地方预算内一般性财政收入(亿元) General Budgetary Revenue of Local Government (100 million yuan) 绝对数 Value	位次 Order
东部地区	**Eastern Region**								
北　京	Beijing	1.7	29	1493	26	895	24	744.5	6
天　津	Tianjin	1.2	30	1024	27	422	27	246.5	18
河　北	Hebei	18.8	12	6809	6	3416	8	407.8	9
辽　宁	Liaoning	14.6	21	4217	14	1952	15	529.6	7
上　海	Shanghai	0.6	31	1742	25	812	25	1106.2	2
江　苏	Jiangsu	10.3	24	7433	5	3720	5	980.5	3
浙　江	Zhejiang	10.2	25	4720	11	3092	9	805.9	5
福　建	Fujian	12.1	23	3511	18	1818	17	333.5	11
山　东	Shandong	15.7	19	9180	2	4940	2	828.3	4
广　东	Guangdong	17.8	15	8304	4	4316	4	1418.5	1
海　南	Hainan	3.4	28	818	28	367	28	57.0	28
中部地区	**Central Region**								
山　西	Shanxi	15.6	20	3335	19	1475	20	256.4	17
吉　林	Jilin	18.7	13	2709	21	1116	22	166.3	24
黑龙江	Heilongjiang	45.4	6	3817	16	1623	19	289.4	14
安　徽	Anhui	14.0	22	6461	8	3453	7	274.6	15
江　西	Jiangxi	16.7	17	4284	13	2040	14	205.8	21
河　南	Henan	16.7	17	9717	1	5587	1	428.8	8
湖　北	Hubei	18.6	14	6016	9	2589	11	310.4	13
湖　南	Hunan	21.2	10	6698	7	3600	6	320.6	12
西部地区	**Western Region**								
重　庆	Chongqing	8.2	26	3144	20	1716	18	200.6	22
四　川	Sichuan	48.5	5	8725	3	4503	3	385.8	10
贵　州	Guizhou	17.6	16	3904	15	2169	13	149.3	26
云　南	Yunnan	39.4	8	4415	12	2401	12	263.4	16
西　藏	Tibet	122.8	2	274	31	135	31	10.0	31
陕　西	Shaanxi	20.6	11	3705	17	1885	16	215.0	20
甘　肃	Gansu	45.4	6	2619	22	1322	21	104.2	27
青　海	Qinghai	72.1	4	539	30	263	30	27.0	30
宁　夏	Ningxia	5.2	27	588	29	298	29	37.5	29
新　疆	Xinjiang	165.0	1	1963	24	744	26	155.7	25
内蒙古	Inner Mongolia	118.3	3	2384	23	1019	23	196.8	23
广　西	Guangxi	23.6	9	4889	10	2649	10	237.8	19

注：1）本表资料来源于2005年《中国统计摘要》，全国及各省数据多为快报数，正式数据以《中国统计年鉴—2005》为准。

2）地方预算内一般性财政收入数据为月度执行情况汇总数。

Note: a) Most of figures in this table are primary statistics from *China Statistical Summary—2005*. The official figures are seen in *China Statistical Yearbook—2005*.

b) The datas of general budgetary revenue of local government refer to the sum of monthly datas.

附录3 续表1 APPENDIX III CONTINUED-1

地 区	Region	地区生产总值(亿元) Gross Domestic Product (100 million yuan) 绝对数 Value	位次 Order	第一产业 Primary Industry	第二产业 Secondary Industry	第三产业 Tertiary Industry	地区生产总值指数(上年=100) Index of GDP (preceding year=100) 绝对数 Value	位次 Order	人均地区生产总值(元) Per Capita GDP (yuan) 绝对数 Value	位次 Order
东部地区	**Eastern Region**									
北 京	Beijing	4283.3	15	102.9	1610.4	2570.0	113.2	10	37058	2
天 津	Tianjin	2931.9	21	102.3	1560.2	1269.4	115.7	2	31550	3
河 北	Hebei	8768.8	6	1370.4	4635.2	2763.2	112.5	15	12918	11
辽 宁	Liaoning	6872.7	8	769.9	3278.9	2823.9	112.8	13	16297	9
上 海	Shanghai	7450.3	7	96.7	3788.2	3565.3	113.6	9	55307	1
江 苏	Jiangsu	15403.2	3	1315.4	8716.1	5371.7	114.9	4	20705	5
浙 江	Zhejiang	11243.0	4	816.0	6045.0	4382.0	114.3	5	23942	4
福 建	Fujian	6053.1	11	777.9	2950.3	2324.9	112.1	21	17218	7
山 东	Shandong	15490.7	2	1778.3	8724.5	4987.9	115.3	3	16925	8
广 东	Guangdong	16039.5	1	1245.4	8890.3	5903.8	114.2	6	19707	6
海 南	Hainan	769.4	28	283.8	180.4	305.1	110.4	31	9450	18
中部地区	**Central Region**									
山 西	Shanxi	3042.4	18	253.4	1810.1	979.0	114.1	7	9150	19
吉 林	Jilin	2958.2	20	561.0	1379.3	1017.9	112.2	18	10932	14
黑龙江	Heilongjiang	5303.0	13	587.8	3155.3	1559.9	111.7	24	13897	10
安 徽	Anhui	4812.7	14	932.4	2169.8	1710.4	112.5	15	7768	26
江 西	Jiangxi	3495.9	16	711.7	1595.7	1188.5	113.2	10	8189	22
河 南	Henan	8815.1	5	1647.5	4515.4	2652.3	113.7	8	9470	17
湖 北	Hubei	6309.9	10	1020.1	2994.7	2295.2	111.3	27	10500	15
湖 南	Hunan	5612.3	12	1155.9	2214.4	2242.0	112.0	22	9117	20
西部地区	**Western Region**									
重 庆	Chongqing	2665.4	24	423.7	1181.2	1060.5	112.2	18	9608	16
四 川	Sichuan	6556.0	9	1394.3	2690.0	2471.8	112.7	14	8113	23
贵 州	Guizhou	1591.9	26	334.1	714.7	543.1	111.4	26	4215	31
云 南	Yunnan	2959.5	19	604.3	1314.2	1041.0	111.5	25	6733	29
西 藏	Tibet	211.5	31				112.2	18	7779	25
陕 西	Shaanxi	2883.5	22	395.0	1416.8	1071.7	112.9	12	7757	27
甘 肃	Gansu	1558.9	27	281.4	758.2	519.4	110.9	30	5970	30
青 海	Qinghai	465.7	29	57.8	227.1	180.9	112.3	17	8606	21
宁 夏	Ningxia	460.4	30	65.1	239.4	155.8	111.0	29	7880	24
新 疆	Xinjiang	2200.2	25	444.7	1010.1	745.4	111.1	28	11199	13
内蒙古	Inner Mongolia	2712.1	23	506.1	1332.5	873.5	119.4	1	11305	12
广 西	Guangxi	3320.1	17	811.4	1288.3	1220.5	111.8	23	7196	28

注：本表绝对数按当年价计算，指数按可比价格计算；人均地区生产总值除北京、天津和上海按"户籍人口"计算外，其他地区按"常住人口"计算。

Note: The absolute figures in this table are calculated at current prices while indices are calculated at comparable prices. Per capita GDP of Beijing, Tianjin and Shanghai are in terms of registration population, whereas other provinces are in terms of resident population.

附录3 续表2 APPENDIX III CONTINUED-2

地 区	Region	农林牧渔业总产值（亿元） Output Value of Farming, Forestry, Animal Husbandry and Fishery (100 million yuan) 绝对数 Value	位次 Order	＃农业 Farming	＃林业 Forestry	＃牧业 Animal Husbandry	＃渔业 Fishery	农林牧渔业总产值指数（上年=100） Index of Gross Output Value of Farming, Forestry, Animal Husbandry and Fishery (preceding year=100)
东部地区	**Eastern Region**							
北 京	Beijing	262.0	26	92.7	12.7	138.7	9.9	100.4
天 津	Tianjin	241.0	28	95.3	1.7	92.6	31.8	104.3
河 北	Hebei	2375.9	4	1135.7	40.0	1037.7	72.1	106.8
辽 宁	Liaoning	1510.5	10	611.3	40.7	548.3	272.2	107.9
上 海	Shanghai	248.9	27	109.3	13.1	70.8	49.9	92.8
江 苏	Jiangsu	2417.6	3	1242.4	40.2	563.4	449.5	108.9
浙 江	Zhejiang	1332.3	11	592.6	78.4	277.9	362.0	104.4
福 建	Fujian	1317.3	12	525.8	86.2	291.7	397.5	105.0
山 东	Shandong	3453.9	1	1891.7	59.5	1022.8	426.1	106.0
广 东	Guangdong	2154.8	6	960.0	61.7	571.1	466.5	104.5
海 南	Hainan	438.7	25	170.9	59.8	83.9	116.6	109.2
中部地区	**Central Region**							
山 西	Shanxi	481.8	23	290.5	19.1	141.2	2.4	106.8
吉 林	Jilin	940.7	17	486.2	32.9	399.1	13.4	105.4
黑龙江	Heilongjiang	1136.6	14	620.2	65.8	400.7	25.0	119.3
安 徽	Anhui	1644.4	9	842.0	71.9	540.8	146.9	108.9
江 西	Jiangxi	1055.0	15	491.0	79.1	325.0	143.2	108.0
河 南	Henan	2963.9	2	1602.9	75.8	1117.2	28.0	112.9
湖 北	Hubei	1695.4	8	921.6	31.8	514.5	205.7	105.5
湖 南	Hunan	1913.3	7	874.0	91.3	796.9	119.9	107.5
西部地区	**Western Region**							
重 庆	Chongqing	612.8	21	333.0	18.5	230.9	21.2	105.7
四 川	Sichuan	2252.3	5	987.7	62.7	1097.6	65.8	107.1
贵 州	Guizhou	524.6	22	317.7	23.2	168.8	7.0	102.6
云 南	Yunnan	965.2	16	516.9	86.4	305.4	19.1	106.8
西 藏	Tibet	62.7	31	26.6	5.7	29.1		107.0
陕 西	Shaanxi	651.2	20	413.7	26.4	179.4	5.1	109.1
甘 肃	Gansu	477.4	24	331.4	16.2	117.7	1.0	107.0
青 海	Qinghai	86.6	30	34.2	1.8	46.5	0.1	105.1
宁 夏	Ningxia	125.5	29	71.3	6.2	41.2	3.6	108.3
新 疆	Xinjiang	750.7	19	515	13.8	187.5	4.3	106.4
内蒙古	Inner Mongolia	851.3	18	411.5	46.6	374.7	6.0	115.0
广 西	Guangxi	1294.5	13	623.1	58.1	460.7	133.8	106.2

注：本表绝对数按当年价计算，指数按可比价格计算。

Note: The absolute figures in this table are calculated at current prices while indices are calculated at comparable prices.

附录3 续表3 APPENDIX III CONTINUED-3

地 区	Region	全部国有及规模以上非国有工业企业（亿元）State-owned and Non-state-owned Industrial Enterprises above Designated Size (100 million yuan)					
		工业增加值 Industrial Value-added		产品销售收入 Sales Revenue	利润总额 Total After-tax Profits	资产合计 Total Assets	负债合计 Total Liabilities
		绝对数 Value	指数(上年=100) Index (preceding year=100)				
东部地区	**Eastern Region**						
北 京	Beijing	1259.5	119.9	5110.8	310.9	6082.4	3138.9
天 津	Tianjin	1395.6	126.5	5494.6	412.5	5113.8	2899.5
河 北	Hebei	2459.2	122.2	8132.2	513.2	7836.2	4883.8
辽 宁	Liaoning	2255.7	123.4	8320.4	389.3	10167.8	5990.8
上 海	Shanghai	3427.0	119.0	13863.3	1003.5	13684.8	6876.8
江 苏	Jiangsu	6447.5	123.4	24492.3	1111.4	20227.3	12580.4
浙 江	Zhejiang	4173.4	121.1	16693.5	942.8	15222.1	8802.9
福 建	Fujian	1845.8	123.5	6212.7	350.6	5815.9	3069.7
山 东	Shandong	6498.3	126.5	21055.1	1383.6	17620.4	10307.4
广 东	Guangdong	7086.4	122.4	26691.4	1274.3	21798.1	12666.9
海 南	Hainan	102.7	118.4	348.1	27.7	477.2	260.0
中部地区	**Central Region**						
山 西	Shanxi	1242.8	121.2	3295.3	218.4	5318.5	3548.4
吉 林	Jilin	994.3	118.6	3190.8	178.7	3981.4	2403.3
黑龙江	Heilongjiang	1619.6	115.3	3613.1	760.2	4684.5	2705.0
安 徽	Anhui	1082.2	125.1	3605.0	175.3	4428.8	2687.6
江 西	Jiangxi	617.8	126.1	2117.1	72.2	2519.4	1642.7
河 南	Henan	2332.7	123.6	7065.3	376.5	7413.9	4782.9
湖 北	Hubei	1664.7	122.8	5097.0	279.8	7766.6	4507.8
湖 南	Hunan	1198.1	124.1	3452.4	156.5	4173.8	2653.2
西部地区	**Western Region**						
重 庆	Chongqing	588.3	125.3	2108.8	115.6	2718.3	1653.7
四 川	Sichuan	1546.5	125.8	4542.7	200.1	6747.6	4269.6
贵 州	Guizhou	438.4	120.1	1188.1	60.4	2036.7	1345.7
云 南	Yunnan	881.2	116.6	1953.0	189.1	3211.0	1764.2
西 藏	Tibet	14.4	114.1	19.2	3.0	80.5	20.7
陕 西	Shaanxi	870.7	122.9	2497.0	245.3	4164.9	2642.2
甘 肃	Gansu	505.1	115.7	1537.3	64.2	2391.1	1456.9
青 海	Qinghai	132.4	124.8	360.0	40.1	958.2	680.6
宁 夏	Ningxia	147.0	125.8	507.4	15.8	796.7	512.9
新 疆	Xinjiang	616.9	114.4	1382.9	227.2	2291.9	1309.4
内蒙古	Inner Mongolia	776.8	138.5	2064.0	123.9	3030.9	1854.6
广 西	Guangxi	595.6	122.8	1834.9	121.8	2502.8	1620.3

注：本表绝对数按现价计算，指数按可比价格计算。

Note: The absolute figures in this table are calculated at current prices while indices are calculated at comparable prices.

附录3 续表4 APPENDIX III CONTINUED-4

地　区	Region	全部国有及规模以上非国有工业企业 State-owned and Non-state-owned Industrial Enterprises above Designated Size					
		综合指数 Comprehensive Index of Economic Efficiency	总资产贡献率（%） Ratio of Total Assets to Industrial Output Value	资产负债率（%） Ratio of Liabilities to Assets	流动资产周转次数（次） Turnover Ratio of Annual Circulating Funds (time)	全员劳动生产率（元/人） Overall Labor Productivity (yuan/person)	产品销售率（%） Ratio of Sales to Products
东部地区	**Eastern Region**						
北　京	Beijing	179.8	9.9	51.6	1.8	129781	97.8
天　津	Tianjin	193.3	13.4	56.7	2.3	120916	99.1
河　北	Hebei	169.9	13.5	62.3	2.5	90525	98.4
辽　宁	Liaoning	150.0	9.1	58.9	1.9	91234	98.1
上　海	Shanghai	203.1	12.6	50.3	2.0	147707	99.1
江　苏	Jiangsu	166.4	11.5	62.2	2.4	103197	97.9
浙　江	Zhejiang	155.9	13.3	57.8	2.2	74129	97.7
福　建	Fujian	155.2	11.8	52.8	2.3	76500	97.5
山　东	Shandong	185.8	15.5	58.5	2.8	100694	98.1
广　东	Guangdong	155.9	11.1	58.1	2.4	87230	97.6
海　南	Hainan	184.5	13.2	54.5	1.7	115447	97.4
中部地区	**Central Region**						
山　西	Shanxi	143.7	11.2	66.7	1.6	66992	97.9
吉　林	Jilin	162.7	10.8	60.4	2.0	99038	99.2
黑龙江	Heilongjiang	283.8	25.0	57.7	2.0	122393	98.0
安　徽	Anhui	145.4	10.8	60.7	2.0	75790	98.9
江　西	Jiangxi	130.3	10.3	65.2	2.1	62399	98.8
河　南	Henan	148.8	12.3	64.5	2.2	71786	98.5
湖　北	Hubei	149.4	8.9	58.0	1.8	85879	97.9
湖　南	Hunan	149.8	12.9	63.6	2.2	75203	99.8
西部地区	**Western Region**						
重　庆	Chongqing	140.9	10.6	60.8	1.8	65329	99.9
四　川	Sichuan	132.9	8.8	63.3	1.6	73164	98.5
贵　州	Guizhou	135.5	10.7	66.1	1.5	66299	96.2
云　南	Yunnan	227.3	19.4	54.9	1.5	148841	98.7
西　藏	Tibet	188.3	13.1	25.7	0.8	81315	91.6
陕　西	Shaanxi	165.5	12.4	63.4	1.5	75455	96.9
甘　肃	Gansu	131.0	9.2	60.9	1.7	66054	97.8
青　海	Qinghai	170.5	8.9	71.0	1.2	95967	98.4
宁　夏	Ningxia	119.4	7.6	64.4	1.6	62470	97.1
新　疆	Xinjiang	264.6	16.7	57.1	2.2	154335	97.6
内蒙古	Inner Mongolia	164.3	10.8	61.2	2.1	96351	97.6
广　西	Guangxi	149.8	12.0	64.7	2.0	68518	96.8

注：全员劳动生产率按不变价工业增加值计算。

Note: The overall labor productivity is on basis of industrial value-added at constant prices.

附录3 续表5 APPENDIX III CONTINUED-5

地 区	Region	农产品产量 Output of Farm Products			工业产品产量 Output of Industrial Products				
		粮食（万吨） Grain (10 000 tons)	油料（万吨） Oilbearing Crops (10 000 tons)	肉类（万吨） Meat (10 000 tons)	原煤（万吨） Coal (10 000 tons)	发电量（亿千瓦小时） Electricity (100 million kwh)	成品钢材（万吨） Steel Products (10 000 tons)	水泥（万吨） Cement (10 000 tons)	汽车（万辆） Motor Vehicles (10 000 vehicles)
东部地区	**Eastern Region**								
北 京	Beijing	70.2	2.9	70.8	908.4	150.6	851.0	1128.0	53.9
天 津	Tianjin	122.8	1.6	53.7		337.7	1493.5	537.0	22.3
河 北	Hebei	2480.1	154.3	534.0	7156.2	1255.6	4697.8	7825.5	14.4
辽 宁	Liaoning	1720.0	45.9	318.4	6232.5	888.7	2598.1	2472.1	14.2
上 海	Shanghai	106.3	7.4	12.5		766.2	1818.4	665.0	56.0
江 苏	Jiangsu	2829.1	238.4	346.8	2747.0	1488.4	3749.9	7993.2	24.4
浙 江	Zhejiang	834.9	48.8	161.8	56.3	1115.2	626.4	8191.6	10.1
福 建	Fujian	736.5	27.8	151.3	1076.1	659.6	568.4	2245.3	6.6
山 东	Shandong	3516.7	369.7	696.5	14646.2	1640.3	2011.7	12363.8	14.7
广 东	Guangdong	1390.0	77.5	360.5	219.4	2022.5	1141.7	7785.3	27.7
海 南	Hainan	190.1	9.1	52.3		66.5	17.6	418.7	6.7
中部地区	**Central Region**								
山 西	Shanxi	1062.0	28.2	66.6	37231.6	1049.3	1102.6	1923.2	0.1
吉 林	Jilin	2510.0	38.1	243.5	2396.5	374.1	430.9	1376.3	64.6
黑龙江	Heilongjiang	3001.0	46.0	165.3	7162.6	550.1	197.8	1128.1	21.1
安 徽	Anhui	2743.0	299.7	333.7	7868.1	606.9	945.7	3235.5	21.8
江 西	Jiangxi	1663.0	74.5	217.7	1232.6	327.8	774.9	2976.1	18.4
河 南	Henan	4260.0	408.7	641.5	14445.5	1185.6	966.0	5393.6	3.0
湖 北	Hubei	2100.1	314.4	309.3	395.6	1105.9	1334.3	3767.7	33.6
湖 南	Hunan	2640.0	139.6	517.1	3036.2	605.2	802.1	3358.2	4.6
西部地区	**Western Region**								
重 庆	Chongqing	1144.6	41.8	167.0	1738.2	232.8	288.1	1906.2	43.4
四 川	Sichuan	3146.7	226.3	609.1	4429.9	881.8	1012.0	3819.9	6.3
贵 州	Guizhou	1149.6	82.7	148.0	9756.6	713.0	203.2	1428.8	0.1
云 南	Yunnan	1509.5	33.4	277.8	1718.6	513.5	345.5	2151.0	5.1
西 藏	Tibet	96.0	5.4	20.8	1.6	11.7		96.0	
陕 西	Shaanxi	1040.0	46.1	101.6	8426.0	481.0	201.3	1800.5	5.0
甘 肃	Gansu	805.8	48.5	76.6	3083.8	455.4	295.3	1353.0	0.1
青 海	Qinghai	88.5	28.9	24.8	418.8	173.4	37.4	342.8	
宁 夏	Ningxia	290.5	13.8	24.4	2354.6	252.9	14.1	582.8	
新 疆	Xinjiang	796.5	44.5	128.1	2219.6	244.1	233.1	1190.3	0.2
内蒙古	Inner Mongolia	1505.3	103.7	201.3	17171.4	815.4	601.4	1182.4	0.6
广 西	Guangxi	1398.5	58.3	210.5	521.3	338.1	376.1	2679.5	28.5

附录3 续表6 APPENDIX III CONTINUED-6

地区	Region	全社会客运量（万人） Passenger Traffic (10 000 persons)		＃铁路	＃公路	全社会旅客周转量（亿人公里） Passenger-kilometers (100 million person-km)		＃铁路	＃公路
		绝对数 Value	位次 Order	Railway	Highway	绝对数 Value	位次 Order	Railway	Highway
东部地区	Eastern Region								
北 京	Beijing	46900	17	5437	41463	232	25	74	158
天 津	Tianjin	3956	30	1499	2457	109	27	85	24
河 北	Hebei	77770	8	5270	72500	945	4	479	466
辽 宁	Liaoning	57637	13	9626	47370	575	11	372	195
上 海	Shanghai	7683	27	4076	2465	123	26	46	72
江 苏	Jiangsu	128394	4	6085	122218	1084	2	228	855
浙 江	Zhejiang	150743	2	6255	142177	795	6	216	572
福 建	Fujian	53513	14	1754	50862	372	16	84	287
山 东	Shandong	89407	7	3876	84290	748	7	267	476
广 东	Guangdong	141747	3	8459	131435	1383	1	308	1066
海 南	Hainan	25791	24	16	24981	85	28		83
中部地区	Central Region								
山 西	Shanxi	39207	19	3411	35688	285	19	105	180
吉 林	Jilin	27088	23	4687	22293	237	24	147	90
黑龙江	Heilongjiang	51263	15	8860	42170	399	15	173	226
安 徽	Anhui	68837	9	3406	65075	709	8	282	427
江 西	Jiangxi	39536	18	3778	35312	555	12	356	198
河 南	Henan	90795	6	5695	85016	938	5	542	395
湖 北	Hubei	67105	10	3456	63127	623	10	283	337
湖 南	Hunan	106310	5	5563	99975	949	3	497	450
西部地区	Western Region								
重 庆	Chongqing	64675	11	2346	60833	321	17	60	226
四 川	Sichuan	158608	1	4945	150176	641	9	170	468
贵 州	Guizhou	58707	12	1855	56077	278	21	126	151
云 南	Yunnan	38653	20	1739	36502	278	21	50	227
西 藏	Tibet	256	31		256	15	31		15
陕 西	Shaanxi	35350	21	3231	31763	450	14	256	194
甘 肃	Gansu	16479	26	1194	15050	282	20	185	96
青 海	Qinghai	4568	29	364	4193	42	30	19	23
宁 夏	Ningxia	6654	28	295	6359	59	29	21	38
新 疆	Xinjiang	22340	25	985	21355	289	18	102	187
内蒙古	Inner Mongolia	28652	22	3142	25510	256	23	101	155
广 西	Guangxi	48078	16	1639	45578	516	13	103	411

附录3 续表7 APPENDIX III CONTINUED-7

地 区	Region	全社会货运量（万吨） Freight Traffic (10 000 tons) 绝对数 Value	位次 Order	#铁路 Railway	#公路 Highway	全社会货物周转量（亿吨公里） Freight ton-kilometers (100 million ton-km) 绝对数 Value	位次 Order	#铁路 Railway	#公路 Highway
东部地区	**Eastern Region**								
北 京	Beijing	31321	24	2065	29256	538	27	455	82
天 津	Tianjin	36237	20	6113	19650	11223	1	360	72
河 北	Hebei	83672	7	15744	66227	4029	4	2221	659
辽 宁	Liaoning	89625	6	15014	70164	2948	6	1160	327
上 海	Shanghai	62986	10	1284	31554	10012	2	42	71
江 苏	Jiangsu	99132	5	5262	69058	2348	8	438	387
浙 江	Zhejiang	118074	3	3663	78540	2702	7	288	354
福 建	Fujian	38253	17	4722	25964	1399	13	218	216
山 东	Shandong	129024	1	14850	106887	4753	3	1081	596
广 东	Guangdong	114790	4	8169	81792	3848	5	342	605
海 南	Hainan	8577	28	468	6168	236	29	3	52
中部地区	**Central Region**								
山 西	Shanxi	121633	2	48929	72621	1418	12	1051	367
吉 林	Jilin	33286	22	6552	26659	596	26	500	96
黑龙江	Heilongjiang	57011	15	15143	40712	1097	16	875	204
安 徽	Anhui	58893	13	9009	43468	1456	11	869	350
江 西	Jiangxi	31924	23	5723	23223	870	20	613	179
河 南	Henan	72730	8	13668	58147	2107	9	1650	422
湖 北	Hubei	43879	16	5036	31584	1383	14	687	236
湖 南	Hunan	70320	9	6043	60291	1552	10	877	514
西部地区	**Western Region**								
重 庆	Chongqing	38168	18	3731	31515	721	23	196	128
四 川	Sichuan	60155	11	8084	49143	837	21	584	231
贵 州	Guizhou	19439	27	5504	13541	611	25	521	84
云 南	Yunnan	59081	12	4534	54326	651	24	284	365
西 藏	Tibet	246	31		246	23	31		23
陕 西	Shaanxi	37961	19	7810	30038	964	18	768	195
甘 肃	Gansu	25686	26	4181	21460	878	19	748	130
青 海	Qinghai	6211	30	1075	5136	137	30	92	45
宁 夏	Ningxia	7853	29	2527	5326	243	28	178	65
新 疆	Xinjiang	28760	25	4985	23775	728	22	446	282
内蒙古	Inner Mongolia	57436	14	14739	42697	1312	15	1042	270
广 西	Guangxi	34486	21	5232	25822	998	17	616	236

附录3 续表8 APPENDIX III CONTINUED-8

地区	Region	固定资产投资额(亿元) Investment in Fixed Assets (100 million yuan) 绝对数 Value	位次 Order	#房地产开发投资 Real Estate Development	房地产开发企业房屋竣工面积(万平方米) Commercial Buildings' Floor Spaces Completed of Real Estate Development Corporations (10 000 sq.m)	房地产开发企业房屋销售面积(万平方米) Commercial Buildings' Floor Spaces Sold of Real Estate Development Corporations (10 000 sq.m)	商品房销售额(亿元) Sales Revenue of Commercial Buildings (100 million yuan)
东部地区	**Eastern Region**						
北　京	Beijing	2528.3	10	1473.3	3067.0	2472.0	1249.1
天　津	Tianjin	1256.7	21	263.9	1108.1	847.0	263.8
河　北	Hebei	3215.3	5	315.9	820.7	864.9	138.8
辽　宁	Liaoning	2979.6	8	701.1	2064.4	1748.8	421.8
上　海	Shanghai	3050.2	7	1175.5	3443.0	3300.8	1932.6
江　苏	Jiangsu	6496.0	2	1269.8	3906.3	3178.9	842.9
浙　江	Zhejiang	5756.2	4	1295.2	3195.3	2794.3	868.5
福　建	Fujian	1893.1	14	477.8	1523.9	1384.8	354.5
山　东	Shandong	6971.8	1	764.8	2396.9	2525.2	516.5
广　东	Guangdong	5765.6	3	1355.8	3407.8	3346.0	1164.9
海　南	Hainan	329.6	29	56.0	105.3	125.8	30.2
中部地区	**Central Region**						
山　西	Shanxi	1442.8	20	125.8	477.1	399.1	72.0
吉　林	Jilin	1171.6	24	159.9	484.6	401.9	75.6
黑龙江	Heilongjiang	1460.8	19	214.1	942.9	857.1	166.2
安　徽	Anhui	1919.4	13	350.3	1685.0	1429.2	254.7
江　西	Jiangxi	1723.7	16	242.8	1155.7	1168.9	135.2
河　南	Henan	3099.4	6	258.8	1135.3	1043.5	164.1
湖　北	Hubei	2265.1	11	337.3	1532.4	1342.9	224.5
湖　南	Hunan	2072.8	12	334.9	1459.1	1188.8	179.6
西部地区	**Western Region**						
重　庆	Chongqing	1621.9	17	405.1	1586.0	1329.3	232.8
四　川	Sichuan	2856.8	9	510.1	2398.7	2102.0	330.5
贵　州	Guizhou	861.2	26	121.7	644.5	554.3	76.8
云　南	Yunnan	1244.3	23	149.9	473.2	538.1	106.4
西　藏	Tibet	167.8	31	5.4	9.2	9.6	2.6
陕　西	Shaanxi	1508.6	18	231.2	538.4	509.4	88.2
甘　肃	Gansu	733.9	27	72.1	321.3	261.5	45.9
青　海	Qinghai	291.5	30	26.2	149.9	93.9	14.9
宁　夏	Ningxia	373.9	28	67.2	428.3	308.2	58.0
新　疆	Xinjiang	1138.7	25	104.7	557.0	643.4	102.0
内蒙古	Inner Mongolia	1788.0	15	111.4	614.4	654.0	91.6
广　西	Guangxi	1247.0	22	192.3	884.5	820.4	170.8

注：本表各省数不包括跨区投资。

Note: Data of each province excludes investment of transregions in this table.

附录3 续表9 APPENDIX III CONTINUED-9

地 区	Region	社会消费品零售总额（亿元） Total Retail Sales of Consumer Goods (100 million yuan) 绝对数 Value	位次 Order	市 City	县 County	县以下 Below County Level	社会消费品零售总额指数（上年=100） Index of Retail Sales of Consumer Goods (preceding year=100)
东部地区	**Eastern Region**						
北 京	Beijing	2191.8	11	1746.4	109.5	335.9	114.4
天 津	Tianjin	1052.7	19	982.9	39.3	30.5	114.1
河 北	Hebei	2522.9	8	1240.6	486.4	795.9	115.8
辽 宁	Liaoning	2642.8	7	2223.6	127.6	291.6	113.4
上 海	Shanghai	2454.6	9	2117.7	18.7	318.2	110.5
江 苏	Jiangsu	4159.7	3	2968.6	242.1	949.0	116.6
浙 江	Zhejiang	3645.4	4	2313.0	407.1	925.3	15.5
福 建	Fujian	1995.8	13	1239.9	248.6	507.4	114.7
山 东	Shandong	4483.4	2	2903.7	445.5	1134.3	113.9
广 东	Guangdong	6370.4	1	4268.2	310.5	1791.6	113.6
海 南	Hainan	220.2	28	148.6	19.9	51.7	114.9
中部地区	**Central Region**						
山 西	Shanxi	884.8	24	563.5	168.9	152.4	121.3
吉 林	Jilin	1252.6	16	976.3	86.9	189.4	112.8
黑龙江	Heilongjiang	1555.4	14	1159.3	205.7	190.3	113.0
安 徽	Anhui	1503.1	15	768.9	319.7	414.4	112.9
江 西	Jiangxi	1059.9	18	533.3	232.8	293.8	114.8
河 南	Henan	2808.2	5	1480.8	558.9	768.4	115.7
湖 北	Hubei	2667.5	6	1829.4	250.4	587.7	113.1
湖 南	Hunan	2069.8	12	1145.6	382.1	542.2	114.0
西部地区	**Western Region**						
重 庆	Chongqing	1061.5	17	653.2	120.1	288.1	127.0
四 川	Sichuan	2384.0	10	1130.1	425.9	827.9	114.0
贵 州	Guizhou	517.6	26	308.1	98.6	110.9	112.8
云 南	Yunnan	884.9	23	482.1	204.1	198.7	113.1
西 藏	Tibet	63.7	31	28.2	27.4	8.1	109.3
陕 西	Shaanxi	966.5	21	647.8	163.7	155.0	113.3
甘 肃	Gansu	535.8	25	349.5	84.9	101.4	112.9
青 海	Qinghai	115.6	30	75.0	27.4	13.2	112.6
宁 夏	Ningxia	137.8	29	94.7	22.9	20.2	114.1
新 疆	Xinjiang	482.1	27	362.8	54.1	65.2	114.5
内蒙古	Inner Mongolia	892.0	22	563.8	200.4	127.8	122.7
广 西	Guangxi	973.4	20	531.0	187.0	255.3	113.5

附录3 续表10 APPENDIX III CONTINUED-10

地区	Region	海关进出口总额(按经营单位所在地分)(亿美元) Value of Imports and Exports (by location of foreign trade managing units) (USD 100 million) 绝对数 Value	位次 Order	# 出口额 Exports	实际利用外商直接投资额(万美元) Foreign Direct Investment Actually Utilized (USD 10 000)	国际旅游人数(万人次) Number of International Tourists (10 000 person-times)	旅游外汇收入(亿美元) Foreign Exchange Earnings from Tourism (USD 100 million)
东部地区	**Eastern Region**						
北　京	Beijing	946.6	4	205.8	255974	315.5	31.734
天　津	Tianjin	420.4	8	208.6	172091	61.6	4.125
河　北	Hebei	135.3	10	93.4	69954	58.1	1.904
辽　宁	Liaoning	344.4	9	189.2	540677	108.1	6.128
上　海	Shanghai	1600.2	3	735.1	631087	385.5	30.412
江　苏	Jiangsu	1708.6	2	875.0	894830	306.6	17.634
浙　江	Zhejiang	852.3	5	581.6	573256	276.7	13.005
福　建	Fujian	475.5	7	294.0	192384	172.9	10.651
山　东	Shandong	606.7	6	358.5	866423	119.3	5.666
广　东	Guangdong	3571.3	1	1915.6	1001158	1563.7	53.782
海　南	Hainan	34.0	26	10.9	11926	30.9	0.816
中部地区	**Central Region**						
山　西	Shanxi	53.8	19	40.4	9022	29.6	0.812
吉　林	Jilin	67.9	13	17.2	19237	32.4	0.960
黑龙江	Heilongjiang	67.9	13	36.8	33917	73.3	3.022
安　徽	Anhui	72.1	11	39.4	42850	50.1	1.407
江　西	Jiangxi	35.3	25	20.0	204487	28.8	0.798
河　南	Henan	66.2	16	41.8	42211	45.0	1.600
湖　北	Hubei	67.7	15	33.8	174441	61.2	1.924
湖　南	Hunan	54.3	18	31.0	141803	55.3	3.131
西部地区	**Western Region**						
重　庆	Chongqing	38.6	21	20.9	40508	43.4	2.031
四　川	Sichuan	68.7	12	39.8	36503	96.6	2.889
贵　州	Guizhou	15.1	28	8.7	6271	23.1	0.802
云　南	Yunnan	37.5	22	22.4	14153	110.1	4.225
西　藏	Tibet	2.0	31	1.3		9.6	0.366
陕　西	Shaanxi	36.4	24	24.0	14132	80.0	3.614
甘　肃	Gansu	17.7	27	10.0	3539	23.7	0.438
青　海	Qinghai	5.8	30	4.6		2.9	0.091
宁　夏	Ningxia	9.1	29	6.5	6704	0.7	0.017
新　疆	Xinjiang	56.4	17	30.5	3996	31.7	0.911
内蒙古	Inner Mongolia	37.2	23	13.6	34297	80.0	2.533
广　西	Guangxi	42.8	20	23.9	29579	117.6	2.879

附录3 续表11 APPENDIX III CONTINUED-11

地 区	Region	在岗职工年平均工资（元）Annual Average Wages of Staff and workers at Post (yuan)		城镇居民人均可支配收入（元）Per Capita Disposable Income of Urban Households (yuan)		农村居民人均纯收入（元）Per Capita Net Income of Rural Households (yuan)		恩格尔系数（%）Engle Coefficients	
		绝对数 Value	位次 Order	绝对数 Value	位次 Order	绝对数 Value	位次 Order	城镇居民 Urban	农村居民 Rural
东部地区	**Eastern Region**								
北 京	Beijing	29674	3	15637.8	2	6170.3	2	32.2	32.4
天 津	Tianjin	21754	6	11467.2	5	5019.5	4	37.2	38.5
河 北	Hebei	12925	24	7951.3	17	3171.1	10	36.8	42.5
辽 宁	Liaoning	14921	10	8007.6	16	3307.1	9	40.4	46.4
上 海	Shanghai	30085	2	16682.8	1	7066.3	1	36.4	34.6
江 苏	Jiangsu	18202	7	10481.9	7	4753.9	5	40.0	44.0
浙 江	Zhejiang	23506	4	14546.4	3	5944.1	3	36.2	39.5
福 建	Fujian	15603	9	11175.4	6	4089.4	7	41.6	46.7
山 东	Shandong	14332	15	9437.8	8	3507.4	8	34.6	41.9
广 东	Guangdong	22116	5	13627.7	4	4365.9	6	37.0	48.8
海 南	Hainan	12652	25	7735.8	20	2817.6	15	46.9	58.9
中部地区	**Central Region**								
山 西	Shanxi	12943	22	7902.9	18	2589.6	18	33.9	45.8
吉 林	Jilin	12431	27	7840.6	19	2999.6	12	35.9	45.6
黑龙江	Heilongjiang	12557	26	7470.7	27	3005.2	11	35.4	40.9
安 徽	Anhui	12928	23	7511.4	24	2499.3	22	43.9	47.5
江 西	Jiangxi	11860	30	7559.6	23	2786.8	16	43.0	53.7
河 南	Henan	12114	29	7704.9	22	2553.2	19	35.0	48.6
湖 北	Hubei	11855	31	8022.8	15	2890.0	13	39.3	51.5
湖 南	Hunan	13928	17	8617.5	13	2837.8	14	36.0	54.1
西部地区	**Western Region**								
重 庆	Chongqing	14357	14	9221.0	9	2510.4	21	37.8	56.0
四 川	Sichuan	14063	16	7709.9	21	2518.9	20	40.2	55.7
贵 州	Guizhou	12431	28	7322.1	29	1721.6	31	41.1	58.2
云 南	Yunnan	14581	12	8870.9	11	1864.2	28	42.4	54.0
西 藏	Tibet	30873	1	9167.4	10	1861.3	29	46.0	64.0
陕 西	Shaanxi	13024	21	7492.5	26	1866.5	27	35.9	42.4
甘 肃	Gansu	13623	18	7376.7	28	1852.2	30	37.1	48.0
青 海	Qinghai	17229	8	7319.7	30	1957.7	26	35.7	48.5
宁 夏	Ningxia	14620	11	7217.9	31	2320.1	23	37.0	42.0
新 疆	Xinjiang	14484	13	7503.4	25	2244.9	25	36.1	45.2
内蒙古	Inner Mongolia	13324	20	8123.0	14	2606.4	17	32.6	42.7
广 西	Guangxi	13579	19	8690.0	12	2305.2	24	42.3	54.3

重庆统计年鉴

贰零零伍

chongqing statistical

yearbook 2005

重庆统计年鉴·二零零五

如何浏览年鉴

两种浏览方式：为方便用户浏览和使用年鉴，本书提供了EXCEL表格（超文本模式）和PDF（电子阅读）两种浏览方式。默认为EXCEL格式，方便查阅和临时性计算。同时提供安装Acrobat Reader软件，方便阅读PDF文书。

How to browse the yearbook

Two modes to browse: In order to browse and use the yearbook easily, two modes-EXCEL (HTML form) and PDF form are offered. EXCEL mode is acquiescent, which provides more convenient consultation and temporary calculation. Acrobat Reader is provided to read PDF.

重庆市统计局　编
CHONGQING MUNICIPAL BUREAU OF STATISTICS